IMPERIAL RUSSIA

A Source Book, 1700–1917

THIRD EDITION

Edited by
BASIL DMYTRYSHYN
Professor Emeritus, Portland State University

Holt, Rinehart and Winston, Inc.

Fort Worth Chicago San Francisco Philadelphia
Montreal Toronto London Sydney Tokyo

To
Virginia

Publisher	Charlyce Jones Owen
Acquisitions Editor	David Tatom
Developmental Editor	Martin Lewis
Production Manager	Kenneth A. Dunaway
Art & Design Supervisor	Impressions Publishing Services, Inc.
Text Designer	Impressions Publishing Services, Inc.
Cover Designer	Nancy Turner

Library of Congress Cataloging-in-Publication Data

Dmytryshyn, Basil, 1925–
Imperial Russia : a source book, 1700–1917 / edited by Basil Dmytryshyn. — 3rd ed.
p. cm.
Includes bibliographical references.
ISBN 0-03-033419-5
1. Russia—History—Sources. I. Title.
DK3.D55 1990 89-26824
CIP

Address for editorial correspondence: Holt, Rinehart and Winston, Inc.,
301 Commerce Street, Suite 3700,
Fort Worth, TX 76102

Address for orders: Holt, Rinehart and Winston, Inc., 6277 Sea Harbor Drive,
Orlando Florida 32887.
1-800-782-4479, or 1-800-433-0001 (in Florida)

PRINTED IN THE UNITED STATES OF AMERICA

0 1 2 3 090 9 8 7 6 5 4 3 2 1

Holt, Rinehart and Winston, Inc.
The Dryden Press
Saunders College Publishing

Preface to the Third Edition

The main objective of this new edition is the same as that of its two predecessors, namely, to make available to the student, the general reader, and the scholar who is not a specialist extensive illustrative source material on political, social, economic, religious, educational, rural, urban, and foreign policy problems Imperial Russia faced between 1700 and 1917.

The new edition includes more than fifty new entries. Ten of these entries deal with the eighteenth century, thirty with the nineteenth century, and the remainder with the twentieth century. Several of the new selections shed light on Russia's colonial ambitions in the North Pacific and in North America; a few deal with the empire's non-Russian subjects; some offer illuminating statistical information on the military, schools, and serfs; others provide excerpts from the works of Russian literary figures; and a number present Imperial Russia's involvement in World War I (1914 1917).

To accommodate the new material, it was necessary to delete a few entries and to abridge, without sacrificing their quality, some lengthy entries of the second edition. The challenge was enormous, and it is hoped that the users of this new edition will be pleased with the final product.

I wish to express my gratitude to the editors of Holt, Rinehart and Winston, Inc. for suggesting that I prepare the third edition. In particular, I would like to thank David Tatom, History Editor and Martin Lewis, Developmental Editor, for their encouragement, patience and understanding. My thanks also go to my colleagues who, over the years, offered ideas and specific suggestions for new entries. Unfortunately, space limitations prevented the incorporation of many of their excellent suggestions. Finally, I wish to thank copy editor Barbara Hughett, whose efficiency eliminated a number of inconsistencies.

I dedicate this edition to my wife Virginia who, as she has done before, helped me to proofread the new material and expertly put it through the word processor.

Basil Dmytryshyn

Green Valley, Arizona

List of Reviewers for
Dmytryshyn, *Imperial Russia*, Third Edition

Audrey Alstadt, Central Connecticut State University
Orysia Karapinka, University of Pittsburgh
Martin Miller, Duke University
Richard Robbins, University of New Mexico
Azade-Ayse Rorlich, University of Southern California
Peter Viereck, Mount Holyoke College

Preface to the Second Edition

The main purpose of this new edition is to include, in accordance with a number of suggestions, documentary material dealing with Russia's foreign relations. In pursuit of that goal texts of twenty-five major treaties, which the government of Imperial Russia negotiated with its neighbors, have been included. It is hoped that the inclusion of this and other new material will make this volume more meaningful and useful to all interested students of the history of Imperial Russia.

To avoid chronological confusion, all dates are given here by the Gregorian Calendar. In the eighteenth century that calendar was eleven days ahead of the Julian Calendar used in Russia; in the nineteenth century the difference was twelve days; and in the twentieth it was thirteen days.

Basil Dmytryshyn

Portland, Oregon
January 14, 1973

Preface to the First Edition

The purpose of *Imperial Russia* is similar to that of the companion volume *Medieval Russia*; namely, to make available to the student, the general reader, and the scholar who is not a specialist a collection of basic sources on political, social, economic, and cultural life in Russia from 1700 to 1917. It is neither a text nor a substitute for a text but an attempt to furnish what a text cannot offer: extensive illustrative source material to amplify and enrich the text.

The selections included in this volume have been drawn from such diverse sources as official decrees, proclamations, instructions, treaties, letters, memoirs, political programs, charters, and literary classics. Many of the selections are fairly long, in order to allow an adequate acquaintance with the documents chosen. For the sake of convenience they are arranged in chronological order. Each of the selections has been provided with a brief introduction to indicate the source from which it was taken and to place it in its proper historical perspective.

In dealing with a subject as complex and controversial as the history of Imperial Russia, the task of selecting representative documents to illuminate some of the more significant aspects of the country's life and development has not been easy, and some readers may feel that their areas of interest are under-represented. The selections included, however, were chosen because they seem to be genuine sources for the understanding of Imperial Russia.

Wherever possible I have used existing translations of documents. Except where indicated in the introductions, such translations are reproduced here in their original form. Because there is no uniform way to transliterate from Cyrillic to Roman characters, the selections that different scholars have translated show a diversity in the spellings of certain Russian names.

Many documents of this collection, however, appear here in English for the first time. In my translations I have aimed for accuracy rather than elegant rendition, and with only minor exceptions I have adhered to the system of transliteration used by the Library of Congress. Thus, all Russian proper names ending in **ий** have been rendered as -ii- (Speranskii); the **Ю** has been rendered throughout as -iu- (Iurii); and the Russian **я** has been rendered as -ia- (Iaroslav). An exception to this rule is the word **бояр**, which, because of the widely used English spelling, has been rendered as *boyar*. All apostrophes have been excluded, and plurals of nontranslatable Russian words *(boyars, gubernias)* have been anglicized.

It is a pleasant custom among scholars to thank all those who have in any way made possible the appearance of a work. I acknowledge my indebtedness to the following institutions and individuals: the Research Committee of Portland State College for financial assistance that helped to defray travel expenses for the selection of material from the Russian collection at the University of California at Berkeley; the library personnel at the University of Illinois and at Portland State College for their friendly cooperation; the publishers who kindly permitted me to reprint selections from previously translated material (individually acknowledged under each item); my colleagues at Portland State College for their sustained interest in and encouragement of this project; and Mrs. Nikki Owens and Mrs. Nancy Maurer, who volunteered their typing services.

My special thanks go to my wife, Virginia, who, now as in the past, has been my most conscientious critic as well as my best proofreader.

Basil Dmytryshyn

Portland, Oregon
June 1967

Contents

Maps

1

The Revolt and Punishment of the Streltsy *in 1698: An Eyewitness Account*

During the reign of Peter the Great (1682–1725) Russia underwent a profound transformation. The moving force behind this change was the tsar himself, who opened the country to Western European influence and forced many fundamental economic, social, financial, and cultural changes. Many of his innovations were accepted without opposition, but others were imposed brutally, without regard for the fate of those who objected.

The first to experience Peter's wrath were the *streltsy,* a corps of musketeers of the Russian army whom the young tsar had held in contempt since boyhood. A rebellion of the *streltsy* took place in 1698 while Peter was touring Western Europe. They were dissatisfied with their conditions, and when they were denied answers to their petitions, they mutinied. Loyal forces crushed the mutiny in a single encounter, captured a number of the leaders, executed some, and imprisoned others. When he learned of the rebellion, Peter interrupted his tour, returned to Moscow, and began reprisals against the *streltsy.* Some two thousand of the *streltsy* were executed, many more subjected to inhuman tortures, and the remainder dismissed from service forever.

Four regiments of the *streltsy* which lay upon the frontier of Lithuania had nefariously plotted to change the sovereignty. The Theodosian Regiment abandoned Viazma, the Athanasian Regiment quit Belaia, the Ivanov left Rzhev-Vladimirov, and the Tikhonian quit Dorogobuzh, in which places they were in garrison. They drove away the loyal officers that happened to be among them, distributed military rank among themselves—the readiest for crime being held the fittest for command. At once they menaced death to all in their next neighborhood, if they would not freely join their party or should resist their design. . . .

From Johann Georg Korb, *Diary of an Austrian Secretary of Legation at the Court of Czar Peter the Great.* Translated from the original Latin and edited by Count MacDonnell (London: 1863), vol. 2, pp. 70–92, 101–114. Words in brackets are mine. Spellings have been modernized to facilitate reading.

The [loyal] regiments of the guards [in Moscow] got notice to hold themselves in readiness to march at an hour's notice, and that those who should decline to act against the sacrilegious violators of the Majesty of the Crown would be held guilty of misprision of their crime—that no ties of blood or kindred held binding when the salvation of the sovereign and the state were at stake—nay, that a son might slay his father if he rose to ruin his fatherland. General [Patrick] Gordon [1635–1699] strenuously executed this Spartan measure, and exhorted the troops entrusted to him to perform their noble task, telling them how there could be no more glorious need than to have saved the sovereign and the state. Nor was the circumstance of this expedition against the mutineers being undertaken on the very festival of Pentecost, devoid of happy omen that the spirit of truth and justice would confound the councils of the wicked—as the event clearly showed. For there was discord between the three principal chiefs of the rebellion, which delayed their march for three days, and so gave the loyal army time to encounter the traitor *streltsy* at the monastery dedicated to the most Holy Resurrection which some call Jerusalem. For the stupendous nature of their crime brought dread, delay, and divided counsels; the concord that is sworn for crime is seldom indeed lasting. Had the rebels reached that monastery but one hour sooner, safe within its strong defenses, they might perhaps have worn out the loyal troops with such long and fruitless labor that they might have lost heart, and victory, hostile to loyalty, might have set her garland upon the brow of treason. But fortune denied to their turbulent counsels the object that they sought. A slender stream not far distant waters the rich land hereabouts. On its hither banks the tsar's troops, and on the opposite the rebel columns had begun to appear. The latter were trying the ford and if they had been really determined to pass, the tsar's force could hardly have hindered them. Fatigued with a long march, and still without sufficient force, Gordon, setting wisdom in the place of strength, strolled along to the bank to talk with the *streltsy*. He found them deliberating about crossing, and dissuaded them from their undertaking with words like these: "What did they mean to do? Whither were they going? If they were thinking of Moscow, the night was too close at hand to admit of their reaching it—there was not room for them all on the hither bank; they would do much better to remain at the other side of the river and give the night to thinking sensibly of what they ought to do on the morrow." The seditious multitude could not resist such friendly advice; they were too much fatigued in body to have stomach for a fight where they did not expect one.

Meantime, Gordon having well examined all the advantages of the ground, occupied an advantageous height with his troops. Shein[1] consenting, he distributed the posts, and fortified himself, leaving nothing undone that could contribute to his own defense and security or to the detriment and damage of the enemy. With equal loyalty and resolution the imperial colonel of artillery, de Grage, bravely performed his part. He made a lodgement upon the height, placed his great guns in advantageous position, and distributed all in such excellent order that almost the whole success that attended the affair was due to the artillery. At the first dawn of day, by command of General Shein, General Gordon went again to parley with the *streltsy,* and after blaming somewhat the disobedience of the regiments, he discoursed largely of the Tsar's clemency, telling them that it was not by sedition and mobbing together that the desires of soldiers should be made known to the Tsar. Why, contrary to their usual dutiful behavior, contrary to the sanction of discipline, had they deserted the places that had been entrusted to their loyal keeping? Why should they have driven away their officers, and have broken out in designs of violence? Let them rather propose their requests peaceably, and, mindful of the loyality they owned, return to their appointed stations, that should he see them yield to their duty, should he hear them beg for it, he would get them both satisfaction for their requests, and pardon, when they confessed it, for their shameful conduct. But Gordon's speech did not move the now hardened stubbornness of the false traitors; and they only saucily answered that they would not go back to their appointed quarters until they had been allowed to kiss their darling wives at Moscow, and had received the arrears of their pay.

Gordon related to Shein the perfectly determined wickedness of the *streltsy.* But as the latter was unwilling to despair altogether of the repentance of the criminals, Gordon did not decline to try a third time to mollify the fierce passions of the rebels with offers of payment of their arrears, and pardon for the crime they were bent upon. Not only was the advice utterly fruitless, but they were in such a state of exasperation that the negotiator was near to have paid dearly for his pains. Already they loudly upbraided and rebuked this man of grave authority, their former general; they warned him to be off forthwith, and not to waste his words to no purpose, unless he wanted a bullet to chastise his marvellous audacity; that they recognized no master, and would listen to orders from nobody; that they would not go back to their quarters; that they must be admitted into Moscow; that if they were forbidden, they would open the road with force and cold steel. Their unexpected fierceness stung Gordon, and he deliberated with Shein and the other military officers present what was to be done. There was no difficulty in deciding the course that should be adopted against men that were predetermined to try the strength of their arms. Everything was made ready, consequently, for the onset and the fight, as the stubborn unanimity of the traitors forced on that last resort. Nor were the *streltsy* less busy; they drew up their array, pointed their artillery, dressed their ranks, and, as if the strife in which they were about to mingle was a struggle with a foreign foe, they preceded it with the customary prayers and invocation of God. . . .

Countless signs of the cross being made on both sides, the attack began on both sides from a distance. The first reports of cannon and small arms proceeded from the lines of General Shein, by whose command none of the pieces were loaded with ball; for he entertained a secret hope that the reality of resistance might terrify them into submissive return to obedience. But the first volley passing without wound or slaughter only added courage to guilt. Vastly emboldened, they responded by a discharge, by which some were laid lifeless, and several were bloodily wounded. When death and wounds had given a sufficient lesson that stronger remedies must be applied, Colonel de Grage was no longer required to dissemble his stout will, and allowed to discharge his great guns, fraught with deadly lead and iron. Colonel de Grage had been anxiously waiting for this command, and lost no time in firing with such precision into their rebel ranks that their furious passions were checked, and the strife of resistance and skirmishing of the mutineers was changed into a piteous slaughter.

When they saw that some were stretched lifeless, courage and fierceness at once deserted the terror-stricken *streltsy,* who broke into disorder. Those that retained any presence of mind endeavored by the fire of their own artillery to check and silence that of the Tsar; but all in vain; for Colonel de Grage had anticipated that design, and directing the fire of his pieces upon the artillery of the seditious mob, whenever they would go to their guns, vomited such a perfect hurricane upon them that many fell, numbers fled away, and none remained daring enough to return to fire them. Still Colonel de Grage did not cease to thunder from the heights into the ranks of the flying. The *streltsy* saw safety nowhere; arms could not protect them; nothing was more appalling to them than the ceaseless flash and roar of the artillery showering its deadly bolts upon them from the German right. And the same men who, but an hour before, had spat upon proferred pardon, offered in consequence to surrender—so short is the interval that separates victors from vanquished. Suppliant, they fell prostrate, and begged that the artillery might cease its cruel ravages, offering to do promptly whatever they were ordered. The suppliants were directed to lay down their arms, to quit their ranks, and obey in everything that would be enjoined to them. Though they at once threw down their arms, and proceeded to the places to which they were ordered, nevertheless, for a little while, the fire of the artillery was kept up, lest with the cessation of the cause of their terror, their rash daring should return, and the mutinous strife be renewed. But when they were truly and thoroughly frightened, they were treated with contemptuous impunity. Thousands of men allowed themselves to be fettered, who, if they had but rather instead have tried their real strength, would, beyond the least doubt, have become the victors of those that vanquished them. . . .

When the ferocious arrogance with which they were swollen had been made to subside completely, in the manner we have just narrated, and all the accomplices of the mutiny had been cast into chains, General Shein instituted an inquiry, by way of torture, touching the causes, the objects, the instigators, the chiefs, and the accomplices of this perilous and impious machination. For there was a very serious suspicion that more exalted people were at the head of it. Every one of them freely confessed himself deserving of death; but to detail the particulars of the nefarious plot, to lay bare the objects of it, to betray their accomplices, was what no person could persuade any of them to do. The rack was consequently got in readiness by the executioner, as the only means left to elicit the truth. The torture that was applied was of unexampled inhumanity. Scourged most savagely with the cat, if that had not the effect of breaking their stubborn silence, fire was applied to their backs, all gory and streaming, in order that, by slowly roasting the skin and tender flesh, the sharp pangs might penetrate through the very marrow of their bones, to the utmost power of painful sensation. These tortures were applied alternately, over and over again. Horrid tragedies to witness and to hear. In the open field above thirty of these more than funeral pyres blazed at the same time, and thereat were these most wretched creatures under examination roasted amidst their horrible howlings. At another side resounded the merciless strokes of the cat, while this most savage butchery of men was being done in this very pleasant neighborhood.

After numbers had been proved by the torture, at last the obstinacy of a few was found to yield; and one of them detailed the following particulars of this most perverse plot. He said that he was not unaware how great their fault was, that all had deserved to lose their lives, and that perhaps none would be found that would shirk death. That had fortune attended their undertaking, they would have decreed the same penalty against the *boyars* as, now that they were vanquished, they expected themselves; for that they had the intention to set on fire, sack, and ruin the whole German suburb, and when all the Germans, without exception, had been got rid of by massacre, to enter Moscow by force, to murder all that would make resistance, taking the rest with them to aid in their nefarious deeds; that they meant to inflict death upon some of the *boyars,* exile upon others, and to drag them all down from their offices and dignities, in order the more easily to conciliate to themselves the sympathies of the masses. That some *popes* [Orthodox priests] were to carry an image of the Blessed Virgin, and another of St. Nicholas, before them, in order that it might appear they had been driven to take up arms by the necessity of defending the faith, and not out of malice. That when they had got possession of authority they meant to scatter papers among the public, to assure the people that the Tsar's majesty, who had gone abroad, in consequence of the pernicious advice of the Germans, had died beyond seas. But that lest the barque of the state should be buffeted at hazard by the billows to perish a wreck upon the first rock, that Princess Sophia Alexeevna [Peter's half-sister and regent from 1682 to 1689] was to be raised to the throne until the Tsarevich [Peter's son Alexei, born in 1690] should have attained his majority and the strength of manhood. That Basil Golitsyn was to have been recalled from exile to aid Sophia with prudent advice.

Now, as any one of the points of this confession was of itself weighty enough to merit death, General Shein had the sentence that was drawn up against them promulgated and executed. Numbers were condemned to be hanged and gibbeted; many laid their heads upon the fatal block and died by the axe; many were reserved to certain vengeance and laid in custody in places in the environs. It was contrary to General Gordon's and Prince Masalskii's advice that the General proceeded to execute the rebels; as in this manner the chiefs of the revolt may, without sufficient examination, have been removed by premature death from further inquest. . . .

[The news of the *streltsy* rebellion reached Peter in Vienna]; he took the quick post, as his ambassador suggested, and in four weeks' time, he had got over about three hundred [German] miles[2] without accident and arrived [in Moscow] on the 4th of September [1698], a monarch for the well-disposed but an avenger for the wicked. His first anxiety after his arrival was about the rebellion. In what it consisted? What the insurgents meant? Who had dared to instigate such a crime? And as nobody could answer accurately upon all points, and some pleaded their own ignorance, others the obstinacy of the *streltsy,* he began to have suspicions of everybody's loyalty, and began to cogitate about a fresh investigation. The rebels that were kept in custody, in various places in the environs, were all brought in by four regiments of the guards to a fresh investigation and fresh tortures. Prison, tribunal, and rack, for those that were brought in, was in Preobrazhenskoe [the village where Peter spent his youth]. No day, holy or profane, were the inquisitors idle; every day was deemed fit and lawful for torturing. As many as there were accused there were knouts, and every inquisitor was a butcher. Prince Feodor Iurevich Romadonovskii showed himself by so much more fitted for his inquiry, as he surpassed the rest in cruelty. The very Grand Duke himself [Peter], in consequence of the distrust he had conceived of his subjects, performed the office of inquisitor. He put the interrogatories, he examined the criminals, he urged those that were not confessing, he ordered such *streltsy* as were more pertinaciously silent to be subjected to more cruel tortures; those that had already confessed about many things were questioned about more;

those who were bereft of strength and reason, and almost of their senses, by excess of torment, were handed over to the skill of the doctors, who were compelled to restore them to strength, in order that they might be broken down by fresh excruciations. The whole month of October [1698] was spent in butchering the backs of the culprits with knout and with flames; no day were those that were left alive exempt from scourging or scorching, or else they were broken upon the wheel, or driven to the gibbet, or slain with the axe—the penalties which were inflicted upon them as soon as their confessions had sufficiently revealed the heads of the rebellion.

The Chiefs of the Rebellion

Major Karpakov was said to be as far beyond the other rebels in treason as he was in official rank. So after being knouted, fire was applied to roast his back to such a degree that he lost both speech and consciousness; and then, as it was feared that death might remove him prematurely, he was commended to the skill of the Tsar's physician, Dr. Carbonari, that he might apply such remedies as would have the effect of restoring his expiring strength, and as soon as he was in some degree restored, he was subjected to the question anew, and fainted away under the sharpest tortures.

Vaska Girin, the insurgent ringleader, after undergoing four times the most exquisite tortures, confessing nothing, was condemned to be hanged. But on the very day appointed for his execution, there was led out of prison, with the rebel *streltsy,* to the question, a certain youth of twenty years of age, on being confronted with whom, he, of his own accord, broke his stubborn silence, and revealed the counsels of the traitors, with all the circumstances. Now that youth of twenty had fallen in by chance with these rebels near the borders of Smolensk, and being forced to wait on the principal instigators of the mutiny, they took no notice of his listening, nor was his presence forbidden even when they used to deliberate about the success of their nefarious enterprise. When he was dragged along with the rebels before the tribunal, he, in order to prove his innocence the more easily, cast himself at the judge's feet, and with the most ardent sighs implored not to be subjected to the torture—that he would confess all that he knew with the most exact truth. Vaska Girin, who was condemned to the halter, was not hanged before having made his judicial confession; for he was one of the prime rebels, and an excellent witness of what he very truly detailed. . . .

Certain *popes* that were connected with the *streltsy* became sharers in their treason. For they put up prayers to God to favor the efforts of treason, and it was they who carried the images of the Blessed Virgin and Saint Nicholas among armed men, and who had promised to draw the people to the side of the revolt, under the pretense of the marked justice of the cause, and of true piety. Hence one of them was hanged by the Tsar's buffoon, near the high church dedicated to the most Holy Trinity; another, being first beheaded with the axe, was set upon the wheel near the same place. *Dumnoi diak* [a high state official] Tikhon Moscovich (whom the Tsar calls his patriarch) was forced to be the butcher of the latter. . . .

[Sophia] was interrogated by the Tsar himself, touching these attempts, and it is still uncertain what she answered. But this much is certain—that in this act the Tsar's Majesty wept for his own lot and Sophia's. Some will have it the Tsar was on the point of sentencing her to death, and used this argument: "Mary of Scotland was led forth from prison to the block, by command of her sister Elizabeth, Queen of England—a warning to me to exercise my power over Sophia." Still once more the brother pardoned a sister's crime, and, instead of penalty, enjoined that she should be banished to a greater distance, in some monastery. . . .

The First Execution, 10th October, 1698

To this exhibition of avenging justice the Tsar's Majesty invited all the ambassadors of foreign sovereigns, as it were to assert anew on his return that sovereign prerogative of life and death which the rebels had disputed with him.

The barracks in Preobrazhenskoe end in a bare field which rises to the summit of a rather steep hill. This was the place appointed for the executions. Here were planted the gibbet stakes, on which the foul heads of these confessedly guilty wretches were to be set, to protract their ignominy beyond death. There the first scene of the tragedy lay exposed. The foreigners that had gathered to the spectacle were kept aloof from too close approach; the whole regiment of guards was drawn up in array under arms. A little further off, on a high *tumulus* in the area of the place, there was a multitude of Moscovites, crowded and crushing together in a dense circle. A German Major was then my companion; he concealed his nationality in a Moscovite dress, besides which he relied upon his military rank and the liberty that he might take in consequence of being entitled by reason of his being in the service of the Tsar to share in the privileges of the Moscovites. He mingled with the thronging crowd of Moscovites, and when he came back announced that five rebel heads had been cut off in that spot by an axe that was swung by the noblest arm of all Moscovy [*viz.,* Peter the Great]. The river Iauza flows past the barracks in Preobrazhenskoe, and divides them in two.

On the opposite side of this stream there were a hundred criminals set upon those little Moscovite carts which the natives call *vozok,* awaiting the hour of the death they had to undergo. There was a cart for every criminal, and a soldier to guard each. No priestly office was to be seen, as if the condemned were unworthy of that pious compassion. But they all bore lighted tapers in their hands, not to die without light and cross. The horrors of impending death were increased by the piteous lamentations of their women, the sobbing on every side, and the shrieks of the dying that rung upon the sad array. The mother wept for her son, the daughter deplored a parent's fate, the wife lamenting a husband's lot bemoaned along with the others, from whom the various ties of blood and kindred drew tears of sad farewell. But when the horses, urged to a sharp pace, drew them off to the place of their doom, the wail of the women rose into louder sobs and moans. As they tried to keep up with them, forms of expression like these bespoke their grief, as others explained them to me: "Why are you torn from me so soon? Why do you desert me? Is a last embrace then denied me? Why am I hindered from bidding him farewell?" With complaints like these they tried to follow their friends when they could not keep up with their rapid course. From a country seat belonging to General Shein one hundred and thirty more *streltsy* were led forth to die. At each side of all the city gates there was a gibbet erected, each of which was loaded with six rebels on that day.

When all were duly brought to the place of execution, and the half dozen were duly distributed at their several gibbets, the Tsar's Majesty, dressed in a green Polish cloak, and attended by a numerous suite of Moscovite nobles, came to the gate where, by his Majesty's command, the Imperial Lord Envoy [the envoy of the Holy Roman Emperor] had stopped in his own carriage, along with the representatives of Poland and Denmark. Next to them was Major-General de Carlowitz, who had conducted his Majesty on his way from Poland, and a great many other foreigners, among whom the Moscovites mingled round about the gate. Then the proclamation of the sentence began, the Tsar exhorting all the bystanders to mark well its tenor. As the executioner was unable to dispatch so many criminals, some military officers, by command of the Tsar, came under compulsion to aid in this butcher's task. The guilty were neither chained nor fettered; but logs were tied to their legs, which hindered them from walking fast, but still allowed them the use of their feet. They strove of their own accord to ascend the ladder, making the sign of the cross towards the four quarters of the world; they themselves covered their eyes and faces with a piece of linen (which is a national custom); very many putting their necks into the halter sprang headlong of themselves from the gallows, in order to precipitate their end. There were counted two hundred and thirty that expiated their flagitious conduct by halter and gibbet.

Second Execution, 13th October, 1698

Although all those that were accomplices of the rebellion were condemned to death, yet the Tsar's Majesty would not dispense with strict investigation. The more so as the unripe years and judgment of many seemed to bespeak mercy, as they were, as one may say, rather victims of error than of deliberate crime. In such case the penalty of death was commuted into some corporal infliction—such as, for instance, the cutting off of their ears and noses, to mark them with ignominy for life—a life to be passed, not as previously, in the heart of the realm, but in various and barbarous places on the frontiers of Moscovy. To such places fifty were transported today, after being castigated in the manner prescribed.

Third Execution, 17th October, 1698

Only six were beheaded today, who had the advantage of rank over the others, if rank be a distinction of honor in executed criminals.

Fourth Execution, 21st October, 1698

To prove to all the people how holy and inviolable are those walls of the city, which the *streltsy* rashly meditated scaling in a sudden assault, beams were run out from all the embrasures in the walls near the gates, on each of which two rebels were hanged. This day beheld about two hundred and fifty die that death. There are few cities fortified with as many palisades as Moscow has given gibbets to her guardian *streltsy.*

Fifth Execution, 23rd October, 1698

This differed considerably from those that preceded. The manner of it was quite different, and hardly credible. Three hundred and thirty at a time were led out together to the fatal axe's stroke, and embrued the whole plain with native but impious blood; for all *boyars,* senators of the realm, *dumnoi diaks,* and so forth, that were present at the council constituted against the rebel *streltsy* had been summoned by the Tsar's command to Preobrazhenskoe and enjoined to take upon themselves the hangman's office. Some struck the blow unsteadily, and with trembling hands assumed this new and unaccustomed task. The most unfortunate stroke among all the *boyars* was given by him [probably Prince Alexei Golitsyn] whose erring sword struck the back instead of the neck, and thus chopping the *strelets* almost in halves, would have roused him to desperation with pain, had not Alexei reached the unhappy wretch a surer blow of an axe on the neck.

Prince [Michael G.] Romadonovskii, under whose command previous to the mutiny these four regiments were to have watched the turbulent gatherings in Poland on the frontier, beheaded, according to order, one out of each regiment. Lastly to every *boyar* a *strelets* was led up, whom he was to behead. The Tsar, in his saddle, looked on at the whole tragedy.

Seventh Execution, 27th October, 1698

Today was assigned for the punishment of the *popes,* that is to say, of those who by carrying images to induce the serfs to side with the *streltsy,* had invoked the aid of God with the holy rites of his altars for the happy success of this impious plot. The place selected by the judge for the execution was the open space in front of the church of the most Holy Trinity, which is the high church of Moscow. The ignominious gibbet cross awaited the *popes,* by way of reward in suit with the thousands of signs of the cross they had made, and as their fee for all the benedictions they had given to the refractory troops. The court jester, in a mimic attire of a *pope,* made the halter ready, and adjusted it, as it was held to be wrong to subject a *pope* to the hands of the common hangman. A certain *dumnoi diak* struck off the head of another *pope,* and set his corpse upon the ignominious wheel. Close to the church, too, the halter and wheel proclaimed the enormity of the crime of their guilty burden to the passersby.

The Tsar's Majesty looked on from his carriage while the *popes* were hurried to execution. To the populace, who stood around in great numbers, he spoke a few words touching the perfidy of the *popes,* adding the threat, "Henceforth let no one dare to ask any *pope* to pray for such an intention." A little while before the execution of the *popes,* two rebels, brothers, having had their thighs and other members broken in front of the Castle of the Kremlin, were set alive upon the wheel; twenty others on whom the axe had done its office lay lifeless around these wheels. The two that were bound upon the wheel beheld their third brother among the dead. Nobody will easily believe how lamentable were their cries and howls, unless he has well weighed their excruciations and the greatness of their tortures. I saw their broken thighs tied to the wheel with ropes strained as tightly as possible, so that in all that deluge of torture I do believe none can have exceeded that of the utter impossibility of the least movement. Their miserable cries had struck the Tsar as he was being driven past. He went up to the wheels, and first promised speedy death, and afterward proffered them a free pardon, if they would confess sincerely. But when upon the very wheel he found them more obstinate than ever, and that they would give no other answer than that they would confess nothing, and that their penalty was nearly paid in full, the Tsar left them to the agonies of death, and hastened on to the Monastery of the Nuns, in front of which monastery there were thirty gibbets erected in a quadrangular shape, from which there hung two hundred and thirty *streltsy*. The three principal ringleaders, who presented a petition to Sophia, touching the administration of the realm, were hanged close to the windows of that princess, presenting, as it were, the petitions that were placed in their hands, so near that Sophia might with ease touch them. Perhaps this was in order to load Sophia with that remorse in every way, which I believe drove her to take the religious habit, in order to pass to a better life.

Last Execution, 31st October, 1698

Again, in front of the Kremlin Castle two others, whose thighs and extremities had been broken, and who were tied alive to the wheel, with horrid lamentations throughout the afternoon and the following night, closed their miserable existence in the utmost agony. One of them, the younger of the two, survived amidst his enduring tortures until noon the following day. The Tsar dined at his ease with the *boyar* Lev Kirilovich Naryshkin, all the representatives and the Tsar's ministers being present. The successive and earnest supplications of all present induced the monarch, who was long reluctant, to give command to that Gabriel who is so well known at his court that an end might be put with a ball to the life and pangs of the criminal that still continued breathing.

For the remainder of the rebels, who were still guarded in places round about, their respective places of confinement were also their places of execution, lest by collecting them all together this torturing and butchery in the one place of such a multitude of men, should smell of tyranny. And especially lest the minds of the citizens, already terror-stricken at so many melancholy exhibitions of their perishing fellow men should dread every kind of cruelty from their sovereign.

But considering the daily perils to which the Tsar's Majesty was hitherto exposed, without an hour's secutity, and hardly escaping from many snares, he was very naturally always in great apprehension of the exceeding treachery of the *streltsy,* so that he fairly concluded not to tolerate a single *strelets* in his empire—to banish all of them that remained to the farthest confines of Moscovy after having almost extirpated the very name. In the provinces, leave was given to any that preferred to renounce military service forever, and with the consent of the *voevodas* [provincial administrators] to addict themselves to domestic services. Nor were they quite innocent; for the officers that were quartered in the camp at Azov to keep ward against the hostile inroads of the enemy told how they were never secure, and hourly expected an atrocious outbreak of treason from the *streltsy*; nor was there any doubt but that they had very ambiguous sympathies for the fortunes of the other rebels. All the wives of the *streltsy* were commanded to leave the neighborhood of Moscow, and thus experienced the consequences of the crimes of their husbands. It was forbidden by *ukaz* [an imperial decree], under penalty of death, for any person to keep any of them or afford them secret harbor, unless they would send them out of Moscow to serve upon their estates. . . .

Notes

1. General Alexei Shein acted in Peter's absence as Commander-in-Chief of the Russian forces.
2. A German mile equals about five English miles.

2

Reorganization of Russia by Peter the Great

Following the punishment of the *streltsy,* Peter made a determined effort to modernize Russian society, and toward that end made many innovations. One of the earliest of these was the introduction of the Julian Calendar in 1699, which continued in official use in Russia until February 1918. Another was the creation in 1711 of a new governing body, the Senate, which assumed many of the young tsar's powers when he was absent from the country. The Senate subsequently evolved into Russia's highest tribunal and remained so until the Bolshevik seizure of power in November 1917.

For Russian society to be modern, Peter believed that at least its upper stratum had to be educated. He sent many young Russians to study abroad and opened schools at home for others. However, since education

---

The following four items are from *Polnoe Sobranie Zakonov Russkoi Imperii . . .* [*Complete Collection of the Laws of the Russian Empire*], 1st series. "A Decree on a New Calendar," from vol. 3, no. 1736, pp. 681–682; "Decrees on the Duties of the Senate," from vol. 4, no. 2321, p. 627, and no. 2330, p. 643; "Decrees on Compulsory Education," from vol. 5, no. 2762, p. 78, and no. 2778, p. 86; "A Decree on Primogeniture," from vol. 5, no. 2789, pp. 91–94. Translation mine. Words in brackets are mine.

committed the Russian nobles to lifelong state service, they chose to shun these opportunities. Early in 1714 Peter forced the reluctant young nobles into schools and shortly thereafter, by decreeing primogeniture, put an end to yet another way of evading service to the state. Previously, the equal division of estates among sons had made each son a service-exempt "breadwinner." Individuals or groups that obeyed the tsar's orders were rewarded with rights and privileges and those who defied him were relegated to obscurity.

A Decree on a New Calendar, December 20, 1699

The Great Sovereign has ordered it declared: the Great Sovereign knows that many European Christian countries as well as Slavic peoples are in complete accord with our Eastern Orthodox Church, namely: Wallachians, Moldavians, Serbs, Dalmatians, Bulgars, and subjects of our Great Sovereign, the Cherkessy [Ukrainians] and all Greeks from whom we accepted our Orthodox faith—all these peoples number their years from eight days after the birth of Christ, that is from January 1, and not from the creation of the world. There is a great difference in those two calendars. This year is 1699 since the birth of Christ, and on January 1 it will be 1700 as well as a new century. To celebrate this happy and opportune occasion, the Great Sovereign has ordered that henceforth all government administrative departments and fortresses in all their official business use the new calendar beginning January 1, 1700. To commemorate this happy beginning and the new century in the capital city of Moscow, after a solemn prayer in churches and private dwellings, all major streets, homes of important people, and homes of distinguished religious and civil servants should be decorated with trees, pine, and fir branches similar to the decoration of the Merchant Palace or the Pharmacy Building—or as best as one knows how to decorate his place and gates. Poor people should put up at least one tree or a branch on their gates or on their apartment [doors]. These decorations are to remain from January 1 to January 7, 1700. As a sign of happiness on January 1, friends should greet each other and the New Year and the new century as follows: when the Red Square will be lighted and shooting will begin—followed by that at the homes of *boyars*, courtiers, and important officials of the tsar, military and merchant classes—everyone who has a musket or any other firearm should either salute thrice or shoot several rockets or as many as he has. . . .

Decrees on the Duties of the Senate

This *ukaz* [decree] should be made known. We have decreed that during our absence administration of the country is to be [in the hands of] the Governing Senate [consisting of the following persons]: Count Musin Pushkin, *gospodin* [Lord] Strezhnev, Prince Peter Golitsyn, Prince Michael Dolgoruky, *gospodin* Plemiannikov, Prince Gregory Volkonskii, *gospodin* Samarin, *gospodin* Vasili Opukhtin, [and] *gospodin* Melnitskii; Anisim Shchukin [is to act as] the Senate's Chief Secretary. Vasili Ershov is to administer the Moscow *Gubernia* [administrative unit] and to report [on it] to the Senate; the position of Prince Peter Golitsyn is to go to *gospodin* Kurbatov. The Military *prikaz* [department] is to be replaced by a Military Board [and is to be] attached to the above mentioned Senate.

Each *gubernia* is to send two officials to advise the Senate on judicial and legislative matters. . . .

In our absence the Senate is charged by this *ukaz* with the following:

1. To establish a just court, to deprive unjust judges of their offices and of all their property, and to administer the same treatment to all slanderers.
2. To supervise governmental expenditures throughout the country and cancel unnecessary and, above all, useless things.
3. To collect as much money as possible because money is the artery of war.
4. To recruit young noblemen for officer training, especially those who try to evade it; also to select about 1000 educated *boyars* for the same purpose.
5. To reform letters of exchange and keep these in one place.
6. To take inventory of goods leased to offices or *gubernias.*
7. To farm out the salt trade in an effort to receive some profit [for the state].
8. To organize a good company and assign to it the China trade.
9. To increase trade with Persia and by all possible means to attract in great numbers Armenians [to that trade]. To organize inspectors and inform them of their responsibilities.

Decrees on Compulsory Education of the Russian Nobility, January 12 and February 28, 1714

Send to every *gubernia* some persons from mathematical schools to teach the children of the nobility—except those of freeholders and government clerks—mathematics and geometry; as a penalty [for evasion] establish a rule that no one will be allowed to marry unless he learns these [subjects]. Inform all prelates to issue no marriage certificates to those who are ordered to go to schools. . . .

The Great Sovereign has decreed: in all *gubernias* children between the ages of ten and fifteen of the nobility, of government clerks, and of lesser officials, except those of freeholders, must be taught mathematics and some geometry. Toward that end students should be sent from mathematical schools [as teachers], several into each *gubernia*, to prelates and to renowned monasteries to establish schools. During their instruction these teachers should be given food and financial remuneration of three *altyns* and two *dengas*[1] per day from *gubernia* revenues set aside for that purpose by personal orders of His Imperial Majesty. No fees should be collected from students. When they have mastered the material, they should then be given certificates written in their own handwriting. When the students are released, they ought to pay one ruble each for their training. Without these certificates they should not be allowed to marry nor receive marriage certificates.

A Decree on Primogeniture, March 23, 1714

We, Peter I, Tsar and Autocrat of All Russia, etc., issue this *ukaz* for the knowledge of all subjects of Our state, regardless of their social status.

The division of estates upon the death of the father causes great harm to Our state and state interests and brings ruin to subjects and the families concerned; namely:

1. *On Taxes.* A man, for instance, had 1000 households and five sons, had a fine manor, good food, and a sound relationship with the people; if after his death this property is divided among his children, each would receive 200 households; those children, remembering the fame of their father and the honor of their family, would not wish to live the life of an orphan; everyone can see that poor subjects will have to supply five instead of one table, and 200 households cannot carry the burden previously carried by 1000 (including state taxes). Does not this practice bring ruin to the people and harm to state interests? Because 200 households cannot pay as punctually to the state and to the nobleman as was possible from 1000 households, because (as noted above) one lord will be satisfied with 1000 (but not with 200) and the peasants, having better conditions, will be able to pay taxes punctually both to the state and to the lord. Consequently, division of estates brings great harm to the government treasury and ruin to subject people.

2. *On Families.* And should each of those five sons have two sons, each son will receive 100 households, and should they further multiply, they will be so impoverished that they may turn into one-household owners, with the

result that [the descendants of] a famous family, in place of fame, will turn into villagers, a problem which has often occurred among the Russians.

3. On top of these two harmful practices, there is yet another problem. Anyone who receives his bread gratuitously, regardless of its amount, will neither serve the state without compulsion nor try to improve his conditions: on the contrary, each will try to live in idleness, which (according to Holy Scripture) is the mother of all evil.

In contrast to Item 1 [On Taxes]: If all immovable property were to be handed down to one son and the others were to inherit only movable property, then state revenues would be sounder; the nobleman would be better off even if he should collect small amounts [from his subjects]; there will be only one manor (as stated above); and his subjects will not be ruined.

Regarding Item 2 [On Families]: Families will not decline but shall remain stable in all their glory, and their manors shall remain famous and renowned.

Regarding Item 3: The remaining [members of the family] will not be idle because they will be forced to earn a living through service, teaching, trade, and so forth. And whatever they do for their own living will also benefit the state. Because this [system] is intended to bring prosperity, the following rules should be followed:

(a) All immovable property, namely hereditary, service, and purchased estates, as well as homes and stores, should neither be sold nor mortgaged but retained in the family in the following manner:

(b) Whoever has sons must will his immovable property to one who will inherit all; other children of both sexes will be rewarded by movable property which either the father or mother will divide for both sons and daughters in the amount they wish, except that the one who inherits the immovable property [will be excluded]. If an individual does not have sons, but daughters only, he should then divide [his property] in the same manner. If an individual fails to assign [his property], a government decree will assign the immovable property to the eldest son in inheritance, while movable property will be divided equally among the others; the same procedure is to apply to daughters.

(c) Whoever is childless will give his immovable property to one of the members of his family, whomever he wishes, and the movable [property] to his relatives or even to strangers. And if he fails to do this, both of these properties will then be divided by a decree among the members of the family; immovable to the nearest member of the family and the rest to all others equally. . . .

*An Instruction to Russian Students Abroad Studying Navigation**

1. Learn [how to draw] plans and charts and how to use the compass and other naval indicators.

2. [Learn] how to navigate a vessel in battle as well as in a simple maneuver, and learn how to use all appropriate tools and instruments; namely, sails, ropes, and oars, and the like matters, on rowboats and other vessels.

3. Discover as much as possible how to put ships to sea during a naval battle. Those who cannot succeed in this effort must diligently ascertain what action should be taken by the vessels that do and those that do not put to sea during such a situation [naval battle]. Obtain from [foreign] naval officers written statements, bearing their signatures and seals, of how adequately you [Russian students] are prepared for [naval] duties.

4. If, upon his return, anyone wishes to receive [from the Tsar] greater favors for himself, he should learn, in addition to the above enumerated instructions, how to construct those vessels aboard which he would like to demonstrate his skills.

5. Upon his return to Moscow, every [foreign-trained Russian] should bring with him at his own expense, for which he will later be reimbursed, at least two experienced masters of naval science. They [the returnees] will be assigned soldiers, one soldier per returnee, to teach them [what they have learned abroad]. And if they do not wish to accept soldiers, they may teach their acquaintances or their own people. The treasury will pay for transportation and maintenance of soldiers. And if anyone other than soldiers learns [the art of navigation], the treasury will pay 100 rubles for the maintenance of every such individual. . . .

A Decree on the Right of Factories to Buy Villages, January 18, 1721†

Previous decrees have denied merchants the right to obtain villages. This prohibition was instituted because those people, outside their business, did not have any establishments that could be of any use to the state. Nowadays,

*From *Pisma i bumagi imperatora Petra Velikogo* [*Letters and Papers of Emperor Peter the Great*]. St. Petersburg: 1887, vol. 1, pp. 117–118. Translation mine. Words in brackets are mine.

†The following three items are from *Polnoe Sobranie Zakonov Russkoi Imperii . . .* [*Complete Collection of the Laws of the Russian Empire*], 1st series. "A Decree on the Right of Factories to Purchase Villages," from vol. 6, no. 3711, pp. 311–312; "Table of Ranks," from vol. 6, no. 3890, pp. 486–493; "A Decree on the Founding of the Academy," from vol. 7, no. 4443. Translation mine. Words in brackets are mine.

thanks to Our decrees, as everyone can see, many merchants have companies and many have succeeded in establishing new enterprises for the benefit of the state; namely, silver, copper, iron, coal, and the like, as well as silk, linen, and woolen industries, many of which have begun operations. As a result, by this Our *ukaz* aimed at the increase of factories, We permit the nobility as well as merchants to freely purchase villages for these factories, with the sanction of the Mining and Manufacturing College, under one condition: that these villages be always integral parts of these factories. Consequently, neither the nobility nor merchants may sell or mortgage these villages without the factories . . . and should someone decide to sell these villages with the factories because of pressing needs, it must be done with the permission of the Mining and Manufacturing College. And whoever violates this procedure will have his possessions confiscated.

And should someone try to establish a small factory for the sake of appearance in order to purchase a village, such an entrepreneur should not be allowed to purchase anything. The Mining and Manufacturing College should adhere to this rule very strictly. Should such a thing happen, those responsible for it should be deprived of all their movable and immovable property.

Table of Ranks, January 24, 1722

Military Ranks		*Civilian Ranks*	*Grades*
Naval Forces	*Land Forces*		
General-Admiral	Generalissimo Field Marshal	Chancellor or Active Privy Counselor	I
Admiral	General of Artillery General of Cavalry General of Infantry	Active Privy Counselor	II
Vice Admiral	Lieutenant General	Privy Counselor	III
Rear Admiral	Major General	Active State Counselor	IV
Captain-Commander	Brigadier	State Counselor	V
First Captain	Colonel	Collegial Counselor	VI
Second Captain	Lieutenant Colonel	Court Counselor	VII
Lieutenant-Captain of the Fleet Third Captain of Artillery	Major	Collegial Assessor	VIII

Lieutenant of the Fleet Lieutenant-Captain of Artillery	Captain or Cavalry Captain	Titled Counselor	IX
Lieutenant of Artillery	Staff Captain or Staff Cavalry Captain	Collegial Secretary	X
		Secretary of the Senate	XI
Midshipman	Lieutenant	*Gubernia* Secretary	XII
Artillery Constable	Sublieutenant	Registrar of the Senate	XIII
	Guidon Bearer	Collegial Registrar	XIV

The following rules are appended to the above Table of Ranks to inform everyone of how he should apply himself to these ranks.

1. Those princes who are related to Us by blood or those who are married to Our princesses always take precedence and rank over all other princes and high servants of the Russian state.

2. Naval and land commanding officers are to be determined in the following manner: If they both are of the same rank, the naval officer is superior at sea to the land officer; and on land, the land officer is superior to the naval officer, regardless of the length of service each may have in his respective rank.

3. Whoever shall demand respect higher than is due his rank, or shall illegally assume a higher rank, shall lose two months of his salary; if he serves without salary then he shall pay a fine equal to the salary of his rank; one third of that fine shall be given to the individual who reported on him, and the remainder will be given to a hospital fund. The observance of this rank procedure does not apply on such occasions as meetings among friends or neighbors or at social gatherings, but only to churches, the Mass, Court ceremonies, ambassadorial audiences, official banquets, official meetings, christenings, marriages, funerals, and similar public gatherings. An individual will also be fined if he should make room for a person of lower rank. Tax collectors should watch carefully [for any signs of violations of these procedures] in order to encourage service [to the state] and to honor those already in service, and [at the same time] to collect fines from impudent individuals and parasites. The above prescribed fines are applicable to male and female transgressors.

4. An identical penalty will be given to anyone who will demand a rank without having an appropriate patent for his grade.

5. Equally, no one may assume a rank that has been acquired in the service

of foreign state until We approve it, an action that We shall do gladly in accordance with his service.

6. No one may be given a new rank without a release patent, unless We personally have signed that release.

7. All married women advance in ranks with their husbands, and if they should violate the order of procedure they must pay the same fines as would their husbands if they had violated it.

8. Although We allow free entry to public assemblies, wherever the Court is present, to the sons of princes, counts, barons, distinguished nobles, and high servants of the Russian state, either because of their births or because of the positions of their fathers, and although We wish to see that they are distinguished in every way from other [people], We nevertheless do not grant any rank to anyone until he performs a useful service to Us or to the state. . . .

11. All Russian or foreign-born servants who have or who have had the first eight grades have the right forever to pass these grades on to their lawful heirs and posterity; members of ancient [Russian] noble families, even though they may be of lesser status and may never before have been brought into a noble dignity by the Crown or granted a coat of arms, should be given the same merits and preferences [as other nobles]. . . .

15. Those who are not nobles but who serve in the military and who advance to an *ober*-officer [position], will, upon attainment of that rank, receive the status of a nobleman, as will those of their children born *ex post facto*. In case an individual has no children after becoming an *ober*-officer, but has children born earlier, he may petition the Tsar, and the status of a nobleman will be granted to one son in whose behalf the father has petitioned. Children of all other grades whose parents are not nobles, regardless of whether they serve in civil or Court positions, are not considered as nobles. . . .

A Decree on the Founding of the Academy, January 28, 1724

His Imperial Majesty decreed the establishment of an academy, wherein languages as well as other sciences and important arts could be taught, and where books could be translated. On January 22, [1724], during His stay in the Winter Palace, His Majesty approved the project for the Academy, and with His own hand signed a decree that stipulates that the Academy's budget of 24,912 rubles annually should come from revenues, from custom dues and export-import license fees collected in the following cities: Narva, Dorpat, Pernov, and Arensburg. . . .

Usually two kinds of institutions are used in organizing arts and sciences. One is known as a University; the other as an Academy or society of arts and sciences.

1. A University is an association of learned individuals who teach the young people the development of such distinguished sciences as theology and jurisprudence (the legal skill), and medicine and philosophy. An Academy, on the other hand, is an association of learned and skilled people who not only know their subjects to the same degree [as their counterparts in the University] but who, in addition, improve and develop them through research and inventions. They have no obligation to teach others.

2. While the Academy consists of the same scientific disciplines and has the same members as the University, these two institutions, in other states, have no connection between themselves in training many other well-qualified people who could organize different societies. This is done to prevent interference into the activity of the Academy, whose sole task is to improve arts and sciences through theoretical research that would benefit professors as well as students of universities. Freed from the pressure of research, universities can concentrate on educating the young people.

3. Now that an institution aimed at the cultivation of arts and sciences is to be chartered in Russia, there is no need to follow the practice that is accepted in other states. It is essential to take into account the existing circumstances of this state [Russia], consider [the quality of Russian] teachers and students, and organize such an institution that would not only immediately increase the glory of this [Russian] state through the development of sciences, but would also, through teaching and dissemination [of knowledge], benefit the people [of Russia] in the future.

4. These two aims will not be realized if the Academy of Sciences alone is chartered, because while the Academy may try to promote and disseminate arts and sciences, these will not spread among the people. The establishment of a university will do even less, simply because there are no elementary schools, gymnasia, or seminaries [in Russia] where young people could learn the fundamentals before studying more advanced subjects [at the University] to make themselves useful. It is therefore inconceivable that under these circumstances a university would be of some value [to Russia].

5. Consequently, what is needed most [in Russia] is the establishment of an institution that would consist of the most learned people, who, in turn, would be willing: (a) to promote and perfect the sciences while at the same time, wherever possible, be willing (b) to give public instruction to young people (if they feel the latter are qualified) and (c) instruct some people individually so that they in turn could train young people [of Russia] in the fundamental principles of all sciences.

6. As a result, and with only slight modifications, one institution will perform as great a service [in Russia] as the three institutions do in other states. . . .

7. Because the organization of this Academy is similar to that of Paris (except for this difference and advantage that the Russian Academy is also to do what a university and college are doing [in Paris]), I think that this institution can and should easily be called an Academy. Disciplines that can be organized in this Academy can easily be grouped in three basic divisions: The first division is to consist of mathematical and related sciences; the second of physics; and the third of humanities, history, and law. . . .

Notes

1. One *altyn* equalled six *dengas,* or three kopecks; one *denga* equalled one-half kopeck.

The Problem of Imperial Succession: Peter's Relations with His Son Alexei

Peter the Great's relations with his son Alexei, his first child, form a sad chapter of his story. The young tsarevich, who was born in 1690, lived with his mother Eudoxia Lopukhina until 1698, but when amorous interests led Peter to commit his wife to a convent in that year, Alexei's rearing was entrusted to Peter's aunts and foreign tutors. While this education introduced Alexei to Western ideas, he missed his mother and grew to dislike and fear his father. Peter's limitless energy and enthusiasm for military matters, moreover, were unsympathetic to his son's delicate health and deep religious convictions. After his marriage in 1711 to a German princess, Charlotte Wolfenbuttel, Alexei turned to heavy drinking and, while under the influence of alcohol, publicly criticized his father's policies. Although he was seldom at home, Peter nevertheless learned of these criticisms, and in 1715, following the death of Charlotte in giving birth to a son, he sent Alexei a "last warning." Alexei agreed to renounce his right to succession. Shortly thereafter, he went abroad,

---

From Friedrich Christian Weber, *The Present State of Russia . . .* (London: 1723), vol. 2, pp. 97–105, 190–201. Weber was Dutch Minister in Russia from 1714 to 1720. Spellings have been modernized to facilitate reading.

first to Vienna and then to Naples. After he was persuaded to return, Peter ordered an investigation into the motives behind his son's flight. A plot against the tsar was uncovered, which under Russian law was punishable by death, but the sentence was never carried out as Alexei died in 1718 in the Fortress of Peter and Paul.

Peter's Declaration to Alexei, October 11, 1715

Declaration to My Son

You cannot be ignorant of what is known to all the world, to what degree our people groaned under the oppression of the Swedes before the beginning of the present war.

By the usurpation of so many maritime places so necessary to our state, they had cut us off from all commerce with the rest of the world, and we saw with regret that, besides, they had cast a thick veil before the eyes of the clearsighted. You know what it has cost us in the beginning of this war (in which God alone had led us, as it were, by the hand, and still guides us) to make ourselves experienced in the art of war, and to put a stop to those advantages which our implacable enemies obtained over us.

We submitted to this with a resignation to the will of God, making no doubt but it was he who put us to that trial, till he might lead us into the right way, and we might render ourselves worthy to experience, that the same enemy who at first made others tremble, now in his turn trembles before us, perhaps in a much greater degree. These are the fruits which, next to the assistance of God, we owe to our own toil and to the labor of our faithful and affectionate children, our Russian subjects.

But at the time that I am viewing the prosperity which God has heaped on our native country, if I cast an eye upon the posterity that is to succeed me, my heart is much more penetrated with grief on account of what is to happen, then I rejoice at those blessings that are past, seeing that you, my son, reject all means of making yourself capable of well-governing after me. I say your incapacity is voluntary, because you cannot excuse yourself with want of natural parts and strength of body, as if God had not given you a sufficient share of either; and though your constitution is none of the strongest, yet it cannot be said that it is altogether weak.

But you even will not so much as hear warlike exercises mentioned; though it is by them that we broke through that obscurity in which we were involved, and that we made ourselves known to nations, whose esteem we share at present.

I do not exhort you to make war without lawful reasons; I only desire you to apply yourself to learn the art of it; for it is impossible well to govern without knowing the rules and discipline of it, was it for no other end than for the defense of the country.

I could place before your eyes many instances of what I am proposing to you. I will only mention to you the Greeks, with whom we are united by the same profession of faith. What occasioned their decay but that they neglected arms? Idleness and repose weakened them, made them submit to tyrants, and brought them to that slavery to which they are now so long since reduced. You mistake, if you think it is enough for a prince to have good generals to act under his orders. Everyone looks upon the head; they study his inclinations and conform themselves to them: all the world owns this. My brother during his reign loved magnificence in dress, and great equipages of horses. The nation was not much inclined that way, but the prince's delight soon became that of his subjects, for they are inclined to imitate him in liking a thing as well as disliking it.

If the people so easily break themselves of things which only regard pleasure, will they not forget in time, or will they not more easily give over the practice of arms, the exercise of which is the more painful to them, the less they are kept to it?

You have no inclination to learn the war, you do not apply yourself to it, and consequently you will never learn it: And how then can you command others, and judge of the reward which those deserve who do their duty, or punish others who fail of it? You will do nothing, nor judge of anything but by the eyes and help of others, like a young bird that holds up his bill to be fed.

You say that the weak state of your health will not permit you to undergo the fatigues of war: This is an excuse which is no better than the rest. I desire no fatigues, but only inclination, which even sickness itself cannot hinder. Ask those who remember the time of my brother. He was of a constitution weaker by far than yours. He was not able to manage a horse of the least mettle, nor could he hardly mount it. Yet he loved horses, hence it came, that there never was, nor perhaps is there actually now in the nation a finer stable than his was.

By this you see that good success does not always depend on pains, but on the will.

If you think there are some, whose affairs do not fail of success, though they do not go to war themselves; it is true: But if they do not go themselves, yet they have an inclination for it, and understand it.

For instance, the late King of France did not always take the field in person; but it is known to what degree he loved war, and what glorious exploits he performed in it, which made his campaigns to be called the theatre and school of the world. His inclinations were not confined solely to military affairs, he also loved mechanics, manufactures and other establishments, which rendered his kingdom more flourishing than any other whatsoever.

After having made to you all those remonstrances, I return to my former subject which regards you.

I am a man and consequently I must die. To whom shall I leave after me to finish what by the grace of God I have begun, and to preserve what I have partly recovered? To a man, who like the slothful servant hides his talent in the earth, that is to say, who neglects making the best of what God has entrusted to him?

Remember your obstinacy and ill-nature, how often I reproached you with it, and even chastised you for it, and for how many years I almost have not spoken to you; but all this has availed nothing, has effected nothing. It was but losing my time; it was striking the air. You do not make the least endeavors, and all your pleasure seems to consist in staying idle and lazy at home: Things of which you ought to be ashamed (forasmuch as they make you miserable) seem to make up your dearest delight, nor do you foresee the dangerous consequences of it for yourself and for the whole state. St. Paul has left us a great truth when he wrote: If a man know not how to rule his own house, how shall he take care of the church of God?

After having considered all those great inconveniences and reflected upon them, and seeing I cannot bring you to good by any inducement, I have thought fit to give you in writing this act of my last will, with this resolution however to wait still a little longer before I put it in execution, to see if you will mend. If not, I will have you to know that I will deprive you of the succession, as one may cut off a useless member.

Do not fancy, that, because I have no other child but you, I only write this to terrify you. I will certainly put it in execution, if it please God; for whereas I do not spare my own life for my country and the welfare of my people, why should I spare you who do not render yourself worthy of either? I would rather choose to transmit them to a worthy stranger than to my own unworthy son.

Peter

Alexei's Reply, October 27, 1715

Most Clement Lord and Father

I have read the paper your Majesty gave me on the 27th of October, 1715, after the funeral of my late consort.

I have nothing to reply to it, but, that if your Majesty will deprive me of the succession to the Crown of Russia by reason of my incapacity, your will be done; I even most instantly beg it of you, because I do not think myself fit for the government. My memory is very much weakened, and yet it is necessary in affairs. The strength of my mind and of my body is much decayed by the sickness which I have undergone, and which have rendered me incapable of governing so many nations; this requires a more vigorous man than I am.

Therefore I do not aspire after you (whom God preserve many years) to the succession of the Russian Crown, even if I had no brother as I have one at present, whom I pray God preserve. Neither will I pretend for the future to that succession, of which I take God to witness, and swear it upon my soul, in testimony whereof I write and sign this present with my own hand.

I put my children into your hands, and as for myself, I desire nothing of you but a bare maintenance during my life, leaving the whole to your consideration and to your will.

Your most humble servant and son,
Alexei

Peter's Declaration to Alexei, January 19, 1716

My last sickness having hindered me till now from explaining myself to you about the resolution I have taken upon your letter which you wrote to me in answer to my first; at present I answer that I observe you talk of nothing in it but of the succession, just as if I needed your consent to do in that affair what otherwise depends on my will. But whence comes it that in your letter you say nothing of that incapacity wherein you voluntarily put yourself, and of that aversion you have for affairs, which I touched in mine more particularly than the ill state of your health, and which you barely mention. I also remonstrated to you the dissatisfaction your conduct has given me for so many years, and you pass all that over in silence, though I strongly insisted upon it. Thence I judge that those paternal exhortations have no weight with you. I have therefore taken a resolution to write to you once more by this present which shall be the last. If you slight the advices I give you in my lifetime, how will you value them after my death?

Can one rely on your oaths, when one sees you have a hardened heart? David said: All men are liars. But supposing you have at present the will of being true to your promises, those great beards may turn you as they please, and make you break them.

Instead that at present their debauches and sloth keep them out of posts of honor, they are in hopes that one day or other their condition will mend by you who already show much inclination for them.

I do not see that you are sensible of the obligations you have to your father, to whom you owe your very being. Do you assist him in his cares and pains since you have attained the years of maturity? Certainly in nothing; all the world knows it; quite contrary you blame and abhor all the good I do, at the hazard and expense of my own health for the sake of my people and for their welfare, and I have all the reasons in the world to believe you will be the destroyer of it, if you outlive me. And so I cannot resolve to let you live on according to your own will, like an amphibious creature, neither fish nor flesh. Change therefore your conduct, and either strive to render yourself worthy of the succession, or turn monk. I cannot be easy on your account, especially now that my health begins to decay. On sight therefore of this letter, answer me upon it either in writing, or by word of mouth. If you fail to do it, I will use you as a malefactor.

Peter

Alexei's "Confession," June 22, 1718

On the 22nd Day of June 1718, I make this answer to the articles upon which M. Tolstoy interrogated me.

1. Though I was not ignorant that it is not the practice of the world to be disobedient as I was to my father, and to be unwilling to do what pleased him, that this even is a sin and a great shame: Yet this proceeded from my living, when a child, with a governess and young women, of whom I learned nothing but amusements and to play in my chamber, and to act the bigot, to which I was naturally inclined.

The persons who were put about me after my governess was taken from me did not teach me to do better, among others Nikifore Viazemskii, Alexei Basili, and the Naryshkins.

My father taking care of my education, and being desirous that I should apply myself to what might render me worthy of being the Tsar's son, ordered me to learn the High-Dutch tongue and other sciences, to which I had a great deal of aversion. I applied myself to them but with great carelessness, only to pass away the time, nor had I ever any inclination for them.

And as my father, who then was often in the army was far off from me, he ordered the most serene Prince [Alexander] Menshikov [1673–1729] to have an eye upon me. When I was with him, I was obliged to apply myself; but when I was out of the Prince's sight, the said Naryshkins and Viazemskii, seeing that my inclinations run solely upon bigotry, idleness, frequenting priests and monks and drinking with them, not only did not dissuade me from it, but even took delight in doing as I did: As they were persons who had been with me from my infancy, I was used to do what they told me, to fear them and to comply with them in everything; and they more and more alienated me from my father by diverting me with such sort of pleasures, and by degrees I came to abhor not only my father's military affairs and his other actions, but even his very person. This is what made me wish always to be far off from him.

When I was intrusted at Moscow with the government of the empire, seeing myself at full liberty and that I was my own master; far from considering that my father had put it into my hands in order to train me up to it, and to lead me to the succession after him, if I rendered myself capable of it: I gave myself still more up to my usual pleasures among priests and monks, and other people of that stamp. Alexander Kikin made it always his earnest business when he was with me to harden me in those disorders.

My father having compassion for me, and being desirous of rendering me worthy of that state to which I was called, sent me into foreign countries; but as I was already full grown and of a settled age, I changed none of my habits.

It is true however that the stay I made there has been useful to me in some things, but not enough so as to eradicate the bad habits which had taken so deep root in me.

2. The bad character of my wicked mind was the cause why I did not dread my father's corrections for my disobedience: I freely own it: For though I truly feared him, yet it was not with a filial awe, but such an apprehension as made me seek means how to keep away from him, that I might not perform his will. Of this I will give a plain instance.

On my return to my father, coming back from foreign parts to St. Petersburg, he received me very graciously. Among other things he asked me whether I had not forgotten what I had learned: I answered I had not. He ordered me to bring to him some drawings of my own doing: As I had learned nothing, I was afraid he might make me draw something in his presence, and fell a-thinking how to disable my right hand so far as to render it unfit for working. I charged a pistol with a ball, and taking it with the left, I fired it against the palm of the right with a design of shooting it through: The ball missed the hand, but the powder burned it enough to make it sore. The ball flew into the wall of my closet where it may still be seen. My father observing that I was hurt on the hand, asked how it happened. I put some sham or other upon him, but did not tell him the truth. One may see by this, that though I feared my father, it was not with a filial awe.

3. As to my having desired the succession by other means than that of obedience, all the world may easily guess the reason of it; for being once stepped out of the good road, unwilling to imitate my father in anything, I

endeavored to obtain the succession by any other method whatsoever than what was fair. I was for having it by a foreign assistance, and if I had obtained it, and that the Emperor had put in execution what he had promised to me, namely, to procure the Crown of Russia to me even by armed force, I would have stuck at nothing to lay hold of the succession. For instance, if the Emperor had demanded Russian troops against any of his enemies whomsoever, or large sums of money in return for his service, I would have done whatever he had desired, and I would also have made great presents to his ministers and generals. I would have maintained at my own expense the auxiliary forces he should have given me to put me in possession of the Crown of Russia, and in short nothing would have been too dear for me to satisfy my own will.

Official Condemnation of Alexei, June 24, 1718

By virtue of the express ordinance issued by His Tsarist Majesty, and signed with his own hand on the 13th of June last, for trying the Tsarevich Alexei Petrovich, for his transgressions and crimes against his father and his lord, the undersigned Ministers, Senators, States Military and Civil, after having been several times assembled in the Chamber of the Regency of the Senate at St. Petersburg, having more than once heard read the originals and extracts of evidences given against him, as also His Tsarist Majesty's letters of exhortation to the Tsarevich, and his answers to them written with his own hand, and the other proceedings relating to that trial; as also the Tsarevich's criminal examinations, confessions and declarations which he either wrote with his own hand, or made by word of mouth to his Lord and his father, and in presence of the undersigned persons, established by His Tsarist Majesty's authority for this present trial. They have declared and owned, that though according to the laws of the Russian Empire, it never belonged to them, who are natural subjects of His Tsarist Majesty's sovereign dominion, to take cognizance of affairs of this nature, which according to their importance, solely depend on the absolute will of the sovereign, whose power depends but on God alone, and is not limited by any law: Yet submitting themselves to His Tsarist Majesty their sovereign's ordinance aforesaid, who gives them that liberty, after mature reflection and in Christian conscience, without fear, or flattery, and without regard to the person, having nothing before their eyes but the divine laws suiting with the present case, both of the Old Testament and the New, the holy writings of the Gospel and of the Apostles, as also the Canons and Rules of the Councils, the authority of the holy fathers and doctors of the church; taking also instruction from the considerations of the Archbishops and the clergy assembled at St. Petersburg by His Tsarist Majesty's order, as above transcribed, and conforming themselves to the laws of all Russia, especially the Constitutions of this empire, to the military laws and statutes, which are conformable to the laws of many other governments, and chiefly to those of the ancient Roman and Grecian [Byzantine] emperors, and of other Christian princes: The undersigned having put it to the vote, did unanimously, without contradiction, agree and pronounce, *that the Tsarevich Alexei Petrovich deserves death* for his crimes aforesaid, and for his capital transgressions against his sovereign and his father, being His Tsarist Majesty's son and subject; so that, though His Tsarist Majesty did promise to the Tsarevich by the letter he sent to him by M. Privy-Councelor Tolstoy, and the Captain of the Guard Rumiantsev, dated Spa the 10th of July, 1717, to pardon him his evasion if he returned of his own accord and willingly, as the Tsarevich himself has owned with thanks in his answer to that letter, written from Naples on the 4th of October, 1717, saying therein that he thanks His Tsarist Majesty for the pardon that had been given to him only for his voluntary evasion; yet he had since made himself unworthy of it by opposing his father's will and by his other transgressions, which he renewed and continued, as is amply set forth in the manifesto published by His Tsarist Majesty on the 3rd of February of the present year, and because among other things he did not return of his own accord.

And though His Tsarist Majesty upon the Tsarevich's arrival at Moscow with the paper of confession containing his crimes, wherein he asked pardon for them, had commiseration of him, as is natural for a father to have for his son, and that in the audience he gave him in the hall of the castle on the said third day of February, he promised him a pardon of all his transgressions: Yet His Tsarist Majesty made him that promise solely upon this express condition which he explained in the presence of all, namely, that the Tsarevich should declare without any restriction or reserve, all that he had committed and plotted against His Tsarist Majesty till that day, and that he should discover all the persons who advised him, his accomplices, and in general all those who knew anything of his designs and intrigues; but if he concealed any person or any thing, the pardon promised should be void and remain revoked, which the Tsarevich then agreed to and accepted, at least in outward appearance, with tears of thankfulness, and promised upon oath to declare all, without reserve. In confirmation of which he kissed the Holy Cross and the Holy Scriptures in the Cathedral Church.

His Tsarist Majesty also confirmed the same to him with his own hand the next day, in the interrogatory articles inserted above, which he caused to be given to him, having written at the top as follows:

> As you received yesterday your pardon on condition of declaring all the circumstances of your evasion and all that has any relation to it: But that if you

> concealed anything, you should forfeit your life; and as you have already by word of mouth made some declarations, you ought for a more ample satisfaction, and for your own discharge, set them down in writing, according to the points set forth hereafter.

And in the conclusion there was further written with His Tsarist Majesty's own hand in the seventh article:

> Declare all that has any relation to this affair, even though it be not specified here, and clear yourself as at the Holy Confession. But if you hide or conceal anything that is afterwards discovered, do not impute anything to me; for it was yesterday declared to you before everybody, that in this case, the pardon you have received, shall be revoked and void.

Notwithstanding this, the Tsarevich in his answers and confessions, spoke without any sincerity; he concealed and hid not only many persons, but also capital affairs and his transgressions, and in particular his rebellious designs against his father and his Lord, and his wicked practices which he had contrived and carried on for a long time, to attempt the usurpation of his father's throne, even in his lifetime, by diverse wicked means, and under wicked pretexts, grounding his hopes and wishes for the death of his father and his Lord, on the populace's declaring in his favor, with which he flattered himself.

All this was discovered afterwards by the criminal examinations, after he had refused to declare it himself, as appeared above.

And so, it is evident from the whole conduct of the Tsarevich, and from the declarations which he made in writing and by word of mouth, and last of all from that of the 22nd of June of the present year, that it was not his intention the succession to the crown should come to him after his father's death, in the manner his father would have left it to him, according to the order of equity and by the ways and means which God prescribed. But that he desired it, and had the design of getting it, even in the lifetime of his father and his lord, against His Tsarist Majesty's will, and by opposing his father's intentions in everything, and not only by insurrections of rebels which he hoped for, but also by the emperor's assistance and with a foreign army which he flattered himself to have at his disposal, should even the government have been in danger of being overturned, and all have been alienated from the state, that might have been demanded of him for that assistance.

These premises therefore evidently show, that the Tsarevich, in hiding all those pernicious designs, and concealing many persons who were of intelligence with him, as he did till the last examination, and till he was fully convicted of all his machinations, had a view to keep in reserve certain means for resuming his designs afterwards when a favorable occasion should offer, and to carry on the execution of this horrid attempt against his father and his Lord, and this whole empire.

He thereby rendered himself unworthy of the clemency and of the pardon that was promised to him by his Lord and his father, which he also owned himself, as well before His Tsarist Majesty, as in the presence of all the states, ecclesiastical and secular, and publicly before the whole assembly, and he also declared by word of mouth and in writing before the undersigned judges, established by His Tsarist Majesty, that all that is above, is true and manifest by the effects that have appeared of it.

Now, seeing the foresaid laws, divine and ecclesiastical, civil and military, and especially the two latter, condemn to death without mercy, not only those whose attempts against their father and lord have been manifested by evidences, or proved by writings, but even those whose attempts have only been in the intention of rebelling, or who have simply framed designs of killing the sovereign, or to usurp the empire. Therefore such a design of rebellion, the like of which was hardly ever heard of in the world, joined to that of a horrid double parricide against his sovereign, first as father of the country, and next as his father by nature (a most clement father who caused the Tsarevich to be educated from the cradle with more than paternal care, with a tenderness and a goodness that appeared on all occasions, who endeavored to train him up to the government, and to instruct him in the art of war with incredible pains and indefatigable application, in order to render him capable and worthy of the succession to so great an empire), how much more has such a design deserved to be punished with death?

It is with afflicted hearts and eyes full of tears, that we, being servants and subjects, pronounce this sentence, considering it does not belong to us in this quality to enter upon a judgment of so great importance, and particularly to pronounce a sentence against the son of the most sovereign and most clement Tsar, our Lord. However it being his will we shall judge; we by this present declare our true opinion, and we pronounce this condemnation with a conscience as pure and as Christian, as we believe to be able to answer it before the dreadful, just, and impartial judgment of the Great God.

Submitting, as for the rest, this sentence which we give, and this condemnation which we pass, to the sovereign power, will, and clement revision of His Tsarist Majasty, our most clement Monarch.

4

Obligations and Rights of Russian Parish Priests, 1721

Throughout most of its history, the Russian Orthodox Church (and its hierarchy) was closely linked with—indeed, it was an instrument of—those holding secular power. The Church performed many functions, ranging from preaching obedience to the tsar to opposing all contacts with Western Europe and all efforts at modernization. The latter point became critical during the reforming reign of Peter the Great. In order to remove it as an obstacle to his reforms, Peter introduced a series of measures that curbed the influence of the Church and transformed it into an obedient tool of the state.

The most important of these measures was imposed in 1721 when Peter replaced the Patriarchate with the Holy Synod. The Synod was organized along the same structural lines as all other departments of the government. It had an ecclesiastical president, two vice presidents, four counsellors and four assessors who were effectively controlled, however, by the office headed by a lay *Ober*-Procurator who was, in fact, the actual head of church administration. Under this arrangement, which lasted until 1917, each tier of church functionaries was assigned a set of specific obligations and rights. The most interesting were those pertaining to parish priests—the most numerous segment of the clergy—on whose shoulders lay the main burden of trying to control and influence the masses.

Obligations and Rights of Russian Orthodox Parish Priests, Established by Peter the Great, 1721

Because particular weaknesses are to be seen in the parish clergy of our Russian Church, for that reason it is fitting to devise specific improvements, in addition to the previous ones, in accordance with God's word, after the example of the ancient fathers, so that bishops shall then understand what they must watch for in their churchmen and the churchmen shall know the true path of their calling, and so that this grand administration, the Most Holy Synod,

---

Source: *The Spiritual Regulation of Peter the Great.* Translated and edited by Alexander V. Muller (Seattle: University of Washington Press), 1972, pp. 58–72. Reprinted by permission of the University of Washington Press.

shall be better able to function in the general supervision of the ecclesiastical estate.

1. Many do insinuate themselves into the priesthood for no other reason than only for greater freedom and subsistence, and they do not possess any requisite aptitude for their vocation. Accordingly, no one shall be installed as a priest or deacon who has not been instructed in a bishop's household school (about which there was a statement in reference to episcopal matters in Article 10). And until those schools come into being, candidates shall be directed to study books on the faith and Christian law; and a candidate shall not be installed until he has committed them to memory.

2. An arriving candidate shall have, in a deposition, authentic testimony from his parishioners that they know him to be a good person; namely, not a drunkard, not an idler in the maintenance of his household, not a scandalmonger, not a querulous grumbler, not a fornicator, not a brawler, and not accused demonstrably in deception and fraud. For these misdeeds in particular impede the work of a pastor and lend to the clergy a wretched aspect.

3. In that same deposition, there shall be specifically indicated, under the signatures of the parishioners, the prestimony [land allocated to the priest of that parish], and under the signature of the candidate, that he is willing to be satisfied with that prestimony or land.

4. An accepted candidate shall not be immediately installed, but he should first master the books referred to. Meanwhile he shall be tested as to whether he is a bigot and feigns humility, which for an intelligent person it is not difficult to find out. Likewise whether he speaks of his dreams and apparitions concerning himself or anyone else. For what good can be hoped for from such persons except old wives' tales and harmful vagaries among the people instead of salutary teaching?

5. Before his installation into the priesthood, a candidate shall in church publicly condemn specifically all schismatic sects, together with an oath that he shall not shelter by silence whomever he finds in the parish, through their estrangement from the Holy Eucharist or through other signs, to be clandestine schismatics, but shall render a report in writing concerning them to his bishop. Along with the aforementioned oath, he must take an oath of loyalty to his Sovereign, and inform of all opposition, as well as whatever matters he is by the rules ordered to report, which someone may mention even during confession, but of which he does not repent and with respect to which he does not lay aside his intention, as is clearly indicated hereunder in Article 11.

6. Until a candidate's installation into the priesthood, while he is learning the church services in a bishop's house, let him copy for himself these rules for priests inscribed herein if he is unable to have a printed *Regulation*; likewise,

the aforestated rules on general matters from the *Regulation*; and third, the aforestated rules for laymen, so that in the future he shall not excuse himself through ignorance of his obligations. And prior to his release, let there be recorded an acknowledgment in the episcopal chancery that he took with him the rules referred to and that he shall acquit himself in compliance with them, subject to punishment according to the judgment of the bishop. At the time that the bishop visits his eparchy [diocese], he must show these rules to the bishop.

7. Priests must especially know these things: in confession if they encounter someone who is cold and without emotion, how to terrify with God's judgment him who is confessing; if they see someone who is skeptical and inclined to despair, how to restore such a one, and how to strengthen him with the hope of God's mercy and kindness; how to instruct one in the breaking of a sinful habit; how to visit and comfort a sick person; how to sustain and administer to the passing of a dying person with words; and how, especially, to support those who have been sentenced and are being led to death, and reassure them of God's mercy. These are truly the most necessary duties of priests.

But since these cannot be expected from a priesthood that is little educated, for that reason (until God grants to see in Russia complete education), it is fitting to write out the parts serving the aforementioned needs. Then a priest, after having committed them to memory, should either say them or read them to a sick person, a dying person, to one being led to death, and in rendering all his other ministration.

8. To those who come to him for confession, a priest shall not be oppressive. He becomes oppressive when, either at the time of confession, he prides himself and appears stern to him who is confessing, whom he ought to comfort with all humility, or at other times, when he impudently asks for something from his spiritual sons, or as it were, importunes with authority. For example: to request or importune a person in authority that he acquit someone in a judicial action, or that he remit a punishment, even though that would be inequitable to the plaintiffs or detrimental to the people. If such arrogant good-for-nothings appear, the authority of the confessional shall be immediately banned to them.

9. And there is yet even a greater misdeed: if a priest reveals in a quarrel the sins of his spiritual son. For this he shall be divested of the priesthood, and he shall be referred to a lay tribunal for corporal punishment in accordance with the determination of the matter.

10. But every confessor must keep from quarreling with his spiritual children, for whatever he spews against them as being reprehensible, those who are present will think that he knows about it from confession, and thus, a slander will become credible and, for that reason, insufferable. For this, confessors who sin thus are liable to severe punishment.

11. If someone in confession informs his spiritual father of some illegality that has not been committed, but that he yet intends to commit, especially treason or mutiny against the Sovereign or against the state, or evil designs upon the honor or well-being of the Sovereign and upon His Majesty's family, and in informing of such a great intended evil, he reveals himself as not repenting but considers himself in the right, does not lay aside his intention, and does not confess it as though it were a sin, but rather, so that with his confessor's assent or silence he might become confirmed in his intention—what can be concluded therefrom is this: When the spiritual father, in God's name, enjoins him to abandon completely his evil intention, and he, silently, as though undecided or justifying himself, does not appear to have changed his mind, then the confessor must not only not honor as valid the forgiveness and remission of the confessed sins, for it is not a regular confession if someone does not repent of all his transgressions, but he must expeditiously report concerning them, where it is fitting, pursuant to His Imperial Majesty's personal *ukase*, promulgated on the twenty-eighth day of April of the present year, 1722, which was published in printed form with reference to these misdeeds, in accordance with which it is ordered to bring such malefactors to designated places, exercising the greatest speed, even as the result of statements concerning His Imperial Majesty's high honor and damaging to the state. Wherefore a confessor, in compliance with the provisions of that personal *ukase* of His Imperial Majesty, must immediately report, to whom it is appropriate, such a person who thus displays in confession his evil and unrepentant intention. However, in that report, the salient points of what has transpired in confession shall not be disclosed, since in accordance with that *ukase*, it is prohibited to interrogate such malefactors, who appear in connection with making the aforementioned damaging statements, anywhere except in the Privy Chancery or in the Preobrazhensky Central Administrative Office. But in that report shall only be stated secretly that such a person, indicating therein his name and rank, harbors evil ideas and impenitent intent against the Sovereign or against the rest of what was referred to above, from which he desires that there be great harm: Therefore, he must be apprehended and placed under arrest without delay. And whereas, by that same personal *ukase* of His Imperial Majesty, it is ordered to send the informers also, under surety furnished by guarantors, or if there are no guarantors, under escort in honorable arrest, to the aforementioned Privy Chancery or the Preobrazhensky Central Administrative Office for proper arraignment of those malefactors, accordingly a priest who has reported that matter, after giving surety for himself, shall proceed, upon being dispatched, to the prescribed place without postponement or evasion. And there, where investigation is made into such misdeeds, he shall report specifically, without any concealment or indecision, everything that

was heard regarding that evil intention. For, by this report, the confessor does not disclose a genuine confession and does not transgress the canons, but rather fulfills the Lord's teaching. . . .

12. Not only must priests inform of an evil that seeks to be put into action, but also of a scandal that has already been perpetrated against the people. For example: when someone, having imagined it somewhere in some way or having hypocritically contrived it, spreads the news of a false miracle and the ordinary, undiscriminating people accept it as real. Later, if such a fabricator discloses that to be a fantasy of his in confession, but does not display repentance for it and does not promise to make it known publicly (so that the ignorant may not accept that lie as real), that lie, being accepted as real through ignorance, will be added to the number of genuine miracles and in time will for everyone become firmly established in memory and renown. Therefore, a confessor must inform of that, where it is fitting, without delay, so that such a falsehood may be halted and the people, beguiled by that lie, might not sin through ignorance and accept that lie as real. For, by use of such false miracles, not only is contumely of one kind or another perpetuated, but God's commandment, "You shall not take the name of the Lord, your God, in vain," is violated. Those who recount such miracles use God's name in a lie, so that it is not glorified by them, but is taken in vain. And upon the piety of Orthodox believers descends censure from those of other faiths. Accordingly, it is most necessary to halt such illegal and impious activity; and confessors, as was mentioned herein, must inform of such cases without concealment and immediately.

13. Whenever something other than those most important causes for the submission of reports has been confessed with repentance and the intention of atonement, and yet it appears to a confessor as a sin difficult to resolve, that is, as a grievous sin that requires some correction and expiation, the confessor shall go to his bishop, and not naming the penitent, he must set forth the sin in detail and ask for a decision. . . .

15. When a priest comes to a sick person to hear his confession and to administer the Holy Mysteries, he shall hear his confession in private, but shall administer the Holy Mysteries in front of the people of that house and also in front of his own churchmen. This is to be done for the reason that some impious priests, concealing schismatics, pretend that they administer the Holy Mysteries to a sick person in private, so that the schismatic may be concealed by such pretended Communion. For such godlessness, a priest shall be utterly estranged from the priesthood and shall be subject to a civil court for corporal punishment; and all the property of a schismatic who hides in this way shall be seized in favor of the Sovereign.

16. Whoever reports espying a priest acting illicitly in this way with a

schismatic shall be given as a reward one-half or one-third part of the schismatic's confiscated property.

17. The same shall be done with a priest who, having been bought by the schismatics, accepts their children as though for baptism and sends them back without having baptized them. . . .

19. Priests, deacons, and other churchmen shall not venture to go chanting at places reputed to be miraculous that have not been accredited in a council; but they must inform their bishops and prohibit it to the people, subject to severe punishment. A priest shall not permit another priest or a hieromonk [a monk who has been ordained as a priest] to perform the liturgy, or a hierodeacon [a priest-deacon] to assist, if he does not have the attestation of a bishop that he is a regular priest or deacon and that he has been dispatched on a mission or has been given leave of absence. Likewise, during a church service, he must as far as possible tell them to stop and especially forbid them from taking part in the liturgy. Coming forth, he shall speak about this without equivocating or truckling to anyone, regardless of how high in ecclesiastical dignity the other may be.

20. A priest, because he is the pastor of those entrusted to him, must watch whether schismatic monks and teachers, or sycophants and hypocrites, enter the house of any parishioner; and should he see any, he must, under penalty of divestment of the priesthood and civil punishment, seize them and send them to the house of the bishop.

21. Priests should not make a commercial enterprise from the performance of their ministry: for example, baptisms, marriages, funerals, and the like, but should be satisfied with the remuneration willingly given them. This shall be especially watched with respect to the requiem service on the fortieth day after death, for which priests demand great prices even if they are not asked about it. They themselves often do not think of conducting a requiem service on the fortieth day after death, but forcibly extort payments as though they were a duty on death. This is one evil that, if a bishop neglects to suppress it, shall furnish sufficient reason for him to be summoned to the Most Holy Ruling Synod for judgment.

22. Whereas it is His Imperial Majesty's intention to arrange the churches in such a way that a sufficient number of parishioners shall be registered at each one, and to determine what every parishioner shall owe the clergy of his church annually, so that, from their donation, all the clergy may have adequate subsistence, accordingly, in compliance with His Imperial Majesty's ukase, the Most Holy Ruling Synod, concurring with upstanding lay authorities, shall convene a council and enact the intended decree. When this has been accomplished, then priests must not thereafter seek even the smallest remuneration for the religious services that have been assigned to them unless

someone should, of his own free will, wish to present some gift. But even that is not to be offered at the time when the priest is fulfilling some requirement, but after the passage of several weeks.

23. The Fourth Holy Ecumenical Council of Chalcedon, in the sixth canon, forbids the absolute ordination of priests and deacons without their becoming affiliated with a specified church, or the performance of any function related to the priesthood or the diaconate by those who are ordained in this manner. While priests and deacons in Russia are not ordained absolutely, yet many are ordained and affiliated with a single church, beyond the number of priests or deacons required; and many, having left their church, wander hither and yon, which in effect creates the same condition as absolute ordination. In order that henceforth there shall be no such disorder, laymen must not accept such priests and deacons at any kind of church service, and bishops must not ordain more than are needed. Those who have left their church, wherever such are found, shall be seized and punished. And if they should not desire to return to their churches and to serve therein in an orderly manner until death, and that under surety of honest persons, then they shall be divested of the priesthood. No superfluous priests shall be ordained under any conditions, for many are ordained and taken into the clergy who are fleeing from official duty. For this reason, their number shall soon be determined by *ukase*.

24. If a priest or a deacon who has been divested of his ecclesiastical dignity by a bishop for the aforementioned crime, or for some other, should travel about the land in the guise of a priest or deacon and undertake to officiate at sacred services, then, after someone like this has been apprehended, he shall be sent to the Most Holy Ruling Synod, and from the Synod, he shall be referred to civil judgment. A bishop himself is free to refer such a one to civil judgment, where it is fitting.

25. But if a parish becomes so impoverished through some unavoidable exigency that it is quite impossible for a priest, together with the other churchmen, to subsist, then the bishop himself shall take care of them, not permitting them to roam, and he is to assign them where a priest is required.

26. A priest shall not, of his own accord, without his bishop's permission, venture to enlist in a military regiment, and military authorities shall not accept such persons. For violation of this, a priest shall be given over to severe punishment, and bishops shall submit written reports concerning this to the Synod as regards the military authorities (if someone among them errs in this way not on account of a priest's subterfuge, but willfully, and undertakes to defend the priest by force), and from the Synod, justice shall be sought in the Military College.

27. In many churches a priest does not accept outsiders among the churchmen, but fills the vacancies of that office with his sons and kinsmen, sometimes

even exceeding the need, heedless of whether they are suitable or proficient in reading and writing. This, over and above other sufficient reasons, is especially harmful because it is thereby easier for a priest to act unrestrainedly, to be unconcerned with church ritual and order, and to conceal schismatics. Article 11, mentioned above, will not be carried out by such a one. Accordingly bishops must most zealously eliminate this evil and severely punish the priests who act in violation, except that, in accordance with the decision of the parishioners and with the permission of his particular bishop, a priest may install one, and only one, of his sons, who is capable of singing and reading, as a sexton or sacristan, and the rest, who have been well educated, shall be placed in other churches or in some other honest occupation.

28. It is not enough merely to consider these other matters—whether priests, deacons, and other church people are given to disorderly conduct, whether they raise a clamor in the streets when drunk, or what is worse, whether they are drunkenly noisome in the churches, whether they perform public church prayers in two or more parts simultaneously, whether they wrangle at meals like boors, whether they extort regalement while visiting, or whether (and this becomes intolerable shamelessness) they flaunt their bravery in fist fights. For such offenses, they shall be severely punished—but a bishop must diligently command them this, that they maintain a good personal appearance, namely, that their outer clothing, even if it is poor, be clean and only black, not any other color, that they do not go about with their heads uncovered, that they do not lie down to sleep in the streets, that they not drink in taverns, that they not display their prowess and fortitude in drinking while visiting as guests, and so on, in the same vein as this. These indecencies show them to be rogues; yet they are placed among the people as pastors and fathers.

29. Henceforth, all priests shall personally be in possession of books that are customarily called *metriki*, that is, parish registry books, in which are recorded the births and baptisms of the children in their parish, designating the year and day and naming the parents and godparents. Likewise, which children died without receiving baptism, together with an additional statement of the reason why the child was deprived of Holy Baptism. They shall also record in those books the persons of their parish who are united in matrimony. Likewise, those who die and are buried, with a statement that, in accordance with their Christian obligation, they expired in repentance; and if someone was not buried, they shall specifically state the reason why he did not receive a Christian burial, with a designation of the year and day. These books shall be declared to the Episcopal Chancery annually; how many are born and die shall be reported to the Episcopal Chanceries every four months, and written

notification concerning that shall be made from the Episcopal Chanceries to the Synod.

30. There must be thorough study in the Most Holy Ruling Synod about what to do with widowed priests and deacons, especially those who have been widowed in youth.

There existed heretofore the custom of making them monks; but how can such a one pronounce before God the pledge that he does not enter the monastic life out of need? What if he does not feel this vocation in himself and does not especially desire it? It is not necessary to force them, but they may be tonsured and placed on probation if they are freely willing.

5

Pososhkov on Poverty and Wealth

In his efforts to modernize Russia, Peter the Great encountered many opponents but also many supporters. Among those who admired the Tsar's activity was Ivan Tikhonovich Pososhkov (1652–1726). The self-taught son of a peasant, Pososhkov himself through his years of multi-faceted service with the government had become aware of numerous defects in Russian life and of the general corruption among state officials. Unlike many of his contemporaries, he put his impressions and plans for correcting Russia's shortcomings into writing. The most important of his works is *A Book on Poverty and Wealth.* Written for Peter the Great (although it is not known whether Peter actually saw it), the *Book* glorifies Russian autocracy and advocates minute regulation of every phase of the life of the tsar's subjects. It is critical on the other hand, of the ignorance of the Russian clergy, the abuses among officials, the laziness and illiteracy of the peasants, the corruption of the courts, and the disrespect for the merchants. Shortly after Peter's death, Pososhkov was arrested and imprisoned in the Fortress of Peter and Paul, where he died in 1726. In the mid-nineteenth century, the historian M. P. Pogodin (1800–1875) discovered Pososhkov's work and acclaimed it as the first major critique

---

From I. T. Pososhkov, *Kniga o skudosti i bogatstve i drugie sochineniia* [*A Book on Poverty and Wealth and Other Works*] (Moscow: Akademiia Nauk, 1951), pp. 13–14, 113–114, 117–118, 120, 122–125, 134–135, 138, 166, 168, 170–172, 178–179, 182–183. Translation mine. Words in brackets are mine.

of mercantilism, antedating Western European economic writings by at least fifty years—a view that was subsequently accepted by Soviet historians.

The Tsardom's wealth consists not of an abundance of money in the Tsar's treasury, nor is the Tsardom wealthy when [members of] the Tsar's Council wear gold-embroidered clothes; but the Tsardom is wealthy when all the people are wealthy according to their own standards; wealthy in their own domestic resoruces and not as a result of outward appearances or the addition of ornaments. We do not enrich ourselves by ornamenting our apparel, but those states that bring these various ornaments to us do [enrich themselves]. Above material wealth we all ought to concern ourselves with immaterial wealth; that is, genuine truth. . . .

Merchants should not be reduced to insignificance, because without merchants no kingdom, be it large or small, can exist. Merchants are allies of the military; military fight and merchants aid and prepare all the necessities for them.

On account of this it is essential to give them substantial protection. Because, as a soul cannot exist without a body, so the military cannot exist without merchants; it is impossible for the military to exist without merchants and for merchants to live without the military.

The Tsardom is enlarged by the military and is enriched by the merchants. Because of this they ought to be protected from the offenders; it should also be seen that officials cause them no harm. There are many thoughtless people who hold merchants in contempt, despise them, and insult them without any cause. Yet nowhere in the world is there an occupation that has no need for a merchant.

It is worthwhile to protect merchants not only from outside offenders but also to see to it that they do not offend one another. Members of other occupations should not be allowed to join merchants and create for them great difficulties. They [the merchants] should be given free trade to enable them to enrich themselves and to increase the treasury of His Imperial Majesty.

When Russian merchants receive free trade, and neither members of other occupations nor foreigners can interfere in their business, the collection of taxes will be in better condition [than it is now]. I believe that if the present system of collection of taxes were to be employed, two or three times the amount would be collected. Today, however, more than half [of the taxes] is lost due to [the graft of] various officials. . . .

Each occupation should lead an honest life—not to sin before God and not to be indebted to the Tsar. The way a person makes a living [should determine] the kind of service he should render. If he is a soldier, let him be a soldier; those belonging to other occupations should fully protect their own. . . .

And should God will that every member of a respective occupation concern himself with his own affairs, then all occupations will flourish and merchants will prosper so much as to be beyond comparison with the present wealth. And taxes could be collected from them twice as great, and I believe even thrice or more, than are presently collected.

Because today trade is carried on by *boyars*, nobles, and their people, officers, soldiers, and peasants—and because they all trade without paying taxes, merchants also carry on a great deal of trade in these people's name without paying taxes. . . . And if a tax collector recognizes them and wants to collect from them, nobles then forcibly intervene in their behalf with the result that no government official dares approach them. And there are [among these people] wealthy individuals whose trade volume reaches 500 or 600 [*rubles*] but who pay no taxes to the Great Sovereign.

And if all this were corrected, then the merchantry would revive as if from sleep.

The merchants also adhere to an old unjust custom: They harm and cheat each other; and foreigners, as Russians, sell goods that seem outwardly to be good but really are of poor quality or of poor workmanship. Some goods, even very poor, are covered up with good ones and sold dearly. By this device they take advantage of inexperienced people; they cheat them in weight, measures, and price. . . .

Penalties should be imposed for such actions, and government officials should collect them from violators immediately upon discovery. Upon payment of the fine, their names should be entered into an appropriate register and submitted monthly to an appropriate office.

And foreigners who come to fairs without the approval of the Head of the Commerce Administration should not be allowed to trade in large or small quantities. . . .

The strange thing is that after they [foreign merchants] come to us with their trifles they set low prices for our material goods, and double prices or even more for theirs.

As if this were not enough, they even price the money of our Great Tsar, which is none of their business; they should price the money of their sovereigns because they have power over their rulers. But our great Emperor is autocrat in his state, and if he should decree that a *kopeck* is worth a *grivna*, then it can be so. We, in our Tsardom, by the will of our monarch, are free to put a price on commodities they bring to us; if they do not like it they will not sell it; like it or not, we will not forcibly take anything from them. We should make one thing firm: Those commodities that have not been sold, or those that are useless, should not be allowed to be stored ashore; they must be taken back or kept aboard ship.

There was a time when they were arrogant; they took every advantage over us when our monarchs were not interested in trade affairs and empowered the *boyars* with it. When foreigners came, they would bribe important persons with a gift, one or two hundred *rubles* worth, and would in return reap a profit 1000 times that because the *boyars* held the merchantry in contempt and were willing to sell all of merchantry for a penny. . . .

If foreigners should not trade with us because of their pride or intransigence for two or three or even five or six years, then our merchants would benefit greatly because goods that were selling in our Rus for a *ruble* would sell for a half or even less. Foreigners should not be allowed to buy at the lower prices because that price resulted from their intransigence.

Without any justification they placed a high price on their goods and thereby caused great hardship; for this not our but their intransigence is responsible. They found fault with our Russian money which is none of their business. When our money comes to their land, then if they do not take our *kopeck* for even a penny, they are free to do it; it is their land and their freedom. But in our land they have no such authority; here the authority belongs to our monarch by whose will we also have some freedom. But they, having come to our land, have put a price on our money and raised prices on all of their goods. . . . A *pud* of copper formerly sold for three *rubles*, but now it sells for seven or eight *rubles*; tin sold for about three *rubles*, but now it sells for more than six; wax was sold for a *poltina* a *pud*, but now it sells for three times as high. Writing paper that sold for eight *grivnas* per foot now sells for two *rubles*. A glass jar that sold for three *rubles* now sells for ten. They have doubled or tripled the price on all foreign goods, and want thereby to reduce the Russian Tsardom to poverty. They take advantage over us, and instead of material goods they bring us various drinks which they praise highly: "This drink is genuine and very good." They hope that through such praise we will buy more and give them more money. And we drink their drink, and then either vomit or excrete it. They also bring to us glassware so that we would buy it, break it, and throw it away. What we ought to do is to build five or six factories and then flood all of their countries with our glassware. . . .

And if they should refuse to sell their goods at a fair price, then they should be told to take all of their commodities home. And poor quality or useless commodities should not be accepted even at half the price if we are to prevent them from thinking that we are fools and from taking undue advantage of us. . . .

For the sake of national preservation, both monks and merchants should be kept away from excessive drinking and luxurious life; they especially should be kept away from foreign drinks; not only should they not drink themselves, but also they should not bring any into an inn to someone else. I think it would not be a bad idea to extend this prohibition to all government officials, so that they would not develop a habit for foreign drinks and would not lose money easily. . . .

We do not gain anything from foreign drinks except vanity, loss of our Russian wealth, and harm to our health. For it we give them from Russian Tsardom our copper money and foreign currency, and other necessities without which they cannot exist and which make them rich. From the foreigners we get only what we drink, and which we either excrete or vomit, and which in addition endangers our health and shortens our life. . . .

It would also be desirable to introduce among merchants the idea that they should aid and not ruin one another. In case they are unable to improve themselves with their own money, they should be allowed to borrow from the Tsar's treasury or local government agencies a sum of money equal to a portion of their business so that no industrious individual would fall into poverty from a misfortune. . . .

Peasant life is poor for no other reason than of their own laziness, the disconcern of administrators, and finally, oppression by the nobility and non-protection [by the state].

If His Tsarist Majesty's taxes were levied on the land they own on the basis of the amount of land each peasant cultivates, and if these taxes were collected from them during advantageous time, and if the nobles would take nothing from the remainder and would not impose an additional burden on them, but would collect only their own dues, and require of them work for their use of land, and would look after their own peasants so that they would not waste time outside Sundays and holidays but be constantly at work, peasants would never become poor.

And peasants who become lazy should be severely punished, because any peasant who becomes dissolute will never go straight but will lean toward banditry and other thievery.

The peasant should diligently plough land during the summer and work in the forest during the winter. This will provide sufficiently for his domestic needs; and he may even obtain some profit for himself.

And if he has no useful work at his own house, then he should go to places where people work for hired wages so that he will not waste time; and if he should do this no peasant will be poor.

To protect peasant life it is essential to see to it that their homes be rebuilt to enable them to live more freely and peacefully; peasants in poor villages are often ruined because they are very crowded, and whenever one house catches on fire the whole village is burnt and not one house is left standing. Through fire they lose not only homes, but food and cattle, and this reduces them to great poverty. If they were not crowded they would not suffer as much. . . .

Peasants also suffer greatly from bandits; if a village has twenty or thirty or more [peasant homes] and a small band of bandits invades the home of a peasant and begins torturing and burning him and taking his belongings openly on their wagons, his neighbors, although they see and hear all this happening, do not leave their own homes to rescue him. As a result bandits do as they wish and torture many peasants to death. Because of this it is impossible for any peasant to become rich.

To protect them from such ruin it is essential to issue in all villages and settlements a firm decree providing that in case bandits should come to someone, and neighbors in that village or settlement would not come to his rescue and would not pursue the bandits, then all those neighbors should be knouted; and whatever has been taken by the bandits because of their negligence should be restored double by his neighbors.

And if bandits should be numerous so that a given village could not handle them, neighboring villages should be notified, and grown men with arms, hooks, and clubs should go out to apprehend those bandits.

And if peasants from a village should refuse to go, they should be knouted and be forced to help restore the robbed property to the victimized village.

And should someone be tortured to death because of the peasants' unconcern, then a penalty of fifty *rubles* or more should be imposed on all those who failed to come to the rescue.

For if peasants were to live in harmony and were to aid and defend each other, bandits would not dare to attack them suddenly, beat them up, and set [their homes] on fire. And if peasants were to live in harmony and were not to insult each other, they all would be satisfied and would lead holy lives.

Peasants suffer greatly because there are no literate people among them. Villages that have twenty or thirty houses have not one individual that is literate. Any person can come to them with or without an imperial decree and say that he has such a decree and they believe him, and consequently suffer unnecessarily because they all are like the blind who cannot see or understand anything. As a result many individuals come to them without imperial decrees, inflict upon them great losses, and as the peasants cannot argue with them they collect from them money which ruins them.

To protect them from such unjust losses, it seems that it would not be a bad idea to force peasants to send their children ten years of age or younger to governmental clerks to learn how to read and write. I think it would be a good thing if even the smallest village had a literate person. They should be firmly told to let their children be educated, without delay, not less than three to four years. And if they do not let their children be educated, then those children who grow up illiterate should be forced to pay a penalty. For when they learn how to read and write, they will be more useful not only to their nobles but to state interests as well. They will be very useful in the army, and no one will cheat them or illegally take something away from them.

I believe it would also be a good idea to issue a decree for regions of the lower [Volga] to force, if need be, the children of the Mordva people to learn how to read and write. When they learn they will like it, because, as in Russia, their villages are visited by soldiers and other government officials, sometimes with and sometimes without authorization, who do as they please because they [the natives] are illiterate and without any protection. . . .

If their children were to learn how to read and write, they would then be their spokesmen and would not allow them to be harmed as before; on the contrary, they would protect them from all illegal abuses.

Others who would learn reading and writing may learn the Christian faith and may wish to be christened, and little by little those literates could convert to Christianity other of their brethren. . . .

Nobles are not eternal but temporary masters of the peasants; for that reason they do not protect them; their direct master is the autocrat of All-Russia.

Consequently, nobles should not be allowed to ruin peasants; they should be protected by a Tsar's decree stipulating that all peasants are equal because peasant prosperity is the Tsardom's prosperity.

Consequently, it seems to me, it would be desirable to issue a decree for the nobles stipulating how much *corvée* and other obligations they may collect from peasants, and how many days per week they are obliged to work for their nobles and perform other tasks, so that they know clearly how much taxes they must pay to the Emperor, how much to the nobleman, and how much to leave for their own needs. Judges should be instructed to see it that nobles impose nothing in excess of what they are legally entitled to, thus bringing peasants into ruin. . . .

It seems to me that adopting the following [rule] would be very advantageous for the peasants: whenever a peasant completely fulfills his obligation to his noble, his noble cannot demand anything above the agreed amount nor oppress him in any way, but see to it only that he does not waste his time and works as hard as possible to make a living for himself. From such an arrangement those peasants who are astute could make a good living.

And if a peasant should not work on the land, and instead should waste time and not accumulate any surplus, such a peasant should be observed by nobles, government officials, and local officials, and penalized severely in order to prevent other peasants from falling on account of their laziness into poverty, thievery, and drunkenness. . . .

In my judgment, not the nobles but the Tsar should protect the peasants, because the nobles control them only temporarily while the Tsar has them eternally; peasant prosperity means prosperity for the Tsardom, and peasant poverty means poverty for the Tsardom. Because of this the Tsar should concern himself not only with nobles and soldiers but with merchants and peasants as well, in order to prevent them from falling into poverty and to enable them to live in relative abundance.

6

Events Surrounding the Assumption of Power by Empress Anna, 1730

With no successor having been designated, Peter the Great's death in 1725 opened the way to the intrigue, *coups d'état*, and political uncertainty that were to plague Russia until 1762. Between 1725 and 1727 Catherine I, Peter's second wife, was technically the ruler. Power was held, however, by Alexander Menshikov (1673–1729), one of Peter's trusted lieutenants. From 1727 to 1730 the crown belonged to Peter's grandson, Peter II (born in 1715), although the aristocratic Dolgoruky family exercised great influence during this time. The early death of Peter II in 1730 created a new succession crisis, the third in five years. Led by the Golitsyn family, Russian aristocrats invited Anna, the widowed thirty-seven-year-old daughter of Ivan V (who with Peter I had been co-tsar from 1682 to 1696) to rule the empire. The invitation, however, was subject to Anna's acceptance of certain limitations on autocratic powers. Initially Anna accepted the conditions. When on her way to Moscow from her home in Livonia she was informed by representatives of the petty nobility that the terms did not meet with their approval, Anna repudiated the conditions, punished their originators, and, with the aid of her Baltic-German advisers, of whom Ernst von Biron (1690–1771) was the most influential, inaugurated one of the most unenlightened reigns in Russian history.

From Christof Herman von Manstein, *Memoirs of Russia: Historical, Political, Military from the Year 1727–1744* . . . (London: 1770), pp. 25–36. Words in brackets are mine. Certain spellings have been modernized to facilitate reading.

The young Emperor[1] fell sick on the 17th of January [1730] of smallpox. The ignorance of the physicians, who mistook it for merely a violent fever, and the too ungovernable vivacity of this prince were the cause of his death. He would not bear to remain quiet; he opened a window, and the small-pox, which had begun to come out, struck in again, and on the 29th of January (old style) he died in the first of the spring of his youth.

The reign of Peter II had lasted but two years and nine months, and though this Prince was so very young when he died, he was nevertheless, mourned by the whole nation. The Russians of the old stock found in him a prince after their own heart, especially for his having quit Petersburg, and brought back their residence to Moscow. Even at this instance all Russia pronounces this epoch the happiest that it had known for a century past. There was no compulsion to serve in the army, so that everyone could stay at home quietly, enjoy his property, and even improve it. Except a few of the great, who were jealous of the power of the Dolgorukys,[2] all the rest of the nation were content. Universal joy appeared on every face, the treasury was replenishing, and the town of Moscow was lifting its head again out of the ruin into which Peter I had precipitated it by his taste and predilection for Petersburg. There was nothing went amiss but the marines and the army, which would have been entirely ruined if this reign had continued some years more on the same foot.

It would be difficult to define the character of Peter II on the account of his extreme youth. It is generally, however, agreed that he had a good heart, a great deal of vivacity and penetration, and an excellent memory. It was enough for him to hear anything once to retain it; so that, if with so many naturally good qualities he could have profited of the instructions of others, it is likely he would have become a very great Prince. . . .

To the Dolgorukys it was reproached that they had contrived to hide from all the world the danger of the Emperor's sickness as long as they possibly could; and that as soon as they found there were no hopes of his recovery they had framed a will, by which Princess Catherine [Dolgoruky], who had been betrothed to the Emperor, was instituted Empress and Heiress of the Empire; which will Prince Ivan [Dolgoruky] had signed in the name of the Emperor, having been accustomed to sign the name of that Prince during his life, by his order. Accordingly, scarce had Peter II closed his eyes in death when Prince Ivan came out of the chamber with his drawn sword in his hand, flourishing it, and cried out *Long live Empress Catherine*! but no one joining the cry, he saw that his project was miscarrying; upon which, putting his sword up again in his scabbard, he went home immediately and burnt the will. There are, however, many who will have it that no such will was ever made, and that it was merely an invention of the enemies of the Dolgorukys to accomplish the ruin of that family. But as this was inserted in the manifestos which were published against these princes as one of the principal articles of their guilt, I could not well avoid mentioning it; besides, as to the fact above specified of the Prince Ivan's coming out of the apartment with his sword drawn, it is perfectly true; I had it from a man of great veracity; and even from one of the family itself: it is also certain that if the Dolgorukys had not been at variance among themselves, the Princess Catherine would infallibly have mounted the throne, but the disunion that reigned among their chiefs was the destruction of all of them.

The council of state, the senate, and such of the principal generals of the army as were then at Moscow, assembled immediately after the death of Peter II and sat in close committee in a chamber of the palace of Kremlin. The High-Chancellor Golovkin announced to the assembly the death of the Emperor, and as soon as he had done speaking, the Prince Dmitri Mikhailovich Golitsyn[3] got up and said that "since, by the demise of Peter II the whole male line of Peter I was extinct, and that Russia had suffered extremely by despotic power, to the prevalence of which the great number of foreigners brought in by Peter I had greatly contributed, it would be highly expedient to limit the supreme authority by salutary laws and not to confer the imperial crown on the new Empress that should be chosen but under certain conditions"; concluding with putting the question to the whole assembly, whether "they did not approve this proposal?" They all assented to it, without any the least opposition. Upon which the Prince Basil Lukich Dolgoruky proposed the Duchess Dowager of Courland; alleging, that as the crown was now falling to a female, it was but just to prefer the daughter of the Tsar Ivan V, the elder brother of Peter I to those of this emperor; that though the duchess of Mecklenburg[4] was the eldest, it was to be considered that she was married to a foreign Prince, whereas the Duchess of Courland was actually a widow, and not being above thirty-six years of age, might marry, and give heirs to Russia.

The true reason, however, for preferring the duchess of Courland was that she being at Mittau, the remoteness of that place would afford time for the firmer establishment of the republican system.

All the votes then united in her favor, and it was agreed that the council of state, which was at that time constituted of seven members of whom the majority were the Dolgorukys or their relations, should have the whole power, and the assembly framed the following articles:

1. That the Empress Anna was to reign only, in virtue of the resolves, upon deliberation of the privy-council.

2. That she should not declare war nor make peace on her own authority.

3. That she would not lay any new tax, or bestow any post or place of consequence.

4. That she would punish no gentleman with death unless he was duly convicted of his crime.

5. That she should not confiscate anyone's property.

6. That she should not alienate of dispose of any lands belonging to the crown.

7. That she should not marry, nor choose an heir, without asking upon all these points the consent of the privy-council.

The assembly then chose three members to notify to the Empress her accession to the throne, and to propose to her the conditions under which she was to reign.

On the part of the council was deputed the Prince Basil Lukich Dolgoruky; on the part of the senate, the Prince Michael Golitsyn; and on the part of the nobility, the Lieutenant-General Leontev.

In the instructions given to these deputies, it was enjoined to them to require of the Empress that she should sign the above articles, and that she should not bring her favorite with her to Moscow, Biron,[5] gentleman of the chamber. . . .

The council of state imagined they had sufficient precaution against the restoration of despotic government, having exacted from the whole army an oath that it would not serve the Empress but conjointly with the senate. Moreover, before the assembly broke up, they had forbidden, under pain of death, the acquainting the new Empress of anything that had been debated and resolved. She was not to receive advice of her election and of the conditions under which she was to mount the throne but at first hand from the deputies.

Nothwithstanding which the lieutenant-general Iaguzhinskii dispatched that night his aide-de-camp, Mons. Sumarokov to Mittau to apprize the Empress of every thing.

He wrote to her, and entreated her to hasten her departure from Mittau as soon as the deputies should have their audience; to submit to all the conditions that should be required of her; and for the rest, to trust to his counsels: that, in the meanwhile, until her arrival at Moscow, he would use his best endeavors to increase the party of such as were not at all pleased at this government by the council of state; that his father-in-law, the high-chancellor Golovkin, was already on her side, and that after the arrival of her Majesty everything would be terminated to her wish.

Sumarokov had a good deal of difficulty to pass, all the roads round the capital being strictly guarded. Every traveller was diligently searched for papers or letters: however, he disguised himself so well, that he got through all undiscovered. But that was not all; he had the same dangers to encounter at the advanced posts on the confines of Courland, who had orders to stop all persons that should come by the way from Moscow. The apprehension of this made him take such a large circuit that in spite of all obstacles he got safe to Mittau. It is true he had been necessarily so much retarded in his journey that he had barely time to deliver his dispatches to the Empress before the deputies arrived and demanded audience.

The Prince Dolgoruky had, I do not know by what means, discovered that a courier from Moscow had got thither before the deputies, and had had admission to the Empress. Upon this he ordered a strict search to be made for him; and finding that he was just set out on his return, he sent to pursue him, and he was accordingly brought back to Mittau. The deputies then ordered him an unmerciful bastonade; made him he put into irons and carried to Moscow, where the count Iaguzhinskii was also seized, and thrown into close prison. . . .

The Empress consented, without making any difficulty, to the signing of whatever the deputies presented to her on the part of the privy-council. She did not even oppose the leaving her favorite behind her at Mittau, and got immediately in readiness to set out for Moscow.

Her Majesty came on the 20th of February to a village called Sviatskii (or *All Saints*) situated two leagues from Moscow, where she stopped for five days. As soon as she was arrived there, the high-chancellor, at the head of the members of the privy-council, repaired thither, and presented her with the ribbon of St. Andrew, and star, in a gold basin. As soon as the Empress saw it, she said, "It is true, I had forgot to put the '*order on*' "; and taking it with her own hands out of the basin she made one of her attendants put it on her, without suffering any of the members of the privy-council to help her on with it; and when the high-chancellor was beginning to harangue her, she stopped him, and prevented his going on.

On the same day, she appointed the Prince Saltykov, a very near relation to the mother of the Empress, lieutenant-colonel of the guards. This was the first act of authority she took upon her since her accession to the throne. The rest of her conduct, after her arrival at Moscow gave many of the members of the council and senate reason to think that she was satisfied with the restrictions laid on despotic power. She signed anew all that the council of state required and affected to submit cheerfully to all the conditions.

Her secret conduct was very different from this her public one. Her favorite, whom, at the requisition of the council, she had left behind, was arrived at Moscow; and she took all the pains imaginable to form a strong party. She tried to engage the guards by her liberality to those who daily did duty about her person. In short, she left no arts or managements unemployed towards effectuating her purpose of creating misunderstandings among the members of the council of state. Everything succeeded to her wish. It had been remarked to them that the family of the Dolgorukys, and its connections, would be the only persons that would be benefited by the smallness of the Empress's influence; that they had tied up her hands only to establish the more firmly the power which they had acquired under Peter II; that there was already of that family many of the members of the privy-council, and of the senate; that little by little, the number would go on augmenting; and that they ought to reflect on the conduct of that family, after the death of the late Emperor, at which time they had aspired to transmit the imperial crown to their family, in which not having been able to succeed, they had not given up the hope of bringing it about in time, by their circumscription of the supreme power.

Neither was it omitted the instilling a mistrust into the lesser nobility, which is very numerous in Russia, by giving them to understand that none of them stood any chance of obtaining any preferment of the least consequence, while the council of state should have all the power in their hands; as each member would make a point of procuring the most considerable employments for his respective relations and creatures; and that, properly speaking, they would be the slaves of the council: whereas, if the Empress was to be declared sovereign, the least private gentleman might pretend to the first posts of the empire with the same currency as the first Princes: that there were examples of this under Peter I when the greatest regard was paid to true merit; and that if that Prince had done acts of severity, he had been obliged to it; besides, that the lesser nobility had nowise suffered by him; on the contrary, they had recovered their consequence under his reign.

Such hints thrown out with proper discretion did not fail to producing the expected effect. The guards who, even to the private soldiers, are constituted of hardly any but the nobles of the country, formed meetings. Several hundreds of country-gentlemen assembled at the houses of the Princes Trubetskoi, Bariatynskii, and Cherkasskii, as being those in whom they had the greatest confidence, and who were in the interest of the Empress. These did not fail of animating them more and more, till, on the 8th of March, they judged them ripe for the point at which they wanted them. It was then that these Princes, at the head of six hundred gentlemen, went to wait on the Empress; and having obtained an audience, entreated for her to order the council of state and the senate to assemble, for the examination of certain points touching the regency. The Empress having consented, she ordered, at the same time, Count Saltykov, lieutenant-general, and lieutenant-colonel of the guards, to have all the avenues well guarded, and not to permit any one to go out of the palace. The guards were also commanded to have their pieces loaded with ball, and special care was taken to acquaint all those who came to court of the precautions which had been ordered.

While these arrangements were taking, the council of state and the senate were assembled. The Empress gave orders that both these bodies should appear before her. These princes then having repaired to the presence-chamber, or hall with the canopy, the Count Matveev, advancing towards her Majesty, spoke and said that he was deputed by the whole nobility of the empire to represent to her that she had been, by the deputies of the council of state, surprised into the concessions she had made; that Russia having for so many ages been governed by sovereign monarchs, and not by council, all the nobility entreated of her to take into her own hands the reins of government; that all the nation was of the same opinion, and wished that the family of her Majesty might reign over them to the end of time.

The Empress, at this speech, affected great surprise: "How," said she, "was it not then with the will *of the whole nation that I signed the act presented to me at Mittau*?" Upon which the whole assembly answered, "No." At this she turned toward Prince Dolgoruky, and said to him, "*How came you then, Prince Basil Lukich, to impose on me so?*" She then ordered the high-chancellor to go and bring her the writings which she had signed. This being done, she made him read them with an audible voice; and at each article she stopped him, and asked if such an article was for the good of the nation. The assembly having to all and each of them constantly answered "*No*;" she took the deeds out of the hands of the high-chancellor, and tore them saying, "*These writings then are not necessary.*' She declared at the same time, "That as the empire of Russia had *never been governed but by one sole monarch*" she "claimed the same prerogatives as her ancestors had had, from whom she derived her crown by right of inheritance, and not from the election of the council of state, as they had pretended; and that whoever should oppose her sovereignty should be punished, as guilty of high-treason." This declaration was received with applause, and nothing was heard all over the town but acclamations and shouts of joy.

The Empress also gave assurance, "that though she had taken the supreme power into her own hands, she should nevertheless make it her care to govern with all imaginable mildness; that she would have nothing more at heart than the happiness of her people; that she would constantly avail herself of the good counsels of her senate, composed of persons of the greatest experience and the most acknowledged probity; and that she should never have recourse to acts of rigor, unless in the utmost extremity."

To secure her then against any enterprises of the disaffected, there were guards posted in all the streets; the troops took afresh the oath of allegiance; and couriers were dispatched into all the provinces with the notification of the Empress having taken on her the supreme authority.

The lesser nobility and the common people, who had dreaded the government by a council of state, rejoiced much at this alteration of things: but the evening after that this affair had been decided, there was observed an Aurora Borealis, which, overspreading the whole horizon, made it appear all in blood. This phenomenon made such an impression on the superstitious people as to create a general terror; and in the sequence of time the Russians pretended that this presage was but too fatally verified by the streams of blood which Biron caused to be shed in that country.

The consternation of the members of the council, and especially of the Dolgorukys, was extreme, when they were summoned to appear before the Empress. Prince Dmitri Mikhailovich Golitsyn was the only one of them who preserved serenity of countenance, with even some disdain. He said to some of his friends, "*Well! the feast was prepared, but the guests were not worthy of it; I know I shall be the victim of this. Be it so. It is for my country I shall suffer. I feel the end of my career; but those who make me now mourn will have longer cause to mourn than I. . . .*"

Notes

1. Peter II, grandson of Peter the Great, ruled from 1727 to 1730.

2. The Dolgorukys were an ancient and influential family in Russia. Their influence rose to unprecedented heights during the reign of Peter the Great and immediately following his death.

3. Like the Dolgorukys, the Golitsyns were an ancient aristocratic family of Russia.

4. The Duchess of Mecklenburg had left her husband in 1719 and returned to Russia to live.

5. Ernst von Biron (1690–1771), was a close associate of Empress Anna during her reign (1730–1740), and some Russian historians refer to this period as "Bironovshchina," the rule of Biron.

7

Events Surrounding the Assumption of Power by Empress Elizabeth, 1741

Before she died, on October 17, 1740, Anna named as her successor an infant boy, Ivan VI (born in August 1740), the son of her sister's daughter, Anne of Mecklenburg and Prince Anthony Ulrich von Brunswick-Bevern-Lüneburg. She also stipulated that until he reached the age of seventeen her close confidant Biron was to act as regent. These provisions were made without consulting the Senate, the Holy Synod, or any other important institutions and individuals, including the all-powerful Guard Regiments. A conspiracy consequently developed against Biron's regency, led by Field Marshal Burkhard Christoph Munnich (1683–1767), commander of the Russian armies. On November 9, 1740, Munnich arrested Biron, making it possible for Princess Anne, mother of Ivan VI, to proclaim herself regent of Russia with Munnich first minister. Early in March 1741, Munnich was replaced by Count A. I. Osterman (1686–1747), for many years an architect of Russian foreign policy. German in-fighting for control of the Russian crown came to an end on December 5, 1741, when Peter the Great's daughter Elizabeth, with the aid of the guards arrested the entire Brunswick family, deposed Ivan VI, and assumed power.

The day after the decease of the Empress [Anna], the senate, the clergy, and all who were at that time of any consequence in Petersburg, were summoned to the summer-palace, where the Empress had passed the last days of her life; the troops were put under arms, and the duke of Courland [Biron] caused the act to be publicly read by which he was declared regent of the empire of Russia till the Emperor Ivan VI should have completed his seventeenth year. Every one then took the oath of allegiance to the new Emperor, and everything passed off quietly enough for the first days; but as the duke was universally detested, the murmuring soon began to break out.

From Christof Herman von Manstein, *Memoirs of Russia: Historical, Political, Military from the Year 1727 to 1744* . . . (London: 1770), pp. 264–275, 279–281, 308–326. Manstein took an active part in some of these events. Words in brackets are mine. Certain spellings have been modernized to facilitate reading.

The regent [Biron], who had spies everywhere, soon learnt that he was spoken of with contempt; that some officers of the guards, especially of the regiment of Semenevskii, of which Prince Anthony Ulrich was lieutenant-colonel, had said that if the Prince would undertake anything against the regent they would readily assist him. He was also informed that Princess Anne and her spouse resented their being excluded from the regency. Beginning then to be uneasy at this, he caused several officers to be taken up and carried prisoners to the citadel: Grammatin, the adjutant of the Prince, was one of them. The general Ushakov, president of the secret chancery, and the solicitor-general, Prince Trubetskoi, had orders to examine them with all imaginable severity. Some of them had the knout inflicted on them, to bring them to any impeachment of others; in short, hardly a day passed while this regency lasted without some being apprehended. . . .

[On the night of November 18, 1740, there was set in motion a palace revolution masterminded by Marshall Burkhard Munnich (1683–1767) with the assistance of his aide-de-camp, General Christof Herman von Manstein, the author of this account.]

Manstein entered the place; and not to make too much noise, he made the detachment follow him at a distance. All the centinels suffered him to pass in without any opposition; for, as he was personally known to all the soldiers, they imagined he might be sent to the duke upon some affair of consequence, so that he crossed the guards, and got as far as the apartments, without any difficulty. . . . In the chamber he found a great bed, in which the duke [Biron] and duchess were lying buried in a profound sleep. Not even the noise he had made in forcing open the door had waked them. Manstein having got close to the bed, drew the curtains, and desired to speak with the regent. Upon this, both started up in a surprise and began to cry out loud, judging rightly enough that he was not come to bring them any good news. Manstein happening to stand on the side on which the duchess lay, the regent threw himself out of bed, on the ground, certainly with an intention to hide himself under the bed; but this officer springing quickly round to the other side, threw himself upon him, and held him fast embraced till the guards came in. The duke having at length got upon his legs again, and wanting to disengage himself from their hold, distributed blows with his double fist to the right and left, to which the soldiers made no return but with strokes from the butt-end of their muskets; and throwing him down again on the floor, they crammed a handkerchief into his mouth and bound his hands with an officer's sash; then they led him, naked as he was, to the guardroom, where they covered him with a soldier's cloak, and put him into a coach of the marshal's that was waiting for him. An officer was placed in it by the side of him, and he was carried to the winter-palace.

While the soldiers were struggling with the duke, the duchess was got out of bed in her shift, and running after him as far as into the street, when a soldier took her in his arms and asked Manstein what he should do with her. He bid him carry her back to her chamber; but the soldier not caring, it seems, to take the trouble of it, threw her down on the ground, in the midst of the snow, and there left her. The captain of the guard, finding her in this piteous condition, made her clothes be brought to her, and reconducted her to the apartments she had always occupied.

As soon as the duke was thus on the way to the winter-palace, the same colonel, Manstein, was sent to seize his younger brother Gustavus Biron, who was then at Petersburg. He was lieutenant-colonel of the Izmailov regiment of guards. But this expedition required somewhat more of precautionary measures than the first; for Gustavus Biron was beloved in his regiment, and had a guard of it in his house, consisting of a sergeant and twelve men. And, accordingly, the centinels made at first some resistance, but they soon were laid hold of, and threatened with death if they made the least noise. After which Manstein went into the bedchamber of Biron and made him get up, telling him that he had an affair of great consequence to impart to him. Having then drawn him to the window, he acquainted him with his orders of arrest. Biron wanted to open the window, and began to cry out; but he was instantly let to know that the duke was seized, and under confinement, and that himself would be killed on the least resistance. The soldiers, who had waited in the adjoining room, came in directly, and satisfied him that there was nothing for him but to obey. They gave him a furred cloak, put him into a sledge, and he too was carried to the winter-palace. . . .

As soon as the duke was seized, order was sent to all the regiments that happened to be then at Petersburg to be put under arms, and to assemble round the palace. The Princess Anne then declared herself Grand-Duchess of Russia, and regent of the empire during the minority of the Emperor. She at the same time put on the collar of the order of St. Andrew, and everyone took a new oath of fidelity, in which the Grand-Duchess was mentioned by name, which had not been done in that imposed by the regent. There were none that did not make great demonstrations of joy at seeing themselves delivered from the tyranny of Biron; and from that moment every thing was quiet. Even the piquets were taken away, which the duke of Courland had posted in the streets to prevent commotions during his regency; and there were some who, at the very moment of the event, prognosticated that it would not be the last revolution; and that those who had been the most active in bringing this about would be the first that would be overset by another. Time has shown that they were not in the wrong. . . .

On the 22d of November, the Grand-Duchess bestowed several gratifications and made many promotions:

The Prince, her husband, was declared generalissimo of all the forces of Russia, as well by land as by sea;

Count Munnich had the post of prime-minister;

Count Osterman that of high-admiral, which had been many years vacant;

The Prince Cherkasskii was appointed high-chancellor, a post that had not been filled since the death of count Golovkin;

The Count Golovkin, son of the high-chancellor, deceased, was made vice-chancellor.

Several others had great recompences in ready-money, or in lands. All the officers and subalterns, who had been employed in apprehending the duke, were promoted. Lieutenant-Colonel Manstein had a regiment, and some fine lands, which were taken from him again when the Empress Elizabeth mounted the throne. The soldiers of the guard received their gratifications in money.

Marshal Munnich had not thus worked the duke's fall, but in order to raise himself to the highest degree of fortune; he had retained the same views as when he persuaded the duke to make himself regent; that is to say, to draw to himself the whole power, to leave to the duchess nothing but the title of regent, and himself to do all the functions of it; imagining now to himself that no one would dare to undertake any the least thing against him. He was mistaken. . . .

It has been above set forth that the duke of Courland was, on the same day that he was seized, transferred to Schüsselburg. A commission, composed of several senators, proceeded there on his trail and condemned him to death. He had his pardon. The Princess Anne had, from the first moment of the revolution, resolved to banish him to Siberia. An engineer had been sent there to direct the building of a house, expressly designed for his prison. Marshal Munnich gave the first sketch of it with a pencil, little then imagining that it was for himself he was planning.

In the month of May [1741], the duke of Courland was, with his family, transferred from Schlüsselburg to his new habitation. . . .

The court of Petersburg had not failed to notify to the states of Courland that their duke was seized; that he had had his trial and been found guilty of high-treason; that he and all his family were sent to Siberia, where they were to pass the remainder of their lives. . . .

The Princess Elizabeth [daughter of Peter the Great], though far from satisfied during the whole reign of the Empress Anna, had remained quiet till the marriage of the Prince Anthony Ulrich with the Princess Anne was concluded. Then, indeed, she began to take some steps towards forming a party; all which, however, was transacted with such secrecy that nothing of it transpired while the Empress lived. But after her death, and the seizure of Biron, she began to think more seriously of it. . . .

At Petersburg the Princess began with gaining over some soldiers of the guards of the regiment of Preobrazhenskii. The principal of them was one Grunstein, who, from a bankrupt-merchant, had taken on to be a soldier. This man engaged many others, so that little by little there were got as far as thirty grenadiers of the guards to be of the plot. . . . [On December 4, 1741] the Grand-Duchess took the Princess Elizabeth aside, and told her that she had had several intimations concerning her conduct and that, especially, her surgeon [Lestock] had frequent conferences with the French minister [Marquess de la Chetardie], and was plotting treasonable practices against the reigning family; that hitherto, she (the Grand-Duchess) had not wished to give credit to these informations; but that, if they continued, she should be obliged to have Lestock taken up, and that means would be used to force him to confess the truth. The Princess stood out this conversation very well. She protested to the Grand-Duchess that she had never had a thought of undertaking anything against her, or against her son; that she had too much religion to break the oath she had taken; that all these informations were given by enemies, who wanted to make her unhappy; that Lestock had never set his foot in Chetardie the French ambassador's house (which was true, for there had been always a third place chosen for their interviews); that, however, the Grand-Duchess might, if she pleased, have Lestock taken up, which would but serve the more to discover her being guiltless. The Princess Elizabeth shed abundance of tears at this explanation, and succeeded so well in persuading her of her innocence, that the Grand-Duchess (who also wept much) believed her wrongfully accused. . . .

At midnight [of December 5, 1741], the Princess, accompanied by the Vorontsovs and Lestock, repaired to the barracks of the grenadiers of the regiment of Preobrazhenskii; thirty of whom were, as has been observed, personally in the plot. These assembled others, to the number of three hundred, as well subalterns, as private men. The Princess, in a few words, declared her intention to them, and asked their assistance. They all, to a man, consented to sacrifice themselves for her. Their first step of dispatch was to seize the officer of the grenadiers, who lay in the barracks, his name Grews, a Scotchman; after which they took an oath of fidelity to the Princess. She then put herself at the head of them, and marched straight to the winter-palace, and entered, with part of those that followed her, into the guard-rooms, without finding the least resistance. There she told the officers the reason of her coming. They made no show of opposition, and left her to act as she pleased. Centinels were then posted at all the doors and avenues. Lestock and Vorontsov penetrated with a detachment of grenadiers into the apartments of the Grand-Duchess, and made prisoners, her and her husband, her children, and the favorite, that was lodged near them. As soon as this was done, several detachments were sent to seize marshal Munnich, his son, lord steward of the household to the Grand-Duchess; count Osterman, count Golovkin, count Lowenwolde, grand-marshal of the court; baron de Mengden, and some others, persons of less consequence. All these prisoners were carried to the palace of the Princess. She sent Lestock to marshal Lacy, to acquaint him of what she had done; and to declare to him that he had nothing to fear, ordering him at the same time to come directly to her.

The senate, and all the greatest men of the empire that were then at Petersburg, were convened at the palace of the new Empress; and, at break of day all the troops were assembled before it, where, after the declaration to them that the Princess Elizabeth had seated herself on the throne of her father; the oath of fidelity was tendered to them, and taken without any contradiction; so that every thing was presently in as great tranquillity as before.

The same day, the Empress quit the house in which she had resided till then, and took possession of the imperial palace. . . .

On the day of the revolution, the new Empress declared, by a manifesto, that she had ascended her father's throne, in virture of her hereditary right, and that she had caused the usurpers to be seized.

Three days afterwards, another manifesto was published, which was to demonstrate her having an unquestionable title to the imperial crown. It was also therein specified that as neither the Princess Anne nor her husband had any right to the throne of Russia, they should be sent back, with their family, to Germany. They were made to leave Petersburg, with all their domestics, under an escort of the guard, commanded by general Saltykov, who had been at the head of the police in the time of the Empress Anna; they got no father than Riga, where they were stopped from proceeding farther. At first, they were lodged in the citadel, and some months after they were transferred to the fort of Dunamund; and, at length, instead of being permitted to go to Germany, they were brought back into Russia.

They have had different places for their prisons. The Grand-Duchess died in childbed, March 1746. Her body was brought to Petersburg, and buried in the convent of St. Alexander Nevskii. . . .

There was a commission appointed, which was constituted of several senators and others of the Russian nobility, to prepare and conduct their [the prisoners'] trial. They were accused of various crimes. Among others, it was imputed to count Osterman that he had contributed, by his cabals, to the election of the Empress Anna, and that he had suppressed the will of the Empress Catherine.

Count Munnich was charged with having told the soldiers, at the time of his seizing on the duke of Courland, that it was in order to place the Princess Elizabeth on the throne.

Both of them could easily have disproved these accusations, but they were not allowed to make their defense.

The true crimes of all these prisoners were their having incurred the displeasure of the new Empress and their having too well served the Empress Anna.

Besides, the Empress had promised those who assisted her to ascend the throne that she would deliver them from the oppression of foreigners; so that she was obliged to condemn those of them who had been the highest promoted.

The tenor of the sentence was that count Osterman should be broken alive upon the wheel; that marshal Munnich should be quartered; that Count Golovkin, Count Lowenwolde, and the Baron Mengden should be beheaded.

The Empress at once pardoned them all as to their lives; but they were banished into different parts of Siberia. Count Osterman had not his pardon till he was on the scaffold, with his head on the block.

The court caused a manifesto to be published on this occasion, in which all the crimes of which they were accused were specified.

All the fortunes of the exiled, except those that their wives had brought them, were confiscated to the profit of the court, which gratified others with them.

The permission had been indulged to these ladies of going to settle upon their own estates, and of not following their husbands; but not one of them would avail herself of the liberty.

The first care of the Empress, after her getting possession of the imperial power, was to reward those who had served her in this revolution. She began with her favorite, Razumovskii, who was declared chamberlin some months after her coronation. She raised him to the post of grand-master of the hunt, made him a count, and gave him the blue ribbon. Shuvalov, the two Vorontsov brothers, and Balck, who had served the Princess in quality of gentlemen of the chamber, were also made chamberlains.

She declared Lestock actual privy-counsellor, first physician, and president of the college of physicians. The whole company of grenadiers of the regiment of Preobrazhenskii were ennobled and promoted. The private men of them had the rank of lieutenants, and the corporals that of majors; the armourer and quarter-master that of lieutenant-colonels; and the sergeants that of colonels of the army. It was called the company of body-guards. Her Majesty declared herself the captain of it; the Prince of Hesse-Homburg, lieutenant-Captain Razumovskii, and Vorontsov, first lieutenants, with the rank of lieutenants-generals; and the Shuvalovs, lieutenants, with the title of brigadier. . . .

This company committed all imaginable disorders for the first months that the Empress remained at Petersburg. The new noble lieutenants ran through all the dirtiest public-houses, got drunk, and wallowed in the streets. They entered into the houses of the greatest noblemen, demanding money with threats, and took away, without ceremony, whatever they liked. There was no keeping within bounds men who, having been all their lifetime used to be disciplined by drubbing, could not presently familiarize themselves to a more civil treatment. It must have been the work of time to reduce them to good manners. I do not know whether they were ever brought to correct themselves, but the most unruly of them were expelled from the corps and placed as officers in other regiments of the army, where the vacancies were many. An admirable expedient this for procuring excellent officers! . . .

The Empress recalled from Siberia a number of the banished families, of which a great part had been sent thither in the time of the Empress Catherine [I]. All the posts were restored to them which they had occupied before their imprisonment. It was reckoned that since the commencement of the Empress Anna's reign there had been above twenty thousand sent to Siberia. There were five thousand of them of which the habitation could never be discovered, nor any the least news learnt of what was become of them. But as the Empress had recalled all that could be found, there was not a day passed but there were sent at court some new faces of persons who had passed several years successively in the most horrid prisons. . . .

8

Lomonosov's Challenge of the "Normanist Theory," 1749

One of the most controversial issues in Russian history is the question of the origin of the Rus state. The polemic was begun in the eighteenth century by a German philologist and historian, Gottlieb Siegfried Bayer

---

From M. V. Lomonosov, *Polnoe sobranie sochinenii* [Complete Collection of Works] (Moscow: Akademiia Nauk, 1952), vol. 6, pp. 19–25. Translation mine.

(1694–1738), and was later developed by historians Gerhard Friedrich Müller (1705–1783) and August Ludwig von Schlözer (1735–1809). The essence of what subsequently became known as "the Normanist theory" was that everything constructive to be found in the formative stages of the Rus state and its culture—that is, customs, law, political structure, and art—was due entirely to Scandinavian or Norman influence. Like all hypotheses this theory was vulnerable. Its main weakness was that it was largely based on the similarities of some names and terms in the Rus and Scandinavian languages.

The first to challenge the Normanist allegations was Michael V. Lomonosov (171–1765), Russia's greatest eighteenth-century scientist. Though he was not a historian by training and his knowledge of the available sources was scant, Lomonosov assailed the Normanist view and the method of approach employed by its advocates in a series of arguments (the first of which is presented below). He argued that the Rus state had developed long before the Normans came to Rus, and that the Normanists falsified the course of Rus history because their knowledge of the Rus language was insufficient, because they failed to consult native sources, and because they relied too heavily on evidence in foreign languages. With time, these two positions—Normanist and anti-Normanist—led to intensive investigations of the origin of the Rus state and with it to a thorough modification of original premises.

By Her Majesty's decree, the Chancellor's Office of the Academy of Sciences has authorized me to review Professor [Gerhard Friedrich] Müller's [1705–1783] lecture on the origin of the name [Russia] and of the people of Russia, in order to determine whether it contains anything prejudicial to Russia. I have read it several times and having examined it am now submitting to the Chancellor's Office my impressions, which consist of the following points:

1. With respect to sources on which Mr. [*gospodin*] Müller bases his views, the following are quite inappropriate: 1) He promises to rely on foreign authors [only] where native [authors] are not available (p.6)[1] however, contrary to this [pledge] he rejects Russian authors not only summarily but quite frequently and contemptuously, as is explained below in point 9. This he does very unjustly and audaciously. How inadequate foreign authors can be is evident on p. 32, where many falsehoods are stated on the division of the state by Grand Prince Vladimir Sviatoslavich [980–1015]; their [foreign authors'] unfamiliarity with our lands, cities, and princes, is likewise evident throughout his book. Mr. Müller tried in vain to correct and reconcile their gross errors. It is true that our chronicles are not free from fiction interwoven with truth. The history of all ancient peoples in their beginnings is based on mythology. One should not reject the truth along with fiction and then rely exclusively on conjectures. All this shows that he [Müller] did not read many

of the Russian chronicles and consequently *[he]* complains in vain that Russian history has insufficient ancient sources. 2) He uses foreign authors quite inconsistently, and, from a historiographical point of view, inappropriately, for whenever they contradict his own views he considers them unreliable, and when they tend to agree with him he considers them authentic. This can be seen in [his use of] the Saxon Grammar on p. 25 and other places. 3) It is impossible to reach a conclusion from a mere similiarity of names (pp. 7 and 12), but whenever he [Müller] thinks it will benefit him, he does not let the opportunity pass, and interprets the association of names according to his view. On p. 53 he ridiculously made Gostomyl out of Gostomysl. He invented this because he does not understand the Russian language; Gostomyl means anyone who is appreciated by visitors, whereas Gostomysl is one who is thoughtful of visitors.

2. On such erroneous sources [as these], his whole dissertation is based. In it he refutes at first the view about the origin of Moscow from Mosokh and Russians from the River Ross. I read his presentation ten times and could not decide whether he argues against or agrees with these views. Finally I realized that his refutations are indecisive, are intertwined with disorderly arrangement and accordingly resemble a dark night.

3. Mr. Müller writes very little about the Scythians, who should be considered as the first inhabitants of our present-day settlements. Does this [omission] mean that he did not wish to repeat what the late Professor [Gottlieb Siegfried] Bayer [1694–1738] wrote in our "Commentaries."?[2] It would perhaps be more appropriate to think that he did not wish to accept the latter's views because they did not agree with his. I detected here that Mr. Müller omitted one of the best examples for praising the Slavic people, for, as it is known, the Scythians were not afraid of Darius, the Emperor of Persia, or of Macedonian Emperors Philip and Alexander [the Great], or even of the Romans. On the contrary, they not only repelled them but also defeated them. It is easy to conclude from this that the Slavic people must have been very brave because they overcame the mighty Scythians and expelled them from their extensive settlements—an undertaking which could not have been possible without great struggles and important victories. It is true that Mr. Müller says (p. 13) that "your forefathers were known as Slavs because of their famous achievements." But throughout his dissertation he tries to show the opposite, inasmuch as every page reveals how the Russians are beaten, how they are *happily* robbed, how the Scandinavians win, ruin and kill with sword and fire, and how the Huns take Kii with them to war and slavery. All this sounds so strange that if Mr. Müller could write in a more lively style he would turn Russia into such a poor nation as no nation, even the most destitute, has ever been portrayed by any writer.

4. The second main part of his dissertation deals with the Slavic people, whose arrival at their present locations Mr. Müller places rather late, a factor that is contrary to the Slavic names of ancient Russian cities. If Slavs came into the present lands in the fourth century [A.D.], then these cities could not have had Slavic names before Slavs came there. That Slavic people lived within the present-day Russian frontiers, even before the birth of Christ, is not too difficult to prove.

5. Mr. Müller does not consider the Varangians as Slavic people, even though [it is known] that they descended fromt he Roxolans, a Slavic people, who, with the Goths, also a Slavic people, migrated from the Black Sea to the Baltic shores; that they spoke a Slavic language, though somewhat corrupted on account of their association with the old Germans; and that Riurik, with his brothers, was related to Slavic princes, and because of that was invited to Russia to rule. None of this can be deduced from this dissertation, though other sources show this quite clearly.

6. Mr. Müller believes that the Russian name is new, and that it began with Riurik, and from this he then concludes that foreigners did not know it. But how to conclude from this that the Varangians did not consider themselves Rus? The Germans call themselves *Deutsch,* though neither Russians nor French refer to them thusly, even to the present day. The same was true with the Varangians. They descended from the Roxolans and always called themselves Rus, even though other nations did not refer to them so. Nestor's own words show that the Varangians were called Rus, and accordingly, on that account, Novgorodian Slavs and other [Slavic tribes along the Dnieper River] became known as Rus. Is it not rather naive to state, as Mr. Müller does, that the Finns gave the Varangians and the Slavs their name?

7. In addition to these comments, the following of [Müller's] guesses deserve attention: 1) Change of the city of Izborsk into Issaburg is quite inappropriate. This change was devised primarily to refute the ancestors of Gostomysl in Pskov. This [i.e., their presence there], however, is clearly evident in the birth of Olga, the Great Princess, who is called a Pskovian in the *Prolog* and a grand-daughter of Gostomysl by Stryjkowski.[3] 2) Names of princes who descended from the Varangians he [Müller] considers non-Slavic without realizing that Oskold is a Slavic name that means a double ax *(bipennis),* similarly as in Psalm 73, verse 6, [where it states that] it was destroyed by an ax and an *oskord* (or *oskold*). Dir is derived from the word *deru,* that is jack-plane. Olga was named from the relief she gave her mother through her birth. 3) Mr. Müller tries to turn these two princes [Oskold and Dir] into one, using an unsubstantiated guess and failing to realize that the grave of each of them is separately mentioned several times in the Kievan *Synopsis*

[published in 1680]. 4) [Mr. Müller] considers in vain the word *bogatyr* as being of Tartar origin.

8. Because of these unfounded views and empty phrases it is possible to find many contradicting statements [in Müller's work]. In the very beginning of p. 2 and subsequently, he says that through the "Commentaries" we make available the works [of the Academy] to the rest of the world; but on p. 3, in the opening lines, he states that almost no one in the Academy is aware of his own [Müller's] works.

9. On top of this the following [statements] are rather imprudent and prejudicial: 1) The refutation of Kiev's ferry from Nestor's [Chronicle] is presented, as a mere display, for ridicule. 2) He calls Slavic princes Russian Tsars contrary to his own belief and also prejudiciously to the first real Tsars of Russia. 3) Equally and quite inappropriately he calls Slavic princesses Russian Tsarinas. 4) He calls the Novgorodians braggards in order to prove his speculations. 5) He speaks very audaciously and reproachfully of St. Nestor, the chronicler, as for example, *Nestor was wrong,* and this many times.

10. As regards Latin style, a historian, more than other individual, should have an adequate command of Latin, because he must study not only [the views of] ancient Latin historians but also must learn their style. The Russian translation which he himself rendered contains many intolerable errors, which clearly show that he is not that great an expert of the Russian language to be able to correct native Russians as he had boasted about himself in his presumptuous, yet disproving, preface to his history of Siberia, which I think contains as many inadequacies as does the present dissertation.

11. The introduction and conclusion of the dissertation, while full of transgressions against the Russian language, have no though-provoking statements that would bring some cohesion or that would create excitement among the listeners. The entire work of the dissertation is composed without any unity or order, and because of its many disgressions it is very unclear.

12. The end for which this dissertation was completed is this: to bring to our Graceful Sovereign the first fruits of Her Majesty's revitalization of the Academy so that it would be accepted as useful by Russian listeners and by every reader as a new truth. The first [goal] requires seriousness and mag nificence, the second and the third [require] substance, clarity, and originality that had been carefully researched. This lecture does not have these qualities; [on the contrary it] is quite undignified, and for Russian listeners it is ludicrous and provocative, and, in my judgment, it cannot be corrected to the point that it would be dignified enough for public presentation.

Professor Michael Lomonosov reports this.

September 16, 1749

Notes

1. Such references to page numbers refer to Müller's work.
2. "De origine et priscis sedibus Scytharum," *Commentarli Academiae Scientiarum imperialis*, vol. 1 (1728), pp. 385–399.
3. M. O. Stryjkowski, *Kronika Polska, Litewska, Zmodzka; Wszystkiej Rusi*; [*A Chronicle of Poland, Lithuania, Latvia and the Entir Rus*], Krolewiec: 1582.

9

Peter III's Charter to the Nobility, February 18, 1762

The chief beneficiaries during the era of palace revolutions were the nobles. Between 1725 and 1762 they succeeded in reducing their obligations to the state while at the same time retaining all the rights and privileges that went with that service. In 1730, for instance, Anna repealed Peter the Great's decree on primogeniture (see Chapter 2); in 1731 she established a military academy for the sons of the nobility; and in 1736 she reduced the compulsory military service of the nobles to twenty-five years. During Elizabeth's reign (1741–1761) the government established a state bank for the nobles and granted them the right to elect provincial officials with broad executive and judicial powers in local affairs. The nobility's control over their serfs was also expanded. These and other measures helped to weld the heterogeneous Russian nobility into a class-conscious social group. A significant step in that process occurred early in 1762, when the new tsar, Peter III, freed the Russian nobles from all compulsory service to the state. Peter's "friendly gesture," however, failed to save his life. In 1762 he was murdered by his wife's lovers.

All Europe, indeed the greater part of the world, knows what difficulties Peter the Great, wise monarch of immortal memory, Our dear sovereign grandfather

---

From *Polnoe Sobranie Zakonov Russkoi-Imperii . . . (Complete Collection of the Laws of the Russian Empire)*, 1st series, vol. 15, no. 11,444, pp. 912–915. Translation mine. Words in brackets are mine.

and Emperor of all the Russias had encountered in his efforts to bring happiness to his country in instructing the people in military, civil, and political affairs.

To achieve this goal it was essential first to convince the nobles, the chief body of the state, of the great advantages enjoyed by enlightened states over those people who live in ignorance and sloth. Because circumstances then demanded extreme sacrifices from Russian nobles, he [Peter I] did not show any mercy towards them, forced them into military and civil service, induced their youth to study useful arts and sciences, sent them to European countries, and, to achieve the same goal as rapidly as possible, even established various schools in Russia itself.

It is true that in the beginning these innovations were burdensome and unendurable for the nobles, as they were deprived of peace, were forced to leave their homes, were obliged against their will to serve in the army or to perform other service, and were required to register their children [in schools]. Many nobles resented these demands, and some even tried to evade them; but they were fined. Some were even deprived of their property and accused of neglecting their own good as well as that of their children.

These demands, though burdensome in the beginning and accompanied by force, proved to be of much advantage during the reigns of Peter the Great's successors, especially during the reign of Our dear aunt, Empress Elizabeth Petrovna, of glorious memory, who followed in the footsteps of her sovereign father, who supported the knowledge of political affairs and who, by her protection, extended much useful knowledge throughout Russia. We can look with pride at everything that has occurred, and every true son of the country will agree that great advantages have resulted from all this. Manners have been improved; knowledge has replaced illiteracy; devotion and zeal for military affairs has resulted in the appearance of many experienced and brave generals; civil and political concerns have attracted many intelligent people; in a word, noble thoughts have penetrated the hearts of all true Russian patriots who have revealed towards Us their unlimited devotion, love, zeal, and fervor. Because of all these reasons We judge it to be no longer necessary to compel the nobles into service as has been the practice hitherto.

Because of these circumstances, and by virtue of the authority granted to Us by the Almighty, We grant freedom and liberty to the entire Russian nobility, by Our High Imperial Grace, from this moment and forever, to all future generations. They may continue to perform service in Our Empire or in other European countries friendly to Our State on the basis of the following rules:

1. All nobles who are presently in Our service may continue as long as they wish or as long as their health may permit them; those serving in the army should not ask for release or furlough during a campaign or three months

before a campaign; they should wait for release until the end of a war; those serving in the army may request release or retirement permits from their superiors and must wait for these permits; those serving Us in various capacities in the first eight ranks must apply for their release directly to Us; other ranks will released by the departments for which they work.

2. At their retirement We will reward all nobles who serve Us well and faultlessly by promoting them to a higher rank, provided they have served at least one year in the rank from which they retired; those who wish to retire from military service and enter civil service, provided there is a vacancy for them, should be rewarded only if they have served three years in a given rank.

3. Those nobles who have retired or those who have terminated their military or civil service for Us, but who should express a desire to reenter the military service, shall be admitted, provided they prove worthy to those ranks to which they belong and provided they will not be elevated to ranks higher than those of their coservicemen who were equal in rank at the retirement; if they should be elevated in rank this should go into effect from the day they rejoin the service. We issue this rule in order to give preference in promotions to those now in service over those who have retired and also to make it possible for those who have retired from one service to join other services.

4. Those nobles who will be freed from Our service and who would wish to travel to other European countries should immediately receive the necessary passports from Our Foreign College under one condition: namely, that should ever the need demand, those nobles shall return home whenever they are notified. Everyone should fulfill this request as soon as possible; those who fail to comply with it will have their property confiscated.

5. Those Russian nobles who, in addition to serving Us, serve other European sovereigns, may return to their country and enter Our service fully provided there is a vacancy; those nobles who serve foreign sovereigns in various capacities and can prove it will be accepted to Our service as vacancies develop; the same is true of the employment of lesser ranking nobles.

6. By virtue of this manifesto, no Russian nobleman will ever be forced to serve against his will; nor will any of Our administrative departments make use of them except in emergency cases and then only if We personally should summon them; this rule also applies to the nobility of the Smolensk area. An exception to this rule is St. Petersburg and Moscow, where an *ukaz* of the Sovereign Emperor Peter I stipulates that some men from among the retired nobles should be made available for various needs at the Senate and at the [Heraldic] Office; We amend this Imperial rule by decreeing that henceforth there should be selected annually thirty men to serve in the Senate and twenty

to serve in the Office. These men should be chosen by the Heraldic Office from among the nobles living in gubernias and not from those still in service. No one should be designated by name for this duty. Nobles themselves should decide who should be selected in the *gubernias* and provinces. Local officials should forward the names of those so selected to the Heraldic Office and also provide those selected with needed items.

7. Although, by this gracious manifesto we grant forever freedom to all of Our Russian nobles, except freeholders, Our fatherly concern for them as well as for their children will continue. The latter, We decree, should henceforth, whenever they reach twelve years of age, be reported to the Heraldic Office in *gubernias,* provinces, or cities or wherever is most convenient. From their parents or relatives who are bringing them up, information should be obtained about the level of the children's education up to the age of twelve and where they would like to continue their studies, whether within Our State in various institutions We have founded, in European countries, or should the means of their parents allow it, in their own homes by experienced and skillful teachers. No nobleman should keep his children uneducated under the penalty of Our anger. Those noblemen who have under 1000 serfs should report their children to Our Cadet Corps of the Nobility, where they will learn everything befitting a nobleman and where they will be educated with the utmost care. Following his education each nobleman will assume his rank in accordance with his dignity and reward, and subsequently each may enter and continue his service as indicated above.

8. Those nobles who presently are in Our military service as soldiers or lower rank officers below the rank of *Ober*—Officer, that is, those who have failed to attain officer rank, should not be allowed to retire unless they have served twelve years in the army.

9. We grant this gracious act to all of Our nobles for eternity as a fundamental and unalterable law; by Our Imperial word We pledge to observe it in its entirety in the most solemn and irrevocable manner. Our rightful successors should not alter it in any way whatsoever, as their adherence to this decree will serve as an indispensable support for the autocratic throne of All Russia. We hope that in return for this act Russian nobles, realizing what great concern We have shown toward them and toward their descendants, will continue to serve Us loyally and zealously and will not withdraw from Our service; on the contrary, that they will seek the service eagerly and will continue it as long as possible, and will educate their children attentively in useful knowledge; those who will not perform any service will also lead purposeless lives and will not educate their children in any useful subject. Such people, who are not concerned with the general good, We recommend that all Our faithful subjects despise and avoid. We will not allow such people

any access to Our court, nor will We tolerate their presence at public assemblies and festivals.

10

Catherine II's Account of Her Accession to the Throne, 1762

When Elizabeth died in December 1761, the throne of Russia passed to Peter, the son of her sister Anna and the Duke of Holstein. Peter III, whom Elizabeth had brought to Russia in 1742 at the age of fourteen, was one of the few tsars of eighteenth-century Russia to ascend the throne legally and without the aid of a palace clique. This very factor deprived him of the support necessary to prevent his downfall. Chief among the conspirators against his rule was his wife, Catherine (born Princess Sophia Augusta Frederica of Anhalt-Zerbst, on May 2, 1729), whom Elizabeth had selected to be Peter's consort. Since their marriage in 1745 the two had quarreled constantly, were unfaithful to each other, and had even disputed his responsibility for an offspring born in 1754, the future tsar Paul (1796–1801). Peter III antagonized many Russian officers by his open admiration of Frederick the Great of Prussia, with whom the Russians were at war. With the aid of some of the officers, Catherine masterminded the removal of her husband (later he was murdered) and ascended the Russian throne. She ruled the empire as Catherine II, or Catherine the Great, until her death in 1796.

[From a Letter to Poniatowski, August 2, 1762]

I am sending at once Count Keyserling as Ambassador to Poland to declare you King after the death of the present monarch and in the event of his not proving successful so far as you are concerned, I want it to be Prince Adam.

All minds here are still in a state of ferment. I beg you not to come here now, for fear of increasing it.

Reprinted with permission of The Macmillan Company from *The Memoirs of Catherine the Great.* Edited by Dominique Maroger. With an Introduction by G. P. Gooch. Translated from the French by Moura Budberg (New York: Collier Books, 1961), pp. 271–277.

My advent to the throne had been planned for the last six months. Peter III lost what little intelligence he ever had. He shocked and offended everyone; he wanted to disrupt the Guards and sent them campaigning for that purpose, and would have had them replaced by his Holstein troops that were ordered to remain in town. He wanted to change his religion, marry Elizabeth Worontsov, and arrest me. On the day of the peace celebrations, after insulting me publicly at table, he ordered my arrest in the evening. My uncle, Prince George, made him withdraw the order.

From that day I kept my ears open to the offers made to me since the Empress's death. The plan was to lock him up in his room, like Princess Anne and her children. He went to Oranienbaum. We had full confidence in a great number of captains in the Guards regiments. The ins and outs of the secret were in the hands of the three brothers Orlov, the eldest of whom, according to Osten, used to follow me everywhere and committed innumerable follies. His passion for me was openly acknowledged and that is why he undertook what he did. They are all three of them very determined men and loved by most soldiers, having served in the Guards. I have great obligations in regard to them; all Petersburg is witness of it.

The Guards were all prepared and at the end there were thirty or forty officers in the secret and about ten thousand subalterns. There was not one traitor during the three weeks, because the plotters were divided into four separate sections and only the leaders met for the execution of the plan, while the real secret remained in the hands of these three brothers. Panin wanted the declaration to be made in favour of my son, but all the others were against it.

I was in Peterhof. Peter III was living and drinking at Oranienbaum. It was agreed that in case of treason we would not wait for his return but assemble the Guards and proclaim me Empress. Devotion to me acted in place of treason. On the 27th the rumour spread that I had been arrested. A soldier came to a captain called Passek, the leader of a section, and told him that this was no doubt my end. He would not allow himself to be reassured and, still greatly alarmed, went to another officer and told him the same thing. That officer was not in the secret and, horrified that another officer had listened to this soldier without arresting him, reported to the Major, who ordered Passek's arrest. The whole regiment was astir. A report of what had happened reached Oranienbaum during the night and caused alarm among our confederates. They decided to send the second of the Orlov brothers to fetch me back to town while the other two spread the news that I was arriving. The Hetman Volkonski and Panin were in the secret.

I was sleeping peacefully in Peterhof at six in the morning of the 28th. The previous day had been disturbing as I was aware of what was going on.

Alexei Orlov came in very calmly and said: "All is ready for the proclamation, you must get up"; I asked for details, he said: "Passek has been arrested." I hesitated no longer, dressed promptly, without further ado, and got into the carriage in which Orlov had arrived. Another officer was acting as groom at the carriage-door, a third joined us a few miles away from Peterhof. A little further on, the eldest Orlov came to meet me with the younger Bariatinski, who gave me his seat in the coach, for my horses were exhausted. We went on to join the Ismailovski regiment, twelve men and a drummer, who started to beat the alarm. The soldiers rushed to kiss my hands, my feet, the hem of my dress, calling me their saviour. Two of them brought a priest with a cross and started to take the oath. After that I resumed my seat in the carriage, the priest with the cross walked in front, and we went on to the Semionovski regiment. They came to meet us, shouting *"Vivat!"* I alighted at the church of Kazan. Then the Preobrajenski regiment arrived, also shouting *"Vivat"* and saying: "Forgive us for being the last to come, our officers tried to arrest us, but here are four of them, whom we arrested to show you our zeal. We want what our brothers want."

The Horse Guards then came, in such a frenzy of joy as I have never seen before, weeping and shouting that the country was free at last. All this took place between the Hetman's garden and the Kazan Cathedral. The Horse Guards were led by their officers. As I knew that my uncle, to whom Peter III had given this regiment, was hated by his men, I sent word to him, begging him to stay at home, as I feared some accident to his person. But his regiment had already put him under arrest, pillaged his house, and manhandled him.

I then went to the Winter Palace where the Synod and Senate were assembled. A manifesto and the text of the oath were hastily composed. From there I walked to the troops, of which there were about 14,000 men, and was greeted with shouts of joy. Then on the Old Winter Palace to make final arrangements. It was decided to go to Peterhof, where Peter III was to dine. I sent Admiral Talysin to Kronstadt. Chancellor Worontsov arrived loaded with reproaches. He was taken to the church to swear the oath. Then came Prince Trubetskoi and Count Shuvalov with the object of securing the regiments and killing me; they were also taken without offering resistance and made to swear the oath.

Having expedited our messengers and taken all necessary precautions, about ten in the morning I put on the Guard's uniform, having had myself proclaimed Colonel with great jubilations. I rode at the head of the troops to Peterhof and left a few men of every regiment to guard my son, who had remained in town. When we arrived at a little monastery half-way along the road, Vice-Chancellor Galitzine met us with a very flattering letter from Peter

III (I forgot to say that as we left the town three soldiers from the Guards came up to me, sent from Peterhof to spread the manifesto among the people and said: "Take this, it is from Peter III but we are handing it to you and are glad to be able to join our brothers.") Then came a second letter brought by General Ismailov, who, throwing himself on his knees, asked me: "Do you consider me an honest man?" I replied that I did. "Well," he said, "it is a relief to be among intelligent people. The Emperor offers to abdicate. I will bring him to you and avoid a civil war for my country." I agreed to this and Peter III abdicated in perfect freedom at Oranienbaum, surrounded by 1590 Holstein men and then came with Elizabeth Woronstov, Gudovich, and Ismailov to Peterhof where I gave him a guard of six officers and a few soldiers.

As it was St. Peter's Day, at midday we had to have dinner. While that was being prepared, the soldiers took it into their heads that Peter III had been brought by Field-Marshal Prince Trubetskoi to try to work out a reconciliation between us. They began to whisper to anyone within earshot, including the Hetman, the Orlovs and others, that they had not seen me for three hours, that they were terrified that that old rogue Trubetskoi was pulling the wool over my eyes "by making a false peace between me and my husband and thus bringing about my ruin and theirs, too, in which case they would tear him to pieces." I went to Trubetskoi and told him to take the carriage, while I would go round the troops on foot alone. I told him what was being said. He went to town, extremely frightened, and I was received with frenzied cries, after which I sent the deposed Emperor to Ropsha, fifteen miles from Petersburg, under the command of Alexei Orlov, while respectable and comfortable rooms were being prepared for him in Schlüsselburg and also to give time to organize a relay of horses.

But God disposed differently. Fright had given him a colic that lasted three days and passed on the fourth. On that day he drank excessively—for he had everything he wanted, except liberty. The illness affected his brain, it was followed by a great weakness and in spite of all the assistance of physicians, he gave up the ghost, after asking for a Lutheran priest. I had him opened up—but his stomach showed no traces of ill health. The cause of death was established as inflammation of the bowels and apoplexy. He had an inordinately small heart, quite withered. . . .

After he had been dispatched from Peterhof to Ropsha, I was advised to go straight to town. I foresaw that the troops might become alarmed. I spread the rumour about my departure, under the pretext of wanting to know at what time, after three days of fatigue duty, they would be ready to go. They said: "Towards ten in the evening but she must come with us." So I went with them and half-way stopped at Kurakine's estate, where I threw myself on the bed in my clothes. An officer pulled off my boots. I slept for two and one-half hours and then we went on. From Catherinenhof I rode again at the head of the Preobrajenski regiment, a hussar regiment rode in front, then my escort, the Chevalier Guards, then came, immediately before me, my Court. After me came the Guards regiments in order of seniority, and three field regiments. The acclamations were frantic and I moved towards the Summer Palace where my Court, the Synod, my son, and all who attend Court were waiting. I went to church to hear the Te Deum, then came congratulations. I had neither drunk, nor eaten, nor slept from six in the morning on Friday till after dinner on Sunday, and went to bed as soon as possible and slept. At midnight a captain rushed into the room, waking me up and saying: "Our men are terribly drunk, a hussar has shouted to them: 'To arms! Thirty thousand Prusians are coming to take away our mother!' So they have taken up arms and are coming here to see how you really are. They promise to go home quietly if they find you all right. They will listen to no one, not even to the Orlovs."

So I had to get up again and, so as not to alarm my guard in the courtyard—a full battalion—I went to tell them why I was going out at this hour. Then, with two officers, I went to tackle the rioters and told them I was well, that they should go and have some sleep and leave me to have mine, that I was just about to sleep, having not slept for three nights, and that I hoped they would in future obey their officers. They replied that they had been alarmed by the rumour concerning these accursed Prussians and all wanted to die for me. I said: "Thank you, but go back to bed!" They bade me good night and good health and went home like lambs, turning back to look at me. Next day they apologized for having woken me up and said: "If we spend our time wishing to see her, we will only destroy her health and prevent her from working."

A book would not suffice to describe the officers' behaviour. The Orlovs shone by their art of leadership, their prudent daring, by the care introduced in small details, by their presence of mind and authority. They have much common sense and generous courage. Enthusiastically patriotic and honest, passionately attached to me and friends among each other, as brothers rarely are, there are five of them in all, but only three were here. Captain Passek distinguished himself by the fortitude with which he stood his twelve hours' imprisonment. The soldiers opened both windows and doors to him, but he did not wish to arouse alarm in his regiment before my arrival and was patiently waiting to be taken to Oranienbaum to be interrogated. The order came after I arrived. Princess Dashkov, younger sister of Elizabeth Worontsov, (through she wants all the honour of the execution of the plot attributed to her, simply because she knew some of the leaders) was in bad odour on account of her sister, nor did the fact that she was only nineteen years old impress anyone. Though she pretended to be the intermediary through whom everything reached me, everybody had been in touch with me for six months before she even knew their names. It is true that she is intelligent but she behaves ostentatiously and is an intriguer and disliked by our officers; only the heedless and the rash told her what they knew, which was not much more than a few details. I. Shuvalov, the lowest and meanest of men, has, I am told, written to Voltaire that a girl of nineteen has changed the face of the Empire. Please undeceive this great writer. Bariatinski, who concealed the whole matter from his beloved brother, deserves real praise. In the Horse Guards an officer call Khitrov, twenty-two years of age and a petty officer called Potemkin, displayed discernment, courage, and action.

This is in short all that happened. Everything was done, I will not conceal from you, under my own direction and finally I threw cold water on the plan because the departure to the country prevented its execution and things had been more than mature for a fortnight. The dethroned Emperor, when he learnt of the disturbance in town, was prevented by the young women in his retinue from following the advice of old Field-Marshal Munich who advised him to try Kronstadt or join the Army with a few men, and when he finally took a rowing boat to go to Kronstadt, the town was already in our hands, thanks to Admiral Talysin who disarmed General Devier, who was there on the side of the Emperor. An officer in the port threatened the poor Prince of his own accord, saying that he would riddle his boat with bullets. At last, God brought everything to the end He wished and all this is more a miracle than an organized and planned event, for so many favourable circumstances cannot be brought together without the hand of God.

I received your letter. A regular correspondence would be subject to a thousand inconveniences, I have twenty thousand precautions to take and have no time for harmful little love-letters.

I feel very embarrassed. . . . I cannot tell you what it is about, but it is true.

I will do everything for you and your family, rest assured of it.

I have thousands of proprieties and discretions to consider and also to bear the burden of government.

You must know that everything was carried out on the principle of hatred of the foreigner; Peter III himself counted as such.

Goodbye, the world is full of strange situations.

11

The Nakaz, *or* Instruction, *of Catherine II to the Legislative Commission of 1767–1768*

Among the enlightened despots of eighteenth-century Europe, Catherine II of Russia occupies an eminent place. She acquired this position through her associations with such prominent men of letters as Diderot, Grimm, Voltaire, and D'Alembert, through her patronage of education, and through her writings, of which the *Nakaz,* or *Instruction,* to the Legislative Commission of 1767–1768 is the most important. The *Nakaz,* which Voltaire called the finest monument of the century, represents Catherine's ambition to remodel Russia's laws in accordance with the new principles being expounded in Western Europe. Together with its two supplements, it consists of 655 articles, and took two years to prepare. About four-fifths of the articles were taken from Montesquieu's *The Spirit of Laws,* while Beccaria's *Essay on Crimes and Punishments* influenced over 100 of them. To conform with the conditions in Russia, Catherine modified and in some cases even distorted the ideas of Western writers. Although the Commission held 203 sessions, it failed to achieve anything constructive, due as much to the selfish policies of the Russian nobility as to Catherine's failure to follow her own theories in practice. In spite of this, the *Nakaz* remains an outstanding document in Russia's political, economic, and historical literature.

The Instructions to the Commissioners for Composing a New Code of Laws

1. The Christian Law teaches us to do mutual Good to one another, as much as possibly we can.

2. Laying this down as a fundamental Rule prescribed by that Religion, which has taken, or ought to take Root in the Hearts of the whole People; we cannot but suppose that every honest Man in the Community is, or will

---

From *The Grand Instructions to the Commissioners Appointed to Frame a New Code of Laws for the Russian Empire: Composed by Her Imperial Majesty Catherine II . . .* Translated by Michael Tatischeff, (London: 1768), pp. 69–79, 80–82, 85–90, 104–106, 115–118, 126–128, 132–141, 144–150, 159–166, 178–181, 185–196.

be, desirous of seeing his native Country at the very Summit of Happiness, Glory, Safety, and Tranquility.

3. And that every Individual Citizen in particular must wish to see himself protected by Laws, which should not distress him in his Circumstances, but, on the Contrary, should defend him from all Attempts of others that are repugnant to this fundamental Rule.

4. In order therefore to proceed to a speedy Execution of what *We* expect from such a general Wish, *We,* fixing the Foundation upon the above first-mentioned Rule, ought to begin with an Inquiry into the natural Situation of this Empire.

5. For those Laws have the greatest Conformity with Nature, whose particular Regulations are best adapted to the Situation and Circumstances of the People for whom they are instituted.

This natural Situation is described in the three following Chapters. . . .

Chapter I

6. Russia is an European State.

7. This is clearly demonstrated by the following Observations: The Alternations which *Peter the Great* undertook in Russia succeeded with the greater Ease, because the Manners, which prevailed at that Time, and had been introduced amongst us by a Mixture of different Nations, and the Conquest of foreign Territories, were quite unsuitable to the Climate. *Peter the First,* by introducing the Manners and Customs of Europe among the European People in his Dominions, found at that Time such Means as even he himself was not sanguine enough to expect.

Chapter II

8. The Possessions of the Russian Empire extend upon the terrestrial Globe to 32 Degrees of Latitude, and to 165 of Longitude.

9. The Sovereign is absolute; for there is no other authority but that which centers in his single Person that can act with a Vigour proportionate to the Extent of such a vast Dominion.

10. The Extent of the Dominion requires an absolute Power to be vested in that Person who rules over it. It is expedient so to be that the quick Dispatch of Affairs, sent from distant Parts, might make ample Amends for the Delay occasioned by the great Distance of the Places.

11. Every other Form of Government whatsoever would not only have been prejudicial to Russia, but would even have proved its entire Ruin. . . .

Chapter IV

22. There must be a political Body, to whom the Care and strict Execution of these Laws ought to be confided. . . .

26. In Russia the Senate is the political Body, to which the Care and due Execution of the Laws is confided.

27. All other Courts of Judicature may, and ought to remonstrate with the same Propriety, to the Senate, and even to the Sovereign himself, as was already mentioned above. . . .

Chapter V

31. *Of the Situation of the People in general.*

32. It is the greatest Happiness for a Man to be so circumstanced, that, if his Passions should prompt him to be mischievous, he should still think it more for his Interest not to give Way to them.

33. The Laws ought to be so framed as to secure the Safety of every Citizen as much as possible.

34. The Equality of the Citizens consists in this; that they should all be subject to the same Laws.

35. This Equality requires Institutions so well adapted as to prevent the Rich from oppressing those who are not so wealthy as themselves, and converting all the Charges and Employments intrusted to them as Magistrates only to their own private Emolument.

36. General or political Liberty does not consist in that licentious Notion, *That a Man may do whatever he pleases.*

37. In a State or Assemblage of People that live together in a Community, where there are Laws, Liberty can only consist *in doing that which every One ought to do, and not to be constrained to do that which One ought not to do.*

38. A Man ought to form in his own Mind an exact and clear Idea of what Liberty is. *Liberty is the Right of doing whatsoever the Laws allow:* And if any one Citizen could do what the Laws forbid, there would be no more Liberty; because others would have an equal Power of doing the same.

39. The political Liberty of a Citizen is the Peace of Mind arising from the Consciousness that every Individual enjoys his peculiar Safety; and in order that the People might attain this Liberty, the Laws ought to be so framed that no one Citizen should stand in Fear of another; but that all of them should stand in Fear of the same Laws.

Chapter VI

40. *Of Laws in general.*

41. Nothing ought to be forbidden by the Laws but what may be prejudicial, either to every Individual in particular, or to the whole Community in general.

42. All Actions which comprehend nothing of this Nature are in nowise cognizable by the Laws; which are made only with the View of procuring the

greatest possible Advantage and Tranquillity to the People, who live under their Protection.

43. To preserve Laws from being violated, they ought to be so good, and so well furnished with all Expedients, tending to procure the greatest possible Good to the People; that every Individual might be fully convinced that it was his Interest, as well as Duty, to preserve those Laws inviolable.

44. And this is the most exalted Pitch of Perfection which we ought to labour to attain to. . . .

Chapter VII

64. *Of the Laws in particular.*

65. Laws carried to the Extremity of Right are productive of the Extremity of Evil.

66. All Laws, where the Legislation aims at the Extremity of Rigour, may be evaded. It is Moderation which rules a People, and not Excess of Severity.

67. Civil Liberty flourishes when the Laws deduce every Punishment from the peculiar Nature of every Crime. The Application of Punishment ought not to proceed from the arbitrary Will, or mere Caprice of the Legislator, but from the Nature of the Crime; and it is not the Man, who ought to do Violence to a Man, but the proper Action of the Man himself. . . .

Chapter VIII

80. *Of Punishments.*

81. The Love of our Country, Shame, and the Dread of public Censure, are Motives which restrain, and may deter Mankind from the Commission of a Number of Crimes.

82. The greatest Punishment for a bad Action, under a mild Administration, will be for the Party to be convinced of it. The civil Laws will there correct Vice with the more Ease, and will not be under a necessity of employing more rigorous Means.

83. In these Governments, the Legislature will apply itself more to prevent Crimes than to punish them, and should take more Care to instil Good Manners into the Minds of the Citizens, by proper Regulations, than to dispirit them by the Terror of corporal and capital Punishments.

84. In a Word, whatever is termed Punishment in the Law is, in Fact, nothing but Pain and Suffering.

85. Experience teaches us that, in those Countries where Punishments are mild, they operate with the same Efficacy upon the Minds of the Citizens as the most severe in other Places. . . .

87. The People ought not to be driven on by violent Methods, but we

ought to make Use of the Means which Nature has given us, with the utmost Care and Caution, in order to conduct them to the End we propose.

88. Examine with Attention the Cause of all Licentiousness; and you will find that it proceeds from the Neglect of punishing Crimes, not from the Mildness of Punishments. Let us follow Nature, which has given Shame to Man for his Scourge and let the greatest Part of the Punishment consist in the Infamy which accompanies the Punishment. . . .

94. It is unjust to punish a Thief who robs on the Highway in the same Manner as another, who not only robs, but commits Murder. Every One sees clearly that some Difference ought to be made in their Punishment, for the Sake of the general Safety. . . .

96. Good Laws keep strictly a just Medium: They do not always inflict pecuniary, nor always subject Malefactors to corporal Punishment.

All Punishments by which the human Body might be maimed ought to be abolished.

Chapter IX

97. *Of the Administration of Justice in general. . . .*

119. The Laws which condemn a Man upon the Deposition of one Evidence only are destructive to Liberty. . . .

120. Two Witnesses are absolutely necessary in order to form a right Judgment: For an Accuser, who affirms, and the Party accused, who denies the Fact, make the Evidence on both Sides equal; for that Reason, a Third is required in order to convict the Defendant; unless other clear collateral Proofs should fix the Credibility of the Evidence in favour of one of them.

121. The Evidence of two Witnesses is esteemed sufficient for Conviction in every criminal Case whatsoever. The Law believes them, as if they spoke from the Mouth of Truth itself. . . .

123. The Usage of Torture is contrary to all the Dictates of Nature and Reason; even Mankind itself cries out against it, and demands loudly the total Abolition of it. We see, at this very Time, a People greatly renowned for the Excellence of their civil Polity, who reject it without any sensible Inconveniencies. It is, therefore, by no Means necessary by its Nature. *We* will explain this more at large here below.

124. There are Laws which do not allow the Application of Torture, except only in those Cases where the Prisoner at the Bar refuses to plead, and will neither acknowledge himself innocent nor guilty. . . .

127. It is likewise just that some of the Judges should be of the same Rank of Citizenship as the Defendant; that is, his Equals; that he might not think himself fallen into the Hands of such People as would violently over-

rule the Affair to his Prejudice: Of this there are already Instances in the Martial Laws.

128. When the Defendant is condemned, it is not the Judges who inflict the Punishment upon him, but the Law.

129. The Sentence ought to be as clear and distinct as possible; even so far as to preserve the very identical Words of the Law. But if they should include the private Opinion of the Judge, the People will live in Society without knowing exactly the reciprocal Obligations they lie under to one another in that State. . . .

155. If the Laws are not *exactly* and *clearly* defined, and understood *Word by Word*; if it be not the sole Office of a Judge to *distinguish,* and lay down *clearly,* what Action is comformable to the Laws, and what is repugnant to them: If the Rule of *just* and *unjust,* which ought to govern alike the ignorant Clown and the enlightened Scholar, be not a *simple Question* of Matter of Fact for the Judges; then the Situation of the Citizen will be exposed to strange Accidents.

156. By making the *penal* Laws always *clearly* intelligible, *Word by Word,* every one may calculate truly and know exactly the Inconveniences of a bad Action; a Knowledge which is *absolutely* necessary for restraining People from committing it; and the People may enjoy Security with respect both to their Persons and Property; which ought ever to remain so, because this is the *main Scope* and *Object* of the Laws, and without which the Community would be dissolved.

157. If the Power of *interpreting* Laws be an Evil, there is an Evil also which attends the *Obscurity* of them, and lays us under the Necessity of having Recourse to their Interpretation. This Irregularity is still greater when the Laws are written in a Language *unknown* to the People, or expressed in *uncommon* Phrases.

158. The Laws ought to be written in the *common vernacular Tongue*; and the Code, which contains all the Laws, ought to be esteemed as a Book of the utmost Use, which should be purchased at as *small* a Price as the Catechism. If the Case were otherwise, and the Citizen should be ignorant of the Consequences of his own Actions, and what concerns his Person and Liberty, he will then depend upon some few of the People who have taken upon themselves the Care of preserving and explaining them. Crimes will be less frequent in *proportion* as the Code of Laws is more *universally* read, and *comprehended* by the People. And, for this Reason, it must be ordained, That, in all the Schools, Children should be taught to read *alternately* out of the Church Books and out of *those* which contain the Laws. . . .

193. The Torture of the Rack is a Cruelty established and made use of by many Nations, and is applied to the Party accused during the Course of

his Trial, either to extort from him a Confession of his Guilt, or in order to clear up some Contradictions in which he had involved himself during his Examination, or to compel him to discover his Accomplices, or in order to discover other Crimes, of which, though he is not accused, yet he may *perhaps* be guilty.

194. (1) No Man ought to be looked upon as *guilty* before he has received his judicial Sentence; nor can the Laws deprive him of *their* Protection before it is proved that he has *forfeited all Right* to it. What Right therefore can Power give to any to inflict Punishment upon a Citizen at a Time when it is yet dubious whether he is *innocent* or *guilty?* Whether the Crime be known or unknown, it is not very difficult to gain a thorough Knowledge of the Affair by duly weighing all the Circumstances. If the Crime be known, the Criminal ought not to suffer any Punishment but what the Law ordains; consequently the Rack is quite unnecessary. If the Crime be not known, the Rack ought not to be applied to the Party accused; for this Reason, *That the Innocent ought not to be tortured*; and, in the Eye of the Law, every Person is innocent whose Crime is not yet *proved.* It is undoubtedly extremely necessary that no Crime, after it has been proved, should remain unpunished. The Party accused on the Rack, whilst in the Agonies of Torture, is not Master enough of himself to be able to declare the Truth. Can we give more Credit to a Man when he is light-headed in a Fever, than when he enjoys the free Use of his Reason in a State of Health? The Sensation of Pain may arise to such a Height that, after having subdued the whole Soul, it will leave her no longer the Liberty of producing any proper Act of the Will, except that of taking the shortest instantaneous Method, in the very twinkling of an Eye, as it were, of getting rid of her Torment. In such an Extremity, even an *innocent* Person will roar out that he is *guilty,* only to gain *some Respite* from his Tortures. Thus the very same Expedient, which is made use of to distinguish the *Innocent* from the *Guilty,* will take away the *whole Difference* between them; and the Judges will be as uncertain whether they have an *innocent* or a *guilty* Person before them, as they were before the Beginning of this *partial* Way of Examination. The Rack, therefore, is a sure Method of condemning an innocent person of a weakly Constitution, and of acquitting a *wicked Wretch,* who depends upon the Robustness of his Frame. . . .

196. (3) To make use of the Rack for discovering whether the Party accused has not committed *other Crimes*, besides *that* which he has been *convicted* of, is a certain Expedient to *screen every Crime from its proper* Punishment: For a Judge will always be discovering new Ones. Finally, this Method of Proceeding will be founded upon the following Way of reasoning: *Thou art guilty of one Crime, therefore, perhaps, thou hast committed an Hundred others: According to*

the Laws, thou wilt be tortured and tormented; not only because thou are guilty, but even because thou mayest be still more guilty. . . .

220. A Punishment ought to be *immediate, analogous* to the *Nature* of the Crime, and *known* to the Public.

221. The *sooner* the Punishment succeeds to the Commission of a Crime, the *more useful* and *just* it will be. *Just*; because it will spare the Malefactor the torturing and useless Anguish of Heart about the *Uncertainty* of his Destiny. Consequently the Decision of an Affair, in a Court of Judicature, ought to be finished in as little Time as possible. *I have said before that Punishment immediately inflicted is most useful*; the Reason is because the smaller the Interval of Time is which passes between the Crime and the Punishment, the *more* the Crime will be esteemed as a *Motive* to the Punishment, and the Punishment as an *Effect* of the Crime. Punishment must be *certain* and *unavoidable.*

222. The most certain Curb upon Crimes is not the *Severity* of the Punishment, but the absolute Conviction in the People that Delinquents will be *inevitably* punished. . . .

Chapter XII

264. *Of the Propagation of the human Species in a State.*

265. Russia is not only *greatly* deficient in the *number* of her Inhabitants; but at the same Time, extends her Dominion over *immense* Tracts of Land; which are neither peopled nor improved. And therefore, in a Country so circumstanced, *too much* Encouragement can never be given to the *Propagation* of the human Species.

266. The Peasants generally have twelve, fifteen, and even twenty Children by one Marriage; but it rarely happens that one *Fourth* of these ever attains to the *Age* of Maturity. There must therefore be some Fault, either in their Nouriture, in their Way of Living, or Method of Education, which occasions this *prodigious* Loss, and disappoints the *Hopes* of the Empire. How flourishing would the State of this Empire be if we could but ward off, or *prevent* this fatal Evil by proper Regulations!

267. You must add too to *this,* that two Hundred Years are now elapsed since a *Disease* unknown to our Ancestors was imported from America, and *hurried* on the Destruction of the human Race. This Disease spreads *wide its mournful* and *destructive* Effects in *many* of our Provinces. The utmost Care ought to be taken of the Health of the Citizens. It would be highly prudent, therefore, to stop the Progress of this Disease by the Laws.

268. Those of Moses may serve here for an Example. (Leviticus, chap. xiii)

269. It seems too that the Method of exacting their Revenues, *newly*

invented by the Lords, diminishes both the *Inhabitants* and the *Spirit of Agriculture* in Russia. Almost all the Villages are *heavily* taxed. The Lords, who seldom or never *reside* in their Villages, lay an Impost on every Head of one, two, and even five Rubles, without the least Regard to the *Means* by which their Peasants may be able to *raise* this Money.

270. It is highly necessary that the Law should prescribe a Rule to the Lords for a more judicious Method of raising their Revenues; and oblige them to levy *such* a Tax as *tends least* to separate the Peasant from his House and Family; this would be the Means by which Agriculture would become more extensive, and Population be more increased in the Empire.

271. Even now some Husbandmen do not see their Houses for fifteen Years together, and yet pay the Tax annually to their respective Lords; which they procure in Towns at a vast Distance from their Families, and wander over the whole Empire for that purpose.

272. The more happily a People live under a Government, the more easily the Number of the Inhabitants increases.

273. Countries, which abound with Meadow and Pasture Lands, are generally *very thinly* peopled; the Reason is that *few* can find Employment in those Places: But arable Lands are much *more* populous; because they *furnish* Employment for a *much greater* Number of People.

274. Wherever the Inhabitants can enjoy the Conveniencies of Life, there Population will certainly increase.

275. *But a Country which is so overwhelmed with Taxes that the People, with all their Care and Industry, can with the utmost Difficulty find Means for procuring a bare Subsistance, will, in length of Time, be deserted by its Inhabitants. . . .*

Chapter XIII

293. *Of handicraft Trades, and Commerce.*

294. There can be neither skillful Handicraftsmen, nor a firmly-established Commerce, where Agriculture is neglected, or carried on with Supineness and Negligence.

295. Agriculture can never flourish there, where no Persons have any Property of their own.

296. This is founded upon a very simple Rule: *Every Man will take more Care of his own Property, than of that which belongs to another; and will not exert his utmost Endeavours upon that which he has Reason to fear another may deprive him of.*

297. Agriculture is the most laborious Employment a Man can undertake. The *more* the Climate induces a Man to shun this Trouble, the *more* the Laws ought to animate him to it. . . .

299. It would not be improper to give a Premium to those Husbandmen who bring their Fields into better Order than others.

300. And to the Handicraftsmen, who distinguished themselves most by their Care and Skill.

301. This Regulation will produce a Progress in the Arts, in all Parts of the Country. It was of Service, even in our own Times, in establishing very important Manufactories.

302. There are Countries where a Treatise of Agriculture, published by the Government, is lodged in every Church, from which the Peasant may be able to get the better of his Difficulties, and draw proper Advantage from the Instructions it contains.

303. There are Nations inclined to Laziness. In order to exterminate Laziness in the Inhabitants, arising from the Climate, such Laws are to be made as should deprive those who refuse to work, of the Means of Subsistance.

304. All Nations inclined to Laziness are arrogant in their Behaviour; for they who do not work esteem themselves, in some Measure, Rulers over those who labour.

305. Nations who have given themselves up to Idleness are generally proud: We might turn the Effect against the Cause from which it proceeds, and destroy Laziness by Pride itself.. . . .

307. As *Pride* induces some to shun Labour, so *Ambition* impells others to excell all the rest in Workmanship.

308. View every Nation with Attention, and you will find that arrogant Pride and Laziness, most commonly, go Hand in Hand together. . . .

311. A Man is not poor because he has nothing; but because he will do no Work. He who has no Estate, but will work, may live as well as he, who has an annual Income of a Hundred *Rubles*, but will do no Work.

312. A Tradesman who has taught his Children his Art, has given them such an Estate as increases in proportion to their Number.

313. Agriculture is the first and principal Labour which ought to be encouraged in the People: The next is the manufacturing our own Produce.

314. Machines, which serve to shorten Labour in the mechanick Arts, are not always useful. If a Piece of Work, wrought with the Hands, can be afforded at a Price equally advantageous to the Merchant and the Manufacturer; in this Case, Machines which shorten Labour, that is, which diminish the Number of Workmen, will be greatly prejudical to a populous Country.

315. Yet, we ought to distinguish between what we manufacture for our Home consumption, and what we manufacture for Exportation into foreign Countries.

316. Too much Use cannot be made of this Kind of Machines in our Manufactures, which we export to other Nations; who do, or may receive the

same Kind of Goods, from our Neighbours or other People; especially those who are in the same Situation with ourselves.

317. Commerce flies from Places where it meets with Oppression, and settles where it meets with Protection. . . .

319. In many Countries, where all the Taxes are farmed, the *Collection* of the Royal Revenues *ruins* Commerce, not only by its Inequality, Oppression, and extreme Exactions, but also by the *Difficulties* it occasions, and the Formalities it requires. . . .

321. The Liberty of Trading does not consist in a Permission to Merchants of doing whatever they please; this would be rather the *Slavery* of Commerce: What *cramps* the Trader does not *cramp* the Trade. In free Countries the Merchant meets with innumerable Obstacles; but in despotic Governments he is not near so much thwarted by the Laws. England prohibits the Exportation of its Wool; she has ordained Coals to be imported to the Capital by Sea; she has prohibited the Exportation of Horses fit for Stallions; she obliges Ships, which Trade from her Plantations in America into Europe, to anchor first in England. By these, and such like Prohibitions, she *cramps* the Merchant; but it is for the *Benefit* of Commerce. . . .

Chapter XIV

347. *Of Education.*

348. The Rules of Education are the fundamental Institutes which train us up to be Citizens.

349. Each particular Family ought to be governed upon the Plan of the great Family; which includes all the Particulars.

350. It is impossible to give a general Education to a very numerous People, and to bring up all the Children in Houses regulated for that Purpose; and, for that Reason, it will be proper to establish some *general Rules,* which may serve *by Way of Advice* to all Parents.

351. Every Parent is obliged to teach his Children the Fear of God as the Beginning of all Wisdom, and to inculcate into them all those Duties, which God demands from us in the Ten Commandments, and our orthodox Eastern Greek Religion, in its Rules and Traditions.

352. Also to inculcate into them the Love of their Country, and to ensure them to pay due Respect to the established civil Laws, and to reverence the Courts of Judicature in their Country, as those who, by the Appointment of God, watch over their Happiness in this World.

353. Every Parent ought to refrain *in Presence* of his Children, not only from *Actions,* but even *Words* that *tend* to Injustice and Violence; as for Instance, *Quarrelling, Swearing, Fighting, every Sort of Cruelty,* and *such like*

Behaviour; and not to allow those who are about his Children *to set them such bad Examples.*

354. He ought to forbid his Children, and those who are about them, the *Vice* of *lying,* though even *in jest*; for *Lying* is the most pernicious of *all Vices.*

355. We shall add here, for the Instruction of every Man in particular, what has been already printed, and serves as *a general Rule* for the Schools already founded, and which are still founding by *Us,* for *Education,* and for the *whole* Society.

356. *Every one ought to inculcate the Fear of God into the tender Minds of Children, to encourage every laudable Inclination, and to accustom them to the fundamental Rules, suitable to their respective Situations; to incite in them a Desire for Labour, and a Dread of Idleness, as the Root of all Evil, and Error; to train them up to a proper Decorum in their Actions and Conversation, Civility, and Decency in their Behaviour; and to sympathise with the Miseries of poor unhappy Wretches; and to break them of all perverse and forward Humours; to teach them Oeconomy, and whatever is most useful in all Affairs of Life; to guard them against all Prodigality and Extravagence; and particularly to root a proper Love of Cleanliness and Neatness, as well in themselves as in those who belong to them; in a Word, to instill all those Virtues and Qualities which joint to form a good Education; by which, as they grow up, they may prove real Citizens, useful Members of the Community, and Ornaments to their Country.*

Chapter XV

357. *Of the Nobility.*

358. The Husbandmen, who cultivate the Lands to produce Food for People in every Rank of Life, live in Country Towns and Villages. *This is their Lot.*

359. The Burghers, who employ their Time in mechanick Trades, Commerce, Arts, and Sciences, *inhabit the Cities.*

360. *Nobility* is an Appellation of *Honour,* which distinguishes all those who are adorned with it from every other Person of *inferior* Rank. . . .

363. *Virtue* with *Merit raises* People to the Rank of Nobility.

364. Virtue and Honour ought to be the Rules, which prescribe *Love for their Country, Zeal for its Service, Obedience and Fidelity to their Sovereign*; and continually suggest, *never to be guilty of an infamous Action. . . .*

371. The Actions which render a Man unworthy of the Appellation of *Noble* are *Treason, Robbery, Theft* of all Kinds, the *Violation of Oaths,* or his *solemn Word given, false Evidence,* which he either *gave* himself, or *suborned* others to give; *Forgery* of false Deeds, Letters, or any such Kind of Writings:

372. In a Word, *every Fraud* contrary to *Honour,* especially those *Actions* which *degrade* a Man, and bring him into Contempt.

373. And the Preservation of Honour intire, consists in the *Love of their Country,* and *Observance of all its Laws and Duties:* From whence will follow,

374. *Praise* and *Glory,* especially to *that Race* which can reckon up among *their Ancestors more* of such Persons who were *adorned* with *Virtue, Honour, Merit, Fidelity* and *Love to their Country,* and consequently *to their Sovereign.*

375. And the Prerogatives of the Nobility ought to be founded on all the above-mentioned Qualifications, which compose the very *Essence* of the Appellation of *Nobleman.*

Chapter XVI

376. *Of the middling Sort of People.*

377. *I* have mentioned in the XVth Chapter, *that those People who inhabit the Cities apply themselves to handicraft Trades, Commerce, Arts, and Sciences.* In whatever *State* the *fundamental Qualification* for the Rank of Nobility is established, *conformably* with the Rules prescribed in the XVth Chapter, it is no less *useful* to establish the Qualification of Citizens upon *Principles* productive of *Good Manners and Industry,* by which the People we here treat of will *enjoy that Situation.*

378. This Sort of People, of whom we ought now to speak, and from whom the State expects much Benefit, are admitted into the *Middling* Rank, if their *Qualifications* are firmly *established* upon *Good Manners and Incitements to Industry.*

379. People of *this Rank* will enjoy a State of Liberty, without intermixing either with the *Nobility* or the *Husbandmen.*

380. To this Rank of People, we ought to annex all those who are neither *Gentlemen,* nor *Husbandmen*; but employ themselves in *Arts, Sciences, Navigation, Commerce,* or *handicraft Trades.*

381. Besides these, all those who are not of the *Nobility* but have been educated in *Schools* or *Colleges,* of what Denomination soever, *ecclesiastical* or *civil,* founded by *Us* and *Our* Ancestors:

382. Also the Children of People belonging to the Law. But as in that *third Species,* there are different Degrees of Privilege, therefore we shall not enter into a detail of Particulars; but only open the way for a due Consideration of it.

383. As the whole Qualification which intitles People to this *middling* Rank is founded upon good Manners and Industry; the violation of these Rules will serve, on the Contrary, for their Exclusion from it; as for Instance, *Perfidiousness* and *Breach of Promise,* especially if *caused* by *Idleness* and *Treachery. . . .*

493. (c) *Rules necessary, and of great Importance.*

494. In such a State as *Ours,* which extends its Sovereignty over so many

different Nations, to forbid, or not to allow them to profess *different Modes* of Religion, would greatly indanger the Peace and Security of its Citizens.

495. And the most certain Means of bringing back these wandering Sheep to the true Flock of the Faithful is a *prudent Toleration* of other Religions, not repugnant to our orthodox Religion and Polity.

501. (d) *How can we know, when a State approaches to its Fall, and entire Dissolution?*

502. The Corruption of every Government generally begins by the *Corruption of its fundamental Principles.*

503. The fundamental Principles of a Government are not only corrupted, when they extinguish that Idea of the State ingrafted in the Minds of the People by the Law, which may be termed the *Equality* prescribed *by the Laws*; but even then, when this *Idea of Equality* shall take root in the People, and *grow to such* a Pitch of Licentiousness, that every one *aims* at being *equal* to him, who *is ordained* by the Laws *to rule over him.*

504. If they do not shew Respect to the *Sovereign,* to the *Courts of Judicature* and to *Governors*; and if they do not respect the *Ancient,* neither will they respect *Fathers,* nor *Mothers,* nor *Masters*; and the State insensibly will run to ruin.

505. When the fundamental Principles of Government are corrupted, then the *Regulations* introduced in it are termed *Hardships,* or *Severities.* The established *Rules* are termed *Restraints*; what was *Caution* before, is *now* termed *Fear.* The *Property* of particular Persons constituted, in former Times, the *Wealth of the People*; but now the *Wealth of the People* becomes the *Inheritance of particular Persons,* and the Love of their Country vanishes.

506. In order to preserve the *fundamental Principles* of a well-regulated Government inviolate, the State ought to be supported in its present Grandeur; and this State will fall to Decay if its fundamental Principles should be *altered.*

507. There are two Kinds of Corruption; the first is, when the *Laws are not observed*; the second when the *Laws are so bad that they corrupt themselves*; and the Evil then is *incurable*; because the *Remedy* of the Evil is to be found only in *itself.*

508. A State may change also two different Ways; either because the Constitution of it *mends,* or because the *same* Constitution *corrupts.* If the *fundamental* Principles in a State are preserved, the Constitution of it *mends*; but if the fundamental Principles of it are destroyed, the Constitution *changes,* and then it *corrupts.*

509. The *more* capital Punishments increase, the *more* a State is in Danger of Destruction; for capital Punishments *increase* in Proportion to the *Corruption* of Manners, and Corruption of Manners produces the *Ruin* of a State. . . .

511. A Monarchy is destroyed when the Sovereign imagines that he dis-

plays his Power more by *changing* the Order of Things, than by adhering to it, and when he is more found of *his own Imaginations* than of *his Will,* from which the Laws proceed, and have proceeded. . . .

521. All the Examples and Customs of different Nations, which are introduced in this Work, ought to produce no other Effect than to cooperate in the Choice of those Means, which may render the People of Russia, humanly speaking, the *most happy* in themselves of any People upon Earth.

522. Nothing more remains now for the Commission to do but to compare every Part of the Laws with the Rules of these Instructions.

Conclusion

523. *Perhaps some Persons may object, after perusing these Instructions, that they will not be intelligible to every one. To this it may be answered: It is true, they will not be readily understood by every Person after one slight Perusal only; but every Person may comprehend these Instructions, if he reads them with Care and Attention, and selects occasionally such Articles as may serve to direct him, as a Rule, in whatever he undertakes. These Instructions ought to be frequently perused, to render them more familiar: And every one may be firmly assured that they will certainly be understood; because,*

524. Assiduity *and* Care *will* conquer *every Difficulty; as, on the Contrary,* Indolence *and* Carelessness *will* deter *from every laudable Attempt.*

525. *To render this difficult Affair more easy; these Instructions are to be read over once, at the Beginning of every Month, in the Commission for composing the New Code of Laws, and in all the subordinate Committees, which depend upon it; particularly the respective Chapters and Articles instrusted to their Care, till the Conclusion of the Commission.*

526. *But as no perfect Work was ever yet composed by Man; therefore, if the Commissioners should discover, as they proceed, that any Rule for some particular Regulations has been omitted, they have Leave, in such a Case, to report it to Us, and to ask for a Supplement.*

The Original signed with Her Imperial Majesty's *own Hand, thus,*

Moscow, *July* 30, 1767 Catherine

12

Novikov's Thoughts on Catherine II and on Russia

Nikolai I. Novikov (1744–1818) was the most influential Russian publicist of the eighteenth century. Educated first at home and then at the University of Moscow, Novikov commenced his literary activity in 1769 with the publication of the satirical journal *Truten* (*Drone*); following its closure in 1770, on orders of Catherine II, he started three new journals: *Pustomel* (*Chatterbox*), *Zhivopisets* (*Painter*), and *Koshelek* (*Bag*). After authorities closed all three of these journals, Novikov moved his activity from St. Petersburg to Moscow, where, from 1779 to 1789, he established a remarkably successful publishing enterprise. This enterprise attracted talented people, with whose help he published some 1000 titles of books (translations and original works) on a variety of topics. In 1792 Catherine II had Novikov arrested, sentenced him to fifteen years in prison, and ordered the burning of some 20,000 copies of his books. After her death in 1796, Novikov was released from prison and settled on his estate, where he remained inactive for the remainder of his life.

In his prime Novikov was Russia's most ardent promoter of human rights, justice, education, and tolerance. He was also a trenchant critic of serfdom, which he held responsible for all of Russia's problems. Many of Novikov's writings were accounts of interviews. Others were either "letters to the editor" or his own "editorial replies." At one point in his career Novikov had a literary dialogue with Catherine II, who, for a time, edited the journal *Vsiakaia Vsiachina* [*This and That*].

N. I. Novikov's Polemic with Catherine II, June 16, 1769

Mr. Editor:

The Lady [editor] of *This and That* has been displeased with us and

---

Source: I. V. Malyshev, ed., *N. I. Novikov i ego sovremenniki Izbrannye sochineniia* (Moscow: Akademiia Nauk, 1961), pp. 24–25, 67–70. Translation mine.

considers our moral views abusive. But now I think that she is less guilty than I had previously thought. Her whole problem is that she cannot express herself clearly in Russian and therefore cannot understand properly the Russian written word—a problem that is characteristic of many of our current writers.

From the words she has singled out in paragraph 52, a native Russian could not conclude otherwise than that Mr. A. [that is, Novikov] was correct and that the Lady of *This and That* has criticized him unfairly.

In the fifth letter, published in *Drone,* nothing is said against mercy nor against condescendence, as the Lady of *This and That* thinks, and the reading public, to which I am now appealing, can verify this. If I had written that an individual who tries to correct vices is more humane than the one who is indulging in them, then I simply cannot understand how I could have disturbed Her Grace [Catherine II]. It seems that the Lady of *This and That* has become so overwhelmed with flatteries that she now considers as transgression anything that does not praise her.

I do not know why she thinks that my letter is abusive. The term "abusive" means scolding or using vile terms. However, in my previous letter, which apparently has infuriated the heart of this elderly lady, there is no mention of whips, or gallows, or other things that are found in her publication.

The Lady of *This and That* wrote that the fifth letter, which appeared in *Drone,* should be eliminated. But this expression is not good Russian. "To eliminate" means to transform. It is an expression that is peculiar to autocracy, and in such trifles as her letters it would be inappropriate to resort to such measures. The supreme authority can eliminate anything using other measures. It would have been more appropriate for the Lady of *This and That* to say that she despises rather than that she wishes to eliminate my criticism. Many of the pages [of *Drone*] are passed from hand to hand and it would be impossible to eliminate them.

She maintains that I have an evil heart because, in her view, I misrepresent the terms "condescendence" and "mercy." It seems to me that I wrote quite clearly that human follies are worthy of compassion and that they require correction, not connivance. I believe, therefore, that for anyone who knows Russian and who believes in truth, my explanation will not be viewed as being contrary to justice or mercy. I do not know how to respond to her suggestion that perhaps I should get well. I am not sure who needs the cure more: the Lady or I. Having said that she does not wish to reply to the fifth letter that appeared in *Drone,* nevertheless, she has replied to it with all of her heart and reason and her letter includes all of her gall.

Whenever she forgets that, as a humble person, she often gets embroiled in matters that are beyond her capacities, it seems that to clear her mind it would be proper for her to take a cure.

This Lady has labelled my intellect as being dull because I have allegedly failed to understand her morals. I will respond to this as follows: My eyes cannot see anything that is not there. I am quite pleased the Lady of *This and That* has given me the opportunity to be judged by the general public. From our future letters the public will discover who between us was right.

Your Humble Servant,
Pravdoliubov

N. I. Novikov's Perception of Russian Society, January 1770

There is an old saying that is found in all languages, even at the present time: Everyone is seeking happiness. A few find it; the rest complain. Everyone interprets happiness in his own way. A *Miser* seeks happiness in great wealth; a *Pompous Person* in splendor; a *Haughty Person* in the servility of his subordinates; an *Amorous Person* in his lover; and so forth. I will present to my readers a few examples [of such characters].

A *Simpleton* is poorly educated, but nature has bestowed upon him exceptional qualities. In his youth he read many love stories that greatly influenced his thinking. This Simpleton is amorous and believes that of mortals he is the happiest person, especially when his female lover responds to him in the same way. He is delighted by every caress and by every glance. In short, this Simpleton believes that all of his happiness centers in his lover. This happiness, however, cannot endure for a long time, and, obviously, our Simpleton is deceiving himself.

Present-day expression of love differs vastly from that practiced by our ancestors. In our time many women do not consider it as sin to love one man and to deceive six. To say, therefore, that true love requires fidelity or blind devotion from a lover means that a lover must be blind. Present-day young lovers actually behave as follows. They pretend that they believe every word their lovers tell them, even though they think exactly the opposite. Frequently they behave like veteran government ministers. They cheat in order to discover the means to an end. This attitude has, in turn, been responsible for the emergence of an expression, which I know but to which I do not subscribe, that women are more cunning than men. I will leave to my gracious readers to decide who is more cunning: he who thinks he is deceiving and is being deceived, or he who allows himself to be deceived and is deceiving. I will add only that the Simpleton will not be happy in this town [St. Petersburg] and will have to search for his happiness in places located some distance from settlements.

A *Miser* has stemmed from a noble background, but, according to some observers, his blood is 1000 times more vicious than that of all mean peasants. At one time he was a judge in a lucrative office, and plundering and taking bribes were considered then as normal gifts. Consequently, while he ruined many people, he amassed for himself enormous wealth, which he would have increased in direct proportion to the groan of the poor and powerless people had not the Shining Truth that occupies the throne of Russia [Catherine II] in its vastness removed this parasite from his judgeship. But while they removed him from this post, he found, nevertheless, a way to oppress his fellow citizens. He loaned money, which he had accumulated illegally, at illegal rates, and, as his goal of happiness, he sought to increase his wealth, irrespective of the fact that he had no close relatives and could not consume more than one-tenth of his unearned annual income. In short, by practicing daily injustice and illegality, our Miser frequently complains that the government has imposed limits on his income. Albeit illegally, our Miser has found his happiness. But I know that every honest person will not envy him.

A *Pompous Person* has enormous wealth, but he manages it very poorly. Instead of helping the poor and fulfilling his other Christian obligations that plead for fulfillment, our Pompous Person annually purchases additional expensive carriages and accumulates an enormous number of horses, footmen, crews, and so forth. His dining room daily serves forty different dishes, but only fifteen people sit at the table. Our Pompous Person is not satisfied with everything he has. His only concern about his own happiness is that he cannot have it all. Ambition that is neither allowed nor attainable can seldom be realized! In order to increase his pomposity, our Pompous Person would like to acquire the wealth of the entire world. Fortunately, he cannot get that happiness, and I would like for him to be content with what he has and, of course, for him to be happy.

A *Pettifogger* is a person who, by using illegal means in his contracts and leases, has amassed a substantial fortune. He fights to the death for every *kopeck* and increases his wealth daily. At the same time, he sighs every minute and says that he is unhappy; that his children will inherit very little; that he is being constantly offended; that all idlers are happy and that he alone is a very unhappy person. [In our view] the Pettifogger cannot be happy because, although he has happiness within his reach, he does not know how to enjoy it.

Is it ever possible to list all human aspirations? Every human being is trying to seek his happiness in accordance with his individual inclinations. A large majority would like to have what it cannot have. These people will never be happy. Only those can be happy who are satisfied with what they have and whose ambitions know limits. These people aspire only to have what is essential for their well-being and not what they would like to have to satisfy their caprices. It would be very nice if everyone could follow the example of an *Honest Person* who has an annual income of 1000 rubles but who lives on 750 *rubles* and gives the rest to the poor. If that Honest Person desires more income, he desires it only to be able to contribute more to benefit others.

Finally, in accordance with well-established practice, in this New Year I wish happiness for all of my readers.

For the Well-to-Do People

Please be kind to your subordinates and to all of your common people. Arrange your activity and your affairs in such a way that they will consider you their protector and intercessor in their needs and not their tyrant who deprives them of their prosperity at a time when real benefits are being offered them in abundance from the throne. Be virtuous so that you will not think of oppressing the poor. Do good to all of them without exception, and passionately take more care of their well-being than your own. Do not listen to your flatterers because they, while seducing you, take advantage of your weaknesses and use your authority to oppress others. And those who are being oppressed consider this as a terrible blow from your own hand. These flatterers tell you that you are a well-born person. They lie. Behind your back they say that everyone is surprised by your generosity, that you satisfy their needs, that they cheat you; and they call you a dumbbell. Avoid these people because they are your poison. They are a bile that fills your sweet life with bitters.

Be the judge of your own action. Conduct your business impartially and you will discover how honest or deceitful your conduct is. Therein should be the center of your happiness! A truly virtuous person of your standing will obviously call himself happy should he decide to live up to these suggestions. And, frankly, it is not too difficult to remember that a poor person recognizes the virtuous one when the latter does not harm him.

My Appeal to the Middle Classes

Your status requires that you be appreciated by the well-to-do and by the poor because you occupy a middle ground between the high- and the low-born. You should always tell the former the truth without being rude; point out to them their transgressions; and show respect to the virtuous among them, not because of their rank, but because of their just and righteous behavior. Do not hold them in contempt on account of their innocent acts, because human weakness is a natural characteristic of mankind. Do not flatter them, and do not allow yourself to be embroiled in their generosity. Fortunes made in such a way do not last too long.

You should also remind your low-born associates of their obligations and, using your own exemplary behavior, try to encourage them to fulfill them. Finally, while preparing yourself for higher positions, you should also try to condition yourself to be a virtuous person, a characteristic that is very essential for those posts. Your should perform your duties justly and, in accordance with your performance, aspire to higher posts. At the early stage of your career you should become accustomed to bearing the burdens imposed on you by your superiors. Power and responsibility glitter on the outside and, therefore, they have attracted you. Be candid in your dealings with both the high- and the low-born. In your position make friends with everyone, but patronize only those who would tell you the truth even after you have gained a high post and who also would be so virtuous that you could learn something from them. If you cannot encounter such individuals, then you will not find happiness even though you may have a high rank. This is so because a person of high moral quality seldom has a true friend.

My Advice to Petty Bourgeoisie

I wish you continued industriousness and the display of a true sense of justice.

My Advice to the Poor

I wish that you were surrounded with decent and virtuous people and that your superiors would not oppress you. I believe that this would be your greatest happiness!

My Advice to Peasants

I wish that your nobles would behave toward you as your fathers and that you would act as their children. I wish you ample physical strength, good health, and industriousness. When you have these qualities, you will be happy. [And remember], your happiness benefits the entire empire.

[A New Year's Wish for Myself]

Finally, on the occasion of this New Year I would like to express a wish for my own happiness. What would I like? I will leave this to you, my readers, to figure out. But really I wish that all the wishes that I have expressed for my fellow citizens would please and benefit them and that they would not curse me.

13

The Russo-Polish Treaty on the First Partition of Poland, September 18, 1773

In the course of the eighteenth century the international stature of Poland deteriorated very rapidly and the territorially large country became a pawn in the balance-of-power game. In part this deterioration was brought on by such domestic problems as the *liberum veto,* religious dissent, ethnic discontent, and social unrest. In part Poland's problems stemmed from the increased ambition of her neighbors who sought to increase their territories at Poland's expense. The instigator of the territorial dismemberment of Poland was Frederick the Great of Prussia, who sought by this device to "reestablish the balance of power" in Europe. Russia adhered to this concept in 1771 and Austria in 1772. Each power then forced the powerless king of Poland to sign a treaty legalizing the naked aggression. The following is the Russian text of the "treaty."

Article I

Henceforth and forever there will be an inviolable peace, and sincere union and perfect friendship between His Majesty the King of Poland, the Grand Duke of Lithuania, and his successors, as well as the Kingdom of Poland and the Grand Duchy of Lithuania, on the one hand, and Her Majesty the Empress of All the Russias, her heirs and successors, and all her states, on the other hand, on the same basis as established by the Treaty of Warsaw of February 24, 1768, which treaty is renewed by the present treaty in the most authentic fashion, in order to have force, strength and value in all its articles, which have not been changed or restricted by the present treaty.

Article 2

In order to terminate irrevocably all boundary disputes between the two states and to abolish all claims of any nature, His Majesty the King of Poland, for his successors, and the Orders of the States General of the Kingdom of Poland

---

From Le Compte D'Angeberg [Chodzko], *Recueil des traites, conventions et actes diplomatiques concernant la Pologne 1762–1862* (A Collection of Treaties, Conventions and Diplomatic Papers Concerning Poland, 1762–1862) (Paris: 1862), pp. 126–136. Translation mine.

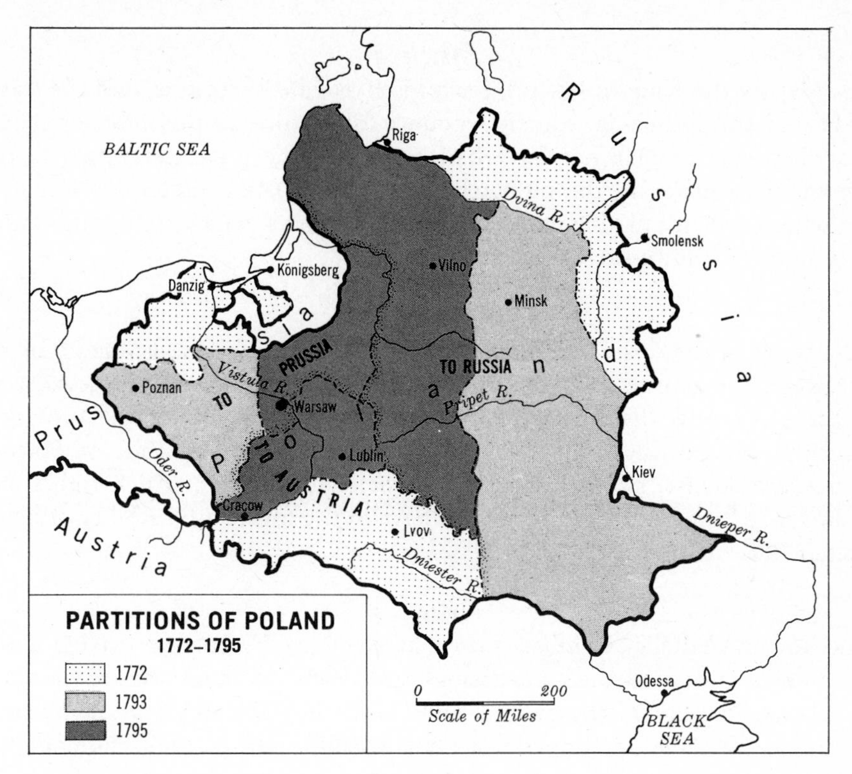

and of the Grand Duchy of Lithuania, cede by the present treaty irrevocably and in perpetuity and without any retraction or revision, to Her Majesty the Empress of All the Russias, her heirs and successors of both sexes, the following countries. . . .

[precise description of the frontier follows.]

His Majesty the King of Poland, and the Orders of the States of the Kingdom of Poland and the Grand Duchy of Lithuania, cede therefore to Her Imperial Majesty of All the Russias, her heirs and successors, all the countries and districts mentioned. According to the agreement thus determined for the new boundaries between the two states, with all property, sovereignty and independence, with all cities, fortresses, villages and rivers, with all vassals, subjects and inhabitants from whom they demand at the same time both the homage and loyalty which they have given to His Majesty and the Crown of Poland, with all the civil, political and spiritual rights, and in general with everything that belongs with the sovereignty of these countries, and they promise never to lay claim under any pretext to these provinces ceded in the present treaty.

Article 3

His Majesty the King of Poland, for himself and his successors, and the states of Poland and Lithuania, equally renounce for all time all the rights or claims that they may or may not have had on any of the provinces which at the present time make up the monarchy of all the Russias, under any denomination, pretext, stipulation of events or circumstances, which rights and claims may never in the future be exercised.

Article 4

As a result of the cession stipulated in Article 2, Her Imperial Majesty of All the Russias renounces, on her part, for all time and for her successors, all rights and claims that she may have or have had on any of the provinces which at the present time comprise the states of the Republic of Poland, under any pretext, stipulation of events or circumstances, which rights and claims may have been legal, or should have in the future a possibility of being exercised.

Article 5

The Roman Catholics *utriusque ritus* shall enjoy, in the provinces ceded under the present treaty, all their possessions and property; as for their civil rights in relation to religion, they will entirely be maintained in *status quo,* that is to say, in the same free exercise of their worship with all their churches and ecclesiastical goods which they possessed at the moment of their passage under the domination of Her Imperial Majesty in September, 1772, and Her Imperial Majesty and her successors shall not use their sovereign rights to jeopardize the *status quo* of the Roman Catholics in the aforementioned countries.

Article 6

Her Imperial Majesty of All the Russias guarantees formally, and in the most firm manner, to His Majesty the King of Poland and his successors, and to the Republic of Poland, all their actual possessions according to the intent of, and as they were after the treaty was entered into by the Serene Republic of Poland and the Empress of Hungary and Bohemia, and the King of Prussia. In the same manner the King and the Republic of Poland guarantee to Her Imperial Majesty of All the Russias and to her successors, according to the extent and in the state in which they now exist, those European possessions transferred after the conclusion of these treaties. And the two high contracting parties declare the same conditions to the new state which they intended to execute thusly in Article 2 of their treaty of 1768.

Article 7

Her Imperial Majesty, having declared her will to contribute by her good offices to establishing a calm and good order in Poland on a solid and permanent basis, will guarantee a constitution, which will be made in perfect agreement with the ministers of the three contracting courts and of the parliament presently assembled in Warsaw under the auspices of a Confederation, and a free, republican and independent form of government for the pacification of the condition of subjects of the religion of Eastern Orthodox non-Uniats and the dissidents of the two evangelic rites; for this purpose there shall be established a separate act under the constitution which will be signed by the ministers and respective commissioners as an integral part of the present treaty and will have the same force and value as if it were here inserted word for word. And the two high contracting parties declare that Articles 3, 4 and 5 of the treaty of 1768, with the separate acts which are contained therein, will not be considered to be a result of what will be arranged in the mentioned separate acts.

Article 8

Everything that will be arranged and stipulated either in the treaties or separate conventions which will take place later and everything that concerns itself with commerce between the two nations and all of their intercourse, will have the same force and value as if it were inserted word for word in the present treaty.

Article 9

Since one cannot include in this treaty everything that might bring close understanding and benefit to both states, other separate acts, which are to be inserted where stipulated and accorded on the part of both, will have the same force and value as if they were a part of this treaty.

Article 10

In order to establish properly the frontiers between the two states, the two high contracting parties declare that they will appoint immediately commissioners for this purpose, and in the case that these commissioners will not be able to agree upon the interpretation of Article 2 of this treaty, they will rely upon the mediation of the two other contracting courts, while in the meantime the work of demarcation will be halted. And if disputes between the two states or their subjects were to arise in the future concerning the boundaries, commissioners from both sides will be appointed who will try to work out an amicable agreement.

Article 11

Because of the disturbances that have agitated the Kingdom of Poland and the war which has arisen between the Russian Empire and the Ottoman Porte, the latter having published a manifesto in which it blames the Republic of Poland for the violation of the Treaty of Karlowitz, and because of the doubts and anxieties that have arisen concerning the effective existence of this peace and the subsequent attitude of the Porte towards the Republic, Her Imperial Majesty of All the Russias promises to work with Her Majesty the Empress of Hungary and Bohemia and His Majesty the King of Prussia to dissuade the Porte from all hostile views against the Serene Republic. . . .

14

The Pugachev Rebellion

When Peter III released Russian nobles from compulsory service to the state in 1762 (see Chapter 9), unfounded rumors began to circulate among the peasants that their own emancipation from the nobility would follow. Peasant expectations were shattered first by the murder of Peter III and then by the increased rigors of serfdom that followed Catherine II's accession to the throne, among them her dissolution of the Legislative Commission and her issuance in August 1767 of a decree prohibiting all complaints by serfs against their masters. The closing of this only avenue of redress increased peasant restlessness and precipitated the peasant revolt of 1773–1774. The leader of this war was an obscure Cossack, Emelian Pugachev (1730–1775), who posed as Emperor Peter III. His forces seized control of vast areas in the Volga Basin, terrorized many nobles, and promised freedom to the lower strata of Russian society. Catherine II tried to calm the panic-stricken nobility through patriotic appeals and through the dispatch of strong military formations against Pugachev. Late in 1774 the tide turned in favor of the government forces and Pugachev was captured, tried, and executed.

Catherine II's Manifesto Against Pugachev, December 23, 1773

By the Grace of God, We, Catherine II, Empress and Autocratrix of All the Russias, etc.

From William Tooke, *The Life of Catherine II, Empress of All the Russians* (Dublin: 1800), vol. 2, pp. 345–346. Spellings have been modernized to facilitate reading.

Make known to all Our faithful subjects that We have learnt, with the utmost indignation and extreme affliction, that a certain Cossack, a deserter and fugitive from the Don, named Emelian Pugachev, after having traversed Poland, has been collecting, for some time past, in the districts that border on the river Ural, in the government of Orenburg, a troop of vagabonds like himself; that he continues to commit in those parts all kinds of excesses, by inhumanly depriving the inhabitants of their possessions, and even of their lives; and that in order to attract to his party, hitherto composed of robbers, such persons as he meets, and especially the unhappy patriots, on whose credulity he imposes, he has had the insolence to arrogate to himself the name of the late Emperor Peter III. It would be superfluous here to prove the absurdity of such an imposture, which cannot even put on a shadow of probability in the eyes of sensible persons; for, thanks to the Divine Goodness, those ages are past in which the Russian Empire was plunged in ignorance and barbarism when Gregory Otrepiev, with his adherents and several other traitors to their country, made use of impostures as gross and detestable to arm brother against brother, and citizen against citizen.

Since those times, which it is grievious to recollect, all true patriots have enjoyed the fruits of public tranquillity, and shudder with horror at the very remembrance of former troubles. In a word, there is not a man deserving of the Russian name, who does not hold in abomination the odious and insolent lie by which Pugachev fancies himself able to seduce and to deceive persons of a simple and credulous disposition, by promising to free them from the bonds of submission, and obedience to their sovereign, as if the Creator of the universe had established human societies in such a manner as that they can subsist without an intermediate authority between the sovereign and the people.

Nevertheless, as the insolence of this vile refuse of the human race is attended with consequences pernicious to the provinces adjacent to that district; as the report of the flagrant enormities which he has committed may affright those persons who are accustomed to imagine the misfortunes of others as ready to fall upon them, and as We watch with indefatigable care over the tranquillity of Our faithful subjects, We inform them by the present manifesto that We have taken, without delay, such measures as are the best adapted to stifle the sedition: and in order to annihilate totally the ambitious designs of Pugachev, and to exterminate a band of robbers, who have been audacious enough to attack the small military detachments dispersed about those countries, and to massacre the officers who were taken prisoners, We have dispatched thither, with a competent number of troops, General Alexander Bibikov [1727–1774], general in chief of Our armies, and major of Our regiment of life guards.

Accordingly, We have no doubt of the happy success of these measures, and We cherish the hope that the public tranquillity will soon be restored, and that the profligates who are spreading devastation over a part of the government of Orenburg will shortly be dispersed. We are moreover persuaded that Our faithful subjects will justly abhor the imposture of the rebel Pugachev, as destitute of all probability, and will repel the artifices of the ill-disposed, who seek and find their advantage in the seduction of the weak and credulous, and who cannot assuage their avidity but by ravaging their country, and by shedding of innocent blood.

We trust, with equal confidence, that every true son of the country will unremittedly fulfill his duty of the contributing to the maintenance of good order and of public tranquillity, by preserving himself from the snares of seduction, and by duly discharging his obedience to his lawful sovereign. All Our faithful subjects therefore may dispel their alarms and live in perfect security, since We employ Our utmost care, and make it Our peculiar glory, to preserve their property, and to extend the general felicity.

Given at St. Petersburg, December 23, 1773.

*Pugachev's "Emancipation Decree," July 31, 1774**

We, Peter III, by the Grace of God Emperor and Autocrat of All-Russia, etc.

This is given for nationwide information.

By this personal decree, with our monarchial and fatherly love, we grant [freedom] to everyone who formerly was in serfdom or in any other obligation to the nobility; and we transfer these to be faithful personal subjects of our crown; [to the Old Believers] we grant the right to use the ancient sign of the Cross, and to pray, and to wear beards; while to the Cossacks [we restore] for eternity their freedoms and liberties; we [hereby] terminate the recruiting system, cancel personal and other monetary taxes, abolish without compensation the ownership of land, forest, pastures, fisheries and salt deposits; and [finally] we free everyone from all taxes and obligations which the thievish nobles and extortionist city judges have imposed on the peasantry and the rest of the population. We pray for the salvation of your souls and wish you a happy and peaceful life here [on earth] where we have suffered and experienced much from the above-mentioned thievish nobles. Now since our name,

*From *Pugachevshchina: Iz arkhiva Pugacheva. Manifesty, ukazy i perepiska (The Pugachev Upheaval: From the Pugachev Archieve. Manifestos, Decrees and Correspondence)*, (Moscow-Leningrad: Tsentarkhiv, 1926), vol. 1, pp. 40–41. Translation mine. Words in brackets are mine.

thanks to the hand of Providence, flourishes throughout Russia, we make hereby known by this personal decree the following: all nobles who have owned either *pomesties*, [estates granted by the state] or *votchinas* [inherited estates], who have opposed our rule, who have rebelled against the empire, and who have ruined the peasantry should be seized, arrested, and hanged; that is, treated in the same manner as these unchristians have treated you, the peasantry. After the extermination of these opponents and thievish nobles everyone will live in a peace and happiness that shall continue to eternity.

Peter Given July 31, 1774

15

The Treaty of Kutchuk Kainardzhi, July 21, 1774

In the eighteenth century the Russian Empire achieved two major ambitions. Early in the century, after some twenty years of fighting, Peter I established Russia as a Baltic Sea power at the expense of Sweden, and by the end of the century, after two wars (1768–1774 and 1787–1792), Catherine II had elevated the empire into a Black Sea power at the expense of the Ottoman Empire. Of the two processes, the later was more spectacular and in the long run more advantageous to Russia. It also created more complications for Russia, for it involved her in a series of prolonged struggles in the nineteenth century, first with the Ottoman, then with the Austrian, English, French, and German empires. One of the basic causes for these complications stemmed from the misinterpretation of the terms of the Treaty of Kutchuk Kainardzhi of July 21, 1774, which, among other things, gave Russia valuable territories, opened the Black Sea and the Straits to navigation, and, under cover of protecting Orthodox Christians throughout the Ottoman Empire, provided Russia with a pretext for intervention in domestic affairs of the Ottoman state.

From *Polnoe Sobranie Zakonov Russkoi Imperii* . . . (Complete Collection of the Laws of the Russian Empire), 1st series, vol. 19, No. 14, 164, pp. 957-67. Translation mine.

Article 1

All hostile activities and enmities that have occurred between the two countries are hereby terminated forever; also forgotten are all hostile activities and oppositions, armed or otherwise, which both sides undertook or resorted to, and under no circumstances should these return; instead there should be an eternal and inviolable peace on land as well as on the sea. Equally let there be sincere agreement, inviolable eternal friendship and the most diligent execution of and adherence to these articles and the unity agreed on by the two contracting parties, Her Illustrious Imperial Majesty and His Majesty the Sultan, and their heirs and descendants, as well as between the Empires, possessions, territories, subjects and citizens of both countries. Henceforth, neither side will undertake against each other, secretly or openly, any hostile act or opposition. As a result of the renewal of such a sincere friendship, both sides will issue amnesties and general pardon to all those subjects, regardless of their status, who transgressed in one way or another against the other country; they will free all those who are chained to the galleys or who are in dungeons; they will allow the exiles to return, and will promise to return to them all of their possessions and titles which they enjoyed previously; they will not allow any uncalled for abuses, losses or insults under any pretext whatsoever. All of them should be allowed to live under the safety and protection of laws and customs of their lands similarly as their fellow countrymen. . . .

Article 3

All Tartar peoples: Crimean, Bug, Kuban, Edisan, Zhambuiluk, and Edichkul, without exception should be recognized by both Empires as free and completely independent from any outside power, and living under the autocratic rule of their own Khan of the line of Ghenghis Khan, elected and elevated by the entire Tartar nation, who in turn will govern them on the basis of old laws and customs without giving any account of his rule to any foreign power. Neither the Russian Court nor the Ottoman Porte will interfere in any election or elevation of the said Khan, nor in domestic, political, civil, and internal matters under any pretext, but will recognize and consider this Tartar nation politically and civilly as any other nation, governed by its own laws, independent of anyone else, except God. In religious matters, however, as Moslems, in the judgment of his Sultanic Majesty as the Supreme Caliph of the Islamic faith, they [the Tartars] must conform to rules stipulated by their faith without the slightest violation, retaining at the same time political and civil liberties. The Russian Empire will surrender to this Tartar nation, excepting the fortresses of Kerch and Eniko with their counties and harbors which the Russian Empire will retain for itself, all cities, forts, villages, lands and ports in the

Crimea and the Kuban which were won during the war; the lands between the Berda River, the Konskie Waters and the Dnieper; and also all the land along the Polish frontier between the Rivers Bug and Dniester, except the fort Ochakov with its old *uezd*, which shall belong to the Sublime Porte. [The Russian Empire] pledges, following the signing of the peace treaty and the exchange of ratifications, to remove all of its forces from Tartar possessions; while the Sublime Porte pledges equally to renounce all of its rights to forts, cities, villages and everything in the Crimea, Kuban, and on the island of Taman; not to station any military units or personnel; and to relinquish these regions to the Tartars, similarly as has the Russian Court, to complete supreme, independent rule and administration. Moreover, the Sublime Porte solemnly undertakes and pledges never in the future to bring into the above mentioned cities, forts, lands, and settlements, any kind of military personnel, or to maintain it there, and will leave all Tartars in full freedom and independence in the same way as the Russian Empire has done. . . .

Article 7

The Sublime Porte pledges to give the Christian faith and its churches firm protection and it grants the Ministers of the Russian Imperial Court [the right] to protect all interests of the church built in Constantinople and mentioned below, in Article 14, and those whom it serves, and it [the Porte] will accept any complaints respectfully, since these are being made by a trusted person of a neighboring and truly friendly country.

Article 8

Both religious and civil subjects of the Russian Empire have permission to journey freely to the holy city of Jerusalem and other solemn places, and from those persons there shall not be collected, either in Jerusalem or other places or along the road, any fee, tax, tribute, or any other payments; on the contrary they should be provided with appropriate passports and decrees similar to those which subjects of other friendly countries use. During their stay in the Ottoman Empire they should not be insulted, even in the slightest way, or offended, but they should be given full protection.

Article 11

For the convenience and advantage of both Empires, there shall be free and unimpeded navigation for the merchant ships belonging to both Contracting Powers, in all the seas which wash their shores; the Sublime Porte permits Russian merchant vessels, such as are universally employed by the other powers for commerce in its ports, free passage from the Black Sea into the White Sea [Aegean], and reciprocally from the White Sea [Aegean] into the Black

Sea; as also permission to enter all the ports and harbors situated either on the seacoasts, or in the passages and channels which join those seas. Likewise, the Sublime Porte allows subjects of the Russian Empire to trade in its territories by land as well as by water, and upon the Danube by ship, in accordance with the rights and privileges specified above in this Article, which are also enjoyed in its territories by other friendly people whom the Sublime Porte favors in trade, such as the French and the English; and the Capitulations of those two nations and others shall, just as if they were here inserted verbatim, serve as a rule equally for commerce as well as Russian merchants, who upon paying the same duties may import and export all kinds of goods and disembark their merchandise at every port and harbor, on the Black as well as on the other seas, including Constantinople.

While granting in the above manner to their respective subjects freedom of commerce and navigation upon all waters without exception, the two Empires at the same time allow merchants to stop within their territories for as long a time as their business requires, and promise them the same security and freedom as are enjoyed by the subjects of other friendly Courts. And in order to be consistent throughout, the Sublime Porte also allows the establishment of Consulates and Vice-Consulates in those places where the Russian Empire may consider it expedient to establish them; they shall be respected equally with the Consuls of other friendly powers. It permits them to have interpreters called *Baratli*, that is, those who have patents, providing them with Imperial patents, and allowing them to enjoy the same prerogatives as those in the service of the said French, English, and other nations.

Similarly, the Russian Empire permits the subjects of the Sublime Porte to trade in its dominions, by sea and by land, with the same prerogatives and advantages as are enjoyed by the most friendly nations, and upon paying the usual duties. In case of accident to the vessels, the two Empires are bound respectively to render them the same assistance as is given in similar cases to other friendly nations; and all necessary things shall be furnished to them at the usual price.

Article 12

Whenever the Russian Imperial Court will wish to enter into a commercial agreement with the African provinces of Tripoli, Tunis and Algeria, the Sublime Porte will use all of its power and trust to realize the aspirations of the above mentioned Court, and will act, for the above mentioned provinces, as a guarantor in the execution of all conditions which may be stipulated in agreements. . . .

Article 14

The Imperial Court of Russia, similarly as other countries, has the right, in addition to a private chapel in the quarters of the Minister, to build in the

Galat Part [of Constantinople] on Bei Ogl Street, a public Greek Orthodox Church, which shall remain always under the protection of Ministers of that Empire, and it shall not be subjected to any persecution or insult. . . .

Article 16

The Russian Empire returns to the Sublime Porte all of Bessarabia, with the cities of Akkerman, Kiliia, Izmail and other settlements, villages and everything which that province possesses; equally the fortress Bendery is being returned. The Russian Empire returns to the Sublime Porte the Wallachian and Moldavian principalities with all of their fortresses, cities, settlements, villages and everything they posses; the Sublime Porte accepts these on the following conditions, which it pledges solemnly to observe: (1) To accord to all citizens of these principalities, regardless of their social status, rank, occupation, or race, without exception, complete amnesty and full forgiveness as stipulated in Article 1 of this treaty, whether they actually committed a felony or were suspected of endangering the interests of the Sublime Porte, and to restore to them their previous dignity, rank, and estates, and return to them the property which was theirs before the present war; (2) Not to interfere in any way with absolute freedom of the Christian faith or with the building of new or repairing of old churches; (3) To restore to monasteries and private people lands and estates which previously belonged to them but which had been, in violation of all justice, taken away from them near Brailov, Khotin, Bendery and other places, which now are known as *rais*; (4) To recognize clergymen and extend the respect which is due them; (5) To allow freedom of movement with all property to those families who wish to leave their country and resettle in other countries; these families will have one year, starting from the ratification date of this treaty, to settle all their affairs before their free departure from their country; (6) No monetary or other obligation for old debts, regardless of their nature, should be collected; (7) No contributions or payments should be demanded from people for the war period; and for the many sufferings and ruins they experienced in the present war, no payments during the next two years following the exchange of ratifications of this treaty should be collected; (8) Upon the expiration of two years [the Sublime Porte] pledges to observe every compassion and generosity in imposing on them monetary taxes, which should be collected every second year by special deputies; because of this regularly collected tax, no official, be he a Pasha or a governor, can either oppress them or demand from them any payments or taxes under any pretext; they [the people] should exercise the same privileges they enjoyed during the reign of Sultan Mehmet IV, of glorious memory, father of the beloved present Sultan; (9) The princes of the two principalities [Wallachia and Moldavia] have the right to maintain at the court of the Sublime Porte Christian representatives of the Greek faith, who will concern themselves with the affairs of these principalities, and who will be treated appropriately by the Sublime Porte; being humans and enjoying full civil rights, they will not be subject to any oppression; (10) It is also agreed that Ministers of the Imperial Court of Russia attached to the Sublime Porte have the right to speak on behalf of both principalities [Wallachia and Moldavia], and it is understood that their interests will be heard with sympathetic and respectful attention.

Article 17

The Russian Empire returns to the Sublime Porte all coastal islands which are under its suzerainty, and the Sublime Porte on its part pledges: (1) To observe solemnly, in the treatment of the inhabitants of those islands, conditions set forth in Article 1 regarding general amnesty and full pardon of all transgressions committed or suspected of having been committed against the interests of the Sublime Porte; (2) Not to subject the Christian faith or its churches to even the slightest oppression, and to place no obstacles in the way of building or repairing of churches; people who serve in these churches shall not be insulted or oppressed; (3) To collect no annual taxes from the people for the time they were under the occupation of the Russian Empire, and for a period of two years following the transfer of those islands to the Sublime Porte, on account of the great suffering they endured in the course of this war; (4) To give to families who wish to leave their country and settle in other places free exit with all their possessions; and so that these families have a chance to settle their affairs they are to have one year beginning with the date of the exchange of ratifications of the treaty to leave freely their country; and (5) Should the Russian fleet need anything on its departure, which is to take place three months after the exchange of ratifications of the treaty, the Sublime Porte will provide it with everything it [the fleet] needs.

Article 18

The Castle Kinburn, located at the mouth of the Dnieper River, with a sizable area on the left bank of the Dnieper and with the angle which comprises the steppe between the Dnieper and the Bug Rivers, will remain under complete, eternal, and direct rule of the Russian Empire.

Article 19

The fortresses of Enikal and Kerch, located on the Crimean peninsula, with their harbors and everything they possess, as well as all counties, starting with the Black Sea and following the old Kerch frontier to the land of Bugak, and from Bugak in a straight line to the Sea of Azov, will remain under complete, eternal, and direct rule of the Russian Empire.

Article 20

The city of Azov with its surroundings, that is, limits stipulated in the treaty of 1700, negotiated by Governor Tolstoy and the Governor of Achug, Hassan Pasha, will eternally belong to the Russian Empire.

Article 21

Both Kabardas, namely Great and Little, because of their proximity to the Tartars have a greater tie with the Crimean Khans; consequently [the question of] their acquisition by the Imperial Court of Russia should be decided by the Crimean Khan, his Council, and his Tartar Elders.

Article 22

Both Empires agree to cancel completely and to forget forever all previous treaties and conventions between them, including the Treaty of Belgrad and conventions stemming from it, and never to claim any rights deriving from them, except the treaty of 1700 between Governor Tolstoy and the Achug Governor, Hassan Pasha, concerning the borders of Azov county and the outlining of the frontiers of Kuban, established by a convention which will remain unaltered. . . .

16

Catherine II's Charter to the Nobility, April 21, 1785

On April 21, 1785, Catherine II granted the Russian nobles a charter of rights and privileges. In part an expression of Catherine's thanks for the support they had given her, the charter also represented the last stage in the general improvement of the nobility's position since the death of Peter I. Under the new charter, the nobles in each *gubernia*, or administrative district, became a privileged class with broad powers of self-government and great administrative influence. Each noble was exempted from state service, the payment of taxes, and army conscription. He

---

From *Polnoe Sobranie Zakonov Russkoi Imperii . . . (Complete Collection of the Laws of the Russian Empire),* 1st Series, vol. 22, no. 16,187, pp. 346–351. Translation mine. Words in brackets are mine.

possessed absolute right of ownership over his land and peasants and was at liberty to pursue trade or industry. The Russian nobles called Catherine's reign their "golden age."

As a result of new gains and the expansion of Our Empire, when We everywhere enjoy every kind of internal and external peace, We direct Our great deed more and more toward an uninterrupted occupation with delivering to Our faithful subjects in all vital branches of internal state administration durable and lasting decrees aimed at the increase of happiness and order for future times; toward that aim We find it appropriate to extend Our solicitude to Our loyal Russian *dvorianstvo* [nobility], in view of the services, zeal, attention, and undeviating faith to All-Russian autocrats—to Ourselves as well as to Our throne—which it [the nobility] has shown during troublesome times, in war as well as peace. And following God's examples of justice, mercy, and grace, which have beautified the Russian throne and glorified our ancestors, and being moved by Our own motherly love and distinct gratitude to the Russian nobility, Our imperial judiciousness and will order, decrees, announces, and approves undeviatingly for eternity, for the benefit of Russian nobility, in Our and imperial service, the following articles:

1. The title of the nobility is hereditary and stems from the quality and virtue of leading men of antiquity who distinguished themselves by their service—which they turned into merit and acquired for their posterity the title of the nobility.

2. It is to the advantage of both the Empire and the Crown, as it is also just, that the respectful title of the nobility be maintained and approved firmly and inviolably; and therefore, as formerly, now and in the future the title of the nobility is irrevocable, hereditary, and belongs to those honorable families who use it; and accordingly:

3. A nobleman transmits his noble title to his wife;

4. A nobleman transmits his noble title to his children hereditarily;

5. Neither a nobleman nor a noblewoman can be deprived of the title of the nobility unless they forfeit it themselves by an act contrary to the standards of noble dignity.

6. The following acts are contrary to the standards of noble dignity and can deprive one of the title: (a) violation of an oath; (b) treason; (c) robbery; (d) thefts of all sorts; (e) deceitful acts; (f) violations which call for either corporal punishment or a deprivation of honor; (g) incitement of others to commit violations—if this be established.

7. But since the title of the nobility cannot be revoked except as a result of violation, and marriage is an honest [institution] set up by divine law, when a noblewoman marries a non-noble man she does not forfeit her title; but she cannot pass on her nobility to her husband or her children.

8. A nobleman cannot be deprived of his title without due process of law.

9. A nobleman cannot be deprived of his honor without due process of law.

10. A nobleman cannot be deprived of his life without due process of law.

11. A nobleman cannot be deprived of his property without due process of law.

12. A nobleman can be judged by his peers only.

13. A nobleman who has committed a crime and is legally liable to be deprived either of his title, honor, or life, cannot be punished without his case being presented before the Senate and then approved by his Imperial Majesty.

14. All criminal acts of a nobleman which for ten years went either unnoticed or had no action taken on them we decree be henceforth forgotten forever. . . .

15. A nobleman cannot be subjected to corporal punishment.

16. Noblemen who serve as junior officers in Our armed forces should be punished according to regulations applicable to senior officers.

17. We confirm freedom and liberty to the Russian nobility on an hereditary basis for eternity.

18. We confirm the right of the nobles now in service to continue their service or to ask freedom from service on the basis of the regulations established for that purpose.

19. We confirm the right of the nobles to enter the service of other European countries friendly to Us and to travel abroad.

20. Since the title and privileges of the nobility in the past, present, and future are acquired by service and work useful to the Empire and the throne, and since the very existence of Russian nobility depends on the security of the country and the throne, whenever Russian autocracy needs the service of the nobility for the general well being, every nobleman is then obligated, the moment the autocratic government calls him, to perform fully his duty and sacrifice his life, if need be, to government service.

21. A nobleman has the right to sign his name not only as lord of his *pomestie* estate, granted to him by the state, but also as owner of his *votchina* estate, inherited from his ancestors or granted through grace.

22. A nobleman has the power and the authority to give away to whomever he wishes the property which he acquired legally as first owner, to bequeath this property in his will, to confer it as dowry, or to sell or give it away for his livelihood. He may, however, dispose of inherited property only in conformity with the provisions of the law.

23. The inheritable property of a nobleman who may be convicted of a serious crime should pass on to his legal heirs.

24. No one should attempt to seize or damage arbitarily a nobleman's property without due process of law or the legal judgement of the appropriate court of justice.

25. If a nobleman has a claim against another nobleman he should bring it before the appropriate court of justice.

26. The nobles have the right to purchase villages.

27. The nobles have the right to sell wholesale whatever their villages grow or their handicrafts produce.

28. The nobles may have factories and mills in their villages.

29. The nobles may build small towns on their estates on which they may organize trade and annual fairs. [This activity must not be] contrary to state laws, must be done with the full knowledge of governor generals and *gubernia* administrations, and must be arranged in such a way as not to conflict with fairs of other local cities.

30. The nobles have the right to have, to build, or to buy homes in cities and to have handicrafts there.

31. In case a nobleman prefers to make use of the municipal code of civil rights, he may subordinate himself to it.

32. The nobles are hereby permitted to sell abroad wholesale the products harvested or made on their property, or to have them exported from the designated harbors.

33. The nobles have the right granted to them by the gracious *ukaz* of June 28, 1782 to ownership of not only the fruits of the land belonging to them, but also all resources found beneath the surface and in waters, and all of their products, as is fully stated in that *ukaz.*

34. The nobles have the right of ownership of forests which grow on their property and of their free utilization as is fully explained in the gracious *ukaz* of September 22, 1782.

35. The homes of the nobility in villages are to be free from quartering of soldiers.

36. A nobleman is personally freed from the soul tax. . . .

37. We grant Our faithful nobles the permission to assemble in the *gubernias* where they live, to organize in every *namestnichestvo* [district] an Association of Nobles, and to enjoy the rights, privileges, distinctions, and preferences stated below.

38. Nobles may assemble in the *gubernia* by and with the permission of the governor-general or governor every three years during the winter for the purpose of electing noble representatives as well as to hear proposals of the governor-general or the governor.

39. The meeting of nobles in the *namestnichestvo* has permission to elect a *gubernia* marshal of the nobility; this election will occur every three years

at which time the names of two marshals of the *uezd* nobility will be submitted to the imperial representative or administrator. The governor-general or the governor will then designate which will be *gubernia* marshal of the nobility for that *gubernia*.

40. By virtue of articles 64 and 211 of the statutes, the *uezd* marshal of the nobility is elected by the nobility of the *uezd* through secret ballot every three years. . . .

47. The Association of Nobles has permission to present its needs and interests to the governor-general or the governor.

48. The Association of Nobles has permission to petition, through its deputies, both the Senate and the Imperial Majesty in accordance with the law. . . .

62. The Association of Nobles cannot elect a nobleman whose annual income from his village is below 200 *rubles*, or who is under twenty years of age, to perform functions of an elective representative of the nobility.

63. A nobleman who either has no village or is under twenty years of age can participate in the Association of Nobles but cannot have an elective voice.

64. A nobleman who never performed any service or who served but did not attain officer rank (even though officer rank was given to him at retirement) may be a member of the Association of Nobles; but he cannot sit in deliberation with the worthy ones or have the right to elect or be elected. . . .

17

Russian Schools In The Eighteenth Century

In the eighteenth century Imperial Russia was profoundly transformed in practically all areas of activity, including—above all—education. Peter I built the foundation of the educational system with the establishment of a number of professionally oriented schools with utilitarian curricula. Under Catherine II, Russia's educational system expanded with the addition of several institutions (state and privately supported) of research

---

Source: *Polnoe Sobranie Zakonov,* First Series, Vol. XXII, No. 16, 421, pp. 646–669. Translation mine.

and learning and with the official chartering of a network of state-sponsored elementary and secondary schools.

On paper, Catherine II's efforts were quite impressive. In practice, however, there was a marked discrepancy between the official intent and the final product. This discrepancy stemmed from the fact that the government failed to allocate the necessary funds for education and never allowed education to enjoy the required freedom of inquiry; and that serfs and indigenous natives, who comprised more than half of the Empire's population, were not legally entitled to education. The net result of this policy was that (with the single exception of the multinational Ottoman Empire) Imperial Russia had the highest illiteracy rate of all major countries of Europe and continued to enjoy that distinction until the twentieth century.

Rules Governing Public Elementary Schools in the Russian Empire, August 5, 1786

Chapter One: Public Elementary Schools

I. Grades in Public Elementary Schools

1. There should be one elementary school in the capital of each *gubernia*. Each such school should consist of four grades or classes where pupils should be taught, in their native language, the following academic and scientific subjects:

2. In the first grade they should be taught reading, writing, the fundamentals of Christian religion, and manners. After they have mastered the alphabet, children should be taught how to group letters together. Then they should read the primer, rules for students, abbreviated catechism, and church history. During the second half of the school year children should be required to copy from books and identify and write letters of the alphabet and Church and Roman numerals. They also should be taught the elementary rules of grammar, which are appended in a table alongside the alphabet in a volume entitled *A Guide for Teachers of the First and Second Grades.*

3. The following books, published on orders of Her Imperial Majesty, are to be used in teaching the subjects to the pupils of the above-mentioned grades: (a) *The Alphabet Table*; (b) *A Table Governing the Connection of Letters*; (c) *The Russian Primer*; (d) *Rules for Students*; (e) *Abbreviated Catechism*; (f) *Church History*; (g) *A Guide Book on Copying*; and (h) *A Guide to Penmanship.*

4. In the second class or grade, while reviewing the same subjects and Christian religion and manners, students should start reading the expanded catechism (minus explanations from the Holy Scriptures); a book on obligations of individuals and citizens; and the first part of arithmetic. They also

should review church history; continue their penmanship; and study the rules of grammar that are found in the table on proper articulation of letter connection, reading, and orthography in the above-mentioned volume, *A Guide for Teachers of the First and Second Grades.* In this grade pupils should be introduced to drawing.

5. The following books, published on orders of Her Imperial Majesty, are to be used in this grade: (a) *Expanded Catechism*; (b) *Church History*; (c) *A Book on Obligations of Individuals and Citizens*; (d) *A Guideline for Calligraphy*; (e) *A Book on Copying*; and (f) *The First Part of Arithmetic.*

6. The third grade curriculum should include the following: drawing; reading of excerpts from the New Testament; review of the expanded catechism with examples from the Bible; the second part of arithmetic; the first part of world history; introduction to general European geography and a preliminary survey of the Russian Empire; and Russian grammar with exercises in orthography.

7. The following books, published on orders of Her Imperial Majesty, are to be used in this grade: (a) *The Expanded Catechism*; (b) *Excerpts from the New Testament*; (c) *The Second Part of Arithmetic*; (d) *The First Part of World History*; (e) *General Geography and Geography of the Russian Empire*; (f) *A General Outline of Europe, Asia, Africa, America and the Russian Empire*; (g) *The Terrestrial Globe*; and (h) *Russian Grammar.*

8. In the fourth grade students should review the following subjects: Russian geography; drawing; world history; and Russian grammar. They also should be exposed to the works that have practical application to correspondence, accounting, drawing and the like. Also in this grade lectures should be given on Russian history and on general and applied geography with map exercises, and on foundations of geometry, mechanics, physics, natural history, and public architecture. The first year of mathematics should emphasize geometry and architecture, while the second should stress mechanics, physics, architectural drawing, and designing.

9. The following books, published on orders of Her Imperial Majesty, are to be used in this grade: (a) *Russian Grammar*; (b) *Russian Geography*; (c) *General World Geography*, including an introduction to the understanding of the mathematical concepts of the globe; (d) *Russian History*; (e) *World History* (Part II); (f) *General Outlines of the World*, that is, Europe, Asia, Africa, America, and Russia; (g) *The Globe*; (h) *Geometry*; (i) *Architecture*; (j) *Mechanics*; (k) *Physics*; and (l) *An Outline of Natural History.*

10. Furthermore, each elementary school [in *gubernia* capitals] will have a program enabling those who wish to, to become teachers in elementary schools. Those interested in pursuing it must study teaching methods, and,

after successfully passing their examinations, each will receive a teaching certificate from the Director of Public Education.

II. The Study of Foreign Languages in Public Elementary Schools

11. All public elementary schools, in addition to teaching basic rules of the Russian language as the principal national language, should also teach basic rules of Latin for those wishing to continue their education in higher institutions of learning, namely in gymnasia or universities. In addition they should teach foreign languages of countries that border on the given *gubernia* in which the elementary school is located in order to utilize its graduates in future public life. . . .

III. The Teaching Resources of Public Elementary Schools

14. Because not everyone can have them at home, teaching resources, for those who teach and study in public elementary schools in Russia, should consist of the following:

15. A library containing foreign and Russian books, especially those pertaining to subjects taught in public elementary schools and maps used in the study of geography.

16. A collection of natural samples from the three kingdoms of nature [animal, vegetable, mineral] essential for explaining and understanding natural history, especially the features native to the *gubernia* where the public elementary school is located.

17. A collection of geometric forms, instruments for teaching physics, maps, and other models essential to explaining architecture and mechanics.

IV. The Number of Teachers in Public Elementary Schools and Their Teaching Load

18. Each public elementary school should have six teachers who must teach the following subjects: one teacher who, in the third grade, teaches the second part of arithmetic, Russian grammar and Latin, and who, in the fourth grade, continues to teach Russian grammar and Latin, and who also lectures on geometry, architecture, mechanics, and physics—for a total of a twenty-three-hour teaching load per week.

19. One teacher responsible for world and Russian history and world and Russian geography and natural history in the third and fourth grades—for a total of a twenty-three-hour teaching load.

20. One second-grade teacher to teach twenty-nine hours per week of subjects in his grade and who also must provide explanations of the New Testament and of the *Expanded Catechism* in the third grade.

21. One first-grade teacher who will devote twenty-seven hours per week to subjects taught in his grade.

22. One teacher of drawing who will teach four hours per week in the second, third and fourth grades and an additional two hours on Wednesday and Saturday afternoons.

23. One teacher of foreign languages who will teach eighteen hours per week. . . .

Statistical Data on Russian Public Schools, *1782–1800*

Year	*Number of Schools*	*Boys*	*Girls*	*Total*	*Number of Teachers*
1782	8	474	44	518	26
1783	9	654	77	731	28
1784	11	1,082	152	1,234	33
1785	12	1,282	209	1,491	38
1786	165	10,230	858	11,088	394
1787	218	11,968	1,571	13,539	525
1788	227	13,635	924	14,559	520
1789	225	13,187	1,202	14,389	516
1790	269	15,604	921	16,525	629
1791	288	16,723	1,064	17,787	700
1792	302	16,322	1,178	17,500	718
1793	311	16,165	1,132	17,297	738
1794	302	15,540	1,080	16,620	767
1795	307	16,035	1,062	17,097	716
1795	307	16,035	1,062	17,097	716
1796	316	16,220	1,121	17,341	744
1797	285	14,457	1,171	15,628	644
1798	284	15,396	1,405	16,801	752
1799	277	15,754	1,561	17,315	705
1800	315	18,128	1,787	19,915	790

Source: Russia, Ministry of Public Education, *Sbornik materialov dlia istorii prosveshcheniia v Rossii.* St. Petersburg: 1893, Vol. I, pp. 339–340. Translation mine.

18

Radishchev's Journey from St. Petersburg to Moscow

In 1790 Alexander N. Radishchev (1749–1802), a Leipzig-educated Russian revolutionary, published *A Journey from St. Petersburg to Moscow.* In it this first great disciple of European enlightenment in Russia crusaded for a humane government, the rule of law, and freedom of speech and press. He championed the downtrodden and the rights of individual citizens, indicted the autocratic state machine and its two basic pillars—the nobles and the clergy—and expressed abhorrence for militarism and colonial conquest. The book contained such rich descriptions of peasant field work, the transportation system, an auction sale of serfs, the recruiting system, forced marriages, and other aspects of eighteenth-century Russia that its reprinting was barred in Russia for over a hundred years. Although Radishchev was tried and sentenced to death, Catherine II commuted the sentence to exile in Siberia. He returned to Russia after her death in 1796. Below are reproduced two passages from this remarkable book: *An Ode on Liberty,* wherein Radishchev indicts the Russian political system through the words of his "travelling companion," and a description of the recruiting system in Russia in the 1780s.

I

O blessed gift of the heavens, source of all great deeds, O Liberty, Liberty, priceless gift! Permit a slave to sing of you. Fill my heart with your fire; with the stroke of your mighty arms, transform serfdom's night into light. Let Brutus and Tell wake once more, and let kings enthroned in [tyrannous] might be dismayed at your voice.

This stanza was condemned for two reasons: first, because the verse 'transform serfdom's night into light' is very stiff and hard to pronounce on account of the frequent repetition of the letter 'T' and the piling up of too many consonants. In 'serfdom's night' there are ten consonants to three vowels, whereas it is possible to write as melodiously in Russian as in Italian—.

Reprinted by permission of the publishers from Aleksandr Nikolaevich Radishchev, *A Journey From St. Petersburg to Moscow.* Translation by Leo Wiener. Edited with an Introduction and Notes by Roderick Page Thaler (Cambridge, Mass.: Harvard University Press, 1958, by the President and Fellows of Harvard College), pp. 194–212.

Agreed—although some thought this verse successful, finding in the roughness of the verse an onomatopoetic expression of the very laboriousness of the action—. The second objection: 'Let kings be dismayed at your voice.' To wish a king dismay is to wish him evil, consequently—. But I do not want to tire you with all the remarks made about my verses. Many of them, I must confess, were justified. Let me read it to you.

2

I came into the world and you with me. . . .

We shall omit this stanza. Its theme is: man is free in all things from birth—.

3

But what stands in the way of my freedom? Everywhere I behold a barrier to my yearnings; a communal power has arisen in the people, the source of power everywhere. Society obeys it in everything, and is everywhere of one accord with it. No limits are set to the general welfare. In the power of all I see my lot: in doing the will of all, I do my own: this is what law in society means.

4

Amidst a fertile dale, amidst fields heavy with grain, where tender lilies bloom, in the shade of peaceful olive trees, whiter than Parian marble, brighter than the rays of the brightest day, stands a temple open to every view. There no false sacrifice swirls up in smoke, there the fiery inscription may be seen: 'Have done with the miseries of the innocent!

5

Crowned with an olive branch, seated upon a hard stone, dispassionate and cold, a deaf divinity. . . .

And so forth. Law is represented in the form of a divinity within a temple whose guards are Truth and Justice.

6

He lifts up his stern countenance, and spreads joy and terror around him; he looks with equanimity upon all persons, neither hating nor loving. He ignores flattery, subservience, high descent, eminence, wealth; and despises mortal offerings; he knows neither ties of blood nor of friendship, and distributes rewards and punishments impartially: he is the image of God on earth.

7

Behold a horrible monster, hydra-like, with a hundred heads! It looks mild and its eyes are ever full of tears, but its jaws are full of venom. It tramples upon the earthly powers, and stretches its head up toward Heaven, which it claims as its native home. It sows false phantoms and darkness everywhere, and commands all to believe blindly.

8

It has enshrouded reason in darkness, and everywhere it spreads its creeping poison. . . .

The portrayal of religious superstition, robbing man of sensitiveness, enticing him into the yoke of slavery, and clothing him in the armor of error:

It commands him to fear the truth. . . .

[Tyrannous] power calls this monster Revelation; reason calls it Deceit.

9

Let us look into the vast regions where the tarnished throne of slavery stands; In peace and quiet, religious and political superstition, each supporting the other, join to oppress society. The one tries to fetter reason, the other strives to destroy the will: "For the common good," they say.

10

In the shadow of slavish peace no golden fruit can grow; where everything hinders the spirit's striving, nothing great can thrive.

And all the evil consequences of slavery, such as recklessness, idleness, trickery, hunger, and so forth.

11

Raising his haughty brow and grasping his iron scepter, the king seats himself augustly on the throne of terror and sees his people only as base creatures. Holding life and death in his hands, he says: "At will I can spare the evildoer or delegate my power. When I laugh, all laugh; if I frown threateningly, all are confounded. You live only so long as I permit you to live."

12

And we look on calmly . . .

as the ravenous dragon, reviling all, poisons their days of joy and happiness. But though all stand before your throne with bended knees, tremble, for, lo, the avenger comes, proclaiming liberty. . . .

13

Everywhere martial hosts will arise, hope will arm all; everyone hastens to wash off his shame in the blood of the crowned tormentor. Everywhere I see the flash of the sharp sword; death, flying about in various forms, hovers over the proud head. Rejoice, fettered peoples! The avenging law of nature has brought the king to the block.

14

Having rent the curtain of deceptive night with a mighty thunderbolt, having overthrown the enormous idol of haughty and stubborn power, having fettered the hundred-armed giant, it drags him to the throne, where the people now sit. "Violator of the power I granted you! Speak, villain whom I crowned, how dared you rise against me?

15

"I clad you in the purple that you might preserve equality in society, watch over the widow and orphan, save innocence from calamity and be its loving father, but an implacable enemy of vice, the lie, and calumny; that you might reward merit with honor, forestall evil through order, and maintain purity of morals.

16

"I have covered the sea with ships. . . .

I have provided means for achieving wealth and well-being. I desired that the peasant should not be a captive in his field, and that he should bless you. . . .

17

"Ruthlessly, out of my own blood, I raised up a mighty host; I cast the brazen cannon with which to punish your external enemies. I commanded them to obey you and with you to strive for glory. For the common good, all things are permitted me. I tear up the bowels of the earth and extract the glittering metal for your adornment.

18

"But you, forgetting the oath you swore to me, forgetting that I had chosen you, came to think that you had been crowned for your own pleasure, and that you were the master, not I. With the sword you destroyed my laws; you silenced all rights; you made truth blush with shame. You have opened the door to all abominations, you have begun to appeal not to me, but to God, and you thought you could scorn me.

19

"Garnering with bloody sweat the fruit I planted for sustenance, dividing my crumbs with you, I did not spare my strength. But to you all treasures are insufficient! Tell me, what did you lack, to justify your tearing the rags off my back? To reward a sycophantic courtier or a woman lost to honor! Or have you made gold your god?

20

"You gave to the arrogant the token of distinction established to reward the deserving; you brandished against the innocent my sword, sharpened against evildoers. The hosts brought together for the defense of the homeland—are you leading them into glorious battle to avenge suffering humanity? You fight in bloody fields so that tipsy Athenians, yawning, may call you a hero.

21

"O evildoer, worst of all evildoers . . .

You have combined all crimes in yourself and have directed your sting against me. . . .

Die, then, die a hundred deaths."

So spake the people. . . .

22

O great man full of perfidy, hypocrite, flatterer, blasphemer! You alone might have given the world a great example of benevolence. I consider you, Cromwell, a criminal, because, having power in your hands, you destroyed the citadel of freedom. But you have taught generation after generation how nations can avenge themselves; you had Charles executed by due process of law.

23

The voice of freedom resounds on all sides. . . .

The whole nation streams to the assembly; it destroys the iron throne, and, as Samson did of yore, it pulls down the perfidious palace. It builds the citadel of nature on the foundation of the law. Thou art great, aye great indeed, Spirit of Liberty; creative as God Himself!

24

The next eleven stanzas consist of an account of the kingdom of Liberty and its achievements, that is, security, peace, well-being, greatness. . . .

34

But the passions that goad men to madness . . .

turn the civil peace into disaster. . . .

stir the father up against the son, tear asunder the bonds of marriage,

and bring all the dread consequences of boundless lust for power. . . .

35, 36, 37

Description of the ruinous consequences of luxury. Civil discord. Civil war. Marius, Sulla, Augustus. . . .

> He put troublesome freedom to sleep, and wound flowers around the iron scepter. . . .

Thence came slavery. . . .

38, 39

This is the law of nature: from tyranny, freedom is born; from freedom, slavery. . . .

40

Why marvel at this, for man, too, is born to die. . . . The following eight stanzas contain prophecies about the future fate of our country, which will fall into separate parts—all the sooner, the greater it grows. But the time for that has not yet come. When it comes, then

> The heavy fetters of night will break.

Even in its death throes, stubborn Power will set up a guard against free speech, and gather all its strength for its expiring effort to crush rising freedom. . . .

49

But humanity will roar in its fetters, and, moved by the hope of freedom and the indestructible law of nature, will push on. . . . And tyranny will be dismayed. Then the united force of all despotism, of all oppressive power

> Will in a moment be dispersed. O chosen day of days!

50

> Even now I hear the voice of nature, the primal voice, the voice of the Godhead.

The dark citadel totters, and liberty shines forth with a glorious radiance.

"That's the end," the newfangled poet said. I was very glad of it, and wanted to say something to him, perhaps raise an unpleasant objection to his verses, but the bell reminded me that in traveling it is better to make reasonable haste with post nags than to climb on Pegasus when he is mettlesome.

Gorodnya

As I drove into this village, my ears were assailed not by the melody of verse, but by a heart-rending lament of women, children, and old men. Getting out of my carriage, I sent it on to the post station, for I was curious to learn the cause of the disturbance I had noticed in the street.

Going up to one group of people, I learned that a levy of recruits was the cause of the sobs and tears of the people crowded together there. From many villages, both crown and manorial, those who were to be drafted into the army had come together here.

In one group an old woman fifty years of age, holding the head of a lad of twenty, was sobbing. "My dear child, to whose care are you committing me? To whom will you entrust the home of your parents? Our fields will be overgrown with grass, our hut with moss. I, your poor old mother, will have to wander about begging. Who will warm my decrepit body when it is cold, who will protect it from the heat? Who will give me food and drink? But all that does not weigh so heavily upon my heart as this: who will close my eyes when I die? Who will receive my maternal blessing? Who will return my body to our common mother, the moist earth? Who will come to remember me at my grave? Your warm tears will not fall upon it; I shall not have that consolation."

Near the old woman stood a grown-up girl. She, too, was sobbing. "Farewell, friend of my heart; farewell, my shining sun. I, your betrothed, will never know comfort or joy again. My friends will not envy me. The sun will not rise for me in joy. You are leaving me to pine away, neither a widow nor a wedded wife. If our inhuman village elders had only let us get married, if you, my darling, could have slept but one short night on my white breast. Perhaps God would have taken pity on me and given me a little son to comfort me."

The lad said to them: "Stop weeping, stop rending my heart. Our Sovereign calls us to service. The lot fell on me. It is the will of God. Those not fated to die will live. Perhaps I will come home to you with the regiment. I may even win rank and honors. Dear Mother, do not grieve. Take care of my Praskov'yushka." This recruit was drafted from an Economic village.[1]

From another standing nearby I heard altogether different words. Amidst them I saw a man of about thirty, of medium size, standing erect and looking happily at the people around him.

"The Lord has heard my prayers," he said. "The tears of an unfortunate man have reached the Comforter of all men. Now I shall at least know that my lot may depend on my own good or bad behavior. Heretofore it depended on the arbitrary whims of a woman. I am consoled by the thought that hereafter I shall not be flogged without a fair trial!"

Having gathered from what he said that he was a manorial serf, I was curious to learn the cause of his unusual joy. To my question he replied: "Dear sir, if a gallows were placed on one side of you and a deep river ran on the other, and you, standing between these two perils, could not possibly escape going either to the right or to the left, into the noose or into the water, which would you choose? Which would sense and impulse make you prefer? I think everyone would rather jump into the river, in the hope of escaping from peril by swimming to the other shore. No one would willingly investigate the strength of the noose by putting his neck into it. This was my situation. A soldier's life is a hard one, but better than the noose. Even that would be all right, if that were the end, but to die a lingering death under the cudgel, under the cat-o'nine-tails, in chains, in a dungeon, naked, barefooted, hungry, thirsty, under constant abuse—my lord, although you look upon your peasants as your property, often less regarded than cattle, yet, unfortunately, they are not without feeling. You appear to be surprised to hear such words from the lips of a peasant; but why, when you hear them, are you not surprised at the cruelty of your brothers, the noblemen?"

And in very truth I had not expected such words from a man dressed in a gray caftan and with his head shaven. But wishing to satisfy my curiosity, I asked him to tell me how, being of such a low estate, he had arrived at ideas which are frequently lacking in men improperly said to be nobly born.

"If it will not tire you to hear my story, I will tell you: I was born in slavery, the son of my master's former valet. How happy I am to think that they will never again call me Van'ka or any other offensive name, that they will never again call me like a dog by whistling. My old master, a kindhearted, reasonable, and virtuous man, who often lamented the fate of his slaves, wanted, on account of my father's long service, to do something special for me; so he gave me the same education as his son. There was hardly any difference between us, except that the cloth of his coat was perhaps better. Whatever they taught the young master, they taught me, too; our instruction was exactly the same, and I can say without boasting that in many things I did better than my young master.

" 'Vanyuasha,' the old master said to me, 'your happiness depends entirely on you. You have more of an inclination for learning and morality than my son. He will be rich by inheritance and will know no want, while you have known it from birth. So try to be worthy of the pains I have taken for you.' When my young master was in his seventeenth year, he and I were sent to travel abroad with a tutor, who was told to look upon me as a traveling companion, not a servant. As he sent me away, my old master said to me: 'I hope that you will return to give me and your parents joy. You are a slave within the borders of this country, but beyond them you are free. When you return, you will not find fetters imposed upon you because of your birth,' We were away for five years and then returned to Russia, my young master happy at the thought of seeing his father, and I, I must confess, flattering myself that I would obtain what I had been promised. My heart was atremble as I again entered the borders of my country. And indeed my foreboding was not false. In Riga my young master received the news of his father's death. He was deeply moved by it; I was thrown into despair. For all my efforts to win his friendship and confidence had been in vain. Not only did he not love me, but—perhaps from envy, as is characteristic of small souls—he hated me.

"Observing the anxiety produced in me by the death of his father, he told me he would not forget the promise that had been made to me, if I would be worthy of it. It was the first time he had ventured to tell me so, for, having received control of his property through the death of his father, he had dismissed his tutor in Riga, paying him liberally for his labors. I must do justice to my former master: he has many good qualities, but timidity of spirit and thoughtlessness obscure them.

"A week after our arrival in Moscow, my master fell in love with a pretty girl, but one who with her bodily beauty combined a very ugly soul and a hard and cruel heart. Brought up in the conceit of her station, she respected only external show, rank, and wealth. In two months she became my master's wife, and I became her slave. Until then I had not experienced any change in my condition and had lived in my master's house as his companion. Although he never gave me any orders, I generally anticipated his wishes, as I was aware of his power and of my position. Scarcely had the young mistress crossed the threshold of the house, in which she was determined to rule, before I was made aware of my hard lot. On the first evening after the wedding and all next day, when I was introduced to her by her husband as his companion, she was occupied with the usual cares of a bride; but in the evening, when a fairly large company came to the table and sat down to the first supper with the newly married pair, and I sat down in my usual place at the lower end of the table, the new mistress said to her husband in a fairly loud voice that if he wished her to sit at the table with the guests, he must not permit any serfs to sit there. He looked at me and, at her instance, sent word to me that I should leave the table and eat supper in my room. Imagine how deeply this humiliation hurt me! I suppressed the tears that came to my eyes, and withdrew. I did not dare to make my appearance the next day. They brought me my dinner and supper without saying anything to me. And so it went on succeeding days. One afternoon, a week after the wedding, the new mistress inspected the house, and, after apportioning the duties and living quarters to all the servants, entered my rooms also. They had been furnished for me by my old master. I was not at home. I will not repeat what she said there, to ridicule me, but when I returned home they gave me her order, whereby I was sent down to a corner on the ground floor with the unmarried servants, where my bed and my trunk, with my clothes and linens, had already been placed; all my other things she had left in my former rooms, in which she installed her serving maids.

"What took place in my soul when I heard this is easier to feel, if you can, than to describe. But so as not to detain you with superfluous details: my mistress, after taking control of the house and finding that I had no aptitude for service, made me a lackey and decked me out in livery. The least, imaginary remissness in my duties led to my ears being boxed, beatings, and the cat-o'-nine-tails. O, my lord, it would have been better if I had never been born! How many times did I complain against my dead benefactor for having fostered a responsive soul in me. It would have been better for me if I had grown up in ignorance and had never learned that I am a man, equal to all others. Long, long ago I would have freed myself from my hateful life, if I had not been held back by the prohibition of our Supreme Judge. I determined to bear my lot patiently. And I endured not only bodily wounds, but also those which she inflicted upon my soul. But I almost broke my vow and cut short the miserable remains of my woeful life as a result of a new blow to my soul.

"A nephew of my mistress, a youngster of eighteen years, a sergeant of the Guards, educated in the fashion of Moscow dandies, became enamored of a chambermaid of his aunt's, and, having quickly won her ready favors, made her a mother. Although he was usually quite unconcerned in his amours, in this case he was somewhat embarrassed. For his aunt, having learned about the affair, forbade the chambermaid her presence, and gently scolded her nephew. She intended, after the fashion of benevolent mistresses, to punish the one whom she had formerly favored by marrying her off to one of the stable boys. But since they were all married already, and since, for the honor of the house, there had to be a husband for the pregnant woman, she selected me as the worst of all the servants. In the presence of her husband, my mistress informed me of this as though it were a special favor. I could not stand this abuse any longer. 'Inhuman woman!' I cried. 'You have the power to torment me and to wound my body; you say the laws give you the right to do this. I hardly believe it, but I know full well that no one can be forced to marry.' She listened to my words in ominous silence. Then I turned to her husband and said: 'Ungrateful son of a generous father, you have forgotten his last will and testament, you have forgotten your own promise; but do not drive to despair a soul nobler than yours! Beware!' I could say no more, because, by command of my mistress, I was taken to the stable and whipped mercilessly with the cat-o'-nine-tails. The next day I could hardly get up out of bed from the beating; but I was brought before my mistress again. 'I will forgive you your impudence of yesterday,' she said; 'marry my Mavrushka; she begs you to, and I want to do this for her, because I love her even in her transgression.'

'You heard my answer yesterday,' I said; 'I have no other. I will only add that I will complain to the authorities against you for compelling me to do what you have no right to.' 'Then it's time for you to become a soldier!' my mistress screamed in fury.—A traveler who has lost his way in a terrible desert will rejoice less when he finds it again than I did when I heard these words. 'Take him to be a soldier!' she repeated, and the next day it was done. Fool! She thought that being made a soldier would be a punishment for me, as it is for the peasants. For me it was a joy, and as soon as they had shaved my forehead, I felt like a new man. My strength was restored. My mind and spirit began to revive. O hope, sweet solace of the unfortunate, remain with me!" A heavy tear, but not a tear of grief and despair, fell from his eyes. I pressed him to my heart. His countenance was radiant with new joy. "All is not yet lost," he said; "you arm my soul against sorrow by making me feel that my misery is not endless."

From this unfortunate man I went to a group in which I saw three men fettered in the strongest irons. "It is amazing," I said to myself as I looked at these prisoners, "now they are downcast, weary, timid, and they not only do not want to become soldiers, but the greatest severity is required to force them into that status; but as soon as they become accustomed to the execution of their hard duty, they grow alert and spirited, and even look with scorn upon their former condition." I asked one of the bystanders who, to judge from his uniform, was a government clerk: "No doubt you have put them in such heavy fetters because you are afraid they will run away?"

"You guessed it. They belonged to a landed proprietor who needed money for a new carriage and got it by selling them to crown peasants, to be levied into the army."

I. —"My friend, you are mistaken. Crown peasants can't purchase their brothers."

He. —"It isn't done in the form of a sale. Having by agreement received the money, the master sets these unfortunates free; they are presumed to be 'voluntarily' registered as crown peasants of the commune which paid the money for them; and the commune, by common consent, sends them to be soldiers. They are now being taken with their emancipation papers to be registered in our commune."

Free men, who have committed no crime, are fettered, and sold like cattle! O laws! Your wisdom frequently resides only in your style! Is this not an open mockery? And, what is worse, a mockery of the sacred name of liberty. Oh, if the slaves weighed down with fetters, raging in their despair, would, with the iron that bars their freedom, crush our heads, the heads of their inhuman masters, and redden their fields with our blood! What would the country lose by that? Soon great men would arise from among them, to take the place of the murdered generation; but they would be of another mind and without the right to oppress others. This is no dream; my vision penetrates the dense curtain of time that veils the future from our eyes. I look through the space of a whole century. I left the crowd in disgust.

But the fettered prisoners are free now. If they had any fortitude, they could put to naught the oppressive intentions of their tyrants. Let us go back to them. —"My friends," I said to the captives, these prisoners of war in their own country, "do you know that if you do not freely wish to enter the army, no one can now compel you to do so?" "Stop making fun of poor wretches, sir. Even without your jesting, it was hard enough for us to part, one from his poor old father, another from his little sisters, a third from his young wife. We know that our master sold us as recruits for a thousand rubles."

"If you did not know it before, you must know now that it is against the law to sell men as recruits, that peasants cannot legally buy men, that your master has set you free, and that the purchasers intend to register you in their commune, as though of your own free will."

"O, sir, if that is really so, we do thank you. When they line us up for muster, we will all say that we do not want to become soldiers and that we are free men."

"Add to it that your master sold you at a time when such a sale was not legal, and that they are delivering you up as recruits in violation of the law."[2] One can easily imagine the joy that lighted up the faces of these unfortunates. Leaping up from their places and vigorously shaking their fetters, they seemed to be testing their strength, as though they would shake them off. But this conversation could have gotten me into serious trouble, for the recruiting officers, having heard what I said, rushed toward me in violent anger, and said, "Sir, don't meddle with other people's business, and get away while the getting's good!" When I resisted, they pushed me so violently that I was forced to leave this crowd as fast as I could.

As I approached the post station, I found another gathering of peasants, surrounding a man in a torn coat. He seemed to be somewhat drunk. He was making faces at the people, who laughed till the tears came, watching him. "What is it all about?" I asked a boy. "What are you laughing at?"

"Well, the recruit is a foreigner and can't speak a word of Russian." From the few words he spoke, I gathered that he was a Frenchman. That made me still more curious; I wanted to find out how a foreigner could be offered as a recruit by the peasants. I asked him in his native tongue: "My friend, by what fate did you get here?"

Frenchman. —"Fate wanted it so. Where things go well, there one should stay."

I. —"How did you become a recruit?"

Frenchman. —"I love a soldier's life. I've known it before, and I wanted it."

I. —"But how does it happen that you are sent from a village? Usually they take only peasants, and Russians at that, as soldiers from the villages; but I see that you are neither a peasant nor a Russian."

Frenchman. —"It happened this way. As a child I was apprenticed to a hairdresser in Paris. I left for Russia with a gentleman whose hair I dressed for a whole year in Petersburg. He had no money to pay me; so I left him and almost starved to death, looking for a job. Luckily, I got a berth as a sailor on a ship flying the Russian flag. Before putting to sea, I had to take an oath as a Russian subject; then we set off for Lübeck. On the way the bosun often beat me with a rope's end for being lazy. Through my carelessness I fell from the rigging to the deck and broke three fingers, which ruined me for ever dressing hair again. When we got to Lübeck I fell in with Prussian recruiting officers and served in various regiments. They often took the stick to me for being lazy or drunk. When I was stationed in the garrison at Memel, I got drunk one day and stabbed a fellow; so I had to get out of there in a hurry. Remembering that I had taken my oath in Russia and that I was a faithful son of the fatherland, I started out for Riga, with two *thalers* in my pocket. One the way I lived on charity. In Riga my good luck and skill served me in good stead. I won some twenty *rubles* in a tavern. bought myself a good overcoat for ten, and went off with a Kazan' merchant as his lackey. As we were going along a street in Moscow, I met two of my countrymen, who advised me to leave my master and look for a teaching job in Moscow. I told them I could hardly read, but they said, 'You talk French—that's enough.' My master did not see me leaving him on the street, and kept on his way, while I stayed in Moscow. My countrymen soon found me a teaching job paying a hundred and fifty *rubles* a year, plus a pood of sugar, a *pood* of coffee, ten pounds of tea, my board, a servant, and carriage. But I had to live in the country. So much the better. There they didn't find out for a whole year that I couldn't write. But some one of my master's in-laws, who was living at the same place, gave my secret away to him, and they took me back to Moscow. I couldn't find such another fool, I couldn't dress hair with my broken fingers, and I was afraid I'd starve to death; so I sold myself for two hundred *rubles*. They registered me as a peasant, and now they're sending me as a recruit. I hope," he said with an important air, "that as soon as a war comes along, I'll get to be a general; and if there isn't any war, I'll stuff my pockets (if possible), and, crowned with laurel, return to my country for a well-earned rest."

More than once I shrugged my shoulders as I listened to this rogue, and with a heavy heart I lay down in my carriage and continued on my journey.

Notes

1. A village of serfs, formerly belonging to a monastery, but after the secularization of monastic lands by the Emperor Peter III in 1762, belonging to the government and administered by the Economic College.

2. During the time of a levying of recruits, it is against the law to make any contract for the sale of serfs.

19

Suvorov's Comments on Military Conduct and Leadership

Eighteenth-century Imperial Russia gained international respect and influence primarily through territorial growth that was essentially a product of military might. Initially, much of that might derived from the transfer of European technology, experience, and skilled personnel. Aided by this infusion, the Russians soon developed their own tactics, strategy, and military leaders. One of the most colorful of these was Field Marshal Alexander V. Suvorov (1730–1800). His tactics, strategy, and heroic exploits made an enormous contribution to Russian military successes against Turkish, Polish, and French forces.

In 1797 Suvorov presented his views on warfare and the training of troops in a treatise entitled *The Science of Conquest.* This treatise, the essence of which Suvorov distilled for a letter to his godson, became a basic manual for all imperial commanders, and later for Soviet military commanders. Emperor Alexander I erected a statue to Suvorov's memory in recognition of his contributions to Russia's military successes, and during World War II the Supreme Soviet of the USSR established the Suvorov Medal as the highest military decoration for gallantry in combat.

Source: S. Glinka, ed. *Zhizn Suvorova im samim napisanaia* (Moscow: 1819), Part II, pp. 62–66. Translation mine.

A. V. Suvorov's Letter to His Godson, A. Karachai, Concerning Military Conduct and Leadership, 1796

Alexander, my Dear Godson!

As a military man, study diligently the works of Vauban, Cogorne, Kurass, and Hubner. Also, familiarize yourself with theology, physics, and the fundamentals of morals. Read attentively the works of Eugene (Count of Savoy), Turenne, the *Commentaries* of Julius Caesar and Frederick II (King of Prussia); the first volumes of world history by Rollene and *Reminiscences* by Moritz, Count of Saxony. Likewise, study languages that have useful application to literature, and practice horseback riding and fencing.

Military virtue consists of the following: daring of the soldier, bravery of the officer, and courage of the general. Guided by order and discipline, the commander of the army rules with the help of vigil and foresight.

Always be frank with your comrades. Be moderate in urgency and impartial in your conduct. Always exhibit an ardent zeal in the service of your sovereign. Respect genuine glory, but always distinguish flattery from arrogance and pride.

As soon as possible, develop the habit of forgiving the mistakes of others but never forget your own mistakes.

Fervently teach your subordinates and set for them your own example. Study constantly and be aware that others may discern at a glance what has made you a great military leader. Learn how to utilize the environment. Be patient in military matters. Do not allow yourself to be dejected by temporary setbacks. Learn how to anticipate wrong or doubtful developments. Do not succumb to temporary passions.

Preserve in your memory the names of great individuals and follow their actions with prudence in your own campaigns. Never underestimate your enemy regardless of whom he may be. Try to familiarize yourself with his weapons and tactics and know how he employs them and how he fights. Know your own strengths and his weaknesses.

Get accustomed to indefatigable activity. Always take advantage of a lucky opportunity because often a twinkling of the eye brings victory. Always strive to gain Caesar's agility. He was able to capture his adversary, even in daylight, by encircling him and attacking him at a place and time of his own choice. Always try to cut off all supplies of your enemy and try to gain complete knowledge of his military art so that your own forces will never be deficient in supplies.

May God elevate you to the courageous achievements of Karachai, your famous father.

Alexander Suvorov

20

The Law of Succession of 1797

In theory, imperial succession in eighteenth-century Russia was based on the right of primogeniture, that is, the throne was to pass from father to eldest male heir. In practice, that procedure was constantly abused. Only one eighteenth-century tsar, Peter I, ruled by right of primogeniture. Six others, who ruled from 1725 to 1796, ascended the throne either through coups or various machinations.

When he assumed power in 1796, Catherine II's son, Paul, resolved to put an end to the succession intrigues by promulgating a law that would reestablish the principle of primogeniture. The new succession law passed its first test in 1801, when Paul's eldest son, Alexander, succeeded, following Paul's murder by drunken officers. In December 1825, after Alexander's death, the 1797 law of succession precipitated a crisis when, thanks to a secret arrangement that had been made between Alexander and his next-eldest brother, Constantine, the youngest brother, Nicholas, and not Constantine, ascended to the throne. That succession crisis helped to spark the Decembrist Revolt.

Paul's Law on Imperial Succession, April 5, 1797

We, Paul, Heir, Tsarevich, and Grand Prince, and We, Maria, his wife and Grand Princess.

In the name of the Father, the Son, and the Holy Spirit.

Based on Our free and mutual consent, and being of sound mind and calm spirit, We have formulated this Our public act by virtue of which, because of Our love for the country, We are designating, in accordance with natural law, Our eldest son, Alexander, as Our successor after My, Paul's, death, and after him all his male heirs. Should his male line expire, then the succession will be transferred to the line of My second son, where it will follow the pattern stated for My eldest son, and so on, should I have more sons. This [rule of succession] is known as primogeniture.

Source: *Polnoe Sobranie Zakonov*, First Series XXIV, No. 17,910, pp. 587–89. Translation mine.

Upon extinction of the last male line of My sons, the succession shall remain in the last line, but this time in the female line of the last reigning male, as the closest to the throne, in order to avoid difficulties of transition from one family to another. Should that happen, the order of succession should prefer male over female heirs. Nevertheless, it is essential to note here once and forever that this right of succession does not deprive the female who may have acquired that right directly. Upon extinction of that line, the succession is to be transferred to the female line of descendants of My eldest son, and, should that be impossible, then to the male or female who is to take his place, observing the rule, however, that the male line is preferred over the female, as stated above. This [form of succession] is known as intercession.

Upon the extinction of these lines the right of succession is to be transferred to the female line of My remaining sons following the same order, and then to the line of male descendants of my eldest daughter, and upon its extinction to her female descendants, observing the same rule of succession that has been set forth for the female line of My sons. Upon extinction of both male and female lines of My eldest daughter the succession right is to be transferred to the male and then to the female line of My second daughter, and so on. The following rule should be observed here: A younger sister, even though she may have sons, should not take the right [of succession] from her elder sister who may still be single, because the latter may still marry and have children. A younger brother, however, must be preferred in succession over his older sister.

Having established these rules of succession, We must explain the reasons behind them. They are as follows: that the empire never be without [a rightful] heir; that the successor always be designated by law; that there never be even the slightest doubt of who should succeed whom; that the right of succession of families be preserved without violating natural law; and that all difficulties be avoided in the transition from one family line to another. . . .

21

Conditions of Peasants in the Eighteenth Century

In contrast to the improvement in the position of Russian nobles during the eighteenth century (see Chapters 9 and 16), the condition of Russian peasants deteriorated steadily. So unbearable was their lot that many left their native villages in search of improvement elsewhere, even abroad. These flights, which often involved whole villages, hurt the interests of the state, and both Peter the Great and Anna issued decrees aimed at halting them. When this avenue of escape was closed, the peasants rose in the violent rebellion led by Pugachev (see Chapter 14.) It was not until the end of the eighteenth century that the government formally relaxed obligations of peasants to their masters. It was also at the end of the eighteenth century that newspaper advertisements for the sale of peasants began to appear in Russia.

Peter I's Decree Against Peasant Flights, April 5, 1707

Last year, 1706, fugitives and peasants appeared in Moscow and other cities; on settlements, crown villages and on the estates of the patriarch, bishops, monasteries, church and other clergy; these fugitives and peasants, with their wives, children, and belongings, should be returned to their previous *pomeshchiks and votchinniks* from whom they fled within half a year from the date of this *ukaz*. Whoever retains these fugitives and peasants beyond that date and will not return them to their rightful owners will lose half of his estate to the Great Sovereign, the other half going to those to whom the fugitives or peasants belong. And should those fugitives and peasants who were sent to their original places be unable to reach them because of interference by other nobles, stewards, elders, or peasants who would like to have them

---

The following four items are from *Polnoe Sobranie Zakonov Russkoi Imperii . . . (Complete Collection of the Laws of the Russian Empire)*, 1st Series. "Peter I's Decree Against Peasant Flights" from vol. 4, no. 2147, pp. 378–379. "Anna's Decree Against Peasant Flights" from vol. 9, no. 6951, pp. 809–810. "Catherine II's Decree on Deportation of Serfs" from vol. 17, no. 12,311, p. 10. "Paul's Decree on Reduction of Work Days for Serfs" from vol. 24, no. 17,909, p. 587. Translation mine. Words in brackets are mine.

for themselves, should this be established beyond doubt, then . . . this will be contrary to the sovereign's *ukaz*. The Great Sovereign was informed this year, 1707, that many nobles have lost the fear of God, have overlooked the *ukaz* of the Great Sovereign, and have kept the fugitives and peasants and sent other people away from their estates, but not to the original places; while some nobles do not allow them [the fugitives] to reach their destination by taking them in. The Great Sovereign, Peter Alekseevich, Tsar and Grand Prince, Autocrat of all Great, Little and White Russia, by this personal *ukaz* orders that these nobles, stewards and elders who keep the old fugitives and peasants, or who take on new ones, or do not return them to their rightful destination . . . will be punished without delay. *Voevodas* [administrative leaders] should go into villages and collect information from nobles, stewards, and elders as to whether they have fulfilled their duties or not; and in each small village they should collect from five to six, and in large [villages] from ten to fifteen, good respectable men, testimony sworn on the penalty of death about the above mentioned fugitive peasants. Copies of this *ukaz* of the Great Sovereign should be posted on all gates, and be distributed in cities and offices for everyone to remember.

Anna's Decree Against Peasant Flights, May 6, 1736

According to an *ukaz* of February 23, 1721, issued by Emperor Peter the Great, Our uncle of blessed and eternal memory, anyone who [without fulfilling his obligations] flees and then is caught is to be punished severely by a public whipping, in order to discourage others from doing the same. But while this *ukaz* calls for a severe punishment of all those who flee—as the crime is the same—there is nevertheless a great difference.

1. Anyone who flees, committing beforehand a robbery or a murder, or fled a long time ago and during his absence let his taxes be paid by other peasants, should be subjected to the most severe punishment.

2. Anyone who flees on account of hunger or because of rumors he did not understand, and then having realized his mistake returns shortly thereafter, and no one as a consequence is forced to pay his taxes, such individuals—unlike the first—according to the rules of natural law should be punished less severely.

Consequently We decree that throughout Our state this *ukaz* be made known so that all those who have fled be punished by knout, whip, lash, or stick upon their apprehension. Administrators of the crown, church, bishopric, and monastery lands should determine which punishment should be applied to their peasants; [on the estates of the nobility] the nobles or their stewards should determine their cases.

Catherine II's Decree on Deportation of Serfs to Hard Labor, January 17, 1765

We herewith make it publicly known:

Following Her Imperial Majesty's confirmation, which on January 17, [1765] was presented to the Senate, it was decreed that in case any landowner wants to deliver for better disciplining in hard labor his serfs who, because of very impudent behavior, deserve a just punishment, the Board of Admiralty will take charge of them and use them for heavy work as long as the landlord concerned desires it. During this whole period these people, together with convicts, will be provided with food and clothing from the treasury. When the landlord shall want them back, they [serfs] are to be returned without question, but under one condition: the clothes and shoes of the people, if they are not completely worn out, are to be collected again for the treasury.

Paul's Decree on Reduction of Work Days for Serfs, April 5, 1797

We make known to all Our faithful subjects:

God's law, as it is given to us in the form of the Ten Commandments, teaches us that we offer the seventh day to Him; in this day, the holy day of Christianity and the day in which We decided to accept the holy anointment and the coronation on Our dynastic throne, We feel that it is Our duty before the Creator and the Giver of all blessings to emphasize that throughout Our empire this law be adhered to exactly and infallibly. I am hereby instructing everyone to observe [this law] and [am informing everyone] not to force under any pretext whatsoever the peasants to work on Sundays. For agricultural works there are six days in the week. These should be divided equally, [three] for the peasants [to work on their own land, and three] to work for the nobleman. [If this division] is properly organized it will be sufficient to fulfill all agricultural needs.

*Newspaper Advertisements for the Sale of Serfs, 1797**

1

For sale well behaved menial craftsmen: two tailors, a shoemaker, a watchmaker, a cook, a coach maker, a wheeler, an engraver, a night workman, and two coachmen. They may be seen and the price [for them] may be ascertained from their own *pomeshchik* [landlord] in the Third Part, Fourth Quarter, No. 51. There, too, are available for sale three young racing horses, one stallion, two geldings, and a herd of hunting dogs, about fifty, which will be one year old in January or February.

2

There is for sale, in the Fifteenth Part, Second Quarter, No. 183, in the parish of Adrian and Natalia, in the Second Meshchanskaia Street near the Church, a menial man. He is twenty-five years old, a trained woman's shoe maker who knows his profession exceptionally well; in addition he performs all domestic, coachman's, and footman's tasks, as well as waiting at the table. He has a pregnant wife twenty-two years old who sews, irons, starches, waits on the lady of the house, and cooks. They have a three year old daughter.

3

For sale a thirty-five year old peasant, with his wife about the same age, and three young children. Those who wish to purchase may learn the price from their owner at the Tenth Part, in Nicholas parish, on Bolvanovka, No. 529.

4

In Part Twelve, an officer has for sale a sixteen year old girl, formerly belonging to a poor house, who knows how to knit, sew, iron, starch, and dress a lady; she has a nice figure and pretty face.

*From A. K. Dzhivelegov, S. P. Melgunov and V. I. Picheta, eds. *Velikaia Reforma: Russkoe obshchestvo i krestianskii vopros v proshlom i nastoiashchem (The Great Reform: Russian Society and the Peasant Problem in the Past and at Present)* (Moscow: 1911), vol. 1, p. 258. Translation mine. Words in brackets are mine.

22

Russian Explorations in the North Pacific in the Eighteenth Century

In the eighteenth century Imperial Russia brought enormous territories under its control. In Europe this acquisition occurred at the expense of Sweden, the Ottoman Empire, and the Polish-Lithuanian Commonwealth. In the Far East and in the North Pacific area the expansion stemmed from a series of remarkably successful Russian explorations sponsored by state and private entrepreneurs.

Acquisition of numerous islands in the North Pacific transformed the North Pacific Ocean into an exclusive Russian preserve. The entire undertaking was a mixture of skillfully intertwined scientific, imperialistic, and private-enterpreneurial motives and designs. The Russians cloaked their activity in secrecy and were extremely reluctant to share information with other nations. This reluctance generated rumors, curiosity, and suspicion and brought immediate responses from such leading maritime powers as Spain, England, France, and the United States. The combined efforts of these Western powers produced the first and most reliable information about the region, its resources, and its inhabitants. The Russians continued, however, to maintain their control and claim on the area and used it subsequently to establish bases in Alaska, California, and Hawaii.

A Statement from the Admiralty College to the Senate Concerning the Purpose of the Bering Expedition October 16, 1732

In accordance with the instructions from His Imperial Majesty, Peter the Great of blessed and eternally deserving memory, instructions which he personally gave to Captain Commander [Vitus] Bering while Bering was in St. Petersburg, the expedition made a search to find whether the land of Kam-

---

Source: The following five entries are from Basil Dmytryshyn, E. A. P. Crownhart-Vaughan and Thomas Vaughan, eds., *Russian Penetration of of the North Pacific Ocean, 1700–1797: A Documentary Record* (Portland: Oregon Historical Society Press, 1988), pp. 96–100, 159–60, 190–91, 321–24, 334–35. Reprinted with the permission of the Oregon Historical Society.

chatka might be joined to America. However, as Bering reports, he followed that instruction and sailed along the land from Kamchatka north and east to 67° latitude, and as he has indicated on the map he prepared in conjunction with that expedition, there is no joining of the land in that latitude with the coast of America. All information on the map above that latitude, from there north and west to the mouth of the Kolyma River, Bering has taken from earlier maps and records.

Bering indicates on this map that he found no juncture between the two lands. Nevertheless, it must be strongly emphasized that even though he suggests there is no juncture, this has not been proven and should not be accepted as fact. Also, it is possible to voyage along the [Siberian] coast from the Ob River to the Lena and beyond. Nothing is known about some of these places, and consequently it is impossible to describe them precisely because there are no reliable maps or reports. Further, no observations or descriptions have been made about the islands near Japan and a route to the east. Consequently, to fulfill the desire of His [late] Imperial Majesty [Peter] and to bring benefit to the Empire and to enhance the interests of Her Imperial Majesty, the Admiralty College believes with Captain Commander Bering that this matter lies within the jurisdiction of the Admiralty College and submits the following opinion.

On the strength of the above mentioned instructions given by the late Sovereign Emperor Peter the Great, of blessed memory, and by the desire of Her Imperial Majesty, a detailed observation and search should be undertaken, even though Bering has shown that the coast of Kamchatka does not appear to be joined to the coast of America. This should nevertheless be studied in detail, and the American coast should be visited by a naval expedition and explored as thoroughly as possible. Further, a voyage should be made to the islands near Japan, where observations and explorations should be made. The entire expedition should be undertaken in the following manner:

1. To secure first hand information as to whether the land of Kamchatka is joined to America, as well as whether there is a sea route from the mouth of the Ob River to the Enisei and Lena rivers, there should be constructed in sites described below, sloops with 24 oars and a deck. One should be built near Tobolsk on the Irtysh River, and two on the Lena River near Iakutsk, because in regard to local travel and peoples, these places can be most useful. The vessels should be armed with falconets. The one built at Tobolsk should sail to the mouth of the Ob River and then from the mouth east along the coast [of the Arctic Ocean] as far as the mouth of the Enisei. Of those built in Iakutsk, one should go on the Lena River to its mouth and from there west along the coast to the mouth of the Enisei, toward the one instructed to sail [east] from the mouth of the Ob. The other one built in Iakutsk should

proceed from the mouth of the Lena River east along the coast to the mouth of the Kolyma River. From the mouth of the Kolyma it should continue east along the coast and round the point which the map indicates is in 73° latitude, and from there, continue along the coast to the mouths of the Anadyr and Kamchatka rivers. Thus the entire [Arctic] coastline from Arkhangelsk will be surveyed in detail. For that purpose another ship should be sent out from Arkhangelsk to survey the coast to the Ob River. Thus, by making several expeditions, the time required for this survey will not be too great.

2. In regard to the exploration of the American coastline: if in Okhotsk, in accordance with point no. 18 of the Proposition submitted to the Senate by General Cavalier Pavel I. Iaguzhinskii, the ships are either being built or are completed, they should be inspected. If they are ready for such a voyage, two should be dispatched. If construction has begun but the ships are not yet completed, then oversee their completion. But if construction has not begun, or if it has commenced but the ships will not be suitable for such a voyage, then do not build others in Okhotsk because of the shortage of trees there. Instead, following Captain Commander Bering's suggestion, since there is a good roadstead in the Kamchatka River and an abundance of good shipbuilding timber there, build two packetboats [three-masted sailing vessels] on the Kamchatka River. Then if, God forbid, one should be shipwrecked, the other could provide assistance and information. However, if one ship has been started in Okhotsk and appears suitable for the voyage, then finish it and build another packet-boat in Kamchatka. Arm them with guns and outfit them fully, as required. Both should proceed east as winds will permit, even as far as 67° northern latitude. Search for the American coast or islands with great diligence and effort.

The expedition should be undertaken with good judgment so the men can return to Kamchatka as they did previously, and will not be so delayed that they might be trapped in the ice. For this reason the expedition should set out immediately after the spring breakup of ice and there should be no delay.

3. For use in exploring and discovering a route to the Japanese islands, there should be built on the Kamchatka River a suitable decked vessel and two sloops, each with 24 oars and a deck. Once these are built and armed, they are to proceed on the designated voyage in accordance with instructions. If there is a vessel left from the previous expedition, in sufficiently good condition that a voyage can safely be undertaken, then there will be no need to build a new decked vessel. It will then only be necessary to build the two sloops.

4. These vessels, according to the judgment of their commanding officers, should proceed toward America under Captain Commander Bering on one ship and Captain Lieutenant Chirikov on the other. As noted above, they

should sail together. During the voyage they are to act in mutual agreement. For that reason they should be given joint instructions. Captain Spanberg is to proceed toward the Japanese islands in command of the ship and the two double sloops which Bering used on his previous expedition. The Admiralty College feels that both Spanberg and Chirikov are completely qualified to undertake this expedition.

Bering's subordinates should be sent to survey the [Arctic] coast from the Ob River to the Lena and beyond, from Tobolsk to the mouth of the Enisei, from Iakutsk to the mouth of the Enisei, and from Iakutsk and the mouth of the Ob [sic Lena?] east along the coast to the Kolyma and around the cape [Chukotsk peninsula] to the mouths of the Anadyr and Kamchatka rivers.

Each of these vessels should be staffed as required with subordinate senior and junior naval officers and enlisted men of various ranks. The Governing Senate will receive a special list indicating these assignments. The crew has already been appointed. In accordance with an ukaz from the Governing Senate, some of the ranks have already been sent to Siberia. The names of those who have already been sent are included in the present list, so no others are required for those positions.

5. Captain Commander Bering and the other commanders on these vessels, while at sea, are to receive special instructions from the Admiralty College on their conduct at sea. The Admiralty College will submit these instructions, when they are ready, to the Governing Senate for their review.

6. While Captain Commander Bering is on land during this expedition, he is to proceed as follows. When the expeditions reach the Japanese islands, when they survey the American coastline or islands located near America, and when as they sail from the western [Siberian] rivers and from Arkhangelsk they encounter islands on their way, they should anchor near shore and find out everything possible about the natives there and how to deal with them.

When Captain Spanberg returns to Okhotsk from Japan either he or a staff officer is to return here [to St. Petersburg] with detailed information and a description and a map. The rest of the crew is to remain in Okhotsk until an *ukaz* is issued. The Admiralty College will transmit all this information to the Governing Senate for its consideration.

7. In this regard the Admiralty College will submit to the Governing Senate its opinion as to whether the construction of the designated ships will be accomplished on time so that artillery and other supplies which can be secured in those towns can be prepared in a reasonable length of time.

In addition, adequate provisions are to be prepared in Iakutsk for the servitors who are sent to Kamchatka and Okhotsk. The Admiralty College will submit a list of the amount of provisions, artillery and other supplies which will be necessary for the ships. On the basis of that list, *ukazes* are to be sent to those places ordering that all necessary items be prepared in good time. Vessels must be built in Iakutsk to transport these supplies by water. The Admiralty College believes that naval officers should be sent to Iakutsk now to build these vessels and make all necessary preparations. They would have joint responsibility with the local commanding officers for carrying out these instructions without delay, and should send these provisions and supplies on to Okhotsk so that when Captain Commander Bering arrives, everything will be ready for him . . .

A Decree from the Senate Appointing Missionaries to Kamchatka to Convert the Kamchadal Natives to Orthodox Christianity, January 2, 1742

In order to enable the local [native] population of the Kamchatka territory to have the opportunity to hear the Word of God, and to convert them and enable them to understand Christian morality, Arkhimandrit Ioasaf Zankevich of Spaskii Monastery in Tobolsk is to proceed there. To assist him in baptizing the natives, two church-servitor priests and one *diakon* [deacon] who have been exiled to Okhotsk [are to be sent there]. Also, five priests, two other *diakons*, ten *diachoks* [reader-assistants] and a *ponomar* [sexton] will be sent to the Kamchatka, Okhotsk and Anadyrsk *ostrogs* to conduct church services. Her Imperial Majesty, at the request of the Holy Synod, has designated the following salaries for them: 300 *rubles* for the Arkhimandrit for the first year, to be taken from *gubernia* revenues in Tobolsk; 150 *rubles* apiece for the two assisting priests; 100 *rubles* for the *diakon* [from Okhotsk]; 80 *rubles* apiece for the other priests; 60 *rubles* apiece for the other *diakons*; 40 *rubles* apiece for the *prichetnik* [minor churchman], *diachoks* and *ponomar*.

The following supplies are also to be issued to them for the church: sacramental wine, wax, palm branches and flour for the holy wafers. All of this is to come out of revenues from Okhotsk *ostrog*, if they are sufficient. If not, then Iakutsk is to provide these things every year without any delay so they will not suffer need and hunger in such a distant land without resources for food, and so they can conduct church liturgy and carry on church affairs without delay.

Arkhimandrit Zankevich should be provided transportation and a guide. He is also to be issued sufficient travel funds for the journey from Tobolsk to Irkutsk, and from there, for himself and for the church supplies, to Iakutsk and on to Okhotsk. From that place he and the designated church servitors are to be sent across the sea [of Okhotsk] to Kamchatka aboard an appropriate vessel, taking with them everything else needed for the *iconostasis* and the church furnishings.

If the Siberian *gubernia* office failed to send with the previous *igumen*, Filevskii, any items specified in the *ukaz* issued by the Governing Senate in 1732, these things are also to be sent now without any further delay. A guard of three reliable soldiers who can read, taken from church lists, are to be sent with Arkhimandrit Zankevich from the Tobolsk garrison for his protection and assistance. They are to receive appropriate compensation and remain with him constantly as long as he is proselytizing in Kamchatka. They are to obey him implicitly. Wherever necessary, the *arkhimandrit* is to receive guides and interpreters. Such persons are to be reliable and to have sworn the oath.

Any necessary *ukazes* regarding this assignment are to be issued and the Holy Synod is to be kept informed of progress. The Holy Synod will decide the question of what financial reward those who choose to be baptized will receive, and the Holy Synod will inform the Governing Senate. Upon receiving Senate approval, the Holy Synod will issue a statement so that the Office for the Newly Baptized in Kazan will issue the appropriate amount of money.

A Decree from the Senate Sending an Infantry Colonel and Other Officers to Siberia to Investigate Abuses and Mistreatment of Natives by Russian Iasak *Collectors, September 24, 1745*

This decree is to be announced in Siberia for general information.

1. In accordance with an *ukaz* of Her Imperial Majesty, Colonel Wolf of the Kabardinsk Infantry Regiment is being dispatched to Siberia with senior and junior officers to investigate the protection of the loyal subjects of Her Imperial Majesty, especially the Kamchadals, against officials assigned there to collect *iasak*, and from their subordinates who inflict abuse and ruin upon these people. This is to be done so that in the future no one, under any circumstances, will inflict abuse and ruin on local people (except for the collection of Treasury-imposed obligations).

Likewise, henceforth no one is to take any of the newly baptized or unbaptized natives into forced servitude under the pretext of punishment for debt, forgery or any other false accusation. Anyone who takes such baptized or unbaptized persons into servitude, or who has written acknowledgements of indebtedness, [is to be informed that] such debts are not to be recovered through force except for those which have been incurred through obligations during normal trade transactions, and which, upon careful examination, are seen to be bona fide. Such obligations can and should be enforced. In the future, however, any illegal statements of debt are not to be contracted.

If in the future, subsequent to this prohibition, anyone should hold such persons as slaves, or should have any written document of indebtedness, he will be treated as a violator of this *ukaz*.

2. If any local natives have been abused, they should submit their petitions to Colonel Wolf. In these petitions they should state the simple truth, without any embroidery. Upon receipt of the petitions, Wolf is authorized to investigate, in accordance with this *ukaz*, without exception. If investigations show that anyone has collected any additional [*iasak*] from local natives, this is to be confiscated from the usurious person, and returned to the natives from whom it was taken, without delay.

3. This generosity on the part of Her Imperial Majesty is extended to the local natives, as loyal subjects of Her Imperial Majesty, so they will not be impoverished. In return, those people, as subjects of Her Imperial Majesty, receiving such generosity from Her Imperial Majesty, are forever to perform loyal service to Her Imperial Majesty, and unhesitatingly pay the *iasak* imposed on them into the Treasury.

A Memorandum from Count Aleksandr R. Vorontsov, and Count Aleksandr A. Bezborodko, Concerning Russia's Rights to the Islands and Coasts of North America, December, 1786

On the basis of a memorandum from Major-General [P. P.] Soimonov to the President of the College of Commerce, concerning trade and hunting in the Pacific Ocean, Her Imperial Majesty has instructed us to submit our view to Her Imperial Majesty, which we have most humbly formulated and hereby submit.

The Northwest Coast of America and the islands in the archipelagos between there and Kamchatka, and from the peninsula to Japan, were discovered long ago by Russian seafarers. Their detailed notes bear witness to this. Major-General Soimonov has prepared an extract of these accounts, which extract is hereby dutifully appended.

According to a generally accepted rule, the first nation to discover an unknown land has the right to claim it. This has been true in earlier ages, and has been the general practice since the discovery of America. Thus when a European country discovered a previously unknown land, they claimed it. Indeed the popes of Rome, on behalf of Roman Catholic rulers, would issue papal bulls to reaffirm such a discovery and thereby finalize the right of possession.

Based on this precedent it is indisputable that the following should belong to Russia: (1) the American coast from 55°21′ north to the latitudes reached by captains Bering and Chirikov and other Russian seafarers; (2) all the islands near the mainland and the Alaskan peninsula, which were discovered by Bering and which [Captain James] Cook named after Montague—these include Sv. Stefan, Sv. Dalmatiia, Evdokiia, Shumagin, and others which lie between the sailing course of our seafarers and the mainland; (3) all the islands west of these in the archipelagos known as the Fox and Aleutian islands, and others to the north which Russian *promyshlenniks* visited every year; (4) the archipelago of the Kuril Islands which extends to Japan, which islands were discovered by captains Spanberg and Walton.

For this reason there is no foundation to the claim of the English under the leadership of Captain Cook to a river which he named but which had previously been discovered by Captain Chirikov. Cook claimed this river under the jurisdiction and in the name of the English king, raised a flag and ordered that some English coins be buried in the land there. There is also no basis for his claim to Prince William Sound and the island of Kay. This is clearly documented by the naval journals of captains Bering and Chirikov, who sailed for a great distance along that coast. This can be more clearly seen in the map Major-General Soimonov has prepared.

The acquisition of all these previously unknown islands to Your Majesty's Empire is founded on the right of first discovery by the Russians. This was accomplished with great effort on the part of the government and also on the part of Your Majesty's individual subjects who were encouraged by their great profits from the fur trade and went on to make more and more discoveries. However, these acquisitions have not yet been officially claimed by the government. Thus in our view it is necessary that Your Majesty issue an Imperial decree, through Russian ministers accredited to the Courts of all European seafaring nations, announcing that these lands which Russians have discovered must form an integral part of Russia as part of our Empire. For that reason the Empire cannot allow foreign seafarers and ships to sail there, just as other seafaring powers do not permit foreign nations into their settlements outside of Europe, considering these places as reserved exclusively for trade for their own subjects. For greater clarification they should be provided with the above mentioned map, which should be published and made available under the watchful supervision of Major-General Soimonov.

However, since such a declaration will be inadequate without considerable support, and might in some ways even undermine the dignity of the Court, we, the undersigned, humbly submit to Your Imperial Majesty that it would be most beneficial if Your Majesty would decree that several naval vessels be sent into these regions belonging to Your Empire. A number of capable naval officers should be stationed abroad these vessels, as well as the appropriate number of lower ranking naval personnel, in order to be able to enforce the prohibition which would extend to all alien ships belonging to any European power who might proceed there to establish their own control or to carry on trade with the local people.

After such a declaration, out of respect for Your Imperial Majesty neither the English Court nor any other like naval power would dare send their naval vessels there; however one should not assume that private merchants or privileged East Indian Company personnel or others would cease their efforts. This was evidenced by the fact that not long ago an English naval sloop belonging to private merchants attempted to trade in those regions to realize large profit through the fur trade. Although we too have commercial vessels, it is doubtful that they are equipped and built in such a manner that they could successfully prevent these private entrepreneurs from coming, without Your Majesty's mighty naval protection.

Secret Instructions from Lieutenant General Ivan V. Iakobii, Governor General of Siberia, To Agents of Grigorii I. Shelikhov, to Establish Russia's Claim to Newly Discovered Parts of Alaska, June 21, 1787

First. When you receive the packet which contains fifteen insignia of the Russian Empire and ten iron plates, on which are a bronze cross and bronze letters proclaiming "This land belongs to the Russian Empire," immediately try to emplace these on land in that part of western America known as Alaska. It is desirable that the insignia be placed in the same location where an English ship anchored in the year 1784 and engaged in a rich and profitable trade. To the best of our knowledge that location is in 50° 40′.

2. Wherever you emplace one of these insignia, within a few paces you are to bury one of the plates as well, on which are to be described not only the location but also a statement on which side of the insigne it has been placed, and also the depth.

3. Use every possible means to chart the coastline. Note where bays and inlets are located, their depth, names, and configuration.

4. Try to bury the plates in such a manner that not only will they not be seen by the natives, but so they are hidden from all of our Russian workmen. This secret is to be preserved and the fact that the plates have been buried is to be erased from the memory of the natives.

5. If it should happen that ships of other nations should reach those regions for the same purpose, you are empowered to declare that the land and the commerical rights belong to the Russian Empire and that the land was first discovered by Russian seafarers.

6. The Company representative, [G. I.] Shelikhov, has asked me for permission for the Company to hire workers from among the native inhabitants

because of the shortage of Russian workmen. I find no objection to this and so give my permission on this condition: that every man be compensated for his work with decent pay, and that each be treated not only in a manner which human beings deserve, but in a manner which will also carry out the wish and intent of the wise and humane Autocrat. By treating them justly and giving them honest pay for their labor, you will not only provide the Company with help needed in the business, but you will also use this as a means of making them contented subjects of Russia under the wise administration of our great Empress, and will inspire in them the desire to become subjects of the Russian scepter.

7. Whenever a special expedition is sent to a place you have discovered, when vessels carrying our *promyshlenniks* go there, you should instruct them to try diligently to find new places, places not previously discovered. Thus not only may they claim the discovery of these new areas and thereby gain better trade opportunities for themselves, but also their efforts may be recognized by the Crown with praise and respect. This will also eliminate the constant complaints from one company or another, and the abuse of native inhabitants. Further, it will eliminate the need to search for transgressors, which is required by law, if companies do not remain in one place.

8. Send a detailed description of all vegetation in areas your company visits. If you are in a forested area, identify the trees, state whether there are berries, whether there are fruit trees. Describe the animals and birds that live in that climate. Also describe the quality of the soil and state whether or not it may be possible to develop agriculture there.

[Signed] Ivan Iakobii

23

Czartoryski's Account of the Events Surrounding the Assassination of Paul, 1801

One of the most tragic rules of eighteenth-century Russia was Tsar Paul (1796–1801). Though he was her first son, Catherine II never showed any love for him, viewed him as hopelessly incapable, and even allowed her numerous favorites to insult him. Paul resented this treatment and blamed Catherine for the death of Peter III. The antipathy between mother and son became so intense that when Paul ascended the throne in 1796 he sought to undo most of Catherine's work. He dismissed many of her favorites and rehabilitated her enemies, including Radishchev. He introduced a strict new law on imperial succession and even sought to improve the condition of the serfs. By these actions Paul, who was inexperienced in the art of government, alienated important groups and caused a great deal of confusion, irritation, and uncertainty. Early in 1801 a conspiracy developed against him. It was masterminded by Count Nikita P. Panin, a vice chancellor; Joseph Ribas, a Spanish soldier of fortune and an admiral in the Russian navy; and Count Peter Pahlen, military governor of St. Petersburg. Paul was murdered and was succeeded by his son, Alexander I (1801–1825), who had been Catherine's choice in the first place.

Then he [Alexander I] spoke to me of his father's death with inexpressible grief and remorse. We often returned to this subject, and Alexander gave me full details of it, which I shall repeat below, together with information communicated to me by other actors in the tragedy. . . .

Alexander told me that the first man who spoke to him about the plans of the conspirators was Count Panin, and he never forgave him. This personage seemed destined more than anyone else to play an important part in the affairs

---

From Memoirs of *Prince Adam Czartoryski and His Correspondence with Alexander I.* Edited by Adam Gielgud (London: Remington and Co., 1888), vol. 1, pp. 227–248, 251–255. Prince Adam Czartoryski (1770–1861) was for a number of years one of Alexander's closest associates.

of the Empire, and he had all that was wanted for such an undertaking; a celebrated name, uncommon talents, and much ambition. . . . As will be seen further on, Panin was one of the chief leaders of the conspiracy which brought about Paul's death, though he did not actually take part in it. . . .

The two Counts Panin and Pahlen were at that time the strongest heads of the Empire. They saw further and more clearly than the other members of Paul's Council, to which both of them belonged; and they agreed to initiate Alexander into their plans. It would not have been prudent to attempt anything without being assured of the consent of the heir to the crown. Devoted fanatics or enthusiasts might no doubt have acted otherwise. By not implicating the son in the dethronement of his father, by exposing themselves to a certain death, they would have better served both Russia and the prince who was to be called upon to govern her; but such a course would have been almost impracticable, and it would have demanded an audacity and antique virtue which in these days very few men possess. Pahlen, as Governor of St. Petersburg, had easy means of access to the Grand-Duke, and obtained from him a secret audience for Panin; their first interview took place in a bath. Panin represented to Alexander the evils from which Russia was suffering and would continue to suffer if Paul continued to reign. He said that Alexander's most sacred duty was to his country, and that he must not sacrifice millions of people to the extravagant caprices and follies of a single man, even if that man was his father; that the life, or at least the liberty, of his mother, of himself, and of the whole of the Imperial family was threatened by Paul's inconceivable aversion for his wife, from whom he was entirely separated; that this aversion increased from day to day, and might prompt him to the most outrageous acts; and that it was therefore necessary to save Russia, whose fate was in Alexander's hands, by deposing Paul, which would be the only means of preventing him from inflicting greater calamities on his country and his family, and securing to him a quieter and more happy life. This speech produced a great impression on Alexander but it did not convince him. It required more than six months to enable his tempters to obtain his consent to their plans. Pahlen had at first left all the speaking to Panin, who was an adept at specious arguments; but when the latter was sent to Moscow, Pahlen completed the work of his colleague by hints and allusions, intelligible only to Alexander himself, which were so skilfully introduced with a military frankness which he made almost as effective as eloquence, that Alexander became more and more persuaded that the aims of the conspiracy were just and good.

It was a thousand pities that a prince so anxious and so well qualified to be a benefactor to his country did not hold entirely aloof from a conspiracy which resulted almost inevitably in his father's assassination. Russia certainly suffered much under the almost maniacal Government of Paul, and there are no means in that country of restraining or confiding a mad sovereign; but Alexander felt and exaggerated in his own mind all his life the sombre reflection of the crime committed on his father, which had fallen on himself, and which he thought he could never wipe out. This ineffaceable stain, although it was brought about solely by his inexperience and his total and innocent ignorance of Russian affairs and the Russian people, settled like a vulture on his conscience, paralyzed his best faculties at the commencement of his reign, and plunged him into a mysticism sometimes degenerating into superstition at its close.

At the same time it must be admitted that the Emperor Paul was precipitating his country into incalculable disasters and into a complete disorganisation and deterioration of the Government machine. Paul governed intermittently, without troubling himself about the consequences, like a man who acts without reflection according to the impulse of the moment. The higher classes, the principal officials, the generals and other officers of rank—all, in a word, who thought and acted in Russia—were more or less convinced that the Emperor had fits of mental alienation. His reign became a rule of terror. He was hated even for his good qualities, for at bottom he desired justice, and this impulse sometimes led him to do a just thing in his outburst of rage; but his feeling of justice was blind, and struck at all without discrimination of circumstances; always passionate, often capricious and cruel, his decrees were constantly suspended over the heads of the military and civil officers, and made them detest the man who thus filled their lives with uncertainty and terror. The conspiracy had the sympathy of all, for it promised to put an end to a regime which had become intolerable. A sovereign may commit grave mistakes, bring evils on his country, cause its wealth or its power to decline, without exposing himself to death as a punishment for his misdeeds. But when the sovereign authority weighs at every moment on each individual in the State, and continually disturbs like a fever the peace of families in the ordinary relations of life, passions are excited which are much more formidable than those produced by evils which, though affecting the entire community, are little felt by individuals. This was the real motive of Paul's assassination. I utterly disbelieve the story that English money contributed to this event. For even supposing—and I am sincerely convinced there is no foundation for such a belief—that the English Government of that day was devoid of all feelings of morality, such an expenditure would have been totally unnecessary. The deposition, if not the murder, of Paul had become inevitable in the natural course of events. Even before my departure from St. Petersburg it was the fashion among the young men of the Court to talk freely on this subject, to make satirical epigrams on Paul's eccentricities, and to suggest all kinds of absurd plans for getting rid of him. The universal aversion to his rule was shown, often without any attempt at concealment, on every possible occasion; it was a State secret which was confided to all, and which no one betrayed, though the people lived under the most redoubted and the most suspicious of sovereigns, who encouraged espionage, and spared no means of obtaining exact information not only of the actions, but of the thoughts and intentions of his subjects. The wish to get rid of the Emperor Paul showed itself more strongly the nearer one approached the Court and the capital, but it did not really become active until almost at the moment of its execution. Notwithstanding the extreme favour with which the conspiracy was regarded in the most distinguished society of the Empire, it could not have attained its objects, and would probably have been discovered, if the appointment of Governor-General of St. Petersburg, which placed at his disposal the garrison and the police, had not been in the hands of the chief promoter of the enterprise.

One day the Emperor said, with a scrutinizing glance at Pahlen: "I hear a conspiracy is being formed against me." "Such a thing is impossible, Sire," replied the General with his frank and good-natured smile; "it cannot be formed unless I belong to it." This reassured Paul, though it is said that his suspicions were aroused by anonymous letters, and that on the eve of his death he had sent for General Araktcheyeff to give him the place of Governor-General of St. Petersburg, after dismissing Pahlen. If Araktcheyeff had come in time, St. Petersburg would have been the scene of many tragic events; he was a man inbued with a strong sentiment of order and with an energy which sometimes grew into ferocity. His return would probably have been followed by that of Count Rostopchin, and Paul might then have been saved. . . .

Although everybody sympathised with the conspiracy, nothing was done until Alexander had given his consent to his father's deposition. The men who undertook to carry out the plan were Pahlen and the two Zuboffs, whom Paul had recalled from exile and loaded with favours, thinking he had nothing to fear from them now he was in his new castle. Their first step was to induce a number of Generals and other officers of rank who were their friends to come under various pretexts to St. Petersburg; and this was rendered more easy by the fact that Paul himself had invited many high functionaries and Generals to be present at the fêtes he was about to give on the marriage of one of his daughters. Pahlen and the Zuboffs took steps to enlist the services of some of the more eminent of the Generals, without stating positively what they intended to do. But it was necessary to act at once, for the slightest imprudence or revelation might place the Emperor in possession of their secret, and he was already so suspicious that he might at any moment take some step which would be their ruin. It was not known whether he had already sent for Araktcheyeff and Rostopchin. The former lived at twenty-four hours' journey from St. Petersburg and might come at any moment. Doubtless he and Rostopchin would endeavour to moderate the Emperor's excesses, but their influence would probably not be sufficient to put a stop to the severities he wished to exercise with regard to several members of the Imperial family. It was evident that any further delay or vacillation would be most dangerous, and might be the cause of incalculable calamities; and the conspirators accordingly decided to strike the blow on the 3rd of March, 1801.

On that evening Plato Zuboff gave a grand supper, to which were invited all the Generals and other officers of rank who were supposed to approve of the objects of the conspiracy. These were only now clearly explained to them, as the only way to secure the enterprise against accidents was for two or three leaders to prepare it, and not to announce it to the others who were to take part in it until the moment for its execution should arrive.

Zuboff represented to his guests the deplorable condition in which Russia was placed by the insanity of her sovereign, the dangers to which both the State and each individual citizen were exposed, and the probability that new and more outrageous excesses might at any moment be expected. He pointed out that the insane act of a rupture with England was contrary to the essential interests of the Russian nation, dried up the sources of its wealth, and exposed the Baltic ports, and the capital itself, to the gravest disasters; and that none of those whom he addressed could be sure of their fate on the morrow. He enlarged on the virtues of the Grand-Duke Alexander, and on the brilliant destinies of Russia under the sceptre of a young Prince of such promise, whom the Empress Catherine, of glorious memory, had regarded as her successor, and had intended, if she had not been prevented by her death, to place on the throne. He concluded by declaring that Alexander, rendered desperate by the misfortunes of his country, had decided to save it; and that all that was now necessary was to depose the Emperor Paul, to oblige him to sign a deed of abdication, and, by proclaiming Alexander Emperor, to prevent his father from ruining both himself and his Empire. Pahlen and both the Zuboffs repeated to the assembled guests the assurance that the Grand-Duke Alexander approved of their plan. They were careful not to say how much time it took them to persuade him, and with what extreme difficulty and with how many restrictions and modifications his consent was finally obtained. The last point was left vague, and everyone probably explained it after his own fashion.

When the company had been made to understand that Alexander's consent had been given there was no further hesitation. Meanwhile champagne was drunk freely and there was general excitement. Pahlen, who had gone away for a short time on business connected with his functions as Governor-General, came back from the Court and announced that the Emperor did not seem to suspect anything, and had said goodnight to the Empress and the Grand-Dukes as usual. Those who had been at supper in the palace afterwards said they recollected that Alexander, when he took leave of his father, did not change countenance or show that he was conscious of the scene which was preparing. Probably they did not look at him, for he has often told me how agitated he was, and certainly the risks he ran not only for himself, but for his mother, his family, and many others were enough to make him sad and anxious. The Grand-Dukes were always obliged to maintain an attitude of strict reserve before their father, and this constant habit of concealing their emotions and thoughts may explain why at this grave and supreme moment no one perceived in Alexander's countenance what was passing in his mind.

At the Zuboffs' house the guests had become so convivial that time went fast. At midnight the conspirators set out for the Emperor's palace. The leaders had drunk but moderately, wishing to keep their heads clear, but the majority of those who followed them were more or less intoxicated; some could hardly even keep their legs. They were divided into two bands, each composed of some sixty generals and other officers. The two Zuboffs and General Bennigsen were at the head of the first band, which was to go to the palace direct; the second was to enter through the garden, and was under the command of Pahlen. The aide-de-camp in waiting, who knew all the doors and passages of the palace, as he was daily on duty there, guided the first band with a dark lantern to the entrance of the Emperor's dressing-room, which adjoined his bedroom. A young valet who was on duty stopped the conspirators and cried out that rebels were coming to murder the Emperor. He was wounded in the struggle which ensued, and rendered incapable of further resistance. His cries waked the Emperor, who got out of bed and ran to a door which communicated with the Empress's apartments and was hidden by a large curtain. Unfortunately, in one of his fits of dislike for his wife, he had ordered the door to be locked; and the key was not in the lock, either because Paul had ordered it to be taken away or because his favourites, who were opposed to the Empress, had done so, fearing lest he should some day have a fancy to return to her. Meanwhile the conspirators were confused and terrified at the cries of Paul's faithful defender, the only one he had at a moment of supreme danger when he believed in his omnipotence more than ever and was surrounded by a triple line of walls and guards. Zuboff, the chief of the band, lost heart and proposed to retire at once, but General Bennigsen (from whom I obtained some of these details) seized him by the arm and protested against such a dangerous step. "What?" he said, "You have brought us so far, and now you want to withdraw? We are too far advanced to follow your advice, which would ruin us all. The wine is drawn, it must be drunk. Let us march on."

It was this Hanoverian that decided the Emperor's fate; he was one of those who had only that evening been informed of the conspiracy. He placed himself at the head of the band, and those who had most courage, or most hatred for Paul, were the first to follow him. They entered the Emperor's bedroom, went straight to his bed, and were much alarmed at not finding him there. They searched the room with a light, and at last discovered the unfortunate Paul hiding behind the folds of the curtain. They dragged him out in his shirt more dead than alive; the terror he had inspired was now repaid to him with usury. Fear had paralyzed his senses and had deprived him of speech; his whole body shivered. He was placed on a chair before a desk. The long, thin, pale, and angular form of General Bennigsen, with his hat on his head and a drawn sword in his hand, must have seemed to him a terrible spectre. "Sire," said the General, "you are my prisoner, and have ceased to reign; you will now at once write and sign a deed of abdication in favour of the Grand-Duke Alexander." Paul was still unable to speak, and a pen was put in his hand. Trembling and almost unconscious, he was about to obey when more cries were heard. General Bennigsen then left the room, as he has often assured me, to ascertain what these cries meant, and to take steps for securing the safety of the palace and of the Imperial family. He had only just gone out the door when a terrible scene began. The unfortunate Paul remained alone with men who were maddened by a furious hatred of him, owing to the numerous acts of persecution and injustice they had suffered at his hands, and it appears that several of them had decided to assassinate him, perhaps without the knowledge of the leaders or at least without their formal consent. The catastrophe, which in such a case was, in a country like Russia, almost inevitable, was doubtless hastened by the cries above referred to, which alarmed the conspirators for their own safety. Count Nicholas Zuboff, a man of herculean proportions, was said to be the first that placed his hand on his sovereign, and thereby broke the spell of imperial authority which still surrounded him. The others now saw in Paul nothing but a monster, a tyrant, an implacable enemy—and his abject submission, instead of disarming them, rendered him despicable and ridiculous as well as odious in their eyes.

One of the conspirators took off his official scarf and tied it round the Emperor's throat. Paul struggled, the approach of death restoring him to strength and speech. He set free one of his hands and thrust it between the scarf and his throat, crying out for air. Just then he perceived a red uniform, which was at that time worn by the officers of the cavalry guard, and thinking that one of the assassins was his son Constantine, who was a colonel of that regiment, he exclaimed: "Mercy, your Highness, mercy! Some air, for God's sake!" But the conspirators seized the hand with which he was striving to prolong his life, and furiously tugged at both ends of the scarf. The unhappy

Emperor had already breathed his last, and yet they tightened the knot and dragged along the dead body, striking it with their hands and feet. The cowards who until then had held aloof surpassed in atrocity those who had done the deed. Just at that time General Bennigsen returned. I do not know whether he was sincerely grieved at what had happened in his absence; all he did was to stop the further desecration of the Emperor's body.

Meanwhile the cry "Paul is dead!" was heard by the other conspirators, and filled them with a joy that deprived them of all sentiment of decency and dignity. They wandered tumultuously about the corridors and rooms of the palace, boasting to each other of their prowess; many of them found means of adding to the intoxication of the supper by breaking into the wine cellars and drinking to the Emperor's death.

Pahlen, who seems to have lost his way in the garden, came to the palace with his band immediately after the deed had been consummated. It is said that he had delayed his arrival on purpose, so as to be able to profess to have come to the Emperor's assistance in case his colleagues should have failed. Be this as it may, he was extremely active directly he arrived, giving the necessary orders during the rest of the night, and omitting nothing which could give him a claim to reward as the prime mover and commander of the enterprise.

It will be seen from the above narrative how easy it would have been for the undertaking to have been foiled by an accident, notwithstanding the precautions which had been taken to ensure its success. The conspiracy had the sympathies of the higher classes and most of the officers; but not of the lower ranks of the army. The persons who suffered from Paul's insane fits of rage and severity were usually the higher military and civil officials; his caprices very seldom affected men of the lower ranks, who, moreover, were continually receiving extra pay and rations of bread, wine, and brandy when they were on drill or on a parade. The punishments to which the officers were exposed did not therefore produce any unpleasant impression on the common soldier; on the contrary, they were a sort of satisfaction to him for the blows and ill-treatment he constantly had to endure. Moreover, his pride was flattered by the great improtance attached to his calling, for to Paul nothing could be more important than a foot raised too soon on the march, or a coat badly buttoned on parade. It amused and pleased the soldiers to see their Emperor dispensing endless punishments and severities among the officers while he took every opportunity to afford to the men ample compensation for the work and trouble that was required of them. The soldiers of the Guard, many of whom were married, lived with their families almost in opulence, and both they and those of the other regiments were satisfied with and attached to the Emperor. General Talyzin, one of the principal conspirators, who was very popular among the soldiers, had undertaken to bring to the palace one of the battalions of the first regiment of the Guard which was under his command. He assembled the men after leaving Zuboff's supper, and began to tell them that their fatigues were about to cease, and that they would now have an indulgent and kind sovereign who would not impose upon them the rigorous duties they had hitherto had to perform. He soon perceived, however, that his words were not listened to with favour; the soldiers preserved a gloomy silence, their faces had a sombre expression, and some murmurs were heard. The General cut short his speech, uttered in a sharp tone of command the words "Right wheel—march," and the battalion, which had now again become a machine, marched to the palace, all the outlets from which it occupied.

Count Valerian Zuboff, having lost a leg in the Polish War, could not belong to either of the bands of the conspirators. He entered the palace soon after the death of the Emperor became known, and then went to the guard-room to sound the opinions of the soldiers. He congratulated them on having a new and a young Emperor; but this compliment was ill received, and he was obliged to leave the room hastily to avoid disagreeable manifestations. All this shows how easy it would have been for Paul to crush the conspirators if he had been able to escape them for a moment and to show himself to the guards in the courtyard. It also shows how illusory and impracticable was Alexander's plan of keeping his father in confinement. If Paul's life had been saved, blood would have flowed on the scaffold, Siberia would have been crowded with exiles, and his vengeance would probably have extended to his sons.

I will not describe what happened during this terrible night in the part of the palace which was inhabited by the Imperial family. The Grand-Duke Alexander knew that his father would in a few hours be called upon to abdicate, and without undressing he threw himself on his bed full of anxiety and doubt. About one o'clock he heard a knock at his door, and saw Count Nicholas Zuboff, his dress in disorder, and his face flushed with wine and the excitement of the murder which had just been committed. He came up to Alexander, who was sitting on his bed, and said in a hoarse voice: "All is over." "What is over?" asked Alexander in consternation. He was somewhat dead, and perhaps he feared to misunderstand what was being said to him, while Zuboff on his side feared to state exactly what had been done. This somewhat prolonged the conversation; Alexander had not the least idea that his father was dead, and did not therefore admit the possibility of such a thing. At length he perceived that Zuboff, without clearly explaining himself, repeatedly addressed him as "Sire" and "Your Majesty," while Alexander thought he was merely Regent. This led to further questioning, and he then learnt the truth. Alexander was prostrated with grief and despair. This was not surprising, for even ambitious men cannot commit a crime or believe themselves the cause of one without repulsion, while Alexander was not at all ambitious. The idea of having caused the death of his father filled him with horror, and he felt that his reputation had received a stain which could never be effaced. As for the Empress, directly the news reached her and she dressed hastily, rushing out of her apartments with cries of despair and rage. Perceiving some grenadiers, she said to them repeatedly: "As your Emperor has died a victim to treason, I am your Empress, I alone am your legitimate sovereign; follow me and protect me." General Bennigsen and Count Pahlen, who had just brought a detachment of men whom they could trust to the palace to restore order, strove to calm her and forced her with difficulty to return to her room. She had scarcely entered it, however, than she wished to go out again, although guards had been placed at her door. At first she seemed determined at all risks to seize the reins of government and avenge her husband's murder. But though she was generally respected, she was not capable of inspiring those feelings of enthusiastic devotion which cause men to act impulsively and without weighing the consequences. Her appeals to the soldiers (which were perhaps rendered somewhat ridiculous by her German accent) produced no effect, and she retired in confusion, vexed at having uselessly disclosed her ambitious views.

I never heard any details of the first interview between the Empress and her son after Paul's assassination. Subsequently they came to an understanding with each other; but during the first terrible moments Alexander was so absorbed by his remorse that he seemed incapable of saying a word of thinking of anybody. His mother, on the other hand, was in a passion of grief and animosity; the only member of the Imperial family that retained her presence of mind was the young Empress. She did her utmost to console Alexander and give him courage and self-reliance. She did not leave him during the whole of the night, except when she went for a few moments to calm her mother-in-law and persuade her to stop in her room and not expose herself to the fury of the conspirators. While in this night of trouble and horror some were intoxicated with triumph and others plunged in grief and despair, the Empress Elizabeth alone exercised a mediatory influence between her husband, her mother-in-law, and the conspirators.

During the first years of his reign, Alexander's position with regard to his father's murderers was an extremely difficult and painful one. For a few months he believed himself to be at their mercy, but it was chiefly his conscience and a feeling of natural equity which prevented him from giving up to justice the most guilty of the conspirators. He knew that there was a general sympathy for the objects of the conspiracy, and that those who had personally taken part in their realization had only decided to do so when they were assured of his consent. It would have been difficult under these circumstances to distinguish between degrees of guilt; every member of the society of St. Petersburg was more or less an accomplice in the fatal deed, for those who wished Paul to be deposed must have known that his deposition, if resisted, might have involved his death. If the assassins alone had been brought to trial, they would certainly have accused the other conspirators and have referred to Alexander's consent in justification of their action, though the crime had been committed against his express wish. Moreover, he did not for many years know who they were, as all the conspirators were interested in keeping the secret. The assassins all perished miserably, including Count Nicholas Zuboff, who, not daring to show himself at Court, died in retirement, consumed by illness, by remorse, and by disappointed ambition. . . .

The views of the Zuboffs as to the conspiracy were communicated to me by Count Valerian Zuboffs a few days after my return to St. Petersburg. He complained that the Emperor did not declare himself for his true friends, who had placed him on the throne and had not feared any danger they had incurred in his service. The Empress Catherine had acted otherwise; she had always supported those who had helped her, and had not hesitated to maintain them in power. By this wise and sagacious conduct, said Zuboff, she had been able always to reckon on their devotion. No one hesitated to make a sacrifice for her, as such sacrifices were always rewarded; but Alexander was exposing himself by his vacillating conduct to the most serious consequences, and was discouraging his best friends. Zuboff added that the Empress Catherine had expressly enjoined him and his brother to look upon Alexander as their only legitimate sovereign, and to serve him alone with unshaken zeal and fidelity. This they had done, and what was their reward? He said this to exculpate his brother and himself in the eyes of the young Emperor with regard to the assassination of his father, and to prove to him that their conduct was the necessary result of the engagements Catherine had demanded of them as to her grandson. But they did not know that Alexander, and even his brother Constantine, by no means regarded their grandmother's memory with veneration or attachment. During this conversation, which lasted more than an hour, I several times interrupted the Count to explain the young Emperor's conduct. It was evident that the Zuboffs wished me to communicate their views to the Emperor, and though I did not promise, I considered it my duty to do so. Their statements produced but little impression on Alexander, but they showed that the conspirators were still very proud of their achievement, and that they felt convinced they had done a great service to Russia, had a right to Alexander's gratitude and confidence, and were necessary to the security and prosperity of the new reign. They even hinted that their discontent might be dangerous to him. Alexander, however, was deaf both to their arguments and their threats. He could not look with favor on his father's murderers, or give himself up into their hands. Moreover, he had already dismissed Pahlen, who was perhaps the only one of the conspirators who by his ability, his connections, his boldness, and his ambition, could inspire serious fear or become really dangerous. Alexander also dismissed other leaders of the conspiracy who were not dangerous, but the sight of whom was odious and disagreeable to him. The only leader who remained at St. Petersburg was Count Valerian Zuboff, who was a member of the Imperial Council. His amiability and frankness pleased Alexander and inspired him with confidence; and this feeling was confirmed by the attachment which the Count professed (I think sincerely) to have for the Emperor personally, and also by his indolence, his unwillingness to take appointments to which onerous duties were attached, and especially by his amours, which occupied nearly the whole of his time.

The punishment of Pahlen and the other leaders of the conspiracy was the most painful that could have been inflicted on them, and Alexander punished himself with more severity than the others. His grief and the remorse which he was continually reviving in his heart were inexpressibly deep and touching. In the midst of the pomp and the festivals of the coronation, the yound Emperor was reminded of the similar ceremonies which had been passed through by his father, and he saw in imagination Paul's mutilated and blood-stained body on the steps of the throne which he was now himself to ascend. This brilliant display of supreme power, instead of rousing his ambition or flattering his vanity, increased his mental tortures, and he was never, I think, more unhappy. He remained alone for hours, sitting in silence with fixed and haggard looks.

With me, as the confidant of his secret thoughts and troubles, he was most at his ease, and I sometimes entered his room when he had been too long under the painful influence of these fits of despair and remorse. I tried to recall him to his duties; he acknowledged that a painful task was before him, but the severity of his condemnation of his own conduct deprived him of all energy. He replied to all my exhortations and words of encouragement and hope: "No, it is impossible, there is no remedy. I must suffer. How can I cease to suffer? This cannot change."

Those who approached him often feared that his mind would be affected, and as I was then the only person who could speak to him freely I was constantly urged to do so. I think I was of some use in preventing Alexander from succumbing under the weight of the terrible thought that pursued him. Some years later, the great events in which he took a leading and glorious part gave him some consolation and for a time, perhaps, absorbed all his faculties; but I am certain that towards the end of his life it was the same terrible thought that so depressed him, filling him with a disgust of life and a piety which was perhaps exaggerated, but which is the sole possible and real support in the most poignant grief. When we returned to this sad topic, Alexander often repeated to me the details of the plan he had formed to establish his father in the Palace of St. Michael and afterwards to enable him as much as possible to reside in the Impeial Palaces in the country. "The Palace of St. Michael," he said, "was his favourite residence, and he would have been happy there. He would have had the whole of the winter garden to walk and ride in." Alexander intended to attach a riding school and a theatre to the palace, so as to bring together within its precincts everything that could have amused the Emperor Paul and made his life happy. He judged of his father by himself. There was always in his noble character a feminine element, with its strength and weakness. He often used to make plans which could not be realised, and on this idealistic foundation he raised complete structures which he made as perfect as possible. Nothing was more impracticable—especially in Russia—than the romantic means which Alexander had devised of rendering his father happy, while depriving him of his crown and of the possibility of tormenting and ruining the country. Alexander was not only young and inexperienced; he had almost the blind and confiding inexperience of childhood, and this characteristic remained with him for some years until it was destroyed by the realities of life.

I have not concealed anything in regard to the catastrophe which inaugurated his reign, for this was the best way of doing him justice. The complete truth, without any restriction, exculpates him up to a certain point from an odious accusation, and explains how he was led into an action which he abhorred and why he seemed not to have punished the assassins with sufficient rigour. I have shown how inexperienced and unambitious he was, and what were the plausible and even honourable motives by which he was actuated. We may pity Alexander, but we must hesitate to condemn him.

24

Karamzin's Thoughts on Patriotism and Book Publishing in Russia

Nikolai M. Karamzin (1766–1826) is known primarily as a leading conservative nineteenth century Russian historian. He gained this reputation thanks to publication (between 1816 and 1829) of his monu-

---

Source: I. V. Malysher, ed. *N. I. Novikov i ego soveremenniki. Izbrannye sochinenniia* (Moscow: Akademiia Nauk, 1961), pp. 406–411, 415–417. Translation mine.

mental twelve-volume work entitled *A History of the Russian State*. Written in vivid Russian and employing a highly effective style, that work secured a permanent place as a literary monument and as a major defense of Russian autocracy. Karamzin expressed the same spirit in his *Note on Ancient and Modern Russia* (published in 1811).

In addition to being a great historian, Karamzin was a translator, a journalist, a writer of short stories, and essayist, a traveller, a keen observer of human follies, an ardent proponent of enlightenment and a vicious critic of ignorance and superstition. All this is evident from two essays he published in 1802. One dealt with the meaning and nature of patriotism; the other offered a highly perceptive view of the growing importance of book publishing in Russia and its impact on Russian society.

N. M. Karamazin's View on Love of One's Country and National Pride, 1802

Love of country may be *physical, moral, and political.* Every human being loves the place of his birth and of his upbringing. This attachment is common to all people of all nations. This is a matter of nature and should be called *physical* attachment. The native country is dear to one's heart, not because of the beauty of its landscapes, its clear sky, or its pleasant climate, but because of its fascinating memories that enfold, so to say, the dawn and cradle of mankind. There is nothing more precious in the world than life. It is the first blessing. And the beginning of every aspect of our well-being commands a certain special charm for our imagination. Consequently, tender lovers and friends cherish the memory of the first day of their love and friendship. A Laplander, born almost in the grave of nature, nevertheless loves the cold bleakness of his land. While you may move him to happy Italy, his eyes and heart will turn to the north as does a magnet. The bright radiance of the sun will not rouse in his soul the same sweet feelings as will the bleak day, the howling of the storm and the falling of the snow. They all remind him of his native land! The very arrangement of the nerves formed in every human, which seems to be based on climate, links us with our country. It is not without reason that physicians sometimes recommend an air cure. It is not without reason that an inhabitant of Switzerland, when removed from his snowy mountains, becomes depressed and falls into melancholy and revives when he returns to the wild Unterwalden or the rough Glarus. Every vegetation thrives better in its own climate. This natural law also applies to humans. I do not imply that natural beauties and benefits of one's country exert no influence on its love. Some countries that have been richly endowed by nature can be very dear to their inhabitants. All I am saying is that these beauties and benefits do not represent the basic foundation of people's physical attachment to their own country. Otherwise this attachment would not be common.

We get attached to those with whom we grew up and with whom we live. Their soul *conforms* to ours, becomes a kind of mirror of it, serves as the object or means of our moral satisfactions, and becomes the object of the heart's inclinations. This affection for fellow citizens or people with whom we grew up, were educated, and live, represents the second or moral love of country. It is as common as the first, that is, the local or physical love, but at times it is even stronger, because time reinforces habit. One needs only to see two fellow countrymen who encounter each other in a foreign land. With what pleasure they embrace and hasten to pour out their souls in intimate conversation! They may be seeing each other for the first time, but already they are acquainted and are on friendly terms, forging their personal ties through whatever links them to their country! It seems to them that although they may converse in a foreign language, they nevertheless understand each other better than they understand others. This is because there is always some commonness in the character of fellow countrymen, and the citizens of the same state always form, so to speak, an electric circuit that transforms the same impression via the most remote coils or links. Along the shores of the most beautiful lake in the world [Lake Geneva], that mirrors a bountiful nature, I happened to meet a Dutch patriot who, out of hatred for the Stadholder and the followers of the House of Orange, had left his country and settled in Switzerland between Nyon and Rolle. He had a beautiful little house, a physics laboratory, and a library. Seated at his window he could view the most splendid panorama of nature. Walking past the little house, I envied the owner without knowing him. And when I got to know him in Geneva I told him about it. The response of the phlegmatic Dutchman surprised me by its animation. "No one can be happy," he said, "outside his own country, where his heart has learned to understand his own people and where he has formulated habits close to it. No people of any other country can replace one's fellow countrymen. I am not living with those with whom I lived for forty years, nor am I living now the way I lived for forty years. It is difficult to adjust oneself to new habits, and I am weary!"

But the physical and moral attachment to one's country, the effect of nature and of human qualities still do not constitute the great virtue for which the Greeks and Romans were renowned. Patriotism is love of one's country, well-being, and fame, and the desire to promote them in every way possible. It requires the ability to reason and therefore not everyone possesses it.

The best philosophy is that which bases man's duties on his happiness. This philosophy tells us that we should love everything that benefits our country because our own well-being is inseparable from it. It tells us that the country's enlightenment offers us many pleasures in life; that its peace and virtues serve as a shield of family joys; that its glory is our glory; and that, if it is humiliating for a man to call himself the son of a contemptible father, it is no less humiliating for a citizen to call himself the son of a contemptible country. In this way, love of our own well–being awakens in us a love for country, and personal self–esteem develops in us the national pride on which patriotism rests. For that reason the Greeks and the Romans perceived themselves as the first nations and considered all others as barbarians. For that reason, too, the English, who in modern times pride themselves for patriotism more than other [nations], think more of themselves than do others.

I dare not think that in Russia we do not have many patriots. But it seems to me that we are unduly *humble* in our thinking about our national dignity. Humility can be harmful in politics. He who has no respect for himself will certainly not receive respect from others.

I do not say that love of one's own country should blind us and make us believe that we are better than all others in every respect. However, every Russian should be aware of his own worth. Let us agree that, in general, some nations are more enlightened than we are because their circumstances have been more favorable. But we should also be aware of all the benefits fate has bestowed on the Russian nation. Let us stand boldly alongside the others, clearly speak our name, and repeat it with noble pride.

Unlike the Greeks or the Romans, we do not need to resort to fables and fiction to extol our origins. Glory was the cradle of the Russian nation and victory the herald of its existence. The Roman empire discovered that there were Slavs because they [Slavs] came and destroyed their legions. Byzantine historians speak of our ancestors as being a wonderful people whom nothing could resist, and who differed from other peoples of northern [Europe], not only in their bravery but also in a certain knightly graciousness. In the ninth and tenth centuries our heroes amused themselves by terrorizing the then–new capital of the world. They needed only to appear before the walls of Constantinople to receive tribute from Greek emperors. In the eleventh century the Russians, who were always preeminent in bravery, also stood second to no other European nation in enlightenment, because of their close religious links with Constantinople, which shared with us the fruits of its learning. In the time of Iaroslav [the Wise, 1015–1054] many Greek books were translated into the Slavic language. The stalwart Russian character is proud that Constantinople was never able to secure political influence over our fatherland. Our princes appreciated the wisdom and the knowledge of the Greeks, but they were always ready to punish them by force of arms for the slightest sign of audacity.

The division of Russia into many principalities and the discord among its princes paved the way for the triumph of the descendants of Genghis Khan and for our prolonged misfortunes. Great men as well as great nations are subject to the blows of fate, but even in the midst of disaster they reveal their greatness. Thus, Russia, tormented by a cruel enemy, was perishing in glory. Whole towns preferred certain annihilation to the shame of slavery. The inhabitants of Vladimir, Chernigov, and Kiev sacrificed themselves to the national pride, and in so doing saved the Russian name from defamation. Overwhelmed by those unhappy times that resembled a frightening, barren desert, the historian rests on the graves and finds consolation in mourning the death of many worthy sons of the fatherland.

And which European nation can boast of a better fate? Which one among them has not been shackled several times? In any case, our conquerors terrified both East and West. Occupying the throne of Samarkand, Tamerlane perceived himself Emperor of the world.

And which nation broke its shackles so gloriously? And which so gloriously took revenge on its ferocious enemies? All that was needed was to have a resolute and courageous sovereign on the throne. After some drowsiness, national strength and bravery announced their awakening with thunder and lightning.

The Time of Troubles [1601–1613] presents again a sorrowful picture of sedition. But soon love for the country kindled the heart. Townsmen and rural folk demanded a military leader and [Prince Dmitrii Z.] Pozharskii, known to have serious wounds, arose from his sickbed. The virtuous [Kuzma Z.] Minin, served as an example. And those who could not give their lives for the country, gave all of their possessions . . . Neither ancient nor modern history of nations can show us anything more moving than this general, heroic patriotism. In the reign of Alexander [I] it would be fitting for the Russian heart to wish that a worthy monument be erected in Nizhnii Novgorod (where the voice of love for the country was first heard) to revive in our memory a glorious period of Russian history. Such monuments elevate the spirit of the nation. The modest monarch will not forbid us to inscribe on this monument [a statement] that it was built during his *fortunate* time.

Peter the Great, who *linked* us with Europe and showed us the advantages of enlightenment, did not for long degrade the national pride of the Russians. We glanced at Europe, so to speak, and at once we appropriated the fruits of her long labors. Barely had the great sovereign told his soldiers how to use their new weapons than they grasped them and rushed forth to fight the foremost army of Europe [that is, Sweden]. Generals appeared on the scene. At the time they still were pupils who subsequently became examples for their teachers. Soon other [nations] could and had to borrow from us. We demonstrated how to defeat the Swedes, the Turks and, finally, the French.

These famous republicans, who talk better than they fight, and who so often boast about their frightful bayonets, fled in Italy at the first brandishing of Russian bayonets. Because we know that we are braver than many, we also know who is braver than we. Courage is a great quality of the soul. A nation distinguished by it should be proud of itself.

We have accomplished more in the art of warefare than in other arts because we have been involved in it more in order to reinforce the existence of our empire. However, we can boast not only of our military laurels. In wisdom our governmental institutions equal the institutions of states that have been enlightened for several centuries. Our humaneness, the manners of our society, and our lifestyle surprise foreigners who come to Russia with a false notion of a people who were considered barbarians early in the eighteenth century.

Those who envy the Russians say that we have only a very high degree of *imitativeness.* But is this not a sign of an exceptional development of our soul? It is said that Leibnitz's teachers also found in him *imitativeness.*

In the sciences we still lag behind others because, and only because, we study them less than others, and because in our country the stature of a scholar does not command the same respect as, for example, in Germany, England or elsewhere. If our young nobles, *who study, were able to complete their studies* and would dedicate themselves to sciences, we could already have had our own Linneuses, Hallers, and Bonnets. The achievements of our literature (which requires less learning but, I dare say, much more intelligence than the so-called sciences) reveal the great talent of the Russians. How long has it been since we have known what style pertains to poetry or to prose? In some areas we already equal foreigners. Already in the sixteenth century the French had their Montaigne, who was philosophizing and writing. Is it any wonder, therefore, why they write better than we? Should the wonder not rather be that some of our works compare well with their best in vividness of thought and fine nuances of style? Let us be candid, dear fellow-citizens, and we will recognize our own worth. We will never become wise using foreign wisdom and will never become famous with foreign fame. French and English authors can do without our praise. Russian writers, however, need at the very least the attention of Russians. Thank God, the disposition of my soul is opposed to a satirical or quarrelsome spirit. Nevertheless, I would like to reproach many of our ardent readers who, while better acquainted with all the works of French literature than are the Parisians, still are unwilling to look at a Russian book. Do they wish to have foreigners inform them about Russian talents? Let them read critical French and German journals which, judged by some translations, do justice to our talents. For example, the worst French translation of [M. V.] Lomonosov's odes and various passages from [A. P.] Sumarokov received the attention and praise of foreign journalists. Who would not be ashamed to be like D'Alembert's nurse, who, while taking care of him, learned from others to her surprise that he was a wise man? Some excuse themselves on account of their poor knowledge of the Russian language. This excuse is worse than the guilt itself. Let us leave it to our dear society ladies to declare that the Russian language is crude and unpleasant, that *charmont* and *seduisant* [charming and seductive], *expansion* and *vapeurs* [candid and fanciful] cannot be expressed in it, and that, in a word, it is not worth the effort of knowing. Who can dare to prove to the ladies that they are wrong? But men do not have such an amiable right to judge unjustly. Our language is capable not only of expressing lofty eloquence and high-sounding, picturesque poetry, but also tender simplicity and the sound of heart and feelings. It is richer in harmony than French; it is more capable of expressing the effusion of the soul in its sounds; and it offers more *analogical* words, that is, words conforming to the action expressed. The latter characteristic is peculiar only to basic languages! Our misfortune is that we want to speak French and are oblivious to cultivating our own language. It is not obvious, therefore, that in our conversation we are unable to express some subtle nuances?

In my presence one foreign diplomat said that "our language must be very obscure because the Russians who speak it," he felt, "do not understand each other and immediately turn to speaking French." Do we not ourselves give ground for such absurd conclusions? The language is important for the patriot. And I admire Englishmen because, when conversing with their tender lovers, they prefer to *whistle* and *whisper* in English rather than speak in a foreign language which almost every one of them knows well.

There is a limit and a measure to all things. Like an individual, a nation always begins with imitation. But in due time *it ought to be itself*, so to speak. *I do exist morally!* Presently we already have accumulated so much knowledge and taste of life that we could live without asking: How do they live in Paris or in London? What do they wear there? What are their means of transportation? And how do they furnish their homes? The patriot tries to secure for his country what is beneficial and necessary, but he rejects slavish imitation in trifles that is humiliating to national pride. It is proper and necessary to learn. But woe to a human being or nation that forever remains a pupil!

Until now Russia has steadfastly progressed politically and morally. One may say that Europe respects us more from year to year. And we still are only in the middle of our glorious course! A [careful] observer sees everywhere new *branches of learning and discoveries,* He sees many fruits and even more blossoms. Our symbol is an ardent youth whose heart is full of life, who loves activity, and whose motto is: *work and hope!* Victories have cleared the way for us to prosperity. Glory is the right to happiness.

N. M. Karamzin's Comments on the Book Business in Russia, 1802

Twenty years ago there were only two bookstores in Moscow. Their annual sales amounted to less than 10,000 rubles. Now there are twenty bookstores and their total annual sales amount to about 200,000 rubles. How many ardent readers has Russia gained? Those who wish reason to triumph, and who believe that love of reading is the most useful way to reach that goal, will be very pleased by this development.

Mr. [N. I.] Novikov served in Moscow as the principal disseminator of books. After he leased the University Press he modernized the mechanics of book publishing, expanded translation of books, opened bookstores in other towns, sought in every way to attract the public to read, and set the general taste without losing sight of the particular inclination. He sold books as a wealthy Dutch or English merchant would sell his goods from all lands, that is, with intelligence, insight and far-sightedness. Previously, Moscow newspapers had had a circulation of fewer than 600 copies. Mr. Novikov made their content richer by adding diverse articles to the political ones. Finally, as a free supplement to the *Vedomosti*, he published *Detskoe Chtenie*, which the public liked because of the novelty of its subject and the variety of its material, in spite of the amateurish translations of many items. The number of subscribers increased annually and in ten years it reached 4000. In 1797 newspapers became important for the Russians because they included imperial decrees and other governmental news. Presently [that is, 1802] the circulation of Moscow newspapers is about 6000. Doubtless, considering the size of the empire, this is not enough. But compared with the earlier circulation it is quite large. And in no other country has the number of readers grown as fast as in Russia. It is, of course, true that many nobles, even the well-to-do ones, still do not subscribe to newspapers. In contrast, merchants and townspeople like to read them. Even the poorest people subscribe to them, and the totally illiterate want to know *what is reported from foreign countries!*

One of my acquaintances had an opportunity to observe several pastry makers who gathered around a man and listened very attentively to his describing aloud of a battle between the Austrians and the French. He inquired and learned that five of them had pooled their resources and subscribed to the *Moskovskie Vedomosti*, even though four of them were illiterate. The fifth read out the words while the rest listened.

Our book trade cannot compare to the German, French or English trade. Yet, judged by the annual progress of our book trade, can we not expect [good results] in time? There are bookstores now in practically every *gubernia* capital. Along with other goods, [merchants] bring the riches of our literature to every trade fair. For example, during the Makariev Trade Fair [near Nizhnii Novgorod] rural noble ladies acquire ample supplies not only of mob–caps but of books as well. In earlier days merchants travelled through villages with ribbons and rings; now they travel with *learned goods.* And while most of them are unable to read, they tell the contents of novels and comedies in their own amusing way in order to entice the rustics. I know noblemen whose annual income is less than 500 *rubles* but who, in their own words, have said that they are collecting *little libraries* and are delighted by them. And while we often toss around fine editions of Voltaire and Buffon, they do not allow even a speck of dust to fall on a copy of Miramond. They read every book several times and reread it with renewed pleasure.

A curious person will doubtless want to know what kinds of books are most popular in our country. I myself raised this question with many book dealers. All of them, without hesitation, replied "Novels." That is not surprising since this genre of works captivates a large body of the reading public. It captivates their heart and imagination, presents a picture of society and of people like ourselves in interesting situations and depicts the strongest and at the same time the most ordinary passion in its diverse forms. Not everyone can philosophize or place himself in the position of the heroes of history. But everyone loves, has loved, or has wished to love, and so he discovers himself in the hero of the novel. The reader believes that the author speaks to him in the language of his own heart. In one reader the novel nourishes hope; in another it rekindles pleasant memories. As is well known, in our country this genre of literature has many more translations than original works and, as a result, the fame of foreign authors outshines that of the Russians. At present [August von] Kotzebue is very fashionable. And, as at one time Parisian bookdealers wanted from every author *Parisian Letters* [by Montesquieu], so now our bookdealers demand from translators, and even from authors, Kotzebue, the one and only Kotzebue! It makes no difference whether it is a novel, a tale, good or bad—as long as the title page bears the name of the famous Kotzebue!

I do not know what others think, but I rejoice. If only people read! The most mediocre novels, even those written[by authors] without any talent, contribute somewhat to enlightenment. Anyone who is fascinated by *Nikanor, the Unfortunate Nobleman* [by Matvei Komarov] is intellectually below the author's level. At the same time, he does well to read this novel because doubtless he will learn something from its ideas or the way they are presented. As soon as a great gulf develops between the author and the reader, the former cannot exert a strong influence on the latter no matter how intelligent he may be. Everyone needs something close to him. One person needs Jean Jacques [Rousseau]; another Nikanor. As physical taste in general tells us whether a given food will satisfy our need, so [the reader's] moral taste will reveal the true relationship between the subject and his mind. However, this mind can gradually lift itself up, and whoever starts with *The Unfortunate Nobleman* often reaches *[Sir Charles] Grandison* [by Samuel Richardson].

All pleasant reading exerts an influence on the intellect. Without it the heart cannot feel and the imagination cannot function. Even the poorest novels contain some logic and rhetoric. Whoever reads them will be a more eloquent and more coherent speaker than the complete ignoramus who has never opened a book in his life. Moreover, contemporary novels are rich in all sorts of knowledge. When an author has decided to write three or four volumes he uses every means to fill them, including all branches of science. He may describe, for instance, an American island, using Busching; or he may explain the nature of the island's flora, varifying it with [the work by] Bomar. As a result the reader learns about geography and natural history. I am convinced that in some German novel the [recently discovered] planet Piazzi will soon be described more thoroughly than in the *Petersburgskie Vedomosti.*

They are mistaken who think that novels can be harmful to the heart, because usually they either glorify virtue or stress a mortal point. It is true that some characters of novels are both attractive and depraved. But, precisely, how are they attractive? By some good traits with which the author has painted over their bleakness. As a result the good triumphs in the evil itself. Our moral nature is such that the heart will never accept the positive portrayal of villains. They can never be transformed into our favorites. What novels do the people prefer? Usually the sentimental ones. Readers always shed tears from love of the good and they nourish it. No, no. Bad people never read novels. Their mean soul prevents them from accepting the gentle feeling of love, and it does not concern itself with the fate of tenderness. Can a vile cheater or an egoist find himself as the loving hero of a novel? What interest does he take in others? It is indisputable that novels turn the heart and imagination . . . *romantic.* There is no harm in it. Indeed, for us, inhabitants of the cold and iron north, it is quite beneficial! There is not doubt that the cause of the evil in the world, about which we hear complaints everywhere, are not the romantic hearts, but the rough and cold–blooded [reality] that acts as its opposite! The romantic heart brings upon itself more grief than harm to others; at the same time it loves its grief and would not exchange it for the pleasure of the egoists.

In short, it is good that our public reads novels.

25

The Franco-Russian Arrangements at Tilsit, July 7, 1807

One of the most outstanding features of the early reign of Alexander I was his struggle with Napoleon. Alexander entered the conflict in the spring of 1805, when he joined England, Austria, and Sweden to form the Third Coalition against France. The Coalition performed very badly from its inception, and late that year the Austro-Russian forces suffered a great disaster at Austerlitz that induced Austria to withdraw from the Coalition. Early in 1806 Prussia replaced Austria after the latter's untimely exit. The new combination also experienced a number of disasters culminating in the battle at Friedland, June 14, 1807, where the Russians suffered a decisive defeat. On June 22, 1807, Napoleon and Alexander signed an armistice, and three days later both Emperors met near Tilsit, on a raft in the middle of the Nieman River, to negotiate peace. On July 7, 1807, these negotiations produced several agreements that provided a number of advantages to both Empires.

The Franco-Russian Treaty of Peace and Friendship, July 7, 1807

Article 1

From the day of exchanging ratifications of the present treaty, peace and genuine friendship shall prevail between His Majesty the Emperor of All Russia, and His Majesty the Emperor of France and King of Italy.

Article 2

Both parties shall immediately cease all hostilities at all points by sea and land, as soon as the news of the signing of the present treaty shall be officially received.

The High Contracting Parties shall promptly dispatch [this news] through special couriers to their respective generals and commanders.

From USSR. Ministerstvo Inostrannykh Del. *Vneshniaia politika Rossii XIX i nachala XX veka* (Foreign Policy of Russia in the 19th and early 20th Century) (Moscow: 1963), III, 631–646. Russian and French texts. Translation mine.

Article 3

All ships of war and other vessels belonging to the High Contracting Parties or their subjects, which may have been seized after the signing of this treaty, shall be returned [to their rightful owners] and in case these vessels were sold, the sale price shall be returned.

Article 4

Out of esteem for His Majesty the Emperor of all Russia and to provide him with proof of His sincere desire to unite both nations in a tie of immutable confidence and friendship, His Majesty Emperor Napoleon wishes to restore to His Majesty the King of Prussia, an ally of His Majesty the Emperor of All Russia, all conquered countries, towns, and territories, namely:

A portion of the Duchy of Magdeburg, located on the right bank of the Elbe River;

The Mark of Prignitz, the Uker Mark, the Middle and the New Mark of Brandenburg, except for the District of Kotbus, in Lower Lusatsia, which will belong to His Majesty the King of Saxony;

The Duchy of Pomerania;

The Upper, the Lower and the New Silesia, and the County of Glatz;

A portion of the district of Netze, located north of the main road between Driessen and Schneidemühl through Waldau to the Vistula and following the boundary of the Bromberg district; the navigation of the Netze River and of the Bromberg Canal, from Driessen to the Vistula and back, will become open and free of all tolls; Pomerelia, the Nogat Island, the territories located along the right bank of the Nogat and of the Vistula, west of Old Prussia and to the north of the Kulm and the Ermerland Districts, and, finally, the Kingdom of Prussia as it was on January 1, 1772, together with the fortresses of Spandau, Stettin, Küstrin, Glogau, Breslau, Schweidnitz, Neisse, Brieg, Kosel, and Glatz, and generally all fortresses, citadels, castles, and strongholds, other than those listed above, in the same condition in which those fortresses, citadels, castles, and strongholds may be at present; and in addition to the above, the city and citadel of Graudentz.

Article 5

Those provinces which on January 1, 1772, formed a part of the former Kingdom of Poland and since have at various times been brought under Prussian rule, shall become, except for the territories named or designated in the preceding article, or those which will be listed in Article 10 [of the present treaty], the possessions and sovereignty of His Majesty the King of Saxony under the name of the Duchy of Warsaw, and shall be governed by laws that will guarantee freedom and privileges of the peoples of this Duchy and which shall be consistent with the security of neighboring states.

Article 6

The City of Danzig with a territory of two miles around it shall be restored to its [former] independence under the protection of His Majesty the King of Prussia and His Majesty the King of Saxony and shall be governed by those laws with which it was governed at the time of its independence.

Article 7

To be able to communicate between the Kingdom of Saxony and the Duchy of Warsaw, His Majesty the King of Saxony shall have free use of a military road through the possessions of His Majesty the King of Prussia. This road, the number of troops which shall be allowed to pass at any given time, and the place they may rest and secure food, shall be determined by a special agreement between the two named sovereigns under the mediation of France.

Article 8

Neither His Majesty the King of Prussia, nor His Majesty the King of Saxony, nor the city of Danzig, shall have the right to interfere in any way whatsoever with free navigation on the Vistula nor to hinder it through the institution of any kind of tolls, taxes or duties. . . .

Article 10

In order to deliniate as much as possible the natural frontiers between Russia and the Duchy of Warsaw, the region, which is partly surrounded by the present frontiers of Russia, extending from the Bug to the mouth of the Lossosna along the *Thalweg* of that river and that of the Bobra up to its mouth, along the *Thalweg* of the Narew from the above mentioned place to the Surazh, along the *Thalweg* of the Lisa to its source near the Village Mien, along the *Thalweg* of the canal which begins near the said village and empties into the Nurchik, along the Nurchik to its mouth beyond Nur, and, finally, along the *Thalweg* of the Bug upwards to the present frontiers of Russia, shall forever be annexed to the Russian Empire.

Article 11

No person of any rank or estate whatever who resides or has property in the area delineated in the above-mentioned article, or in provinces which comprised the ancient Kingdom of Poland and which are now transferred to His Majesty the King of Prussia, or individuals who live now in the Duchy of Warsaw but who have in Russia immovable property, pensions and other forms of income, shall be molested, or have his immovable or movable property, pension, and other income confiscated. No person shall be deprived of his rank or status, or be subjected to some other form of punishment on account of his participation in military or political affairs of the present war. . . .

Article 14

His Majesty Emperor Napoleon accepts the mediation of His Majesty the Emperor of All Russia to negotiate and conclude the final peace treaty between France and England, on condition that England will equally accept the mediation within one month following the exchange of ratifications of the present treaty.

Article 15

His Majesty the Emperor of All Russia, being desirous on His part of establishing intimate and lasting relations between the two empires, recognises His Majesty Joseph Napoleon as King of Naples and His Majesty Louis Napoleon as King of Holland.

Article 16

His Majesty the Emperor of All Russia equally recognizes the Confederation of the Rhine, the present status of authority of each of the rulers comprising this Confederation, and their titles, which many of them have received by the Act of Confederation as well as by subsequent treaties of accession.

His Majesty the Emperor of All Russia also promises that, in accordance with information which His Majesty Emperor Napoleon will communicate to Him, He will acknowledge those rulers who will become members of the Confederation of the Rhine stipulated by the Act of Confederation.

Article 17

His Majesty the Emperor of All Russia cedes to His Majesty the King of Holland all of His property and sovereignty to the Seigniorage of Jever in East Frieseland.

Article 18

The present treaty of peace and friendship shall be mutually binding on their Majesties the Kings of Naples and Holland, and on the rulers of the Confederation of the Rhine, who are allies of His Majesty Emperor Napoleon.

Article 19

His Majesty the Emperor of Russia equally recognizes His Highness Prince Jerome Napoleon as King of Westphalia.

Article 20

The Kingdom of Westphalia shall consist of provinces ceded by His Majesty the King of Prussia on the left bank of the Elbe and those presently in the possession of His Majesty Emperor Napoleon.

Article 21

His Majesty the Emperor of All Russia pledges to recognise the changes which His Majesty Emperor Napoleon shall make in pursuance of Article 20, and cessions of His Majesty the King of Prussia (His Majesty the Emperor of All Russia shall be informed about these changes), and the state of sovereignty that shall accrue to these Sovereigns in whose behalf these changes shall have been made.

Article 22

All hostilities shall cease immediately at all points on land and sea between the forces of His Majesty the Emperor of All Russia and those of His Majesty the Sultan as soon as the news of the signing of the present treaty shall be officially received.

The High Contracting Parties shall without delay dispatch special couriers to convey this news as soon as possible to the respective generals and commanding officers.

Article 23

Russian forces shall withdraw from the principalities of Wallachia and Moldavia, but the said provinces shall not be occupied by the forces of His Majesty [the Sultan] prior to the ratification of the future final peace treaty between Russia and the Ottoman Porte.

Article 24

His Majesty the Emperor of All Russia shall accept the mediation of His Majesty the Emperor of France and King of Italy, to negotiate and conclude a peace advantageous and honorable equally to both Empires.

Authorized plenipotentiaries shall be dispatched to a place designated by the interested parties to start and proceed with these negotiations.

Article 25

The time within which the High Contracting Parties shall withdraw their forces from places they are to evacuate, pursuant to the above stipulations, similarly as the manner in which different articles contained in the present treaty shall be executed, shall be determined by a special agreement.

Article 26

His Majesty the Emperor of All Russia and His Majesty the Emperor of France and King of Italy mutually pledge to respect the integrity of their own possessions and those of states that participate in the present peace treaty in the state in which they exist now, and in which they may exist pursuant to the above stipulations.

Article 27

Prisoners of war taken by the Contracting Parties or states participating in the present Peace treaty shall be mutually repatriated simultaneously and without any discrimination.

Article 28

Commercial relations between the Russian Empire on the one hand and the French Empire, the Kingdoms of Italy, Naples, and Holland, and the Confederation of the Rhine on the other, shall be reestablished on the same footing as they were before the war.

Article 29

The ceremonial between the two courts—that of St. Petersburg and the Tuilleries—with respect to each other and also with respect to their ambassadors, ministers, and envoys mutually accredited to each other, shall be based on the rights of complete reciprocity and equality. . . .

Secret Articles, July 7, 1807

Article 1

Russian forces shall surrender to French forces the land known as Catarro [Kotor].

Article 2

Seven islands [of that territory] shall become personal property of His Majesty Emperor Napoleon.

Article 3

His Majesty the Emperor of France and King of Italy agrees neither to punish nor to persecute directly or indirectly any subject of the Sublime Porte, and especially the Montenegrins, for their participation in whatever capacity in hostile actions against French forces as long as they shall remain peaceful from here on.

Article 4

His Majesty the Emperor of All Russia pledges to recognise His Majesty the King of Naples Joseph Napoleon as King of Sicily as soon as King Ferdinand IV shall be compensated either by the Baleric Islands, or the Island of Candie, or some other possession of the same value.

Article 5

If, during the subsequent peace with England, Hanover should be united with the Kingdom of Westphalia, then the territory which His Majesty the King of Prussia has ceded along the left bank of the Elbe, with a population between 300,000 and 400,000, shall be separated from that Kingdom and shall be restored to Prussia.

Article 6

The present heads of [the ruling] houses of Hesse-Kassel, Brunswick-Wolfenbuttel, and Nassau-Orange shall receive annual subsidies. These subsidies shall be applicable to the princes and to their wives as well, should they survive them.

The subsidy for the head of the Hesse-Kassel House shall be 200,000 Dutch *florins*.

The subsidy for the head of the Brunswick-Wolfenbuttel House shall be 100,000 Dutch *florins*.

These subsidiaries shall be paid by His majesty the King of Westphalia.

The subsidy for the head of the Nassau-Orange House shall be 60,000 Dutch *florins* and shall be paid by His Highness the Grand Duke of Berg.

Her Serene Highness the Dowager Princess of Anhalt-Zerbst, who has the right to maintenance from revenues of the Seignioralty of Ever, shall be compensated with an annual pension of 60,000 Dutch *florins* to be paid by His Majesty the King of Holland.

Article 7

The above separate secret articles shall have the same force and significance, word for word, as if they were included in the open treaty concluded today, and they shall be ratified with it. . . .

The Franco-Russian Secret Defensive and Offensive Alliance, July 7, 1807

Article 1

His Majesty the Emperor of All Russia and His Majesty the Emperor of France and King of Italy bind themselves to act jointly on land as well as on sea, or simultaneously on land and sea, in any war that France or Russia may be forced to undertake, or in a war against any other European power.

Article 2

Should the opportunity for such a joint action materialize, and whenever it should become a reality, the High Contracting Parties shall agree by a special convention what kind of forces each should supply against the common enemy, and at what locations these forces should be deployed, although they now bind themselves, should conditions so require, to deploy all of their land and naval forces.

Article 3

All military operations shall be undertaken jointly, and neither of the Contracting Parties shall under any circumstances enter into separate peace negotiations without the consent of the other Party.

Article 4

Should England not accept Russia's mediation, or having accepted it should she then decide not to conclude peace by next November 1 [1807], then [France and Russia], having agreed that flags of all nations should equally enjoy freedom of the sea, and having acknowledged that conquests made by her [England] against France and her allies from 1805 on, when Russia joined her, should be restored, in the said month of November [1807], the Envoy of His Majesty the Emperor of All Russia will deliver a note to the Government of St. James. Alongside the expressed concern which the said Imperial Majesty has for the peace of the world and His intention to use all powers of His Empire to secure for mankind prolonged peace, that note shall include a positive and clear statement that in case England should refuse to conclude peace on the above mentioned terms, His Majesty the Emperor of All Russia will act jointly with France. Should the Government of St. James fail to supply Him with a categorical and satisfactory answer by December 1 [1807], then the Russian Ambassador will be instructed to request his passport by a specified day and to leave England immediately.

Article 5

Should the developments foreseen in the preceding article materialize, the High Contracting Parties will jointly and simultaneously request the Courts of Copenhagen, Stockholm, and Lisbon to close their harbors to the English, to recall their envoys from London, and to declare war against England. Should any of the three Courts refuse to comply with this request, the High Contracting Parties will deal with them as with the enemy, and should Sweden refuse, then Denmark will be induced to declare war against her.

Article 6

Equally, the High Contracting Parties will act jointly and exert pressure on the Court of Vienna to adhere to the terms stipulated in Article 4, [namely] that it too close its harbors to the English, recall its envoy from London, and declare war against England.

Article 7

Should, however, England conclude peace on the stipulated terms in the prescribed time (His Majesty the Emperor of All Russia shall use His influence to induce her to do it), then Hanover shall be restored to the King of England in compensation for French, Spanish, and Dutch colonies.

Article 8

Equally, if, as a result of changes that have transpired in Constantinople, the Porte should refuse to accept French mediation, or should it fail, after having been accepted, to produce a satisfactory result within a three months' period from the start of negotiations, then France shall act jointly with Russia against the Ottoman Porte, and the two High Contracting Parties will agree to liberate from the Turkish yoke and oppression all provinces of the Ottoman Empire in Europe, except Constantinople and the Province of Rumelia.

Article 9

The present treaty shall be kept secret and shall neither be made public nor revealed to any government by one of the High Contracting Parties without the consent of the other.

It will be ratified and its ratifications will be exchanged in Tilsit within four days.

Tilsit, July 7, 1807.

26

Speranskii's Proposed Brief Outline of State Organization, 1809

Alexander I's achievements as tsar can be traced to the influence of three associates. At the beginning of his reign most of his ideas were stimulated by his Swiss tutor, Frédéric C. La Harpe (1754–1838). Between 1806 and 1812 Alexander's dreams were inspired by Michael M. Speranskii (1772–1839). After 1812 General Aleksei Arakcheev (1769–1834) influenced many of his actions. While each left a distinct imprint on Alexander I's reign, of the three men the influence of Speranskii is perhaps the most interesting. The son of a village priest, Speranskii was a self-made man. He developed a familiarity with contemporary political and economic theories and had been exposed to the harsh realities of Russian life. With this rare combination of the theoretical and the practical Speranskii was invaluable to Alexander I, who selected him as his chief adviser from 1806 to 1812. In this capacity Speranskii prepared a plan for the reorganization of the empire. Had Alexander accepted the plan, Russia might have evolved into a constitutional monarchy, but such was not the case. Soon after the proposal was presented, Alexander, frightened by the excesses of the French Revolution and influenced by the opponents of change, dismissed Speranskii and sent him to Siberia.

Basic Components

State power is represented in three branches—legislative, judicial, and executive.

The [State] Council coordinates all activity and passes it on to the sovereign.

The State Duma is entrusted with lawmaking.

The Senate is entrusted with courts.

Ministries are entrusted with administration.

From M. M. Speranskii, *Property i zapiski (Projects and Notes)*, Edited by A. I. Kopanev, M. V. Kukushkina and C. N. Valka (Moscow-Leningrad: Akademiia Nauk, 1961), pp. 222–231. Translation mine. Words in brackets are mine.

Organization of the [State] Council

Departments within the Council	*Competence*
I. Legal	Review of laws, statutes, and proposals presented by commissions and ministries.
II. Military Affairs	Affairs pertaining to the Ministries of War and Navy.
III. State Economy	Internal affairs, land and water communication system. Finance and Treasury. Ministry of Enlightenment.
IV. Civil and Religious Affairs	Police, Justice, and Religious Departments.
Institutions within the Council	
State Chancellery	General central execution of all affairs that come before the State Council.
Legislative Commission	Preparation of state laws.
Commission on Petitions	Review of petitions addressed to the sovereign.

Main Components

The [State] Council consists of members appointed by the sovereign. Ministers are members of the Council in accordance with rank. Every department has a chairman appointed every six months. All matters enter departments through ministries. Important matters from departments are brought before a general meeting. In the general meeting the chairman is appointed annually. Nothing emanates from the Council without the approval of the sovereign.

Organization of the State Duma

Composition	*Competence*
The State Duma consists of deputies elected from all free classes at the *gubernia* dumas.	Proposed laws are presented by the government, are considered by the Duma, and are approved by the sovereign.

Chairman of the Duma is chosen from among three candidates after the Duma is elected. The Duma has a Chancellor who supervises its rules, archives, and the conduct of its affairs.	The Duma receives ministerial reports; in case of an open violation of the State Constitution, the Duma has the right to demand a reply from ministeries and to present its view to the sovereign.

Main Components

No new law can be issued without being considered by the Duma. Imposition of new taxes, duties, and obligations is considered by the Duma.

A law that has been considered in the Duma is presented for the sovereign's approval. A legislative measure that has been rejected by a majority of votes [in the Duma] is considered invalid.

For a detailed review of a legislative project the Duma selects temporary committees from among its members.

Organization of the Senate

Composition	*Competence*
The Senate consists of elected senators who will gradually replace the current members.	All court matters are entrusted to the Senate.
[The Senate] is divided into departments. Within the Senate there is organized a High Criminal Court in which members of the [State] Council, the Duma, and the Senate participate.	This High Court has jurisdiction over ministries, members of the [State] Council, senators and governor-generals.
In the Senate there is established the position of a Chancellor of Justice.	He supervises publications and documents of the Senate. He is Minister of Justice in the High Criminal Court.
Minister of Justice	He supervises legal forms and legal procedures both within the Senate and in other courts.

Organization of Ministries

Ministries	*Ministers*	*Competence*
Foreign Affairs	Minister of Foreign Affairs	Foreign Relations
Military	Minister of War	Land Forces
Naval	Minister of Navy	Naval Forces
Internal Affairs	Minister of Internal Affairs	Agriculture, Industry, Domestic Trade, Posts
	Chief Director of Communication	Communication
	Minister or Chief Director of Schools	Administration of schools
Finances	Minister of Finances	Revenues: collection of taxes and dues; administration of mines, forests, customs, etc.
	Minister of the Treasury	Circulation of capital and credit. Administration of currency, banks, etc.
	Minister or Chief Director of Accounting	Control of all accounts
Justice	Minister of Justice	Supervision and protection of courts
Religious Affairs	*Ober*-Procurator of the Synod	Department of Religious Affairs
Police	Minister of Police	Protection of internal security. State Police

Main Components

Every Ministry has as many departments as there are chief parts. Every department has a director. These directors comprise the Council of the Ministry.

All ministers have a general instruction that determines the picture of their activity, their relation to the Council, and degrees of their power and responsibility.

Matters that require a general meeting of ministers are introduced to the Committee of Ministers.

Organization of the Legislative Order in Gubernias

Composition	*Competence*
Volost dumas are organized in *volosts* from all owners of immovable property and from officials of state *volosts.*	To elect deputities to the *okrug* duma. To elect judges to *volost* courts. To elect members of the Council attached to *volost* administration. To elect a certain number of more distinguished citizens to organize a census in the *volost.* To account *volost* expenses and to redistribute new tax obligations. To present needs of the *volost.*
Okrug dumas are composed of a determined number of deputies elected by the *volost* dumas.	To elect deputies to the *gubernia* dumas, to the *okrug* court, to the council attached to the *okrug* administration; to elect a definite number of more distinguished citizens from *volost* rosters to give an account of *okrug* taxes and to distribute same, and to present needs of the *okrug.*
Gubernia dumas.	Election of deputies to the State Duma, to *gubernia* courts, to councils attached to the *gubernia* administration, and so forth.

Main Components

The *volost* dumas represent the first, so to speak, element of legislative order, which, emerging in the *volost* gradually rises as a result of elections of deputies, every three years, and forms the State Duma.

All dumas have chairmen.

The lists of all *gubernia* dumas are to be submitted to the Chancellor of the [State] Duma. From these lists then is prepared a state list, from which are recruited officials, approved by public opinions, for the performance of certain administrative tasks.

Organization of the Executive Administration in *Gubernias*

Composition	*Competence*
The *gubernia* administration The chief official in the *gubernia* is the governor (wherever no governor-general exists). *Gubernia* administration branches are divided into offices: each office has its own chief. Chiefs of these branches under the chairmanship of the governor form the *gubernia* administration. Important matters are decided at a general meeting; current [matters] in the offices. The governor has an instruction determining the degree of his authority and responsibility. At the *gubernia* administration is located a Council of Disputes of the *gubernia* duma for the distribution of annual obligations, for accounting and for presenting needs [of the *gubernia*]. It meets once a year.	All matters of police, treasury collections, and taxes and general well being, are subjects of the *gubernia* administration.

The *Okrug* Administration

The chief of the *okrug* is the vice-governor; the government is divided into offices similar to those in the *gubernia* administration. Chiefs of the expeditions under chairmanship of the vice-governor comprise an *okrug* administration. Attached to it is an *okrug* council, consisting of deputies of the *okrug* duma. Local *uezd* police stations, city mayors, and district police officers are part of the *okrug* administration. Through them the *okrug* administration reaches *uezds*.	The same problems as in the *gubernia* administration, except that they are smaller in scope.

The Volost Administration

It is organized along the same lines as the *okrug* administration, with smaller competence.	The same problems, except smaller in scope.

27

The War of 1812

The most eventful episode in the reign of Alexander I (1801–1825) was Napoleon's invasion of Russia in 1812. Napoleon decided to undertake the campaign after Alexander's official withdrawal from the Continental System in December 1810. If successful, the undertaking would have eliminated the last obstacle in Napoleon's attempt to control Europe. His past record seemed to assure quick success, and to make his victory certain Napoleon assembled a force of over 600,000 men and led them into Russia in June 1812. But the Russian strategies of retreat and scorched earth upset Napoleon's plans, making it impossible for him to defeat the enemy or even to provision his own armies. The only engagement, the battle of Borodino, was costly and indecisive, as the Russians retreated in orderly fashion toward Moscow, which Napoleon's forces occupied in September 1812. Late in October, to avoid wintering his overextended forces in Moscow, Napoleon ordered the retreat, which has remained a classic military horror. The Grand Army lost some 400,000 men to battle casualties, exposure, and starvation, and about 100,000 were imprisoned. The Russian success was due in large measure to favorable natural circumstances, the strategy of Marshal M. I. Kutuzov, and the aroused patriotism which the tsar helped to stimulate by appealing to his subjects to defend the country, the Orthodox religion, and "liberty."

From General Sir Robert Wilson, *Narrative of Events During the Invasion of Russia by Napoleon Bonaparte and the Retreat of the French Army, 1812*. Edited by Herbert Randolf. 2d ed. (London: 1860), pp. 46–48, 368–369.

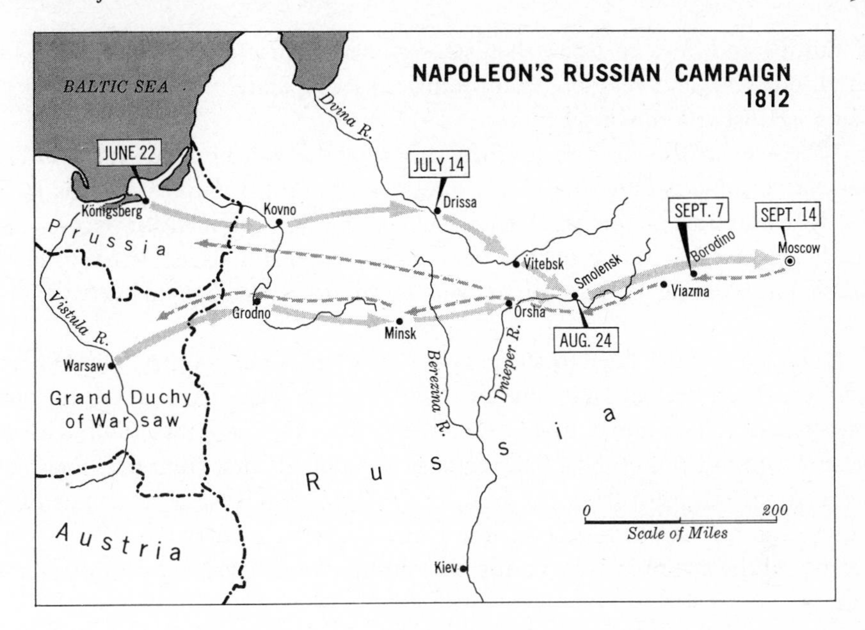

Alexander's Proclamation to the Nation, July 18, 1812

The enemy has passed the frontiers and carried his arms into the interior of Russia. Since perfidy cannot destroy an empire which has existed with a dignity always increasing for so many generation, he has determined to attack it by violence, and to assault the empire of the Czars with the forces of the continent of Europe.

With treason in the heart and loyalty on the lips, he flatters the ears of the credulous and enchains their arms; and if the captive perceives fetters under the flowers, the spirit of domination discovers itself, and he calls forth war to assure the work of treason! But Russia has penetrated his views. The path of loyalty is open to her: she has invoked the protection of God; she opposes to the plots of her enemy an army strong in courage, and eager to drive from her territory this race of locusts who consume the earth, and whom the earth will reject, finding them too heavy a burden to sustain.

We call out sufficient armies to annihilate the enemy. Our soldiers who are under arms are like lions who dart on their prey; but we do not disguise from our faithful subjects that the intrepid courage of our warriors actually under arms needs to be supported by an interior line of troops. The means ought to be proportioned to the object; and the object placed before you is to overthrow the tyrant who wishes to overthrow all the earth.

We have called on our ancient city of Moscow, the first capital of our empire, to make final efforts, and she is accustomed to make them, by sending her sons to the succour of the empire. After her, we call on all our subjects of Europe and Asia to unite themselves for the cause of humanity! We call on all our civil and religious communities to cooperate with us by a general rising against the universal tyrant.

Wherever in this empire he turns his steps he will be assured of finding our native subjects laughing at his frauds, scorning his flattery and his falsehoods, trampling on his gold with the indignation of offended virtue, and paralyzing, by the feeling of true honour, his legions of slaves. In every noble Russian he will find a Pojarskoi, in every ecclesiastic a Palitsyn, in every peasant a Minin.

Nobles! You have been in all ages the defenders of our country! Holy Synod! And you members of our Church! You have in all circumstances by your intercession called down upon our empire the Divine protection! Russian people! Intrepid posterity of Sclavonians! It is not the first time that you have plucked out the teeth from the head of the lion, who sprung on you as upon a prey, and met his own destruction! Unite yourselves! Carry the cross in your hearts and the sword in your hands, and human force never can prevail against you.

I have delegated the organization of the new levies to the nobles of every province; and I have charged with the care of assembling the brave patriots who will present themselves of their own accord for the defence of the country the gentlemen amongst whom the officers will be chosen. The number of those who will be assembled ought to be sent to Moscow, where they will be made acquainted with the commander-in-chief.

Given at our camp of Polotzk, the 18th of July, 1812.

Alexander

M. I. Kutuzov's Report to Alexander I Concerning the Evacuation of Moscow, September 16, 1812

After a very bloody, although for us victorious, battle of August 26 [1812], I was forced to abandon our positions at Borodino for reasons I have already had the honor of reporting to Your Imperial Majesty. As a result of that battle the [main] army was in great confusion while the second [reserve] army was greatly weakened. In such conditions we were approaching Moscow, where daily we encountered increased activity of the enemy's advanced units. Because of the close proximity [to Moscow] there was no desirable terrain where I could meet the enemy. Russian forces that we hoped to join were unable to link with us. The enemy organized two new columns: one was advancing

Source:N. M. Korobkov, ed. *Feldmarshal M. I. Kutuzov. Sbornik Dokumentov i materialov.* (Moscow: Gospolitizdat, 1947), pp. 177–78. Translation mine.

link with us. The enemy organized two new columns: one was advancing along the Borovsk highway, the other along the Zvenigorod, in order to harass the rear of my forces that were retreating to Moscow. For that reason I could not dare to have another battle whose outcome would have resulted not only in the the destruction of my army, but also in a bloody peril to and turning of Moscow itself into ashes. In such a critical situation, after consulting with my leading generals, some of whom disagreed with my assessment of the situation, [it was decided that] I was to allow the enemy to proceed to Moscow from where all treasures, the arsenal, and practically all movable property, both state and private, were to be evacuated and where not one inhabitant was to be left behind.

I dare to report humbly to You, Most Merciful Sovereign, that the entry of the enemy into Moscow does not mean the subjugation of Russia. On the contrary, I am moving with my army along the Tula highway. This will enable me to protect the supplies that were prepared in our rich *gubernias*. Any other decision would have prevented me from achieving this goal, and would have denied me the opportunity of establishing contact with the armies of [Generals] Tormasov and Chichagov. While I am not minimizing the fact that the occupation of the capital could be a deeply felt wound, nevertheless, I do not waver between selecting this development and the results that may benefit us in saving our armies. Using all of my forces, I am currently preparing a counter-offensive along the Tula and Kaluga highways, whose aim is using my units to cut the enemy's entire communication line between Smolensk and Moscow. At the same time I am deploying every means to attack the enemy's rear guard units and, by attracting the enemy's attention, I hope to force him to abandon Moscow and to alter his operations. I have ordered General Winzingerode to hold his positions along the Tver highway. He has a cossack regiment at his disposal to guard the Iaroslav highway and to protect the inhabitants against enemy raids. Presently, I have assembled my forces not far from Moscow, and with firm resolve am expecting the enemy. As long as the army of Your Imperial Majesty is safe and is inspired by its well-known bravery and our diligence, the temporary loss of Moscow does not mean the loss of the Fatherland. I sincerely hope that Your Imperial Majesty will agree that these consequences are inseparably linked with the loss of Smolensk.

Prince [M. I.] Kutuzov
General of the Infantry

Alexander's Victory Proclamation to the Army, January 13, 1813

Merecz, 13th January 1813

Soldiers,

The year has ended—a year forever memorable and glorious—one in which you have trampled in the dust the pride of the insolent aggressor.

The year has passed, but your heroic deeds survive.

Time will not efface their trace. They are present to your contemporaries—they will live with their posterity.

You have purchased at the price of your blood the deliverance of your country from the hostile powers leagued against its independence.

You have acquired rights to the gratitude of Russia and to the admiration of mankind. You have proved by your fidelity, your valour, and your perseverance, that when hearts are filled with the love of God, and devotion of their Sovereign, the efforts of the most formidable enemies resemble the furious waves of the ocean, which break in impotent lashings against indestructible rocks, and leave behind only confused sounds.

Soldiers! Desirous of distinguishing all those who have participated in these immortal exploits, I have ordered medals of silver to be struck, which have been blessed by our holy Church. They bear the date of the memorable year 1812; suspended to a blue ribbon, they will decorate the warrior breasts which have served as bucklers of the country.

Each individual of the Russian army is worthy to bear this honourable recompense of valour and constancy.

You have all shared the same fatigues and dangers; you have had but one heart, one mind; you will all be proud to wear the same distinction; it will proclaim every where that you are the faithful children of Russia—children on whom God the Father will pour His benedictions.

Your enemies will tremble on seeing these decorations; they will know that under these medals hearts are beating, animated with unconquerable valour, and imperishable, because it is not based upon ambition or impiety, but on the immutable foundation of patriotism and religion.

Alexander

Russian Losses (Human and Animal) in the War of 1812

Gubernia	*Human Losses*	*Animal Losses*
Kaluga	2,230	7,355
Moscow	58,811	31,664
Smolensk	172,566	128,739

Vilno	92,243	12,778
Bialystok *oblast*	321	734
Total	430,707[Sic]	230,677

December, 1812
A. Balashev
Minister of Police

Source: *Memuary sovremennikov i ochevidtsev* (Moscow: 1912), p. 105. Translation mine.

28

Russo-Polish Relations, 1815–1835

The three partitions of Poland (by Russia, Austria and Prussia in 1772, 1793, and 1795) terminated the independent existence of that kingdom. Thereafter, although each partitioning power tried to integrate former Polish territories into its administrative, political, social, cultural, and economic system, the Poles tried every means to regain their political independence.

Because Russia had acquired the largest portion of Poland, relations between the two peoples (which historically were never friendly) became very tense. The Russians tried to pacify the Poles by granting them a fairly liberal constitution in 1815. Unfortunately, the constitution benefited only a small area of former Poland. In addition, in day-to-day operations Russian authorities seldom adhered to the constitutional provisions. This behavior antagonized many Poles, spawned tensions and conspiracies, and, in 1830–31, exploded in a violent anti-Russian rebellion. At the height of their initial successes, the Poles officially re-

---

From Le Comte D'Angeberg [Chodzko], *Recueil des traites, conventions et actes diplomatiques concernant la Pologne 1762–1862 (A Collection of Treaties, Conventions and Diplomatic Papers Concerning Poland, 1762–1862)* (Paris: 1862), pp. 707–724. Translation mine.

nounced their allegiance to Russia and dethroned Nicholas I as their constitutional monarch. Nicholas I responded with military force and with total integration of "constitutional Poland" into the Russian Empire where it remained until 1917.

Polish Freedoms under the Constitution of 1815

Article 1

The Kingdom of Poland is united in perpetuity to the Russian Empire. . . .

Article 3

The crown of the kingdom of Poland is hereditary in Our person and in those of Our descendants, heirs, and successors, on the basis of the order of succession established for the imperial throne of Russia.

Article 4

The constitutional charter established the mode and the principles of sovereignty.

Article 5

The king, in his absence, shall nominate a lieutenant who shall reside in the kingdom. The lieutenant is revocable at will. . . .

Article 8

Foreign policy relations of Our empire are the same as those of the kingdom of Poland.

Article 9

The sovereign alone shall have the right to decide whether the kingdom of Poland shall take part in the wars of Russia, as well as in the treaties of peace or of commerce that that power may conclude.

Article 10

In case Russian troops should be brought to Poland or Polish troops to Russia, or in case of transit of those troops through a province of the two states, their maintenance and cost of transportation will be borne by the state to which they belong. The army of Poland shall never be employed outside Europe.

Article 11

The Roman Catholic religion, professed by the majority of the inhabitants of the kingdom of Poland, shall receive the most careful attention from the government, without in any way diminishing the freedom of other sects, which without exception shall be allowed to worship freely and publicly, and shall enjoy the protection of the government. Whatever distinction there may be between Christian sects, there shall be no distinction in the enjoyment of civil and political rights. . . .

Article 16

Freedom of the press is guaranteed. The law shall regulate the ways and shall repress abuses.

Article 17

The law shall protect equally all citizens without regard to their class or their status . . .

Article 19

No person shall be arrested otherwise than according to procedures established by the law. . . .

Article 24

Every Pole is free to move his person and his property in accordance with procedures established by the law.

Article 25

All convicts shall be punished for their crimes in the kingdom; no person shall be deported except when banishment is provided by the law.

Article 26

All property, regardless of its nature, . . . is declared sacred and inviolable. . . .

Article 28

All administrative, judicial, and military public business, without any exception, shall be conducted in the Polish language.

Article 29

Public offices, civil and military, may be occupied only by Poles. The positions of presidents of courts of first instance, presidents of palatinal commissions and of courts of appeal, members of palatinal councils, the offices of nuncios and deputies of the Diet, and those of senators, may be given only to landowners. . . .

Article 31

The Polish nation shall have in perpetuity a national representative body. The latter will consist of a Diet composed of the king and two houses. The Senate will be the first house; Chamber of Nuncios and Deputies of the Communes will form the second house. . . .

Article 33

Any foreigner who shall have acquired property, become naturalized, and shall have learned the Polish language shall be eligible to hold public office after five years residence, if his conduct be irreproachable.

Article 34

Nevertheless, the king may at his pleasure, or upon request of the Council of State, admit foreigners distinguished for their abilities to any public office except those designated in Article 90.

Article 35

The government is inherent in the person of the king. He exercises in all their fullness the functions of the executive power. All executive or administrative authority can emanate only from him.

Article 36

The person of the king is sacred and inviolable. . . .

Article 40

The right to declare war and to conclude all treaties and conventions whatsoever is reserved to the king.

Article 41

The king nominates senators, ministers, state councilors, *les maîtres des requêtes,* presidents of local commissions, presidents and judges of various courts, diplomatic and commercial agents, and all other administrative officials who are subordinate to him or to authorities to whom he had delegated the power.

Article 42

The king nominates archbishops and bishops of different cults, suffragan bishops and prelates.

Article 43

The right to pardon is reserved exclusively to the king. He alone has the power to commute punishment.

Article 44

The sovereign enjoys the right to issue statutes and to publish civil and military orders. . . .

Article 46

The right to grant titles of nobility, to naturalize and to distribute honorary titles, belongs exclusively to the king. . . .

Article 86

The legislative power rests in the person of the king and in the two legislative chambers in conformity with the provisions of Article 31.

Article 87

The Diet shall meet every two years in Warsaw at a time stated in the summons issued by the king. The sessions shall last for thirty days. The king alone may prorogue, adjourn, or dissolve it.

Article 88

The king may convoke an extraordinary Diet if he sees a need for it.

Article 89

A member of the Diet, so long as he shall be a member, may not be arrested nor judged by a criminal court, save by vote of the Chamber to which he belongs. . . .

Article 138

The judicial system is constitutionally independent. . . .

Article 140

The courts consist of judges nominated by the king and of judges selected in conformity with the organic statute.

Article 141

Judges nominated by the king are irremovable for life; judges selected are equally irremovable for the duration of their functions. . . .

Polish Dethronement of Nicholas I, 1831

I. A Proposal by Polish Deputy, R. Soltyk

A. By declaring its unconditional independence [from Russia], the Polish nation considers the Romanov Dynasty to have lost its right to the Polish Crown and renounces its [the Dynasty's] supreme right vis-a-vis the Polish nation.

Source: *Istoriia Rossii v XIX veke.* (Moscow: Granat, 1910), vol. I, p. 318. Translation mine.

B. The Polish nation renounces its earlier loyalty oath [to Russia and its Romanov Dynasty] because that oath was extracted [by force] and was, therefore, contrary to international law.

C. Finally, the Polish nation solemnly declares that the source of all authority resides in the people, and that the people who, by the Revolution of November 29 [1830], have regained their independence and rights, have thereby assumed their inalienable rights to determine their political destiny and to organize their best possible form of government.

II. The Act of Dethronement

All solemn and sacred agreements are inviolable as long as they are observed by both sides. Our long sufferings are universally well known. Numerous violations of freedoms which both monarchs [Alexander I and Nicholas I] had pledged to uphold, have freed the Polish nation from owing an allegiance to the present reigning monarch. The words, which Emperor Nicholas has expressed, that our first shot will be a signal for complete destruction [of Poland] have dashed all of our hopes of securing justice and have greatly disappointed us. Accordingly, represented by its *sejm* [that is, parliament] the Polish nation hereby declares its independence [from Russia] and expresses its right to bestow the Crown of Poland upon anyone worthy to wear it who will also offer solemn and safe guarantees and will pledge that he will sacredly and inviolably preserve our rights.

A Statement by Nicholas I to Polish Representatives, October, 1835

Gentlemen, I am aware that you want to address me. I even know the content of your statement. To free you from telling a lie, I would wish that it not be expressed in my presence. Gentlemen, yes, I wish to free you from telling me a lie, because I know that your personal feelings are entirely different from those you are trying to express to me.

How can I believe in your statements since you told me the same thing at the start of the revolution [of 1830–31]? Are you not the same individuals who, five or eight years ago, told me of your allegiance and devotion to me and gave me solemn assurances of your loyalty? And then, shortly thereafter, you violated your oaths and committed many horrors. . . .

Gentlemen, you have two options: you may persist in your determination to have an independent Poland; or you may live peacefully and be my loyal subjects.

Source: *Russkaia Starina,* vol. VII (1873), pp. 679–80. Translation mine.

Should you insist on cherishing the goal of being an independent nationality, that is, an independent Poland with all of its fantasies, then you will invite great misfortune upon yourself. I have decreed that a citadel be built in Warsaw [Alexander's Citadel], and I would like to inform you that, at the slightest provocation, I will order that your city be destroyed. I will destroy Warsaw and, obviously, will not rebuild its foundations.

It hurts me to tell you this because it is very difficult for a sovereign to talk in this manner to his subjects. But I am telling you this for your own benefit. Gentlemen, it is up to you to forget the past. You can achieve it only by your conduct and by your loyalty to my government. . . .

You can accomplish it be educating your children properly, and by instilling in them the fundamentals of religion and loyalty to their sovereign.

In spite of all the current upheavals that trouble Europe and in spite of all the ideas that threaten the social fabric of society, Russia is the only major power that is unaffected by them.

Gentlemen, believe me, to be a part of Russia and to be able to benefit by her protection is a singular happiness. If you behave properly and if you fulfill your obligations to me, then my fatherly concern will extend to all of you irrespective of what has transpired before. My government will always express concern about your well-being.

Please remember well what I have just told you.

29

The Question of Imperial Succession

One of the most tragic problems in the history of Imperial Russia is the question of succession. A major concern of Peter the Great (see Chapter 3), it was also of importance in the reigns of Anna (see Chapter 6), Elizabeth (see Chapter 7), and Catherine II (see Chapter 10). To prevent palace revolutions or unlawful usurpations of power, Tsar Paul, soon after

---

The following three items are from Paul Lacroix, *Hist ire de la vie et du regne de Nicholas Ier Empereur de Russie (History of the Life and of the Reig i of Nicholas I, Emperor of Russia)* (Paris: 1864), vol. 1, pp. 238–239, 244–247, 395–399. Translation mine.

his ascension, issued a new law of succession (see Chapter 20), by which the throne of Russia was to pass from the father to the eldest son and, if there were no sons, to the next eldest brother of the tsar. Paul's death in 1801 (see Chapter 23) placed his eldest son Alexander I on the throne.

Because Alexander I had no sons to succeed him, under the 1797 law the throne was to pass at his death to his brother Constantine (1779–1831). Early in 1822, however, Constantine, who lived in Warsaw with his morganatic wife, renounced his right to succession in favor of his younger brother, Nicholas (1796–1855). The arrangement was made with such secrecy that when Alexander died late in 1825 there followed a strange comedy of errors that helped to precipitate the Decembrist Revolution.

Constantine's Renunciation of His Right to the Throne, January 26, 1822

Sire!

Encouraged by all the proofs of the infinitely sympathetic disposition of Your Imperial Majesty toward me, I am once more laying at your feet, Sire, a most humble prayer.

Not finding in myself either the genius, or the talents, or the force necessary to be elevated to the sovereign dignity to which I have the right by virtue of my birth, I beg Your Imperial Majesty to transfer this right to whomever follows after me, and thus to assure forever the security of the empire. As for myself, I will add by this renunciation a new guarantee and a new force to the engagement which I have voluntarily and solemnly contracted on the occasion of my divorce from my first wife.

All the circumstances of my own situation, bearing more and more upon this measure, prove to the Empire and to the entire world the sincerity of my views.

Sire, accept with good will my prayer; help me secure the consent of our Imperial Mother to this plan and sanction it with your Imperial assent.

In the sphere of private life, I shall pledge myself always to serve as an example to your faithful subjects, and to all those who are animated by a love for our dear country.

I am with profound respect for your Majesty, your most faithful subject and brother,

St. Petersburg, 26 January, 1822 Tsarevich Constantine

Alexander I's Manifesto on the Succession, August 28, 1823

By the Grace of God, We, Alexander I, Emperor and Autocrat of all the Russias, etc., hereby make known to all Our faithful subjects:

From the moment of Our coming to the throne of all the Russias, We have constantly felt that it was Our duty toward All Mighty God not only to guarantee and increase during Our life the happiness of Our beloved country and Our people, but also to prepare and assure their security and their well being after Us by a clear and precise designation of Our successor in accordance with the laws of Our Imperial House and the interests of the Empire. We were unable to designate him immediately, as Our predecessors had done, because We waited in the hope that it would perhaps please Divine Providence to give Us an heir to the throne in a direct line. But as the years have passed, it has more and more seemed to Us Our duty to place Our throne in such a position that it will not remain vacant even for a moment.

While We bear this anxiety in Our heart Our well beloved brother, Tsarevich and Grand Duke Constantine, following the dictates of his own conscience, has addressed to Us, the request that We transfer his right to the sovereign dignity, a position to which he would one day be elevated by virtue of his birth, to a person who might possess this right after him. He revealed at the same time his intention to give new force to the additional act relative to the succession to the throne which We promulgated in 1820, an act freely and solemnly recognized by him insofar as that act concerned him.

We are profoundly moved by the sacrifice which Our beloved brother has felt that he should make in his own interests for the consolidation of the fundamental laws of Our Imperial House, and the unshakable peace of the Empire of all the Russias.

Having invoked the aid of God, having seriously reflected upon a subject as dear to Our heart as it is vital for the Empire, and finding that the statutes which exist on the order of succession to the throne do not deprive those who have the right of the power to renounce it, and because in this special circumstance it does not present any difficulty in the order of hereditary succession to the throne, with the consent of Our noble Mother, who is the supreme head of the Imperial family to which We belong, and by the absolute power which We possess from God Himself, We ordered and shall order:

First, the voluntary act by which Our younger brother, Tsarevich and Grand Duke Constantine, renounces his rights to the throne of all the Russias shall be irrevocable. The said act of renunciation shall be, in order to insure knowledge of its existence, preserved in the Cathedral of the Assumption in Moscow and in the three high Courts of Our empire; in the Holy Synod, in the Council of the Empire, and in the Governing Senate. Secondly, on the basis of the strict provision of the statute on succession to the throne, be it known that Our successor shall be Our second brother, Grand Duke Nicholas.

As a result, We have the well founded hope that on the day it shall please the King of Kings to recall Us, following the common law of all mortals, from Our temporal reign to eternity, the properly constituted authorities of the Empire, to whom We have made known Our irrevocable wish in this matter, will hasten to swear submission and allegiance to the emperor whom We have just designated as heir to the indivisible crown of the Empire of all the Russias, of the Kingdom of Poland, and of the Grand Duchy of Finland. As for Ourselves, We ask that all Our faithful subjects, with the same feeling of love with which We have considered Our first responsibility on earth to be the care given to their constant prosperity, address fervent prayers to Our Lord Jesus Christ, that He might deign, in His infinite sympathy, to receive Our souls into His eternal kingdom.

Given at Tsarskoe-Selo, August 28, year of Grace 1823, and of Our reign the 23rd.

Alexander

Nicholas I's Manifesto upon Ascending the Throne, December 24, 1825

By the Grace of God, We, Nicholas, Emperor and Autocrat of all the Russias, etc., make known to all Our faithful subjects:

In the sorrow of Our heart, in the midst of the general sadness which surrounds Us, We, Our Imperial house, and Our dear country, humble Ourselves before the unalterable decrees of the All-Mighty, and seek from Him alone Our strength and Our consolations. He has just called to Him Emperor Alexander I, of glorious memory, and We have all lost a father and a sovereign, who, for twenty-five years, has worked for the well-being of Russia and of Us.

When, on December 9, We learned the news of this sad event, We took pains, even in this moment of sadness and tears, to perform a sacred duty and follow only the impulse of Our heart, and We took the oath of allegiance to Our beloved brother Tsarevich Grand Duke Constantine as the legitimate heir to the throne of Russia by the right of primogeniture.

We had just discharged this sacred obligation when We were notified by the Council of Empire that on October 15, 1823, there had been placed in their hands a packet, sealed with the sign of the Emperor, on which there had been written in the hand of His Imperial Majesty himself: "To hold in the Council of Empire until I order otherwise; and in the case of my death to be opened at an extraordinary session, before proceeding to any other act." This sovereign order had been executed by the Council and the following items had been found in the said packet: (1) A letter of Tsarevich Grand Duke Constantine, dated January 26, 1822, addressed to the Emperor, by which his Imperial Highness renounced his succession to the throne which belonged to him by the right of primogeniture; (2) a manifesto of August 28, 1823, signed by his Imperial Majesty's own hand, by which, after having expressed his agreement to the renunciation of Tsarevich and Grand Duke Constantine, it is stated that, being next in age after him, We are, by virtue of the fundamental law, the proper heir to the throne. We were informed at the outset that identical documents had been deposited with the Holy Synod and in the Cathedral of the Assumption in Moscow.

The above mentioned facts did in no way change the determination which We had made. We recognize the acts of renunciation made by His Imperial Highness during the life of the Emperor and confirmed by the assent of His Imperial Majesty; but We have neither the wish nor the right to consider this renunciation as irrevocable since it has neither been published nor transformed into law. We wish thus to show Our respect for the first fundamental law of Our country on the unchanging order of succession to the throne; and faithful to the oath which We have taken, We insist that the entire Empire follow Our example. In this grave circumstance Our desire is not to contest the validity of the resolutions expressed by His Imperial Highness. He has again besought Us not to oppose the wishes of the later Emperor, Our father and common benefactor, wishes which We shall always hold sacred; We seek only to guarantee the letter of the law which rules the order of succession to the throne, to reveal fully the loyalty of Our intentions, and to preserve Our dear country in a moment of uncertainty over the person of the legitimate sovereign. This determination, conceived in the purity of Our conscience before God who reads the depths of Our hearts, was blessed by Her Imperial Majesty Marie, Our beloved Mother.

However, the sad news of the death of His Majesty, the Emperor, was taken directly from Taganrog to Warsaw on December 7, two days sooner than it was received here. Immovable in his resolution, Tsarevich and Grand Duke Constantine confirmed it on the following day by two acts, dated December 8, which he entrusted Our beloved brother Grand Duke Michael to bring to Us. These acts consist: first, of a letter addressed to her Imperial Majesty, Our beloved mother, a letter in which—renewing his earlier decision and resting upon a rescript of the late Emperor, dated February 14, 1822, which served as a response to his act of renunciation of which there was a copy attached—His Imperial Highness renounced definitively and solemnly all his rights to the throne, and on the basis of the order established by fundamental law, made them known to Us as well as to Our heirs; second, a letter addressed to Us, in which His Imperial Highness reiterates the first expression of his determination, gives to Us the title of Imperial Majesty, reserving only for himself that of Tsarevich which he bore formerly, and calls himself the most faithful of Our subjects.

Regardless of how decisive these acts may have been, and regardless of their certainty up to that time, the evidence was clear that the decision of His Imperial Highness was absolute and irrevocable and the nature of the problem and Our feelings in the matter caused Us to defer the publication of the said acts until such time as His Imperial Highness had manifested his desires relative to the oath which We rendered to him as well as to that of the entire Empire. . . .

As a result of all these acts, and by virtue of the fundamental law of the Empire on the order of succession, with a heart full of respect for the unalterable decrees of Providence which guides Us, We ascend the throne of Our ancestors, the throne of the empire of all the Russias, and those of the kingdom of Poland and the Grand Duchy of Finland, which are inseparable, and We order:

1. That the oath of allegiance be taken to Us and to Our heir, His Imperial Highness Grand Duke Alexander, Our well beloved son;

2. That the time of Our accession to the throne be dated from December 1, 1825.

Finally We ask all Our faithful subjects to raise with Us their fervent prayers toward the All-Mighty that He grant Us the power of His support for the burden which Divine Providence has imposed upon Us, that He sustain Us in Our firm intentions to live only for Our beloved country and to follow in the footsteps of the monarch who preceded Us. Then Our reign will be only a continuation of his, and We shall be able to accomplish all the wishes which he conceived for the well being of Russia, he whose sacred memory nourishes in Us the desire and hope to merit the blessings of heaven and the love of Our people!

Given in Our imperial residence at St. Petersburg, December 24, in the year of Grace, 1825, and of Our reign the first.

Nicholas

30

The Decembrist Movement

After the victorious campaigns against Napoleon, many Russian officers returned home with boxes crammed with books and heads full of ideas for improving their country. Small secret groups were organized, of which the most important was the Union of Salvation. In 1818 this group, composed of a southern and a northern branch, changed its name to the Union of Welfare. The southern branch, led by Colonel Paul I. Pestel (1793–1826), advocated, in the Jacobin tradition, drastic changes in Russia's social, economic, and political structure. The northern branch, headed by such men as Prince Sergei P. Trubetskoi (1790–1860) and Nikita M. Muraviev (1795–1826), proposed a more moderate plan. The first Russian revolution began on December 26, 1825, at the height of confusion within the imperial family over the succession following the death of Alexander I. The revolt proved a dismal failure, for many reasons. Many of the more resolute leaders were arrested and the others failed to act decisively; the expected popular uprising failed to materialize; and, finally, the armed forces remained loyal to the regime. The attempts of the Decembrists, as this group is commonly called, became an ideal of self sacrificing struggle against autocracy for later generations of Russian revolutionaries.

Statute of the Union of Welfare

Book One. Aims of the Union of Welfare

1. Convinced that good morals represent the firm foundation of national welfare and valor, and that all the efforts of the government to attain them will fail unless the governed take active part in realizing these well-intentioned aims, the Union of Welfare believes that it is its sacred obligation to disseminate the true rules of morality and enlightenment among fellow citizens, and to assist the government in elevating Russia to the level of greatness and welfare to which the Creator has predestined it.

From I. Ia. Shchipanov, ed. *Izbrannye sotsialno-politicheskie i filosofkie proizvedeniia dekabristov* (Selected Socio-Political and Philosophical Works of the Decembrists) (Moscow: Gospolitizdat, 1951), vol. 1, pp. 241–250, 299–319. Translation mine. Words in brackets are mine.

2. Because its aim is the *welfare of the country,* the Union does not conceal it [its aim] from well-meaning citizens, but in order to avoid the censure of malice and jealousy its activity must be conducted in secrecy.

3. Because in all of its actions it will strive to observe strictly the rules of justice and virtue, the Union will not try to expose those wounds which it cannot remedy immediately, inasmuch as it is guided neither by lust for glory nor similar motives, but by a desire for the common welfare.

4. The Union hopes to receive benevolent support from the government; this hope is based on the following statements of the *Nakaz* by the late Empress Catherine II: "If their minds are inadequately prepared for them (the laws), then assume the responsibility of preparing them and you will accomplish thereby a great deal." And in another place: "That policy is bad which corrects through law what should have been corrected through manners."

5. The following four basic fields constitute the aim of the Union: (1) philanthropy; (2) education; (3) justice; and (4) national economy.

6. *First Field: Philanthropy.* The Union supervises all philanthropic institutions in the state, such as hospitals, orphanages, etc., and also those places where mankind is suffering, namely, dungeons, prisons, etc. With zeal that befits its noble aim, the Union will seek to survey, and if possible to improve, the above mentioned institutions and to establish new ones. It will bring to the attention of the government all inadequacies and abuses that have been detected in those institutions. [The Union] is fully convinced that it [the government] is genuinely sympathetic with all of this, and that it is ready to extend a helping hand to all those who suffer. The Union also is concerned that invalids be cared for in appropriate places.

7. *Second Field: Section 1. Dissemination of moral principles.* The Union will attentively disseminate among all estates of the population genuine principles of virtue and will remind and explain to all their obligations toward faith, neighbors, the country, and existing authorities. It will point out the unbreakable tie that exists between the people's virtue, that is, good morals, and its welfare, and will use every means to eradicate the vices that have entered our hearts, especially preference for personal rather than public gains, baseness, vile passions, hypocrisy, extortion, and cruelty toward subordinates. In short, by enlightening all about their duties, it [the Union] will try to reconcile and to persuade all classes, ranks, and races in the state, and to encourage them to strive unanimously toward the government's aim: the *common good,* so that a general public opinion will emerge as a true tribunal of morality whose beneficent influence will complete the formation of good habits and thereby will place on a firm and indestructible foundation the welfare and virtue of the Russian people.

The Union will achieve this end through publication of periodical works consonant with the educational level of each class, [and] writing and translation of books pertaining to man's obligations. Personal examples and words [of members] will also contribute to this aim. Clergymen, belonging to the Union, are especially obligated to enlighten their parishioners, without exception, about their duties. Those clergymen who are not members of the Union should be encouraged to do the same.

8. *Section 2: Education of youth* The education of youth represents also a permanent aim of the Union of Welfare. Under its supervision should be placed without exception all national educational institutions. The Union should inspect them, improve them, and establish new ones. As far as the education of youth is concerned, special effort must be made to arouse in it a love for everything virtuous, useful, and elegant, and contempt for everything that is imperfect and low, in order to stop the strong impulse of the passions by the firm but just reminder of an enlightened reason and conscience.

With respect to private education, the Union should try subtly to persuade the parents to instill the principles of virtue in their children and to support all deserving educators; those, however, who under the guise [of educators] creep into households to sow dissension and debauchery the Union will try not only to expel, but will try to deprive them, as corrupters of youth's morals, from earning their daily bread in this profession. The Union will especially supervise foreigners who, in addition to sowing dissension and corruption in households, instill in the children contempt for [everything that is] native and an attachment to [things that are] foreign. The Union will seek to dissuade parents from education their children in foreign countries. The education of the female sex, as a source of virtue in private education, is also of concern to the Union.

The Union will use the following means to attain this end: its own example, the spoken word, and periodical publications, which, among others, should include methods of education, names of recognized good educators, and books useful for that purpose.

9. *Section 3: Dissemination of knowledge* By all available means the Union will fight ignorance and will seek to instill genuine enlightenment by directing the minds to useful occupations and especially toward a knowledge of the fatherland. To this end it will write and translate books—good textbooks as well as those that will aid useful learning. It will try to disseminate education among the common people. It will use satire to divert people away from books that are contrary to the aims of the Union, or those that have no impact. Only the truly elegant will be allowed in literature and everything that is either bad or mediocre will be eliminated.

10. *Third Field: Justice* Next to good morals, justice is, without doubt,

one of the main aspects of national welfare and is therefore an integral part of the aim of the Union. The Union will supervise the execution of governmental measures; will encourage civil and religious officials to fulfill their duties; will keep informed of all pending cases, and will seek to direct everything to the path of justice; will support poor but honest and trusted officials; will compensate for losses incurred in the cause of justice; will promote genuinely deserving individuals; will try to direct the dishonest and depraved into a proper path, and, in case of a failure, will try to deprive them of the opportunity to do harm. The Union will also try to limit and eradicate the lust for power and disregard for human rights which we acquired during our up-bringing, and will try to convince everyone of the truth that *the general prosperity of the people is infallibly based on private* [prosperity] *and that every individual, regardless of his estate, has the right to use it.*

11. *Fourth Field: National economy* National economy as the foundation of national wealth should be the aim of the Union—because through trade and industry it unites not only all estates but all vast areas of the state, and because transfer of wealth from one hand to another equalizes fortunes and thereby provides everyone with the hope that through industriousness he can enjoy that part of prosperity he has envied in others. The Union will pay particular attention to agriculture and to all forms of cultivation of the soil in order to develop useful produce; it will support every useful industry in the state; it will supervise foreign and domestic trade and will seek to develop it, and through it to vitalize the unproductive regions of the country; it will support and call to the attention of the government that it [should] reward those merchants and industrialists who distinguish themselves in trying to do things for the general good; it will single out honest merchants, and will try to turn dishonest [ones] to their duties; and in general it will seek that more honesty be introduced in trade. The Public Treasury is also an object of interest of the Union.

Book Two. General Laws of the Union of Welfare

1. *Qualifications of the candidates* Having as its aim the *general welfare,* the Union of Welfare invites to membership all those who, by their honest life, have earned for themselves a good name in society, and who, feeling the nobility of the aim of the Union, are prepared to endure all the hardships that are associated with its attainment.

2. The Union does not consider differences in occupation and estates: all Russian citizens—nobles, clergy, merchants, townsmen, and free men—who agree with the above, who profess the Christian faith, and who are at least eighteen years old, are eligible for membership in the Union of Welfare.

Note: The Union considers to be Russian citizens those who were born in Russia and who speak Russian. Foreigners who left their country to serve a foreign state [Russia] do not deserve confidence by this act, and consequently cannot be considered Russian citizens. The Union considers worthy of this honor only those foreigners who have rendered important services to our country and who are passionately attached to it.

3. Women will not be admitted to the Union. Efforts should be made, however, to bring them subtly to organize philanthropic and *private societies,* whose aims are similar to those of the Union.

4. Anyone known to be a dishonest individual, and who has not improved his reputation, cannot be admitted to the Union of Welfare. In general, all those who are depraved, vicious, and subject to vile passions, are precluded from participating in the Union.

5. *Duties of the members* Every member, upon joining the Union, is required, depending on his qualifications, to enroll in one of the fields listed in the aims [of the Union] and contribute as much as possible to [the success of] its work.

6. Every member is unquestionably required to obey all lawful orders of the Union authorities, diligently execute all of their assignments, and cheerfully submit to all the reprimands which these authorities may impose for failure to carry out obligations.

7. Members of the Union not only should not avoid public obligations, but as true sons of the Fatherland, should accept them with pleasure and execute them with zeal; and by their faultless conduct, justice, and nobility, elevate the prestige of their position in the eyes of others.

8. In every occupation, in every position, a member of the Union is obligated to aid others, to show respect for virtuous and distinguished people and to try to establish contact with them, keeping the Union informed about it. He must oppose the evil and the depraved by all means, without violating public order.

9. Members of the Union should aid one another in public life; members of the nobility are obligated to aid members from among the merchants, townsmen, and husbandmen, while members from these classes must act in a similar manner among themselves and towards nobles. Members of the civil service must defend those in the military and the military must speak for the civilians. All this, however, should not be contrary to truth or to the benefit of vice or crime. In general, every [member] must disseminate this truth: that every class and service is useful to the state, must be equally respected by true sons of the Fatherland, and that only those persons who deviate from their obligations and perfer vice to virtue deserve contempt.

10. Every member, under the penalty of punishment, is obligated to report

to the authorities of the Union all illegal and shameful acts of his fellow members.

11. Other obligations of the Union members stem naturally from the aims of the Union. To the extent of his abilities, every member is obligated to accelerate the attainment of these aims. By his own example and word he must encourage everyone to virtue, disseminate ideas consonant with the aims of the Union, and speak the truth and defend it fearlessly; in short, he must strive to build a moral wall that will protect the present as well as future generations from all misfortunes of vice, and thereby erect an everlasting and unshakable foundation for the greatness and welfare of the Russian people.

12. Every member, upon joining the Union, must contribute annually *one twenty-fifth* of his income to the common treasury. In this matter the Union depends completely on the honesty of every member, because no other feeling than virtue induces everyone to contribute to the common good.

13. *Rights of the members* The difference in civil positions and ranks is abolished in the Union and is replaced by submission to the authorities of the Union. This, however, should not preclude normal respect for officials: a member of the Union must always and everywhere fulfill zealously his public obligations.

14. Every member has the right as well as the duty to participate within the legal framework in administration and legislation of the Union. He also has the right to submit in writing his views on any problem to lower as well as to higher authorities of the Union.

15. No member [of the Union] may be accused on grounds of suspicion alone; he may not be punished until sufficient evidence against him has been presented.

16. Every member has the right to organize or be a member of any society approved by the government, but he must inform the Union of everything that transpires in them and should subtly direct them to the aims of the Union. Members are prohibited from joining societies that are not approved by the government, because the Union, acting for the good of Russia, and for the aims of the government, does not wish to arouse the latter's suspicion.

17. No one may speak with outsiders about the work and affairs of the Union without specific permission; no one has the right, without special permission, to expound his thought in writing either against or in behalf of the Union; on the contrary, every member is obligated to refrain from revealing to non-members any disagreement within the Union; if there is a need he must defend the Union and its members with appropriate dignity.

18. If it should happen that some people, even those who have some virtue, and who have become fully acquainted with the aims and the per-

manent procedures of the Union, decide to leave it . . . the Union allows them to withdraw on condition that they keep secret everything they know.

Rules of Conduct for the United Slavs, 1820's

1. Do not rely on anyone except your close friends and your [weapons]. Your friends will help you and [your weapons] will protect you.

2. Do not aspire to have a slave if you do not wish to be a slave.

3. Everyone will hold you in high esteem if you will not seek pride and affluence.

4. Simplicity, sobriety, and humility are guardians of freedom and they will guarantee your peace of mind.

5. Do not aspire to have more than you have now and you will be independent.

6. Let the goddess of Enlightenment be your pennant and allow your kind disposition to prevail in your home.

7. Study sciences, arts, and crafts. Express your interest and enthusiasm for them and your friends will admire you.

8. Do not alienate your children through haughtiness, vanity or fanaticism. The latter are signs of the evil spirit of Beelzebub.

9. You must tolerate all religions and customs of all other nations but you are required to accept only the best [they have to offer].

10. You will try to eliminate all prejudices, and especially those pertaining to class distinctions, and the moment you acknowledge the existence of another human being, you yourself will become a human being.

11. You will become a virtuous person, and virtue in your entire life will give you the crown of peace for your conscience.

12. You may even use your [weapons], should it be required to defend innocent people from injustice, and you will not suffer as a result because your friends will protect you.

13. Using your wise judgment and your weapons, you will assist your friends and they, in turn, will assist you.

14. If you will remain loyal to these goals, the haughtiness of tyranny with its vanity will kneel before you.

15. If you are a [true] Slav, then you will build four fleets along the sea shores that surround you: the Black Sea, the White Sea, the Dalmatian Sea, and the Arctic Sea. In the center of your [Slavic] countries you will [symbolically] erect a statue honoring the goddess of Enlightenment and you will

Source: M. V. Nechkina, *Obshchestvo soedinennykh slavian.* (Moscow: 1927), pp. 96–98. Translation mine.

set her up in the highest esteem. From her you will receive justice which you must respect, because without it you cannot reach the goal you have charted for yourself.

16. Trade and naval power will flourish in your Slavic ports, and justice will prevail in your inland cities.

17. Do you wish to have all of the above? If the answer is yes, then join your brothers who have been alienated from you because of the ignorance of your ancestors. You should set aside one-tenth of your annual income and you will dwell in the hearts of your friends. *"L'esprit de servitude parait naturellement ampule comme celui de la liberte est nerveux et celui de la vraie grandeur est simple, voila que vous devez observer,"* that is, "The spirit of servility usually appears as arrogant, the spirit of freedom as good, and the spirit of true greatness as simple characteristics. You should remember this."

Project for a Constitution by Nikita M. Muraviev: Second Draft

Chapter I. The Russian People and Government

1. The Russian people are free and independent, and consequently are not, and cannot be, the property of any individual or family.

2. The source of *supreme power* is the people, who have the exclusive right to make *fundamental laws* for themselves.

Chapter II. Citizens

3. *Citizenship* is the right to participate, in accordance with the rules set forth in this Constitution, in the government—either *indirectly,* that is, through the election of officials or electors, or *directly,* that is, through being elected to any public office of the *legislative, executive* or *judicial branches.*

4. *Citizens* are those inhabitants of the Russian Empire who enjoy the abovementioned rights.

5. To be a citizen a person must meet the following qualifications:
   (a) Be twenty-one years old.
   (b) Have a known and permanent residence.
   (c) Possess a healthy mind.
   (d) Have personal freedom.
   (e) Pay public obligations on time.
   (f) Be unimpeached before the law.

6. An alien who was not born in Russia, but who has resided there continuously for seven years, has the right to petition *the court* for Russian citizenship, provided he has renounced under oath his association with the government whose subject he previously had been.

7. An alien who has not been granted Russian citizenship cannot perform any public or military duty in Russia, has no right to serve as a soldier in the Russian army, and cannot acquire lands.

8. Twenty years after the promulgation of this Constitution of the Russian Empire no person who has not become literate in the Russian language may be recognized as a citizen.

9. The right of citizenship can be lost *temporarily* through:
  (a) Court declaration of insanity.
  (b) Court-imposed prison sentence.
  (c) *Temporary deprivation* of rights by a court.
  (d) Declaration of bankruptcy.
  (e) Embezzlement of public funds.
  (f) Personal servitude.
  (g) Lack of permanent home, occupation, and means of livelihood.

  [The right of citizenship may be lost] *forever* through:
  (a) Entering the service of another state.
  (b) Accepting service or obligation in a foreign country without the consent of his [the Russian] government.
  (c) Decision of a court for dishonorable punishment, which carries *the loss* of the citizenship rights.
  (d) Acceptance without the approval of the parliament, of a gift, pension, a sign of distinction, [or a] title, whether honorary or one which brings him gain, from a foreign government, sovereign, or people.

Chapter III. Status, Personal Rights, and Obligations of Russians

10. All Russians are equal before the law.

11. All native inhabitants of Russia, and Russian-born children of foreigners who are of age, are considered to be Russians until they announce that they do not wish to enjoy this privilege.

12. Everyone must fulfill his public obligations, obey the laws and authorities of the Fatherland, and come to the defense of the country whenever the law should require it.

13. Serfdom and slavery are abolished; any slave who reaches Russian soil becomes free. No distinction is recognized between noblemen and commoners, because this is contrary to our faith, according to which all men are *brothers,* all *well-born* by divine will, all born *for the good,* and all simply men: because all are weak and imperfect.

14. Everyone has the right to express freely his thoughts and feelings and communicate them through print to his countrymen. Books, similarly as all other acts, may be brought before the court by other citizens and must be tried before a *jury.*

15. All the existing merchant and craft *guilds* are abolished.

16. Everyone has the right to engage in any occupation he feels will benefit him most: *agriculture, cattle raising, hunting, fishing, handicrafts, industry, trade,* etc.

17. Every litigation involving property exceeding the value of one pound of pure silver (twenty-five silver *rubles*), goes before a jury court.

18. Every criminal case is tried by a jury.

19. Anyone suspected of a crime may be detained by lawfully constituted authorities in accordance with established procedure; however, within twenty-four hours (those responsible for his detention) must inform him in writing of the reason for his detention; otherwise he is set free immediately.

20. Unless he is arrested for a criminal offense, a prisoner is to be set free immediately if *bail* is posted for him.

21. No one may be punished except under terms of a law that had been properly introduced and duly promulgated *before the crime was committed.*

22. This Constitution will outline what officials, and under what circumstances, have the right to issue written orders *to detain* a citizen, *search his home, seize his papers,* and *open his letters.* Equally, it will outline the responsibility for committing such offenses.

23. The right to property, especially movable property, is sacred and inviolable.

24. The land belongs to landowners. The houses of villagers and their gardens, together with all of their agricultural implements and cattle belonging to them, are their property.

25. Economic and appanage peasants will be called *common owners,* as are *free agriculturists,* because the land on which they now live will be given to them in *common possession* and recognized as their property. The Appanage Administration is abolished.

26. Subsequent legislation will determine how these lands will be transferred from a *common to private ownership* of each of the villagers, and the rules that will determine the division of common land among them.

27. Villagers living on leased estates are also *freed,* but the land remains in the possession of the lessees for the duration of the lease.

28. *Military colonies* are abolished forthwith. Members of settled battalions and squadrons, and their families, join the class of common *owners.*

29. The division of men into fourteen classes is terminated. Civil ranks that were borrowed from the Germans, and which differ very little among themselves, are abolished in conformity with the ancient customs of the Russian people. Such titles and classes as freeholders, merchants, nobles, and *eminent citizens* are replaced by *citizen* or Russian.

30. The clergy will continue to receive their salaries. They are, however, freed from quartering and carting duties.

31. Nomadic tribes do not enjoy the rights of citizens. They have, however, the right to take part in the election of a *volost elderman.*

32. Citizens have the right to organize different societies and associations without requesting permission or authorization from anyone, provided their actions are not illegal.

33. Each of such societies has the right to make its own bylaws, provided the latter are not contrary to this Constitution or to public laws.

34. No foreign-based society can have a subordinate branch or a subsidiary in Russia.

35. No violation of the law may be excused by reference to orders from superiors. *The violator* of the law is punished first, then whoever authorized the illegal act.

36. Citizens have the right to address their complaints or petitions to the National Assembly, the Emperor, and the governing bodies of the states [of the Empire].

37. Underground dungeons and casements, and in general all the so-called state prisons, are abolished. No one may be imprisoned except in public prisons, designated for this purpose.

38. *Accused* should not be imprisoned in the same place together with *convicts,* nor should those imprisoned for debts or minor offenses be put together with criminals and villians.

39. Citizens should elect prison officials from among people of good conscience, who would be accountable for every illegal and inhuman act against prisoners.

40. The present police officials are released from duty and are to be replaced by officials elected by the inhabitants.

41. Any citizen who would violate free election of *national representatives,* by violence or bribery, will be brought before the court.

42. No one may be prevented from the exercise of his religion according to his conscience and feelings, as long as he does not violate the laws of nature and morality.

Chapter IV. On Russia

43. For legislative and executive purposes Russia is divided into thirteen states, two regions, and 569 districts or parishes. . . .

	State	*Capital*
I.	State of Bothnia	Helsingfors
II.	State of Volkhov	City of St. Peter
III.	Baltic State	Riga
IV.	Western State	Vilno
V.	State of the Dnieper [River]	Smolensk
VI.	Black Sea State	Kiev
VII.	Caucasian State	Tiflis
VIII.	Ukrainian State	Kharkov
IX.	Trans-Volga State	Iaroslavl
X.	State of the Kama [River]	Kazan
XI.	State of the Lower Steppe	Saratov
XII.	State of the Ob [River]	Tobolsk
XIII.	State of the Lena [River]	Irkutsk
	Moscow Region	Moscow
	Don Region	Cherkassk. . . .

Chapter VI. National Assembly

59. *The National Assembly,* consisting of the *Supreme Duma* and the *Chamber of People's Representatives,* is invested with all legislative power.

Chapter VII. The Chamber of Representatives, Number, and Election of Representatives

60. The Chamber of Representatives consists of members elected for two years by the citizens of the States.

61. At the time of his election a representative must reside in the state that elects him.

62. Until they have fulfilled them, individuals who have public works contracts cannot serve as representatives. . . .

Chapter VIII. The Supreme Duma

73. The Supreme Duma consists of three citizens from every state, two from the Moscow Region, and one from the Don Region, a total of forty-two members. Members of the Supreme Duma are elected by the governing institutions of the states and regions, that is, by *State Dumas* and the *Chambers of Electors* at joint sessions.

74. Immediately upon arrival in the capital, members of the Supreme Duma are divided into three equal groups. Members of the first group will terminate their position in the Duma in two years; members of the second group after four years; and members of the third group after six years. Thus, one-third of the membership of the Duma will be elected every two years. . . .

75. Criteria indispensable for membership in the Supreme Duma are: thirty years of age; nine years of Russian citizenship for a [naturalized] foreigner; residence in the state that elects him; immovable property worth 1500 pounds of pure silver, or movable property worth 3000 pounds of pure silver. . . .

77. Within the competence of the Supreme Duma belongs the impeachment of ministers, supreme court justices, and all other officials of the Empire who have been accused by people's representatives. No one can be sentenced except by the judgment of two-thirds of the members present. The Duma has no authority to impose any other sentence except to declare that *the accused is guilty and to deprive him of the seat and position he occupies*. . . .

Jointly with the Emperor, the Duma participates in the conclusion of peace, in the appointment of judges to superior courts, commanders-in-chief of land and naval forces, corps commanders, chiefs of squadrons, and chief keeper of the order. Consent by two-thirds of the members of the Duma are required for this.

Chapter IX. Power and Prerogatives of the National Assembly, and the Law-making Process

78. The National Assembly meets at least once a year. . . .

79. Each Chamber decides on the rights and credentials of its members . . .

80. Each Chamber has the right to censure its members for unbecoming conduct or in case of crime, *but never for expressing an opinion*; it may expel a member by a *decision* of two-thirds of the members.

81. The sessions of both Chambers are public. At the Emperor's request, however, both Chambers may deliberate behind closed doors, having removed [from the premises] all unauthorized persons. . . . Women and minors under 17 years of age are not admitted to the sessions of either Chamber.

82. Each Chamber keeps minutes of its daily proceedings and publishes them periodically, except those that they decide to keep secret. . . .

83. Members of the Supreme Duma and representatives are remunerated from the State Treasury for each day of their service. . . .

84. In no instance, except *treason,* or transgressions or violations of public order, may members of the National Assembly be arrested during the session, or during their trip to the capital, or during their return home. Never should they be threatened for what they have said in their Chambers, and no one

has the right to demand that they explain their speeches. A member accused of transgression is suspended by his Chamber until a court verdict.

85. No official in public service may be a member of either Chamber as long as he retains his official position.

86. No member of the Duma or a Representative may be appointed to any government office during the entire term for which he has been elected. . . .

89. To attain force of *law,* each bill passed by the Duma and the Chamber of Representatives must be submitted to the Emperor. If the Emperor approves the bill, he signs it; if he disapproves, he sends it back with his comments to the Chambers where it was initiated; the Chamber enters into its minutes all of the Emperor's comments against the bill and reopens debate on it. If, after this second debate on a bill, two-thirds of the members favor it, then the bill goes with all of the Emperor's comments to the other Chamber where it is debated anew, and if a *majority* approves it, then the bill becomes law. . . .

92. The National Assembly has the power to make and annual laws dealing with the judiciary and the executive; that is:

(a) Issue a civil, criminal, commercial, and military code for Russia . . .
(b) Declare through a law, in case of invasion or rebellion, that a given region is on a war footing and under *martial law.*
(c) Make public the law of *amnesty . . .*
(d) Declare war.
(e) [Supervise] taxes, loans, auditing of expenditures, pensions, grants, all revenues and expenditures; in short, [have control over] all financial matters. But it cannot approve a budget for more than two years.
(f) [Concern itself with] all governmental measures pertaining to industry, national wealth, postal service, maintenance of old and creation of new land and water ways, and establishment of banks.
(g) Protect sciences and useful arts, and grant authors and inventors exclusive right to derive benefits from their works and inventions for a specific number of years. . . .
(h) Receive reports from ministers in case of physical or mental illness of the Emperor, and on his death or abdication declare a regency or proclaim the heir Emperor.
(i) Elect governors of states.

93. The National Assembly has no power to make new *constitutional laws,* or annul the existing ones; it has no right to issue measures on any matter not listed as belonging within its competence.

94. The *National Assembly,* composed of men elected by the Russian people and representing them, assumes the character of their majesty. . . .

98. The National Assembly does not have authority to establish or to

prohibit any denomination or sect. Faith, conscience, and views of citizens, so long as they do not violate any law, are not within the competence of the National Assembly. . . . The National Assembly has no authority to infringe freedom of speech or press. . . .

100. . . . Powers which this Constitution does not delegate to any of the herein designated assemblies or officials belong to the entire Russian people.

Chapter X. The Supreme Executive Power

101. The Emperor is the Supreme official of the Russian government. His rights and privileges are as follows:

(a) His power is hereditary in direct line from father to son, but from the father-in-law it passes to the son-in-law.
(b) In his person he concentrates the entire executive power.
(c) He has the right to halt the action of the legislative branch and to compel it to review the law.
(d) He is commander-in-chief of land and naval forces.
(e) He is the supreme chief of any branch of militia on active duty for the Empire.
(f) He may demand a written statement from chief officials of any executive department on any matter related to their duties.
(g) He negotiates and concludes peace treaties with foreign states with the advice and consent of two-thirds of the voting members of the Supreme Duma. A treaty concluded in this manner becomes a supreme law.
(h) He appoints ambassadors, ministers, and consuls, and represents Russia in all of her relations with foreign states. He appoints all officials not listed in this Constitution.
(i) He may not include in treaties any article that would violate rights and property of citizens within the Fatherland. Equally, without the consent of the National Assembly he may not include any provision to attack a country or to relinquish any territory belonging to Russia.
(j) He appoints judges to Supreme Court vacancies with the advice and consent of the Supreme Duma. . . .
(k) During the session of both Chambers, he must present before the National Assembly a report on the state of Russia, and recommend to it adoption of measures which in his view are either indispensable or desirable.
(l) He has the right to call both Chambers into session, and [to convene] the Supreme Duma in case of treaty negotiations or impeachment.

(m) He may not use military forces inside Russia, in case of rebellion, without submitting a request concerning it to the National Assembly, which must satisfy itself through an immediate inquiry of the need for a state of siege. . . .

(n) He receives ambassadors and plenipotentiaries of foreign governments.

(o) He supervises the strict execution of public laws.

(p) He grants titles to all officials of the Empire.

(q) He is entitled His Imperial Majesty; no other title is permitted. . . .

(r) At his assumption of the reign, the Emperor takes the following oath in the National Assembly:

I solemnly swear that I will faithfully execute the duties of Russian Emperor, and with all my might shall preserve and defend this Constitution of Russia.

(s) Members of the Imperial family are not distinguished from other individuals; they are subject to the same rules and the same acts of the government as all other [citizens], and enjoy no special rights or privileges. . . .

105. The ruler of the Empire cannot be absent from it without creating serious difficulties. . . .

106. The Emperor's departure from Russia is considered tantamount to his abandoning it and abdicating his imperial title; in such cases the National Assembly immediately proclaims the heir Emperor.

Excerpts from Pestel's Testimony

Until the age of twelve I was brought up in the home of my parents. In 1805, with my brother who is now Colonel in the Regiment of the Cavalier Guard, I went to Hamburg, and from there to Dresden, from where I returned in 1809 to my parents' home. During our absence from the fatherland, our education was guided by a certain Seidel, who, upon entering Russian service, was on the staff of General [Nicholas] Miloradovich in 1820. In 1810 I was assigned to the Corps of Pages, from which I graduated in 1811 as a lieutenant of the Lithuanian Life Guard [Regiment], which now is called the Moscow Life Guard Regiment. Until I began preparing for entrance to the Corps of Pages, I had not the slightest conception of political sciences, whose under-

From I. Ia. Shchipanov. ed. *Izbrannye sotsialno-politicheskie i filosofskie proizvedeniia dekabristov (Selected Socio-Political and Philosophical Works of the Decembrists)* (Moscow: Gospolitizdat, 1951), vol. 2, pp. 163–169, 187–188. Translation mine. Words in brackets are mine.

standing was required for admission to the upper class. I studied them then under Professor and Academician [Karl F.] Hermann [1767–1838], who at that time taught these sciences in the Corps of Pages.

After I left the Corps of Pages, military and political sciences interested me most, but I was fascinated primarily by political and then by military [matters].

During the winter of 1816–1817 I attended a course in political science [offered] by Professor and Academician Hermann in his quarters on Vasilevskii Island. I learned from him then very little that was new, because in his lectures he presented almost the same material that I already had heard from him at the Corps of Pages. The format of his lectures was different, but the subject matter was the same.

I cannot name any single individual who was responsible for imbuing me with free thinking and liberal ideas. Nor can I state definitely the time when these began to emerge, because this did not happen suddenly but little by little and in the beginning without making any great impression on me. I have the honor now to tell the [Investigating] Committee honestly and with complete frankness [how it all occurred]. After I received the fundamentals of political science I became infatuated. I had a burning desire and with all my heart I wished to do good. I saw that prosperity and disaster of kingdoms and peoples depends to a great extent on governments, and this belief directed me increasingly to those studies that discuss these problems and show the way to them. But in the beginning I was preoccupied with these studies as well as with the reading of political works in a good natured manner and without any free-thinking, and with but just one aim: to be sometimes at an appropriate time and place, a useful servant of the sovereign and of the fatherland.

This activity later induced me to think whether in the structure of the Russian government the rules of political science were observed or not. I did not question yet the supreme power, but thought only of ministers, of local government, of individual officials, and similar problems. I then discovered that there were many contradictions within the rules of political science, as I understood them, and I began to study various problems in depth; namely, what kind of decrees could change, supplement, or improve them. I also directed my thoughts and attention to the condition of the people, and serfdom affected me always very strongly, similarly as did the privileges enjoyed by the aristocracy. I considered the latter as a kind of wall between the monarch and the people—a wall which, for the sake of its own advantages, tried to hide from the monarch the true condition of the people. With time I began to develop thoughts on diverse topics and doctrines: namely, privileges of the annexed provinces; rumors about military colonies, the decline of trade, industry and general prosperity; lack of justice, and corruption of the courts and other departments; the burden of military service for soldiers; and many similar topics which, in my judgment, could contribute to individual dissatisfaction; and when I put these [problems] together I saw the whole picture of national poverty. Then a grumbling against the government began to emerge within me.

I believe that the turning point in my political views, understanding, and thinking, was the restoration of the House of Bourbon on the French throne. As I reflected on this development I began to realize that a majority of the basic propositions introduced by the revolution were not only retained at the restoration but were even acknowledged as useful; this in spite of the fact that everybody, including myself, had always been opposed to revolution. This led me to conclude that a revolution is really not as bad as they say, and that it can even be quite valuable. This thought led me, in turn, to another proposition; namely, that those states that did not have any revolution were deprived of similar privileges and institutions. These thoughts began then to merge with those noted earlier, and simultaneously they gave birth to constitutional and revolutionary thoughts. The constitutional [thoughts] were fully monarchial, while the revolutionary [thoughts] were rather weak and unclear. Slowly the former became fixed and clear, while the latter became strong. The reading of political books strengthened and developed within me all those thoughts, views, and understanding. The horrible consequences that occurred in France during the revolution forced me to seek means to prevent their occurrence [in Russia], and this led me to develop the idea of a provisional government as a necessary means to prevent civil war.

I moved from monarchial-constitutional to republican thinking as a result of the following facts and reflections: The work of Destute de Tracy [1754–1836], in French, exerted a powerful influence on me. He shows that every government wherein one person is the head of state, especially if it is hereditary, will inevitably end in despotism. All newspapers and political works so strongly applauded the growth of prosperity in the United States of America, attributing it to the governmental structure, that it appeared to me as a clear indication that the republican form of government was superior [to all other forms].

[M. I.] Novikov [1777–1822] spoke to me about his republican constitution for Russia, but at the time I still favored monarchy; subsequently I began to recall his views and agreed with them. I recalled the glorious time of Greece when it was a republic and its pitiful condition thereafter. I compared the mighty glory of Republican Rome with its lamentable fate under the rule of the emperors. The history of Great Novgorod likewise strengthened in me republican ideas. I discovered that in France and England, constitutions are only covers that in no way prevent English ministers of French kings from doing what they want. Because of this I preferred autocracy to such constitutions, for I thought that under the autocratic form of government the unlimited power [of the ruler] is open for everyone to see. In constitutional monarchies, on the other hand, there also exists limitless power, but it acts slowly, and as a result cannot quickly correct a mistake. As for the two chambers, they exist only as mere covers.

It seemed to me that the main trend of our times was the struggle between popular masses and all kinds of aristocracies, whether based on wealth or on hereditary rights. I thought that these aristocracies would ultimately emerge stronger than any monarch, as was true in England, that they represented the main obstacle to the prosperity of the state, and that they could be removed only by a republican form of government. Developments in Naples, Spain, and Portugal then exerted a profound influence on me. I found in them the irrefutable proof of the instability of monarchial constitutions and sufficient causes for distrusting the sincerity of the monarchs who accepted them. The latter considerations greatly strengthened my republican and revolutionary thinking.

From all that has been said, the Committee will note that I was influenced in developing my views by reading of books, by thinking of various developments, and also by exchanging my ideas with those of other members of the Society. All this led me to become a convinced republican, and I could not visualize any greater prosperity or higher aspiration for Russia than a republican form of government. When I discussed this problem with other members of the Society who asked my thoughts, visualizing the whole picture of happiness which Russia, in our judgment, would then enjoy, we all were excited to the point of ecstasy, and I and the other members were willing not only to agree to try everything but to do everything possible to strengthen and realize our system. We were very cautious to remove or to prevent every form of political chaos, disorder, or civil war, which I always considered to be an implacable enemy.

Having openly and candidly presented the development of my liberal and free-thinking ideas, it is appropriate now to add that during the entire year 1825 my ideas became weak and I began to view things somewhat differently. It was, however, too late to turn back. I could not write the *Russkaia Pravda* [Russian Justice] as easily as before. They demanded that I finish it. I tried, but the work produced no results and I did not write anything during the entire year, but only corrected here and there what had already been written before. I was very frightened of civil war and internal chaos, and this problem cooled me off as it did also our aim. In our conversations I still would get excited, but only for a short time; everything was different than it formerly was. Finally, the fear that our Society had been discovered by the government brought me back into the movement. I did nothing serious, however, and remained with the regiment in complete inactivity until my arrest [on December 25, 1825]. . . .

In 1816 or 1817—I do not recall exactly where—during a discussion about the [Welfare] Society with me and Nikita Muraviev, [M. S.] Lunin spoke of executing a regicide on the road to Tsarkoe Selo, to be carried out by a group of masked members when the time should arrive to start the action. Whether Lunin or Nikita Muraviev informed anyone else about this I truly do not know. During meetings of the Society itself, Lunin's suggestion was never mentioned while I was present. I paid no attention to this suggestion at the moment because I thought that the time to begin a revolution was quite distant, and because I believed that it was first essential to prepare a constitution, and then write various decrees and regulations so that simultaneously with the outbreak of the revolution the new order could be fully introduced. I did not yet entertain any idea of a provisional government. On account of my beliefs, Lunin facetiously suggested that I planned to write an encyclopedia first and then start a revolution.

I was preoccupied with the elaboration of my constitution, more than with the realization of a revolution itself, though I frequently gave thoughts to that problem as well.

In conclusion I would like to state before the Committee that all the inadequacies that the Committee has noticed or may notice [in my testimony] are exclusively my own. They stem either from my perplexity or from lack of memory. They are not by-products of dishonesty, because with all my fortitude I have always tried to present all the facts very frankly and am now undeniably prepared to reveal everything that pertains to me. The proof that I always did everything candidly has never been more strongly demonstrated than now.

A Manifesto of Prince Trubetskoi

Lord save Thy people and give [them] Thy blessing.

A Manifesto of the Senate makes hereby known that:

1. The old government has been overthrown.

2. A Provisional Government has assumed authority, pending elections and formation of a new government.

From *Vosstanie dekabristov. Materialy* (The Decembrist Uprising. Sources) (Moscow-Leningrad: Gosizdat, 1925), vol. 1, pp. 107–108. Translation mine. Words in brackets are mine.

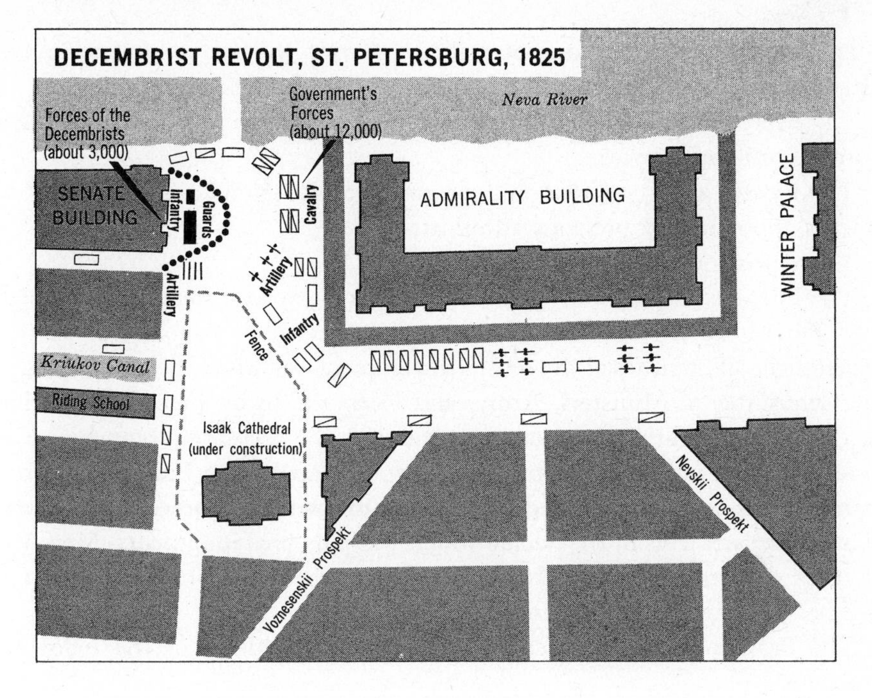

3. Freedom of the press [is hereby established] and accordingly censorship is abolished.

4. Freedom of religious worship is extended to all religious faiths.

5. Slavery is [hereby] abolished.

6. Equality before the law of all social strata [is hereby established], and accordingly military courts and all kinds of judicial commissions whose decisions are brought before civil courts are hereby abolished.

7. Every citizen has the right to make such a living as he wants, and therefore a nobleman, a merchant, city inhabitant, and a peasant have the right to serve in the army, civil service, clergy, and engage in wholesale or retail trade upon payment of established sales taxes. [Everyone] has the right to acquire property such as land and homes in cities as well as villages. [Everyone] has the right to enter into relations with another and bring him [in case of a violation] before the court of justice.

8. Collection of soul taxes is hereby discontinued.

9. Monopolies on salt and hard liquor are hereby abolished, and accordingly free distilling and salt extraction is established with a tax on the amount of salt and of vodka produced.

10. Recruiting systems and military colonies are hereby abolished.

11. Reduction of the military service for lower social ranks is hereby es-

tablished. The exact amount of military service will be set following the equalization of military obligation among all social strata.

12. Everyone without exception who has served fifteen years will be released from the military service.

13. *Volost, uezd, gubernia* and *oblast* administrations are to replace all officials appointed by previous administration.

14. Open courts are hereby established.

15. Introduction of jurors in criminal and civil courts is hereby established.

A Provisional Government of two or three persons is established. To this government all branches of the central government—all Ministries, the Council, the Committee of Ministers, Army, and Fleet—are to be subordinated; that is, the entire executive but not the judicial or the legislative branches. The judicial branch will have its own ministry, subject to the Provisional Government, but cases not decided by lower courts will be handled by civil and criminal departments of the Senate which will pass final judgments. Members of these departments, until the new elected government shall take control, will be the same as they are now.

The Provisional Government is charged with solution of the following problems:

1. Equalization of the rights of all layers of society.
2. Organization of local *volost, uezd, gubernia* and *oblast* administrations.
3. Organization of domestic militia.
4. Organization of the judicial branch of the government with jurors.
5. Equalization of recruiting obligations among all social strata.
6. Abolition of the permanent army.
7. Devising of a system of election for the legislative branch, whose members will decide on the composition of the government and the nature of the fundamental law.

A. S. Pushkin's Poem, "To Siberia," Honoring the Decembrists, 1827

Deep in the Siberian mines,
Keep your patience proud;
Your bitter toil shall not be lost,
Your noble thought will remain unbowed.

Source: A. S. Pushkin, *Polnoe sobranie sochinenii* (Moscow: 1936), vol. II, p. 24. Translation mine.

Hope, the true companion of human fate,
In your gloomy dungeon's cells,
Will awaken your courage and joy,
And the welcome day will come.

Love and friendship will then reach you,
Through the gloomy dungeon bars;
The same way my free voice is now reaching you,
In your current prison cells.

Then the heavy chains will fall,
The dungeons will crumble at a word;
And freedom will greet you at the gate,
And brothers will give you back the sword.

A. I. Odoevskii's Response to A. S. Pushkin's Poem, 1827

The ardent sounds of your prophetic words
Have reached our ears;
Our hands reached out for swords,
But were stopped by heavy chains.

You, bard, be assured that we
Are proud of our fate;
And behind the prison gate
Continue to defy the tsars as before.

Our bitter toil will not be lost!
From a spark a fame will grow,
And our well-informed people
Will gather under the sacred banner.

Then we will forge swords from our chains,
Will rekindle the flame of freedom,
Will surprise and challenge the tsars,
And all nations will sigh with joy!

Source: A. I. Odoevskii, "Stikhotvoreniia," *Sovetskii pisatel,* 1936, p. 44. Translation mine.

31

Russian Treatment of their Siberian Subjects

One of the most momentous historic, economic, political, cultural and geopolitical events in Russian history was Moscow's conquest of northern Asia. That conquest not only brought under Moscow's control a vast territory, rich in natural resources and inhabited by peoples of diverse ethnic backgrounds and cultures, but it also transformed the hitherto East European, Orthodox, Slavic, Muscovite state into a powerful, multinational and multicultural Eurasian Russian colonial empire.

Initially, that is, in the seventeenth and eighteenth centuries, the Russians exploited indiscriminately the peoples and resources of their newly-acquired colonial empire. That practice soon produced many undersirable results, however, including massive native discontent, which forced the Russians to adopt new *modus operandi.* The new rules, some of which are reproduced below, were formulated by leading statesman Mikhail M. Speranskii (1772–1839) and they remained in force throughout the entire nineteenth century.

Regulations Governing Natives of Siberia, July 22, 1822

PART I.
RIGHTS OF INDIGENOUS NATIVES

Chapter I.
Divisions of Indigenous Natives

1. All native tribes inhabiting Siberia, which until now have officially been called the *iasak–paying people*, are henceforth, on the basis of their diverse levels of education and their current way of life, divided into three basic categories. The first includes the settled peoples, that is those who live in settlements and towns; the second encompasses nomads who live in specific regions but who annually move from one place to another; and the third includes migratory peoples or hunters who are constantly on the move along the rivers and overland.

Source: *Polnoe Sobranie Zakonov,* First Series, vol. XXXVIII, No. 29,126, pp. 394–417. Translation mine.

2. The first category, or settled natives, includes: a) [Russian] subject merchants of Bokhara and Tashkent and their agents; b) agricultural Tatars and Bukhtarmintsy and several former *iasak-paying* native tribes of Biisk and Kuznetsk krai; c) small numbers of [native] families who live alongside Russian settlers; and d) indigenous natives who have lived with and worked for Russian settlers for a long time.

3. The second category, or nomadic natives, includes: a) nomadic agriculturist Buriat, Khorinsk, Seleginsk, Alarsk, Kudinsk and Verkholensk natives and several Kochin tribes and a portion of other former *iasak–paying peoples* of the Biisk and Kuznetsk region; b) southern cattle herders and *promyshlenniki* [trappers and hunters], namely the Sagai and such Biisk and Kuznetsk *iasak–paying* Buriats as: Tunkinsk, Kitoisk, and Olkhonsk as well as the Nizhneudinsk Buriats and Tungus, the Nerchinsk natives, the Seleginsk Tungus and others; and c) such northern reindeer herders and hunters as the Iakuts, the Narym Ostiaks, natives of the Berezovo and Ob region, the Pelym Voguls, and the Tungus of the Enisei, Ob, Barguzin, Kiren and other areas.

Note: Nomadic Kirghiz-Kaisaks are included in the category of nomadic natives, but they are governed by their own special charters.

4. The third category of indigenous natives or migratory hunters includes: the Obdorsk Samoeds, the Turukhan and Karaga natives, natives of the lower Iakutsk oblast, namely, the Koriaks, the Iukagirs, the Lamuts and other natives of the Okhotsk, Gizhinga and Kamchatka regions.

5. Because their relations with the Russians differ from that of other Siberian natives, the Chukchi and the Zhiungorsk tribute payers form a special category.

6. Natives of the Kuril and the Aleutian archipelago, as well as coastal inhabitants of North America who currently are subjects of the Russian-American Company, also form a special category.

7. Based on this general division the indigenous natives have the following rights and obligations:. . . .

Chapter II.
General Rights of Settled Natives

12. Settled natives who profess Christian faith are not distinguished in any way from Russians. Those among them who profess paganism or Islam are known as settled natives of different faith [*ossedlye inovertsy*] to differentiate them from the rest.

13. All other settled natives have the same rights and obligations as the corresponding Russian classes. They are governed in accordance with general laws and regulations. . . .

Chapter IV.
The Rights of Settled Agriculturists

17. All natives of different faiths who live in their own settlements and are engaged in their own settlements and are engaged in their own agriculture are included in the category of [Russian] state peasants.

18. These natives of different faiths are subject to the same taxes and obligations [as are Russian state peasants], but they are freed from military service.

19. Those among the natives of different faiths who are known as cossacks remain in the cossack group, and they are governed by a special cossack code.

20. Properties, which the natives of different faiths currently have, belong to them in accordance with their ancient rights. Those among them who have an insufficient amount of land should receive parcels from the nearby empty lands, as provided by regulations governing state peasants. . . .

Chapter V.
General Rights of Nomadic Natives

24. Nomadic natives comprise a special category, similar to peasants, but are subject to a different form of administration.

25. These natives enjoy their ancient rights. They should be informed that, with the expansion of agriculture, they will not be included against their will in the category of peasants, and that, without their own request, they will not be assigned to any other category.

26. Nomadic natives who profess different faiths have at their disposal specially designated properties for each of their generations.

27. The distribution of these properties is to be apportioned by the nomads themselves in accordance with the fair share rule or their other customs. . . .

29. Nomadic natives have full freedom to engage in agriculture, livestock herding, and other local enterprises, based on water or land that [Russian authorities] have allocated to them. . . .

34. Nomadic natives are administered by their own tribal leaders who comprise their local administration.

35. All nomads are administered in accordance with local laws and customs of their tribes.

36. In all criminal cases, all nomads are to be tried in Russian courts in accordance with the prevailing state laws.

37. Criminal cases pertaining to the indigenous natives are: sedition, premeditated murder, theft and violence, counterfeiting, and, in general appropriation of Treasury and public property. . . .

40. Nomads are subject to all regulations of *gubernia* authorities as provided in a special regulation.

41. All nomads are obligated to fulfill the terms of their charters.

42. All nomads are freed from military service.

43. Cossack regiments that have been organized among the nomads for the purpose of protecting [Russian] frontiers are governed by their old regulations. . . .

Chapter VI.
Rights of Migratory Natives

61. Rights of migratory natives or hunters who live far away from inhabited places are, in general, the same as those enjoyed by other nomads.

62. The following are exceptions and limitations:

a) All migratory natives are excluded from owning special tribal lands and from owning designated parcels of that land. Wherever possible they will receive large sections of territory that will extend to the lands inhabited by the settled people or by other migratory natives;

b) Nomadic natives will not be subject to any financial levies by *gubernia* authorities and they will not pay any taxes to maintain the Steppe Administration;

c) In regions they inhabit, all migratory natives are free to move for hunting purposes from one *uezd* to another and from one *gubernia* to another without any interference by Russian or tribal authorities.

Chapter VII.
Native Titles

63. All natives, who within their tribes have such titles as: princeling, *toion, taisha, zaisan, shulenga,* and the like, may keep and use them in areas where their customs and steppe laws prevail.

64. Hereditary titles are to remain hereditary; elective titles are to remain elective. . . .

32

Reactionary and Repressive Policies of Nicholas I

The reign of Emperor Nicholas I (1825–1855) is best remembered for its anti-revolutionary spirit abroad and its quasi-military dictatorship at home. The dictatorship expressed itself in various forms, ranging from extensive use of ad hoc secret committees to suppression of all forms of dissent. Authorities dealt harshly with not only the Decembrists, but also with peasants, intellectuals, and national and religious minorities. These measures, however, failed to produce the desired results. The harsh treatment of the Decembrists, for example, produced a generation of dedicated followers. The firm stand on maintaining serfdom resulted in over 700 peasant uprisings, half of them serious enough to require the deployment of military forces to suppress them. Censorship of intellectuals and of the press gave birth to student circles, "thick journals," and the "Golden Age" of Russian literature. Finally, official attempts to impose Russian values on the non-Russian peoples of the empire led to the emergence of local nationalisms. In short, the reactionary and repressive policies of Nicholas I were a disaster because they ran counter to Russia's national and vital interests.

Nicholas I's Manifesto on Peasant Unrest, May 2, 1826

Governors have called to Our attention that in some settlements peasants of the state and of the nobility, misled by malicious rumors and evil talk, digress from normal order and think that the former, that is, state peasants, will be freed from tax payments, while the latter, that is, peasants of the nobility, [will be freed] from their obligations to their masters.

Feeling sorry about the misleading of these villagers, and wishing to direct them to the truth by means of the kindness natural to Our fatherly mercy, I am ordering announced everywhere:

1. That all talk about freedom of state peasants from the payment of taxes and of the nobility peasants and household people from obligations to their

---

From *Polnoe Sobranie Zakonov Russkoi Imperii . . . (Complete Collection of the Laws of the Russian Empire)* 2nd series, vol. 1, no. 330, p.455. Translation mine. Words in brackets are mine.

masters is a malicious rumor conceived and spread by ill-intended people for a profit motive, that is, to enrich themselves at peasant expense.

2. All social strata within the state, including state and nobility peasants and household people, should fulfill all of their obligations according to the law and obey their appointed superiors submissively.

3. After this declaration has been published, should there occur among state or nobility peasants or household people some disturbance based on a false rumor about freedom from payment of taxes or legal authority of the nobility, the guilty ones will invite Our anger and will be punished immediately to the fullest severity of the law.

4. Governors are hereby authorized to keep continuous vigilance and to bring the spreaders of such rumors or talk before the court without delay and deal with them likewise to the fullest severity of the law.

5. And inasmuch as We have received weekly petitions from peasants written on the basis of the above mentioned rumors and talk, to terminate this evil and to preserve safety and order, We decree that the composers or writers of such petitions be brought before the court as disturbers of general peace and punished to the fullest severity of the law.

The Governing Senate will make an appropriate regulation for the publication of Our order for universal knowledge, causing it to be read in churches on Sundays and Holy Days, at fairs and markets for a period of six months from the day this manifesto is received in the *gubernia.* Governors are, in addition, instructed to keep continuous vigilance in execution of Our order, as they will be personally responsible for any disorder that may occur.

Nicholas

A Memorandum to Emperor Nicholas I from Admiral A. S. Shishkov Concerning his Views on Censorship, December 12, 1826

Most Merciful Sovereign!

Everyone knows and no one doubts that the French Revolution, which occurred at the end of the last century, was prepared and was caused by inadequate governmental supervision of book publishing. The prime reason for this was the presence [in France] of highly educated and at the same time most impious individuals, namely, Voltaire, D'Alembert, Diderot and many others. Their sharp minds and their trenchant pens, agitated by a sense of

Source: *Chteniia v obshchestve istorii i drevnostei rossiiskikh,* vol. III (1868), pp. 121–27. Translation mine.

pride and selfishness, implanted seeds which, when ripened, multiplied free thought and immorality and then destroyed the faith and the throne. After it suffered great privation, weary France recognized its mistake and returned to its religion and government. Someone has said, erroneously to be sure, that while it died in France, the French Revolution, nevertheless, will not be extinguished until it has affected all other nations. We already have witnessed the result of this prophecy [in 1820] in Spain, in Naples, and in other countries.

Russia was unaffected by it in the past. However, we are now seeing some signs of this plague. Loose talk, which never existed here about religion, freedom, and government, has multiplied sects and dissidents among us, has stirred up common people, and has implanted in the inexperienced heads and hearts of young people the audacity to form a governmental system based on their dreams. This has been verified not only by rumors but by real events. Many developments and reports show that free thinking and atheism is on the rise. . . .

We are witnessing now things that did not exist before; namely, frequent incitement of peasants against nobles and the resolute demand for freedom which, in their view, consists of parasitic behavior and licentiousness. We have witnessed with horror the development of last December [1825]. Its participants were not common people, but officials, princes, nobles, and writers, who called themselves enlightened, who were endowed with keen minds and a worldly outlook. There developed—and I would like to emphasize it—a treasonous and ill-intentioned phenomenon based on delusion and unbelief and which had never existed among the people belonging to that class. . . . In France, as well as among us, all of them stemmed from the circulation and reading of mystic, immoral books and journals, which, because of the lack of proper review, passed the weak system of censorship.

To stop this trend, the Sovereign Emperor of blessed memory [that is, Alexander I] was pleased to appoint me as Minister of Public Education [in January, 1824] with the understanding that I would erect a barrier against the entrenched and gradually spreading evil known as *the spirit of the time.* He empowered me to do it with these strong words. The *ukaz* he gave me stated, among other things: "I am authorizing you to begin a resolute supervision [of publications] so that in the works that have already been published and in those that may be published in the future, as well as in translations [of foreign books], especially those intended *to be used in schools,* there be included nothing that would disturb our faith and morals. National well-being could suffer a great deal from this [disturbance] and, therefore, you are obligated before God and Us to employ indefatigable supervision in eliminating and exposing all evil thoughts that are currently being disseminated through books, and you are not to allow them to appear in any form in the future. . . ."

I do not know whether in these difficult times and circumstances the existing weak censorship that has allowed this to happen should continue to function, or whether I should submit for Your Majesty's approval a new set of strict censorship rules that would erect barriers to evil thoughts without endangering the content of morally-written literary works. In the previous censorship code there was an article providing that if there was a double meaning [in the text of a work], the author was favored; that is, it allowed every evil-minded writer, by using clever skills, to disseminate dishonesty and lewdness freely. Whether similar provisions should be incorporated in the revised Code, which is currently being prepared, or whether they should be deleted altogether, it is imperative that every precaution be taken to make impossible in the future the development of any nation-wide disturbances. . . .

A Restriction on Educational Opportunities for Nonprivileged Members of Russian Society, August 1827

It has been brought to Our attention that serfs belonging to rural nobles and to [well-to-do] peasants frequently are allowed to study in *gymnasia* and other institutions of higher learning. This practice causes two-fold harm. On the one hand, these young people, after receiving elementary schooling from their masters or from their careless relatives, enter institutions of higher learning with harmful habits which they then either transmit to their classmates, or else they prevent children of diligent parents from attending those institutions.

On the other hand, depending on their academic progress, the capable youngsters of this group become exposed to a life, thoughts, and ideas that are beyond their social status. The resulting burden becomes unbearable for them and they frequently fall into a dangerous depresion or develop low self-esteem. To prevent these harmful tendencies from developing in the future, We feel obligated to decree as follows:

1. That in all universities and all other institutions of higher learning, both state and private, which are under the jurisdiction of the Ministry of Public Education, as well as in *gymnasia* and similar institutions of instruction, only members of [the legally] free classes be allowed to attend lectures. This rule applies to those who currently are registered in the free category and who are able to provide satisfactory evidence [concerning their free status], even though

Source: *Polnoe Sobranie Zakonov,* Second Series, vol. II, No. 1,308, pp. 675–7. Translation mine.

they may not yet have been assigned to the category of merchants or townsmen or have a [bona fide] profession.

2. Serfs belonging to nobles or household serfs are allowed as before to attend church and *uezd* schools as well as private institutions of learning whose curricular offerings are identical with those of *uezd* schools.

3. Serfs may be allowed to attend special institutions of learning that have already been founded or that may be established for them in the future either by the state or by private individuals, where they may study agriculture, horticulture, or skills essential to their well-being so they can then improve agricultural, handicraft, and other enterprises. In these institutions the following restrictions will apply to them: subject matters that are not essential to mastering crafts and industrial know-how are to be the same as those taught in *uezd* schools.

33

The Eastern Question, 1828–1833

The reign of Nicholas I (1825–1855) is best remembered for his suppression of the Decembrists, the subsequent maintenance of autocratic firmness at home, and his preoccupation with the Eastern Question in the realm of foreign policy. By Eastern Question is meant Russia's attempt to dislodge the Ottoman control of the Balkan peninsula and of the Straits and replace it with Russian control. It was not a new policy because its foundations were laid down in the Treaty of Kutchuk Kainardzhi in 1774. Nicholas I sought to obtain the objectives of this policy with greater vigor and determination than did his predecessors. He involved Russia in a major war against the Ottoman Turks in 1828, and in the Treaty of Adrianople extracted numerous concessions from them. In 1833

The following selected documents depicting Russian interest in the Eastern Question were taken from Sir Edward Hertslet, *The Map of Europe by Treaty . . .* (London: Butterworth, Harrison and Sons, 1875), II, pp. 813–823, 925–928. To facilitate reading and recognition the spelling of certain names has been modernized. Thus, Servia has been rendered throughout as Serbia. In other cases modern geographical spellings have been placed in parenthesis wherever they differ from the original.

he gained additional advantages for Russia through negotiations that culminated in the Treaty of Unkiar Skelessi. Finally, to dislodge Ottoman power in the area completely, he involved Russia from 1853 to 1856 in a major war, the Crimean War, not only against the Turks, but the French and the British as well. The Crimean War ended in a great disaster and humiliation for Russia.

The Treaty of Adrianople, September 14, 1829

Article 1

All hostility and dissention which, up to the present time, have existed between the two Empires shall cease from the date hereof, as well by land as by sea, and there shall be perpetual Peace, amity, and good intelligence between His Majesty the Emperor and Padisha of All the Russias, and His Highness the Emperor and Padisha of the Ottomans, their heirs and successors to the Throne, as well as between their respective Empires. The two High Contracting Powers will employ a special attention for preventing all that may cause the renewal of any misunderstanding between their respective subjects. They will scrupulously fulfill all the conditions of the present Treaty of Peace, and will use all their vigilance to prevent its being contravened in any manner, either directly or indirectly.

Article 2

His Majesty the Emperor and Padisha of All the Russias, desirous of giving His Highness the Emperor and Padisha of the Ottomans a proof of the sincerity of his amicable disposition, restores to the Sublime Porte the Principality of Moldavia, with the same limits which that Principality had before the commencement of the War which has just been terminated by the present Treaty. His Imperial Majesty likewise restores the Principality of Wallachia, the Banat of Crajova (Craiova), without any exception whatsoever, Bulgaria and the country of Dobrudgia (Dobrudzha), from the Danube as far as to the sea, . . . and lastly, all the cities, towns, and villages, and, in general, all the places which the Russian troops have occupied in Rumelia.

Article 3

The Pruth shall continue to form the Boundary of the two Empires, from the point where that River touches the Territory of Moldavia as far as its confluence with the Danube. From this place the frontier line shall follow the course of the Danube as far as the embouchure of St. George, so that while leaving all the Islands formed by the different branches of this River in the possession of Russia, the right bank will remain, as heretofore, in that of the Ottoman Porte. . . . The merchant-vessels of the two Powers shall be competent to navigate the Danube throughout its whole course, and those which bear the Ottoman flag may freely enter the Kilia and Souline (Sulina) embouchures, that of St. George remaining common to the war and merchant flags of the two Contracting Powers. But the Russian Ships of War must not, in sailing up the Danube, go beyond the place of its junction with the Pruth.

Article 4

Georgia, Imeritia, Mingrelia, Gouriel (Guria), and several other provinces of the Caucasus, having been for a long time and in perpetuity annexed to the Empire of Russia, and this Empire having moreover acquired by the Treaty concluded with Persia at Tourkmantchai (Turkmanchai), on the 10th–22nd of February, 1828, the Khanates of Erivan (Erevan) and Naktchivan (Nakhichevan), the two High Contracting Powers have been convinced of the necessity of establishing between their respective States, throughout the whole of this line, a well-defined frontier and such as shall prevent all future misunderstanding. . . . In consequence whereof it has been agreed to recognize henceforth for the frontier between the States of the Imperial Court of Russia and those of the Sublime Ottoman Porte in Asia, the line which, following the present boundary of the Province of Gouriel (Guria), from the Black Sea, ascends to that of Imeritia, and thence in the most direct line to the point where the frontiers of the Pashalics of Akhaltzik (Akhaltsikhe) and of Kars unite with those of Georgia, leaving, in this manner, to the north and within this line the city of Akhaltzik (Akhaltsikhe) and the fort of Alkhalkhaliki (Akhalkalaki), at a distance which must not be less than two hours. All the countries situated to the south and west of this line of demarcation towards the Pashalics of Kars and of Trebizond, together with the greater part of the Pashalic of Akhaltzik (Akhaltsikhe), shall remain in perpetuity under the dominion of the Sublime Porte, whilst those which are situated to the north and east of the said line, towards Georgia, Imeritia, and Gouriel (Guria), as well as the whole of the coast of the Black Sea, from the mouth of the Kouban (Kuban) as far as the port of St. Nicholas inclusively, shall remain in perpetuity under the dominion of the Empire of Russia. . . .

Article 5

The Principalities of Moldavia and Wallachia having been in consequence of a Capitulation placed under the Suzerainty of the Sublime Porte, and Russia having guaranteed their prosperity, it is understood that they shall preserve all the privileges and immunities which have been granted to them either by their Capitulations, or by the Treaties concluded between the two Empires, or by the Hatti-Sherifs promulgated at different times. In consequence whereof, they shall enjoy the free exercise of their Worship, perfect security, an independent national Government and full liberty of Commerce. . . .

Article 6

The circumstances which have occurred since the conclusion of the Convention of Akkermann, not having allowed the Sublime Porte to occupy itself immediately with the carrying into execution the clauses of the Separate Act relative to Serbia, and annexed to Article 5 of the said Convention; it undertakes in the most solemn manner to fulfill them without the least delay, and with the most scrupulous exactitude, and to proceed especially to the immediate restitution of the six districts detached from Serbia, so as to secure forever the tranquility and welfare of that faithful and devoted nation. . . .

Article 7

Russian subjects shall enjoy, throughout the whole extent of the Ottoman Empire, as well by land as by sea, the full and entire freedom of trade secured to them by the Treaties concluded heretofore between the two High Contracting Powers. This freedom of trade shall not be molested in any way, nor shall it be fettered in any case, or under any pretext, by any prohibition or restriction whatsoever, nor in consequence of any regulation or measure, whether of public government or internal legislation. Russian subjects, ships, and merchandise shall be protected from all violence and imposition. The first shall remain under the exclusive jurisdiction and control of the Russian Minister and Consuls; Russian ships shall never be subjected to any search on the part of the Ottoman authorities, neither out at sea nor in any of the ports or roadsteads under the dominion of the Sublime Porte; and all merchandise or goods belonging to a Russian subject may, after payment of the Customhouse dues imposed by the tariffs, be freely sold, deposited on land in the warehouses of the owner or consignee, or transshipped on board another vessel of any nation whatsoever, without the Russian subject being required, in this case, to give notice of the same to any of the local authorities, and much less to ask their permission so to do. It is expressly agreed that the different kinds of wheat coming from Russia shall partake of the same privileges, and that their free transit shall never, under any pretext, suffer the least difficulty or hindrance.

The Sublime Porte engages, moreover, to take especial care that the trade and navigation of the Black Sea, particularly, shall be impeded in no manner whatsoever. For this purpose it admits and declares the passage of the Strait of Constantinople and that of the Dardanelles to be entirely free and open to Russian vessels under the merchant flag, laden or in ballast, whether they come from the Black Sea for the purpose of entering the Mediterranean, or whether, coming from the Mediterranean, they wish to enter the Black Sea: such vessels, provided they be merchant ships, whatever their size and tonnage, shall be exposed to no hindrance or annoyance of any kind, as above provided. The two Courts shall agree upon the most fitting means for preventing all delay in issuing the necessary instructions. In virtue of the same principle the passage of the Strait of Constantinople and of that of the Dardanelles is declared free and open to all the merchant ships of Powers who are at Peace with the Sublime Porte, whether going into the Russian ports of the Black Sea or coming from them, laden or in ballast, upon the same conditions which are stipulated for vessels under the Russian flag.

Lastly, the Sublime Porte, recognizing in the Imperial Court of Russia the right of securing the necessary guarantees for this full freedom of trade and navigation in the Black Sea, declares solemnly, that on its part not the least obstacle shall ever, under any pretext whatsoever, be opposed to it. Above all, it promises never to allow itself henceforth to stop or detain vessels laden or in ballast, whether Russian or belonging to nations with whom the Ottoman Porte should not be in a state of declared war, which vessels shall be passing through the Strait of Constantinople and that of the Dardanelles, on their way from the Black Sea into the Mediterranean, or from the Mediterranean into the Russian ports of the Black Sea. And if, which God forbid, any one of the stipulations contained in the present Article should be infringed, and the remonstrances of the Russian Minister thereupon should fail in obtaining a full and prompt redress, the Sublime Porte recognizes beforehand in the Imperial Court of Russia the right of considering such an infraction as an act of hostility, and of immediately having recourse to reprisals against the Ottoman Empire. . . .

Article 14

All the Prisoners of War, of whatsoever nation, condition, and sex they may be, who are in the two Empires, must, immediately after the exchange of the Ratifications of the present Treaty of Peace, be delivered up and restored without the least ransom or payment. Exception is made in favour of the Christians who, of their own free will, have embraced the Mahometan religion, in the States of the Sublime Porte, and of the Mahometans, who in like manner, of their own free will, have embraced the Christian religion in the States of the Empire of Russia.

The same shall be observed with respect to the Russian Subjects, who, after the signing of the present Treaty of Peace, may have, in any manner, fallen into captivity, and who are in the States of the Sublime Porte. The

Imperial Court of Russia promises, on its part, to act in the same manner towards the subjects of the Sublime Porte.

No reimbursement of the sums which have been expended by the High Contracting Powers for the maintenance of the Prisoners of War, shall be required. Each of them shall provide all that is necessary for them during their journey to the frontier, where they will be exchanged by Commissioners appointed respectively.

Article 15

All the Treaties, Conventions, and Stipulations, entered into and concluded at different epochs, between the Imperial Court of Russia and the Sublime Ottoman Porte, excepting the Articles which have been modified or changed by the Present Treaty of Peace, are confirmed in all their force and integrity, and the two High Contracting Powers engage to observe them religiously and inviolably. . . .

The Treaty of Unkiar Skelessi, July 8, 1833

In the name of Almighty God.

His Imperial Majesty, the Most High and Most Mighty Emperor and Autocrat of All the Russias, and His Highness the Most High and Most Mighty Emperor of the Ottomans, being equally animated with the sincere desire of maintaining the system of peace and good harmony happily established between the two Empires, have resolved to extend and strengthen the perfect friendship and confidence which reign between them by the conclusion of a Treaty of Defensive Alliance. . . .

Article 1

There shall be for ever Peace, Amity, and Alliance between His Majesty the Emperor of All the Russias and His Majesty the Emperor of the Ottomans, their Empires and Their Subjects, as well by land as by sea. This Alliance having solely for its object the common defence of their dominions against all attack, their Majesties engage to come to an unreserved understanding with each other upon all the matters which concern their respective tranquility and safety, and to afford to each other mutually for this purpose substantial aid, and the most efficacious assistance.

Article 2

The Treaty of Peace concluded at Adrianople on the 14th September, 1829, as well as all the other Treaties comprised therein, as also the Convention signed at St. Petersburg on the 26th April, 1830 and the Arrangement relating to Greece, concluded at Constantinople on the 21st July, 1832, are fully confirmed by the present Treaty of Defensive Alliance, in the same manner as if the said transactions had been inserted in it word for word.

Article 3

In consequence of the principle of conservation and mutual defence, which is the basis of the present Treaty of Alliance, and by reason of a most sincere desire of securing the permanence, maintenance, and entire Independence of the Sublime Porte, His Majesty the Emperor of All the Russias, in the event of circumstances occuring which should again determine the Sublime Porte to call for the naval and military assistance of Russia, although, if it please God, that case is by no means likely to happen, engages to furnish, by land and by sea, as many troops and forces as the two High Contracting Parties may deem necessary. It is accordingly agreed, that in this case the Land and Sea Forces, whose aid the Sublime Porte may call for, shall be held at its disposal.

Article 4

In conformity with what is above stated, in the event of one of the two Powers requesting the assistance of the other, the expense only of provisioning the Land and the Sea Forces which may be furnished, shall fall to the charge of the Power who shall have applied for the aid.

Article 5

Although the two High Contracting Parties sincerely intend to maintain this engagement to the most distant period of time, yet, as it is possible that in process of time circumstances may require that some changes should be made in this Treaty, it has been agreed to fix its duration at eight years from the day of the exchange of Imperial Ratifications. The two parties, previous to the expiration of that term, will concert together, according to the state of affairs at that time, as to the renewal of the said Treaty.

Separate Article

In virtue of one of the clauses of Article 1 of the Patent Treaty of Defensive Alliance concluded between the Imperial Court of Russia and the Sublime Porte, the two High Contracting Parties are bound to afford to each other mutually substantial aid, and the most efficacious assistance for the safety of their respective dominions. Nevertheless, His Majesty the Emperor of All the Russias, wishing to spare the Sublime Ottoman Porte the expense and inconvenience which might be occasioned to it by affording substantial aid, will not ask for that aid if circumstances should place the Sublime Porte under the obligation of furnishing it, the Sublime Ottoman Porte, in place of the aid which it is bound to furnish in case of need, according to the principle of reciprocity of the Patent Treaty, shall confine its action in favour of the Imperial Court of Russia to closing the Strait of the Dardanelles, that is to say, to not allowing any Foreign Vessels of War to enter therein under any pretext whatsoever. . . .

34

Chaadaev's Comments on Russian History and Culture

Peter Ia. Chaadaev (1794–1856) came from an influential noble background. Although young, he participated in the War of 1812, and, upon its conclusion he became fascinated, as did many of his contemporaries, by the movement that eventually culminated in the Decembrist Revolt. He was not an active participant in the movement; in fact, during the mushrooming of the conspiracy, Chaadaev was in Western Europe, which was then engulfed in romanticism, liberalism, and an assortment of other "isms."

Because he sympathized with the Decembrists, Russian authorities arrested Chaadaev upon his return to Russia in 1826, but released him for lack of evidence of any apparent involvement in the conspiracy. Chaadaev then settled in Moscow where, thanks to his writings, he emerged as one of Russia's most controversial nineteenth century thinkers. His literary heritage is modest. It consists of a few essays and a number of letters—all written in French, "the language of polite and polished society." Chaadaev became an instant sensation in 1836 when the Moscow *Telescope* published one of his letters in which he praised West European experience and criticized Russian history and its Orthodox–influenced culture. Authorities suppressed the journal, exiled its editor, dismissed

---

Source: Reprinted by permission of The University of Tennessee Press. From Peter Yakovlevich Chaadayev, *Philosophical Letters and Apology of a Madman.* Translated with an Introduction by Mary-Barbara Zeldin (Knoxville, Tennessee: The University of Tennessee Press, 1969), pp. 34–43.

the censor, and, on Nicholas I's order, declared Chaadaev insane and placed him under police and medical supervision for a year.

Peter Ia. Chaadaev's Critical Comments on Russian History and Culture, 1829

. . . One of the worst features of our unique civilization is that we have not yet discovered truths that have elsewhere become truisms, even among nations that in many respects are far less advanced than we are. It is the result of our never having walked side by side with other nations; we belong to none of the great families of mankind; we are neither of the West nor of the East, and we possess the traditions of neither. Somehow divorced from time, we have not been touched by the universal education of mankind. That wonderful interconnection of human ideas in the succession of the centuries, that history of the human mind which brought man to the state in which he is today in the rest of the world, has had no influence upon us. That which elsewhere has long constituted the foundation of society and life is still for us but theory and speculation. . . .

Look about you. Don't you think that we are very restless? We all resemble travelers. Nobody has a definite sphere of existence; we have no proper habits; there are no rules, there is no home life, there is nothing to which we could be attached, nothing that would awaken our sympathy or affection—nothing durable, nothing lasting; everything flows, everything passes, leaving no traces either outside or within you. In our own houses we seem to be camping, in our families we look like strangers, in our cities we look like nomads, even more than the nomads who tend their herds on our steppes, for they are more attached to their wastelands than we to our cities. And do not think that this is not important, Poor souls that we are, let us not add to our other afflictions that of not understanding ourselves, let us not aspire to the existence of pure intelligences; let us learn to live sensibly within our given reality. But, first, let us talk a while longer about our country; this will not lead us away from the subject. Without such a preamble, you could not understand what I have to say.

Every nation has its period of stormy agitation, of passionate unease, of hasty activities. In such a period men become wanderers over the world, both in body and spirit. This is a time of great passions, strong emotions, great national undertakings. At such times nations toss about violently, without any apparent object, but not without benefit for future generations. All societies have gone through such phases. Such periods provide them with their most vivid memories, their legends, their poetry, their greatest and most productive ideas; such periods represent the necessary basis of every society. Otherwise societies would have nothing valuable or cherished in memory; they would value only the dust of the earth they inhabit. This fascinating phase of the history of nations represents their adolescence, the age when their faculties develop most vigorously, and whose remembrance brings both joy and wisdom to their maturity. But we Russians, we are devoid of all this. At first brutal barbarism, then crude superstition, then cruel and humiliating foreign domination, the spirit of which was later inherited by our national rulers—such is the sad history of our youth. We had none of that period of exuberant activity, of the fervent turmoil of the moral forces of nations. Our period of social life which corresponds to this age was filled with a dull and gloomy existence, lacking in force and energy, with nothing to brighten it but crime, nothing to mitigate it but servitude. There are no charming remembrances, no graceful images in the people's memory; our national tradition is devoid of any powerful teaching. Cast a look upon the many centuries in our past, upon the expanse of soil we inhabit, and you will find no endearing reminiscence, no venerable memorial, to speak to you powerfully of the past, and to reproduce it for you in a vivid and colorful manner. We live only in the narrowest of presents, without past and without future, in the midst of a flat calm. And if we happen to bestir ourselves from time to time, it is not in the hope, nor in the desire, of some common good, but in the childish frivolousness of the infant, who raises himself and stretches his hands toward the rattle which his nurse presents to him. . . .

Our first years, spent in immobile brutishness, have left no traces on our minds; we have nothing that is ours on which to base our thinking; isolated by a strange fate from the universal development of humanity, we have also absorbed none of mankind's ideas of traditional transmission. Yet it is on those ideas that the life of nations is founded; it is from those ideas that their future develops and that their moral growth derives. If we want to have an outlook similar to that of other civilized nations, we have somehow to repeat the whole education of mankind. In this we can be assisted by the history of [other] nations, and we have before us the products of the ages. No doubt this task is difficult, and possibly it is not given to one man to exhaust this vast subject; but, first of all, we must know what we are talking about, what is this education of mankind and what is the place which we occupy in the general order of things.

Nations live but by the mighty impressions which past centuries have left in their minds and by contact with other nations. In this way every man is conscious of his ties with the whole of mankind. "What is the life of man," Cicero asked, "if the memory of past events does not come to bind the present to the past?" But we Russians, like illegitimate children, come to this world without patrimony, without any links with people who lived on the earth before us; we have in our hearts none of these lessons which have preceded our own existence. Each one of us must himself once again seek to tie the broken thread in the family. What is habit, instinct, among other peoples we must get into our heads by hammerstrokes. Our memories go no further back than yesterday; we are, as it were, strangers to ourselves. We walk through time so singly that as we advance the past escapes us forever. This is a natural result of a culture based wholly on borrowing and imitation. There is among us no inward development, no natural progress; new ideas throw out the old ones because they do not arise from the latter, but come among us from Heaven knows where. Since we accept only ready–made ideas, the indelible traces which a progressive movement of ideas engraves on the mind and which gives ideas their forcefulness makes no furrow on our intellect. We grow, but we do not mature; we advance, but obliquely, that is, in a direction which does not lead to the goal. We are like children who have never been made to think for themselves; once they have come of age they have nothing of their own; all their knowledge is on the surface of their being, their whole soul is on the outside. This is exactly our situation.

Nations are moral beings in the same way as individuals are. As years make the education of persons, so centuries make theirs. In a way, one can say that as a people we are an exception to the rule. We belong to that number of nations which do not seem to make up an integral part of the human race, but which exist only to teach the world some great lesson. The lesson which we are destined to give will, naturally, not be lost; but who knows when we shall find ourselves once again in the midst of humanity, and what afflictions we shall experience before we accomplish our destiny?

The peoples of Europe have a common aspect, a family resemblance. In spite of the general division of these peoples into Latin and Teutonic branches, into southern and northern, there is a common link which unites them into a fasces, clear to anyone who has studied their general history. You know that even recently all Europe was called Christendom, and that this word had its place in public law. In addition to this general character, each of these peoples has a particular character, which, however, consists of no more than history and tradition.

It is what makes up the hereditary intellectual patrimony of these peoples. Every individual has a right to it; each assimilates during his lifetime, without fatigue or labor, these notions scattered in his society, and profits by them. You can draw the parallel yourself and see how many elementary ideas we can thus pick up through simple give-and-take, to make use of them as best we can to direct our lives. And observe that this is not a matter of study or reading, of anything literary or scientific, but simply of the contact of minds, of those ideas which invade a child in the cradle, which surround him in the midst of his play, which his mother breathes on him in her caresses; finally, these are ideas which, in the guise of divers feelings, enter into the marrow of his bones with the very air he breathes, and which have already formed his moral being before he is delivered out into the world and society.

Do you wish to know what ideas these are? They are the ideas of duty, of justice, of right, of order. They were brought forth by the very events which set up societies; they are integral elements in the social life of these nations. Such is the atmosphere of the West; this is more than history, more than psychology; it is the physiology of a European. What have we to substitute for this in our country? . . .

You will find that, as a result, a certain poise, a certain method in our thoughts, a certain logic is lacking to us all. The Western syllogism is unknown to us. There is more than frivolity in our best minds. But the best ideas are no more than sterile visions and remain paralyzed in our brains owing to lack of connection and succession. It is a trait of human nature that a man gets lost when he can find no means to bind himself to what has come before him and what will follow upon him. Then all consistency, all certainty escapes him. Lacking the guiding sense of continuous duration he finds himself lost in the world. There are lost souls in every country; but in ours it is a general characteristic. I do not mean the lightness with which one used to reproach the French—actually but an easy manner of conceiving things which did not exclude either depth or breadth of mind and which gave infinite grace and charm to their social intercourse—I mean the flightiness of a life totally lacking in experience and foresight, a flightiness which results simply from the ephemeral existence of an individual detached from the species. Such a life holds dear neither the honor nor the progress of any community of ideas or interests, not even a traditional family outlook or that mass of prescriptions and perspectives which compose, in a state of things founded on memory of the past and awareness of the future, both public and private life. There is absolutely nothing general in our heads; everything in them is individual, and everything is transitory and incomplete. Even in our very expressions I find something strangely vague, cold, uncertain, something which resembles to an extent the aspect of people at the lowest rung of the social ladder. When I was abroad, particularly in the South where faces are so animated and expressive, I often compared the faces of my compatriots with those of the natives, and I was struck by this expressionlessness in our faces.

Foreigners have praised in us a sort of careless rashness which one finds particularly in the lower classes of our nation, but, since they could observe only certain isolated effects of our national character, they could not judge the whole. They did not see that the same principle which makes us sometimes so daring makes us also ever incapable of depth and perseverance. They did not see that what renders us so indifferent to the hazards of life renders us indifferent also to all good, all evil, all truth, all deceit, and that it is precisely this which deprives us of all those powerful motives which lead men to perfect themselves. They did not see that it is precisely this lazy boldness which is responsible for the fact that in our country not even the upper classes, painful though it be to say this, are exempt from the vices which elsewhere exist only among the very lowest. They did not see, finally, that, although we have some of the virtues of a young people not much advanced in civilization, we have none of the virtues of a mature, highly cultured people.

I do not mean, certainly, that we have only vices, while European peoples have only virtues; God forbid! But I do say that in order to judge peoples fairly we must study the general spirit that constitutes their life, for that spirit alone, and not any other specific trait of character, can lead them on the road toward greater moral perfection and indefinite progress.

The masses are subject to certain forces which themselves exist in the top social group. They do not think for themselves; there are among them a certain number of thinkers who think for them, who give the impulse and put in motion the collective intelligence of a nation. While the small number thinks, the rest feels and the general motion occurs. This is true of all races on earth, except for some brutish ones in whom there remains of human nature but the physical form. The primitive peoples of Europe, the Celts, the Scandinavians, the Germans *[Germains]*, had their druids, their scalds, their bards; these were, in their way, powerful thinkers. Look at those peoples of North America which the materialistic civilization of the United States is so busily destroying; there are among them men of remarkable profundity. Well, I ask you, where are our wise men, where are our thinkers? Who has ever thought for us? Who thinks for us now?

And yet, situated between the two great divisions of the world, between East and West, with one elbow leaning on China and the other on Germany, we should have combined in us the two great principles of intelligent nature, imagination, and reason, and have united in our civilization the past of the entire world. But this is not the part which Providence has assigned to us. Far from it, she seems wholly to have neglected our destiny. Suspending, where we were concerned, her beneficial action on the human mind, she left us completely to ourselves, she wished to have nothing to do with us, she wished to teach us nothing. Historical experience does not exist for us. To behold us it would seem that the general law of mankind had been revoked in our case. Isolated in the world, we have given nothing to the world, we have taken nothing from the world; we have not added a single idea to the mass of human ideas; we have contributed nothing to the progress of the human spirit. And we have disfigured everything we touched of that progress. From the very first moment of our social existence, nothing has emanated from us for the common good of men; not one useful thought has sprouted in the sterile soil of our country; not a single great truth has sprung from our midst; we did not bother to invent anything, while from the inventions of others we borrowed only the deceptive appearances and the useless luxuries.

Strange. Even in the world of science, which touches on all fields, our history makes no connection, explains nothing, proves nothing. If the barbarian hordes which threw the world into confusion had not crossed the land we inhabit before swooping down on the West, we would hardly have provided a chapter to world history. For people to notice us, we have had to stretch from the Bering Straits to the Oder. Once, a great man [Peter the Great] wanted to educate us, and in order to make us eager for enlightenment, he threw us the mantle of civilization: we picked up the mantle but did not touch civilization. Another time, another great Prince [Alexander I], associating us to his glorious mission, led us victorious from one end of Europe to the other: returning home from this triumphal march across the most civilized countries in the world, we brought back nothing but evil ideas and baneful errors which resulted in an immense calamity that set us back by half a century. We have something in our blood which drives off all true progress. In a word, we have lived and we live but to be a great lesson to such distant posterity as will be aware of it; today, whatever anyone says, we mark a void in the intellectual sphere. I cannot tire of marveling at this void and this strange solitude of our social existence. It is due, certainly, in part to some singular destiny, but doubtless in part, too, to man, as is true in all moral events. Let us question history still further; it is history which explains a people.

What were we doing at the time when, from the midst of the struggle between the energetic barbarism of the northern peoples and the high idea of religion, the edifice of modern civilization was being built up? Driven by a baneful fate, we turned to Byzantium, wretched and despised by those nations, for a moral code that was to become the basis of our education. Only a moment earlier an ambitious mind [Patriarch Photius] had removed this household from the universal brotherhood; what we got was thus the idea as it had been disfigured by human passion. At the time, in Europe everything was animated by the vivifying principle of unity. All emanated from it and all converged upon it. The whole intellectual movement of those times tended to build up the unity of human thought, and all incentive had its source in this powerful need to arrive at a universal idea which is the genius of modern times. Strangers to this marvelous principle, we became the prey of conquerors, and when, freed from foreign yoke, we could, had we not been separated from the common family, have profited from the ideas which had blossomed during this time among our Western brothers, we fell instead into an even harsher servitude, sanctified as it was by the fact of our deliverance.

Many glowing rays were already then illuminating Europe, flashing out from the apparent darkness with which it was covered. The greater part of the knowledge in which man prides himself today was already anticipated by individual minds; society already had assumed a definite character; and, by turning back to pagan Antiquity, the Christian world had found the forms of beauty which it lacked up to then. But we locked ourselves up in our religious separatism, and nothing reached us of what was happening in Europe. We had no dealings with the great project of the world. The outstanding qualities with which religious had endowed modern peoples and which, in the opinion of a healthy mind, raises them as much above the Ancients as they in turn were above the Hottentots and the Lapps; these new forces with which it had enriched human mind; these customs which submission to a disarmed authority rendered as gentle as they had at first been brutal, none of this had taken place among us. While the Christian world marched on majestically along the road marked out for it by its divine Creator, carrying along generations, we, although called Christians, stuck to our place. The entire world was being rebuilt, while we built nothing: as before, we hibernated in our hovels built of logs and straw. In a word, the new destiny of mankind was not being fulfilled in our country. We were Christians, but the fruits of Christianity were not ripening for us.

35

Belinskii's Letter to Gogol, July 15, 1847

The period of uncompromising reaction, as the reign of Nicholas I is commonly known, witnessed great literary creativeness and a deep philosophical search for answers to questions of Russia's future. In literature the giant was Nikolai V. Gogol (1809–1852), author of *Dead Souls* and

---

Reprinted from V. G. Belinsky, *Selected Philosophical Works* (Moscow: Foreign Languages Publishing House, 1948), pp. 503–512.

Inspector General— masterly portrayals of social, economic, and bureaucratic ills of Russian life. In criticism the leader was Vissarion G. Belinskii (1810–1848), Russia's greatest literary critic. Initially one of Gogol's warmest admirers, Belinskii introduced him to the Russian reading public as a realist who was clearly in touch with Russia's social and political conditions. However, when in 1847 Gogol published a collection of moralizing sermons entitled *Selected Passages from a Correspondence with Friends* advocating a return to conservative virtues and defending such Russian institutions as serfdom and autocracy, Belinskii broke with Gogol and denounced him bitterly. Belinskii's death in 1848 saved him from official persecution, but his letter to Gogol circulated widely and the Russian reading public came to know it by heart.

You are only partly right in regarding my article as that of an angered man: that epithet is too mild and inadequate to express the state to which I was reduced on reading your book. And you are entirely wrong in ascribing that state to your indeed none too flattering references to the admirers of your talent. No, there was a more important reason for this. One could suffer an outraged sense of self-esteem, and I would have had sense enough to let the matter pass in silence were that the whole gist of the matter; but one cannot suffer an outraged sense of truth and human dignity; one cannot keep silent when lies and immorality are preached as truth and virtue under the guise of religion and the protection of the knout.

Yes, I loved you with all the passion with which a man, bound by ties of blood to his native country, can love its hope, its honor, its glory, one of the great leaders on its path of consciousness, development and progress. And you had sound reason for at least momentarily losing your equanimity when you forfeited that love. I say that not because I believe my love to be an adequate reward for a great talent, but because I do not represent a single person in this respect but a multitude of men, most of whom neither you nor I have ever set eyes on, and who, in their turn, have never set eyes on you. I find myself at a loss to give you an adequate idea of the indignation which your book has aroused in all noble hearts, and of the wild shouts of joy which were set up on its appearance by all your enemies—both the non-literary—the Chichikovs, the Nozdrevs, and the mayors . . . and by the literary, whose names are well known to you. You see yourself that even those people who are of one mind with your book have disowned it. Even if it had been written as a result of deep and sincere conviction, it could not have created any other impression on the public than the one it did. And it is nobody's fault but your own if everyone (except the few who must be seen and known in order not to derive pleasure from their approval) received it as an ingenious but all too unceremonious artifice for achieving a sheerly earthly aim by celestial means. Nor is that in any way surprising; what is surprising is that you find it surprising. I believe that is so because your profound knowledge of Russia is that of an artist but not of a thinker, whose role you have so ineffectually tried to play in your fantastic book. Not that you are not a thinker, but that you have been accustomed for so many years to look at Russia from your *beautiful far-away*; and who does not know that there is nothing easier than seeing things from a distance the way we want to see them; for in that *beautiful far-away* you live a life that is entirely alien to it, you live in and within yourself or within a circle of the same mentality as your own which is powerless to resist your influence on it. Therefore you failed to realize that Russia sees her salvation not in mysticism, nor asceticism, nor pietism, but in the successes of civilization, enlightenment and humanity. What she needs is not sermons (she has heard enough of them!) or prayers (she has repeated them too often!), but the awakening in the people of a sense of their human dignity lost for so many centuries amid the dirt and refuse; she needs rights and laws conforming not with the preaching of the church but with common sense and justice, and their strictest possible observance. Instead of which she presents the dire spectacle of a country where men traffic in men, without even having the excuse so insidiously exploited by the American plantation owners who claim that the Negro is not a man—a country where people call themselves not by names but by sobriquets, such as Vanka, Vaska, Steshka, Palashka; a country where there are not only no guarantees for individuality, honor, and property, but even no police order, and where there is nothing but vast corporations of official thieves and robbers of various descriptions! The most vital national problems in Russia today are the abolition of serfdom and corporal punishments and the strictest possible observance of at least those laws which already exist. This is even realized by the government itself (which is well aware of how the landowners treat their peasants and how many of the former are annually done away with by the latter), as is proven by its timid and abortive half-measures for the relief of the white Negroes and the comical substitution of the single-lash knout by a cat-o'-three tails.

Such are the problems which prey on the mind of Russia in her apathetic slumber! And at such a time a great writer, whose beautifully artistic and deeply truthful works have so powerfully contributed towards Russia's awareness of herself, enabling her as they did to take a look at herself as though in a mirror—comes out with a book in which he teaches the barbarian landowner in the name of Christ and Church to make still greater profits out of the peasants and to abuse them still more. . . . And you would expect me not to become indignant? . . . Why, if you had made an attempt on my life I could not have hated you more than I do for these disgraceful lines. . . . And after this, you expect people to believe the sincerity of your book's intent!

No! Had you really been inspired by the truth of Christ and not by the teaching of the Devil, you would certainly have written something entirely different in your new book. You would have told the landowner that since his peasants are his brethren in Christ, and since a brother cannot be a slave to his brother, he should either give them their freedom, or, at least, allow them to enjoy the fruits of their own labour to their greatest possible benefit, realizing as he does, in the depths of his own conscience the false relationship in which he stands towards them.

And the expression: *"Oh, you unwashed snout, you!"* From what Nozdrev and Sobakevich did you overhear this, to give to the world as a great discovery for the edification and benefit of the *muzhiks*, whose only reason for not washing is that they have let themselves be persuaded by their masters that they are not human beings? And your conception of the national Russian system of trial and punishment, whose ideal you have found in the foolish saying that both the guilty and innocent should be flogged alike? That, indeed, is often the case with us, though more often than not it is the man who is in the right who takes the punishment, unless he can ransom himself, and for such occasions another proverb says: *guiltlessly guilty!* And such a book is supposed to have been the result of an arduous inner process, a lofty spiritual enlightenment! Impossible! Either you are ill—and you must hasten to take a cure, or . . . I am afraid to put my thought into words! . . .

Proponent of the knout, apostle of ignorance, champion of obscurantism and Stygian darkness, panegyrist of Tatar morals—what are you about! Look beneath your feet—you are standing on the brink of an abyss! . . . That you base such teaching on the Orthodox Church I can understand: it has always served as the prop of the knout and the servant of despotism; but why have you mixed Christ up in this? What in common have you found between Him and any church, least of all the Orthodox Church? He was the first to bring to people the teaching of freedom, equality, and brotherhood and set the seal of truth to that teaching by martyrdom. And this teaching was men's *salvation* only until it became organized in the Church and took the principle of Orthodoxy for its foundation. The Church, on the other hand, was a hierarchy, consequently a champion of inequality, a flatterer of authority, an enemy and persecutor of brotherhood among men—and so it has remained to this day. But the meaning of Christ's message has been revealed by the philosophical movement of the preceding century. And that is why a man like Voltaire who stamped out the fires of fanaticism and ignorance in Europe by ridicule, is, of course, more the son of Christ, flesh of his flesh and bone of his bone, than all your priests, bishops, metropolitans, and patriarchs! Do you mean to say you do not know it! It is not even a novelty now to a schoolboy. . . . Hence, can it be that you, the author of *Inspector General* and

Dead Souls, have in all sincerity, from the bottom of your heart, sung a hymn to the nefarious Russian clergy which you rank immeasurably higher than the Catholic clergy? Let us assume that you do not know that the latter had once been something, while the former had never been anything but a servant and slave of the secular powers; but do you really mean to say you do not know that our clergy is held in universal contempt by Russian society and the Russian people? Of whom do the Russian people relate obscene stories? Of the priest, the priest's wife, the priest's daughter and the priest's farm hand. Does not the priest in Russia represent for all Russians the embodiment of gluttony, avarice, servility, and shamelessness? Do you mean to say that you do not know all this? Strange! According to you the Russian people are the most religious in the world. That is a lie! The basis of religiousness is pietism, reverence, fear of God. Whereas the Russian man utters the name of the Lord while scratching himself somewhere. He says of the icon: *if it isn't good for praying it's good for covering the pots.*

Take a closer look and you will see that it is by nature a profoundly atheistic people. It still retains a good deal of superstition, but not a trace of religiousness. Superstition passes with the advances of civilization, but religiousness often keeps company with them too; we have a living example of this in France, where even today there are many sincere Catholics among enlightened and educated men, and where many people who have rejected Christianity still cling stubbornly to some sort of god. The Russian people is different; mystic exaltation is not in its nature; it has too much common sense, a too lucid and positive mind, and therein, perhaps, lies the vast scope of its historic destinies in the future. Religiousness with it has not even taken root among the clergy, since a few isolated and exclusive personalities distinguished for such cold ascetic reflectiveness prove nothing. The majority of our clergy has always been distinguished for their fat bellies, scholastic pedantry, and savage ignorance. It is a shame to accuse it of religious intolerance and fanaticism; rather could it be praised for an exemplary indifference in matters of faith. Religiousness with us appeared only among the Schismatic sects who formed such a contrast in spirit to the mass of the people and were so insignificant before it numerically.

I shall not dilate on your panegyric to the affectionate relations existing between the Russian people and its lords and masters. I shall say point-blank that panegyric has met sympathy nowhere and has lowered you even in the eyes of people who in other respects stand very close to you in outlook. As far as I am concerned, I leave it to your conscience to admire the divine beauty of the autocracy (it is both safe and profitable), but continue to admire it judiciously from your *beautiful faraway:* at close quarters it is not so attractive, and not so safe. . . . I would remark but this: when a European, especially a Catholic, is seized with a religious ardour he becomes a denouncer of iniquitous authority, similar to the Hebrew prophets who denounced the iniquities of the great ones of the earth. With us on the contrary: no sooner is a person (even a reputable person) afflicted with the malady which is known to psychiatrists as *religiosa mania* than he begins to burn more incense to the earthly god than the heavenly one, and so overshoots the mark in doing so that the former would fain reward him for his slavish zeal did he not perceive that he would thereby be compromising himself in society's eyes. . . . What a rogue our fellow the Russian is! . . .

Another thing I remember you saying in your book, claiming it to be a great and incontrovertible truth, that literacy is not merely useless but positively harmful to the common people. What can I say to this? May your Byzantine God forgive you that Byzantine thought, unless, in committing it to paper, you knew not what you were saying. . . . But perhaps you will say: "Assuming that I have erred and that all my ideas are false, why should I be denied the right to err and why should people doubt the sincerity of my errors?" Because, I would say in reply, such a tendency has long ceased to be a novelty in Russia. Not so very long ago it was drained to the less by Burachok and his fraternity. Of course, your book shows a good deal more intellect and talent (though neither of these elements is very richly represented) than their works; but then they have developed your common doctrine with greater energy and greater consistence, they have boldly reached its ultimate conclusions, have rendered full meed to the Byzantine God and left nothing for Satan, whereas you, wanting to light a taper to each of them, have fallen into contradiction, upholding for example, Pushkin, literature and the theatre—all of which, in your opinion, if you were only conscientious enough to be consistent, can in no way serve the salvation of the soul but can do a lot towards its damnation. . . . Whose head could have digested the idea of Gogol's identity with Burachok? You have placed yourself too high in the regard of the Russian public for it to be able to believe you sincere in such convictions. What seems natural in fools cannot seem so in a man of genius. Some people have been inclined to regard your book as the result of mental derangement verging on sheer madness. But they soon rejected such a supposition, for clearly that book was not written in a single day, or week, or month, but very likely in one, two or three years; it shows coherence; through its careless exposition one glimpses premeditation, and the hymn to the powers that be nicely arranges the earthly affairs of the devout author. That is why a rumour has been current in St. Petersburg to the effect that you have written this book with the aim of securing a position as tutor to the son of the heir-apparent. Before that, your letter to Uvarov became known in St. Petersburg, wherein you say that you are grieved to find that your works about Russia are misinterpreted; then you evince dissatisfaction with your previous works and declare that you will be pleased with your own works only when the tsar is pleased with them. Now judge for yourself, is it to be wondered at that your book has lowered you in the eyes of the public, both as a writer and still more as a man? . . .

You, as far as I can see, do not properly understand the Russian public. Its character is determined by the condition of Russian society, in which fresh forces are seething and struggling for expression; but, weighed down by heavy oppression and finding no outlet, they induce merely dejection, weariness and apathy. Only literature, despite the Tatar censorship, shows signs of life and progressive movement. That is why the title of writer is held in such esteem among us, that is why literary success is easy among us even for a writer of small talent. The title of poet and writer has long since eclipsed the tinsel of epaulettes and gaudy uniforms. And that especially explains why every so-called liberal tendency, however poor in talent, is rewarded by universal notice, and why the popularity of great talents which sincerely or insincerely give themselves to the service of orthodoxy, autocracy, and nationality declines so quickly. A striking example is Pushkin who had merely to write two or three verses in a loyal strain and don the *kamer-junker's* livery to suddenly forfeit the popular affection! And you are greatly mistaken if you believe in all earnest that your book has come to grief not because of its bad trend, but because of the harsh truths alleged to have been expressed by you about all and everybody. Assuming you could think that of the writing fraternity, but then how do you account for the public? Did you tell it less bitter home truths less harshly and with less truth and talent in *Inspector General* and *Dead Souls?* Indeed the old school was worked up to a furious pitch of anger against you, but *Inspector General* and *Dead Souls* were not affected by it, whereas your latest book has been an utter and disgraceful failure. And here the public is right, for it looks upon Russian writers as its only leaders, defenders, and saviours against Russian autocracy, orthodoxy, and nationality; and therefore, while always prepared to forgive a writer a bad book, will never forgive him a pernicious book. This shows how much fresh and healthy intuition, albeit still in embryo, is latent in our society, and this likewise proves that it has a future. If you love Russia rejoice with me at the failure of your book! . . .

I would tell you, not without a certain feeling of self-satisfaction, that I believe I know the Russian public a little. Your book alarmed me by the possibility of its exercising a bad influence on the government and the censorship, but not on the public. When it was rumoured in St. Petersburg that the government intended to publish your book in many thousands of copies, and to sell it at an extremely low price, my friends grew despondent; but I told them there and then that the book, despite everything, would have no success and would soon be forgotten. In fact it is now better remembered for the articles which have been written about it than for the book itself. Yes, the Russian has a deep, though still undeveloped instinct for truth.

Your conversion may conceivably have been sincere, but your idea of bringing it to the notice of the public was a most unhappy one. The days of naive piety have long since passed, even in our society. It already understands that it makes no difference where one prays, and that the only people who seek Christ and Jerusalem are those who have never carried Him in their breasts or who have lost Him. He who is capable of suffering at the sight of other people's sufferings and who is pained at the sight of other people's oppression, bears Christ within his bosom and has no need to make a pilgrimage to Jerusalem. The humility which you preach is, first of all, not novel, and, secondly, savours on the one hand of prodigious pride, and on the other of the most shameful degradation of one's human dignity. The idea of becoming a sort of abstract perfection, of rising above everyone else in humility, is the fruit of either pride or imbecility, and in either case leads inevitably to hypocrisy, sanctimoniousness, and Chinaism. Moreover, in your book you have taken the liberty of expressing yourself with gross cynicism, not only of other people (that would be merely impolite) but of yourself—and that is vile, for if a man who strikes his neighbour on the cheek evokes indignation, the sight of a man striking himself on the cheek evokes contempt. No, you are not illuminated, you are simply beclouded; you have failed to grasp either the spirit or the form of Christianity of our time. Your book breathes not the true Christian teaching but the morbid fear of death, of the devil, and of hell!

And what language, what phrases? "Every man hath now become trash and a rag"—do you really believe that in saying *hath* instead of *has* you are expressing yourself biblically? How eminently true it is that when a man gives himself wholly up to lies, intelligence and talent desert him. Did not this book bear your name, who would have thought that this turgid and squalid bombast was the work of the author of *Inspector General* and *Dead Souls?*

As far as it concerns myself, I repeat: you are mistaken in taking my article to be an expression of vexation at your comment on me as one of your critics. Were this the only thing to make me angry I would have reacted with annoyance to this alone and would have dealt with all the rest with unruffled impartiality. But it is true that your criticism of your admirers is doubly bad. I understand the necessity of sometimes having to rap a silly man whose praises and ecstasies make the object of his worship look ridiculous, but even this is a painful necessity, since, humanly speaking, it is somehow awkward to reward even false affection with enmity. But you had in view men who, though not brilliantly clever, are not quite fools. These people, in their admiration of your works, have probably uttered more ejaculations than talked sense about them; still, their enthusiastic attitude toward you springs from such a pure and noble source that you ought not to have betrayed them neck and crop to both your common enemies and accused them into the bargain of wanting to misinterpret your works. You, of course, did that while carried away by the main idea of your book and through indiscretion, while Vyazemsky, that prince in aristocracy and helot in literature, developed your idea and printed a personal denunciation against your admirers (and consequently mostly against me). He probably did this to show his gratitude to you for having exalted him, the poetaster, to the rank of great poet, if I remember rightly for his "pithless, dragging verse." That is all very bad. That you were merely biding your time in order to give the admirers of your talent their due as well (after having given it with proud humility to your enemies)—I was not aware; I could not, and, I must confess, did not want to know it. It was your book that lay before me and not your intentions: I read and reread it a hundred times, but I found nothing in it that was not there, and what was there deeply offended and incensed my soul.

Were I to give free rein to my feelings this letter would probably grow into a voluminous notebook. I never thought of writing you on this subject though I longed to do so and though you gave all and sundry printed permission to write you without cermony with an eye to the truth alone. Were I in Russia I would not be able to do it, for the local "Shpekins" open other people's letters not merely for their own pleasure but as a matter of official duty, for the sake of informing. This summer incipient consumption has driven me abroad, [and Nekrasov has forwarded me your letter to Salzbrunn which I am leaving today with Annenkov for Paris via Frankfort-on-Main]. The unexpected receipt of your letter has enabled me to unburden my soul of what has accumulated there against you on account of your book. I cannot express myself by halves, I cannot prevaricate; it is not in my nature. Let you or time itself prove to me that I am mistaken in my conclusions. I shall be the first to rejoice in it, but I shall not repent what I have told you. This is not a question of your or my personality, it concerns a matter which is of greater importance than myself or even you; it is a matter which concerns the truth, Russian society, and Russia. And this is my last concluding word: If you have had the misfortune of disowning with proud humility your truly great works, you should now disown with sincere humility your last book, and atone for the dire sin of its publication by new creations which would be reminiscent of your old ones.

Salzbrunn, July 15, 1847.

36

Russo-Ukrainian Relations in the Nineteenth Century

Russo-Ukrainian relations have for years been one of the most misunderstood, not only by Russians and Ukrainians themselves, but even more importantly by the outside world. Misconception on all sides has stemmed primarily from a mistaken belief that the two peoples are the same; that is, both are Slavic, both are predominantly Orthodox in faith, and since the middle of the seventeenth century they have had political, administrative, and economic links.

These simplistic perceptions (that have some adherents even today) were first seriously challenged in the nineteenth century when, influenced by a rising tide of national awakening, Ukrainians began to search for their national roots as the first step to independent political existence. This search assumed numerous forms, including organization in the 1840's of the Saints Cyril and Methodius Society. Russian authorities became greatly alarmed by Ukrainian aspirations for independent (or even equal) existence, since they were well aware that the loss of Ukraine, rich in natural resources, would create catastrophic economic and geopolitical consequences for Russia. For that reason harsh measures were taken against any manifestation of "Ukrainophilism," including prohibition of publishing anything in the Ukrainian language. It goes without saying that it was an ill-advised and short-sighted policy.

Statute and Rules of the Cyril-Methodius Society

Main Ideas

1. We believe that spiritual and political unity of Slavs is their true destiny toward which they all should strive.

2. We believe that after the unification each Slavic nation should have its own independence. We recognize the following [Slavic] nations: South Russians, North Russians and Belorussians, Poles, Czechs and Slovaks, Lusatians, Illirian Serbs and Croats, and Bulgars.

3. We believe that every nation should have its own national government

---

The following text of the program of the Society of Saints Cyril and Methodius and two of its appeals are from *Byloe (The Past),* No. 2 (February 1906), pp. 66–68. Translation mine. Words in brackets are mine.

and should subscribe to complete equality of citizens regardless of their birth, religious belief, or social status.

4. We believe that governments, laws, right of private property, and education of all the Slavs should be based on the teachings of the Holy religion of Our Lord Jesus Christ.

5. We believe that under such equality both education and moral standards should serve as a basis for participation in the affairs of government.

6. We believe that there should exist a general Slavic Assembly consisting of representatives of all [Slavic] nations.

Basic Rules of the Society

1. We are organizing a society whose basic aim is to disseminate the above stated ideas, primarily through the education of youth, through literature, and through the increase of membership of the society. The society selects as its patrons the saintly educators Cyril and Methodius, and accepts as its symbol a chain link and an icon with the name or image of these saints.

2. Upon joining the society every member will take an oath pledging gifts, work, fortune, and public contacts to attain the aims of the society; and should he undergo persecution or even tortue for ideas advocated by the society, after taking the oath, no member is allowed to compromise other members who are his brothers.

3. In case a member falls into enemy hands and leaves behind a needy family the society will help it.

4. Every member who joins the society can opt a new member without revealing to him the names of other members of the society.

5. Slavs of all nations and occupations are eligible to become members of the society.

6. Absolute equality must prevail among members of the society.

7. Because Slavic nations currently profess diverse religious faiths and have national prejudices against each other, the society will strive to remove all national and religious animosities among them and will disseminate among them the idea that differences among Christian churches may possibly be accommodated.

8. The society will strive to eliminate at the earliest possible moment serfdom and all other forms of discrimination against lower classes, and at the same time will seek to spread literacy everywhere.

9. The society as a whole and every member individually should base their activity on Christian principles of love, kindness, and suffering. The society considers godless the maxim that the end justifies the means.

10. Those members of the society who live in a given area may hold their

own meetings and adopt their own rules to guide their activity. These rules, however, should not contradict the basic ideas and rules of the society.

11. No members shall reveal the existence and composition of the society to those who are neither joining it nor have expressed any desire of joining it.

Appeals of the Society

Brother Ukrainians!

We present for your consideration the following statements. Consider whether these points are beneficial:

1. We believe that all Slavs should unite.

2. But [at the same time we believe that] every nation should be an independent republic and should govern itself independently; that every nation should use its own language and its literature; and that it should have its own political system. We recognize the following nations [in the future Pan-Slav Union]: Great Russians, Ukrainians, Poles, Czechs, Lusatians, Croats, Illirian Serbs and Bulgars.

3. There should be organized a parliament or a Slavic Assembly where deputies would come from all Slavic republics and would deliberate and decide on matters that affect the entire Slavic Union.

4. Every republic should have its own administrator elected for a specified period of time. The union as a whole should have a similar administrator also elected for a specified period of time.

5. Universal equality and freedom should prevail in every republic and classes should be abolished everywhere.

6. Elected representatives and other officials [in every republic] should be chosen by the people not on the basis of birth or property qualification but by virtue of their intelligence and education.

7. Christian belief should be the foundation for legislation and public order in the Union as a whole as well as in every republic.

Here, brother Ukrainians, inhabitants of the Ukraine on both sides of the Dnieper [River], we offer you this for your consideration. Read it carefully and let each individual decide how best to accomplish all this or even to improve it. There is a proverb that says where there are many heads there is also much wisdom. Think seriously about all this, and when the time comes for you to express yourself God will endow you with reason and understanding.

Great Russian and Polish Brothers!

This appeal to you comes from the Ukraine, your younger sister whom you have crucified and divided, but who not only wants to forget this evil but who actually sympathizes with your misfortunes and is ready to shed the blood of her children for your freedom. Read this brotherly appeal, consider the vital matter of your own salvation, and awake from your dream and drowsiness. Eliminate in your hearts the foolish hatred toward one another, as this hatred was implanted there by the tsars and masters in order to eliminate our freedom. Become ashamed of the yoke which you carry on your shoulders, become ashamed of your corruption. Place a curse on the sacrilegious name of the earthly tsar and the landlord. Abandon the spirit of distrust which you have acquired from German and Latin nations. Abandon the spirit of stubbornness which the Tartars have implanted in you. Adopt Slavic natural love toward mankind, and remember also your brothers who are still oppressed either in the silk chains of the Germans or under the rule of the Turks. Let the following be the aim of life of every one of you: Slavic Union, universal equality, brotherhood, peace and love of our Lord Jesus Christ. Amen.

A Report to Nicholas I by Count A. F. Orlov, Chief of Gendarmes, Concerning the Activity of the Saints Cyril and Methodius Society, May 1848

Your Majesty!

It was discovered recently that young scholars in Kiev, almost all of whom are natives of Little Russia [that is, Ukraine], have organized the Ukrainian Slavic Society of Saints Cyril and Methodius. The organizers of the society include: Collegial Secretary [P.] Hulak[-Artemovskii], Adjutant [N.] Kostomarov, and Candidate Belozerskii. With them are also other young people, mostly students of Saint Vladimir University [in Kiev].

The principal aim of the Society is to help unite other Slavic nations to Russia, but their methods call for arousing their spirit of self–esteem. They hope to accomplish this goal by removing from their customs and traditions all foreign influences, by eliminating all hostilities and discords among them, by promoting the Orthodox faith among them, and by organizing schools among them and publishing books for common people.

A statute was found among some followers of this Ukrainian Slavic Society, who were not actual members. Its provisions call for the establishment among all Slavs of a national representative government. Also found was a manuscript whose treasonable content elaborated on the statute, and another manuscript called "God's Commandments" or *Podnestrianka*, which represents a paraphrase of [Adam] Mickiewicz's *Pilgrims*, and abounds in revolutionary and

Source: *Borba Klassov*, No. 1–2 (1924), pp. 253–255. Translation mine.

communist slogans, seditious appeals to other Slavic nations, and other treasonous statements.

It is essential to note that the idea of trying to introduce an independent language and literature for each Slavic nation, and the suggestion that all Slavic peoples be united in one nation is not the work of individuals actually associated with this Society. It is the effort of many scholars [called Slavophiles] who are currently engaged in studying the Slavs.

In Kiev and throughout Little Russia this Slavophilism is being transformed into Ukrainophilism. There, young people are seriously trying to establish [an independent] language, literature and customs for Little Russia. They even hope to return to the earlier times of Cossack freedoms and to the Hetman state.

All of those who are associated with the Ukrainian Slavic Society are natives of Little Russia, and are also Ukrainophiles. All of them, including artist[-poet Taras] Shevchenko, and his former teachers Kulish and Kostomarov, have expressed in their works an erroneous view on current conditions in Ukraine. They argue that Ukraine is presently in a sad situation and they speak with great enthusiasm about the earlier days of Little Russia and attribute great significance to her. They portray her history as the most illustrious of all nations and describe the raids of the *haidamaks* as a manifestation of their knighthood. Finally, they also cite examples of their former freedoms, noting that this spirit of freedom has not vanished and that it is hidden within them.

Shevchenko's poetry in the Little Russian language, and especially such of his manuscripts as "The Dream," "A Message for the Living and the Dead," "The Three Souls," and others embody libelous and, to a considerable extent, insolent content, while the rest is really outrageous.

1. In accordance with [an earlier] imperial decree concerning this Ukrainian Slavic Society, all guilty persons have been severely punished and, in addition, it has been resolved that the following works, which already have been published, not be allowed to be distributed or sold: Shevchenko's *Kobzar* (1840); Kulish's *Ukraine* (1843), and *A History of the Ukrainian People* (1846); and Kostomarov's *Ukrainian Ballads* (1839), and his *A Branch,* published in 1840 under the pseudonym of Jeremiah Halka.

2. Adjutant-Generals Bibikov [in charge of Kiev, Podolie, and Volyn *Gubernias*] and Kokoshkin [in charge of Kharkov, Poltava, and Chernigov *Gubernias*] should be instructed that distribution of Shevchenko's poetry as well as the manuscript "God's Commandments" and similar disgraceful works not be allowed to be distributed [in those regions]. The same prohibition should apply to the idea of earlier [Ukrainian] freedoms, to the Hetman state and to the alleged right [of Ukraine] to an independent existence. They should

also be instructed to pay attention to the activities of everyone who is conducting research on the antiquity, history, and literature of Little Russia, and to use every subtle way and means, but without revealing any obvious evidence of persecution, to curtail every manifestation or abuse of inquiry in those areas without antagonizing the natives of Little Russia.

3. The Minister of Public Education, who already has taken appropriate steps in guiding scholarly research to deal with the nationality problem, the language, [and] the literary works of native Russians, should be instructed by an imperial decree that henceforth teachers and writers, acting in conformity with the spirit and intent of the policy of our government, should not introduce in their lectures, books, or articles any notion of Russia's trying to annex other Slavic nations; that they should not discuss any problem that is within the sphere of governmental and not of scholarly competence; that, as much as possible, they should avoid discussing the nationality and language problems concerning Little Russia and all other subject nations of Russia without giving preference to the love of family over that of country or empire; that they should avoid everything that in any way could harm affection for the empire, especially in light of current deplorable conditions and the alleged idyllic times [Russia's] subjects enjoyed in the past; that no research by scholars and popular writers should be allowed to depict Little Russia, Poland, and other countries as entities distinct from the Russian Empire and the unity it represents; and that all censors should pay very careful attention to works published in Moscow, Kiev, and Kharkov and to all books published in the Slavophile spirit which these people use and which, while containing no outright evil intentions, nevertheless may persuade some individuals with evil designs to conclude that there are some reasons for independence and freedoms for Russia's subjects.

An Anonymous Appeal to the Citizens of Kiev to Rebel, 1848

The hour of freedom has arrived at last. Finally we have an opportunity to take revenge against our oppressors and tyrants. All enlightened nations have thrown off their oppressive yokes. Now it is our turn to do the same in order to become, like them, free and happy. Freedom and equality, which have been emphasized in the Bible, have now been established in all states of Europe. Now Rus too is thinking of implementing this sacred goal.

Great people, take courage! You, too, will soon be freed from your shackles. All you have to do is gather your strength and move against your enemies with full determination and belief in the sanctity of your cause. Because God is with you, no human force is capable of stopping you.

Source: A. S. Nifontov, *Rossiia v 1848 godu* (Moscow: 1949), p. 85. Translation mine.

Citizens of Kiev! We are directing our message especially to you. You live in a holy and good city which has fallen into the hands of a vicious Tatar servant named Bibikov [who, in 1848, was Governor-General of Kiev *Gubernia*]. With the help of his favorite and flatterer, [named] Pisarev, he is oppressing you in every possible way. He is even ready to drink your blood if you do not wake up and terminate his impudence.

Do not be afraid of bayonets or guns with which they may threaten you. Russian soldiers will not rise against Russian compatriots. On the contrary, they will join their own people and in concert they will rebel against the common enemies of the fatherland and of our faith. Russian warriors! Your superiors are directing you against many other nations, chiefly because those nations wish your well-being and freedom. For that reason do not believe the perfidious promises of your leaders and do not forget that when you suppress [other nations], you are actually creating for yourselves new shackles and new oppression.

An Anonymous Appeal to Ukrainian Peasants to Rebel, 1862

An Appeal to All Decent People!

Dear People! Every day you see fires [around you]. Every day you see that villages and towns are set on fire. Do you know what causes them? Nobles want to deprive the poor people of everything so they would then be forced to work for them to earn their daily bread; they know that when the poor have nothing, when they are unable to heat their homes, and when they are unable to replenish their livestock, they will be in a desperate situation to make a living. When that happens, these nobles will set their own prices and will even lend them money in order to enslave the poor again. We will witness a repetition of the same process that affected your ancestors who originally were free but who later became serfs.

Good people! Nobles may even poison your livestock. They have the power to do it. The resolve, however, is yours, not theirs. When villages that belong to nobles are sometimes set on fire, these fires are the work of the enemies of nobles. And nobles are your enemies. Good people, rise up! Ask the oldtimers to tell you what the *haidamaks* did to nobles, how things were then, and how the *haidamaks* thanked nobles. Do what your ancestors did. This will reveal your strength, your will and your justice. When all of you

Source: Fedir Savchenko, *The Suppression of the Ukrainian Activities in 1876.* Reprint of the Kiev 1930 edition with an editor's preface . . . by Omeljan Pritsak and with an introduction by Basil Dmytryshyn. Harvard Series in Ukrainian Studies (Munich: Wilhelm Fink Verlag, 1970), pp. 350–351. Translation mine.

rise at once, no one will be able to stop you. You have numerical superiority. Rebel at once, and neither nobles nor the Muscovites will be able to stop you! There are more of you and justice is on your side. Nobles are unwilling to surrender their land to you. Yet the land is yours. Your grandfathers either fought for it or purchased it with their blood.

How long will you allow these exploiters to torture you? Good people, listen to me! Wait until everyone is ready and then rise in common—all of you—that is, serfs, cossacks, townsmen, and all honest people. If you will not rise, you will perish. Your masters, your eternal enemies, will reenserf you. They are responsible for fires. They hire Germans, they place shackles on you, they incite the Muscovites against you, and they beat you up! And they will do all of this for quite some time because you are afraid and because you do not have intestinal fortitude. This is exactly what local nobles like very much. Corrupt nobles tell you to be quiet because God allegedly wills it so! Good people! Do you believe that God wants to deceive people so cheaply?

Has the cossack glory disappeared [from your midst]? Do you want to become old men and see your children enslaved? What do you prefer? To be enslaved by nobles or to be masters in your own homes? Think carefully what is written in this appeal. Is this statement in any way a lie? I am telling you the honest truth. The time will come soon when we will cry like little children. Take a common oath and struggle against nobles for justice, for freedom, and for cossack glory. Fight against inequity because the end is near for nobles. All of you are free. All of you are equal. Your land, your right, your freedom is the kingdom of God! Tell each other what you have learned from this proclamation and make certain that nobles do not see it; because if they should discover it, they would put you in shackles and send you to Siberia, since they are very skilled in such matters. Nobles are afraid of dangerous souls and will try to prevent people from learning the truth. But, before you act, be aware most of all of local officials. Keep the content of this proclamation among yourselves, but do not wait too long because next year nobles will destroy all of you. . . .

A Project for Official Restrictions Against Ukrainian Publications, 1875

In order to stop an activity of the Ukrainophiles that is dangerous for the Empire, it appears that it would be desirable to adopt, pending further review, the following measures:

Source: Fedir Savchenko, *The Suppression of the Ukrainian Activities in 1876.* Reprint of the Kiev 1930 edition with an editor's preface . . . by Omeljan Pritsak and with an introduction by Basil Dmytryshyn. Harvard Series in Ukrainian Studies (Munich: Wilhelm Fink Verlag, 1970), pp. 381–83. Translation mine.

A. By the Ministry of Internal Affairs

1. All books that have been published abroad in the Little Russian dialect [that is, Ukrainian language] should not be allowed to enter into the Empire without first receiving a special import permit from the Main Department for Printed Matters.

2. Within the Empire there should be issued a decree prohibiting the publication in that dialect of all original works or translations, except historical documents, provided that if the latter are a part of the oral national tradition (such as songs, stories or proverbs) they may be published only in accordance with the rules of Russian orthography (and they cannot be published in accordance with the rules of the so-called "Kulishovka") [that is, Ukrainian orthography popularized by Panteleimon Kulish, a well-known nineteenth century Ukrainian writer and scholar].

Note I: Adoption of these measures would not be more than an expansion of the Imperial Resolution of July 3, 1863, which allowed the publication in the Little Russian dialect of only those works which were in the realm of belle-lettres literature. All other printed material in that dialect, whether of religious content or instructional, and that intended for elementary schools, was ordered to be terminated.

Note II: While keeping in force the intent of the Imperial Resolution, it still would be possible to allow the publication in the Little Russian dialect of works other than historical documents and belle-lettres, provided such works adhered to the rules of Russian orthography and received publication permits from the Main Department for Printed Matters upon prior review of each case.

3. All stage plays, librettos to musical composition, and public announcements (which form the current Ukrainophile manifestations) should be denied the opportunity of publication.

4. [The pro-Russian] newspaper *Slovo*, which is currently published in Galicia and which is hostile to the Ukrainophiles, should be supported and perhaps given a small but permanent subsidy [a marginal remark suggested that a sum of 1000 *rubles* annually should be allocated for that purpose], because without such a subsidy that newspaper could not exist and would have to terminate its operations. A Ukrainophile newspaper, *Pravda,* which is quite hostile to Russian interests, is published in Galicia with a substantial subsidy by the Poles [sic].

5. Suspend the publication of the newspaper *Kievskii Telegraf* [a marginal note says: "Because of its harmful effects"]. This action should be justified by the fact that its nominal editor, Snezhko-Blotskii, is totally blind and therefore cannot participate in the editorial activity. As a result the editorial direction of the newspaper is currently manipulated by individuals from a

small circle of people and by the publisher Hohotska, all of whom are very hostile [to Russian interests].

B. By the Ministry of Public Education

6. Increased official supervision of local educational districts should be instituted in order to prevent the use of the Little Russian dialect in teaching any subject matter in elementary schools. [A marginal note observed: "This is not essential"].

7. A thorough purge of libraries in all elementary and secondary schools in all Little Russian *gubernias* should be conducted for the purpose of removing books and pamphlets that have been mentioned in Point 2 of the present project.

8. Very serious attention should be given to the lecturing personnel in the educational districts of Kharkov, Kiev, and Odessa. We should request that the principals of these districts submit the names of all lecturers, indicating the loyalty of each concerning Ukrainophile tendencies. [The Ministry of Public Education] should have the right to transfer all teachers disloyal and semi-disloyal [to Russia] to Russian *gubernias* and to replace them with bona fide Russian teachers.

9. In the future, the selection of teachers in the mentioned school districts should be based on their moral qualities and should be made decisively by appropriate officials and their performance should be judged not only by words but by deeds.

Note I. There still exist two Imperial decrees of the late Sovereign Nikolai Pavlovich, which have neither been challenged nor rejected by the Supreme Authority [that is, the Imperial Senate, which acted as the highest court of the land]. These decrees, which presently have the force of law, imposed a strict obligation on the superintendents of all school districts and, in general, on all officials of education not to tolerate in their schools individuals with undesirable thoughts, not only among teachers but among students as well. It would be useful to reemphasize the content of these decrees.

Note II. It would also be desirable to adopt as a standard rule that teachers in all schools in the Kharkov, Kiev, and Odessa educational districts be primarily Russian and that Little Russians be assigned to the St. Petersburg, Kazan, and Orenburg districts.

10. The Kiev Branch of the Imperial Geographic Society should be closed (in the same manner that the Political-Economic Committee that emerged in the latter Society within the Statistical Department was closed in the 1860s). Future operation of the branch could be allowed only with the approval of the local Governor-General, provided all individuals who in any way were suspected of harboring anti-Russian tendencies were barred from associating

with it. [A marginal note stated: "The Ministry of Internal Affairs should determine how this rule should be implemented."]

C. By the Third Department of His Imperial Chancery

11. [M.] Drahomanov and [P.] Chubinskii should immediately be expelled [from the Russian Empire] for being incorrigible and therefore very dangerous agitators in the country. [A marginal note stated: "They should be expelled and their possible future return to the capitals of southern *gubernias* should receive strict secret supervision."]

37

Herzen's Commentaries on the Russian Scene, 1849–1855

Nineteenth century Russian society produced a galaxy of dedicated revolutionaries and profound revolutionary thinkers. The most honored and respected among the latter is Alexander I. Herzen (1812–1870). The son of a wealthy nobleman, Herzen attended the University of Moscow where he actively participated in student debates and where he emerged as a forceful spokesman for the Russian Westernizers. Herzen's early radical views were variously influenced by the ideas of the French enlightenment, French utopian socialism, and German idealistic philosophy. To escape persecution Herzen went into voluntary exile in 1847, first to Paris, then to Italy, London, Geneva, and again to Paris, where he died on January 21, 1870. His writings exerted a strong influence on Russian political thought, and it has been reported that Alexander II himself (1855–1881) read Herzen's newspaper, *Kolokol* (The Bell), which was published in London. While in exile Herzen became acquainted with many of the leading European revolutionaries, debated various issues with them and, under the impact of the experience, evolved his theory of Russian socialism based on the peasant commune. This theory laid the ideological foundation for the revolutionary populism which, until 1917, inspired much of the activity of the Russian radical intelligentsia

---

Source: Alexander Herzen, *Selected Philosophical Works* (Moscow: Foreign Languages Publishing House, 1956), pp. 340–347.

Herzen's Letter from Paris to His Friends in Moscow, March 1, 1849

Our separation will continue for a long time, perhaps forever. At the present moment I do not wish to return, and I do not know whether I will have a chance to do so later. You have been expecting me and I am in duty bound to explain the situation. If I owe anyone at all an explanation for my absence, or for my conduct, it is, of course, to you, my friends.

An insurmountable repugnance and a strong inner voice, a prophetic voice, forbids me from crossing the borders of Russia, particularly now when the monarchy, exasperated and frightened by all that is going on in Europe, redoubles its fury in suppressing every intellectual movement, and brutually curtains off sixty million people from mankind liberating itself, barring out its black, iron hand, covered with Polish blood, the last ray of light faintly illuminating a small number of them. No, my friends, I cannot cross the boundary of this kingdom of darkness, arbitrariness, silent torpor, secret murders, gagged torture. I shall wait until the power, weary with fruitless efforts and enfeebled by the resistance it has provoked, recognizes *something* in the Russian individual worthy of respect.

Please, don't misunderstand me; it is not pleasure nor diversion, nor even personal safety that I have found here. Indeed, I do not know who could, today in Europe, find either pleasure or diversion. . . . You could sense the sorrow in every line of my letters; life here is very difficult. Venomous hatred is intermingled with love; gall with tears; a feverish agitation saps the whole organism. The time of illusion and hopes is over. There is nothing here in which I believe save a handful of people, a few ideas and the fact that the movement cannot be stopped. I see the inevitable downfall of the old Europe and regret nothing that exists, neither the heights attained by her education, nor her institutions. There is nothing in this world that I love more than that which it chastises, nothing that I respect more than that which it executes and yet I stay here only to suffer doubly—from my own grief and from its grief and to perish, perhaps, at its downfall and ruin towards which it is rushing headlong.

Why then do I stay here?

I stay because that struggle is going on *here*. Here, in spite of the blood and tears, social problems are being worked out; and painful and burning as the suffering here is, it is articulate. The struggle is open and above-board. No one hides. Woe betide the vanquished but at least they will have given battle. They are not gagged before they have had their say. The tyranny is great but the protest is thundering; the warriors are often sent to the galleys, chained hand and foot—but with head upraised and their right to free speech not denied them. Where the word has not been lost, the cause has not yet been lost. It is this open struggle, this free speech that keeps me here. For its sake I am willing to sacrifice everything. I give up you, my friends, part of my fortune and, perhaps, my very life to march in the ranks of the vigorous minority "persecuted, but invincible."

It is for this free word that I have broken, or rather, for a time, loosened my blood ties with the people in whom I found such rich response to all that is light and dark in my heart, whose tongue and songs are my tongue and songs, and I stay in a country where only the bitter cry of the proletariat and the desperate bravery of its friends arouse my deep sympathy.

This decision has cost me dear. You know me—and will believe me. I have stifled my heartache. My heart has been torn by the struggle, and I have made my decision not as a hot-headed youth but as a man who has long reflected over the step taken, weighing all that he loses. It took me many months of hesitation and deliberation to arrive at a decision and I have finally decided to sacrifice everything

to human dignity,
to free speech.

I cannot let myself be influenced by consideration of the consquences. They lie beyond my power. They depend rather on the power of autocratic caprice which goes to the lengths of its arbitrary compass which has traced not only our words, but our steps as well. It lay, however, within my power not to obey, and I did not.

To go against one's convictions when it can be avoided is immoral. Passive submission now becomes almost impossible. I have witnessed two revolutions. I have too long been a free man to suffer myself again to be enchained. I have lived through popular movements and have grown accustomed to free speech. Am I again to become a serf? Never, not even for the sake of suffering together with you! If it were necessary to prevail over myself for the sake of a common cause, I might have found the strength. But where is this common cause of ours at the moment? There, at home, you have no ground on which a free man can stand. So how can you call me back? To a struggle—I gladly agree! But to martyrdom, to futile silence, to submission—under no circumstances! Ask anything you like of me, but don't ask me to be double-faced; don't compel me to act the loyal subject. Respect in me the liberty of the individual.

Personal freedom is a magnificent thing; *by it and by it alone* can a nation achieve its true freedom. Man must respect and honor his freedom in himself no less than in his neighbour or in the people at large. If you are convinced of this then you will agree that it is my right and my duty to remain here;

that it constitutes the only way in which an individual in our country can voice his protest; that it is the sacrifice he must make for the sake of human dignity. But if you will qualify my staying here as desertion, and forgive me only because you love me, that will mean that you have not yet completely liberated yourselves.

I am well aware what objection may be raised from the point of view of sentimental patriotism and civic affectation; but I cannot accept these superannuated views. I have outgrown them. I have extricated myself from them and it is precisely against them that I am fighting. This rehash of Roman and Christian reminiscences interfere most of all with the establishment of true conceptions of freedom—conceptions that are sound, clear and mature. Fortunately, customs and long evolution in Europe compensate for some of the absurd theories and absurd laws. People here live on soil fertilized by two civilizations; the path, trodden by their ancestors in the course of two and a half thousand years, was not futile, and much that is human has sprung up in spite of externalities and the official system.

In the worst days of European history we find some respect for the individual and a certain recognition of his independence, certain rights conceded to talent, to genius. Vile as the German Government of those days was, Spinoza was not exiled. Lessing was not flogged nor forced into the army. In this respect shown not only to sheer physical force, but to moral force as well, in this involuntary recognition of the individual lies one of the greatest humanistic principles of life in Europe. Europe never regarded its citizens residing abroad as criminals or anyone emigrating to America as a traitor.

Not so in our country. The individual at home ever oppressed and neglected has never made as much as an attempt to get a hearing. Free expression of opinion at home was always regarded as an insolence; independence as sedition. The individual was absorbed in the state; was dissolved in the commune. The revolution effected by Peter I replaced the antiquated landlord rule of Russia by the European bureaucratic system. Everything that could be transferred from the Swedish and German codes was; everything that could be transplanted from Holland, a land of free municipalities, to an autocatic government of rural communes was borrowed. But the unwritten, moral restraints on the government, the instinctive recognition of the rights of individuals, the right of thought, of truth, could not be transplanted and were not. Slavery in Russia increased with education; the state grew, improved, but the individual in no way profited by the process. Indeed, the stronger the state grew, the weaker did he become. The European forms of administration and of the judiciary, military and civil organization have developed into a monstrous, hopeless despotism. If Russia were not so vast and that borrowed system of government had not been built so haphazardly and amorphously, one could then say without exaggeration that not a soul with any sense of personal dignity could have remained in Russia.

Corrupted by the complete absence of resistance, power went on occasions to outrangeous lengths, unparalleled in the history of any other country. You know the extent of it from stories about Emperor Paul, a poet of his craft. Discard the capricious, the fantastic in Paul and you will see that he is by no means original and the principles inspiring him are exactly those to be found not only in all the tsars but in every governor, police inspector or landlord. All fourteen ranks of the famous bureaucratic hierarchy are becoming ever more drunk with the certainty of their own immunity. Every act of power, every relation of a superior to a subordinate is a flagrant exhibition of gross insolence, of the humiliating certainty that the individual will stand for anything—the recruitment repeated for three times, the law on foreign passports, flogging in the school for engineers. Thus Little Russia [Ukraine] accepted serfdom in the eighteenth century; thus all Russia, finally, believed that people could be sold and resold without a question, without even being asked by anybody on what legal grounds all this was done, not even by those who were being sold. The government at home is more self-assured and unrestrained than it is in Turkey or in Persia. There is nothing to restrict it, no traditions of the past: for it has disowned its own past, and has no concern for that of Europe. It has no respect for its people, knows nothing of the general culture of mankind, and battles against the present. Hitherto, at least, the government was ashamed of its neighbours and looked up to them; now it sets itself up as an example to all oppressors and aspires to be their mentor.

We saw the worst possible period of the imperial regime. We grew up under terror, under the black wings of the secret police, and were mutilated by hopeless oppression. We have barely survived. But is that not too little? Has the time not come to loosen our hands and tongue for activity which would serve as an example? Has the time not come to awaken the slumbering consciousness of the peoples? And surely it is impossible to awaken it by whispering, or remote allusions, when shouting and blunt words are barely audible? Open, frank acts are required: December 14 [1825] made so violent an impression on young Russia precisely because it took place in Saint Isaac's Square. But now not only the square, but the written word, or the lecturer's chair have all grown impossible in Russia. An individual working in secrecy or his protest from afar is all that is now left open to us.

I stay here not only because I find it repugnant to allow myself to be pinioned on crossing the borders, but also in order to work. I cannot live with folded arms anywhere; here I have no other work but that of *our cause.*

He who has, for more than twenty years, nurtured in his breast a single thought, suffered for it and lived for it; he who has wandered from prison to prison, from one place of exile to another, who owes to this thought the finest moments of his life, the most inspiring meetings, will not abandon it. Nor will he make it dependent on external factors and the degree of longitude and latitude. Quite the other way round. Here I am more useful. Here I am your uncensored speech, your free press, your chance representative.

All this seems new and unusual only to us; actually it has had many precedents. In all countries, faithful and active people used to emigrate at the beginning of a revolution, when thought was still feeble and the material power unbridled; their free words came from afar and this fact in itself lent their words weight and authority, for behind the words you could see the self-sacrificing deeds. The force of their words grew with the distance, as does the impetus of a stone, dropped from a high tower. Emigration is the first symptom of the approaching revolution.

Besides, Russians abroad have one more task to fulfill. It is indeed time to acquaint Europe with Russia. Europe does not know us; she knows our government, our facade and nothing more; conditions are extremely propitious for accomplishing this. It would not become Europe to drape herself majestically in the robes of disdainful ignorance. *Das vornehme Ignorieren* of Russia would not become Europe now that she has felt the despotism of the petit bourgeoisie and the Algerian Cossacks, now that she has been kept in a state of siege from the Danube to the Atlantic Ocean, and her prisons and galleys have been filled with people persecuted for their convictions. Let Europe become more closely acquainted with a nation whose youthful strength she felt in battles even though she eventually emerged the victor; let us tell Europe of this mighty and still enigmatic people which has so unobtrusively formed a country of sixty million and has grown so strong and tremendously large without departing from the principle of communal organization, and was the first to preserve it through the various stages of state development; about a people which, in some astonishing way, was able to come out intact from under the yoke of the Mongolian hordes and of German bureaucrats, from under the disciplinary stick of the corporal of the barracks and from under the degrading whip of the Tatars, a people which retained its fine character, clear mind and vigorous nature in spite of the oppression of serfdom, and which responded to the tsar's edict to promote education within a century with the genius of Pushkin. Let the Europeans become acquainted with their neighbour; they only fear him. It would be well for them to know what they fear.

Hitherto we have been unpardonably modest and conscious of our enslaved condition. We were apt to forget all that was good, full of hope and promise in the life of our people. We waited for a German [Baron August von

Haxthausen, who wrote a controversial book on Russia's agrarian system] in order to introduce ourselves to Europe. Is that not a disgrace?

Will I have the time to accomplish something? I don't know—I hope so!

Farewell, my friends, for long—give me your hands and your help. I need both the one and the other. And then, who knows? So much has happened in recent times! Perhaps that day when we shall gather as of old in Moscow and clink our glasses unafraid "To Russia and blessed liberty," *is not so far off* as it seems.

My heart refuses to believe that that day will not come; it is wrung at the thought of eternal separation, at the thought that I shall not see those streets which I paced so often full of my youthful dreams, those houses which are so interwoven with my memories, our Russian villages, our peasants whom I missed so much at the southernmost part of Italy. . . . No, it cannot be. But what if it is so? Then I bequeath my toast to my children. Dying in an alien land, I shall preserve my faith in the future of the Russian people, and bless it from my place of voluntary exile!

Herzen's Appeal to Russian Nobles, June 1853

Let this first free Russian word from abroad be addressed to you. Inspired by the entire intellectual activity of the last century, there has evolved in your midst a need for independence and a desire to be free. There also exists in your midst a self-denying minority which may redeem Russia in the eyes of other nations and in its own eyes.

From your midst came [such Decembrists as] Muraviev and Pestel, Ryleev and Bestuzhev. From your midst also came Pushkin and Lermontov. Finally, I, too, having left the country in order to disseminate free Russian thought abroad, have stemmed from your midst. For that reason I turn first to you. I do so not with any words of reproach, not at this moment with an impossible appeal to carry on the struggle, but with friendly talk about a common grief, about a common shame, and with brotherly counsel.

It is both painful and shameful to be a slave. But it is even more distressing and painful to acknowledge that our slavery is necessary and normal and that it is a natural phenomenon. A great sin rests on our souls. We have inherited it but are not responsible for it. We are keeping our inheritance unjustly. Like a heavy rock it pushes us to the bottom, and with it around our necks we cannot swim.

We are slaves because our forefathers sold their human dignity for inhuman

Source: A. I. Herzen, *Sobranie sochinenii v 30-ti tomakh* (Moscow: Akademiia Nauk, 1957), vol. 12, pp. 80–86. Translation mine.

rights which we now enjoy. We are slaves because we are the masters. We are slaves because we are nobles, that is, nobles without any faith in our rights. We are slaves because we hold our brothers in slavery. They are our equals in birth, blood, and language. We will never enjoy freedom as long as the wretched conditions of serfdom oppress us and as long as the hideous, shameful, and totally unjust slavery of our peasants exists among us.

On Saint George's Day [November 26] new life should begin in Russia. On Saint George's Day our freedom should commence. It is impossible to be a free man and have household serfs purchased like a commodity and sold like an animal herd. It is impossible to be a free man and have the right to beat peasants and send household serfs to a police station. It is impossible to speak about human rights and at the same time be the owner of human souls.

The tsar may ask you: "Why do you want to be free? You collect taxes from your peasants, appropriate their work, take their children to your mansions, cheat them out of their land, sell, purchase, resettle, beat and flog them, and, whenever you get tired of doing all this, you send them to my police stations where I thrash them willingly for you. Is this not enough for you? You should know your honor! Our ancestors surrendered to you a portion of Our autocracy. They gave you [the right] to enslave free people. They tore away half of their own purple and gave it to your fathers to make them [morally] poor. You have not complained about this arrangement. Indeed, you seem to enjoy it and you live with it. What kind of talk about freedom can there be between us? Remain firm and loyal to the tsar as long as your Orthodox peasants are loyal to you. Why should nobles wish to be free?"

It is possible that the tsar may be right. In the past many of you have expressed a desire to free your peasants, and Pestel and his associates made freeing them their first priority. Initially they disagreed on whether they should give peasants their freedom with or without land. Later they realized the absurdity of the idea of trying to free them without any land, thereby transferring them into a perpetual hungry and migratory condition. Then there emerged the question of the amount of land [each peasant should get] and the remuneration [each noble should receive].

In *gubernias* where nobles predominate, namely in Penza, Tambov, Iaroslav, Vladimir, Nizhnii Novgorod, and, finally, in Moscow, the idea of freeing peasants was viewed sympathetically and never encountered opposition similar to that voiced by American owners of black slaves. Nobles of Tula submitted a project. Ten other *gubernias* held meetings and made proposals. But then, [in 1848] both nobles and government officials became frightened and their trembling hands dropped all beneficial initiatives. There was nothing to fear. The upheaval of 1848 was rather mild. Since then everything has become dormant. What has happened to the minority that made a noise in restaurants of St. Petersburg and Moscow about the freeing of peasants? What has happened to the committees, deliberations, projects, plans, and proposals? . . .

Our inactivity, our indolent self-control, and our passive compliance have brought on melancholy and despair. Because we lack self-discipline, we have reached a condition where the government does not persecute us; it only frightens us. If it were not for the young people, full of courage, and the celebrated affair of Petrashevskii and his friends, it would not have been possible to think that you had made an agreement with [Tsar] Nikolai Pavlovich.

Meanwhile, discontent is growing in villages. Peasants look gloomy. Household serfs are disobeying. All kinds of rumors circulate among them. One says that a noble and his family perished in an arson-caused fire; another was killed with a flail and a pitchfork; women smothered an overseer in the field; and a chamberlain was beaten with birch rods and was forced to agree to remain silent.

Obviously, serfdom has made peasants sick, but they do not know yet what appropriate steps they should take in order to terminate it. You, however, know that without freeing peasants no progress is possible. Hopefully, this step depends on you. It should happen today because we do not know what will happen tomorrow. What are you waiting for? Permission from the government? It gave you a cunning as well as a double-meaning hint in 1842 [a decree of April 2, 1842], but you failed to take advantage of it. . . .

Study our words and remember them. Presently you have more than the right; you have the power. . . . I am not suggesting, as Christ did to Nicodemus, that you dispose of your wealth on account of selflessness. I am not offering you paradise in return for this sacrifice. I despise phraseology and do not believe at all in generosity or class selflessness. On August 4, 1792, [sic] French nobles acted more realistically than selflessly.

Select what is more advantageous for you: the freeing of peasants with land with your participation, or the struggle against emancipation with the government's participation. Select what is more beneficial for you; start a new, free Rus and solve amicably the difficult problem jointly with peasants, or commence a crusade against them with a firearm in one hand and a rod in the other. *Peasants will be emancipated if there is a future for Rus and for the Slavic world. . . .*

Or Russia will vanish in its tracks, marked by unnecessary bloodshed and savage victories; it will slowly fade away like the Tatar yoke . . . An empire that cannot distance itself from such a gruesome sin that so deeply affects its internal structure does not have the right to education, to future development, and participation in history. Yet, neither you nor I believe in such an awful future. You and I feel and know that the freeing of peasants is unavoidable, irrefutable, and inescapable. Even if you can do nothing for them, they still will be free, either because of the tsarist grace or the grace of a Pugachev-type upheaval. In both instances you will perish and with you will perish the enlightenment for which you have labored so hard, using demeaning servility and gross injustice.

It will be very painful if emancipation originates with the Winter Palace. Should that happen, tsarist authority will justify itself before the public and, after crushing you, autocracy will be greatly strengthened. A Pugachev-type rebellion is also frightening because if the emancipation of peasants cannot be achieved by other means, then that price is not very high. Gruesome transgressions bring gruesome results. . . .

You have read the history of the Pugachev rebellion. . . . My heart is saddened by the thought of innocent victims for whom I weep. But, bowing my head I declare: Let the awesome fate manifest itself because no one knew about it or wanted to stop it. If I were convinced that this problem is unsalvageable, I would not have addressed you. If that were the case I know that my words would have been fruitless or they would have been dismissed with ridicule. Fortunately, it is the opposite. I am convinced that there is no need to bring national progress paved with human corpses. . . .

Learn while there is still time. I believe in you. You gave me your pledge and my heart has not forgotten it. That is why I am turning to you, to my unfortunate brothers, in order to bolster your strength of which you are unaware, to show you the means of which you are ignorant, to reveal to you your weaknesses. . . .

Prevent great calamities as long as it is in your power. Save yourselves from serfdom and peasants from bloodshed. Have mercy on your children. Have mercy on the poor Russian people. Please hurry because time is running out. You should not waste even one hour. Sympathetic air that has recently been circulating in Europe is bringing change to Rus. . . .

The forthcoming transformation is not alien to the Russian heart. While the word socialism is unknown to our people, its meaning is very close to the soul of every Russian who spends his entire life in his village or in his working *artel* [group]. In socialism Rus will meet its revolution.

Such gigantic currents cannot be stopped by customs barriers or by birch [flails]. . . . Step aside if you do not wish to sink or swim with the current. Perhaps some of you who do not want emancipation think that the tsar will help you. Those who think so have been accustomed to the use of violent military pacifications, to playing the role of the executioner, which the government willingly assumes at the request of a nobleman. They have become accustomed to the government's silence about peasant grievances, about the illegal sale of serfs, exhorbitant taxes, the compulsory employment of peasants outside their villages. . . .

It is possible that the tsar may help you by employing methods which his predecessor of blessed memory [Alexander I] applied in organizing military colonies and in killing every tenth, every twentieth man. Perhaps . . . However, if you decide to join peasants and jointly reject this form of tsarist protection, you will feel good and you will also be pleased. . . . And remember this: If the hereditary Austrian Emperor, who abdicated on account of his incompetence, found a way to common ground with Shela [leader of Polish peasants in Galicia], what will Nikolai Pavlovich and his heir do for you?

Herzen's Statement of Dedication to His Son Alexander of His Book From the Other Shore, *January 1, 1855*

Sasha, My Dear Boy:

I dedicate this book to you because I have written nothing better and, in all likelihood, never shall; because I love this book as a testimonial of the struggle in which I have sacrificed much, but not the courage to know; because, finally, I am not in the least afraid to turn over into your adolescent hands this protest, in places impetuous, of an independent personality, against views that are absolete, slavish, and false, against preposterous idols which do not belong to our times but still linger among us, interfering with some and frightening others.

I do not want to deceive you. Know the truth as I know it. Learn this truth without experiencing either the tormenting errors or the deadening disillusionments, but simply by the right of inheritance.

You, too, will have to face and solve different conflicts. You will have your share of hardships, and of labour. You are fifteen years old and you have already felt the impact of terrible blows.

Do not search for any solutions in this book. You will not find them. Indeed, the period possesses none. That which has been decided is finished, while the coming revolution is in its infancy.

We do not build, we destroy; we do not proclaim new discoveries but discard old falsehoods. The man of today, that unhappy *pontifex maximus,* only lays the bridge; some stranger, belonging to the future, will pass over it. You, perhaps, will see it. Don't stay behind on this *shore.* Better perish with the revolution than seek sefety in the alms-house of reaction.

Source: Alexander Herzen, *Selected Philosophical Works* (Moscow: Foreign Languages Publishing House, 1956), pp. 336–337.

The religion of the revolution, of the great social reformation, is the only religion which I bequeath to you. It has no other paradise or rewards but your sense of right, your own conscience. . . . When the time comes to back home, to our own people, to preach it. Once there was a time when they appreciated my speech and, perhaps, they will remember me.

I give you my blessing on this path in the name of human reason, personal freedom and fraternal love.

Your father Twickenham, January 1, 1855

Herzen's letter to Emperor Alexander II, March 10, 1855

It's possible, my boy, that the Creator
Has designated you for the crown.
Love your people, respect the law,
Study hard to become tsar.
For your own sake reverse the voice of true freedom
And discard the negative spirit
Of servility and injustice . . .

An Ode to Grand Prince Alexander Nikolaevich
by K. Ryleev, August 30, 1823

Sovereign!

Your reign commences under an unusually lucky constellation. You have no bloody stains, nor do you suffer the pangs of remorse.

You have not received news of the death of your father from assassins. You were not asked to walk across a square covered with Russian blood to be seated on the throne. You did not have to use force to inform the nation of your assumption of power.

There is not one precedent in your dynasty of such a clean start. But that is not all.

The people expect from you gentleness and human kindness. Indeed, you are a very fortunate person!

Fate and coincidence have joined to assist you. Among all of your relatives you are the only one who was born in Moscow, and you were born at the time when the city began to emerge to new life after the devastating fire [of 1812]. Your birth was announced from the Kremlin Wall by shots fired by the Borodino and Tarutino cannons that had just returned from abroad and were covered with Parisian dust. I was five years old then, but I remember it well.

Source: A. I. Herzen, *Sobranie Sochinenii* (Moscow: Akademiia Nauk, 1957), vol. 12, pp. 272–274. Translation mine.

Ryleev greeted you with advice. Can you not accept the advice of the the heroic defenders of freedom and the promoters of their convictions? Why, indeed, did your center-stage position compel him to write such a meek and peaceful verse? What prophetic voice told him that your then-childish head would, in due time, inherit the crown?

You were educated by a poet [V. A. Zhukovskii] who was greatly admired by Russia. When you came of age the fate of our martyrs improved slightly. As is evident, you are a lucky person.

Then came your journey through Russia. I saw you; indeed, I remember it well. Because of your presence my own geographic fate improved. They transferred me from Viatka to Vladimir. I have not forgotten it.

Exiled in a far-away Trans-Volga town, I observed the genuine affection with which the common people welcome you and I though "How will he respond to this affection?"

Well, the time for repayment has arrived, and for you it is very simple! Let your heart be free. You seem to love Russia truly. And you really can do so much, very much, for the Russian people.

I, too, love the Russian people. I left them on account of love. I could not keep my hands folded, remain silent and witness those horrors perpetrated on them by nobles and officials.

My departure has not altered my feelings in the midst of foreign surroundings and horrors brought on by [the Crimean] war. I did not change my banner. Recently, [February 27, 1855] the English people publicly greeted the Russian people.

Obviously, my banner is not yours. I am an incorrigible socialist. You are an autocratic emperor. Nevertheless, between your emblem and mine there is one common bond, namely, love for the same people.

I am ready to sacrifice a great deal on their behalf. Neither prolonged years of persecution, nor prison, nor exile, nor painful wandering from one country to another has altered my resolve. I have done all of this on account of my love of the people.

I am prepared to wait, to disappear, or to speak about other matters, if only I could have a real assurance that you will do something for Russia.

Sovereign. Please grant freedom of expression to Russia. Our senses experience constraints. Our thoughts are poisoning our hearts because of the absence of freedom. We suffer on account of the shackles of censorship. Grant us free speech . . . We have plenty to say to the world and to ourselves.

Give land to peasants. It belongs to them. Remove from Russia the disgraceful blot of serfdom. Heal the wounds on the backs of our brothers. They are awesome signs of human persecution.

On his deathbed your father—please do not be afraid, I know that I am talking to his son—acknowledged that he was unable to do everything that he wanted for all of his subjects . . . In the last moments of his life serfdom struck his conscience.

During thirty years of his reign he was unable to free peasants. Please hurry! Free the peasant from future villainous acts, save him from shedding the blood he will be forced to spill. . . .

I am ashamed that we, as people, are content with trivia. We want material things. You, as everyone else, may have some serious reservations about this. Nevertheless, we are content with this.

It is possible that in the post you presently occupy, and being surrounded by a horde of flatterers, you will be shocked by my audacity. You may even laugh at this little grain of sand that represents seventy million grains of souls that represent our granite foundation.

Please do not ridicule it. I speak only of things that cannot be discussed in Russia. For that reason I have established the first Russian printing press in a free country [England]. It is to serve as an electrometer to indicate the activity and direction of the suppressed force. . . .

[Remember that] a few drops of water that cannot find any outlet are sufficient to break granite.

Sovereign! If those thoughts should reach you, please read them without any malice. Read them alone, and then reflect on them. It is seldom that you have an opportunity to hear the real voice of free Russia.

38

Aksakov's Defense of the Freedom of Expression

Constantine S. Aksakov (1817–1860) was one of the most influential spokesmen of the Slavophile movement. He was a literary critic, historian, political philosopher, and poet. As were many of his like-minded compatriots, Aksakov was inspired by the German romantic movement in general and by Hegel's philosophy in particular. Under their influence he extolled the imaginary virtues of the truly Russian national ways,

---

Source: K. S. Aksakov, *Sochineniia* (Petrograd: 1915), vol. I, pp. 98–99. Translation mine.

viewed the Russian Orthodox Church as a unique source of the country's strength, exaggerated the virtues of the *mir* (peasant commune), admired peasants, and demanded the abolition of serfdom. Aksakov also criticized the "decadent West," deplored the modernizing efforts of Peter I, passionately hated bureaucracy, and, as evident in a poem he published in 1853, he ardently defended freedom of expression and free press.

K. S. Aksakov's Poem "Free Word," 1853

You are the greatest of God's miracles!
You are the beacon and the flame of human thought!
For us you are a heavenly ray on earth,
As well as a banner for humanity.
You drive away the lie of ignorance,
And with your commitment to an everlasting life,
You guide us to light and justice.
You, Free Word!

It is said that spiritual forces grant authority,
And that humans have no power.
But if this view is right it is then contrary to truth,
And it represents justification to lies and vice.
But, regardless of whether free word
Struggles with the lie or
Lives in the new environment,
It always is a threat to injustice!
You, Free Word!

Do not ever bestow on anyone rewards
Based on imposing slavery on peoples;
Because wherever there is slavery,
There also is cause for rebellion and poverty.
Freedom is the surest guarantee against rebellion.
A slave in rebellion is more vicious than an animal,
Because he readily exchanges a knife for his chains . . .
The weapon of a free people is
You, Free Word!

Oh, Free Word, the sacred gift of God!
Whoever desecrates you
Charts a different path for mankind.
He reveals a criminal inclination to slavery!
You need a unique sword
To combat intrigues and hostile talk.
You, Free Word!

39

The Crimean War, 1853–1856

The Crimean War was a watershed, not only in Russian but in European history. Russia entered the war militarily unprepared. Although her armed forces fought bravely (both on land and at sea), incompetent leadership, poor communications, domestic discontent and epidemics, the antiquated political and social system, and weapons that were obsolete and in short supply caused them to suffer heavy casualties. It should be noted that incompetent allied military leadership (Turkish, French, English, and Italian) resulted in heavy allied casualties also. In the end, however, the allies prevailed, and forced the Russians to sign the Treaty of Paris on March 30, 1856.

By exposing her weakness, the Crimean War forced Russia to surrender most of the rights she had won in the Black Sea region since the reign of Peter I. It also compelled her authorities to plunge into a policy of "Great Reforms" that fundamentally altered the course of Russian history. The Crimean War also introduced profound changes elsewhere in Europe. It inflated the importance of France (ruled by Napoleon III), it deflated the stature of the Ottoman Empire, and, in a peculiar way, it contributed to the unifications of Italy and Germany. In short, the Crimean War was a major turning point in European history.

Statistical Data on the Strength of Russia's Armed Forces on the Eve of the Crimean War, 1853

Regular Forces	*Officers*	*Rank & File*
Infantry	15,382	581,845
Cavalry	4,983	86,282
Light Field Artillery	1,784	40,896
Cavalry Artillery	339	8,057
Garrison Artillery	793	40,681
Engineering Units	364	15,944

Source: A. M. Zaionchkovskii, *Vostochnaia voina 1853–1856 . . . Prilozheniia* (St. Petersburg: 1908), vol. I, pp. 476–477. Translation mine.

Other Supporting Units	988	35,302
Internal Security	2,430	144,934
Total	27,009* [Sic]	953,948** [Sic]

Reserves	*Officers*	*Rank & File*
Infantry		121,125
Cavalry	736	24,210
Artillery & Engineers		13,540
Total	736	158,875
Inactive and not part of the Military	—	10,760
Total of Regular Forces	27,745	1,123,583
Total of Irregular Formations	3,647	242,203
Grand Total	31,392	1,365,786 [Sic]

An Inventory of Weapons Available to Russian Forces on January 1, 1853

Types of Weapons	*Should Have Had*	*Actual Number*	*Deficiency*
For Ground Forces			
a) Weapons for Infantry	1,014,959	532,835	482,124
b) Weapons for Cavalry and Cossacks	71,038	20,849	50,189
c) Carbines	69,199	21,167	48,032
d) Rifles	37,318	6,198	31,120
e) Pistols	43,248	7,704	35,544
For Garrisons			
a) For Infantry	49,000	9,907	39,093
b) For Cavalry	500	101	399

*This figure includes 3,267 officers who served in regular formations but were assigned to reserve and supporting units.

**This figure includes 10 cossack formations with 2,044 officers and 78,144 rank-and-file cossacks. All irregular forces on active duty numbered 89,168 rank-and-file men.

An Order by Vice-Admiral V. A. Kornilov Calling for the Sinking of Russian Naval Vessels in Order to Defend Sevastopol, September 11, 1854

Comrades! After a bloody battle with the superior enemy, our armed forces have retreated to Sevastopol in order to defend it with our last breath.

You have sampled the enemy's steamers and have seen his vessels that do not use sails. The enemy has doubled his numbers in order to attack us from the sea. We should abandon the frivolous idea that we can destroy the enemy at sea. We are needed to defend the city where our homes are and where most of our families live.

The commander-in-chief has resolved to sink five old ships in the navigation channel. Temporarily they will block the enemy's entry to raid and at the same time [this action] will free our units to reinforce our defense units.

It is an infamous act to destroy ones own work. We have tried every means to maintain our ships, doomed to be sacrificed soon in unenviable circumstances. Yet we must resign ourselves to the inevitable.

[In 1812] Moscow was burning, but Rus did not perish as a result. On the contrary, it emerged strong. God is merciful! Indeed, He is preparing a new fate for His loyal Russian subjects.

Let us, therefore, pray to God and let us resolve that we will not allow a powerful enemy to conquer us. For over a year he has been gaining new allies and now he has encircled the Russian Empire. Envy is insidious. The Emperor is dispatching a new army to help us and if we do not waver, then the impudence will be punished and the enemy will be crushed.

Peace Treaty of Paris, March 30, 1856

Article 1

From the day of the exchange of the Ratifications of the present Treaty there shall be Peace and Friendship between Her Majesty the Queen of the United Kingdom of Great Britain and Ireland, His Majesty the Emperor of the French, His Majesty the King of Sardinia, His Imperial Majesty the Sultan, on the one part, and His Majesty the Emperor of All the Russias, on the other part; as well as between their heirs and successors, their respective dominions and subjects, in perpetuity.

Source: N. V. Novikov and P. G. Safinov, eds. *Vitse-Admiral Kornilov. Sbornik dokumentov* (Moscow: 1947), p. 258. Translation mine.

Source: Sir Edward Hertslet, ed. *The Map of Europe by Treaty* . . . (London: 1875), vol. II, pp. 1250–1264, 1270–1271, 1266–1269.

Article 2

Peace being happily reestablished between their said Majesties, the Territories conquered or occupied by their armies during the War shall be reciprocally evacuated.

Special arrangements shall regulate the mode of the Evacuation, which shall be as prompt as possible.

Article 3

His Majesty the Emperor of All the Russias engages to restore to His Majesty the Sultan the Town and Citadel of Kars, as well as the other parts of the Ottoman Territory of which the Russian troops are in possession.

Article 4

Their Majesties the Queen of the United Kingdom of Great Britain and Ireland, the Emperor of the French, the King of Sardinia, and the Sultan, engage to restore to His Majesty the Emperor of All the Russias, the Towns and Ports of Sebastopol (Sevastopol), Balaklava, Kamiesch (Kamyshevaia Bukhta), Eupatoria (Evpatoriia), Kertch (Kerch), Jenikale, Kinburn (Kinburin), as well as all other Territories occupied by the Allied Troops.

Article 5

Their Majesties the Queen of the United Kingdom of Great Britain and Ireland, the Emperor of the French, the Emperor of All the Russias, the King of Sardinia, and the Sultan, grant a full and entire Amnesty to those of their subjects who may have been compromised by any participation whatsoever in the events of the War in favour of the cause of the enemy.

It is expressly understood that such Amnesty shall extend to the subjects of each of the Belligerent Parties who may have continued, during the War, to be employed in the service of one of the other Belligerents.

Article 6

Prisoners of War shall be immediately given up on either side.

Article 7

Her Majesty the Queen of the United Kingdom of Great Britain and Ireland, His Majesty the Emperor of Austria, His Majesty the Emperor of the French, His Majesty the King of Prussia, His Majesty the Emperor of All the Russias, and His Majesty the King of Sardinia, declare the Sublime Porte admitted to participate in the advantages of the Public Law and System (*Concert*) of Europe. Their Majesties engage, each on his part, to respect the Independence and the Territorial Integrity of the Ottoman Empire; Guarantee in common the strict observance of that engagement; and will, in consequence, consider any act tending to its violation as a question of general interest. . . .

Article 11

The Black Sea is Neutralized; its Waters and its Ports, thrown open to the Mercantile Marine of every Nation, are formally and in perpetuity interdicted to the Flag of War, either of the Powers possessing its Costs, or of any other Power, with the exceptions mentioned in Articles 14 and 19 of the present Treaty.

Article 12

Free from any impediment, the Commerce in the Ports and Waters of the Black Sea shall be subject only to Regulations of Health, Customs, and Police, framed in a spirit favourable to the development of Commercial transactions.

In order to afford to the Commercial and Maritime interests of every Nation the security which is desired, Russia and the Sublime Porte will admit Consuls into their Ports situated upon the Coast of the Black Sea, in conformity with the principles of International Law.

Article 13

The Black Sea being Neutralized according to the terms of Article 11, the maintenance or establishment upon its Coast of Military-Maritime Arsenals becomes alike unnecessary and purposeless; in consequence, His Majesty the Emperor of All the Russias, and His Imperial Majesty the Sultan, engage not to establish or to maintain upon that Coast any Military-Maritime Arsenal. . . .

Article 15

The Act of the Congress of Vienna, having established the principles intended to regulate the Navigation of Rivers which separate or traverse different States, the Contracting Powers stipulate among themselves that those principles shall in future be equally applied to the Danube and its Mouths. They declare that its arrangement henceforth forms a part of the Public Law of Europe, and take it under their Guarantee.

The Navigation of the Danube cannot be subjected to any impediment or charge not expressly provided for by the Stipulations contained in the following Articles: in consequence, there shall not be levied any Toll founded solely upon the fact of the Navigation of the River, nor any Duty upon the Goods which may be on board of Vessels. The Regulations of Police and of Quarantine to be established for the safety of the States separated or traversed by that River, shall be so framed as to facilitate, as much as possible, the passage of Vessels. With the exception of such Regulations, no obstacle whatever shall be opposed to Free Navigation. . . .

Article 19

In order to insure the execution of the Regulations which shall have been established by common agreement, in conformity with the principles above declared, each of the Contracting Powers shall have the right to station, at all times, Two Light Vessels at the Mouths of the Danube.

Article 20

In exchange for the Towns, Ports, and Territories enumerated in Article 4 of the present Treaty, and in order more fully to secure the Freedom of the Navigation of the Danube, His Majesty the Emperor of All the Russias consents to the rectification of his Frontier in Bessarabia. . . .

Article 21

The territory ceded by Russia shall be Annexed to the Principality of Moldavia, under the Suzerainty of the Sublime Porte.

The Inhabitants of that Territory shall enjoy the Rights and Privileges secured to the Principalities; and during the space of three years, they shall be permitted to transfer their domicile elsewhere, disposing freely of their Property.

Article 22

The Principalities of Wallachia and Moldavia shall continue to enjoy under the Suzerainty of the Prote, and under the Guarantee of the Contracting Powers, the Privileges and Immunities of which they are in possession. No exclusive Protection shall be exercised over them by any of the guaranteeing Powers.

There shall be no separate right of interference in their Internal Affairs.

Article 23

The Sublime Porte engages to preserve to the said Principalities an Independent and National Administration, as well as full liberty of Worship, of Legislation, of Commerce, and of Navigation. . . .

Article 26

It is agreed that there shall be in the Principalities a National Armed Force, organized with the view to maintain the security of the Interior, and to ensure that of the Frontiers. No impediment shall be opposed to the extraordinary measures of defence which, by agreement with the Sublime Porte, they may be called upon to take in order to repel any external aggression.

Article 27

If the Internal Tranquillity of the Principalities should be menaced or compromised, the Sublime Porte shall come to an understanding with the other

Contracting Powers in regard to the measures to be taken for maintaining or reestablishing legal order.

No armed Intervention can take place without previous agreement between those Powers.

Article 28

The Principality of Serbia shall continue to hold of the Sublime Porte, in conformity with the Imperial Hats which fix and determine its Rights and Immunities, placed henceforward under the Collective Guarantee of the Contracting Powers.

In consequence, the said Principality shall preserve its Independent and National Administration, as well as full Liberty of Worship, of Legislation, of Commerce, and of Navigation.

Article 29

The right of garrison of the Sublime Porte, as stipulated by anterior regulations, is maintained. No Armed Intervention can take place in Serbia without previous agreement between the High Contracting Powers.

Article 30

His Majesty the Emperor of All the Russias and His Majesty the Sultan maintain in its Integrity the State of their possessions in Asia, such as it legally existed before the rupture.

In order to prevent all local dispute the Line of Frontier shall be verified, and, if necessary, rectified, without any prejudice as regards Territory being sustained by either Party. . . .

For this purpose a Mixed Commission, composed of two Russian Commissioners, two Ottoman Commissioners, one English Commissioner, and one French Commissioner, shall be sent to the spot immediately after the reestablishment of diplomatic relations between the Court of Russia and the Sublime Porte. Its labours shall be completed within the period of 8 months after the exchange of the Ratifications of the present Treaty.

Article 31

The Territories occupied during the War by the troops of their Majesties the Queen of the United Kingdom of Great Britain and Ireland, the Emperor of Austria, the Emperor of the French, and the King of Sardinia, according to the terms of the Conventions signed at Constantinople on the 12th of March, 1854, between Great Britain, France, and the Sublime Porte; on the 14th of June of the same year, between Austria and the Sublime Porte; and on the 15th of March, 1855, between Sardinia and the Sublime Porte; shall be evacuated as soon as possible after the exchange of the Ratifications of the present Treaty. The periods and the means of execution shall form the object of an arrangement between the Sublime Porte and the Powers whose troops have occupied its Territory.

Article 32

Until the Treaties or Conventions which existed before the War between the Belligerent Powers have been either renewed or replaced by new Acts, Commerce of importation or of exportation shall take place reciprocally on the footing of the regulations in force before the War; and in all other matters their subjects shall be respectively treated upon the footing of the Most Favoured Nation.

Article 33

The Convention concluded this day between their Majesties the Queen of the United Kingdom of Great Britain and Ireland, the Emperor of the French, on the one part, and His Majesty the Emperor of All the Russias on the other part, respecting the Aland Islands, is and remains annexed to the present Treaty, and shall have the same force and validity as if it formed a part thereof. . . .

Convention Between Russia and Turkey, Limiting Their Naval Forces in the Black Sea, Paris, March 30, 1856

Article 1

The High Contracting Parties mutually engage not to have in the Black Sea any other Vessels of War than those of which the number, the force, and the dimensions are hereinafter stipulated.

Article 2

The High Contracting Parties reserve to themselves each to maintain in that Sea six steam-vessels of fifty metres in length at the line of flotation, of a tonnage of 800 tons at the maximum, and four light steam or sailing vessels of a tonnage which shall not exceed 200 tons each.

Convention Respecting the Straits of the Dardanelles and of the Bosphorus, March 30, 1856

Article 1

His Majesty the Sultan, on the one part, declares that he is firmly resolved to maintain for the future the principle invariably established as the ancient rule of his Empire, and in virtue of which it has, at all times, been prohibited for the Ships of War of Foreign Powers to enter the Straits of the Dardanelles and of the Bosphorus; and that, so long as the Porte is at Peace, His Majesty will admit no Foreign Ship of War into the said Straits.

And Their Majesties the Queen of the United Kingdom of Great Britain and Ireland, the Emperor of Austria, the Emperor of the French, the King of Prussia, the Emperor of All the Russias, and the King of Sardinia, on the other part, engage to respect this determination of the Sultan, and to conform themselves to the principle above declared.

Article 2

The Sultan reserves to himself, as in past times, to deliver Firmans of Passage for Light Vessels under Flag of War, which shall be employed, as is usual in the service of the Missions of Foreign Powers.

Article 3

The same exception applies to the Light Vessels under Flag of War, which each of the Contracting Powers is authorized to station at the Mouths of the Danube in order to secure the execution of the Regulations relative to the liberty of that River, and the number of which is not to exceed two for each Power. . . .

40

The Franco-Russian Treaty of Neutrality and Cooperation, March 3, 1859

Russian defeat in the Crimean War (1853–1855) and especially the humiliating restrictions the victors imposed in the Treaty of Paris (March 1856), dealt a heavy blow to Russia's prestige in international affairs. After 1856, therefore, the aim of Russian diplomacy was quite obvious: to gain friends in order to be in a position to undo the harm. Because this aim coincided with the ambitions of Napoleon III to remake the

---

From *Krasnyi Arkhiv* (Red Archive) (1938), vol. 88, Bk. 3, pp. 215–216. Translation mine.

map of Europe, France, and Russia, adversaries in the Crimean War took steps to become allies. Negotiations encountered no major barriers, and by 1858 Tsar Alexander II, in a meeting with the French representative in Warsaw, pledged Russia's full diplomatic cooperation in the French desire to amputate Austria. On March 3, 1859, Alexander's pledge was formalized in a secret treaty, which stipulated, among other things, that in case France were to involve itself in a war with Austria to help bring about Italian unification, Russia would assume a political and military position of benevolent neutrality towards France. To ease French efforts against Austria, the tsar ordered maneuvers of Russian forces along the Austrian frontier on the eve of the French attack against Austria. Russian cooperation assured French victory; however, the French failure to reciprocate brought the Franco-Russian rapprochement to an end.

Article 1

In case of an outbreak of war between France and Sardinia—on the one side, and Austria on the other, His Majesty the Emperor of All-Russia will assume a political and military position of benevolent neutrality towards France.

Article 2

The high contracting parties will reach an agreement on changes in the existing treaties which, in the interest of both states, they will seek jointly during peace negotiations.

Article 3

His Majesty the Emperor of All-Russia will not oppose the extensions of power of the House of Savoy in Italy provided the rights of monarchs who will not take part in the war are observed.

Article 4

His Majesty the Emperor of All-Russia and His Majesty the Emperor of the French agree to explain the situation, which may arise in connection with the war between France and Austria, to their allies and to make them understand that this struggle cannot endanger the interests of great mutual powers, whose balance of power will not be affected.

Article 5

Both high contracting parties pledge to keep secret the present treaty which will be ratified. The exchange of ratification will take place in Paris within a month or sooner if this be possible. . . .

Kisilev. Walewski.

41

The Russo-Chinese Treaties, 1858–1860

From the end of the seventeenth to the middle of the nineteenth century, Russian relations with China were on the whole peaceful. Thereafter they alternated between hostility and friendship. The responsibility for the new direction rested with Count Nikolai N. Muraviev-Amurskii, who, as Governor General of Eastern Siberia, initiated a policy aimed at piecemeal unilateral abrogation of the "eternal treaty of friendship" the two governments had signed in 1689 at Nerchinsk. In 1850 Muraviev-Amurskii ordered Russian occupation of the lower Amur, introduced Russian settlers to the newly-conquered region, and, using military pressure and diplomatic ruse, in May 1858, at Aigun, he secured Chinese consent to Russian control of the area between the Ussuri River and the sea. The Russians expanded these gains by the Treaty of Tientsin (June, 1858), and two years later in the Treaty of Peking they secured additional rights to the newly conquered areas—some 350,000 square miles in fact—and to make their presence there permanent, in 1860 they laid the foundation to the city of Vladivostok.

The Treaty of Aigun, May 28, 1858

Article 1

The left bank of the Amur River, beginning with the Argun River to the mouth of the Amur, shall be under the suzerainty of the Russian Empire, and the right bank [of the Amur River] to its confluence with the Ussuri shall be under the suzerainty of the Ta-Tsing [Chinese] Empire; the territories and places located between the Ussuri River and the Sea, shall, as heretofore, be jointly governed by the Ta-Tsing and the Russian Empires, until the frontier between the two Empires in this area shall be determined. Only vessels of the Ta-Tsing [Chinese] and the Russian Empires may navigate the Amur, Sungari, and the Ussuri Rivers; navigation of those rivers is forbidden to

---

From Russia, Ministerstvo Inostrannykh Del. *Sbornik dogovov Rossii s Kitaem, 1689–1881* (A Collection of Treaties Between Russia and China, 1689–1881) (St. Petersburg: 1889), pp. 110–112, 122–130, 159–172. Russian and French texts. Translation mine.

vessels of all other states. Manchu inhabitants who live on the left bank of the Amur River, from the Zeia River southward to the village Hormoldzin, shall be left in perpetuity in their former settlements under the jurisdiction of the Manchu government, in order that the Russian inhabitants might not injure or oppress them.

Article 2

In the interest of mutual friendship between the subjects of both states, reciprocal trade shall be permitted to the subjects of both Empires who live along the Ussuri, Amur, and the Sungari Rivers, and the authorities must reciprocally protect the merchants of both states on both banks [of the said rivers].

Article 3

The provisions laid down by mutual agreement of the Plenipotentiary of the Russian Empire, Governor-General Muraviev, and the Plenipotentiary of the Ta-Tsing [Chinese] Empire, Commander-in-Chief of the Amur, I-shan, shall be carried out precisely and inviolably in perpetuity. To this effect, Governor-General Muraviev, for the Russian Empire, remitted [a copy of the present treaty], written in the Russian and Manchu languages, to the Commander-in-Chief, I-shan, of the Ta-Tsing [Chinese] Empire, and the Commander-in-Chief I-shan, for the Ta-Tsing [Chinese] Empire, remitted [a copy of the present treaty], written in the Manchu and Mongol languages to Governor-General Muraviev of the Russian Empire. All provisions contained herein shall be made public for the information of the frontier inhabitants of both Empires.

[Signed] May 28, 1858, in the town of Aigun.

Nikolai Muraviev
Petr Perovskii

I-shan
Dziraminga

The Treaty of Tientsin, June 3, 1858

Article 1

The present treaty reconfirms peace and friendship that have existed for many years between His Majesty the Emperor of All Russia and His Majesty the Bogdokhan of the Ta-Tsing [Chinese] Empire and between their respective subjects.

Governments of both Empires shall always protect personal safety and inviolability of property of Russian subjects residing in China and of Chinese subjects residing in Russia.

Article 2

The former right of Russia to send envoys to Peking any time the Russian government shall consider it essential is hereby reconfirmed. . . .

Absolute equality shall also be maintained in correspondence as well as visits between Russian envoys or plenipotentiary ministers and members of the State Council, Ministers of the Court of Peking, and Governor-Generals of frontier and Maritime provinces. On the same basis [of absolute equality] also shall be conducted all relations between frontier Governor-Generals and other frontier officials of both Empires.

If the Russian government should find it necessary to appoint a plenipotentiary minister to reside in one of the open ports, then in his personal and written contacts with highest local authorities as well as with Ministers in Peking, he shall follow general rules currently in use by all foreign powers.

Russian envoys may proceed to Peking, either by way of Kiakhta via Urga, or from Ta-ku at the mouth of the Pei-ho River, or any other way from other open cities and ports of China. Following the receipt of advanced notice, the Chinese government shall be obligated to make necessary arrangements for the safe and swift journey of the envoy and of his suite, as well as their reception in the capital with due honors, securing for them appropriate lodgings and providing them with all necessities.

Financial expenses that may accrue from all of those articles shall be paid by the Russian Government and not at all by the Chinese Government.

Article 3

Henceforth Russia's trade with China may be carried on not only overland in former frontier towns, but by sea as well. For trade purposes, Russian merchant ships may put into the following ports: Shanghai, Ningpo, Fu-chou-fu, Hsiamen [Amoy], Canton, Taiwan-fu, on the Island of Formosa, Kiung-chou, on the Island of Hainan, and other open places for foreign trade.

Article 4

In overland trade no restrictions shall henceforth be placed on the number of individuals who may be engaged in it, on the volume of goods or the available capital.

In maritime commerce, including all of its details, such as presenting of declarations on imported merchandise, paying anchorage fees, and duties based on the existing tariff, and so forth, Russian merchant vessels shall conform to general rules established for foreign commerce in Chinese ports.

Should Russians be engaged in an illegal trade, the goods they have brought shall be subject to confiscation.

Article 5

The Russian Government shall, at its discretion, have the right to appoint Consuls in all the previously mentioned ports.

To maintain order among Russian subjects living in open ports of China, and to support the authority of the Consuls, it [the Russian Government] may dispatch naval warships there.

Rules governing relations between the Consuls and local authorities, granting of a suitable area for the construction of churches, homes, and warehouses, Russian purchase of land from the Chinese upon mutual agreement, and other such problems that are normally within the competence of the Consuls, shall be resolved in accordance with general rules which the Chinese Government has adopted to deal with [other] foreigners.

Article 6

Should a Russian warship or a merchant ship be wrecked along China's coast, then local authorities shall be obligated to take immediate steps aimed at rescuing the endangered crew, saving the property, goods, and the ship itself. They also must take all necessary measures to enable the survivors, their property, and the goods to reach the nearest of open ports, where a Russian Consul, or an agent of any other nation friendly to Russia, is located, or even the [Russo-Chinese] border, should this be possible. Expenses connected with the saving of people and goods shall be paid subsequently by order of the Russian Government.

If, while sailing along the Chinese shores, Russian merchant or naval vessels should require making repairs or providing themselves with water or fresh provisions, they shall be allowed for that purpose to enter into Chinese ports that are closed for trade, and to secure everything they need at prices freely agreed upon, without any interference by local authorities.

Article 7

All disputes between Russian and Chinese subjects in places that are opened for trade shall be resolved by Chinese authorities, only in concert with the Russian Consul or the agent representing the authority of the Russian Government in that place. Should Russian subjects be accused of a crime or a misdemeanor, they shall be judged according to Russian laws. Equally, for any crime or an attempt against life or property of the Russians, Chinese subjects shall be judged and punished according to laws of their country.

Russian subjects who may penetrate inside China and who may commit there some sort of crime or misdemeanor, must be brought to the [Russo-Chinese] border, or to any of the open ports where a Russian Consul resides, for judgment and punishment according to Russian laws.

Article 8

Having recognized that Christian doctrine facilitates the establishment of order and peace among men, the Chinese Government pledges not to persecute its subjects for their loyal adherence to the Christian faith; on the contrary, it shall protect them on equal terms with those who profess other beliefs that are allowed within the Empire.

Considering Christian missionaries as men of good will who are not seeking personal advantages, the Chinese Government shall allow them to propagate the Christian faith among its subjects, and shall not hinder their penetration from all open ports to the interior of the Empire, and for that purpose Russian Consuls or frontier authorities shall supply certificates to a fixed number of missionaries.

Article 9

The indeterminate parts of the frontier between China and Russia shall be established without delay by representatives of both governments, and their agreement on the frontier line shall form a supplementary article of the present treaty. After the delineation of frontiers shall have been completed, there shall be prepared detailed description and maps of frontier areas which both Governments shall use in the future as in disputable documents on these frontiers.

Article 10

Members of the Russian Ecclesiastical Mission shall not be required to stay in Peking for a fixed period, as has been the custom hitherto, but each, upon the review of the superior authority, may return at any time to Russia via Kiakhta or any other way, and they may be replaced in Peking by other appointees.

All expenses for the maintenance of the [Russian] Mission shall henceforth be paid by the Russian Government, and the Chinese Government shall be freed from the expenses which heretofore were assessed against it.

Travel expenses by members of the Mission, couriers, and other persons dispatched by the Russian government from Kiakhta, or from China's open ports to Peking, and vice-versa, shall be paid by the Russian Government; local Chinese authorities shall be obliged on their part to take all necessary steps to insure that the travel of all the above-mentioned individuals shall be convenient and speedy.

Article 11

For regular communications between Russian and Chinese Governments, as well as for the needs of the [Russian] Ecclesiastical Mission in Peking, a monthly postal service shall be established between Kiakhta and Peking. A

Chinese courier shall be dispatched on a designated day once a month from Peking and from Kiakhta, and he shall in fifteen days or less, deliver the dispatched papers and letters to one of the designated places.

Moreover, once every three months, or four times per year, a parcel post, with packages and other goods, shall be dispatched from Peking and Kiakhta and vice-versa, and the duration of this journey shall be set at one month.

All expenses arising from the dispatching of letter and parcel posts shall be equally shared by the Russian and Chinese Governments.

Article 12

All political, commercial and other rights and privileges which other nations may subsequently acquire, [especially] the most favored nation [status] from the Chinese Government, shall simultaneously be extended to Russia without any necessary negotiations on her part in this regard. . . .

The Treaty of Peking, November 14, 1860

Article 1

In order to corroborate and clarify Article 1 of the Treaty concluded in the town of Aigun, May 16, 1858 (twenty-first day of the fourth Moon of the eighth year of Hien-Fong), and fulfill Article 9 of the Treaty of June 13 (third day of the fifth Moon) of the same year in the city of Tientsin, the following is established:

Henceforth the Eastern frontier between the two Empires, beginning with the confluence of the Shilka and Argun Rivers, shall descend along the course of the Amur River to the confluence of the latter with the Ussuri River. The lands situated on the left bank (north) of the Amur River shall belong to the Empire of Russia, and the lands situated on the right bank (south), as far as the confluence with the Ussuri River, shall belong to the Empire of China. Further, from the confluence of the Ussuri River with Lake Hinkai, the frontier shall follow the Ussuri and Songacha Rivers. The lands situated on the east bank (right) of these rivers shall belong to the Empire of Russia, and on the west bank (left) to the Empire of China. . . .

Article 4

All along the frontier line established by Article 1 of the present Treaty, free barter without tariffs shall be authorized between the subjects of the two Empires. Local frontier officials should give special protection to this barter and to those engaged in it.

Here too, all terms relative to commerce established by Article 2 of the Treaty of Aigun are also confirmed.

Article 5

In addition to the existing commerce at Kiakhta, Russian merchants shall enjoy their ancient right to go from Kiakhta to Peking for trading purposes. Enroute they shall be permitted to trade, but not wholesale, at Urga and at Kalgan. The Russian Government shall have the right to have at Urga a Consul (lin-chi-khuan) and several assistants, and to construct there at its own expense a dwelling for this official. The grant of land for the building, the rules governing its dimensions, and also the grant of pasture shall be negotiated with the Governors of Urga.

Chinese merchants shall be equally authorized to go to Russia to trade if they so desire.

Russian merchants shall have the right to travel in China, at all times, for commercial purposes; they are forbidden to assemble at one place in groups of more than 200; moreover, they must have permits from the Russian frontier authority indicating the name of the head of the caravan, the number of men in it; and the place of its destination. During the trip, these merchants shall have the right to buy and sell whatever they wish. All the expenses of their trip shall be their own responsibility.

Article 6

Commerce shall also be opened on an experimental basis at Kashgar on the same basis as at Ili and at Tarbagatai. At Kashgar the Chinese Government shall cede an area sufficient for the construction of a trading post, with all the necessary buildings, such as dwelling houses, a warehouse for the storing of merchandise, a church, and so forth, as well as space for the cemetary, and a pasture similar to that at Ili and at Tarbagatai. Instructions shall be given immediately to the Governor of the Kashgar area for the concessions of the said needs.

The Chinese Government shall not be responsible for thefts from Russian merchants trading at Kashgar, if such thefts shall have been committed by people who had come from beyond the lines of the Chinese outposts.

Article 7

Russians in China, and Chinese subjects in Russia may, in the places open to commerce, move about freely in their commercial activities, without any restraints by local authorities; they may frequent with the same freedom, and at all times, market places, stores, and homes of local merchants; and they may buy and sell, wholesale and retail, various merchandise, for cash or barter, and extend and receive credit as their mutual confidence shall dictate.

The duration of stay of merchants in places where trade is carried on shall not be limited, and shall depend on their own judgment.

Article 8

Russian merchants in China and Chinese merchants in Russia shall be placed under a special protection of the two Governments. In order to supervise merchants and to prevent any misunderstanding that might occur between them and the natives of the country, the Russian Government may immediately appoint Consuls at Kashgar and at Urga, on the basis of rules adopted for Ili and Tarbagatai. The Chinese Government may equally, if it so desires, appoint its Consuls in the capitals and other cities of the Russian Empire.

The Consuls of both states shall be lodged in buildings constructed at the expense of their respective Governments. However, it is not forbidden for them to rent, if that seems convenient, lodgings from local inhabitants. . . .

Article 9

The present extension of commercial relations between the subjects of the two governments, and the establishment of the new frontiers, shall henceforth invalidate the old rules laid down by the Treaties concluded at Nerchinsk and at Kiakhta, and by supplementary Conventions; equally invalid are relations between frontier authorities and the rules established for the solution of frontier problems, since they no longer reflect the present situation. To replace these rules, the following procedures are hereby established:

Henceforth, in addition to relations along the eastern frontier at Urga and Kiakhta, between the Governor of Kiakhta and the authorities of Urga, and along the western frontier, between the Governor of Western Siberia and the administration of Ili, there shall also be frontier relations between military Governors of the Amur Province and of the Maritime Province, and the Commanders-in-Chief of the Heilung-kiang and Kirin [regions], and between the Commissioner of frontiers of Kiakhta and the *dzarguchei* (pu-yuen), in accordance with the intent of Article 8 of the present Treaty. . . .

Article 10

During an investigation and solution of frontier problems, irrespective of their importance, frontier officials shall follow rules set forth in Article 8 of the present Treaty; inquiries concerning subjects of one or of the other Empire, as well as punishments that should be inflicted upon them, shall be carried out in accordance with the wording of Article 7 of the Treaty of Tientsin, in conformity with the laws of the country to which the guilty party belongs.

In cases involving trespassing, driving away or stealing of cattle across the frontier, as soon as they have been informed, and as soon as the evidence shall be presented to the head of the nearest outpost, local authorities shall send men authorized to conduct a search. Once found, cattle shall be promptly returned to the owner, and if any are missing, reparations shall be made according to the laws, and should an indemnity payment be required it must not be raised to several times the value of the missing beast (as has been the practice heretofore).

Should an individual flee across the frontier, at the first warning measures shall be taken immediately to find the fugitive. The arrested fugitive shall then be returned to the frontier authority without any delay and with all objects he possesses; an examination of the motives of flight and judgment on the matter itself shall be carried out by the local authority of the country to which the fugitive belongs. During the time of his stay abroad, from his arrest until his extradition, the fugitive shall be properly fed, and, in case of need, clothed; guards who accompany him must treat him humanely and must not indulge in any arbitrary acts toward him. The same procedure is applicable toward a fugitive about whom no advance warning was given. . . .

42

Russian Serfs and Their Emancipation in 1861

Like autocracy, Russian serfdom evolved gradually. It was introduced for state interests and, from inception, Russian serfdom generated an extremely complex and, for the most part, unwritten assortment of rights, obligations, and exceptions that varied from place to place. Students of Russian history are agreed that serfdom was one of the principal barriers to Russia's economic, social, cultural, and political progress. It also was a most inhuman institution.

Based on their obligations, Russian serfs fell into three categories: *obrok* (*quitrent*), *barshchina* (*corvee*), and household. Regardless of category, all serfs were human chattel. While their treatment varied from owner to owner, all serfs were required to pay their masters in cash, kind, or labor. They could not complain against their master, and could neither move nor marry without their master's permission. In addition, Russian serfs

Source: I. Ignatovich, *Pomeshchichi krestiane nakanune osvobozhdeniia*. 2nd ed. (Moscow: 1910), p. 62. Translation mine.

paid taxes to the government, served in the military, and performed countless other obligations.

By exposing her backwardness and weakness, Russia's defeat in the Crimean War convinced Emperor Alexander II that the abolishment of serfdom and introduction of the long-overdue reforms could no longer be postponed. The Reform Era, as the period after 1861 is commonly known, began with the Emancipation Manifesto of March 3, 1861. That act shattered the entire structure of Russian society and forced the government to introduce other reforms that affected all aspects of Russian life.

Census Data on the Number of Russian Nobles and Serfs, 1835 and 1858

Figures Based on the Census of 1835

Category of Nobles	*Number of Nobles*	*Number of Serfs*	*Number of Serfs per One Noble*
Nobles without estates	17,763	62,183	3
Nobles with up to 20 serfs	58,457	450,037	8
Nobles with 21 to 100 serfs	30,417	1,500,357	49
Nobles with 101 to 500 serfs	16,740	3,634,194	217
Nobles with 501 to 1000 serfs	2,273	1,562,831	688
Nobles with over 1000 serfs	1,453	3,556,959	2,448
Total	127,103	10,766,561	

Figures Based on the Census of 1858

Category of Nobles	*Number of Nobles*	*Number of Serfs*	*Number of Serfs per One Noble*
Nobles without estates	3,633	12,045	3
Nobles with up to 20 serfs	41,016	327,534	8
Nobles with 21 to 100 serfs	35,498	1,666,073	47
Nobles with 101 to 500 serfs	19,930	3,925,102	197
Nobles with 501 to 1,000 serfs	2,421	1,569,888	648
Nobles with over 1,000 serfs	1,382	3,050,540	2,207
Total	103,880	10,551,182	

The Distribution of *Obrok* and *Barshchina* Serfs in Selected *Gubernias* in 1858

Gubernia	*Percent of* Obrok *Serfs*	*Percent of* Barshchina *Serfs*
Kostroma	87.5	12.5
Iaroslav	87.4	12.6
Vologda	84.0	16.0
Olonets	72.0	28.0
Vladimir	70.0	30.0
Moscow	68.0	32.0
Nizhnii Novgorod	68.0	32.0
Kaluga	55.0	45.0
Novgorod	45.6	54.4
Voronezh	45.0	55.0
Tver	41.0	59.0
Riazan	38.0	62.0
Orel	28.0	72.0
Smolensk	27.0	73.0
Tula	25.0	75.0
Penza	25.0	75.0
Kursk	24.5	75.5
Pskov	23.0	77.0
Tambov	22.0	78.0
Total Average	47.6	52.4

Source: I. Ignatovich, *Pomeshchichi krestiane nakanune osvobozhdeniia.* 2nd ed. (Moscow: 1910), p. 49. Translation mine.

The Emancipation Manifesto, March 3, 1861

By the Grace of God We, Alexander II, Emperor and Autocrat of All Russia, King of Poland, Grand Duke of Finland, and so forth, make known to all Our faithful subjects:

Called by Divine Providence and by the sacred right of inheritance to the throne of Our Russian ancestors, We vowed in Our heart to respond to the mission which is entrusted to Us and to surround with Our affection and Our Imperial solicitude all Our faithful subjects of every rank and condition, from the soldier who nobly defends the country to the humble artisan who works in industry; from the career official of the state to the plowman who tills the soil.

Examining the condition of classes and professions comprising the state, We became convinced that the present state legislation favors the upper and middle classes, defines their obligations, rights, and priviliges, but does not equally favor the serfs, so designated because in part from old laws and in part from custom they have been hereditarily subjected to the authority of landowners, who in turn were obligated to provide for their well-being. Rights of nobles have been hitherto very broad and legally ill defined, because they stem from tradition, custom, and the good will of the noblemen. In most cases this has led to the establishment of good patriarchal relations based on the sincere, just concern and benevolence on the part of the nobles, and on affectionate submission on the part of the peasants. Because of the decline of the simplicity of morals, because of an increase in the diversity of relations, because of the weakening of the direct paternal attitude of nobles toward the peasants, and because noble rights fell sometimes into the hands of people exclusively concerned with their personal interests, good relations weakened. The way was opened for an arbitrariness burdensome for the peasants and detrimental to their welfare, causing them to be indifferent to the improvement of their own existence.

These facts had already attracted the attention of Our predecessors of glorious memory, and they had adopted measures aimed at improving the conditions of the peasants; but these measures were ineffective, partly because they depended on the free, generous action of nobles, and partly because they affected only some localities, by virtue of special circumstances or as an experiment. Thus Alexander I issued a decree on free agriculturists, and the late

From *Polnoe Sobranie Zakonov Russkoi Imperii . . .* (*Complete Collection of the Laws of the Russian Empire*), 2d Series, vol. 36, no. 36,490, pp. 130–134. Translation mine. Words in brackets are mine.

Emperor Nicholas, Our beloved father, promulgated one dealing with the serfs. In the Western *gubernias,* inventory regulations determine the peasant land allotments and their obligations. But decrees on free agriculturists and serfs have been carried out on a limited scale only.

We thus became convinced that the problem of improving the condition of serfs was a sacred inheritance bequeathed to Us by Our predecessors, a mission which, in the course of events, Divine Providence has called upon Us to fulfill.

We have begun this task by expressing Our confidence toward the Russian nobility, which has proven on so many occasions its devotion to the Throne, and its readiness to make sacrifices for the welfare of the country.

We have left to the nobles themselves, in accordance with their own wishes, the task of preparing proposals for the new organization of peasant life—proposals that would limit their rights over the peasants, and the realization of which would inflict on them [the nobles] some material losses. Our confidence was justified. Through members of the *gubernia* committees, who had the trust of the nobles' associations, the nobility voluntarily renounced its right to own serfs. These committees, after collecting the necessary data, have formulated proposals on a new arrangement for serfs and their relationship with the nobles.

These proposals were diverse, because of the nature of the problem. They have been compared, collated, systematized, rectified, and finalized in the main committee instituted for that purpose; and these new arrangements dealing with the peasants and domestics of the nobility have been examined in the Governing Council.

Having invoked Divine assistance, We have resolved to execute this task.

On the basis of the above mentioned new arrangements, the serfs will receive in time the full rights of free rural inhabitants.

The nobles, while retaining their property rights on all the lands belonging to them, grant the peasants perpetual use of their domicile in return for a specified obligation; and, to assure their livelihood as well as to guarantee fulfillment of their obligations toward the government, [the nobles] grant them a portion of arable land fixed by the said arrangements, as well as other property.

While enjoying these land allotments, the peasants are obliged, in return, to fulfill obligations to the noblemen fixed by the same arrangements. In this state, which is temporary, the peasants are temporarily bound.

At the same time, they are granted the right to purchase their domicile, and, with the consent of the nobles, they may acquire in full ownership the arable lands and other properties which are allotted them for permanent use. Following such acquisition of full ownership of land, the peasants will be freed from their obligations to the nobles for the land thus purchased and will become free peasant landowners.

A special decree dealing with domestics will establish a temporary status for them, adapted to their occupations and their needs. At the end of two years from the day of the promulgation of this decree, they shall receive full freedom and some temporary immunities.

In accordance with the fundamental principles of these arrangements, the future organization of peasants and domestics will be determined, the order of general peasant administration will be established, and the rights given to the peasants and to the domestics will be spelled out in detail, as will the obligations imposed on them toward the government and the nobles.

Although these arrangements, general as well as local, and the special supplementary rules affecting some particular localities, estates of petty nobles, and peasants working in factories and enterprises of the nobles, have been as far as possible adapted to economic necessities and local customs; nevertheless, to preserve the existing order where it presents reciprocal advantages, we leave it to the nobles to reach a friendly understanding with the peasants and to reach agreements on the extent of the land allotment and the obligations stemming from it, observing, at the same time, the established rules to guarantee the inviolability of such agreements.

This new arrangement, because of its complexity, cannot be put into effect immediately, a time of not less than two years is necessary. During this period, to avoid all misunderstanding and to protect public and private interests, the order actually existing on the estates of nobles should be maintained until the new order shall become effective.

Towards that end, We have deemed it advisable:

1. To establish in each *gubernia* a special Office of Peasant Affairs, which will be entrusted with the affairs of the peasant communes established on the estates of the nobility.

2. To appoint in every district justices of the peace to solve all misunderstandings and disputes which may arise from the new arrangement, and to organize from these justices district assemblies.

3. To organize Peace Offices on the estates of the nobles, leaving the village communes as they are, and to open *volost* offices in the large villages and unite small village communes under one *volost* office.

4. To formulate, verify, and confirm in each village commune or estate a charter which would enumerate, on the basis of local conditions, the amount of land alloted to the peasants for permanent use, and the scope of their obligations to the nobleman for the land as well as for other advantages which are granted.

5. To put these charters into practice as they are gradually approved on

each estate, and to put them into effect everywhere within two years from the date of publication of this manifesto.

6. Until that time, peasants and domestics must be obedient towards their nobles, and scrupulously fulfill their former obligations.

7. The nobles will continue to keep order on their estates, with the right of jurisdiction and of police, until the organization of *volost* and of *volost* courts.

Aware of the unavoidable difficulties of this reform, We place Our confidence above all in the graciousness of Divine Providence, which watches over Russia.

We also rely upon the zealous devotion of Our nobility, to whom We express Our gratitude and that of the entire country as well, for the unselfish support it has given to the realization of Our designs. Russia will not forget that the nobility, motivated by its respect for the dignity of man and its Christian love of its neighbor, has voluntarily renounced serfdom, and has laid the foundation of a new economic future for the peasants. We also expect that it will continue to express further concern for the realization of the new arrangement in a spirit of peace and benevolence, and that each nobleman will realize, on his estate, the great civic act of the entire group by organizing the lives of his peasants and his domestics on mutually advantageous terms, thereby setting for the rural population a good example of a punctual and conscientious execution of state regulations.

The examples of the generous concern of the nobles for the welfare of peasants, and the gratitude of the latter for that concern, give Us the hope that a mutual understanding will solve most of the difficulties, which in some cases will be inevitable during the application of general rules to the diverse conditions on some estates, and that thereby the transition from the old order to the new will be facilitated, and that in the future mutual confidence will be strengthened, and a good understanding and a unanimous tendency towards the general good will evolve.

To facilitate the realization of these agreements between the nobles and the peasants, by which the latter may acquire in full ownership their domicile and their land, the government will lend assistance, under special regulations, by means of loans or transfer of debts encumbering an estate.

We rely upon the common sense of Our people. When the government advanced the idea of abolishing serfdom, there developed a partial misunderstanding among the unprepared peasants. Some were concerned about freedom and disconcerned about obligations. But, generally, the common sense of the country has not wavered, because it has realized that every individual who enjoys freely the benefits of society owes it in return certain positive obligations; according to Christian law every individual is subject to higher authority (Romans, chap. xiii., 1); everyone must fulfill his obligations, and, above all, pay tribute, dues, respect, and honor (*Ibid.,* chap. xiii., 7). What legally belongs to nobles cannot be taken away from them without adequate compensation, or through their voluntary concession; it would be contrary to all justice to use the land of the nobles without assuming responsibility for it.

And now We confidently expect that the freed serfs, on the eve of a new future which is opening to them, will appreciate and recognize the considerable sacrifices which the nobility has made on their behalf.

They should understand that by acquiring property and greater freedom to dispose of their possessions, they have an obligation to society and to themselves to live up to the letter of the new law by a loyal and judicious use of the rights which are now granted to them. However beneficial a law may be, it cannot make people happy if they do not themselves organize their happiness under protection of the law. Abundance is acquired only through hard work, wise use of strength and resources, strict economy, and above all, through an honest God-fearing life.

The authorities who prepared the new way of life for the peasants and who will be responsible for its inauguration will have to see that this task is accomplished with calmness and regularity, taking the timing into account in order not to divert the attention of cultivators away from their agricultural work. Let them zealously work the soil and harvest its fruits so that they will have a full granary of seeds to return to the soil which will be theirs.

And now, Orthodox people, make the sign of the cross, and join with Us to invoke God's blessing upon your free labor, the sure pledge of your personal well being and the public prosperity.

Given at St. Petersburg, March 3, the year of Grace 1861, and the seventh of Our reign.

Alexander

43

Katkov's Views on the Polish Situation, 1863

After he ascended the throne in 1855, Alexander II made it known that he would improve not only the position of peasants but that of some of Russia's minority groups as well. Most excited at this prospect were the Poles, who, since the three partitions of Poland at the end of the eighteenth century, had presented Russian officialdom and the educated public of Russia with the most immediately troublesome aspect of their national problem. Polish hopes for independence were further stimulated by sympathies in their behalf expressed abroad in England and France. When, by 1863, the Russians had failed to satisfy Polish ambitions, the Poles rebelled. Russian forces crushed the uprising and in the process committed a number of excesses. These received much attention and additional sympathy for the Poles abroad, but the anti-Russian sentiment, in turn, aroused Russian nationalism. Its spokesman was Michael N. Katkov (1818–1887). As editor of the *Russkii Vestnik* (The Russian Herald), Katkov bitterly assailed foreign interference in Russo-Polish relations and denounced those Russian revolutionaries who sympathized with the Polish cause. Though in his youth he subscribed to moderately liberal views, after 1863 Katkov's name came to be synonymous with reaction in Russian political and literary history.

Nothing is more deceitful in the realm of politics than general rules and abstract formulas. By their very nature they are either dead or have a double meaning. Being abstract, they may simultaneously apply to diametrically opposed circumstances; and two hostile sides may, quite often with equal right, place the same slogans on their banners. Because of this it is dangerous to judge life by abstract maxims. In reality, everything forever and ever is definite and particular. Everything requires a definite viewpoint and special appraisal, and our views will be valid in such an appraisal only if we are able to approach the fact and familiarize ourselves with all of its peculiarities. Without this ability, our views will be opened but we will be unable to see.

Lately in Europe one has been hearing quite frequently and loudly stated views about rights of nationalities and the principle of non-interference. Rights

---

From *Russkii Vestnik,* no. I (1863). Translation mine. Words in brackets are mine.

of nationalities and the principle of non-interference are quite good concepts deserving a prominent place in the realm of ideas. Nothing can be said against them; on the contrary, one only wishes that they could acquire an increasing force and clarity in peoples' minds. It is one thing to acknowledge the existence of a rule, and it is another thing to use it to appraise given phenomena. Understanding is one thing; judgment is another matter. We may have beautiful understanding but our judgments can be grossly invalid. To have valid judgments it is not enough to have beautiful understanding; it is essential that our beautiful views correspond to the fact. Two and two without any doubt make four; and if in this sum, which our facts give us, there should appear other numbers, no matter how much we should argue, the inescapable truth remains that two and two make four and nothing else. If there be something else we must correct the figures and those that do not belong must be discarded.

The problem of the rights of nationalities was lately awakened and defended, primarily due to the Italian situation. Who is not familiar with the circumstances in which this matter was resolved? Who is unaware of what caused its success and why it received sympathy everywhere? As a consequence of this affair, the idea of non-interference into the domestic affairs of an independent state was restated with added emphasis. Because in its own right this idea is quite basic, and because the popular view was everywhere sympathetic to the Italian problem, all manifestions of these principles with respect to the Italian situation were everywhere approved without reservations. Whether Emperor Napoleon III or a minister of Her Britannic Majesty referred in this matter to the principle of nationalities or to the theory of non-interference, the result was always quite satisfactory, even though frequently the same sound rule was declared by the adversaries with a diametrically opposed meaning.

The theory of non-interference did not prevent Western states from interfering quite actively in the course of the Italian problem; neither did the principle of nationality hinder France from annexing Nice; which, according to this principle, belongs really to Italy, similarly as does Venice. Right of nationalities and the principle of non-interference are now knocking in vain at the gates of Rome; French armies are not leaving the Eternal City. The theory of non-interference has not prevented England from administering Turkish affairs and from controlling the Greek revolution; rights of nationalities have not prevented her from killing Turkish Slavs whenever they raised their heads, not only in the name of nationality, but even when they petitioned because of burdensome oppression. Montenegrins were neither subjects nor tributaries of the Sultan; yet the same British minister, who earlier had announced the principle of nationalities, treated the Montenegrins as rebels.

Ships with volunteers and war supplies were dispatched from English ports to Italy when the struggle was in full progess, and no one paid any attention to this, but now heated debate goes on to discover by what right Serbia received arms with Tula markings. All this means that power centers not in general ideas but in their application. It means that power centers in the particularity of every situation, in its circumstances and in its pecularities. The English government found it appropriate to apply the theory of non-interference and the rights of nationalities to the Italian situation, but finds it inappropriate to apply the same theory to the Turkish situation; equally as France considers it inappropriate to apply it to the problem of Rome. . . .

You should never talk to an Englishman about minority rights in India; he will consider you an insane person; a Frenchman will consider you similarly if you should talk to him about minority rights in Algeria. They will raise all sorts of objections. Neither will you gain much if you think to carry on a conversation with an Englishman about granting rights to the Celtic people in Ireland, or with a Frenchman about the possibility of an independent political existence of the same people in Britanny. In vain will you expound the theory of rights that belong to each nationality; in vain, too, will you talk about independent existence; no one will listen to you. They will tell you that you speak of utterly impossible things. They will tell you that you are applying the theory unintelligently; that the theory as such is very meritorious but that it cannot be applied to cases of your own choosing; that not every nationality is entitled to aspire to an independent political existence; and that great chaos would result if one should suddenly endorse such pretentious aspirations. They will tell you that only that nationality has that right which has proven it by its own history and which knows how to maintain and protect it. They will tell you that this right centers not in the letter, not in a word, not in a phrase, but in the reality, in existing conditions, and in given interpretations of vital forces. They will tell you that reality is the best and the only verifiable measure of real rights; and that, until such a verification, outside sympathies and verdicts decide nothing. Public opinion will side with one or the other view on the basis of various impulses or interests, which often have no bearing whatsoever on the rights of minorities. If a man whom we do not like has a heated argument with another, and we know very little about the cause of their argument, then unwittingly we will side with his adversary. As can individuals, so people and states can become an object of sympathy or antipathy; just as in the case of an argument between two individuals, public opinion is capable of siding with one or the other on the basis of its own mood, irrespective of the nature of the arisen argument. Sometimes the cause of prejudice is the very power of the victorious people, and public opinion will sympathize with the weaker side even over an unrealizable and desperate cause. While England struggled with the bloody Sepoy rebellion in India, did not European journalists howl about the rights of nationalities and did it not express its sympathies with the victims of perfidious and mighty Albion? Was not public opinion in France ready to applaud every success of Indian mutineers, including their violent excesses? If one could imagine a serious attempt in Ireland to separate from Great Britain, would they not rejoice in France even over a slight success in such a desperate case, and would not they raise throughout the world protests of indignation over the ultimate British victory, and would not they beat on a drum all possible tunes about the rights of nationalities? But this uproar would not produce any impression in England; the affair would take its own course and not one Englishman would attach any significance to these shouts and howls, just as now no Yankee in North America is disturbed by the Englishman's opinions of the bloody discord in the secessionist states; he is not confused by the hostile criticism from abroad; he snaps at his critics, and for each cruel word he responds with ten or twelve harsher ones. Meanwhile he goes on with his business and fights to the exhaustion of his strength in order to restore the seceding parts of his country.

Everyone knows that every case can be seen from different viewpoints and that contradicting interests will view differently the same situation. The Englishman does not count on French sympathy and the Frenchman in turn does not count on English sympathy in their respective successes or failures. They both find in foreign sympathy or indifference exactly that which is alien to them; both will try to understand their respective problems with their own intellect and appraise and judge them with their own feelings; neither one nor the other will stop perplexed and listen to someone else's opinion in order to define for themselves the line of action; both will operate from the position of their own strength, interests, and incentives. It is possible to imagine that in case of a struggle or of a crisis, both would try to assess themselves with a foreign yardstick, or, God forbid, with the yardstick of their enemies?

In this uninterrupted struggle for existence which we call life, and even call history, every cause has its defenders and its opponents. If there were no defenders then there would be no causes; and if there were no opponents then one would be unable to manifest oneself and to show ones own strength, and ones own right to existence and development. In the midst of this struggle called life and history, all truth is relative and all interest is unilateral. If there are defenders, then there must be opponents; if there are opponents, then there must also be defenders. And both opponents and defenders have their own more or less valid interests, their own more or less valid rights. Life and history show that whose power is mightiest his right is most righteous. But in a struggle one cannot support both sides or not support either. Whoever does not want to take a side in the struggle should leave the field, and on the battlefield each must be either a defender or an opponent of the given cause.

What causes the English or the French to seek truths in an argument between the Russians and the Poles? An outside observer will judge the affair guided not by the causes of the affair, but by his own personal sympathies or his own interests, should he ever become involved in some one else's argument. It is quite natural that neither an Englishman nor a Frenchman burns with zeal for Russian interests and would not be chagrined if a Russian cause suffered a setback somewhere. Not long ago Europe viewed with distrust and fear the Northern colossus, and not too long ago she feared its military despotism. Now these fears have abated. Russia has stopped being a bugbear. But, while no one is particularly afraid of her power, no one would grieve if an external or internal misfortune should afflict her. No foreigner has asked himself this serious question: is this power that has so dangerously and slowly emerged in the wastes of North Eastern Europe true, or is it a meteor, an apparition, that rose accidentally, and which must vanish? No one, except a Russian, is obligated, and no one can, take to his heart the Russian cause—no one can suffer for it, hope for it, and die for it. Our historical destiny, our national character, our fortunes, our sufferings and triumphs are unable to get any sympathetic consideration anywhere except here in Russia among ourselves. Every cause has two endings, every cause has both defenders and opponents and not one Russian cause can have better defenders than Russians themselves, while it can have a multitude of opponents everywhere.

This Polish problem is as much Russian as it is Polish. The Polish problem will always be a problem of Russia. Since ancient times history has placed the fatal question of life and death between these two related peoples. Both states were not simply rivals, but enemies unable to exist side by side—enemies to the very end. Between them the question was no longer that of who would take the priority or who would be more powerful: the question between them was which of them should exist. Sovereign Poland was unable to get along with an independent Russia. Agreements were impossible; either one or the other had to renounce its political independence and its pretensions to a mighty and independent state. And it was not Russia but Poland who felt the pressure of this vital question. It was Poland who started the historical struggle, and there was a time when Russia vanished, and there was another when Poland disappeared. Will this fatal question keep its momentum forever or will the time come when alongside a powerful and strong Russia an independent Poland will be able to live and flourish? One can meditate about this question at leisure, but in time of crisis, in the midst of a struggle, it is natural for a Pole to advocate the Polish cause and for a Russian to defend the Russian cause. Poland lost its independence, but it has not reconciled itself to its fate;

Polish feeling protests against this decision; feeling for his own people is still alive and vigorous in a Pole; it starts in infancy and is then jealously guarded and supported. It feeds itself and gains its strength on sufferings. The Pole did not repudiate his nationality after he lost his political independence. He is trying to free himself from his captivity and does not want to reconcile himself with any future if that future should not promise him a rebirth of a Polish nation with all of its claims. To him a simple independence is insufficient; he wants predominance. To him it is insufficient to liberate himself from alien domination; he wants the distruction of the opponent over whom he has triumphed. To him it is insufficient to be a Pole; he wants the Russian to become a Pole or else to be pushed beyond the Ural mountain range. He renounces all racial ties with us, turns us into a phantom of history, and in place of present Russia he does not want to see any one except Poles and degenerate Chuds and Tartars. What is neither Polish nor Tartar must be banished to Siberia, and in place of present powerful Russia there must arise a powerful Poland, up to Kiev, and Smolensk—Poland from the Baltic to the Black Sea. Are we to blame or condemn a Polish patriot for holding such pretensions? There is no need to blame and condemn the talk! Logical arguments will lead nowhere in such a controversy; no amount of eloquence can assist its settlement. In such an argument only events can speak, because only they possess persuasive eloquence and irresistible logic. In such controversy not words but facts decide, and facts have already decided. Be that as it may, reasonable or not, Polish pretensions are understood by and are natural with a Pole. You may condemn and dispute them, you may contest them with both word and deed, but you will agree that in its extremity, even in its own madness, Polish patriotism nevertheless is a natural phenomenon in a Pole. Events have decided, but the Pole is appealing. He has not lost his hope and is consoling himself with foreign sympathies. He does not try to discover how much sense these sympathies have, or more specifically how much sympathy there is for him and how much hostility there is for his opponent. They applaud him, they grieve for him, but in the last analysis he alone is able to feel fully the call of his nation. He has no need to subscribe to diverse theories; he doesn't need to be told about the rights of natinalities and varied truths. All he needs is to be called a Pole so that everyone can know what he wants and what he doesn't want. Common sense and experience can teach him how to understand better and clearer the interest of his nationality and how to act in its behalf with greater understanding and advantage. Be he on true or false paths, a Pole is a natural defender of his cause. Who would want to become a Pole if a Pole were not there?

Thus at least it would seem. But fate has not completely severed its ties with Poland. It struck her, but at the same time it predestined her to a rare happiness. In the midst of a battle, a Pole is finding among his adversaries his allies who are ready without any investigation to subscribe to all of his conditions. He finds on the Russian side people who with touching generosity, are prepared to sacrifice the interests of their native land and the unity and political significance of their people. He finds people prepared to serve him honorably as obedient tools, people prepared to repeat with enthusiasm everything that is spoken against the Russian name by her enemies, everything that defames and disgraces the Russian cause, everything that extols and beautifies the enemy side, people who are prepared to be Poles more than the Poles themselves.

On February 19 [1862], the very anniversary of the ascension to the throne of the present reigning Emperor, which also coincided with the first anniversary of the emancipation of so many millions of people from serfdom, there was distributed in Moscow a new product of our underground writers. We thought that this form of amusement had tired out our progressives, but here before us is a new proclamation with the stamp of *Zemlia i Volia* [Land and Liberty]. The authors of this anonymous leaflet, speaking in behalf of the Russian people, make an appeal to our officers and soldiers in Poland, trying to convince them to abandon their own flag and to turn their arms against their own motherland. It was impossible to expect such an action even from our progressives! This is worse than fire. One would like to think that this proclamation, like many others, is the work of emissaries of the Polish revolution. It is outrageous and sickening to our national feeling that our enemies think so basely of us, and that they count on the success of such tricks. Is it really possible, indeed that the Russian people gave any ground for such a contemptuous opinion of themselves? However that may be, the fact before our eyes seems to mean that there is something within us that justifies such tactics of our enemies, that we have amidst ourselves shameless elements on whom they can count and, who, by their very existence bring slander upon their country. Polish agitators have organized our domestic revolutionaries, and while they despise them in their souls, they know how to utilize them. These prophets and heroes of the Russian land (as Polish agitators speak of them in flattering their stupidity) are unaware of whose creatures they are. Indeed, think a little: how far would they have been able to advance in our society, what group would they have been able to join, or what position been able to hold? That we have enough stupidity is certainly true. But that one quality alone would have been insufficient to organize people; to arouse them to action; to implant in them a belief that, without rhyme or reason, they are acting in behalf of their own people and in their name, while in reality they are disgracing it and are infringing upon all the foundations of its historical existence. Why have all of these absurdities expressed themselves with such conviction and enthusiasm at a time when the Russian people have started a new life, when every Russian should stand at his post and perform honestly his duties? To do this, stupidity was not enough! It was necessary for the native stupidity to have been joined by an alien influence, and for some kind of adroit hand to hold this delusion, to give support to these absurdities and to galvanize this rot. Such a hand was found. It operated skillfully and it operates even now. But results have deceived it. Our enemies overreached themselves. They were carried away by their own scorn for the Russian people. They operated with deception on weak minds and thus they cruelly deceived themselves. They undertook their bloody trick because they considered Russia not only a "sick colossus," but also a decomposing carcass. They imagined that because they called them their friends, our soldiers would either scatter or join their banner. They relied on diverse proclamations and addresses, allegedly from the Russian army, and, hoping for quick success, they gave the signal to revolt. Who then is to blame for these sorrowful events that are now taking place in Poland?

The authors of the above-mentioned anonymous leaflet reproach the government for the blood that is now being shed there. But whoever they may be, Poles or Russians, let them know that they themselves were immediately responsible for this blood. If, to our shame, they really are Russians, then with their own scornful nihilism they have involved Polish agitators in a delusion disastrous for them concerning the true strength and feelings of the Russian people. If, however, they are Poles, then they put this nihilism on themselves and have deceived themselves by their own work.

The authors of this proclamation do not feel that Poland should remain united with Russia. What right have we, they exclaim, to be masters in Poland, when she herself does not wish it? What right! What kind of metaphysics will our patriots not adopt! They want to blame all the evil in the entire world on our people. They do not inquire why something happens elsewhere. They do not ask by what right Poles did own and now want to own regions that from time immemorial had been settled by the Russian people; they do not ask in what legal code this right is written, or which potentate granted this right to the Poles. This they do not ask. But they ask with a magnanimous indignation: Why do the Russians govern Poland?

They demand that Russia restore to Poland its independence! Return independence to Poland! But what is Poland? Where does it begin and where does it end? Do the Poles themselves know it? Have our patriots asked them about this? If these pitiful creatures would only free themselves from their own stupidity and foreign deception, they would realize that possession of the Kingdom of Poland is not completely a joy for Russia, that it was a necessary evil similar to those sacrifices which the Russian people assumed elsewhere to fulfill their historical destiny. But who said that Polish pretensions confine themselves to the present Kingdom of Poland? Any sober Polish patriot who understands the true interests of his people knows that in its present dimensions the Kingdom of Poland would fare better if it would retain its close ties with Russia, rather than to separate itself from her and form an independent state, insignificant in size, surrounded on all sides by powerful states, and devoid of any opportunity to gain European significance. For a Pole, the separation of Poland has never signified only a separation of the present Kingdom of Poland. No, the very thought of separation arouses pretensions to alter history and to put Poland in place of Russia. Here then is the source of all the present sufferings of the Polish people; here is the root of all of Poland's evils! If Poland were able to free herself from these pretensions, her fortunes would have been completely different, and Russia would not have any necessity to hold Poland with an armed hand. The trouble is that Polish patriotism does not renounce its pretensions: it considers to be Polish all ancient Russian territories where, in former times, Polish dominion and Catholic propaganda were spread with sword and fire.

If the question centered on whether to grant to Poland better institutions or fuller self-government and national administration, then the answer would be easy; then every Russian would be able to sympathize fully with the Poles without becoming a traitor to his motherland. But this is not the case. We know the longing of the best of Polish patriots. We know what demand was made in the name of Polish landowners by Count [Andrew] Zamojski. We also know what Polish nobles demanded in one of the Russian *gubernias* adjacent to Poland. Let foreign politicians express themselves sympathetically for the Polish cause, and let them censure Russia with reproaches. We know without them our own weaknesses and shortcomings. But we also know that with every passing year and day our position is getting brighter, and that on our horizon are unquestionable signs of a better future. No, our struggle with Poland is not a struggle over political foundations; it is a struggle of two nations, and to give in to the pretensions of Polish patriotism would mean signing a death warrant for the Russian people. Let our enemies know this: the Russian people are still alive and know how to stand for one another. If the struggle should assume the dimensions desired by Polish patriotism and our foreign critics, then not one Russian will be found who would not be ready to give his life in this struggle. Let our enemies not deceive themselves by apparitions, and let them not arouse the slumbering strength of the people. This will not serve them any good. As for us, this struggle will be the last test of history, the last consecration of our national destiny. It is easy to understand the proper significance of unfriendly manifestations of public opinion in Europe towards us, and the meaning of the unanimous blaming of

Russia and praise of the Poles that has been expressed in the British House of Commons. Why shouldn't one be able to understand it? Why shouldn't England sympathize now with the Polish cause when there is hope that it may entangle us with our difficulties and thereby place into her hands the whole Eastern question over which we both collide? As for the true aspirations of the Polish people, we view these with greatest sincerity. From the depth of our hearts we wish a better lot for the Poles. But to realize their aspirations it is necessary that the Poles not only stop exciting their pretensions but also quiet and moderate them. With the Poles lies the choice of whether both nations will live in harmony or whether they will carry on a merciless struggle, conducted not just by a government but by the whole great people.

44

Dobroliubov's Definition of "Oblomovism"

N. A. Dobroliubov (1836–1861) was an ardent follower of the literary critic V. G. Belinskii, and of the leader of Russian revolutionary intelligentsia, M. G. Chernyshevskii. In 1857 Dobroliubov became the principal literary columnist of the influential, but radically-oriented, journal *Sovremennik* [Contemporary], which was then edited by Chernyshevskii. Like Belinskii, Dobroliubov believed that literature, poetry, art, and indeed all other intellectual human endeavors, must serve society; that is, they must praise good and condemn evil, advocate progress and criticize status quo, and promote radical and avant guard ideas and oppose conservative and reactionary trends.

The most important of Dobroliubov's writings as a literary critic was his formulation of the theory of social types as represented in nineteenth century Russian literature. He used Oblomov, the lazy principal character in Ivan A. Goncharov's novel, *Oblomov,* as the superfluous man in Russia. Dobroliubov's definition of "Oblomovism" became immediately popular with the radicals and soon was incorporated not only into the Russian language but also into Russian (and later into Soviet) practice and way of life.

Source: N. Dobrolyubov, *Selected Philosophical Essays* (Moscow: 1956), p. 182 ff.

N. *Dobroliubov's Definition of "Oblomovism"*

. . . Oblomov is not altogether a new personage in our literature, but never has he been presented to us so simply and naturally as he is in [Ivan A.] Goncharov's novel [*Oblomov*]. Not to go too far back into the past, we shall say that we find the generic features of the Oblomov type already in [Alexander Pushkin's *Evgenii*] *Onegin*; and then we find them repeated several times in the best of our literary productions. The point is that this is our native, national type, which not one of our serious artists could brush aside. . . .

What are the main features of the Oblomov character? Utter inertness resulting from apathy towards everything that goes on in the world. The cause of this apathy lies partly in Oblomov's external position and partly in the manner of his mental and moral development. The external position is that he is a gentleman: "he has a Zakhar, and another three hundred Zakhars," [Zakhar is Oblomov's personal serf. The "three hundred" are the serfs owned by Oblomov as part of his estate], as the author puts it. Ilya Ilyich (Oblomov) explains the advantages of his position to Zakhar in the following way:

> Do I fuss and worry? Do I work? Don't I have anough to eat? Do I look thin and haggard? Am I in want of anything? Have I not people to fetch and carry for me, to do the things I want done? Thank God, I have never in my life had to draw a pair of stockings on. Do you think I would go to any trouble? Why should I? . . . But I need not tell you all of this. Haven't you served me since childhood? You know all about it. You have seen how tenderly I was brought up. You know that I have never suffered cold or hunger, that I have never known want, that I don't have to earn my bread and, in general, have never done any work.

Oblomov is speaking the absolute truth. The entire history of his upbringing confirms what he says. He became accustomed to lolling about at a very early age because he had people to fetch and carry for him, to do things for him. Under these circumstances he lived the idle life of a sybarite even when he did not want to. And tell me, pray, what can you expect of a man who grew up under the following circumstances:

> Zakhar—as his [Oblomov's] nurse did in the old days—draws on his stockings and puts on his shoes while Ilyusha [that is, diminutive of Ilya], already a boy of fourteen, does nothing but lie on his back and put up one foot and then the other; and if it seems to him that Zakhar has done something not in the right way, he kicks him in the nose. . . . After that Zakhar combs Ilya Ilyich's hair, helps him on with his coat, carefully putting his arms into the sleeves so as not to incommode him too much, and reminds him that he must do so and so and so: on waking up in the morning—to wash himself, and so forth.
>
> If Ilya Ilyich wants anything he has only to make a sign—and at once three

> or four servants rush to carry out his wishes; if he drops anything, if he reaches for something he needs and cannot get it, if something has to be brought in, or if it is necessary to run on some errand—he sometimes, like the active boy he is, is just eager to run and do it himself, but suddenly his mother and his father and his three aunts shout in a quintet: "Where are you going? What for? What are Vaska and Vanka and Zakharka here for? . . . And so Ilya Ilyich is simply not allowed to do anything for himself. . . .

An important factor here is the mental development of the Oblomovs, which, of course, is also moulded by their external position. From their earliest years they see life turned inside out, as it were, and until the end of their days they are unable to understand what their relation to the world and to the people should reasonably be. Later on much is explained to them and they begin to understand something; but the views that were inculcated in them in their childhood remain somewhere in a corner and constantly peep out from there, hindering all new conceptions and preventing them from sinking deep into their hearts. . . . As a result, chaos reigns in their heads: sometimes a man makes up his mind to do something, but he does not know how to begin, where to turn. . . .

Oblomov is not a dull, apathetic type, destitute of ambition and feeling; he too seeks something in life, thinks about something. But the disgusting habit of getting his wishes satisfied not by his own efforts but by the efforts of others developed in him an apathetic inertness and plunged him into the wretched state of moral slavery. This slavery is so closely interwoven with Oblomov's aristocratic habits that they mutually permeate and determine each other, so that it becomes totally impossible to draw any line of demarcation between them. . . .

The whole life of this gentleman [Ilya Ilyich Oblomov] is wrecked because he always remains the slave of another's will and never rises to the level of displaying the least bit of independence. He is the slave of every woman, of every newcomer; the slave of every rascal who wishes to get him under his thumb. He is the slave of his serf Zakhar, and it is hard to say which of them submits more to the power of the other. . . .

The foregoing reflections have brought us to the conclusion that Oblomov is not a being whom nature has completely deprived of the ability to move by his own volition. His indolence and apathy are the results of upbringing and environment. The main thing here is not Oblomov, but Oblomovshchina. Perhaps Oblomov would even have started work had he found an occupation to his liking; but for that he would have had to develop under somewhat different conditions. In his present position he cannot find an occupation to his liking because he sees no meaning in life in general and cannot rationally define his own relations to others. This is where he provides us with the occasion for comparing him with previous types, which the best of our writers have depicted. It was observed long ago that all the heroes in the finest Russian stories and novels suffer from their failure to see any purpose in life and their inability to find a decent occupation for themselves. As a consequence they find all occupations tedious and repugnant, and in this they reveal an astonishing resemblance to Oblomov. . . .

The feature common to all these men is that nothing in life is a vital necessity for them, a shrine in their hearts, a religion, organically merged with their whole being, so that to deprive them of it would mean depriving them of their lives. Everything about them is superficial, nothing is rooted in their natures. They, perhaps, do something when external necessity compels them to, just as Oblomov went visiting the places that Stoltz dragged him to, and bought music and books for Olga and read what she compelled him to read; but their hearts do not lie in the things they do merely by force of circumstances. If each of them were offered gratis all the external advantages that they obtain by their work they would gladly give up working. By virtue of Oblomovshchina, an Oblomov government official would not go to his office every day if he could receive his salary and regular promotion without having to do so. A soldier would vow not to touch a weapon if he were offered the same terms and, in addition, were allowed to keep his splendid uniform, which can be very useful on certain occasions. The professor would stop delivering lectures, the student would give up his studies, the author would give up writing, the actor would never appear on the stage again and the artist would break his chisel and palette, to put it in high-flown style, if he found a way of obtaining gratis all that he now obtains by working. They only talk about lofty strivings, consciousness of moral duty and common interests; when put to the test, it all turns out to be words, mere words. Their most sincere and heartfelt striving is the striving for repose, for the dressing gown, and their very activities are nothing more than an *honourable dressing gown* (to use an expression that is not our own) with which they cover up their vapidity and apathy. Even the best educated people, people with lively natures and warm hearts, are prone in their practical lives to depart from their ideas and plans, very quickly resign themselves to the realities of life, which, however, they never cease to revile as vulgar and disgusting. This shows that all the things they talk and dream about are really alien to them, superficial; in the depth of their hearts they cherish only one dream, one ideal—undistributed repose, quietism, Oblomovshchina. Many even reach such a stage that they cannot conceive of man working willingly, with enthusiasm. . . .

Now, when I hear a country squire talking about the rights of man and urging the necessity of developing personality, I know from the first words he utters that he is an Oblomov.

When I hear a government official complaining that the system of administration is too complicated and cumbersome, I know that he is an Oblomov.

When I hear an army officer complaining that parades are exhausting, and boldly arguing that marching at a *slow pace* is useless, etc., I have not the slighest doubt that he is an Oblomov.

When, in the magazines, I read liberal denunciations of abuses and expressions of joy over the fact that at last something has been done that we have been waiting and hoping for for so long, I think to myself that all this has been written from Oblomovka.

When I am in the company of educated people who ardently sympathize with the needs of mankind and who for many years have been relating with undiminished heat the same (and sometimes new) anecdotes about bribery, acts of tyranny and lawlessness of every kind, I, in spite of myself, feel that I have been transported to old Oblomovka. . . .

45

Russian Colonial Aspirations in the Pacific Rim, 1798–1867

Like many of its contemporary major powers, Imperial Russia in the nineteenth century pursued an active colonial policy in Europe, in Asia and in the Pacific Rim. The principal instrument of colonial adventure in the Pacific Rim was the Russian American Company, which was officially chartered in 1798. The Company was a mixture of private and government interests. Its primary goal was the establishment of Russian presence in Alaska, California, the Kurils, the Aleutians, Sakhalin, and all islands and territories that were not claimed by other major powers.

The proponents of Russian colonial venture in the North Pacific used

---

The following four selections are reproduced by permission of the Oregon Historical Society Press from Basil Dmytryshyn, E. A. P. Crownhart-Vaughan and Thomas Vaughan, eds., *The Russian American Colonies, 1798–1867: A Documentary Record* (Portland: The Oregon Historical Society Press, 1989), pp. 18–23, 159–162, 290–292, 482–484.

every means to achieve their ambition. Communication difficulties, however, together with the emergence of more essential priorities in the European part of the empire, prevented the dream from becoming reality. In 1817 the Russians abandoned their beachhead in Hawaii. In 1841 they sold their colonial outpost in Northern California (Fort Ross). And in 1867 they liquidated their colonial possessions in Alaska with the sale to the United States. The last transaction was a good bargain for both sides. The Russians rid themselves of a faraway territory they could neither supply nor defend, while the Americans acquired a region whose full economic and strategic potentials became clear in the twentieth century.

An Imperial Decree From Emperor Paul I Granting Special Privileges to the Russian American Company for a Period of Twenty Years, December 27, 1799

By the most auspicious grace of God, We, Paul the First, Emperor and Autocrat of All Russia, and so forth, and so forth, and so forth.

We Extend Our Most High Patronage to the Russian American Company.

The benefits and advantages which will accrue to Our Empire from the hunting and trade carried on by Our loyal subjects in the Pacific Ocean and in the land of America have attracted Our Monarchial attention and esteem. For that reason We extend Our imediate partonage to the Company which conducts hunting and trade there and direct that it be named the *Russian American Company.* We further direct that in order to augument the ventures of that Company, all military officers of Our country as well as Our naval forces are to provide support whenever the Company may request it to enable it to conduct its business.

In order to govern, facilitate and encourage the Company, We hereby establish its regulations. By virtue of Our Most Gracious Imperial charter, We hereby grant this Company the following privileges for a period of 20 years:

1. On the basis of the fact that long ago Russian seafarers were the first to discover the coast of America to the northeast [of us], beginning from 55° northern latitude, and the archipelago of islands extending from Kamchatka north to America, and south to Japan, and by Russia's right to possess these lands, We, the All Gracious, permit the company to profit from all hunting and other ventures presently established along the coast of America to the northeast, from the above mentioned 55° to Bering Strait and beyond and likewise on the Aleutian, Kuril, and other islands located in the North Pacific Ocean.

2. The Company may undertake to make new discoveries, not only above 55° northern latitude, but to the south as well; they may occupy lands they discover and claim them as Russian possessions, in accordance with the previously prescribed regulations, provided that these newly discovered territories have not previously been occupied by other nations or have come under their protection.

3. The Company may utilize, without any claims from others, everything above and below ground in places it has already discovered or may in the future discover.

4. We most graciously direct that in the future the Company may rely on its own judgment and, in accordance with need, build settlements and fortified places wherever necessary for the safety of its employees; and without any hindrance whatsoever, it may also send *promyshlenniks* to that region as well as ships carrying goods.

5. In order to increase and strengthen its enterprises, the Company may sail to all nearby nations and enter into trade with all adjacent powers, providing it has their permission and Our Imperial consent.

6. For its voyages, hunting, and other enterprises, the Company may hire people from all walks of life who are free and not under suspicion for some misdemeanor and who hold legal documents permitting them to be hired. Because the places these persons will be sent are so far distant, the *gubernia* [provincial] administration should issued passports valid for seven years to state settlers and free persons from other classes. The Company should not hire peasants and household serfs belonging to *pomeshchiks* [landowners] without permission from the *pomeshchiks* themselves. The Company must pay state taxes for all persons they hire.

7. Although Our Imperial *ukazes* prohibit the cutting of timber without permission from the Admiralty College, nevertheless, considering the distance that separates the Admiralty from the Okhotsk *oblast* [administrative region] where this Company will need to repair ships, and sometimes to build new ships, the Company is to be permitted to [cut and] use lumber without any restrictions.

8. For use in hunting animals, firing sea signals, and all unexpected emergencies that may arise on the American mainland and on the islands, the Company may use its own funds to purchase 40 to 50 *puds* [one *pud* = 36 pounds] of gunpowder per year from the Government artillery depot in Irkutsk, and 200 *puds* of shot from the Nerchinsk factory.

9. If any shareholder of the Company becomes indebted to the Treasury or to private individuals, and has no means with which to repay the debt except for the shares he holds in the Company, in such a case, even though the capital he had invested in the Company is subject to confiscation, never-

theless, on the basis of the regulations of the Company, that capital is to remain untouched in the Company. The creditor cannot demand its release for payment of the debt; as first mortgagee he may only lay claim to the dividends when they are distributed. Upon termination of the Company's privileges, the debtor may claim what is due him in full.

10. Because We have most graciously granted the Company the exclusive rights, for a period of twenty years, to acquire everything necessary to hunt, trade, establish enterprises, and discover new lands, throughout the entire region previously described, we hereby prohibit the enjoyment of these benefits and privileges not only to those who would like to voyage there on their own, but also to all previous *promyshlenniks* engaged in that trade who have ships and enterprises in those places, as well as to those persons who may have participated in the united company as shareholders but did not choose to join the Company. To these latter, in case of disagreements over joining this Company, as stipulated in the Company's regulations, We grant the right to continue their enterprises and enjoy the benefits under the same terms as previously, but only until their vessels return. After that, no one will have these privileges except said Company, under threat of confiscation of all their property.

11. Because the Main Administration of the Russian American Company is under Our Imperial protection, all offices [in the Empire] must note that the Main Administration is in charge of Company business. Should local courts desire information on Company matters, such requests must be directed to the Main Administration of the Company, not to any shareholders.

In concluding this, Our Imperial *gramota* placing the Russian American Company under Our Imperial protection, We instruct all Our military and civil officials and all government offices not to interfere with these privileges We have granted. Further, in case of need or any possible development which may bring loss or harm to the Company, such officials are to warn the Company, and if requested by the Company's Main Administration, to provide every assistance and defense. To add emphasis to this, Our *gramota*, We have signed it personally, and have ordered that it be sealed with Our Imperial Seal.

A Statement from Directors of the Russian American Company Regarding Problems Caused by the Incursion of Bostonians into Waters and Territories Claimed by Russia, April 21, 1808

In the northwestern part of America the Russian American Company has established trade, set up hunting operations, built forts and settlements, constructed ships and undertaken every possible kind of enterprise. Above all, it has persuaded many savage native tribes to accept the sovereign power of Russia over them, and to profess their [Russian Orthodox] religion. The Company constantly attempts to improve and expand these programs; it even hopes to establish educational facilities for native children and charitable homes for impoverished and orphaned girls. But all of these efforts are encountering serious obstructions.

The single most important reason is that ever since 1792, every year ten to fifteen merchant ships come to that region from the North American United States. On these ships come [American] citizens who trade not only with the [Russian American] Company, but with American savages who live in various places on the islands and mainland. The Americans trade for furs to sell in Canton; every year they obtain as many as 15,000 sea otter pelts and 5000 beaver pelts, in addition to other furs. And in exchange for these they bring various goods but especially firearms such as cannon, falconets, guns, pistols, sabers, and other instruments of destruction; they also bring gunpowder; and they even teach the savages how to use these weapons.

The harm to Russian American Company trade in this land, caused by these American citizens includes the following:

In regard to trade: Every year the Americans carry to Canton the above mentioned number of sea otter pelts. They sell the sea otters to the Chinese for 50 *rubles* apiece; beaver pelts fetch five *rubles* each. The Americans take half in cash and the rest in tea, which they obtain for forty *rubles* per *pud* in our currency. If we assume this price, then the sale of this number of sea otters and beavers brings 775,000 *rubles*; and this does not include the sale of furs of other land animals. They snatch this profit right out of the hands of Russian subjects, and right under their eyes. They make a huge profit both from the sale of tea in Europe and from the barter of their goods with the savages. They give the natives a firearm (certainly not the best quality) and ten cartridges and bullets in exchange for one sea otter.

The Chinese, for whom these furs and others from land animals have become indispensable, and who obtain so many of them in Canton [where Russians are prohibited from trading], give us as much lower price for our furs in Kiakhta, which is the only place we can sell them. Further, they buy few from us; each year they buy no more than 2000 to 3000 sea otters and between 80,000 and 100,000 fur seals. And in addition to this problem, in Kiakhta we have to pay duty on these furs as well as on the goods we buy from the Chinese. This expense is a severe impairment to our trade, and because of it we have to resell the Chinese goods at much higher prices each year.

In regard to political and moral matters: The North American republicans expand their operations in places occupied by the Company and induce in the savages actions contrary to the goals of the Company. They instill among them the notion that they should not consider the Russians their oldest, most dependable, and best friends, with the natural right to be their protectors not only against foreign nations but in intertribal quarrels. Such disputes have long been customary among them, and have led to their mutual destruction, with one tribe constantly warring with another over trivial insults. The republicans encourage this depravity by bringing all manner of firearms to exchange with these savages, who by their very natures and lack of education are craven and brutal.

As a result of this the savages have caused a number of unfortunate situations for the Russians who had been friendly and had had commercial relations with them. In addition to the many successful attempts they have made to destroy the Russians in their settlements, in 1801 the Sitka Islanders, reinforced by groups of mainland natives, came in great numbers and attacked our Mikhailovsk fort on that island. They killed the people in the fort with fire, and with swords killed the garrison of Russian *promyshlenniks* who had been there.

On the basis of explanations by some of the savages themselves, the local Chief Administrator, Baranov, believes the Bostonian ships and crews of skippers Crocker *[Jenny]* and [William] Cunningham *[Globe]** were responsible for this disaster, for they not only incited the islanders but gave them gunpowder and guns. After the Russians had been killed the Bostonians took from the savages all the furs the Russians had obtained, which amounted to 3700 sea otter pelts and others, with a value of more than 300,000 *rubles.* They also burned the Company vessels, and were brutal toward any natives who asked a high price for a sea otter or some other pelt during the barter negotiations.

Another incident occurred in 1805 in Yakutat Bay on the mainland where the Company had established a settlement called Slavorossia. Several families lived there, both men and women; they were farmers, artisans, and hunters. They had for some time had friendly relations with the savages, and were confident of their security; however, the savages obtained firearms from the Bostonians; and being inclined to battle and violence, they took the Russians by surprise, as well as Aleuts and other American natives who were loyal to us. They killed them all, burned the settlement, and destroyed the entire enterprise.

*Cunningham, the mate, took command of the ship after her skipper, Bernard Magee, was killed by natives at Skidgate in the Queen Charlotte Islands in October 1801.

That same year the Russians built a settlement for the second time on the island of Sitka. This time, by chance, they found the savages had a wooden fortess equipped with guns and other small weapons traded from the Bostonians. They inflicted considerable harm on us, and if the crew of the ship *Neva* [commanded by Iurii Lisianskii] had not come to our help when they stopped there during their circumnavigation, it would still be in doubt whether that island belonged to us.

Indeed these lawless people, because of a shift [in attitude], suffered the same consequences they had caused us. In 1805 skipper [O.] Porter [*Atahualpa*] was in Milbanke Sound bartering with the savages to acquire some 6000 sea otter pelts. He let the savages who had brought the pelts come aboard his ship, but as soon as they were aboard they shot Porter and several of his crew with pistols obtained from Porter himself. The natives threw the bodies overboard. If it had not been for the bold decision of the navigator Adams [who took command of *Atahualpa*] and the arrival of another Bostonian vessel [*Lydia*] under the command of skipper [Samuel] Hill, who put down the insurrection, Porter's ship and entire crew would have been taken by the savages.

For these reasons, long ago the Company administrator on Kodiak undertook to explain to the Bostonians who came there the forceful instructions he had from his government; he advised them they were not to come to barter with the savages for furs in places that belonged to Russia, and especially they were not to bring them firearms. They were to do all trading with the Company. But even in the face of this advice, the Bostonians would simply reply that they were merchants, free to seek their profit. In regard to any prohibition against trading with the savages, they replied they had not heard of any such prohibition either from their own government or from the Russian government.

These circumstances lead to the conclusion that in order to establish permanent [Russian] settlements in that land, to maintain and increase various institutions in the future, as well as to develop enterprises based solely on the hunting and trade of the dependent peoples, it is necessary that Imperial authority issue a statement that foreigners, and especially the North American republicans, are prohibited there. A similar situation exists in all other European colonies, in both Indies, where no [foreigner] may trade with the savages, but only with the [colonizing] company. This would only apply to Kodiak, the main Russian factory site. They [foreigners] could enter into commercial relations with the Company, and if there is mutual agreement, local trade could be set up with any republicans they wish. This could be established on mutually advantageous terms. Without such a statement, all of the Company's concern about that land will not be sufficient to produce the desired result.

Principal Director and Cavalier [M. M.] Buldakov
Director Benedikt Kramer

A Report from the Main Administration of the Russian American Company to the Minister of Foreign Affairs, Karl V. Nesselrode, Concerning the Hawaiian Islands, August 17, 1817

A few days ago the Main Administration of the Russian American Company had the honor of sending Your Excellency certain information on the [Russian] establishment on the coast of California. The copy herewith appended, of a report received since then from Dr. [Georg] Schäffer, from the island of Kauai, describes the danger which this establishment presently faces from the Spanish.

This report primarily concerns the news that the king of the islands of Kauai and Onecheo has not only given the Russians a cordial reception but that he has made certain commercial arrangements, and has submitted himself unto the sovereignty and protection of His Imperial Majesty. As testimony of this he has presented a formal document to Dr. Schäffer, a copy of which is enclosed. Schäffer reports that he sent the original [to Russia] on a Russian ship.

When this news is submitted to the attention of His Imperial Majesty, it may lead to a superior order and may reach the sloop *Kamchatka* before her departure. If this should be the case, the Main Administration of the Company humbly requests permission to send certain dispatches to its employees.

The English newspaper *Courier* of July 30 [1817] reports this news in an article, which is appended.

The Main Administration of
the Russian American Company
Benedikt Kramer
Andrei I. Severin

[Dr. Schäffer's report:]

The ship *Bering* which belonged to the [Russian American] Company was wrecked on the island of Kauai in the Sandwich Islands, as a result of the malicious deeds of Captain [James] Bennett. I was sent here by Collegiate Counselor Baranov in the capacity of plenipotentiary to investigate this matter and demand the return of the cargo which the Indians salvaged. To my great satisfaction, I carried out this assignment in twenty-four hours. Thus 20,000 Spanish *piasters* worth of goods were saved for the Company.

Baranov also wanted to build a factory in the Sandwich Islands, but King Kamehameha, whose activities were guided by an old English seaman, [John] Young, and by several Americans, firmly rejected this proposal. However, King Tamara of Kauai not only agreed to the establishment of the Russian factory, but even requested protection from the Russian emperor. In a very solemn ceremony, in a written document he entrusted supreme authority over his island to His Imperial Majesty, the Russian Emperor Alexander Pavlovich. I am sending herewith a copy of this document. The original will be sent via Sitka and other points to the Main Administration in St. Petersburg, so it will be presented at the foot of the throne of His Imperial Majesty. [The Company] should request Imperial all-gracious approval and immediately inform me here, via Sitka, by reliable means.

In the name of the Company I concluded a commercial agreement with King Tamara, under the terms of which the Company secures the exclusive right to purchase sandalwood. Further, the King transferred into Company ownership for all time the entire area of Kauai, with a population of some 400 Indian families. We can use the land for plantations, factories and the like. The place also has a maritime harbor called Honolulu. I will send the principal documents to St. Petersburg with a Russian ship, or via Okhotsk. The documents contain the most detailed account of everything.

My only desire is to have dispatched from St. Petersburg to here two good ships with full crews and appropriate armaments. There is not a single reliable ship in Sitka, nor any experienced navigator with the exception of Lieutenant [Iakov] Podushkin. There is everywhere a shortage of labor and of artisans.

Russian settlement in California is threatened with complete destruction by the Spanish. I know very well that the Governor of Monterey has asked permission from the Viceroy of Mexico to do just that. Quite recently he took some thirty *baidaras* [boats], and Aleuts and many Russians, including Dr. Elliot [John Elliot de Castro], into the interior as captives.

Perhaps His Majesty the Emperor will send a frigate to the Pacific. It will render substantial service and be very important for the Russian Empire. I would like to have two 400-ton ships from the Company. The Company ship *Otkrytie,* which brought me here, lost two masts, and we barely escaped with our lives.

Georg Schäffer

The Views of Count Nikolai N. Muravev Regarding the Necessity for Russia to Control the Amur River, 1849–1850

Russia must occupy the mouth of the Amur River and that part of Sakhalin Island which lies opposite, as well as the left bank of the Amur River, for the following reasons.

I. Concern for the eastern frontier of the Empire.

Rumors have for quite some time circulated through Siberia concerning the intentions of the English to occupy the mouth of the Amur River and Sakhalin Island. God forbid they should become entrenched there before we do! In order to establish more through and complete control over trade with China, the English undoubtedly need to control both the mouth of the Amur and the navigation on that river. If the Amur were not the only river flowing from Siberia to the Pacific Ocean, we might not have any objection to their intentions, but navigation via the Amur is the only suitable route to the east. This is a century-old dream of Siberians of all classes; it may be instinctive, but it is no less well grounded.

Upon review of all circumstances known to me, I can state that whoever controls the mouth of the Amur will also control Siberia, at least as far as Baikal, and that control will be firm. It is enough to control the mouth of this river and navigation on it for Siberia, which is increasing in population and flourishing in agriculture and industry, to remain an unalterable tributary and subject of the power which holds the key to it.

II. Strengthening and securing possession of the Kamchatka Peninsula.

Only when we have the left bank of the Amur and the navigation rights on it can we establish communication with Kamchatka, and thus be in a position to establish Russia's firm control over this peninsula. The reason is that the route via Iakutsk and Okhotsk or Aian offers no means of supplying Kamchatka with sufficient military capacity, nor to provide it with proper population, which in and of itself, under the protection of fortresses, would comprise the strength of this distant *oblast* and furnish local land and naval forces with their necessary provisions. With the establishment of steam navigation on the Amur, Kamchatka could be provisioned from Nerchinsk with people and all necessities in no more than two weeks. The Amur River flows from our frontiers to the island of Sakhalin for more than 2000 *versts*, and according to all available information, is navigable for its entire length.

III. Support for our trade with China.

The decrease in the Kiakhta trade already indicates that the intentions of the English in China cannot be beneficial to us. During the first years after their war [Opium War, 1839–42], we did not realize this, because the

Chinese, motivated by their enmity toward the English, preferred to turn to us as their reliable and gracious neighbors. But time and material benefits mitigate the outburst of animosity, and moderate a flame of friendship which does not represent substantial benefits. I believe that the only way to promote our trade with China is to change it from local to widespread, so that by sailing on the Amur we could supply the products of our manufacture to all the northeastern provinces of China, which are more distant from present activities of the English, and consequently, from their competition which is dangerous to our trade.

IV. Maintaining our influence in China.

The English war and peace in China have laid the foundation for the transformation of that populous empire under the influence of the English. But during the lifetime of the late Chinese Emperor, we still hoped he would personally announce that since he had been insulted by them, he could not be favorably disposed toward them and consequently would not allow the spread of English influence in his empire.

Now, with the ascension of his eighteen-year-old son, one can be certain that the English will hasten to turn this event to their advantage with their usual natural entrepreneurial spirit, speed, and persistence, so as to gain control not only of trade, but also of China's politics. I cannot judge whether we can prevent this, when five of China's ports have been not only accessible to the English, but have actually almost become English cities.

I believe it would be prudent for us to have better security along the frontiers with China, to the extent of our domestic needs, so the English will not gain full control there, and thus we must control the Amur. I also think that we must capitalize on current developments in China so we can reveal our plans to them, based on the general benefits to both empires; to wit, that no one but Russia and China should control navigation on the Amur, and that the mouth of that river should be protected, and of course, not by the Chinese.

46

The Russo-German Alliance System, 1863–1890

Between 1863 and 1890 one of the cornerstones of Russian foreign policy in Europe was close cooperation with Bismarck's Germany. That cooperation, based on dynastic ties, adherence to conservatism, and national interests, assumed varied forms and brought many benefits to both countries. Thus for instance, with Russia's "benevolent neutrality," Bismarck unified Germany; while with Bismarck's active support, Russia annulled all restrictions of the Treaty of Paris. The Russo-German close cooperation began in 1863 when the two countries signed a secret agreement, the Alvensleben Convention, aimed at suppressing the Polish rebellion. In May 1873, the two powers signed a secret defensive military convention, and in June 1873, the two Empires were joined by Austria-Hungary in the Schönbrunn Convention (commonly known as the League of the Three Emperors) to maintain peace and status quo in Europe. Late in the 1870's the League was greatly weakened by developments in the Balkans (where Russian and Austrian interests clashed head-on), but it was revived in June 1881 in a series of new agreements. Finally, on June 18, 1887, Bismarck negotiated with the Russians a secret arrangement known as the Reinsurance Treaty, whose terms remained in force until 1890.

Texts of the documents listed in this section came from the following sources: "The Alvensleben Convention" from Karol Lutostanski, *Recueil des actes diplomatique, traites et documents concernant la Pologne* (A Collection of Diplomatic Papers, Treaties and Documents Concerning Poland) (Lausanne: Bureau Polonaise, 1918), I, pp. 598–599. Translation mine; "The Military Convention" of 1873 from *Russko-germanskie otnosheniia.* Sekretnye dokumenty (The Russo-German Relations. Secret Documents) (Moscow: Tsentrarkhiv, 1922), pp. 28–29. Translation mine; and "The Convention of Schönbrunn" of 1873, "The Convention of Berlin" of 1881, and "The Reinsurance Treaty" of 1887, were reprinted by permission of the publishers from Alfred Francis Pribram, ed. *The Secret Treaties of Austria-Hungary, 1879–1914.* English edition by Archibald Cary Coolidge (Cambridge, Mass.: Harvard University Press, 1920), II, pp. 185–187 (alternate pages) and I, pp. 37–47 and 275–281 (alternate pages).

The Alvensleben Convention, February 8, 1863

The Courts of Russia and Prussia, having determined that the recent developments in the Kingdom of Poland pose serious threats to public and private property and can endanger the internal order in the Prussian frontier provinces, are agreed:

That, upon the request of the Commander-in-chief of the Russian army in the Kingdom of Poland or upon that of Infantry General von Werder, Commander-in-chief of the first, second, fifth, and sixth Prussian Army Corps, or at the request of the frontier authorities of the two countries, the commanders of Russian and Prussian detachments are authorized to take common action, and, in case of need, to cross the frontier in pursuit of the rebels who may flee from one country into the other.

Special officers will be sent by each [of the contracting] parties to the General Headquarters of the two armies, as well as to the [headquarters of] the detached corps commanders, to facilitate the practical application of this entente.

These officers will be kept informed of the military dispositions in order that they may communicate these to their respective commanders.

The present arrangement will remain in effect as long as the state of affairs so dictates and so long as the two Courts judge it to be necessary.

Gorchakov von Alvensleben

Secret Article

The Courts of Russia and of Prussia undertake to exchange, by means of their military and civil organs, [all information] concerning the direction of political currents as they affect the Kingdom of Poland or the Grand Duchy of Posen.

Gorchakov von Alvensleben
St. Petersburg, February 8, 1863.

The Military Convention, May 6, 1873

His Majesty the Emperor of All-Russia and His Majesty the Emperor of Germany, in order to give a practical meaning to the idea which they cordially endorse, namely, the strengthening of the presently prevailing peace in Europe and the removal of a possibility of war which could disrupt it, have authorized their Field Marshals, Counts Berg and Moltke, to conclude the following military convention:

Article 1

In the event a European power should attack one of the Empires, the other, in the shortest possible time, would come to its aid with an army of 200,000.

Article 2

This military convention does not have as its aim any hostile intent towards any nation or government.

Article 3

In the event one contracting party should wish to terminate the present military convention it should give a two year notice (twenty-four months) after which time the convention will be considered invalid, in order to give the other side sufficient time to take such measures which it considered essential.

Done at Petersburg, May 6, 1873.

Berg Moltke

We ratify it, May 6, 1873.

Alexander Wilhelm

An Appendix to the Military Convention

The undersigned Field Marshals, in signing the Military Convention which they concluded today, agree that beginning with the day when supporting armies cross the fronties of their own country, the expenses for the food for men, the forage for horses, and for hospitals will be paid by the country which receives the aid.

St. Petersburg, May 6, 1873

Berg Moltke

The Convention of Schönbrunn, June 6, 1873

(a)

His Majesty the Emperor of Austria and King of Hungary and His Majesty the Emperor of All the Russias, desiring to give a practical form to the thought which presides over their intimate understanding, with the object of consolidating the state of peace which exists at present in Europe, and having at heart to reduce the chances of war which might disturb it—convinced that this object could not better be attained than by a direct and personal understanding between the Sovereigns, an understanding independent of the changes which might be made in their administrations, have come into agreement upon the following points:

1. Their Majesties mutually promise, even though the interests of their States should present some divergences respecting special questions, to take counsel together in order that these divergences may not be able to prevail over the considerations of a higher order which preoccupy them. Their Majesties are determined to prevent any one from succeeding in separating them in the field of the principles which they regard as alone capable of assuring, and, if necessary, of imposing the maintenance of the peace of Europe against all subversions, from whatsoever quarter they may come.

2. In case an aggression coming from a third Power should threaten to compromise the peace of Europe, Their Majesties mutually engage to come to a preliminary understanding between themselves, without seeking or contracting new alliances, in order to agree as to the line of conduct to be followed in common.

3. If, as a result of this understanding, a military action should become necessary, it would be governed by a special convention to be concluded between Their Majesties.

4. If one of the High Contracting Parties, wishing to recover its independence of action, should desire to denounce the present Agreement, it must do so two years in advance, in order to give the other Party time to make whatever arrangements may be suitable.

Schönbrunn, May 25 1873 / June 6

Francis Joseph Alexander

The Convention Between Austria-Hungary, The German Empire, and Russia, Berlin, June 18, 1881

(a)

Article 1

In case one of the High Contracting Parties should find itself at war with a fourth Great Power, the two others shall maintain towards it a benevolent neutrality and shall devote their efforts to the localization of the conflict.

This stipulation shall apply likewise to a war between one of the three Powers and Turkey, but only in the case where a previous agreement shall have been reached between the three Courts as to the results of this war.

In the special case where one of them should obtain a more positive support from one of its two Allies, the obligatory value of the present Article shall remain in all its force for the third.

Article 2

Russia, in agreement with Germany, declares her firm resolution to respect the interests arising from the new position assured to Austria-Hungary by the Treaty of Berlin.

The three Courts, desirous of avoiding all discord between them, engage to take account of their respective interests in the Balkan Peninsula. They further promise one another that any new modifications in the territorial status quo of Turkey in Europe can be accomplished only in virtue of a common agreement between them.

In order to facilitate the agreement contemplated by the present Article, an agreement of which it is impossible to foresee all the conditions, the three Courts from the present moment record in the Protocol annexed to this Treaty the points on which an understanding has already been established in principle.

Article 3

The three Courts recognize the European and mutually obligatory character of the principle of the closing of the Straits of the Bosphorus and of the Dardanelles, founded on international law, confirmed by treaties, and summed up in the declaration of the second Plenipotentiary of Russia at the session of July 12 of the Congress of Berlin (Protocol 19).

They will take care in common that Turkey shall make no exception to this rule in favor of the interests of any Government whatsoever, by lending to warlike operations of a belligerent Power the portion of its Empire constituted by the Straits.

In case of infringement, or to prevent it if such infringement should be in prospect, the three Courts will inform Turkey that they would regard her, in that event, as putting herself in a state of war towards the injured Party, and as having deprived herself thenceforth of the benefits of the security assured to her territorial status quo by the Treaty of Berlin.

Article 4

The present Treaty shall be in force during a period of three years, dating from the day of the exchange of ratifications.

Article 5

The High Contracting Parties mutually promise secrecy as to the contents and the existence of the present Treaty, as well as of the Protocol annexed thereto.

Article 6

The secret Conventions concluded between Austria-Hungary and Russia and between Germany and Russia in 1873 are replaced by the present Treaty.

Article 7

The ratifications of the present Treaty and of the Protocol annexed thereto shall be exchanged at Berlin within a forthnight, or sooner if may be. . . .

(b)
The Convention of Berlin, Among Austria-Hungary, the German Empire, and Russia, June 18, 1881.

The undersigned Plenipotentiaries of His Majesty the Emperor of Austria, King of Bohemia, and so forth, and Apostolic King of Hungary,

His Majesty the Emperor of Germany, King of Prussia, and His Majesty the Emperor of All the Russias, having recorded in accordance with Article II of the secret Treaty concluded today the points affecting the interests of the three Courts of Austria-Hungary, Germany, and Russia in the Balkan Peninsula, upon which an understanding has already been reached among them, have agreed to the following Protocol:

1. Bosnia and Herzegovina.

Austria-Hungary reserves the right to annex these provinces at whatever moment she shall deem opportune.

2. Sanjak of Novibazar.

The Declaration exchanged between the Austro-Hungarian Plenipotentiaries and the Russian Plenipotentiaries at the Congress of Berlin under date of July 13/1, 1878, remains in force.

3. Eastern Rumelia.

The three Powers agree in regarding the eventuality of an occupation either of Eastern Rumelia or of the Balkans as full of perils for the general peace. In case this should occur, they will employ their efforts to dissuade the Porte from such an enterprise, it being well understood that Bulgaria and Eastern Rumelia on their part are to abstain from provoking the Porte by attacks emanating from their territories against the other provinces of the Ottoman Empire.

4. Bulgaria.

The three Powers will not oppose the eventual reunion of Bulgaria and Eastern Rumelia within the territorial limits assigned to them by the Treaty of Berlin, if this question should come up by the force of circumstances. They agree to dissuade the Bulgarians from all aggression against the neighboring provinces, particularly Macedonia; and to inform them that in such a case they would be acting at their own risk and peril.

5. Attitude of Agents in the East.

In order to avoid collisions of interests in the local questions which may arise, the three Courts will furnish their representatives and agents in the Orient with a general instruction, directing them to endeavor to smooth out their divergences by friendly explanations between themselves in each special case; and, in the cases where they do not succeed in doing so, to refer the matters to their governments.

6.

The present Protocol forms an integral part of the secret Treaty signed on this day at Berlin, and shall have the same force and validity.. . . .

(c)
Additional Protocol to the Convention of June 18, 1881. Berlin, June 27, 1881.

In order to define still more precisely Paragraph 5 of the Protocol annexed to the secret Treaty of June 18, 1881, the undersigned Plenipotentiaries of His Majesty the Emperor of Austria, King of Hungary, and of His Majesty the Emperor of All the Russias declare that the "local questions" mentioned in the said paragraph do not comprise affairs specially and exclusively interesting either Austria-Hungary or Russia, such as the protection of the respective nationals, commercial questions, claims, rights derived from treaties, etc.

It is understood that friendly cooperation, without being obligatory, may also be asked and accorded reciprocally by the agents of the two States in questions which do not fall under Paragraph 5 of the Protocol.

Berlin, June 27, 1881.

Szëchényi Sabouroff

The Reinsurance Treaty, June 18, 1887

The Imperial Courts of Germany and of Russia, animated by an equal desire to strengthen the general peace by an understanding destined to assure the defensive position of their respective States, have resolved to confirm the agreement established between them by a special arrangement, in view of the expiration on June 15/27, 1887, of the validity of the secret Treaty and

Protocol, signed in 1881 and renewed in 1884 by the three Courts of Germany, Russia, and Austria-Hungary. . . .

Article 1

In case one of the High Contracting Parties should find itself at war with a third great Power, the other would maintain a benevolent neutrality towards it, and would devote its efforts to the localization of the conflict. This provision would not apply to a war against Austria or France in case this war should result from an attack directed against one of these two latter Powers by one of the High Contracting Parties.

Article 2

Germany recognizes the rights historically acquired by Russia in the Balkan Peninsula, and particularly the legitimacy of her preponderant and decisive influence in Bulgaria and in Eastern Rumelia. The two Courts engage to admit no modification of the territorial status quo of the said peninsula without a previous agreement between them, and to oppose, as occasion arises, every attempt to disturb this status quo or to modify it without their consent.

Article 3

The two Courts recognize the European and mutually obligatory character of the principle of the closing of the Straits of the Bosphorus and of the Dardanelles, founded on international law, confirmed by treaties, and summed up in the declaration of the second Plenipotentiary of Russia at the session of July 12 of the Congress of Berlin (Protocol 19).

They will take care in common that Turkey shall make no exception to this rule in favor of the interests of any Government whatsover, by lending to warlike operations of a belligerent power the portion of its Empire constituted by the Straits. In case of infringement, or to prevent it if such infringement should be in prospect, the two Courts will inform Turkey that they would regard her, in that event, as putting herself in a state of war towards the injured Party, and as depriving herself thenceforth of the benefits of the security assured to her territorial status quo by the Treaty of Berlin.

Article 4

The present Treaty shall remain in force for the space of three years, dating from the day of the exchange of ratifications.

Article 5

The High Contracting Parties mutually promise secrecy as to the contents and the existence of the present Treaty and of the Protocol annexed thereto. . . .

(b)
Additional Protocol. Berlin, June 18, 1887

Additional and Very Secret Protocol

In order to complete the stipulations of Articles 2 and 3 of the secret Treaty concluded on this same date, the two Courts have come to an agreement upon the following points:

1.

Germany, as in the past, will lend her assistance to Russia in order to reestablish a regular and legal government in Bulgaria. She promises in no case to give her consent to the restoration of the Prince of Battenberg.

2.

In case His Majesty the Emperor of Russia should find himself under the necessity of assuming the task of defending the entrance of the Black Sea in order to safeguard the interests of Russia, Germany engages to accord her benevolent neutrality and her moral and diplomatic support to the measures which His Majesty may deem it necessary to take to guard the key of His Empire.

3.

The present Protocol forms an integral part of the secret Treaty signed on this day at Berlin, and shall have the same force and validity.

In witness whereof the respective Plenipotentiaries have signed it and have affixed thereto the seal of their arms.

Done at Berlin, the eighteenth day of the month of June, one thousand eight hundred and eighty-seven.

Bismarck
Schouvaloff

47

Turgenev's "Definition" of Nihilism

The emancipation of the serfs in 1861 coincided with the emergence in Russia of a movement known as nihilism. Attracting young Russian radicals who thought of themselves as socialists and democrats, and accordingly were sworn enemies of the bourgeoisie, political liberalism, and aristocracy, the movement was hostile to all forms of authority and sought to destroy superstition. In their efforts to change Russia the nihilists renounced the Russian state and its Orthodox Church. At the same time they maintained a peculiar, almost sacred love for Russia and its people. They idealized education in general and the study of natural science in particular, and through such study they desired earnestly to create a "new man." Because the older generation disapproved of the aims, attitudes, and behavior of the materialistic young radicals, a conflict developed between "fathers and sons." Russia's great novelist Ivan S. Turgenev (1818–1883) depicted this conflict in his novel *Fathers and Sons,* published in 1862. Turgenev's portrayal of the new generation as having blind faith in science at first offended many of them. Later, however, they accepted the name of nihilist for themselves and hailed Bazarov, the hero of the novel, as their ideal of the new man.

"Where's that new friend of yours?" he asked Arkady.

"He's gone out; he's usually up and about early. The main thing is not to pay any attention to him; he doesn't like ceremony."

"Yes, that's obvious," and Pavel Petrovich began leisurely to butter his bread. "Will he be staying here long?"

"It all depends. He's stopping over on his way to his father's."

"And where does his father live?"

"In our *gubernia,* about eighty *versts* from here. He has a little estate there. He used to be an army surgeon."

"Tut, tut, tut! And I've been wondering all the time where I'd heard that name—Bazarov! Nikolai, if I am not mistaken, there was a medical chap in our father's division by the name of Bazarov, wasn't there?"

From Ivan Turgenev, *Fathers and Sons.* Translated from the Russian by Bernard Isaacs (Moscow: Foreign Languages Publishing House, n.d.), pp. 29–35.

"I think there was."

"Why, of course. So that medical fellow is his father, Hm!" Pavel Petrovich twitched his moustache. "Well, and what about Mr. Bazarov himself, what is he?" he said slowly.

"What is Bazarov?" Arkady looked amused. "Shall I tell you what he really is, Uncle?"

"Please do, nephew."

"He is a nihilist."

"A what?" Nikolai Petrovich asked, while Pavel Petrovich stopped dead, his knife with a dab of butter on the tip arrested in mid-air.

"He is a nihilist," Arkady repeated.

"A nihilist," Nikolai Petrovich said. "That's from the Latin *nihil—nothing,* as far as I can judge; does that mean a person who . . . who believes in nothing?"

"Say, 'who respects nothing,' " put in Pavel Petrovich, applying himself to the butter again.

"Who regards everything critically," Arkady observed.

"Isn't that the same thing?" asked Pavel Petrovich.

"No, it isn't. A nihilist is a person who does not look up to any authorities, who does not accept a single principle on faith, no matter how highly that principle may be esteemed."

"Well, and is that a good thing?" Pavel Petrovich broke in.

"It all depends, Uncle. It may be good for some people and very bad for others."

"I see. Well, this, I see, is not in our line. We are men of the old school—we believe that without principles," (he pronounced the word softly, in the French manner, whereas Arkady clipped the word and accentuated the first syllable) "principles taken on faith, as you put it, one cannot stir a step or draw a breath. *Vous avez changé tout cela,* God grant you good health and a generalship, but we'll be content to look on and admire, *Messieurs les* . . . what do you call them?"

"Nihilists," Arkady said distinctly.

"Yes. We used to have *Hegelists,* now we have nihilists. We shall see how you manage to live in a void, in a vacuum; and now please ring the bell, brother Nikolai Petrovich—it's time for my cocoa."

Nikolai Petrovich rang the bell and called, "Dunyasha!" But instead of Dunyasha, Fenichka herself appeared on the terrace. She was a young woman of about twenty-three, all daintily soft and fair-skinned, with dark hair and eyes, childishly full red lips, and delicate little hands. She wore a neat print dress; a new blue kerchief lay lightly upon her rounded shoulders. She carried a large cup of cocoa and having placed it before Pavel Petrovich, stood overcome with bashfulness; the hot blood spread in a deep blush under the delicate skin of her pretty face. She dropped her eyes and stood there by the table, leaning lightly on her finger-tips. She seemed to be ashamed of having come, yet looked as though she felt she was within her rights in coming.

Pavel Petrovich knit his brows sternly, while Nikolai Petrovich felt embarrassed.

"Good morning, Fenichka," he mumbled.

"Good morning, sir," she answered in a clear yet quiet voice, and with a sidelong glance at Arkady, who gave her a friendly smile, she quietly withdrew. She walked with a slightly waddling gait, but even that was becoming to her.

Silence reigned a while on the terrace. Pavel Petrovich sipped his cocoa then suddenly looked up.

"Here comes Mr. Nihilist," he murmured.

Indeed, Bazarov was striding down the garden, stepping over the flower beds. His duck coat and trousers were muddy; a clinging marsh weed was twined round the crown of his old round hat; in his right hand he held a small bag with something alive squirming in it. He quickly approached the terrace and said with a nod, "Good morning, gentlemen; sorry I'm late for tea; I'll be back in a moment; must fix up a place for these captives."

"What have you got there, leeches?" asked Pavel Petrovich.

"No, frogs."

"Do you eat them or breed them?"

"I use them for experiments," Bazarov said indifferently and went into the house.

"He's going to dissect them," Pavel Petrovich said. "He doesn't believe in principles, but he believes in frogs."

Arkady glanced regretfully at his uncle, and Nikolai Petrovich furtively shrugged his shoulders. Pavel Petrovich perceived that his joke had fallen flat, and began talking about the farm and the new steward, who had recently come to him complaining that Foma, one of the hired labourers, was a "rowdy customer" and had completely got out of hand. "That's the kind of Aesop he is," he had said among other things; "he's earned himself a disgraceful 'reputation'; he'll come to a bad end, he will, you mark my words."

Bazarov reappeared, sat down at the table and began hurriedly drinking his tea. The two brothers regarded him in silence, while Arkady's eyes travelled stealthily from Uncle to Father and back again.

"Did you go far?" Nikolai Petrovich presently asked Bazarov.

"You've got a little swamp here, close to the aspen wood. I flushed five snipe; you can shoot them, Arkady."

"Don't you go in for shooting?"

"No."

"You're studying physics, I understand?" Pavel Petrovich asked in his turn.

"Yes, physics; the natural sciences generally."

"The Deutschländer are said to have made considerable progress in this field."

"Yes, the Germans are our teachers in that subject," Bazarov answered casually.

Pavel Petrovich had used the word Deutschländer instead of Germans for the sake of irony, but this had passed unnoticed.

"Do you have as high an opinion of the Germans as all that?" inquired Pavel Petrovich with studied suavity. He was beginning to feel a secret irritation. His aristocratic nature was up in arms at Bazarov's sheer insouciance. This son of an army sawbones, far from being different, answered bluntly and reluctantly, and there was something rude, almost insolent, in the tone of his voice:

"Their men of science are a practical lot."

"So they are. Well, I suppose you have no such flattering opinion about Russian scientists, have you?"

"I suppose so."

"That's very praiseworthy selflessness," retorted Pavel Petrovich, drawing himself up erect and throwing his head back. "But Arkady Nikolaich has just been telling us that you recognize no authorities. Don't you believe them?"

"Why should I recognize them? And what am I to believe in? When anyone talks sense, I agree—that's all."

"Do the Germans all talk sense?" Pavel Petrovich murmured, and his face assumed an expression so impassive and detached as though his thoughts had gone woolgathering.

"Not all of them," Bazarov said stifling a yawn. He was obviously unwilling to continue the word-play.

Pavel Petrovich glanced at Arkady as much as to say: "A polite fellow, this friend of yours, I must say."

"For my part," he went on, not without some effort, "I must plead guilty to disliking the Germans. I say nothing of the Russian Germans: we know that type. But I can't even stomach the German Germans. Those of the old days, well—one could put up with in a pinch; they then had their—well, Schiller, Goethe, you know. . . . My brother, for instance, thinks a lot of them. Now they've all become chemists and materialists . . . "

"A decent chemist is twenty times more useful than any poet," broke in Bazarov.

"Is that so?" commented Pavel Petrovich with a slight lift of his eyebrows, looking as if he were going to doze off. "You don't believe in art then, I suppose?"

"The Art of Making Money, or No More Piles!" Bazarov said with a sneer.

"So, so. You are having your joke, I see. You repudiate everything then, is that it? All right. Does that mean you believe only in science?"

"I've already told you that I believe in nothing; and what is science, science in general? There are sciences, as there are trades and callings; but science in general does not exist at all."

"Very good, sir. But what about the other conventions, those accepted in human society—do you maintain the same negative attitude here as well?"

"What's this, a cross-examination?" Bazarov said.

Pavel Petrovich paled slightly. Nikolai Petrovich deemed it necessary to intervene.

"We shall discuss this matter more fully with you some day, my dear Yevgeny Vasilich; we shall learn your views and let you know our own. For my part, I'm very glad to know you are studying natural science. I hear that Liebig has made some surprising discoveries in soil fertilization. You might help me in my agricultural pursuits; you might be able to give me some useful advice."

"I am at your service, Nikolai Petrovich; but it's a far cry to Liebig! A person has to learn his *abc* first before he can begin to read, whereas we haven't set eyes on our alphabet yet."

"Well, you certainly are a nihilist, I see," thought Nikolai Petrovich.

"Still, I hope you won't mind me bothering you in case of need," he added aloud. "And now, brother, I think it's time for us to be seeing the steward."

Pavel Petrovich stood up.

"Yes," he said, looking at nobody in particular. "It's a sad thing to live five years in the country as we do, enjoying no intercourse with the great minds of the age! You become a silly ass before you know it. Here you are, trying not to forget what you've been taught, when—*lo and behold!*—it turns out to be all tommyrot, and you're told that sensible people no longer waste time on such trifles and that you yourself are an old dunderhead, if you please. Ah, well! The young people are cleverer than us, it seems."

Pavel Petrovich turned slowly on his heel and slowly walked out; Nikolai Petrovich followed him.

"Is he always like that?" Bazarov asked coolly, as soon as the door had closed behind the two brothers.

"Look here, Yevgeny, you handled him rather roughly, you know," Arkady said. "You've insulted him."

"I'll be blowed if I'm going to humor these rustic aristocrats! It's nothing but conceitedness, swell habits, floppery! Why didn't he carry on in St. Petersburg, if that's the way he's made? Well, enough of him! I've found a water beetle, a rather rare speciment—*Dytiscus marginatus*—do you know it? I'll show it to you."

"I promised to tell you his story—"" began Arkady.

"The beetle's?"

"Come, come, Yevgeny. My uncle's story. You'll see he's not at all the man you think he is. He deserves sympathy rather than sneers."

"I'm not denying it, but what makes you harp on him?"

"One must be fair, Yevgeny."

"What's the implication?"

"No, just listen . . . "

And Arkady told him his uncle's story.

48

The Catechism of the Revolutionary, 1868

In its prime, Russian nihilism produced a number of devoted fanatics. In dedication, however, few surpassed the enthusiasm of Michael A. Bakunin (1814–1876) and Sergei G. Nechaev (1847–1882). The prominence of these two men stems largely from their compilation, during exile in Geneva, of practical advice for conspirators entitled *Katekhizis revolutsionera* (The Catechism of the Revolutionary). In it they advocated total destruction of Russia's political, social and economic structure in order to lay the foundation for a new and better state. To attain that aim they felt it was necessary to turn every member-conspirator into a blind instrument of the leader, and accordingly they emphasized that everything which "promotes the success of the revolution is moral and everything which hinders it is immoral."

From A. Shilov, " 'Katekhizis revolutsionera" [K istorii 'nechaevskogo" dela]" (The Catechism of the Revolutionary [The History of the Nechaev Affair]), *Borba Klassov (Class struggle),* no. 1–2 (1924), pp. 268–272. Translation mine.

Paragraph 1

The revolutionary is a doomed man. He has no interests, no affairs, no feelings, no habits, no property, not even a name. Everything in him is wholly absorbed by a single, exclusive interest, a single thought, a single passion—the revolution.

Paragraph 2

In the very depth of his being, not just in words but in deed, he has severed every tie with the civil order, with the educated world, and with all laws, conventions, his personal inclinations dictate, but what the general interests of the revolution demand.

Paragraph 8

For a revolutionary, that individual is dear and friendly who truly supports the revolutionary cause as he himself does. The degree of friendship, trust, and other obligations toward such a friend is determined exclusively by its usefulness to the cause of the all-destructive practical revolution.

Paragraph 9

There is no need to talk about solidarity among revolutionaries. In it centers the entire strength of the revolutionary cause. Revolutionary comrades who equally understand the revolutionary meaning and passion, should if possible discuss all major problems jointly and resolve them unanimously. In the execution of the jointly agreed upon plan, each member should act independently. In the execution of a number of destructive actions, each member must act alone, seeking advice and comradely help only when it is essential to the total success.

Paragraph 10

Every comrade must have under his control several revolutionaries of second and third ranks, those who are not entirely dedicated. He must consider them as a portion of a general revolutionary capital entrusted to his disposal. He must dispose of his part of the capital economically, striving always to get most advantage from it. He considers himself expendable capital designated to the success of the revolutionary cause. He cannot dispose of this capital alone without first consulting all the comrades who are totally dedicated.

Paragraph 11

When a comrade runs into trouble, the question of whether to rescue him or not must be decided by the revolutionary not because of any personal feeling but on the basis of whether such rescue would benefit the revolutionary cause. Therefore, on the one hand, he must weigh the usefulness which the comrade contributes to the cause against, on the other, the losses of revolutionary forces needed for his rescue. Whichever side is weightier gets his decision.

Paragraph 12

The acceptance into the organization of a new member who declares his readiness not in words but in deeds must be resolved unanimously.

Paragraph 13

The revolutionary joins the state, society, and so-called civilized world and lives in it only for the purpose of its more total and speedier destruction. He is not a revolutionary if he feels compassion for something in this world. If he would pause before carrying out a decision affecting any individual of this world, he must always be aware of the fact that he hates everything equally. He would be in jeopardy if he should have family, friends, or love relations. He cannot be considered a revolutionary if such matters could stop his hand.

Paragraph 14

With the aim of merciless destruction, the revolutionary can, and in fact should, often live in society without revealing his true identity. Revolutionaries should infiltrate everywhere into all layers of society: higher, middle, business, church, and estate; the bureaucratic world, the military, the literary, the Third Section, and even the Winter Palace.

Paragraph 15

The whole vile society should be divided into several categories. The first category should consist of those condemned to death. A list of those condemned should be prepared by our organization on the basis of their relative harm to the success of the revolutionary cause and their numbers should come up in order of priority.

Paragraph 16

In preparing such a list as well as in establishing the above-mentioned priority of execution, one should be influenced neither by personal thievery committed by the condemned man nor even by the hatred which he arouses in our organization or among the people. This thievery and this hatred can sometimes even be useful in awakening popular uprising. One should be guided solely by the benefits which his death will bring to the revolutionary cause. Consequently, the first to be destroyed are people who are especially harmful to the revolutionary organization and those whose sudden and violent death will create the greatest fear in the government, since deprivation of its resourceful and energetic statesmen will weaken its power.

Paragraph 17

The second category should consist of those people who have been granted a partial reprieve on their life so that, by their bestial actions, they will provoke people into an inescapable uprising.

Paragraph 18

The third category should include the majority of high placed beasts, individuals who are distinguished neither by their wisdom nor energy, but who possess riches, influence, connections, and power. These should be exploited in every conceivable manner and way. They should be entangled, confused, seized by means of blackmail, and transformed into revolutionary slaves. Their authority, influence, connections, wealth, and power will thus become an inexhaustible source of and a strong support for various revolutionary undertakings.

Paragraph 19

The fourth category should consist of ambitious state bureaucrats and liberals of all shades. The revolutionary should conspire with their programs and pretend that he follows them. While doing this he should gain control of them, seize all of their secrets, compromise them to such an extent that their escape is impossible, and thus with their own hands cause chaos within the state.

Paragraph 20

The fifth category should consist of doctrinaires, conspirators, and revolutionaries of the empty-phrase and paper variety.

Paragraph 21

The sixth category, an extremely vital one, should consist of women, who should be divided into three basic groups.

The first group should be composed of dumb, stupid, and callous women who should be utilized in the same manner as the third and fourth categories of men.

The second group should consist of ardent women, dedicated and practical, but not our own, because they have failed to attain yet the real, phrase-free and factual revolutionary understanding. They should be utilized similarly as the men of the fifth category.

Finally, our own women—those who are completely dedicated and who have accepted our program. They are our comrades. We should consider them as our precious resource without whose aid we cannot succeed.

Paragraph 22

Our organization has no other aim than complete freedom and happiness of the people; that is, the toiling people. Aware that this freedom and the attainment of that happiness is possible only by means of a total popular revolution, our organization will strive with all forces and means at its disposal to publicize and single out those miseries and evils that in the end should lead the people out of sufferings and arouse them to a spontaneous uprising.

Paragraph 23

By popular revolution, our organization understands not a regulated movement in the classical Western pattern—a movement which always has been kept in check by respect for property, tradition, the social order, and the morality of the so-called civilization—a movement which hitherto has limited itself everywhere to the replacement of one political order by another in an effort to create the so-called revolutionary state. The only revolution that can save the people is that revolution which will destroy totally the entire state apparatus and will eliminate all state traditions, orders, and social classes in Russia.

Paragraph 24

Our organization, therefore, has not been destined to superimpose any system upon the people. The future order will emerge without doubt from the popular movement and from life itself. But this problem we leave to future generations. Our task is a passionate, total, universal, and merciless destruction.

Paragraph 25

To accomplish this we must draw closer to the people and above all we must ally ourselves with those elements in people's lives which, ever since the establishment of the power of the Moscovite state, have never stopped protesting, not just in words but in deeds, against everything that is either directly or indirectly associated with the state: against nobles, against officialdom, against priests, against the world of guilds, and against the *kulak*. We must ally ourselves with the evil world of brigands, who in Russia comprise the true and only revolutionaries.

Paragraph 26

To unite this world into a single, invincible, and omnidestructive force is the prime task of our organization, our conspiracy, and our purpose.

49

Demands of the Narodnaia Volia

Throughout the nineteenth century, the Russian revolutionary movement was stalked by the authorities and torn by the inability of its members to resolve the question of whether to use terror as a political instrument. Beginning with the Decembrists, the revolutionaries had been divided on this issue. Many of them favored the unrestrained application of terror, both as a means of self-defense and as a weapon to bring a basic transformation to Russia. The question acquired new dimensions after dismal failure of the populist movement to peacefully penetrate the Russian villages during the mid-1870's. In June 1879, such proponents of terror as Alexander Mikhailov, Michael Grachevskii, Andrei Zheliabov, and Sophia Perovskaia, founded an organization, *Narodnaia Volia* (People's Will). It advocated control of factories for Russian workers and peasant control of land; absolute freedom of thought, speech, press, and assembly; universal suffrage; and the replacement of standing armies by a popular militia. On March 13, 1881, members of the *Narodnaia Volia* assassinated Tsar Alexander II.

The regicide caused the arrest of many members of the terrorist organization, and inaugurated a period of blind and arrogant reaction. Before the reaction set in, members of the executive committee of the *Narodnaia Volia* sent a letter to the new tsar, Alexander III (1881–1894), in which they sought to explain candidly the causes that led to the tragedy.

Program of the Narodnaia Volia, 1879

By fundamental conviction we are socialists and democrats. We are satisfied that only through socialistic principles can the human race acquire liberty, equality, and fraternity; secure the full and harmonious development of the individual as well as the material prosperity of all; and thus make progress. We are convinced that all social forms must rest upon the sanction of the people themselves, and that popular development is permanent only when it proceeds freely and independently, and when every idea that is to be embodied

---

From George Kennan, *Siberia and the Exile System* (London: Century Co., 1891), vol. 2, pp.495–503.

in the people's life has first passed through the people's consciousness and has been acted upon by the people's will. The welfare of the people and the will of the people are our two most sacred and most inseparable principles.

A

1. If we look at the environment in which the Russian people are forced to live and act, we see that they are, economically and politically, in a state of absolute slavery. As laborers, they work only to feed and support the parasitic classes; and as citizens, they are deprived of all rights. Not only does the actual state of things fail to answer to their will, but they dare not even express and formulate their will; they cannot even think what is good and what is bad for them; the very thought that they can have a will is regarded as a crime against the State. Enmeshed on all sides, they are being reduced to a state of physical degeneration, intellectual stolidity, and general inferiority.

2. Around the enchained people we see a class of exploiters whom the state creates and protects. The state itself is the greatest capitalistic power in the land; it constitutes the sole political oppressor of the people, and only through its aid and support can the lesser robbers exist. This bourgeois excrescence in the form of a government sustains itself by mere brute force—by means of its military, police, and bureaucratic organization—in precisely the same way that the Mongols of Genghis Khan sustained themselves in Russia. It is not sanctioned by the people; it rules by arbitrary violence, and it adopts and enforces governmental and economic forms and principles that have nothing whatever in common with the people's wishes and ideals.

3. In the nation we can see, crushed but still living, its old traditional principles, such as the right of the people to the land, communal and local self-government, freedom of speech and of conscience, and the rudiments of federal organization. These principles would develop broadly, and would give an entirely different and more popular direction to our whole history, if the nation could live and organize itself in accordance with its own wishes and its own tendencies.

B

1. We are of opinion, therefore, that it is our first duty, as socialists and democrats, to free the people from the oppression of the present government, and bring about a political revolution, in order to transfer the supreme power to the nation. By means of this revolution we shall afford the people an opportunity to develop, henceforth, independently, and shall cause to be recognized and supported, in Russian life, many purely socialistic principles that are common to us and to the Russian people.

2. We think that the will of the people would be sufficiently well expressed

and executed by a national Organizing Assembly, elected freely by a general vote, and acting under the instructions of the voters. This, of course, would fall far short of an ideal manifestation of the people's will; but it is the only one that is practicable at present, and we therefore think best to adopt it. Our plan is to take away the power from the existing Government, and give it to an Organizing Assembly, elected in the manner above described, whose duty it will be to make an examination of all our social and governmental institutions, and remodel them in accordance with instructions from the electors.

C

Although we are ready to submit wholly to the popular will, we regard it as none the less our duty, as a party, to appear before the people with our program. This program we shall use as a means of propaganda until the revolution comes, we shall advocate it during the election campaign, and we shall support it before the Organizing Assembly. It is as follows:

1. Perpetual popular representation, constituted as above described and having full power to act in all national questions.
2. General local self-government, secured by the election of all officers, and the economic independence of the people.
3. The self-controlled village commune as the economic and administrative unit.
4. Ownership of the land by the people.
5. A system of measures having for their object the turning over to the laborers of all mining works and factories.
6. Complete freedom of conscience, speech, association, public meeting, and electioneering activity.
7. Universal right of franchise, without any class or property limitation.
8. The substitution of a territorial militia for the army.

We shall follow this program, and we believe that all of its parts are so interdependent as to be impracticable one without the other, and that only as a whole will the program insure political and economic freedom and the harmonious development of the people.

D

In view of the stated aim of the party its operations may be classified as follows:

1. *Propaganda and agitation.* Our propaganda has for its object the popularization, in all social classes, of the idea of a political and democratic revolution as a means of social reform, as well as popularization of the party's own program. Its essential features are criticism of the existing order of things,

and a statement and explanation of revolutionary methods. The aim of agitation should be to incite the people to protest, as generally as possible, against the present state of affairs; to demand such reforms as are in harmony with the party's purposes; and, especially, to demand the summoning of an Organizing Assembly. The popular protest may take the form of meetings, demonstrations, petitions, leading addresses, refusals to pay taxes, and so forth.

2. *Destructive and terroristic activity.* Terroristic activity consists in the destruction of the most harmful persons in the Government, the protection of the party from spies, and the punishment of official lawlessness and violence in all the more prominent and important cases in which such lawlessness and violence are manifested. The aim of such activity is to break down the prestige of Governmental power, to furnish continuous proof of the possibility of carrying on a contest with the Government, to raise in that way the revolutionary spirit of the people and inspire belief in the practicability of revolution, and, finally, to form a body suited and accustomed to warfare.

3. *The organization of secret societies and arrangement of them in connected groups around a single center.* The organization of small secret societies with all sorts of revolutionary aims is indispensable, both as a means of executing the numerous functions of the party and of finishing the political training of its members. In order, however, that the work may be carried on harmoniously, it is necessary that these small bodies should be grouped about one common center, upon the principle either of complete identification or of federal union.

4. *The acquirement of ties, and an influential position in the administration, in the army, in society, and among the people.* The administration and the army are particularly important in connection with a revolution, and serious attention should also be devoted to the people. The principal object of the party, so far as the people are concerned, is to prepare them to cooperate with the revolution, and to carry on a successful electioneering contest after the revolution—a contest that shall have for its object the election of purely democratic delegates to the Organizing Assembly. The party should enlist acknowledged partisans among the more prominent classes of the peasantry, and should prearrange for the active cooperation of the masses at the more important points and among the more sympathetic portions of the population. In view of this, every member of the party who is in contact with the people must strive to take a position that will enable him to defend the interests of the peasants, give them and when they need it, and acquire celebrity among them as an honest man and a man who wishes them well. In this way he must keep up the reputation of the party and support its ideas and aims.

5. *The organization and consummation of the revolution.* In view of the oppressed and cowed condition of the people, and of the fact that the Government, by means of partial concessions and pacifications, may retard for a

long time a general revolutionary movement, the party should take the initiative, and not wait until the people are able to do the work without its aid.

6. *The electioneering canvass before the summoning of the Organizing Assembly.* However the revolution may be brought about—as the result of an open revolution, or with the aid of a conspiracy—the duty of the party will be to aid in the immediate summoning of an Organizing Assembly, to which shall be transferred the powers of the Provisional Government created by the revolution or the conspiracy. During the election canvass the party should oppose, in every way, the candidacy of *kuláks* of all sorts, and strive to promote the candidacy of purely communal people.

A Letter from The Revolutionary Executive Committee of the Narodnaia Volia to Alexander III, March 22, 1881

Your Majesty:

Although the Executive Committee understands fully the grievous oppression that you must experience at this moment, it believes that it has no right to yield to the feeling of natural delicacy which would perhaps dictate the postponement of the following explanation to another time. There is something higher than the most legitimate human feeling, and that is duty to one's country—the duty for which a citizen must sacrifice himself and his own feelings, and even the feelings of others. In obedience to this all-powerful duty we have decided to address you at once, waiting for nothing, as will wait for nothing the historical process that threatens us with rivers of blood and the most terrible convulsions.

The tragedy enacted on the Ekaterínski canal was not a mere casualty, nor was it unexpected. After all that had happened in the course of the previous decade it was absolutely inevitable; and in that fact consists its deep significance for a man who has been placed by fate at the head of governmental authority. Such occurrences can be explained as the results of individual malignity, or even of the evil disposition of "gangs," only by one who is wholly incapable of analyzing the life of a nation. For ten whole years—notwithstanding the strictest prosecution; notwithstanding the sacrifice by the late Emperor's Government of liberty, the interests of all classes, the interests of industry and commerce, and even its own dignity; notwithstanding the absolute sacrifice of everything in the attempt to suppress te revolutionary movement—that movement has obstinately extended, attracting to itself the best elements of the country—the most energetic and self-sacrificing people of Russia—and the revolutionists have carried on, for three years, a desperate partisan warfare with the administration.

You are aware, your Majesty, that the Government of the late Emperor could not be accused of a lack of energy. It hanged the innocent and the guilty, and filled prisons and remote provinces with exiles. Tens of so-called "leaders" were captured and hanged, and died with the courage and tranquility of martyrs; but the movement did not cease—on the contrary it grew and strengthened. The revolutionary movement, your Majesty, is not dependent upon any particular individuals; it is a process of the social organism; and the scaffolds raised for its more energetic exponents are as powerless to save the out-grown order of things as the cross that was erected for the Redeemer was powerless to save the ancient world from the triumph of Christianity. The Government, of course, may yet capture and hang an immense number of separate individuals, it may break up a great number of separate revolutionary groups, it may even destroy the most important of existing revolutionary organizations; but all this will not change, in the slightest degree, the condition of affairs. Revolutionists are the creation of circumstances; of the general discontent of the people; of the striving of Russia after a new social framework. It is impossible to exterminate the whole people; it is impossible, by means of repression, to stifle its discontent. Discontent only grows the more when it is repressed. For these reasons the places of slain revolutionists are constantly taken by new individuals, who come forth from among the people in ever-increasing numbers, and who are still more embittered, still more energetic. These persons, in order to carry on the conflict, form an association in the light of the experience of their predecessors, and the revolutionary organization thus grows stronger, numerically and in quality, with the lapse of time. This we actually see from the history of the last ten years. Of what use was it to destroy the Dolgúshintsi, the Chaikóftsi, and the workers of 1874? Their places were taken by much more resolute democrats. Then the awful repressive measures of the Government called upon the stage the terrorists of 1878–1879. In vain the Government put to death the Koválskis, the Dubróvins, the Ossînskis, and the Lisohúbs. In vain it destroyed tens of revolutionary circles. From among those incomplete organizations, by virtue of natural selection, arose only stronger forms, until, at last, there has appeared an Executive Committee with which the Government has not yet been able successfully to deal.

A dispassionate glance at the grievous decade through which we have just passed will enable us to forecast accurately the future progress of the revolutionary movement, provided the policy of the Government does not change. The movement will continue to grow and extend; deeds of a terroristic nature will increase in frequency and intensity, and the revolutionary organization will constantly set forth, in the places of destroyed groups, stronger and more perfect forms. Meanwhile the number of the discontented in the country will grow larger and larger; confidence in the Government, on the part of the people, will decline; and the idea of revolution—of its possibility and inevitability—will establish itself in Russia more and more firmly. A terrible explosion, a bloody hurly-burly, a revolutionary earthquake throughout Russia, will complete the destruction of the old order of things. Upon what depends this terrible prospect? Yes, your Majesty, "terrible" and lamentable! Do not take this for a mere phrase. We understand, better than any one else can, how lamentable is the waste of so much talent and energy, the loss, in bloody skirmishes and in the work of destruction, of so much strength that, under other conditions, might have been expended in creative labor and in the development of the intelligence, the welfare, and the civil life of the Russian people. Whence proceeds this lamentable necessity for bloody conflict? It arises, your Majesty, from the lack in Russia of a real government in the true sense of that word. A government, in the very nature of things, should only give outward form to the aspirations of the people and effect to the people's will. But with us—excuse the expression—the Government has degenerated into a mere camarilla, and deserves the name of a usurping "gang" much more than does the Executive Committee.

Whatever may be the intentions of the Tsar, the actions of the Government have nothing in common with the popular welfare, or popular aspirations. The Imperial Government subjected the people to serfdom, put the masses into the power of the nobility, and is now openly creating the most injurious class of speculators and jobbers. All of its reforms result merely in a more perfect enslavement and a more complete exploitation of the people. It has brought Russia to such a pass that, at the present time, the masses of the people are in a state of pauperism and ruin; are subjected to the most humiliating surveillance, even at their own domestic hearths; and are powerless even to regulate their own communal and social affairs. The protection of the law and of the Government is enjoyed only by the extortionist and the exploiter, and the most exasperating robbery goes unpunished. But, on the other hand, what a terrible fate awaits the man who sincerely considers the general good! You know very well your Majesty, that it is not only socialists who are exiled and prosecuted. Can it be possible that the *Government* is the guardian of such "order"? Is it not rather probable that this is the work of a "gang"—the evidence of a complete usurpation?

These are the reasons why the Russian Government exerts no moral influence, and has no support among the people. These are the reasons why Russia brings forth so many revolutionists. These are the reasons why even such a deed as Tsaricide excites in the minds of a majority of the people only gladness and sympathy. Yes, your Majesty! Do not be deceived by the reports of flatterers and sycophants—Tsaricide, in Russia, is popular.

From such a state of affairs there can be only two exits: either a revolution, absolutely inevitable and not to be averted by any punishments, or a voluntary turning of the Supreme Power to the people. In the interest of our native land, in the hope of preventing the useless waste of energy, in the hope of averting the terrible miseries that always accompany revolution, the Executive Committee approaches your Majesty with the advice to take the second course. Be assured, so soon as the Supreme Power ceases to rule arbitrarily, so soon as it firmly resolves to accede to the demands of the people's conscience and consciousness, you may, without fear, discharge the spies that disgrace the administration, send your guards back to their barracks, and burn the scaffolds that are demoralizing the people. The Executive Committee will voluntarily terminate its own existence, and the organizations formed about it will disperse, in order that their members may devote themselves to the work of culture among the people of their native land.

We address your Majesty as those who have discarded all prejudices, and who have suppressed the distrust created by the actions of the Government throughout a century. We forget that you are the representative of the authority that has so often deceived and that has so injured the people. We address you as a citizen and as an honest man. We hope that the feeling of personal exasperation will not extinguish in your mind your consciousness of your duties and your desire to know the truth. We also might feel exasperation. You have lost your father. We have lost not only our fathers, but our brothers, our wives, our children, and our dearest friends. But we are ready to suppress personal feeling if it be demanded by the welfare of Russia. We expect the same from you.

We set no conditions for you—do not let our proposition irritate you. The conditions that are prerequisite to a change from revolutionary activity to peaceful labor are created, not by us, but by history. These conditions, in our opinion, are two.

1. A general amnesty to cover all past political crimes; for the reason that they were not crimes but fulfillments of civil duty.

2. The summoning of representatives of the whole Russian people to examine the existing framework of social and governmental life, and to remodel it in accordance with the people's wishes.

We regard it as necessary, however, to remind you that the legalization of the Supreme Power, by the representatives of the people, can be valid only in case the elections are perfectly free. For this reason such elections must be held under the following conditions.

1. Delegates are to be sent from all classes, without distinction, and in number are to be proportionate to the number of inhabitants.

2. There shall be no limitations, either for voters or delegates.

3. The canvass and the elections shall be absolutely unrestricted, and therefore the Government, pending the organization of the National Assembly, shall authorize, in the form of temporary measures; (a) Complete freedom of the press; (b) Complete freedom of speech; (c) Complete freedom of public meeting; (d) Complete freedom of election program. This is the only way in which Russia can return to the path of normal and peaceful development.

We declare solemnly, before the people of our native land and before the whole world, that our party will submit unconditionally to the decisions of a National Assembly elected in the manner above indicated, and that we will not allow ourselves, in future, to offer violent resistance to any Government that the National Assembly may sanction.

And now, your Majesty, decide! Before you are two courses, and you are to make your choice between them. We can only trust that your intelligence and conscience may suggest to you the only decision that is compatible with the welfare of Russia, with your own dignity, and with your duty to your native land.

The Executive Committee

50

The Russo–Turkish Treaty of San Stefano, March 3, 1878

After 1856 the prime objective of Russian foreign policy in Europe was to undo the humiliation of the Treaty of Paris. Until 1877 the Russians relied on diplomacy to perform that task. Because the results were not very successful, early in 1877, after careful preparation (military and diplomatic), the Russians resorted to military measures. Turkish unpreparedness and poor leadership enabled Russian armies to roll victoriously

---

From Sir Edward Hertslet, *The Map of Europe by Treaty . . .*, (London: Butterworth, Harrison and Sons, 1875), IV, pp. 2672–2693. To facilitate reading and recognition the spelling of certain names has been modernized. Thus, Servia has been rendered throughout as Serbia; Roumania and Batoum as Rumania and Batum; and Mussulmans as Moslems. Modern geographical spellings have been placed in parentheses wherever they differ from the original.

almost to the gates of Constantinople. Further progress, however, was deemed unwise because Russian victories aroused British opposition and the envy of other interested powers. Afraid of pressing their luck, in March 1878, the Russians signed with the Ottoman Turks the Treaty of San Stefano. By the terms of this treaty, Russia regained her lost influence in the Balkan peninsula. The new situation, however, did not meet with the approval of the powers interested in the fate of the Ottoman Empire—with the result that an international congress met in Berlin to try to resolve the impossible situation.

Article 2

The Sublime Porte recognizes definitely the Independence of the Principality of Montenegro.

An understanding between the Imperial Government of Russia, the Ottoman Government, and the Principality of Montenegro will determine subsequently the character and form of the relations between the Sublime Porte and the Principality as regards particularly the establishment of Montenegrin Agents at Constantinople, and in certain localities of the Ottoman Empire, where the necessity for such Agents shall be recognized, the extradition of fugitive criminals on the one territory or the other, and the subjection of Montenegrins travelling or sojourning in the Ottoman Empire to the Ottoman laws and authorities, according to the principles of international law and the established usages concerning the Montenegrins.

A Convention will be concluded between the Sublime Porte and Montenegro to regulate the questions connected with the relations between the inhabitants of the confines of the two countries and with the military works on the same confines. The points upon which an understanding cannot be established will be settled by the arbitration of Russia and Austria-Hungary.

Henceforward, if there is any discussion or conflict, except as regards new territorial demands, Turkey and Montenegro will leave the settlement of their differences to Russia and Austria-Hungary, who will arbitrate in common.

The troops of Montenegro will be bound to evacuate the territory not comprised within the limits indicated above within ten days from the signature of the Preliminaries of Peace.

Article 3

Serbia is recognized as independent. . . .

Article 4

The Moslems holding lands in the territories annexed to Serbia, and who wish to reside out of the Principality, can preserve their real property by having them farmed out or administered by others. A Turco-Serbian Commission, assisted by a Russian Commissioner, will be charged to decide absolutely, in the course of two years, all questions relating to the verification of real estate in which Moslem interests are concerned. . . .

The Serbian troops shall be bound to evacuate the territory not comprised within the above-mentioned limits within fifteen days from the signature of the Preliminaries of Peace.

Article 5

The Sublime Porte recognizes the Independence of Rumania, which will establish its right to an indemnity, to be discussed between the two countries.

Until the conclusion of a direct Treaty between Turkey and Rumania, Rumanian subjects will enjoy in Turkey all the rights guaranteed to the subjects of other European Powers.

Article 6

Bulgaria is constituted an autonomous tributary Principality, with a Christian Government and a national militia.

The definitive frontiers of the Bulgarian Principality will be traced by a special Russo-Turkish Commission before the evacuation of Rumelia by the Imperial Russian Army. . . .

Article 7

The Prince of Bulgaria shall be freely elected by the population and confirmed by the Sublime Porte, with the assent of the Powers. No member of the reigning dynasties of the great European Powers shall be capable of being elected Prince of Bulgaria.

In the event of the dignity of Prince of Bulgaria being vacant, the election of the new Prince shall be made subject to the same conditions and forms.

Before the election of the Prince, an Assembly of Bulgarian Notables, to be convoked at Philippopolis (Plovdiv) or Tyrnovo (Trnovo), shall draw up, under the superintendence of an Imperial Russian Commissioner, and in the presence of an Ottoman Commissioner, the organization of the future administration, in conformity with the precedent established in 1830 after the Peace of Adrianople, in the Danubian Principalities.

In the localities where Bulgarians are mixed with Turks, Greeks, Wallachians (Koutzo-Vlachs), or others, proper account is to be taken of the rights and interest of these populations in the elections and in the preparation of the Organic Laws.

The introduction of the new system into Bulgaria, and the superintendence of its working, will be entrusted for two years to an Imperial Russian Commissioner. At the expiration of the first year after the introduction of the new system, and if an understanding on this subject has been established between Russia, the Sublime Porte, and the Cabinets of Europe, they can, if it is deemed necessary, associate Special Delegates with the Imperial Russian Commissioner.

Article 8

The Ottoman Army will no longer remain in Bulgaria, and all the ancient fortresses will be razed at the expense of the local government. The Sublime Porte will have the right to dispose, as it sees fit, of the war material and of the other property belonging to the Ottoman Government which may have been left in the Danubian fortresses already evacuated in accordance with the terms of the Armistice of the 19th/31st January, as well as of that in the strongholds of Schoumla (Shumla) and Varna.

Until the complete formation of a native militia sufficient to preserve order, security, and tranquility, and the strength of which will be fixed later on by an understanding between the Ottoman Government and the Imperial Russian Cabinet, Russian troops will occupy the country, and will give armed assistance to the Commissioner in case of need. This occupation will also be limited to a term approximating to two years.

The strength of the Russian army of occupation, to be composed of six divisions of infantry and two of cavalry, which will remain in Bulgaria after the evacuation of Turkey by the Imperial army, shall not exceed 50,000 men. It will be maintained at the expense of the country occupied. The Russian troops of occupation in Bulgaria will maintain their communications with Russia, not only through Rumania, but also by the ports of the Black Sea, Varna and Bourgas (Burgas), where they may organize, for the term of the occupation, the necessary depots.

Article 9

The amount of the annual tribute which Bulgaria is to pay the Suzerain Court, by transmitting it to a bank to be hereafter named by the Sublime Porte, will be determined by an agreement between Russia, the Ottoman Government, and the other Cabinets, at the end of the first year during which the new organization shall be in operation. This tribute will be calculated on the average revenue of all the territory which is to form part of the Principality. . . .

Article 10

The Sublime Porte shall have the right to make use of Bulgaria for the transport by fixed routes of its troops, munitions, and provisions to the provinces beyond the Principality, and *vice versa*. In order to avoid difficulties and misunderstandings in the application of this right, while guaranteeing the military necessities of the Sublime Porte, a special regulation will lay down the conditions of it within three months after the ratification of the present Act by an understanding between the Sublime Porte and the Bulgarian Government.

It is fully understood that this right is limited to the regular Ottoman troops, and that the irregulars, the Bashi-Bazouks, and the Circassians will be absolutely excluded from it.

The Sublime Porte also reserves to itself the right to sending its postal service through the Principality, and of maintaining telegraphic communication. These two points shall also be determined in the manner and within the period of time indicated above.

Article 11

The Moslem proprietors or others who fix their personal residence outside the Principality may retain their estates by having them farmed or administered by others. Turco-Bulgarian Commissions shall sit in the principal centers of population, under the superintendence of Russian Commissioners, to decide absolutely in the course of two years all questions relative to the verification of real property in which either Moslems or others may be interested.

The inhabitants of the Principality of Bulgaria when travelling or sojourning in the other parts of the Ottoman Empire shall be subject to the Ottoman laws and authorities.. . . .

Article 12

All the Danubian fortresses shall be razed. There shall be no strongholds in future on the banks of this river, nor any men-of-war in the waters of the Principalities of Rumania, Serbia, and Bulgaria, except the usual *stationnaires* and the small vessels intended for river-police and Custom-house purposes.

The rights, obligations, and prerogatives of the International Commission of the Lower Danube are maintained intact.

Article 13

The Sublime Porte undertakes to render the passage of Soulina (Sulina) again navigable, and to indemnify the private individuals who have suffered loss by the war and the interruption of the navigation of the Danube, applying for this double charge a sum of 500,000 *francs* from the amount due to the Sublime Porte from the Danubian Commission.

Article 14

The European proposals communicated to the Ottoman Plenipotentiaries at the first sitting of the Constantinople Conference, shall be immediately introduced into Bosnia and Herzegovina, with any modifications which may be agreed upon in common between the Sublime Porte, the Government of Russia, and that of Austria-Hungary. . . .

Article 15

The Sublime Porte engages to apply scrupulously in the Island of Crete the Organic Law of 1868 taking into account the previously expressed wishes of the native population.

An analogous law adapted to local requirements shall likewise be introduced into Epirus, Thessaly, and the other parts of Turkey in Europe, for which a special constitution is not provided by the present Act.

Special Commissions, in which the native population will be largely represented, shall in each province be entrusted with the task of elaborating the details of the new organization, and the result of their labours shall be submitted to the Sublime Porte, who will consult the Imperial Government of Russia before carrying it into effect.

Article 16

As the evacuation by the Russian troops of the territory which they occupy in Armenia, and which is to be restored to Turkey, might give rise to conflicts and complications detrimental to the maintenance of good relations between the two countries, the Sublime Porte engages to carry into effect, without further delay, the improvements and reforms demanded by local requirements in the provinces inhabited by Armenians, and to guarantee their security from Kurds and Circassians.

Article 17

A full and complete amnesty is granted by the Sublime Porte to all Ottoman subjects compromised by recent events, and all persons imprisoned on this account or sent into exile shall be immediately set at liberty. . . .

Article 19

The war indemnity and the losses imposed on Russia which His Majesty the Emperor of Russia claims, and which the Sublime Porte has bound itself to reimburse to him, consist of—

(a) 900,000,000 *rubles* for war expenses (maintenance of the army, replacing of war material, and war contracts).

(b) 400,000,000 *rubles* on account of damage done to the south coast of Russia, to her export commerce, to her industries, and to her railways.

(c) 100,000,000 *rubles* for injuries inflicted on the Caucasus by the invasion; and,

(d) 10,000,000 *rubles* for costs and damages of Russian subjects and establishments in Turkey.

Total: 1,410,000,000 *rubles.*

Taking into consideration the financial embarrassments of Turkey, and in accordance with the wishes of His Majesty the Sultan, the Emperor of Russia consents to substitute for the payment of the greater part of the moneys enumerated in the above paragraph, the following territorial cessions:

(a) The Sandjak of Toultcha (Tulcea), that is to say, the districts (Cazas) of Kilia (Kiliya), Soulina (Sulina), Mahmoudie (Mahmudia), Isaktcha (Isaccea), Toultcha (Tulcea), Matchine (Măcin), Babadagh (Babadag), Hirsowo (Hîrşova), Kustendje (Constanţa), and Medjidie (Medgidia), as well as the Delta Islands and the Isle of Serpents.

Not wishing, however, to annex this territory and the Delta Islands, Russia reserves the right of exchanging them for the part of Bessarabia detached from her by the Treaty of 1856, and which is bounded on the south by the *Thalweg* of the Kilia (Kiliya) branch and the mouth of the Stary-Stamboul.

The question of the apportionment of Waters and Fisheries shall be determined by a Russo-Rumanian Commission within a year after the ratification of the Treaty of Peace.

(b) Ardahan, Kars, Batoum (Batum), Bayazit (Doğubayazit), and the territory as far as the Saganlough. . . .

[An outline of the frontiers follows.]

The definitive limits of the territory annexed to Russia, and indicated on the Map hereto appended, will be fixed by a Commission composed of Russian and Ottoman delegates.

This Commission in its labours will take into account the topography of localities, as well as considerations of good administration and other conditions calculated to insure the tranquillity of the country.

(c) The territories mentioned in paragraphs (a) and (b) are ceded to Russia as an equivalent for the sum of one milliard and one hundred million (1,100,000,000) *rubles.* As for the rest of the indemnity, apart from the 10,000,000 of *rubles* intended to indemnify Russian interests and establishments in Turkey—namely, 300,000,000 of *rubles*—the mode of payment and guarantee of that sum shall be settled by an understanding between the Imperial Government of Russia and that of His Majesty the Sultan.

(d) The 10,000,000 *rubles* claimed as an indemnity for the Russian subjects and establishments in Turkey shall be paid as soon as the claims of those interested are examined by the Russian Embassy at Constantinople and handed to the Sublime Porte.

Article 20

The Sublime Porte will take effective steps to put an amicable end to the lawsuits of Russian subjects pending for several years, to indemnify the latter if need be, and to carry into effect without delay all judgments passed.

Article 21

The inhabitants of the districts ceded to Russia who wish to take up their residence out of these territories will be free to retire on selling all their real property. For this purpose an interval of three years is granted to them, counting from the date of ratification of the present Act.

On the expiration of that time those of the inhabitants who shall not have sold their real property and left the country shall remain as Russian subjects.

Real property belonging to the State, or to religious establishments situated out of the localities aforesaid, shall be sold within the same interval of three years, as shall be arranged by a special Russo-Turkish Commission. The same Commission shall be intrusted with determining how the Ottoman Government is to remove its war material, munitions, supplies, and other State property actually in the forts, towns, and localities ceded to Russia, and not at present occupied by Russian troops.

Article 22

Russian ecclesiastics, pilgrims, and monks travelling or sojourning in Turkey, in Europe or in Asia, shall enjoy the same rights, advantages, and privileges as the foreign ecclesiastics of any other nationality.

The right of official protection by the Imperial Embassy and Russian Consulates in Turkey is recognized, both as regards the persons above-mentioned, and their possessions, religious houses, charitable institutions, and so forth, in the Holy Places and elsewhere.

The monks of Mount Athos, of Russian origin, shall be maintained in all their possessions and former privileges, and shall continue to enjoy in the three convents belonging to them and in the adjoining buildings the same rights and privileges as are assured to the other religious establishments and convents of Mount Athos.

Article 23

All the Treaties, conventions, and agreements previously concluded between the two High Contracting Parties relative to commerce, jurisdiction, and the position of Russian subjects in Turkey, and which had been abrogated by the state of war, shall come into force again, with the exception of the clauses affected by the present Act. The two governments will be placed again in the same relation to one another, with respect to all their engagements and commercial and other relations, as they were in before the declaration of war.

Article 24

The Bosphorus and the Dardanelles shall remain open in time of war as in time of peace to the merchant vessels of neutral states arriving from or bound to Russian ports. The Sublime Porte consequently engages never henceforth to establish at the ports of the Black Sea and the Sea of Azov, a fictitious blockade *(blocus fictif)*, at variance with the spirit of the Declaration signed at Paris on the 4/16th of April, 1856.

Article 25

The complete evacuation of Turkey in Europe, with the exception of Bulgaria, by the Russian army will take place within three months after the conclusion of the Definitive Peace between His Majesty the Emperor of Russia and His Majesty the Sultan.

In order to save time, and to avoid the cost of the prolonged maintenance of the Russian troops in Turkey and Rumania, part of the Imperial army may proceed to the ports of the Black Sea and the Sea of Marmora, to be there shipped in vessels belonging to the Russian Government or chartered for the occasion.

The evacuation of Turkey in Asia will be affected within the space of six months, dating from the conclusion of the definitive peace, and the Russian troops will be entitled to take ship at Trebizond, in order to return by the Caucasus or the Crimea.

The operations of the evaluation will begin immediately after the exchange of ratifications.

Article 26

As long as the Imperial Russian troops remain in the localities which, in conformity with the present Act, will be restored to the Sublime Porte, the administration and order of affairs will continue in the same state as has existed since the occupation. The Sublime Porte will not participate therein during all that time, nor until the entire departure of all the troops.

The Ottoman forces shall not enter the places to be restored to the Sublime Porte, and the Sublime Porte cannot begin to exercise its authority there until notice of each fortress and province having been evacuated by the Russian troops shall have been given by the Commander of these troops to the officer appointed for this purpose by the Sublime Porte.

Article 27

The Sublime Porte undertakes not to punish in any manner, or allow to be punished, those Ottoman subjects who may have been compromised by their relations with the Russian army during the war. In the event of any persons wishing to withdraw with their families when the Russian troops leave, the Ottoman authorities shall not oppose their departure.

Article 28

Immediately upon the ratification of the Preliminaries of Peace, the prisoners of war shall be reciprocally restored under the care of special Commissioners appointed on both sides, who for this purpose shall go to Odessa and Sevastopol. The Ottoman Government will pay all the expenses of the maintenance of the prisoners that are returned to them, in eighteen equal instalments in the space of six years, in accordance with the accounts that will be drawn up by the above mentioned Commissioners.

The exchange of prisoners between the Ottoman Government and the Governments of Rumania, Serbia, and Montenegro will be made on the same bases, deducting, however, in the account, the number of prisoners restored by the Ottoman Government from the number of prisoners that will have to be restored to that Government. . . .

51

Russian Pan-Slavism: Danilevskii's Views

There were many Russian intellectuals in the ninteenth century who applauded the achievements of Western Europe, believed in scientific progress, favored the constitutional form of government, and advocated freedom of thought and of the press. There were also those who were highly critical of "the decadent West" and extolled the virtues of the Slavic and above all of the Russian character. While each of these two positions had numerous spokesmen, few matched Nikolai Ia. Danilevskii (1822-1885) in color and bluntness. A philosopher of Slavophilism and a recognized spokesman of Pan-Slavism, Danilevskii is remembered most

---

From Nikolai Ia. Danilevskii, *Rossiia i Evropa. Vzgliad na kulturnyia i politicheskiia otnosheniia Slavianskogo mira k Germansko-Romanskomu (Russia and Europe. A View on Cultural and Political Relations Between the Slavic and German-Roman Worlds)* (St. Petersburg: 1871), pp. 407–408, 413–414, 421, 426–434, 436–438. Translation mine. Words in brackets are mine.

for his work *Rossiia i Evropa* (Russia and Europe), originally published in 1871. Because the history of Russia was unlike the history of the Latin and Germanic peoples, Danilevskii argued, Russia should remain indifferent to the West and should unite with all Slavs as the first step toward an inevitable confrontation between Europe and the Slavic world. The Slavic union he envisaged was to be under Russian leadership and was to stretch from Stettin in the Baltic to Trieste in the Adriatic, antedating by many years the concept expressed in Winston Churchill's famed Iron Curtain speech of 1946.

[Constantinople has been] the aim of the aspirations of the Russian people from the dawn of our statehood, the ideal of our enlightenment; the glory, splendor and greatness of our ancestors, the center of Orthodoxy, and the bone of contention between Europe and ourselves. What historical significance Constantinople would have for us if we could wrest her away from the Turks regardless of Europe! What delight would our hearts feel from the radiance of the cross that we would raise atop the dome of St. Sophia! Add to this all the other advantages of Constantinople . . . , her world significance, her commercial significance, her exquisite location, and all the charms of the south. One should be cautious, however, that Constantinople, if she should become Russia's capital, should not unduly attract to herself the moral, intellectual, and material forces of Russia, and thereby disrupt her vital balance.

But Constantinople should not become Russia's capital, she should not concentrate [on herself] her national and state life, and consequently she should not become an inseparable part of the Russian state. In order to provide Russia with the above enumerated advantages, without imposing obvious dangers upon her, Constantinople, once freed and transformed into the real Tsargrad, must *ipso facto* be more than just a capital of the Russian state. She cannot have close ties and be a mother image for Russia. Moscow alone has the exclusive prerogative on that. Tsargrad, in a word, should not be the capital of Russia, but the capital of a Pan-Slav Union. . . .

[This] Pan-Slav Union should consist of the following states:

The Russian Empire, to which should be added all of Galicia and Hungarian Rus [present-day Carpatho-Ukraine]; *The Bohemian-Moravian-Slovak Kingdom,* consisting, in addition to Bohemia proper, of that part of Moravia and Northwest Hungary inhabited exclusively or predominantly by Slovaks, with approximately 9,000,000 inhabitants and 1800 square miles;

The Serbo-Croatian-Slovene Kingdom, consisting of the Principality of Serbia, Montenegro, Bosnia, Herzegovina, Old Serbia, Northern Albania, Serbian Voivodina and Banat, Croatia, Slovenia, Dalmatia, the Military Frontiers, the Duchy of Krajna, Hertz, Gradishche, Istria, the Trieste District, two-thirds of Corinthia, and one-fifth of Styria up to the Drava River, with a combined population of about 8,000,000, and a territory of about 4500 square miles.

The Bulgarian Kingdom, with Bulgaria and a large part of Rumelia and Macedonia, with 6,000,000 to 7,000,000 inhabitants, and about 3000 square miles.

The Rumanian Kingdom with Wallachia, Moldavia, a portion of Bukovina, half of Transylvania approximately to the Maros River, and that part of Western Bessarabia inhabited predominantly by the Moldavians. In return for this exchange, Russia should receive the severed part of southern Bessarabia, including the Danube Delta and the Dobrudgea Peninsula. This [Rumanian Kingdom] would comprise about 7,000,000 inhabitants, and more than 3000 square miles.

The Greek Kingdom with the addition to its present territory of Thessaly, Epirus, southwestern parts of Macedonia, all of the islands of the Aegean Archipelago, Rhodes, Crete, Cyprus, and coasts of Asia Minor and of the Aegean Sea, with approximately 2800 or 3000 square miles, and a population of about 4,000,000.

The Magyar Kingdom, with Hungary and Transylvania, excluding those parts which are inhabited by non-Magyar peoples and which should be added to Russia, Bohemia, Serbia, and Rumania, respectively, with a population of about 7,000,000, and 3000 square miles.

The Tsargrad [Constantinople] District, with the adjacent portions of Rumelia and Asia Minor which surround the Bosphorus, the Sea of Marmora, and the Dardanelles with the Gallipoli Peninsula, and Tenedos Island, with approximately 2,000,000 inhabitants.

Such a union, about 125,000,000 strong, consisting largely of peoples homogeneous in spirit and blood who would find in Tsargrad a natural center of their moral and material unity, would provide complete, wise, and therefore the only possible solution of the Eastern problem. Controlling only that which legally belongs to it, not endangering anyone, and not being afraid of any threats, such a union could withstand all storms and adversities and march peacefully along the road of independent development. . . .

The Pan-Slav Union is the only firm ground on which a distinctive Slavic culture can rise—it is the condition *sine qua non* of its development. Such is the general purport, the main conclusion of our entire investigation. Therefore we shall not stop now to cite evidence of the significance, value, and necessity of such an arrangement of the Slavic world from a cultural-historical viewpoint. In this chapter I intend to develop, from a more specialized political viewpoint, the importance, value, and need for unity of the Slavic family in a unified federal system.

We have seen above that from a general cultural-historical viewpoint Russia cannot, either by origin or adoption, be considered an integral part of Europe; that only two possibilities are available to her: either to form a distinct, independent cultural unity with other Slavs, or be devoid of any cultural-historical significance—to be nothing. . . .

Her internal structure being alien to the European world, and in addition being strong and powerful enough to occupy a role as one of the members of the European family and as one of the great European powers, Russia can acquire a distinguished place in history for herself and for Slavdom in no other way than as the leader of a unique, independent political system of states; she would serve as a counterweight to Europe in her totality and unity. These are the advantages, the benefits, and the essence of the Pan-Slav Union for Russia.

The significance of the Union is even more important for Western Slavdom. A Russia which has not become the representative of the Slavic world will inevitably be deprived thereby of the historic goal of her existence. She will present to the world in vast dimensions a pitiful model of the historical ignoramus. Viewed, however, from a more immediate perspective, she still can for a long time—for years and centuries—not only preserve her external independence, but even be a great political force, however, devoid she is of internal meaning and content. For the other Slavic nations the question is put more bluntly. Here the concern is not with the historical essence of their life, nor with their great historical role, but simply with existence—the daily bread of their national life, so to speak. The question of *to be or not to be* presents itself in the most prosaic and therefore in the most fearful and tragic form. We examined this question in sufficient depth in the thirteenth chapter, and there is no need to repeat it here. Here I consider it necessary to advance only those particular, special advantages which must accrue from the Pan-Slav Union for each of the units that should become members.

Let us begin with *Greece*. . . . Let us look at the existing real advantages which will result from her entrance into the Union. Neither topography nor the soil of Greece will permit her to become an agricultural or an industrial state. Trade must serve as the prime basis of wealth and prosperity for the Hellenic peoples. This stems from the natural inclinations of the Greeks, from their long standing habit, and from local conditions of the continental part of Greece, the islands of the Aegean Archipelago, and the Western Coast of Asia Minor. Not only geographic and ethnographic conditions, but historical experience itself, point to this. The prosperity of Greece in glorious times was based on trade. Trade was also the basic preoccupation of the Greeks during the time of their decline and enslavement. Following the restoration of the political independence to a portion of Greece, the Greek people again turned their main activity to that direction.

Trade in the Eastern Mediterranean, in the archipelago and in the Black Sea, is to a large degree in Greek hands and is carried aboard Greek ships. This fact has aroused the envy of England, as evidenced in the Pacifico Affair [in 1850]. The opening of the Suez Canal should immeasurably broaden the trading area of Greece, transforming its significance from local to worldwide. In addition to the Eastern Mediterranean with all of its gulfs and branches, the Red Sea, the Indian Ocean, and the Bay of Bengal will become domestic seas for the Greek merchant fleet. They will be, so to speak, under Greek influence; and no one's trade routes will be shortened to the same degree as the Greeks'. But a voluminous trade (especially in distant seas) can be carried on successfully only if it is supported by a strong navy capable of protecting the merchant flag at all points of the globe. Without it there cannot be necessary confidence and necessary support for trading enterprises. . . . The Pacifico Affair points out quite clearly how vulnerable a country is in its maritime trade if it is not supported by an ample military power. But where is Greece, who has all the prerequisites to become a worldwide maritime nation, to obtain a sufficiently powerful fleet to support her maritime trade? No one can provide her this naval might except a powerful Slavic-Greek Union—the only form under which the Eastern Roman Empire can be resurrected.

A general union of Slavs, headed by Russia, has a particularly real importance for *Bulgaria.* Of all the Slavic nations she is under the most severe oppression because she lives close to her oppressors. Moreover, she least remembers the tradition of statehood and of independent political existence. She feels, however, her oppression, and feels her own uniqueness from her oppressors; therefore she cannot merge with them, she cannot betray her cultural foundations and consequently she aspires for freedom. But how to utilize this freedom, how to make the transition from national to political existence, and to an independent statehood? We have seen similar examples in Greece, Serbia, and Rumania. The Bulgar example therefore is not unique. It is simply a rock that must be avoided in order not to encounter a disaster. The examples of Greece and Serbia differ in many ways from that which is in prospect for Bulgaria. They achieved their independence as a result of prolonged struggles, in the course of which there emerged from the people progressive representatives who lived a national life and who understood the spirit and needs of the people. The people accepted them, and thus the people themselves created essential institutions of public administration. In Serbia even the memory of national representation was preserved—the *skupshchina.* There is nothing of this in Bulgaria. . . .

In order to prevent Bulgaria from falling under an alien influence, she must organize herself under the protective wing of Russia and under the influence of other states of the Slavic Union that are politically more developed. She must develop close relations with them, first as a distinct administrative region and subsequently as a distinct political entity. Such protection and such guardianship of an impartial Russia for all Slavic peoples is especially necessary for Bulgaria for yet another reason; namely, that this country which is inhabited by an independent Slavic people should preserve its independence and not become a victim of the ambitions of neighboring Serbia.

A close connection between Russia and all Slavdom is not less useful for *Serbia* as well, in order to suppress incorrect ambitious instincts within her and to guide these in the proper direction, not toward Bulgaria, but toward the lands under the control of Austria, lands populated by Serbs and the related Croat and Slovene peoples. The vigorous and strong Serbian people must guard against the Polish tradition of eagerness to appropriate what belongs to others while relinquishing their own. The Serbian people can find the necessary strength and hope for success in their struggle against Italianization, Magyarization, and Germanization of their land only in a political union with all the Slavs under the leadership of Russia.

This truism applies to an even greater degree to the *Czech* nation, whose territory juts out into German land like a bastion, inside of which German settlement has achieved great success. Neither the internal struggle with the Germans nor external attacks, which this bone of contention between Slavdom and Germandom cannot escape, can be successfully carried out without a close unity with all Slavdom.

The *Rumanians* can count on the annexation of half of Transylvania, Bukovina, and part of Bessarabia only with the agreement and cooperation of Russia; only under her impartial and peaceful influence is opposition to the usurpation of Magyarism possible. Only by relying on Slavdom, incomparably more kindred to them, can the Rumanians struggle with the corroding Gallomania and the imitativeness of their pitiful intelligentsia.

In the preceding chapter we saw that even *Poland* can find a satisfactory solution to her long torment exclusively in the womb of the Pan-Slav Union, in close unity and friendship with Russia.

For *Hungary* alone, the perspective of such a union that would place a limit on all her ambitions and lofty plans cannot present itself in an optimistic light. But even she can rely on the satisfaction of all of her legal aspirations. She would have to abandon only her illicit love of power.

Such are the advantages for each of the peoples who could and should form independent states in the great Pan-Slav Federation, a union that would unite them. If one should add to all this the brilliant, majestic, universal historical role which such a union promises to all Slavdom, it would seem that such a union must be, if not a spontaneous goal of the ambitions of all

Slavs conscious of their Slavic identity, at least an object of their desires—their political ideal. And we actually cannot recall one famous Slavic name for whom the thought of Slavic unity in one form or another did not represent such an ideal. We will name several who expressed it more or less; as for example, Khomiakov, Pogodin, Hanka, Kollár, and Stur.[1] It is sad that many of the non-Europe oriented Slavs do not regard the political unity of their nations under Russia's leadership with the sympathy that one could and should expect.

The slanders by the Poles and by Europe, with little, and one can even say with absolutely no knowledge of Russia, with no acquaintance with our affairs, are presented in a totally false light, yet have penetrated so deeply that even many of the leading Slavic thinkers, who are fully devoted to the Slavic cause, are frightened by some kind of ghosts. On the one hand they are frightened by the ghost of power-loving Russia, which supposedly desires to destroy the distinctiveness of the Slavic nationalities, to devour them like she devoured Poland; on the other hand, viewing the fate of mankind and civilization in general, they are frightened by the ghost of universal sovereignty, which appears as something terrible for the Slavic heart, saturated with humanism, even if this sovereignty belongs to no one else but the very poor, downtrodden Slavs—whose own oppression horrifies no one and of whom no one says it is incompatible with true humanity. That Slavic independence and the development of Slavic power are not appreciated in Europe is obvious. It would be fruitless and silly on our part or on anyone else's part to try to reassure Europeans of this. But it is sad that Slavs, even the Russians themselves, are able to argue in such a way. As far as possible we will try to dissipate here this unnatural fog, beginning with Russia's love of power.

The facts themselves will serve as an answer and refutation. Nothing will be elaborated here. We will only point to the well known examples of Russia's dealings with regions annexed to her territory. Finland, which had been won from Sweden, was given full autonomy and independence—a separate military force, which has not gone outside the limits of Finland; a separate monetary, trade, and financial system, even a constitution and a parliament; a territorial region which had belonged to Russia for over one hundred years was given to Finland; the Russian language was not introduced in Finnish schools; Orthodoxy did not become the dominant religion; she was not turned into a market for our manufacturers; not one *kopeck* of Finnish revenues went to Russia. In a word, Russia not only did not exploit Finland morally or materially, but to the contrary, she has always extended her a helping hand. The Baltic territory was not only not Russified but, on the contrary, the most powerful agent of Germanization—the Dorpat-German University—was founded and has been maintained by the Russian government. Not only did the Russian government not assist in the Russification of the territory, it placed barriers in opposition to it, even when it was called forth by the natural course of events. All this was done to eliminate the fear of being branded an oppressor of the nationalities who were politically united with Russia. The Polish example itself, so often advanced against Russia, is in essence a good proof of that. Following her unity with Russia, Poland enjoyed statelike independence and a constitutional life; under Russian control Polish influence in Western Russia was extended by means of Vilna University, through a whole system of public education, and much else. Only the obvious, crude attempts of Poles to add West Russia to Poland by force opened our eyes—and that, it seems, only for a time. Although, of course, I do not at all say this in praise of Russia, her government, and her public opinion, these events nonetheless clearly show that no associate of a state that has dealt with the integral parts of its territory in such a manner has anything to fear about its independence, both political and national, or has anything to fear about the violation of the bounds of clearly external-political unified hegemony. Any closer alliance would certainly only allow for that kindred, national sympathy which could not help but draw the members of the Slavic family to one another after the external barriers dividing them were broken and they had undertaken the general historical task.

But this is not enough. If Russia would often act to her own detriment in that way, would she act otherwise when the most obvious, simplest calculation would prompt her to refrain from any interference in the internal affairs of her allies, to touch neither their political nor national independence? . . .

What would Russia achieve if she were to try to destroy the internal independence of Slavic and other powers allied with her by trying to include them in her own state system—even if such a desire proved to be successful? Instead of 40,000,000 loyal, amicably disposed allies, she would acquire 40,000,000 discontented subjects. How much such a situation increases the strength of a state can be seen from abundant examples in the relations of Poland to Russia, Ireland to England, and, above all, Hungary and Venice to Augstia. . . .

Thus, the freedom of the Slavs and the other peoples in the union, amongst themselves and with Russia, would be assured, on the one hand by simple, healthy, political common sense, and by Russia's instinct of self-preservation; on the other hand, the entire past of Russia, the very flaws of Russian and Slavic virtue in general, would serve as a guarantee of the just, inoffensive character of those mutual relations which would develop between the head of the union and its members. He who gave the most can expect the least: he who gave national and even political freedom to the parts comprising a state, as for instance to Finland and even to hostile Poland—having taken it

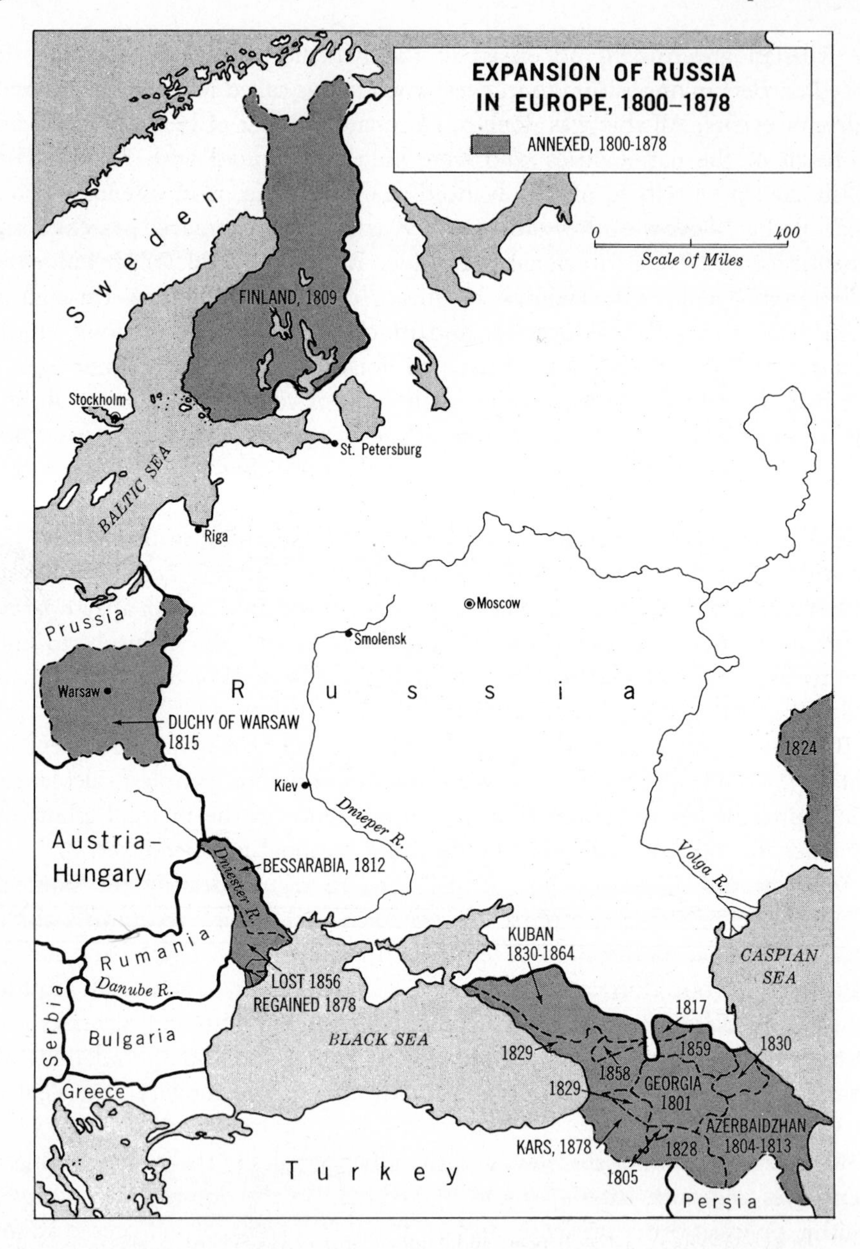

away only after the most senseless, doublecrossing abuse by them and in view of the preservation and securing of the freedom of a part of the Russian people whom the Poles schemed against—will not encroach on the independence of his own allies.

Another scarecrow frightening people away from Pan-Slavism is the fear of a worldwide monarchy, the fear of world sovereignty. It is clear from the above explanation that if such a world sovereignty was the natural, necessary consequence of the Pan-Slav Union, then in any case it would not be especially Russian, but Pan-Slav; and there would be nothing for the Slavs to fear. The thought of world sovereignty did not frighten the ancient Romans; England does not fear the idea of worldwide sovereignty on the seas; the extension of her control, spanning the seas and oceans with a chain of large and small British colonies; the thought of limitless sovereignty from Greenland to the Tierra del Fuego does not frighten America either. What strange modesty—to recoil before a great future, to shun it because of a dread of being too powerful and strong, and even parodying the though of Voltaire about God (that if He did not exist it would be necessary to invent Him), to apply it to Austria in the view of the prevention of such a misfortune?

But this is not the question. The fright itself does not have any basis. The Pan-Slav Union, having assured the freedom of the Slavs and their fruitful interaction on one another, would not be able to threaten the independence of anyone, nor of anyone's legal rights. Again the most simple statistical calculation convinces one of this. The population of only that part of Europe which currently plays an active political role, that is, Germany (with the exclusion of the entire non-German portion of Austria), France, and England, with the addition of only Belgium and Holland (who are surrounded by them, and who must voluntarily or involuntarily follow them), would equal the population of the entire Slavic Union. With the addition of Italy, Spain, Portugal, and the Scandinavian states, there would be at least an excess of fifty million souls on the side of Europe. Consequently, the Slavic system of states would still be significantly weaker than Europe by the amount of its population, and could consider itself invincible only in the defense and protection of Slavic independence and originality. The strength would be only slightly equalized by the previously discussed strategic location of Constantinople and the Czech bastion.

Note

1. Alexander S. Khomiakov (1804-1860), a Russian Slavophile writer; Michael P. Pogodin (1799–1875), a Russian Slavophile historian; Vaclav Hanka (1791–1861), a Czech nationalist; Jan Kolár (1793–1852), a Czech poet; and Ludevit Stur (1815–1856), a Slovak poet. All were outspoken proponents of the Pan-Slav idea.

52

Pobedonostsev's Criticism of Modern Society

The emancipation of the serfs in 1861 profoundly affected all aspects of Russian life. It contributed to the decline of the power of the nobility, discontent among the peasantry, restlessness among the workers, dissatisfaction among the intelligentsia, and increasing reaction among the advocates of autocracy. The principal spokesman of the latter from 1880 to 1905 was Constantine P. Pobedonostsev (1827–1907). A constitutional lawyer by training, Pobedonostsev taught civil law at Moscow University from 1860 to 1865. He left teaching to become first a member of the Senate (Russia's Supreme Court), then a member of the Council of State (a consultative body that advised the tsar in legislative matters), and from 1880 to 1905 he acted as Procurator of the Holy Synod (lay administrator of the Orthodox Church). Since Pobedonostsev was also a tutor in law of Alexander III and Nicholas II, he was, between 1881 and 1905, the most influential member of the government and the prime inspirer of its reactionary policies.

The New Democracy

What is this freedom by which so many minds are agitated, which inspires so many insensate actions, so many wild speeches, which leads the people so often to misfortune? In the democratic sense of the word, freedom is the right of political power, or, to express it otherwise, the right to participate in the government of the State. This universal aspiration for a share in the government has no constant limitations, and seeks no definite issue, but incessantly extends, so that we might apply to it the words of the ancient poet about dropsy: *crescit indulgens sibi.*[1] Forever extending its base, the new Democracy now aspires to universal suffrage—a fatal error, and one of the most remarkable in the history of mankind. By this means, the political power so passionately demanded by Democracy would be shattered into a number of infinitesimal bits, of which each citizen acquires a single one. What will he do with it, then? How will he employ it? In the result it has undoubtedly been shown

---

From K. P. Pobyedonostseff, *Reflections of a Russian Statesman.* Translated from the Russian by Robert Crozier Long (London: Grant Richard, 1898), pp. 23–30, 32–46, 52–54, 62–74.

that in the attainment of this aim Democracy violates its sacred formula of "Freedom indissolubly joined with Equality." It is shown that this apparently equal distribution of "freedom" among all involves the total destruction of equality. Each vote, representing an inconsiderable fragment of power, by itself signifies nothing; an aggregation of votes alone has a relative value. The result may be likened to the general meetings of shareholders in public companies. By themselves individuals are ineffective, but he who controls a number of these fragmentary forces is master of all power, and directs all decisions and dispositions. We may well ask in what consists the superiority of Democracy. Everywhere the strongest man becomes master of the State; sometimes a fortunate and resolute general, sometimes a monarch or administrator with knowledge, dexterity, a clear plan of action, and a determined will, in a Democracy, the real rulers are the dexterous manipulators of votes, with their place-men, the mechanics who so skillfully operate the hidden springs which move the puppets in the arena of democratic elections. Men of this kind are ever ready with loud speeches lauding equality; in reality, they rule the people as any despot or military dictator might rule it. The extension of the right to participate in elections is regarded as progress and as the conquest of freedom by democratic theorists, who hold that the more numerous the participants in political rights, the greater is the probability that all will employ this right in the interests of the public welfare, and for the increase of the freedom of the people. Experience proves a very different thing. The history of mankind bears witness that the most necessary and fruitful reforms—the most durable measures—emanated from the supreme will of statesmen, or from a minority enlightened by lofty ideas and deep knowledge, and that, on the contrary, the extension of the representative principle is accompanied by an abasement of political ideas and the vulgarization of opinions in the mass of the electors. It shows also that this extension—in great States—was inspired by secret aims to the centralization of power, or led directly to dictatorship. In France, universal suffrage was suppressed with the end of the Terror, and was reestablished twice merely to affirm the autocracy of the two Napoleons. In Germany, the establishment of universal suffrage served merely to strengthen the high authority of a famous statesman who had acquired popularity by the success of his policy. What its ultimate consequences will be, Heaven only knows!

The manipulation of votes in the game of Democracy is of the commonest occurrence in most European states, and its falsehood, it would seem, has been exposed to all; yet few dare openly to rebel against it. The unhappy people must bear the burden, while the Press, herald of a supposititious public opinion, stifles the cry of the people with its shibboleth, "Great is Diana of the Ephesians." But to an impartial mind, all this is nothing better than a struggle of parties, and a shuffling with numbers and names. The voters, by themselves inconsiderable unities, acquire a value in the hands of dexterous agents. This value is realised by many means—mainly, by bribery in innumerable forms, from gifts of money and trifling articles, to the distribution of places in the services, the financial departments, and the administration. Little by little, a class of electors has been formed which lives by the sale of votes to one or another of the political organizations. So far has this gone in France, for instance, that serious, intelligent, and industrious citizens in immense numbers abstain from voting, through the difficulty of contending with the cliques of political agents. With bribery go violence and threats, and reigns of terror are organised at elections by the help of which the respective cliques advance their candidates; hence the stormy scenes at electoral demonstrations, in which arms have been used, and the field of battle strewn with the bodies of the killed and wounded.

Organization and bribery—these are the two mighty instruments which are employed with such success for the manipulation of the mass of electors. Such methods are in no way new. Thucydides depicts in vivid colors their employment in the ancient republics of Greece. The history of the Roman Republic presents monstrous examples of corruption as the chief instrument of factions at elections. But in our times a new means has been found of working the masses for political aims, and joining them in adventitious alliances by provoking a fictitious community of views. This is the art of rapid and dexterous generalization of ideas, the composition of phrase and formulas, disseminated with the confidence of burning conviction as the last word of science, as dogmas of politicology, as infallible appreciations of events, of men, and of institutions. At one time it was believed that the faculty of analyzing facts, and deducing general principles, was the privilege of a few enlightened minds and deep thinkers; now it is considered an universal attainment, and, under the name of convictions, the generalities of political science have become a sort of current money, coined by newspapers and rhetoricians. . . .

The Greatest Falsehood of Our Time

That which is founded on falsehood cannot be right. Institutions founded on false principles cannot be other than false themselves. This truth has been demonstrated by the bitter experience of ages and generations.

Among the falsest of political principles is the principle of the sovereignty of the people, the principle that all power issues from the people, and is based upon the national will—a principle which has unhappily become more firmly established since the time of the French Revolution. Thence proceeds the theory of Parliamentarism, which, up to the present day, has deluded much of the so-called "intelligence," and unhappily infatuated certain foolish Russians. It continues to maintain its hold on many minds with the obstinacy of a narrow fanaticism, although every day its falsehood is exposed more clearly to the world.

In what does the theory of Parliamentarism consist? It is supposed that the people in its assemblies make their own laws, and elect responsible officers to execute their will. Such is the ideal conception. Its immediate realization is impossible. The historical development of society necessitates that local communities increase in numbers and complexity; that separate races be assimilated, or, retaining their polities and languages, unite under a single flag, that territory extend indefinitely. Under such conditions direct government by the people is impracticable. The people must, therefore, delegate its right of power to its representatives, and invest them with administrative autonomy. These representatives in turn cannot govern immediately, but are compelled to elect a still smaller number of trustworthy persons—ministers—to whom they entrust the preparation and execution of the laws, the apportionment and collection of taxes, the appointment of subordinate officials, and the disposition of the militant forces.

In the abstract this mechanism is quite symmetrical; for its proper operation many conditions are essential. The working of the political machine is based on impersonal forces constantly acting and completely balanced. It may act successfully only when the delegates of the people abdicate their personalities; when on the benches of Parliament sit mechanical fulfillers of the people's behests; when the ministers of State remain impersonal, absolute executors of the will of the majority; when the elected representatives of the people are capable of understanding precisely, and executing conscientiously the programme of activity, mathematically expressed, which has been delivered to them. Given such conditions the machine would work exactly, and would accomplish its purpose. The law would actually embody the will of the people; administrative measures would actually emanate from Parliament; the pillars of the State would rest actually on the elective assemblies, and each citizen would directly and consciously participate in the management of public affairs.

Such is the theory. Let us look at the practice. Even in the classic countries of Parliamentarism it would satisfy not one of the conditions enumerated. The elections in no way express the will of the electors. The popular representatives are in no way restricted by the opinions of their constituents, but are guided by their own views and considerations, modified by the tactics of their opponents. In reality, ministers are autocratic, and they rule, rather than are ruled by, Parliament. They attain power, and lose power, not by virtue of the will of the people, but through immense personal influence, or the influence of a strong party which places them in power, or drives them from it. They dispose of the force and resources of the nation at will, they grant immunities and favours, they maintain a multitude of idlers at the expense of the people, and they fear no censure while they enjoy the support in Parliament of a majority which they maintain by the distribution of bounties from the rich tables which the State has put at their disposal. In reality, the ministers are as irresponsible as the representatives of the people. Mistakes, abuse of power, and arbitrary acts, are of daily occurrence, yet how often do we hear of the grave responsibility of a minister? It may be once in fifty years a minister is tried for his crimes, with a result contemptible when compared with the celebrity gained by the solemn procedure.

Were we to attempt a true definition of Parliament, we should say that Parliament is an institution serving for the satisfaction of the personal ambition, vanity, and self-interest of its members. The institution of Parliament is indeed one of the greatest illustrations of human delusion. Enduring in the course of centuries the tyranny of autocratic and oligarchical governments, and ignoring that the evils of autocracy are the evils of society itself, men of intellect and knowledge have laid the responsibility for their misfortunes on their rulers and on their systems of government, and imagined that by substituting for these systems government by the will of the people, or representative government, society would be delivered from all the evils and violence which it endured. What is the result? The result is that, *mutato nomine,* all has remained essentially as before, and men, retaining the weaknesses and failings of their nature, have transfused in the new institutions their former impulses and tendencies. As before, they are ruled by personal will, and in the interests of privileged persons, but this personal will is no longer embodied in the person of the sovereign, but in the person of the leader of a party; and privilege no longer belongs to an aristocracy of birth, but to a majority ruling in Parliament and controlling the State.

On the pediment of this edifice is inscribed: "All for the Public Good." This is no more than a lying formula. Parliamentarism is the triumph of egoism—its highest expression. All here is calculated to the service of the ego. In the Parliamentary fiction, the representative, as such, surrenders his personality, and serves as the embodiment of the will and opinions of his constituents; in reality, the constituents in the very act of election surrender all their rights in favour of their representatives. In his addresses and speeches the candidate for election lays constant emphasis upon this fiction; he reiterates his phrases about the public welfare; he is nothing but a servant of the people; he will forget himself and his interests for its sake. But these are words, words, words alone—temporary steps of the staircase by which he climbs to the height he aspires to, and which he casts away when he needs them no longer. Then, so far from beginning to work for soceity, society becomes the instrument of his aims. To him his constituents are a herd, an aggregation of votes, and he, as their possessor, resembles those rich nomads whose flocks constitute their whole capital—the foundation of their power and eminence in society. Thus is developed to perfection the art of playing on the instincts and passions of the mass, in order to attain the personal ends of ambition and power. The people lose all importance for its representative, until the time arrives when they are to be played upon again; then false and flattering and lying phrases are lavished as before; some are suborned by bribery. others terrified by threats—the long chain of manoeuvres spun which forms an invariable factor of Parliamentarism. Yet this electoral farce continues to deceive humanity, and to be regarded as an institution which crowns the edifice of State. Poor humanity! In truth may it be said, *mundus vult decipi, decipiatur.*[2]

Thus the representative principle works in practice. The ambitious man comes before his fellow-citizens, and strives by every means to convince them that he more than any other is worthy of their confidence. What motives impel him to this quest? It is hard to believe that he is impelled by disinterested zeal for the public good.

In our time, nothing is so rare as men imbued with a feeling of solidarity with the people, ready for labour and self-sacrifice for the public good; this is the ideal nature, but such natures are little inclined to come into contact with the baseness of the world. He who, in the consciousness of duty, is capable of disinterested service of the community does not descend to the soliciting of votes, or the crying of his own praise at election meetings in loud and vulgar phrases. Such men manifest their strength in their own work, in a small circle of congenial friends, and scorn to seek popularity in the noisy market-place. If they approach the crowd, it is not to flatter it, or to pander to its basest instincts and tendencies, but to condemn its follies and expose its depravity. To men of duty and honour the procedure of elections is repellent; the only men who regard it without abhorrence are selfish, egoistic natures, which wish thereby to attain their personal ends. To acquire popularity such men have little scruple in assuming the mask of ardour for the public good. They cannot and must not be modest, for with modesty they would not be noticed or spoken of. By their positions, and by the parts which they have chosen, they are forced to be hypocrites and liars; they must cultivate, fraternize with, and be amiable to their opponents to gain their suffrages; they must lavish promises, knowing that they cannot fulfil them; and they must pander to the basest tendencies and prejudices of the masses to acquire majorities for themselves. What honourable nature would accept such a role? Describe it in a novel, the reader would be repelled, but in elections the same reader gives his vote to the living *artiste* in the same role.

Parliamentary elections are a matter of art, having, as the military art, their strategy and tactics. The candidate is not brought into direct relations with his constituents. As intermediary stands the committee, a self-constituted institution, the chief weapon of which is impudence. The candidate, if he is unknown, begins by assembling a number of friends and patrons. Then all together organize a hunt among the rich and weak-minded aristocrats of the neighborhood, whom they convince that it is their duty, their prerogative, and their privilege to stand at the head as leaders of public opinion. There is little difficulty in finding stupid or idle people who are taken in by this trickery; and then, above their signatures, appear manifestos in the newspapers and on the walls and pillars, which seduce the mass, eager always in the pursuit of names, titles, and wealth. Thus are formed the committees which direct and control the elections. They resemble in much public companies. The composition of the committee is carefully elaborated: it contains some effective forces—energetic men who pursue at all costs material ends; while simple and frivolous idlers constitute the ballast. The committees organize meetings, where speeches are delivered, where he who possesses a powerful voice, and can quickly and skillfully string phrases together, produces always an impression on the mass, and acquires notoriety—thus comes out the candidate for future election, who, with favouring conditions, may even supersede him whom he came to help. Phrases, and nothing but phrases, dominate these meetings. The crowd hears only him who cries the loudest, and who with impudence and with flattery conforms most artfully to the impulses and tendencies of the mob.

On the day of polling few give their votes intelligently: these are the individual, influential electors whom it has been worthwhile to convince in private. The mass of the electors, after the practice of the herd, votes for one of the candidates nominated by the committees. Not one exactly knows the man, or considers his character, his capacity, his convictions; all vote merely because they have heard his name so often. It would be vain to struggle against this herd. If a levelheaded elector wished to act intelligently in such a grave affair, and not to give way to the violence of the committee, he would have to abstain altogether, or to give his vote for his candidate according to his conviction. However he might act, he could not prevent the election of the candidate favoured by the mass of frivolous, indifferent, and prejudiced electors.

In theory, the elected candidate must be the favourite of the majority; in fact, he is the favourite of a minority, sometimes very small, but representing an organized force, while the majority, like sand, has no coherence, and is therefore incapable of resisting the clique and the faction. In theory, the election favours the intelligent and capable; in reality, it favours the pushing and impudent. It might be thought that education, experience, conscientiousness in work, and wisdom in affairs, would be essential requirements in the candidate; in reality, whether these qualities exist or not, they are in no way needed in the struggle of the election, where the essential qualities are audacity, a combination of impudence and oratory, and even some vulgarity, which invariably acts on the masses; modesty, in union with delicacy of feeling and thought, is worth nothing.

Thus comes forth the representative of the people, thus he acquires his power. How does he employ it, how will he turn it to advantage? If energetic by nature, he will attempt to form a party; if he is of an ordinary nature, then he joins himself to one party or another. The leader of a party above all things requires a resolute will. This is an organic quality, like physical strength, and does not by any means inevitably accompany moral excellence. With limited intellect, with infinite egoism, and even wickedness, with base and dishonest tendencies, a man with a strong will may become a leader in Parliament, and may control the decisions of a party which contains men far surpassing him in moral and intellectual worth. Such may be the character of a ruling force in Parliament. To this should be joined another decisive force—eloquence. This also is a natural faculty, involving neither moral character, nor high intellectual culture. A man may be a deep thinker, a poet, a skilful general, a subtle jurist, an experienced legislator, and at the same time may not enjoy the gift of fluent speech, while, on the contrary, one with ordinary intellectual capacity and knowledge may possess a special gift of eloquence. The union of this gift with a plentitude of intellectual power is a rare and exceptional phenomenon in Parliamentary life. The most brilliant improvisations, which have given glory to orators, and determined grave decisions, when read are as colourless and contemptible as descriptions of scenes enacted in former times by celebrated actors and singers. Experience shows that in great assemblies the decision does not belong to reason, but to daring and brilliancy; that the arguments most effective on the mass are not the most symmetrical—the most truly taken from the nature of things, but those expressed in sounding words and phrases, artfully selected, constantly reiterated, and calculated on the instinct of baseness always dominant in the people. The masses are easily drawn by outbursts of empty declamation, and under such influences often form sudden decisions, which they regret on cold-blooded consideration of the affair.

Therefore, when the leader of a party combines with a strong will the gift of eloquence, he assumes his first role on an open stage before the whole world. If he does not posses this gift he stands like a stage manager behind the scenes and directs thence all the movements of the Parliamentary spectacle, allotting the parts to others, appointing orators to speak for him, employing in his work all the rich but irresolute intellects of his party to do his thinking for him.

What is a Parliamentary party? In theory, it is an alliance of men with common convictions, joining forces for the realization of their views in legislation and administration. But this description applies only to small parties; the large party, which alone is an effective force in Parliament, is formed under the influence only of personal ambition, and centers itself around one commanding personality. By nature, men are divided into two classes—those who tolerate no power above them, and therefore of necessity strive to rule others; and those who by their nature dread the responsibility inseparable from independent action, and who shrink from any resolute exercise of will. These were born for submission, and together constitute a herd, which follows the men of will and resolution, who form the minority. Thus the most talented persons submit willingly, and gladly entrust to stronger hands the control of affairs and the moral responbility for their direction. Instinctively they seek a leader, and become his obedient instruments, inspired by the conviction that he will lead them to victory—and, often, to spoil. Thus all the important actions of Parliament are controlled by the leaders of the party, who inspire all decisions, who lead in combat, and profit by victory. The public sessions are no more than a spectacle for the mass. Speeches are delivered to sustain the fiction of Parliamentarism, but seldom a speech by itself affects the decision of Parliament in a grave affair. Speech-making serves for the glory of orators, for the increase of their popularity, and the making of their careers; only on rare occasions does it affect the distribution of votes. Majorities and minorities are usually decided before the session begins.

Such is the complicated mechanism of the Parliamentary farce; such is the great political lie which dominates our age. By the theory of Parliamentarism, the rational majority must rule; in practice, the party is ruled by five or six of its leaders who exercise all power. In theory, decisions are controlled by clear arguments in the course of Parliamentary debates; in practice, they in no wise depend from debates, but are determined by the wills of the leaders and the promptings of personal interest. In theory, the representatives of the people consider only the public welfare; in practice, their first consideration is their own advancement, and the interests of their friends. In theory, they must be the best citizens; in practice, they are the most ambitious and impudent. In theory, the elector gives his vote for his candidate because he knows him and trusts him; in practice the elector gives his vote for a man whom he seldom knows, but who has been forced on him by the speeches of an interested party. In theory, Parliamentary business is directed by experience, good sense, and unselfishness; in practice, the chief motive powers are a firm will, egoism, and eloquence.

Such is the Parliamentary institution, exalted as the summit and crown of the edifice of State. It is sad to think that even in Russia there are men who aspire to the establishment of this falsehood among us; that our professors glorify to their young pupils representative government as the ideal of political science; that our newspapers pursue it in their articles and *feuilletons*, under the name of justice and order, without troubling to examine without prejudice the working of the parliamentary machine. Yet even where centuries have sanctified its existence, faith already decays; the Liberal intelligence exalts it, but the people groans under its despotism, and recognizes its falsehood. We may not see, but our children and grandchildren assuredly will see, the overthrow of this idol, which contemporary thought in its vanity continues still to worship. . . .

The prevalent doctrine of the perfection of Democracy and of democratic government stands on the same delusive foundation. This doctrine presupposes the capacity of the people to understand subtleties of political science which have a clear and substantial existence in the minds of its apostles only. Precision of knowledge is attainable only by the few minds which constitute the aristocracy of intellect; the mass, always and everywhere, is *vulgus,* and its conceptions of necessity are vulgar.

Democracy is the most complicated and the most burdensome system of government recorded in the history of humanity. For this reason it has never appeared save as a transitory manifestation, with few exceptions giving place before long to other systems. It is in no way surprising. The duty of the State is to act and to ordain: its dispositions are manifestations of a single will; without this, government is inconceivable. But how can a multitude of men, or a popular assembly act with a single will? The upholder of Democracy takes little trouble over the decision of this question, but evades it by means of those favorite phrases and formulas: "The will of the people," "public opinion," "the supreme decision of the nation," "the voice of the people is the voice of God," and others of a like nature. All these phrases signify that a multitude of men on a multitude of questions may form a common conclusion, and, conformably with their conclusion, arrive at a common decision. This may be possible sometimes, but only on the simplest questions. Where questions present the slightest complexity their decision by a numerous assembly is possible only through the medium of men capable of judging them in all their details, and of persuading the people to accept their judgment. In the number of complex questions may be counted all political questions requiring great concentration of the intellectual forces of the most capable and experienced statemen; on such questions it would be absurd to rely upon unanimity of thought and will in a numerous assembly; the decision of the people could only be ruinous to the State. The enthusiasts of Democracy contend that the people may manifest its will in affairs of State: this is a shallow theory. In reality, we find that popular assemblies are capable only of accepting—through enthusiasm—the opinion expressed by individuals or by a small minority—the opinion, for instance, of the recognised leader of their party, of some local worker of repute, of some organised association, or the impersonal opinion of an influential journal. Thus the discussions which precede decision become an absurd comedy played on a vast stage by a multitude of hands and voices, the greater the multitude the more unintelligible is the comedy, and the more the *dénouement* depends upon fortuitous and disorderly impulses. . . .

The greatest evil of constitutional government lies in the formation of ministries on parliamentary or party principles. Each political party aspires to seize the reins of government at any cost. The chief of the State must submit to the party which commands a majority in Parliament; a ministry is formed from the members of this party, and to maintain itself in power, enters upon a contest with the Opposition, which, in its turn, puts forth its whole strength to overthrow its rivals and take their places. If the chief of the State were to favour the minority and nominate his own ministry from its ranks, the new ministry would dissolve Parliament, and direct all its strength towards gaining a majority at the general election—with the support of this majority being enabled to withstand the Opposition. The placemen of the ministerial party vote always for the Government, not for the sake of upholding authority, not from intimate community of opinions, but because this Government in its turn supports the members of its party in power, and in its concomitant privileges, advantages, and emoluments. The natural instinct of all parties is to support their own in all circumstances, either on account of common interests, or simply by virtue of that gregarious instinct which impels mankind to unite in societies and to march into battle side by side.

It is evident, then, that unanimity of opinion has little influence, and that the pretended solicitude for the public welfare serves as the concealment of motives and instincts in no way related to it. This is the ideal of parliamentary government! It is a gross delusion to regard it as a guarantee of freedom. The absolute power of the sovereign is replaced by the absolute power of Parliament, with this difference only, that the person of the sovereign may embody a rational will, while in Parliament all depends upon accident, as the decisions of Parliament are brought about by the majority. But as, by the side of the majority constituted under the influence of party gambling, a powerful minority exists, the will of the majority is in no way the will of Parliament. Still less can it be regarded as the will of the people, the healthy mass of which abstains from participation in the comedy of parties, and turns away from it with abhorrence. On the other hand, the corrupt part of the population mingles willingly in politics, and thereby is driven to a worse corruption, for the chief motive of this comedy is appetite for power and plunder. Political freedom becomes a fiction maintained on paper by the paragraphs and phrases of the constitution; the principles of monarchical power disappear; the Liberal Democracy triumphs, bringing into society disorder and violence with the principles of infidelity and materialism, and proclaiming Liberty, Equality and Fraternity—where there is place neither for Liberty nor for Equality. Such conditions inevitably lead to anarchy, from which society can be saved alone by dictatorship—that is, by the rehabilitation of autocracy in the government of the world. . . .

The Press

From the day that man first fell, falsehood has ruled the world—ruled it in human speech, in the practical business of life, in all its relations and institutions. But never did the Father of Lies spin such webs of falsehood of every kind as in this restless age when we hear so many falsehoods uttered everywhere on Truth. With the growing complexity of social problems increases the number of relations and institutions pervaded with falsehood through and through. At every step appears some splendid edifice bearing the legend, "Here is Truth." Do you enter—you tread on falsehoods at every step. Would you expose the falsehoods which have angered you, the world will turn on you with anger greater still, and bid you trust and preach that this is truth, and truth unassailable.

Thus we are bidden to believe that the judgments of newspapers and periodicals, the judgments of the so-called Press, are the expression of public opinion. This, too, is a falsehood. The Press is one of the falsest institutions of our time.

But who will dare to stand against the forces of *opinion*—the opinion of the world on men and institutions? Such is the nature of man that each one of us, whatever his words or actions may be, takes care that he shall conform with the opinions of the people. The man is yet unborn who can truly boast himself free from his servility.

In our age the judgment of others has assumed an organised form, and calls itself Public Opinion. Its organ and representative is the Press. In truth, the importance of the Press is immense, and may be regarded as the most characteristic fact of our time—more characteristic than our remarkable discoveries and inventions in the realm of technical science. No government, no law, no custom can withstand its destructive activity when, from day to day, through the course of years, the Press repeats and disseminates among the people its condemnations of institutions or of men.

What is the secret of this strength? Certainly not the novelties and sensations with which the newspaper is filled, but its declared policy—the political and philosophical ideas propagated in its articles, the selection and classification of its news and rumors, and the peculiar illumination which it casts upon them. The newspaper has usurped the position of judicial observer of the events of the day; it judges not only the actions and words of men, but affects a knowledge of their unexpressed opinions, their intentions, and their enterprises; it praises and condemns at discretion; it incites some, threatens others; drags to the pillory one, and others exalts as idols to be adored as examples worthy of the emulation of all. In the name of Public Opinion it bestows rewards on some, and punishes others and the severity of excommunication. The question naturally occurs: Who are these representatives of this terrible power, Public Opinion? Whence is derived their right and authority to rule in the name of the community, to demolish existing institutions, and to proclaim new ideals of ethics and legislation?

But no one attempts to answer this question; all talk loudly of the liberty of the Press as the first and essential element of social well-being. Even in Russia, so libelled by the lying Press of Europe, such words are heard. Our so-called Slavophiles, with amazing inconsistency, share the same delusion, although their avowed object is to reform and renovate the institutions of their country upon a historic basis. Having joined the chorus of Liberals, in alliance with the propagandists of revolution, they proclaim exactly in the manner of the West: "Public Opinion—that is, the collective thought, guided by the natural love of right in all—is the final judge in all matters of public interest; therefore no restriction upon freedom of speech can be allowed, for such restriction can only express the tyranny of the minority over the will of the mass."

Such is the current proposition of the newest Liberalism. It is accepted by many in good faith, and there are few who, having troubled to analyse it have discerned how it is based upon falsehood and self-deception.

It conflicts with the first principles of logic, for it is based on the fallacious premise that the opinions of the public and of the Press are identical.

To test the validity of this claim it is only needful to consider the origin of newspapers, and the characters of their makers.

Any vagabond babbler or unacknowledged genius, any enterprising tradesman, with his own money or with the money of others, may found a newspaper, even a great newspaper. He may attract a host of writers and *feuilletonists*, ready to deliver judgment on any subject at a moment's notice; he may hire illiterate reporters to keep him supplied with rumors and scandals. His staff is then complete. From that day he sits in judgment on all the world, on ministers and administrators, on literature and art, on finance and industry. It is true that the new journal becomes a power only when it is sold in the market—that is, when it circulates among the public. For this talent is needed and the matter published must be attractive and congenial for the readers. Here, we might think, was some guarantee of the moral value of the undertaking—men of talent will not serve a feeble or contemptible editor or publisher; the public will not support a newspaper which is not a faithful echo of public opinion. This guarantee is fictitious. Experience proves that money will attract talent under any conditions, and that talent is ready to write as its paymaster requires. Experience proves that the most contemptible persons—retired money lenders, Jewish factors, newsvendors, and bankrupt gamblers—may found newspapers, secure the services of talented writers, and place their editions on the market as organs of public opinion. The healthy taste of the public is not to be relied upon. The great mass of readers, idlers for the most part, is ruled less by a few healthy instincts than by a base and despicable hankering for idle amusement; and the support of the people may be secured by any editor who provides for the satisfaction of these hankerings, for the love of scandal, and for intellectual pruriency of the basest kind. Of this we meet with evidence daily: even in our own capital no search is necessary to find it; it is enough to note the supply and demand at the newsvendors' shops, and at the railway stations. All of us have observed the triviality of conversation in society; in provincial towns, in the government capitals, the recreations of the people are well known—gambling, scandal, and anecdotes are the chief. Even conversation on the so-called social and political questions takes in a great measure the form of censure and aphorisms, plentifully supplemented with scandal and anecdote. This is a rich and fruitful soil for the tradesmen of literature, and there, as poisonous fungi, spring up organs of calumny, ephemeral and permanent, impudently extolling themselves as organs of public opinion. The great part which in the idle life of government towns is played by anonymous letters and lampoons, which unhappily, are so common among us, is played in the newspaper by "correspondence," sent from various quarters or composed in the editorial offices, by the reports and rumors invented by ignorant reporters, and by the atrocious practice of blackmailing, often the strongest weapon of the newspaper press. Such a paper may flourish, attain consideration as an organ of public opinion, and be immensely remunerative to its owners, while no paper conducted upon firm moral principles, or founded to meet the healthier instincts of the people, could compete with it for a moment.

This phenomenon is worthy of close inspection, for we find in it the most incongruous product of modern culture, the more incongruous where the principles of the new Liberalism have taken root, where the sanction of election, the authority of the popular will, is needed for every institution, where the ruling power is vested in the hands of individuals and derived from the suffrages of the majority in the representative assemblies. For the journalist with a power comprehending all things, requires no sanction; he derives his authority from no election, he receives support from no one. His newspaper becomes an authority in the State, and for this authority no endorsement is required. The man in the street may establish such an organ, and exercise the concomitant authority with an irresponsibility enjoyed by no other power in the world. That this is in no way exaggeration there are innumerable proofs. How often have superficial and unscrupulous journalists paved the way for revolution, fomented irritation into enmity, and brought about desolating wars! For conduct such as this a monarch would lose his throne, a minister would be disgraced, impeached, and punished; but the journalist stands dry above the waters he has disturbed, from the ruin he has caused he rises triumphant, and briskly continues his destructive work.

This is by no means the worst. When a judge has power to dishonor us, to deprive us of our property and of our freedom, he receives his power from the hands of the State only after such prolonged labour and experience as qualify him for his calling. His power is restricted by rigorous laws, his judgments are subject to revision by higher powers, and his sentence may be altered or commuted. The journalist has the fullest power to defame and dishonour me, to injure my material interests, even to restrict my liberty by attacks which force me to leave my place of abode. These judicial powers he has usurped; no higher authority has conferred them upon him; he has never proven by examination his fitness to exercise them; he has in no way shown his trustworthiness or his impartiality; his court is ruled by no formal procedure; and from his judgment there lies no appeal. Its defenders assure us that the Press itself heals the wounds it has inflicted; but any thinking mind can see that these are mere idle words. The attacks of the Press on individuals may cause irreparable injury. Retractions and explanations can in no way give them full satisfaction. Not half of those who read the denunciatory article will read the apology or the explanation, and in the minds of the mass of frivolous readers insulting or calumnious suggestions leave behind an ineffaceable stain. Criminal prosecution for defamation is but the feeblest defense, and civil action seldom succeeds in exposing the offender, while it subjects the offended to fresh attack. The journalist, moreover, has a thousand means of wounding and terrifying individuals without furnishing them with sufficient grounds for legal prosecution.

It is hard to imagine a despotism more irresponsible and violent than the despotism of printed words. Is it not strange and irrational, then, that those who struggle most for the preservation of this despotism are the impassioned champions of freedom, the ferocious enemies of legal restrictions and of all interference by the established authority. We cannot help remembering those wise men who went mad because they knew of their wisdom. . . .

There is nothing more remarkable in this century of advancement than the development of journalism to its present state as a terribly active social force. The importance of the Press first began to increase after the Revolution of July 1830, it doubled its influence after the Revolution of 1848; since then it has grown in power not only year by year but day by day. Already Governments have begun to measure their strength against this new force, and it has become impossible to imagine not only public but even individual life without the newspaper; so that the suppression of newspapers, if it were possible, would mean as much to daily life as the cessation of railway communications. Without doubt, the newspaper serves the world as a powerful instrument of culture. But while we acknowledge the convenience and profit derived from the dissemination of knowledge among the people, and from the interchange of thought and opinion, we cannot ignore the dangers imminent from the unbounded growth of the Press; we cannot refuse to recognize with a feeling of terror, the fatal, mysterious, and disintegrating force which threatens the future of humanity.

Every day the newspaper brings us a mass of varied news. How much of this is of real use to our lives, and to our educational development? How much is it fit to feed in our souls the sacred flame of aspiration unto good? How much is there not to flatter our baser instincts and impulses? We are told that the newspaper gives what the taste of readers demands, that its level reaches the level of the reader's taste. But to this we may reply that the demand would not be so great were the supply less energetically pushed.

If news alone were published the case would be different; but no, it is offered in a special form, embellished with personal opinions, and accompanied by anonymous but very decided commentaries. Papers controlled by serious persons of course exist, but such are few, while to the making of newspapers there is no end; and no morning passes without some writer, unknown to me, whom, perhaps, I should not care to know, obtruding upon me his views, expressed with all the authority of public opinion. What is graver still, however, is that this newspaper addresses not only a single class, but all men, some of whom can barely spell out a page of print, and offers to each a ready-made judgment upon everything, in such a seductive form that, little by little, by force of habit, the reader loses all wish for, and feels absolved from the duty of, forming his own opinions. Some have no ability for forming opinions, and accept mechanically the opinions of their newspapers; while others, born with a capacity for original thought in the trials and anxieties of daily life have not the time to think, and welcome the newspaper which does their thinking for them. The harm that results from this is too visible, especially in our time when powerful currents of thought are everywhere in action, wearing down the corners and distinctions of individual thought, reducing to uniformity the so-called public opinion, and weakening all independent development of thought, of will, and of character. Moreover, for many of the people the newspaper is the only source of education—a contemptible, pretended education—the varied mass of news and information found in the newspaper being taken by its readers as real knowledge, with which he proceeds to arm himself complacently. This we may take as one of the reasons why our age brings forth so few *complete* individuals, so few men of character. The modern Press is like the fabled hero who, having inscribed upon his visor some mysterious characters, the symbols of divine truth, struck all his enemies with terror, till one intrepid warrior rubbed from his helm the mysterious letters. On the visor of our Press today is written the legend "Public Opinion," and its influence is irresistible.

In the present constitution of society the Press has become an *institution* which cannot be ignored, but which must be considered side by side with the existing institutions which constitute the State and are subject to control and responsibility, for there is no institution which may be accounted uncontrolled and irresponsible. The greater the growth of the Press, the more clearly appear, side by side with the apparent advantages of rational and conscientious publicity, those social dangers which it creates. One of these dangers is the production and multiplication of a class of journalists, adventurers, and writers, who feed and grow fat upon the pen. The more serious workers on the serious Press never cease to complain bitterly of the multiplication of these fellows, with whom they are ashamed to be associated, even in name. In all the great States, in all the great markets, out of this rabble of scribbling brethren springs a class of men whom it is no exaggeration to describe as parasites on society.

In fact, these men stand on a special footing in relation to the general welfare, which should unite and inspire all institutions. They are in no way directly interested in the preservation of social order, in the reconciliation of opposing minds and contending parties. This is in the nature of things. The newspaper lives and is nourished by daily events and news. In troubled times its circulation increases; then its energies are expended in the dissemination of rumours and sensations which alarm and irritate the minds of the people; while on the other hand in times of quietude its circulation is sensibly diminished. Hardly has trouble begun when the streets are flooded with new publications which discord nourishes till peace returns, when they vanish as quickly as they appeared. But even in quiet times some must live, and for that end, new agitations are fomented, new interests developed, and sensations invented or exaggerated.

Those journals which pretend to seriousness find matters in the consideration of political questions and in the frothy polemics which daily appear. The journalist is ready at a moment's notice to decide any imaginable political question; and by his position he is bound to consider and decide it immediately, for he is a servant not of thought, or of reason, but a servant of the actual day. No sooner does the thought occur than it flies to paper, thence to the printing press; there must be no delay, no time is allowed for the ripening of this thought. You ask these men are they ashamed. Not at all. They would laugh in your face at such a question; they are persuaded that they render great services to society. They resemble in this the ancient augurs who made merry both over themselves and over their dupes.

If the journalist is to attract attention, he must raise his voice to a scream. This his trade requires, and exaggeration capable of passing into pathos becomes for him his second nature. When he enters upon a controversy he is ready to denounce his adversary as a fool, a rascal, or a dunce, to heap upon him unimaginable insults—this costs his conscience nothing; it is required by journalistic etiquette. His cries resemble the protestations of a trader in the market-place when he cheats his customers.

These are the practices and qualities which unhappily flourish in the Press and among its workers. It would be very laughable were it not so harmful. It is harmful because the Press now occupies an arena in which are discussed and decided the gravest questions of internal and external policy—questions of economy and administration indissolubly bound with the vital interests of peoples. For all this passion is but a weak equipment; sage reasoning and maturity and sanity of thought are also needed; needed, too, is knowledge of the history of peoples, and of practical life. Yet in Europe things have gone so far that from the ranks of journalism rise orators and statesmen who, together with the advocates with whom they share the capacity for abusive language, constitute in Parliament an overwhelming force. In the French Chamber there are but twenty-two representatives of large and fifty of small property, while all the talking strength belongs to journalists, of whom there are fifty-nine, and to advocates, of whom there are a hundred and seven.

And these are the representatives of their country, and the judges of the lives and requirements of the people! The people groan at this confusion of legislators. But it cannot deliver itself. . . .

Notes

1. "It grows as it indulges itself."
2. "The world wishes to be deceived, let it be deceived."

53

Program of Plekhanov's Group for the Emancipation of Labor, 1884

Until the early 1880s the Russian revolutionary movement was predominantly oriented toward the peasant and his commune. This was natural, as Russia's economy was agricultural, her society rural, and the bulk of her population peasant of one kind or another. The emancipation in 1861, mainly because of its resulting inequities and inadequacies, intensified this orientation, with the result that two vocal and active revolutionary groups emerged: *Zemlia i Volia* (Land and Liberty) and *V Narod* (To the People) The aim of the groups was simple: to educate Russian peasants as the first step toward instilling in them self-confidence while at the same time acquainting them with the revolutionary message. This goal, however, was frustrated by the alertness of the police and by the peasant's suspicion and misunderstanding of the motives of the young revolutionaries. While painful, the failure was not catastrophic for, following their disappointment with the peasants, some of the Russian revoluntionaries turned their attention to the rapidly emerging Russian industrial proletariat and to Marxism. The man most responsible for the shift was George V. Plekhanov (1856–1918), who is known as "the father of Russian Marxism." A prolific writer and an original thinker, Plekhanov embraced Marxism shortly after he fled from Russia to Geneva, where in 1884 he prepared the first program of the Group for the Emancipation of Labor. From this group evolved the future Russian Social Democratic Worker's party (the present Communist party of the Soviet Union). While Plekhanov was primarily a Marxist, his program nevertheless advocated a separate path of development for Russia.

The *Emancipation of Labor* group sets itself the aim of spreading socialist ideas in Russia and working out the elements for organizing a Russian workers' *socialist party.*

The essence of its outlook can be expressed in the following few propositions:[1]

From G. V. Plekhanov, *Selected Philosophical Works* (Moscow: Foreign Languages Publishing House, 1959), vol. 1, pp. 400–405.

1. The economic emancipation of the working class will be achieved only by the transfer to collective ownership by the working people of the means and products of production and the organization of all the functions of social and economic life in accordance with the requirements of society.

2. The modern development of technology in civilized societies not only provides the *material possibility* for such an organization but makes it *necessary and inevitable* for solving the contradictions which hinder the quiet and all-round development of those societies.

3. This radical economic revolution will entail most fundamental changes in the entire constitution of social and international relationships.

Abolishing the class struggle by destroying the classes themselves; making the economic struggle of individuals impossible and unnecessary by abolishing commodity production and the competition resulting from it; briefly, putting an end to the struggle for existence between individuals, classes and whole societies, it renders unnecessary all those social organs which have developed as the weapons of that struggle during the many centuries it has been proceeding.

Without falling into utopian fantasies about the social and international organization of the future, we can already now foretell the abolition of the most important of the organs of chronic struggle inside society, namely, *the state as a political organization opposed to society* and safeguarding mainly the interests of the ruling section. In exactly the same way we can already now foresee the international character of the impending economic revolution. The contemporary development of international exchange of products necessitates the participation of all civilized societies in this revolution.

That is why the socialist parties in all countries acknowledge the international character of the present-day working-class movement and proclaim the principle of international solidarity of producers. The *Emancipation of Labor* group also acknowledges the great principles of the former *International Working Men's Association* and the identity of interests among the working people of the whole civilized world.

4. Introducing *consciousness* where *blind economic necessity* now dominates, replacing the modern mastery of the product over the *producer* by that of the *producer* over the *product,* the socialist revolution simplifies all social relationships and gives them a purpose, at the same time providing each citizen with the real possibility of participating directly in the discussion and decision of all social matters.

This direct participation of citizens in the management of all social matters presupposes the abolition of the modern system of political representation and its replacement by *direct popular legislation.*

In their present-day struggle, the socialists must bear in mind this necessary political reform and aim at its realization by all means in their power.

This is all the more necessary as the political self-education and the rule of the working class are a necessary preliminary condition of its economic emancipation. Only a completely *democratic* state can carry out the economic revolution which conforms to the interests of the producers and demands their intelligent participation in the organization and regulation of production.

At present the working class in the advanced countries is becoming increasingly clear on the necessity of the social and political revolution referred to and is organizing into a special labour party which is hostile to parties of exploiters.

Being accomplished according to the principles of the *International Working Men's Association,* this organization, however, has mainly in view the achievement by the workers of political domination within each of the respective states. "The proletariat of each country must, of course, first of all settle matters with its own bourgeoisie."

This introduces an element of variety into the programmes of the socialist parties in the different states, compelling each of them to conform to the social conditions in its country.

It goes without saying that the practical tasks, and consequently the programmes of the socialists, are bound to be more original and complicated in countries where capitalist production has not yet become dominant and where the working masses are oppressed under a double yoke—that of rising capitalism and that of obsolescent patriarchal economy.

In those countries, the socialist must at the same time organize the workers for the struggle against the bourgeoisie and wage war against the survivals of old-prebourgeois social relationships, which are harmful both to the development of the working class and to the welfare of the whole people.

That is precisely the position of the Russian socialists. The working population of Russia is oppressed directly by the whole burden of the enormous police-despotic state and at the same time suffers all the miseries inherent in the epoch of capitalist *accumulation*; and in places—in our industrial centers—it suffers from the oppression of capitalist *production* which is not yet limited by any decisive intervention of the state or by the organized resistance of the workers themselves. Present-day Russia is suffering—as Marx once said of the West European continent— not only from the development of capitalist production, but also from insufficiency of that development.

One of the most harmful consequences of this backward state of production was and still is the underdevelopment of the middle class, which, in our country, is incapable of taking the *initiative* in the struggle against absolutism.

That is why our socialist intelligentsia has been obliged to head the present-day emancipation movement, whose direct task must be to set up free political institutions in our country, the socialists on their side being under the obligation to provide the working class with the possibility to take an active and fruitful part in the future political life of Russia.

The first means to achieve this aim must be agitation for a democratic constitution guaranteeing:

(a) The right to vote and to be elected to the Legislative Assembly as well as to provincial and village self-government bodies for every citizen who has not been sentenced by court to deprivation of political rights[2] for certain *shameful* activities strictly specified by law.

(b) A money payment fixed by law for the representatives of the people, which will allow them to be elected from the poorest classes of the population.

(c) Inviolability of the person and home of citizens.

(d) Unlimited freedom of conscience, speech, the press, assembly and association.

(e) Freedom of movement and of employment.

(f) Complete equality of all citizens irrespective of religion and racial origin[3]

(g) The replacement of the standing army by general arming of the people.

(h) A revision of all our civil and criminal legislation, the abolition of division according to estates and of punishments incompatible with human dignity.

But this aim will not be achieved, the political initiative of the workers will be unthinkable, if the fall of absolutism finds them completely unprepared and unorganized.

That is why the socialist intelligentsia has the obligation to organize the workers and *prepare* them as far as possible for the struggle against the present-day system of government as well as against the future bourgeois parties.

The intelligentsia must *immediately set to work to organize* the workers in our industrial centers, as the foremost representatives of the whole working population of Russia, in secret groups, with links between them and a definite social and political program corresponding to the present-day needs of the entire class of producers in Russia and the basic task of socialism.

Understanding that the details of such a program can be worked out only in the future and by the working class itself when it is called on to participate in the political life of the country and is united in its own party, the *Emancipation of Labor* group presumes that the main points of the economic section of the worker's program must be the *demands:*

(a) Of a radical revision of our agrarian relations, that is, the conditions for the redemption of the land and its distribution to peasant communities. Of the right to renounce allotments and leave the community for those peasants who find this convenient for themselves, and so forth.

(b) Of the abolition of the present system of dues and the institution of a progressive taxation system.

(c) Of the legislative regulation of relations between workers (in town and country) and employers, and the organization of the appropriate inspection with *representation* of the *workers.*

(d) Of state assistance for production *association* organized in all possible branches of agriculture, the mining and manufacturing industries (by peasants, miners, factory and plant workers, craftsmen, and so forth).

The *Emancipation of Labor* group is convinced that not only the success but even the mere possibility of such a purposeful movement of the Russian working class depends in a large degree upon the work referred to above being done by the intelligentsia among the working class.

But the group assumes that the intelligentsia themselves must as a preliminary step adopt the standpoint of modern scientific socialism, adhering to the *Narodnaya Volya* [People's Will] traditions only inasmuch as they are not opposed to its principles.

In view of this, the *Emancipation of Labor* group sets itself the aim of spreading modern socialism in Russia and preparing the working class for a conscious social and political movement; to this aim it devotes all its energies, calling upon our revolutionary youth for help and collaboration.

Pursuing this aim by all means in its power, the *Emancipation of Labor* group at the same time recognizes the necessity for terrorist struggle against the absolute government and differs from the *Narodnaya Volya* party only on the question of the so-called seizure of power by the revolutionary party and of the *tasks of the immediate activity of the socialists among the working class.*

The *Emancipation of Labor* group does not in the least ignore the peasantry, which constitutes an enormous portion of Russia's working population. But it assumes that the work of the intelligentsia, especially under present-day conditions of the social and political struggle, must be aimed first of all at the most developed part of this population, which consists of the industrial workers. Having secured the powerful support of this section, the socialist intelligentsia will have far greater hope of success in extending their activity to the peasantry as well, especially if they have by that time won freedom of agitation and propaganda. Incidentially, it goes without saying that the distribution of the forces of our socialists *will have to be changed if an independent revolutionary movement becomes manifest among the peasantry*, and that even at present people who are in direct touch with the peasantry could, by their work among them, render an important service to the socialist movement in Russia. The *Emancipation of Labor* group, far from rejecting such people, will exert its efforts to agree with them on the basic propositions of the program.

Notes

1. We by no means regard the program which we submit to the judgement of the comrades as something finished and complete, not subject to partial changes or additions. On the contrary, we are ready to introduce into it any kind of corrections, provided they do not contradict the basic concepts of scientific socialism and that they correspond to the practical conclusions following from these concepts concerning the work of the socialists in Russia.

2. Such actions may include, for example, *bribing at elections*, outrageous repression of workers by employers, and so forth.

3. This point is logically included in item 4, which requires among other things, complete freedom of conscience; but we consider it necessary to set it in relief in view of the fact that there are in our country whole sections of the population, for instance the *Jews*, who do not even enjoy the wretched "rights" made available to other "residents."

54

The Franco-Russian Military Convention, August 27, 1891

From 1863 to about 1890 Russian foreign policy in Europe had a strong "pro-German" orientation. That orientation was determined partly by dynastic ties, partly by Bismarck's wisdom, and partly by Russia's fear of the revolutionary France and liberal England. By 1890 some of these determinants disappeared. In 1890 Kaiser Wilhelm II dismissed Bismarck, inaugurated a close dialogue with the British, and deliberately failed to renew the Reinsurance Treaty with the Russian government. The sudden disruption of "lines of communication" between St. Petersburg and Berlin paved the way for the establishment of a dialogue between St. Petersburg and Paris. The initial Franco-Russian *rapprochement* took the form of massive French financial assistance to help Russia's industrialization program. This was followed by exchange visits of naval

---

From France. *Ministère des affaires ètranères. Documents diplomatiques. L'Alliance Franco-Russe* (Paris: Impimerie Nationale, 1918), p. 92. Translation mine.

squadrons, and in August 1891, it culminated in a secret military understanding between the two powers. The consummation of that entente brought Bismarck's nightmare to reality and indirectly paved the way to World War I.

Animated by a common desire to preserve the peace, and having no other aim than to prepare for the necessities of a defensive war provoked against either of them by an attack by the forces of the Triple Alliance, France and Russia have agreed upon the following provisions:

1. If France is attacked by Germany, or by Italy supported by Germany, Russia shall employ all her available forces to fight Germany.

If Russia is attacked by Germany, or by Austria supported by Germany, France shall employ all her available forces to fight Germany.

2. In case the forces of the Triple Alliance, or of one of the Powers which comprise it, should be mobilized, France, and Russia, at the first indication of the event, and without a previous agreement being necessary, shall mobilize all their forces immediately and simultaneously, and shall transport them as near to the frontiers as possible.

3. The forces available which must be employed against Germany shall be for France, 1,300,000 men; for Russia, from 700,000 to 800,000 men. These forces shall begin complete action with all speed, so that Germany will have to fight at the same time in the east and in the west.

4. The Staffs of the armies of the two countries shall constantly plan in concert in order to prepare for and facilitate the execution of the above measures. They shall communicate to each other in time of peace all the information regarding the armies of the Triple Alliance which is in or shall come into their possession. The ways and means of corresponding in time of war shall be studied and arranged in advance.

5. France and Russia shall not conclude peace separately.

6. The present convention shall have the same duration as the Triple Alliance.

7. All the clauses enumerated above shall be kept absolutely secret.

Obruchev Boisdeffre

55

The Russo-Chinese Secret Treaty of Alliance, June 3, 1896

In 1894 the Japanese military machine humiliated China on the battlefield, and in April 1895, Japanese diplomats humbled the Chinese at the peace table at Shimonoseki. Beause these developments upset the status quo in the Far East, all powers interested in China were greatly alarmed. The Russians expressed the greatest concern at these far-reaching changes. They did this not because they wanted to defend the territorial integrity of the Chinese Empire, but because the sudden Japanese thrust into the Asia mainland blocked their own ambitions in China, and in addition threatened their own position in Northeast Asia. To counter the "threat", the Russians (with French and German support) forced the Japanese to give up control of the Liaotung Peninsula, floated a loan on China's behalf, and in December 1895, with French financial help, founded the Russo-Chinese Bank. On June 3, 1896 the sudden pro-Chinese attitude culminated in the conclusion of a secret treaty of alliance by whose terms both countries bound themseles to assist each other militarily against future Japanese territorial ambitions in Korea, China, and East Asia. On the basis of this alliance the Russians then secured a number of significant concessions for construction of their Trans-Siberian Railroad, as well as the use of Chinese harbor facilities.

Article I

Every aggression directed by Japan, whether against Russian territory in Eastern Asia, or against the territory of China or that of Korea, shall be regarded as necessarily bringing about the immediate application of the present treaty.

In this case the two High Contracting Parties engage to support each other reciprocally by all the land and sea forces of which they can dispose at that moment, and to assist each other as much as possible for the victualling of their respective forces.

Reprinted with the permission of The Johns Hopkins University Press from Ernst B. Price, *The Russo-Japanese Treaties of 1907–1916 Concerning Manchuria and Mongolia* (Baltimore: The Johns Hopkins University Press, 1933), pp. 101–102.

Article 2

As soon as the two High Contracting Parties shall be engaged in common action no treaty of peace with the adverse party can be concluded by one of them without the assent of the other.

Article 3

During the military operations all the ports of China shall, in case of necessity, be open to Russian warships, which shall find there on the part of the Chinese authorities all the assistance of which they may stand in need.

Article 4

In order to facilitate the access of the Russian land troops to the menaced points, and to ensure their means of subsistence, the Chinese Government consents to the construction of a railway line across the Chinese provinces of the Amour [that is, Heilungkiang] and of Kirin in the direction of Vladivostok. The junction of this railway with the Russian railway shall not serve as a pretext for any encroachment on Chinese territory nor for any infringement of the rights of sovereignty of his Majesty the Emperor of China. The construction and exploitation of this railway shall be accorded to the Russo-Chinese Bank, and the clauses of the contract which shall be concluded for this purpose shall be duly discussed between the Chinese Minister in St. Petersburg and the Russo-Chinese Bank.

Article 5

It is understood that in time of war, as indicated in Article 1, Russia shall have the free use of the railway mentioned in Article 4, for the transport and provisioning of her troops. In time of peace Russia shall have the same right for the transit of her troops and stores, with stoppages, which shall not be justified by any other motive than the needs of the transport service.

56

Father Gapon's Petition to Nicholas II, January 22, 1905

The Pobedonostsev-directed reaction and persecution, designed to maintain autocracy intact, succeeded in driving the revolutionaries underground, where they became more active, and in increasing popular discontent. This discontent increased sharply following Russia's involvement with Japan in a war which the people neither supported nor understood and which inflicted several military and naval disasters (Port Arthur, Tsushima, Mukden) on Russian forces. In the midst of these reverses, *zemstvo* representatives (representatives of local self-governing districts which had emerged in 1864) unanimously called for a reform of Russian political life. They demanded what other revolutionaries had insisted on: civil rights; freedom of speech, assembly, press, thought, and conscience; equality before the law; and a parliamentary system of government. Official rejection of these modest proposals widened the existing gulf between government bureaucracy and the people, and on January 22, 1905, the tension exploded in a crisis known as "Bloody Sunday." A priest, George A. Gapon (1870–1906), led a peaceful procession of striking workers of St. Petersburg toward the Winter Palace, bearing a petition to Nicholas II listing their grievances and wishes. Instead of the expected audience with the tsar, the petitioners met with police bullets that killed scores and wounded hundreds. The incident caused a great public indignation, intensified the existing radicalism, led to nationwide antigovernment strikes and demonstrations, and triggered the 1905 Revolution.

Sovereign!

We, the workers and the inhabitants of various social strata of the city of St. Petersburg, our wives, children, and helpless old parents, have come to you, Sovereign, to seek justice and protection. We are impoverished; our employers oppress us, overburden us with work, insult us, consider us in-

---

From N. S. Trusova, A. A. Novoselskii and L. N. Pushkarev, eds., *Nachalo pervoi Russkoi revolutsii, ianuar-mart, 1905 goda (The Beginning of the First Russian Revolution, January-March, 1905)*, (Moscow: Akademiia Nauk, 1955), p. 28-31. Translation mine. Words in brackets are mine.

human, and treat us as slaves who must suffer a bitter fate in silence. Though we have suffered, they push us deeper and deeper into a gulf of misery, disfranchisement, and ignorance. Despotism and arbitrariness strangle us and we are gasping for breath. Sovereign, we have no strength left. We have reached the limit of endurance. We have reached that terrible moment when death is preferable to the continuance of unbearable sufferings.

And so we left our work and informed our employers that we shall not resume work until they meet our demands. We do not demand much; we only want what is indispensable to life and without which life is nothing but hard labor and eternal suffering. Our first request was that our employers discuss our needs jointly with us. But they refused to do this; they even denied us the right to speak about our needs, saying that the law does not give us such a right. Also unlawful were our requests to reduce the working day to eight hours; to set wages jointly with us; to examine our disputes with lower echelons of factory administration; to increase the wages of unskilled workers and women to one *ruble* per day; to abolish overtime work; to provide medical care without insult; to build shops in such a way that one could work there and not die because of awful drafts, rains, and snow.

Our employers and factory administrators considered all this to be unlawful; they regarded every one of our requests as a crime and interpreted our desire to improve our condition as audacity.

Sovereign, there are thousands of us here; outwardly we resemble human beings, but in reality neither we nor the Russian people as a whole enjoy any human right, have any right to speak, to think, to assemble, to discuss our needs, or to take measures to improve our conditions. They have enslaved us and they did it under the protection of your officials, with their aid and with their cooperation. They imprison and [even] send into exile any one of us who has the courage to speak on behalf of the interests of the working class and of the people. They punish us for our good heartedness and sympathy as if for a crime. To pity a downtrodden, disfranchised, and oppressed man is to commit a major crime. All the workers and the peasants are at the mercy of bureaucratic administrators consisting of embezzlers of public funds and thieves who not only disregard the interests of the people, but also scorn these interests. The bureaucratic administration has brought the country to complete ruin, has brought upon it a disgraceful war, and continues to lead it further and further into destruction. We, the workers and the people, have absolutely nothing to say in the matter of expenditure of huge taxes that are collected from us. In fact, we do not know where or for what the money collected from the impoverished people goes. The people are deprived of the opportunity to express their wishes and their demands and to participate in determining

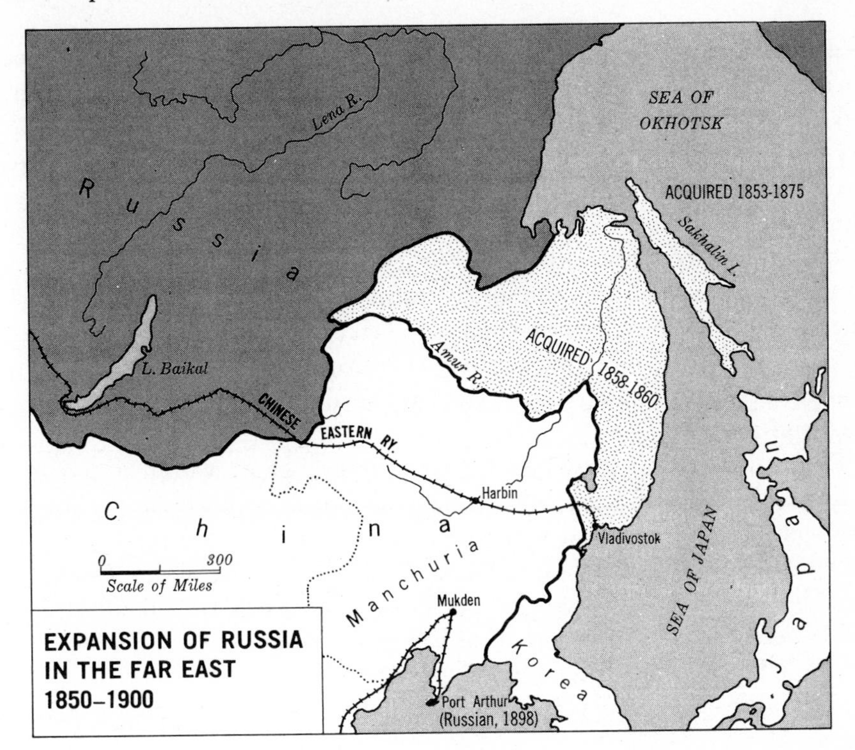

taxes and expenditures. The workers are deprived of the opportunity to organize themselves in unions to protect their interests.

Sovereign! Is all this compatible with God's laws, by the grace of which you reign? And is it possible to live under such laws? Wouldn't it be better for all of us if we, the toiling people of all Russia, died? Let the capitalist-exploiters of the working class, the bureaucratic embezzlers of public funds, and the pillagers of the Russian people live and enjoy themselves. Sovereign, these are the problems that we face and these are the reasons that we have gathered before the walls of your palace. Here we seek our last salvation. Do not refuse to come to the aid of your people; lead them out of the grave of disfranchisement, poverty, and ignorance; grant them an opportunity to determine their own destiny, and remove from them the unbearable yoke of bureaucrats. Tear down the wall that separates you from your people and let them rule the country with you. You have been placed [on the throne of Russia] for the happiness of the people; the bureaucrats, however, pull this happiness out of our hands and hence it never reaches us; we receive only grief and humiliation. Sovereign, examine our requests attentively and without any anger; they are intended not for any evil but for a good [cause] for both of us. It is not arrogance that forces us to speak but the realization of the need to escape from a situation unbearable for all of us. Russia is too great, her needs too diverse and numerous to be administered by bureaucrats only. It is essential to have a popular representation; it is essential that the people help themselves and that they govern themselves. Only they know their real needs. Do not spurn their help; accept it; decree immediately to summon at once representatives of the Russian land from all classes, from all strata, including workers' representatives. Let there be present a capitalist, a worker, a bureaucrat, a priest, a doctor, and a teacher—let everyone regardless of who they are elect their own representatives. Let everyone be equal and free to elect or be elected, and toward that end decree that the elections to the Constituent Assembly be carried out on the basis of universal, secret, and equal suffrage.

This is our chief request because everything is based within it and upon it; this is the main and the only bandage for our painful wounds; without it they will bleed severely and will soon cause our death.

One measure, however, cannot heal all of our wounds. Other [measures] are indispensable and, Sovereign, we speak about them to you directly and openly, as to our father, in behalf of the entire toiling class of Russia.

[The following measures] are indispensable:

1. Measures to eliminate the ignorance and disfranchisement of the Russian people.
   (a) The immediate release and return [from exile] of all those who have suffered because of their political or religious beliefs, or because of strikes or peasant disturbances.
   (b) An immediate declaration of freedom and inviolability of person, freedom of speech and press, freedom of assembly, and freedom of conscience.
   (c) Universal and compulsory public education, financed by the state.
   (d) Responsibility of Ministers before the people and a guarantee of a law abiding administration.
   (e) Equality before the law for everyone, without exception.
   (f) Separation of the church from the state.
2. Measures to eliminate the poverty of the people.
   (a) Abolition of indirect taxes and the substitution of a direct progressive income tax.
   (b) Abolition of redemption payments, [introduction of] low interest rates, and the gradual transfer of the land to the people.
   (c) Placement of military and naval orders in Russia, not abroad.
   (d) Termination of the war by the will of the people.
3. Measures to eliminate the oppression of labor by capital:
   (a) Abolition of the institution of factory inspectors.

(b) Establishment at the factories and mills of permanent committees elected by the workers which, jointly with the management, would consider complaints of individual workers. The dismissal of a worker would not take place other than by the decision of this committee.
(c) Immediate freedom for consumer and trade unions.
(d) An eight-hour working day and standardization of overtime work.
(e) Immediate freedom for the struggle between labor and capital.
(f) Immediate standardization of a minimum wage.
(g) Immediate and continued participation of representatives of the working classes in the preparation of legislation for a state insurance for workers.

Here, Sovereign, are our principal needs with which we came to you. Only if and when they are fulfilled will it be possible to free our country from slavery and poverty; will it be possible for it to flourish; will it be possible for the workers to organize themselves to protect their interests against the insolent exploitation of the capitalists and the thievish government of bureaucrats who strangle the people. Decree and swear that you will realize these [requests] and you will make Russia happy, famous and will imprint forever your name in our hearts and in the hearts of our descendants. And if you will not decree it, if you will not respond to our plea, we shall die here, in this square, before your palace. We have nowhere else to go and it is useless to go. We have only two roads open to us: one leading to freedom and happiness, the other to the grave. Let our life be a sacrifice for suffering Russia. We do not regret this sacrifice. We offer it willingly.

George Gapon, Priest
Ivan Vasimov, Worker

57

Concessions of Nicholas II in the Revolution of 1905

The "Bloody Sunday" massacre had an electrifying effect on all segments of Russian society. It intensified radicalism, increased agitation, and brought on clashes with authorities; it precipitated strikes and demands for a constitutional government, equal rights, and autonomy for minorities; and even led to mutiny. Under the mounting nationwide radicalism, which was accompanied by critical military reverses in the war with Japan, Nicholas II was forced to yield. On October 30, 1905, he issued a manifesto (drafted by Sergei J. Witte) which granted the people of the Empire "personal inviolability, freedom of conscience, speech, assembly and association," and promised to allow the disfranchised elements of society to participate in the election to the Duma. Finally, it established as an "unbreakable rule" that no law should be promulgated without the sanction of the Parliament. The October Manifesto marked the end of absolute monarchy in Russia.

Then on November 16, 1905, the tsar canceled peasant redemption payments, which since the emancipation in 1861 had been one of the main deterrents to progress in the Russian villages. The cancellation paved the way to the agrarian reform commonly known as the Stolypin Land Reforms (1906–1911). These concessions, while failing to satisfy the extreme radicals, pacified the liberals and the majority of the people, thus enabling the authorities to restore order and direct Russia to a period of "constitutional experiment."

The October Manifesto, October 30, 1905

By the Grace of God, We Nicholas II, Emperor and Autocrat of all Russia, Tsar of Poland, Grand Duke of Finland, etc.

Make known to all Our loyal subjects: Rioting and disturbances in the capitals and in many localities of Our Empire fill Our heart with great and

---

The following two items are from *Polnoe Sobranie Zakonov Russkoi Imperii . . . (Complete Collection of the Laws of the Russian Empire),* 3d Series, vol. 25. "The October Manifesto" from no. 26,803, pp. 754–755. "The Cancellation of Redemption Payments" from no. 26,871, p. 790. Translation mine. Words in brackets are mine.

heavy grief. The well-being of the Russian Sovereign is inseparable from the national well-being; and the national sorrow is His sorrow. The disturbances which have appeared may cause a grave national tension that may endanger the integrity and unity of Our state.

By the great vow of Tsarist service We are obligated to use every resource of wisdom and Our authority to bring a speedy end to an unrest dangerous to Our state. We have [already] ordered the responsible authorities to take measures to terminate direct manifestations of disorder, lawlessness, and violence, and to protect peaceful people who quietly seek to fulfill the duties incumbent upon them. To successfully fulfill general measures which We have designed for the pacification of state life, We feel it is essential to coordinate the activity of the higher government.

We impose upon the government the duty to execute Our inflexible will:

1. To grant the population the inviolable foundations of civic freedom based on the principles of genuine personal inviolability, freedom of conscience, speech, assemblies, and associations.

2. Without postponing the scheduled elections to the State Duma, to admit in the participation of the Duma insofar as possible in the short time that remains before its scheduled meeting all those classes of the population which presently are completely deprived of voting rights, and to leave further development of general elective law to the future legislative order;

3. To establish as an unbreakable rule that no law shall become effective without the confirmation by the State Duma, and that the elected representatives of the people shall be guaranteed an opportunity of real participation in the supervision of the legality of the acts by authorities whom We shall appoint.

We summon all loyal sons of Russia to remember their duties towards their country, to assist in terminating this unprecedented unrest, and together with Us to make every effort to restore peace and tranquility in Our native land.

Given in Peterhof, October 30, the year of Our Lord 1905, and eleventh of Our reign.

Nicholas

The Cancellation of Redemption Payments, November 16, 1905

By the Grace of God, We, Nicholas II, Emperor and Autocrat of All-Russia, Tsar of Poland, Grand Duke of Finland, and so forth.

Make known to all Our loyal subjects: Our heart is filled with deep sorrow over disturbances that have developed in villages of certain districts where the peasants have resorted to violence. We can tolerate neither violation of the law nor high-handed actions, and have instructed Our military and civil authorities to use every means to prevent and terminate the disorder and to punish the guilty.

We have the needs of the peasants close to Our heart and do not ignore them. Violence and crime do not, however, aid the peasant; [on the contrary] they may bring much sorrow and misery to the country. The only way to permanently improve the well-being of the peasant is through peaceful and legal means; to improve his condition has always been one of Our first concerns. We have lately issued orders to gather and submit to Us information concerning the measures that might be adopted immediately to benefit the peasants. After consideration, We have decided:

1. To reduce by half, from January 1, 1906, and to terminate completely after January 1, 1907, [redemption] payments from peasants for land which prior to the Emancipation belonged to nobles, state, and Crown.

2. To increase the resources of the Peasant Land Bank, in order to enable it to offer better terms for loans to petty peasants to buy additional land.

We have issued special instructions to realize these measures. We are convinced that if We unite Our efforts with those of the best men to be elected in Russia by Our loyal subjects, including peasants, We shall succeed in satisfying the other peasant needs without harming the interests of nobles.

We hope that the peasant population, which is so dear to Our heart, will follow Christian teachings of love and good and will listen to Our Tsarist call to maintain peace and order and to not violate the laws and rights of others.

Given at Tsarskoe Selo, November 16, the year of Our Lord, 1905, and the twelfth of Our reign.

Nicholas

58

The Fundamental Laws of Imperial Russia, 1906

Until the Revolution of 1905, imperial Russia's autocratic tsars embodied the executive, the legislative, and the judicial branches of the government. Moreover, since each tsar was also nominal head of the Russian Orthodox Church, his power was not only absolute but divine as well. The tsars jealously guarded their prerogatives and rebuffed all suggestions—even the most moderate ones—to alter this arrangement.

The Revolution of 1905 changed the situation. In his October Manifesto Nicholas II granted Russia a parliament, and by April 1906, when the country received its first constitution, imperial Russia had begun its slow development from an autocratic to a constitutional regime. It was an erratic process because the country lacked many necessary prerequisites for a constitutional system: established political parties, a literate population, the experience of self-government, and an atmosphere of mutual trust between the elected legislators and government bureaucrats. The transition was painful also because the tsar, as the following articles indicate, still retained power over matters which in parliamentary countries belonged within the competence of the legislative branch of government. He retained, for instance, his historic title of Autocrat (Article 4), and under Article 45 he had the right to issue imperial decrees in emergencies between sessions of the parliament, which later, however, were to be submitted for approval by the legislature. No longer was he an absolute monarch.

The Fundamental Laws

1. The Russian state is unified and indivisible.

2. The Grand Duchy of Finland, while comprising an inseparable part of the Russian state, is governed in its internal affairs by special decrees based on special legislation.

From *Polnoe Sobranie Zakonov Russkoi Imperii . . . (Complete Collection of the Laws of the Russian Empire),* 3d Series, vol. 26, no. 27,805, pp. 456–461. Translation mine. Words in brackets are mine.

3. The Russian language is the official state language and its use is obligatory in the Army, the Fleet, and in all state and public institutions. The use of local languages and dialects in state and public institutions is determined by special laws.

Chapter I. The Essence of the Supreme Autocratic Power

4. The All-Russian Emperor possesses the supreme autocratic power. Not only fear and conscience, but God himself, commands obedience to his authority.

5. The person of the Sovereign Emperor is sacred and inviolable.

6. The same supreme autocratic power belongs to the Sovereign Empress, should the order of succession to the throne pass to a female line; her husband, however, is not considered a sovereign; except for the title, he enjoys the same honors and privileges reserved for the spouses of all other sovereigns.

7. The Sovereign Emperor exercises the legislative authority jointly with the State Council and the State Duma.

8. The Sovereign Emperor enjoys the legislative initiative in all legislative matters. The State Council and the State Duma may examine the Fundamental State Laws only on his initiative.

9. The Sovereign Emperor approves laws; and without his approval no legislative measure can become law.

10. The Sovereign Emperor possesses the administrative power in its totality throughout the entire Russian state. On the highest level of administration his authority is direct; on subordinate levels of administration, in conformity with the law, he determines the degree of authority of subordinate branches and officials who act in his name and in accordance with his orders.

11. As supreme administrator, the Sovereign Emperor, in conformity with the existing laws, issues decrees for the organization and functioning of diverse branches of state administration as well as directives essential for the execution of the laws.

12. The Sovereign Emperor alone is the supreme leader of all foreign relations of the Russian state with foreign countries. He also determines the direction of foreign policy of the Russian state.

13. The Sovereign Emperor alone declares war, concludes peace, and negotiates treaties with foreign states.

14. The Sovereign Emperor is the Commander-in-Chief of the Russian Army and of the Fleet. He possesses supreme command over all the land and sea forces of the Russian state. He determines the organization of the Army and of the Fleet, and issues decrees and directives dealing with the distribution of the armed forces, their transfer to a war footing, their training, the duration of service by various ranks of the Army and of the Fleet, and all other matters

related to the organization of the armed forces and the defense of the Russian state. As supreme administrator, the Sovereign Emperor determines limitation on the rights of residence and the acquisition of immovable property in localities that have fortifications and defensive positions for the Army and the Fleet.

15. The Sovereign Emperor has the power to declare martial law or a state of emergency in localities.

16. The Sovereign Emperor has the right to coin money and to determine its physical appearance.

17. The Sovereign Emperor appoints and dismisses the Chairman of the Council of Ministers, Ministers, and Chief Administrators of various departments, as well as other officials whose appointment or dismissal has not been determined by law.

18. As supreme administrator the Sovereign Emperor determines the scope of activity of all state officials in accordance with the needs of the state.

19. The Sovereign Emperor grants titles, medals and other state distinctions as well as property rights. He also determines conditions and procedures for gaining titles, medals, and distinctions.

20. The Sovereign Emperor directly issues decrees and instructions on matters of property that belongs to him as well as on those properties that bear his name and which have traditionally belonged to the ruling Emperor. The latter cannot be bequeathed or divided and are subject to a different form of alienation. These as well as other properties are not subject to a different form of alienation. These as well as other properties are not subject to levy or collection of taxes.

21. As head of the Imperial Household, the Sovereign Emperor, in accordance with Regulations on the Imperial Family, has the right to issue regulations affecting princely properties. He also determines the composition of the personnel of the Ministry of the Imperial Household, its organization and regulation, as well as the procedure of its administration.

22. Justice is administered in the name of the Sovereign Emperor in courts legally constituted, and its execution is also carried out in the name of His Imperial Majesty.

23. The Sovereign Emperor has the right to pardon the accused, to mitigate the sentence, and even to completely forgive transgressions, including the right to terminate court actions against the guilty and to free them from trial and punishment. Stemming from royal mercy, he also has the right to commute the official penalty and to generally pardon all exceptional cases that are not subject to general laws, provided such actions do not infringe upon civil rights or the legally protected interests of others.

24. Statutes of the *Svod Zakonov* (Vol. I, part 1, 1892 edition) on the

order of succession to the throne (Articles 3–17), on the coming of age of the Sovereign Emperor, on government and guardianship (Articles 18–30), on the ascension to the throne and on the oath of allegiance (Articles 31–34 and Appendix V), on the sacred crowing and anointing (Articles 35 and 36), and on the title of His Imperial Majesty and on the State Emblem (Articles 37–39 and Appendix I), and on the faith (Articles 40–46), retain the force of the Fundamental Laws.

25. The Regulation on the Imperial Family (*Svod Zakanow,* Vol. I, part 1, 1892 edition, Articles 82–179 and Appendices II-IV and VI), while retaining the force of the Fundamental Laws, can be changed or amended only by the Sovereign Emperor personally in accordance with the procedure established by him, provided these changes or amendments of these regulations do not infringe upon general laws or provided they do not call for new expenditures from the treasury.

26. Decrees and commands that are issued directly or indirectly by the Sovereign Emperor as supreme administrator are implemented either by the Chairman of the Council of Ministers, or a subordinate minister, or a department head, and are published by the Governing Senate.

Chapter II. Rights and Obligations of Russian Subjects

27. Conditions for acquiring rights of Russian citizenship, as well as its loss, are determined by law.

28. The defense of the Throne and of the Fatherland is a sacred obligation of every Russian subject. The male population, irrespective of social status, is subject to military service determined by law.

29. Russian subjects are obliged to pay legally instituted taxes and dues and also to perform other obligations determined by law.

30. No one shall be subjected to persecution for a violation of the law except as prescribed by the law.

31. No one can be detained for investigation otherwise than prescribed by law.

32. No one can be tried and punished other than for criminal acts considered under the existing criminal laws, in force during the perpetration of these acts, provided newly enacted laws do not exclude the perpetrated criminal acts from the list of crimes.

33. The dwelling of every individual is inviolable. Breaking into a dwelling without the consent of the owner and search and seizure are allowed only in accordance with the legally instituted procedures.

34. Every Russian subject has the right to freely select his place of dwelling and profession, to accumulate and dispose of property, and to travel abroad without any hindrance. Limits on these rights are determined by special laws.

35. Private property is inviolable. Forcible seizure of immovable property, should state or public need demand such action, is permissible only upon just and decent compensation.

36. Russian subjects have the right to organize meetings that are peaceful, unarmed, and not contrary to the law. The law determines the conditions of meetings, rules governing their termination, as well as limitations on places of meetings.

37. Within the limits determined by law everyone can express his thoughts orally or in writing, as well as distribute these thoughts through publication or other means.

38. Russian subjects have the right to organize societies and unions for purposes not contrary to the law. Conditions for organization of societies and unions, their activity, terms and rules for acquiring legal rights as well as closing of societies and unions, is determined by law.

39. Russian subjects enjoy freedom of religion. Terms to enjoy this freedom are determined by law.

40. Foreigners living in Russia enjoy the rights of Russian subjects, with limitations established by law.

41. Exceptions to the rules outlined in this chapter include localities where martial law is declared or where there exist exceptional conditions that are determined by special laws.

Chapter III. Laws

42. The Russian Empire is governed by firmly established laws that have been properly enacted.

43. Laws are obligatory, without exception, for all Russian subjects and foreigners living within the Russian state.

44. No new law can be enacted without the approval of the State Council and the State Duma, and it shall not be legally binding without the approval of the Sovereign Emperor.

45. Should extraordinary circumstances demand, when the State Duma is not in session, and the introduction of a measure requires a properly constituted legal procedure, the Council of Ministers will submit such a measure directly to the Sovereign Emperor. Such a measure cannot, however, introduce any changes into the Fundamental Laws, or to the organization of the State Council or the State Duma, or to the rules governing elections to the Council or to the Duma. The validity of such a measure is terminated if the responsible minister or the head of a special department fails to introduce appropriate legislation in the State Duma during the first two months of its session upon reconvening, or if the State Duma or the State Council should refuse to enact it into law.

46. Laws issued especially for certain localities or segments of the population are not made void by a new law unless such a voiding is specifically intended.

47. Every law is valid for the future, except in those cases where the law itself stipulates that its force is retroactive or where it states that its intent is to reaffirm or explain the meaning of a previous law.

48. The Governing Senate is the general depository of laws. Consequently, all laws should be deposited in the Governing Senate in the original or in duly authorized lists.

49. Laws are published for general knowledge by the Governing Senate according to established rules and are not legally binding before their publication.

50. Legal decrees are not subject to publication if they were issued in accordance with the rules of the Fundamental Laws.

51. Upon publication, the law is legally binding from the time stipulated by the law itself, or, in the case that such a time is omitted, from the day on which the Senate edition containing the published law is received locally. The law itself may stipulate that telegraph or other media of communication be used to transmit it for execution before its publication.

52. The law cannot be repealed otherwise than by another law. Consequently, until a new law repeals the existing law, the old law retains fully its force.

53. No one can be excused for ignorance of the law once it is duly published.

54. Regulations governing combat, technical, and supply branches of the Armed Forces, as well as rules and orders to institutions and authorized personnel of the military and naval establishments are, as a rule, submitted directly to the Sovereign Emperor upon review by the Military and Admiralty Councils, provided that these regulations, rules, and orders affect primarily the above mentioned establishments, do not touch on matters of general laws, and do not call for new expenditures from the treasury; or, if they call for new expenditure, are covered by expected savings by the Military or Naval Ministries. In cases where the expected saving is insufficient to cover the projected expenditure, submission of such regulations, rules, and orders for the Emperor's approval is permitted only upon first requesting, in a prescribed manner, the necessary appropriation.

55. Regulations governing military and naval courts are issued in accordance with Regulations on Military and Naval Codes.

Chapter IV. The State Council, State Duma, and the Scope of Their Activity

56. The Sovereign Emperor, by a decree, annually convenes the session of the State Council and of the State Duma.

57. The Sovereign Emperor determines by a decree the length of the annual session of the State Council and of the State Duma, as well as the interval between the sessions.

58. The State Council is composed of members appointed by His Majesty and of elected members. The total number of appointed members of the Council called by the Emperor to deliberate in the Council's proceedings cannot exceed the total number of the elected members of the Council.

59. The State Duma consists of members elected by the population of the Russian Empire for a period of five years, on the basis of rules governing elections to the Duma.

60. The State Council examines the credentials of its members. Equally, the State Duma examines the credentials of its members.

61. The same person cannot serve simultaneously as a member of the State Council and as a member of the State Duma.

62. The Sovereign Emperor, by a decree, can replace the elected membership of the State Council with new members before its tenure expires. The same decree sets new elections of members of the State Council.

63. The Sovereign Emperor, by a decree, can dissolve the State Duma and release its members from their five-year tenure. The same decree must designate new elections to the State Duma and the time of its first session.

64. The State Council and the State Duma have equal rights in legislative matters.

65. The State Council and the State Duma enjoy the constitutional right to submit proposals to repeal or to amend the existing laws as well as to issue new laws, except the Fundamental Law whose review belongs exclusively to the Sovereign Emperor.

66. The State Council and the State Duma have a constitutional right to address questions to Ministers and heads of various departments, who legally are under the jurisdiction of the Governing Senate, on matters that stem from violations of laws by them or by their subordinates.

67. The jurisdiction of the State Council and of the State Duma includes those matters that are listed in the Rules of the Council and of the Duma.

68. Those legislative measures that are considered and approved by the State Duma are then submitted to the State Council for its approval. Those legislative measures that have been initiated by the State Council are reviewed by the Council and, upon approval, are submitted to the Duma.

69. Legislative measures that have been rejected either by the State Council or by the State Duma are considered defeated.

70. Those legislative measures that have been initiated either by the State Council or by the State Duma [and approved by both], but which have failed to gain Imperial approval, cannot be resubmitted for legislative consideration

during the same session. Those legislative measures that have been initiated by either the State Council or by the State Duma and are rejected by either one of the Chambers, can be resubmitted for legislative consideration during the same session, provided the Emperor agrees to it.

71. Legislative measures that have been initiated in and approved by the State Duma and then by the State Council, equally as the legislative measures initiated and approved by the State Council and then by the State Duma, are submitted by the Chairman of the State Council to the Sovereign Emperor.

72. Deliberations on the state budget [by the State Council and/or by the State Duma] cannot exclude or reduce the set sums for the payment of state debts or other obligations assumed by the Russian state.

73. Revenues for the maintenance of the Ministry of the Imperial Household, including institutions under its jurisdiction that do not exceed the allocated sum of the state budget for 1906, are not subject to review by either the State Council or the State Duma. Equally not subject to review are such changes in specific revenues as stem from decisions based on Regulations of the Imperial Family that have resulted from internal reorganizations.

74. If the state budget is not appropriated before the appropriation deadline, the budget that had been duly approved in the preceding year will remain in force with only such changes as have resulted from those legislative measures that became laws after the budget was approved. Prior to publication of the new budget, on the decision of the Council of Ministers and rulings of Ministries and Special Departments, necessary funds will be gradually released. These funds will not exceed in their totality during any month, however, one-twelfth of the entire budgetary expenditures.

75. Extraordinary budgetary expenditures for wartime needs and for special preparations preceding a war are unveiled in all departments in accordance with existing law on the decision of highest administration.

76. State loans to cover both the estimated and non-estimated expenditures are contracted according to the system established to determine state budgetary revenues and expenditures. State loans to cover expenditures in cases foreseen in Article 74, as well as loans to cover expenditures stipulated in Article 75, are determined by the Sovereign Emperor as supreme administrator. Time and conditions to contract state loans are determined on the highest level of government.

77. If the State Duma fails to act on a proposal submitted to it reasonably in advance on the number of men needed for the Army and the Fleet, and a law on this matter is not ready by May 1, the Sovereign Emperor has the right to issue a decree calling to military service the necessary number of men, but not more than the number called the preceding year.

Chapter V. Council of Ministers, Ministers, and Heads of Various Departments

78. By law, the Council of Ministers is responsible for the direction and coordination of activities of Ministers and Heads of various departments on matters affecting legislation as well as the highest state administration.

79. Ministers and Heads of various departments have the right to vote in the State Council and in the State Duma only if they are members of these institutions.

80. Binding resolutions, instructions, and decisions issued by the Council of Ministers, and Ministers and Heads of various departments, as well as by other responsible individuals entitled by law, should not be contrary to existing laws.

81. The Chairman of the Council of Ministers, Ministers, and Heads of various departments, are responsible to the Sovereign Emperor for State administration. Each individual member is responsible for his actions and decisions.

82. For official misconducts in office, the Chairman of the Council of Ministers, Ministers and Heads of various departments are subject to civil and criminal punishment established by law.

59

Programs of Russian Political Parties

The Russian revolutionaries relied on careful political planning methods as well as terror and agitation to attain their objectives. This planning led sometimes to brief appeals to the people, sometimes to elaborate programs for social, economic, and political reforms. In either case the aim was to capture the imagination of the Russian populace. Because open discussion of political issues was not possible before 1905, many of the revolutionary leaders lived, dreamed, and conspired abroad. The

---

The following four items are from V. Ivanovich, ed. *Rossiiskiia partii, soiuzy i ligi (Russian Parties, Unions, and Leagues)* (St. Petersburg: 1906), pp. 3–7, 8–13, 14–18, 117–122. Translation mine. Words in brackets are mine.

Revolution of 1905 changed the situation. When, in the October Manifesto, Tsar Nicholas II promised a constitutional form of government he unintentionally triggered a political ferment and several new political parties appeared. Some of these subscribed to the ideas of the extreme Left (Bolsheviks, Socialist Revolutionaries, Mensheviks); others advocated a moderate program (Cadets, Octobrists); still others supported tsarism (Monarchists, Union of the Russian People); and some favored an autonomous national existence (various Polish, Finnish, and Ukrainian parties, and the Jewish Bund). Regardless of their aims, the rise of political parties in Russia at the beginning of the twentieth century—each operating openly and each trying to attract followers by its appeals—was a new phenomenon. It was not only a sign of mounting dissatisfaction with autocracy, but a manifestation of the developing political restlessness.

Program of the Russian Social Democratic Workers' Party (Bolshevik), August 1903

The development of exchange has created such close ties among all the peoples of the civilized world that the great proletarian movement toward emancipation was bound to become—and has long since become—international.

Considering itself one of the detachments of the universal army of the proletariat, Russian social democracy is pursuing the same ultimate goal, as that for which the social democrats in other countries are striving. This ultimate goal is determined by the nature of contemporary bourgeois society and by the course of its development. The main characteristic of such a society is production for the market on the basis of capitalist production relations, whereby the largest and most important part of the means of production and exchange of commodities belongs to a numerically small class of people, while the overwhelming majority of the population consists of proletarians and semiproletarians who, by their economic conditions, are forced either continuously or periodically to sell their labor power; that is, to hire themselves out to the capitalists, and by their toil to create the incomes of the upper classes of society.

The expansion of the capitalist system of production runs parallel to technical progress, which, by increasing the economic importance of large enterprises, tends to eliminate the small independent producers, to convert some of them into proletarians, to reduce the socio-economic role of others and, in some localities, to place them in more or less complete, more or less open, more or less onerous dependence on capital.

Moreover, the same technical progress enables the entrepreneurs to utilize to an ever greater extent woman and child labor in the process of production and exchange of commodities. And since, on the other hand, technical improvements lead to a decrease in the entrepreneur's demand for human labor power, the demand for labor power necessarily lags behind the supply, and there is in consequence greater dependence of hired labor upon capital, and increased exploitation of the former by the latter.

Such a state of affairs in the bourgeois countries, as well as the ever growing competition among those countries on the world market, render the sale of goods which are produced in greater and greater quantities ever more difficult. Overproduction, which manifests itself in more or less acute industrial crises—which in turn are followed by more or less protracted periods of industrial stagnation—is the inevitable consequence of the development of the productive forces in bourgeois society. Crises and periods of industrial stagnation, in their turn, tend to impoverish still further the small producers, to increase still further the dependence of hired labor upon capital and to accelerate still further the relative, and sometimes the absolute, deterioration of the condition of the working class.

Thus, technical progress, signifying increased productivity of labor and the growth of social wealth, becomes in bourgeois society the cause of increased social inequalities, of wider gulfs between the wealthy and the poor, of greater insecurity of existence, of unemployment, and of numerous privations for ever larger and larger masses of toilers.

But together with the growth and development of all these contradictions inherent in bourgeois society, there grows simultaneously dissatisfaction with the present order among the toiling and exploited masses; the number and solidarity of the proletarians increases, and their struggle against the exploiters sharpens. At the same time, technical progress, by concentrating the means of production and exchange, by socializing the process of labor in capitalist enterprises, creates more and more rapidly the material possibility for replacing capitalist production relations by socialist ones; that is, the possibility for social revolution, which is the ultimate aim of all the activities of international social democracy as the class-conscious expression of the proletarian movement.

By replacing private with public ownership of the means of production and exchange, by introducing planned organization in the public process of production so that the well being and the many sided development of all members of society may be insured, the social revolution of the proletariat will abolish the division of society into classes and thus emancipate all oppressed humanity, and will terminate all forms of exploitation of one part of society by another.

A necessary condition for this social revolution is the dictatorship of the proletariat; that is, the conquering by the proletariat of such political power as would enable it to crush any resistance offered by the exploiters. In its effort to make the proletariat capable of fulfilling its great historical mission, international social democracy organizes it into an independent political party in opposition to all bourgeois parties, directs all the manifestations of its class struggle, discloses before it the irreconcilable conflict between the interests of the exploiters and those of the exploited, and clarifies for it the historical significance of the imminent social revolution and the conditions necessary for its coming. At the same time, it reveals to the other sections of the toiling and exploited masses the hopelessness of their condition in capitalist society and the need of a social revolution if they wish to be free of the capitalist yoke. The party of the working class, the social democracy, calls upon all strata of the toiling and exploited population to join its ranks insofar as they accept the point of view of the proletariat.

On the road toward their common final goal, which is determined by the prevalence of the capitalist system of production throughout the civilized world, the social democrats of different countries must devote themselves to different immediate tasks—first, because that system is not everywhere developed to the same degree; and second, because in different countries its development takes place in a different socio-political setting.

In Russia, where capitalism has already become the dominant mode of production, there are still preserved numerous vestiges of the old pre-capitalist order, when the toiling masses were serfs of the landowners, the state, or the sovereign. Greatly hampering economic progress, these vestiges interfere with the many-sided development of the class struggle of the proletariat, help to preserve and strengthen the most barbarous forms of exploitation by the state and the propertied classes of the millions of peasants, and thus keep the whole people in darkness and subjection.

The most outstanding among these relics of the past, the mightiest bulwark of all this barbarism, is the tsarist autocracy. By its very name it is bound to be hostile to any social movement, and cannot but be bitterly opposed to all the aspirations of the proletariat toward freedom.

By reason of the above, the first and immediate task put before itself by the Russian Social Democratic Workers' Party is to overthrow the tsarist authority and to replace it with a democratic republic whose constitution would guarantee the following:

1. The sovereignty of the people; that is, the concentration of all supreme state power in the hands of a legislative assembly, consisting of people's representatives, and forming one chamber.

2. Universal, equal, and direct suffrage for all male and female citizens, twenty years old or over, at all elections to the legislative assembly and to the various local organs of self-government; the secret ballot at elections; the right of every voter to be elected to any representative institution; biennial parliaments; salaries to be paid to the people's representatives.

3. Broad local self-government; home rule for all localities where the population is of a special composition and characterized by special conditions of life.

4. Inviolability of people and dwelling.

5. Unlimited freedom of religion, speech, press, assembly, strikes, and unions.

6. Freedom of movement and occupation.

7. Abolition of classes; equal rights for all citizens, irrespective of sex, religion, race, or nationality.

8. The right of any people to receive instruction in its own language, to be secured by creating schools at the expense of the state and the local organs of self-government; the right of every citizen to use his native language at meetings; the introduction of the use of the native language on a par with the state language at all local, public, and state institutions.

9. The right of self-determination for all nations included in the composition of the state.

10. The right of any person to sue any official before a jury in the regular way.

11. Election of judges by the people.

12. Replacement of the standing army by a general armament of the people.

13. Separation of church and state, and of school and church.

14. Free and compulsory general and professional education for all children of both sexes up to the age of sixteen; provision by the state of food, clothing, and school supplies for poor children.

As a basic condition for the democratization of our *state economy* the Russian Social Democratic Workers' Party demands the abolition of all indirect taxes and the establishment of a progressive tax on income and inheritances.

In order to *safeguard the working class* against physical and moral degeneration, as well as to insure the development of its power to carry on the struggle for freedom, the party demands the following:

1. Eight-hour working day for all hired labor.

2. A law providing a weekly uninterrupted forty-two-hour respite for all hired labor, of both sexes, in all branches of the national economy.

3. Complete prohibition of overtime work.

4. Prohibition of night work (from 9 p.m. to 6 a.m.) in all branches of the national economy, with the exception of those in which this is absolutely necessary because of technical considerations approved by labor organizations.

5. Prohibition of the employment of children of school age (up to sixteen) and restriction of the working day of minors (from sixteen to eighteen) to six hours.

6. Prohibition of female labor in those branches of industry which are

injurious to women's health; relief from work four weeks before and six weeks after childbirth, with regular wages paid during all this period.

7. Establishment of nurseries for infants and children in all shops, factories, and other enterprises that employ women; permission for freedom of at least a half-hour's duration to be granted at three-hour intervals to all nursing mothers.

8. Old-age state insurance, and insurance against total or partial disability; such insurance to be based on a special fund formed from a tax levied on the capitalists.

9. Prohibition of payment of wages in kind; establishment of regular weekly pay days when all wages shall be paid in money in absolute conformity with all the agreements relating to the hire of workers; wages to be paid during working hours.

10. Prohibition of deductions by employers from workers' wages, on any ground or for any purpose (fines, spoilage, and so forth).

11. Appointment of an adequate number of factory inspectors in all branches of the national economy and extension of their supervision to all enterprises employing hired labor, including government enterprises (domestic service also to be within the sphere of their supervision); appointment of special women inspectors in those industries where female labor is employed; participation of representatives, elected by the workers and paid by the state, in supervising the enforcement of the factory laws, the fixing of wage scales, and in accepting or rejecting the finished products and other results of labor.

12. Control by organs of local self-government, together with representatives elected by the workers, over sanitation in the dwellings assigned to the workers by the employers, as well as over internal arrangements in those dwellings and the renting conditions—in order to protect the workers against the employers' interference with their life and activity as private citizens.

13. Establishment of properly organized sanitary control over all establishments employing hired labor, the medico-sanitary organization to be entirely independent of the employers; in time of illness, free medical aid to be rendered to the workers at the expense of the employers, with the workers retaining their wages.

14. Establishment of criminal responsibility in the case of employers' infringement upon the laws intended to protect the workers.

15. Establishment in all branches of the national economy of industrial courts to be composed of representatives of workers and employers in equal numbers.

16. Imposition upon the organs of local self-government of the duty of establishing employment agencies (labor exchanges) to deal with the hiring

of local and out-of-town labor in all branches of industry, and participation of workers' and employers' representatives in their administration.

In order to *remove the vestiges of serfdom* that fall directly and heavily upon the peasants, and to encourage the free development of the class struggle in the *village,* the party demands above all:

1. Abolition of redemption payments and quit rents as well as all obligations which presently fall on the peasanty, the tax-paying class.

2. Repeal of all laws which restrict the peasant in disposing of his land.

3. Return to peasants of money collected from them in the form of redemption payments and quit rents; confiscation of monastery and church properties as well as property belonging to princes, government agencies, and members of the royal family; imposition of a special tax on lands of nobles who have sold it on loan terms; transfer of the money thus procured into a special reserve fund to meet cultural and charitable needs of villages.

4. Organization of peasant committees: (a) to return to villages (by means of expropriation . . .) those lands which were taken away from the peasants at the emancipation, and which are held by the nobles as a means of enserfment of peasants; (b) to transfer to peasant ownership those lands in the Caucasus which they use now on a temporary basis; (c) to eliminate the remnants of serfdom still in effect in the Urals, the Altai, the Western Provinces, and other parts of the country.

5. Grant to the courts the right to lower unusually high rents and to annual those contracts which contain slave characteristics.

To attain its immediate goals, the Russian Social Democratic Workers' Party will support every opposition and revolutionary movement directed against the existing social and political system in Russia. At the same time it rejects all reformist projects whose aim is to extend or to consolidate bureaucratic-police protection over the toiling classes.

On its own part, the Russian Social Democratic Workers' Party is firmly convinced that a full, consistent, and thorough realization of the indicated political and social changes can only be attained by the overthrow of autocracy and by the convocation of a Constituent Assembly freely elected by the entire people.

Program of the Socialist Revolutionary Party, 1905

In its cultural and social relations, contemporary Russia increasingly enters into closer and closer ties with the advanced countries of the civilized world, while at the same time it preserves a number of peculiarities that have been formulated by the course of its past history, its local conditions, and its international situation.

All the advanced countries of the civilized world, parallel to the growth of the population and its basic needs, experience the growth of man's power over nature, the improved means of utilizing its natural forces, and the increase of creative power of human work in all the spheres of activity. This growth is an indispensable condition for social progress and for the struggle toward a balanced and harmonious development of human individuality.

But this growth of human control over nature takes place in contemporary society under a condition of bourgeois competition of uncoordinated economic units, of private control of the means of production, of transformation of the latter into capital, and of advance exploitation of the direct producers or their indirect subordination to capital. Parallel to the development of the foundations of contemporary society, society itself increasingly transforms itself into two classes: a class of exploited toilers who receive increasingly lower rewards for the wealth their work creates, and a class of exploiters who have a monopoly on the control of natural forces and the social means of production.

As long as in those narrow frames of bourgeois capitalist relations there develop—albeit one sided and incomplete—forms of collective labor and mass production, so long will the contemporary economic development reveal positive, creative aspects, because it prepares certain material elements for a higher socialist system of life and unites in a compact social force the industrial armies of hired workers.

However, since bourgeois capitalist forms tend to narrow, limit, and impede the development of collective forms of labor and socially productive forces, the contemporary economic development strengthens its negative, destructive aspects: the anarchy of commodity production and competition; sterile waste of its economic forces; crises which shatter the national economy to its foundation; the growth of exploitation; dependence and insecurity of the toiling masses; the corrupting power of money on all moral standards; the selfish struggle of all against all for existence and privileged position.

Mutual relations between the positive and negative aspects of contemporary economic development vary from one branch of industry to another and from one country to another. They are relatively good in more advanced branches of industry and in countries of classical capitalism; they become less and less good in other branches of industry, especially in agriculture, and in countries situated less advantageously in the international economic struggle.

But, regardless of those distinctions, the incompatibility and contradiction between the positive and the negative aspects of contemporary economic development represents a general and growing fact fraught with serious historical consequences.

With the growth of social division between the exploiters and the exploited, with the growth of contradictions between the productivity of labor and the inconsequential reward of workers for their products, and with the increase of the norms of their exploitation, there also grows dissatisfaction among the exploited with their conditions in contemporary society.

Because of the spontaneous process of intensifying class relations there is developing, with systematic tactics, a conscious and planned interference into attempts at organizing collective forces in the name of one or another social ideal or the ultimate goal. This expediently directed struggle encompasses simultaneously all aspects of life—economic, political, and spiritual.

The exploiting classes are trying to perpetuate the basis of their existence—exploitation through rent, profit on capital in all of its forms, and increased taxes of the toiling masses. By means of syndicates, cartels, and trusts they are trying to control, for their egoistic gains, the means of production as well as consumption. They are trying to appropriate for their class interest all the institutions of the contemporary state and to transform it completely into a weapon of their rule and impoverishment of the exploited. Finally, they are striving to subjugate spiritual and material literature, art, science, and public opinion in order to keep the toiling masses not only in economic but in intellectual dependence as well.

Not possessing any other resources, or having lost them already in the struggle, they are joining hands with the reactionary forces of the dead past, are resurrecting racial and religious animosity, are poisoning national consciousness with chauvinism or nationalism, and are entering into alliances with the remnants of monarchial and Church-clerical institutions.

The bourgeois system has gradually abandoned its former progressive content, has brought intellectual sterility to its ruling classes, has caused the alienation of the intellectual and moral flower of the nation, and has left it to suffer in the hostile camp of the oppressed and the exploited.

The exploited classes naturally are trying to protect themselves from the pressing burden, and in proportion to the growth of their consciousness they are uniting themselves in this struggle and are directing it against the very foundations of bourgeois exploitation. International by its nature, this movement is becoming increasingly a movement of the great majority in the interest of the great majority, a factor that represents the key to its victory.

International revolutionary socialism represents a conscious expression, scientific illumination, and formulation of this movement. Its aim is intellectual, political, and economic emancipation of the working class. It advances above all as an initiating revolutionary minority, as the fighting vanguard of the toiling masses, trying constantly at the same time to merge with the masses and incorporate them into its ranks. Its basic practical aim is to make all layers of the toiling and exploited people awake that they are one working class, that that class is the only hope of their freedom by means of a planned, organized struggle to create a socio-revolutionary upheaval that consists of:

1. Freeing of all public institutions from control of the exploiting classes.
2. Eliminating, alongside private property in natural forces and in public means of production, the very division of the society into classes.
3. Eliminating the contemporary, stratified, compulsory, repressive nature of public institutions while at the same time preserving and developing their normal cultural functions; that is, planned organization of public work for public good.

The realization of this program will make possible an uninterrupted, free, and unhampered development of all spiritual and material forces of mankind. It will also turn the growth of public wealth from a source of dependence and oppression of the working class into a source of prosperity and balanced harmonious development of human dignity. It will also halt the degeneration of mankind from uselessness and superfluity on the one hand, and, on the other, the presence of excessive work and semi-starvation. Finally, only through the introduction of a free socialist society will mankind be able to develop fully its physical, mental, and moral capabilities and introduce realism, truth, and solidarity ever fully into the social life. Consequently, the essence of contemporary socialism is the freeing of all mankind. It seeks elimination of all forms of civil strife among peoples, of all forms of violence and exploitation of man by man; instead, it seeks to introduce freedom, equality and brotherhood of all regardless of sex, race, religion, or nationality.

The Socialist Revolutionary Party of Russia views its task as an organic, component part of a universal struggle of labor against the exploitation of human dignity, against all barriers that prevent its development into social forms, and conducts it in the spirit of general interests of that struggle in ways that are determined by concrete conditions of Russian reality.

The mutual cooperation between the patriarchal nobility-bureaucratic autocracy and new bourgeois exploitation intensifies the social problem in Russia. The development of capitalism reveals here, more than anywhere else, its dark aspects and, less than anywhere else, it balances the organized creative influence of the growth of public productive forces. The abnormally growing bureaucratic apparatus of the state, as a result of the emancipation of serfs and the development of the *kulak* system in all of its aspects and forms, increasingly paralyzes the productive forces of the village. The toiling peasantry is forced to a large degree to seek help either in subsidiary enterprises or hired labor, and receives from all of its labor an earning that corresponds to the lowest wage earning of an industrial worker. This factor also limits and undermines the domestic market of industry, which in addition suffers from shortages of foreign markets. Surplus population and the capitalist surplus labor force progressively increase, which, because of the competition, lowers the living standards of the city proletariat. The labor movement is forced to develop in conditions of an autocratic regime based on the all-embracing police protection and suppression of individual and public initiative. The class of great industrialists and merchants, more reactionary than everywhere else, depends increasingly on the support of autocracy against the proletariat, and against the toiling masses of the village. In the interest of self-preservation the autocracy has intensified the oppression of the subjugated nationalities of Imperial Russia, has paralyzed their spiritual renaissance, has imposed national, racial, and religious antagonism in order to becloud the understanding of socio-political interests of the toiling masses. The existence of autocracy represents an irreconcilable and progressively intensifying contradiction with all of the economic, socio-political and cultural growth of the country. As a reliable ally and pillar of the most exploiting and parasitical classes in Russia, beyond its frontiers Russian autocracy is also one of the main bulwarks of reaction and a great danger to the cause of the freedom struggle of the working parties of other countries. Its overthrow should be the immediate and undelayed objective of the Socialist Revolutionary Party, not only as the first indispensable condition for the solution of the social problem in Russia, but also as a major factor of international progress.

The burden of the struggle with autocracy, irrespective of the liberal-democratic opposition, which primarily includes middle class elements of the "educated society," falls on the proletariat, the toiling peasantry, and the revolutionary-socialist intelligentsia. The immediate task of the Socialist Revolutionary Party, which assumes the leading role in this struggle, is to broaden and deepen the social and property changes to pave the way thereby for the overthrow of autocracy.

To realize fully its program, namely the expropriation of capitalist property and the reorganization of production and of the entire social system on socialist foundations, it is essential that there be a complete victory of the working class, organized by the Socialist Revolutionary Party, and, in case of need, that there be established a temporary revolutionary dictatorship.

So long as the organized working class, as the revolutionary minority, can exert only partial influence on the change of the social system and legislation, the Socialist Revolutionary Party must see to it that the working class is not blinded by its partial gains and does not lose sight of its ultimate goal; that by its revolutionary struggle the proletariat would seek in this period such changes that would develop and strengthen its solidarity and ability to fight for freedom, would help to elevate its intellectual and cultural needs, and would strengthen its fighting position and eliminate barriers that hinder its organization.

Since the process of the transformation of Russia is led by nonsocialist forces, the Socialist Revolutionary Party, on the basis of the above principles, will advocate, defend, and seek by its revolutionary struggle the following reforms:

In the Realm of Politics and Legislation

The establishment of a democratic republic with broad autonomy for *oblasts* and communes, both urban and rural; increased acceptance of federal principles in relations between various nationalities; granting them unconditional right to self-determination; direct, secret, equal, and universal right to vote for every citizen above twenty years of age regardless of sex, religion, or national origin; proportional representation; direct popular legislation (referenda and initiatives); election, removability at all times, and accountability of all officials; complete freedom of conscience, speech, press, meetings, strikes, and unions; complete and general civil equality; inviolability of the individual and home; complete separation of the church from the state and declaration that religion is a private affair for every individual; introduction of a compulsory, equal-for-all general public education at government expense; equality of languages; free justice; abolishment of permanent armies and their replacement by a people's militia.

In the Realm of National Economy

1. In the matter of labor legislation the Socialist Revolutionary Party sets as its aim the safeguarding of spiritual and material forces of the working class and increasing its capability of further struggle to whose goals should be subordinated all expedient, direct, local, and professional interests of the diverse working strata. In this sphere the Party will advocate: a reduction of the working time in order to relieve surplus labor; establishment of a legal maximum of working time based on norms determined by health conditions (an eight-hour working norm for most branches of industry as soon as possible, and lower norms in dangerous or harmful-to-health work); establishment of a minimum wage in agreement between administration and labor unions; complete government insurance (for accident, unemployment, sickness, old age, and so on), administered by the insured at the expense of the state and employers; legislative protection of labor in all branches of industry and trade, in accordance with the health conditions supervised by factory inspection commissions elected by workers (normal working conditions, hygienic conditions of buildings; prohibition of work for youngsters below sixteen years of age, limitation of work for youngsters, prohibition of woman and child labor in some branches of industry and during specified periods, adequate and uninterrupted Sunday rest, and so forth); professional organization of

workers and their increased participation in determining internal rules in industrial enterprises.

2. In matters of agricultural policy and land relations, the Socialist Revolutionary Party sets its task to be, in the interests of socialism and the struggle against the bourgeois property system, the utilization of the communal as well as the labor views, the traditions and forms of life of Russian peasantry, and especially their views on land as the public property of all the toilers. Consequently, the Party will support socialization of all privately owned lands; that is, their transfer from private property of individual owners to public domain and administration by democratically organized communes and territorial associations of communes on the basis of equalized utilization. Should this basic demand of the agrarian minimum program not be realized at once as a revolutionary measure, the Socialist Revolutionary Party in its future agrarian policy will be guided by consideration of a possible realization of this demand in its entirety, advocating such related measures as: broadening of the rights of communes and their territorial associations in expropriating privately owned lands; confiscation of lands belonging to monasteries, princes, ministers, and so forth, and their transfer, together with state properties, to communes, in order that they would have an adequate amount, and also for the needs of resettlement and redistribution; limiting of payments for the use of land to the amount of clear profit from the farm (less gross revenue of the cost of production and normal remuneration for labor); reimbursement for improvements on land when it is transferred from one user to another; conversion of rent through a special tax into a source of revenue for the communes and self-governing institutions.

3. In matters of financial policy the Party will agitate for the introduction of a progressive tax on income and inheritance, and for complete freedom from taxation of small incomes below an established norm; it will agitate for the elimination of indirect taxes (except luxury taxes), protective duties, and all other taxes that burden labor.

4. In matters of municipal and land economy, the Party will support the development of all kinds of public services, land agronomy organizations, communalization of water supply, education, ways and means of communication, and so forth; will support the granting of broad powers to urban and rural communes to tax immovable property as well as the right to confiscate it if this be necessary to improve the living standards of the toiling population; will support communal and *zemstvo* as well as governmental policy aimed at helping the development of cooperatives on solid democratic foundations.

5. With respect to various measures aimed at nationalization of one or another sectors of the national economy within the framework of a bourgeois state, the Socialist Revolutionary Party will support these measures, provided

they are accompanied by a democratization of the political system, by a change in social forces, and that the very nature of these measures themselves would provide sufficient guarantee against the increase of dependence of the working class on ruling bureaucracy. In general the Socialist Revolutionary Party warns the working class against "state socialism," which is partly a system of half measures for the strengthening of the working class . . . and partly a peculiar type of state capitalism that concentrates various branches of production and trade in the hands of the ruling bureaucracy for their financial and political aims.

The Socialist Revolutionary Party, in commencing its direct revolutionary struggle with autocracy, agitates for the calling of the *Zemskii Sobor* [Constituent Assembly] freely elected by the people regardless of sex, social status, nationality, or religion, to liquidate the autocratic regime and to reform all present systems. The Party will support its program of reform in the Constituent Assembly and it will also try to realize it directly during the revolutionary period.

Program of the Russian Constitutional Democratic Party (Cadet), 1905

I. Basic Rights of Citizens

1. All Russian citizens, irrespective of sex, religion, or nationality, are equal before the law. All class distinctions and all limitations of personal and property rights of Poles, Jews, and all other groups of the population, should be repealed.

2. Every citizen is guaranteed freedom of conscience and religion. No persecution for religious beliefs or convictions, or for change or refusal to accept religious indoctrination, can be allowed. The celebration of religious and church ceremonies and the spread of beliefs is free, provided these activities do not include any general transgressions contrary to the criminal code of law. The Orthodox Church and other religions should be freed from state protection.

3. Anyone who wishes to express his thoughts orally or in writing has the right to publish and spread them through printing or any other media. Censorship, both general and special, regardless of its name, must be abolished and cannot be reinstituted. For their oral or written transgressions the guilty ones will answer before the court.

4. All Russian citizens have the right to organize public or private meetings, in dwellings as well as in the open air, to examine any problem they wish.

5. All Russian citizens have the right to organize unions or societies without needing permission for it.

6. The right to petition is granted to every citizen as well as to all groups, unions, gatherings, and so forth.

7. The person and home of every individual should be inviolable. Entering of a private dwelling, search, seizure, and opening of private correspondence, are allowed only in cases permitted by law or on order of the court. Any individual detained in cities or places where courts are located should be freed within twenty-four hours; in other localities of the Empire not later than three days, or be brought before the court. Any detention undertaken illegally, or without proper grounds, gives a detained person the right to be compensated by the state for losses suffered.

8. No one can be subjected to persecution or punishment except on the basis of law by court authorities in a legally constituted court. No extraordinary courts are allowed.

9. Every citizen has freedom of movement and travel abroad. The passport system is abolished.

10. All the above mentioned rights of citizens must be incorporated into the Constitution of the Russian Empire and be guaranteed by courts.

11. The Constitution of the Russian Empire should guarantee all the minorities inhabiting the Empire, in addition to full civil and political equality enjoyed by all citizens, the right of cultural self-determination, namely: full freedom of usage of various languages and dialects in public, the freedom to found and maintain educational institutions and meetings of all sorts having as their aim the preservation and development of the language, literature, and culture of every nationality.

12. The Russian language should be the official language of the central administration, army, and fleet. The use of local languages alongside the official language in state and public institutions and educational establishments supported by the state or organs of local self-government is determined by general and local laws, and, within their competence, by the institutions concerned. The population of each locality should be guaranteed education in the native language in elementary schools, and possibly in subsequent education.

II. Government Apparatus

13. The constitutional system of the Russian state will be determined by the constitution.

14. People's representatives are elected by a general, equal, direct, and secret ballot, irrespective of their religion, nationality or sex.

The party allows within its midst a difference of opinion on the question of national representation, consisting of one or two chambers in which case the second chamber should consist of representatives of the local organs of self-government, organized on the basis of a general vote and spread throughout all of Russia.

15. National representation participates in the realization of legislative power, in the determination of government revenues and expenditures, and in control of the legality and expedience of actions of higher and lower organs of administration.

16. No decision, decree, *ukaz*, order, or a similar act not based on the legislative measure of national representation, regardless of its name or place of origin, can have the force of law.

17. A government inventory, which should include all revenues and expenditures of the state, should be established by law, every year. No taxes, dues, and collections for the state, as well as state loans, can be established other than by legislation.

18. Members of national representative assemblies should have the right of legislative initiative.

19. Ministers are responsible to the representatives of the national assembly, and the latter have the right of questioning and interpellation.

III. Local Self-Government and Autonomy

20. Local self-government should be extended throughout the entire Russian state.

21. Representatives in the organs of local self-government, being close to the population by virtue of the organization of small self-governing units, should be elected on the basis of universal, equal, direct, and secret ballot, regardless of sex, religion, and nationality, while the assemblies of higher self-governing units can be selected by lower assemblies. *Gubernia zemstvos* should have the right to enter into temporary or permanent unions among themselves.

22. The competence of the organs of local self-government should include the entire field of local administration, including police, but excluding only those branches of administration which, under the condition of present state life, must be located in the hands of the central government. Organs of the local self-government should receive partial support from sources which now go to the budget of the central government.

23. The activity of representatives of the central government should be limited to supervision of the legality of acts of the organs of local self-government; the final decision on any disputes or doubts is reserved for the courts.

24. Following the establishment of rights of civil freedom and proper representation with constitutional rights for the entire Russian state, there should be opened a legal way within the framework of state legislation for the establishment of local autonomy and *oblast* representative assemblies, with

the right to participate in the realization of legislative authority on familiar matters in accordance with the needs of the population.

25. Immediately following the introduction of the imperial democratic government with constitutional rights, there should be established in the Polish kingdom an autonomous administration with a *sejm* [Parliament] elected on the same basis as the state parliament of Russia, preserving its state unity and participation in the central parliament on an equal footing with other parts of the Empire. Frontiers between the Polish kingdom and neighboring *gubernias* shall be established in accordance with the native population and desires of the local population. In the Polish kingdom there should be instituted national guarantees of civil freedom and rights of nationalities on cultural self-determination as well as protection of the rights of minorities.

26. *Finland.* The Finnish Constitution, which safeguards its special state status, should be fully reinstated. All future measures common to the Empire and the Grand Duchy of Finland should be solved by an agreement between legislative branches of the Empire and the Grand Duchy.

IV. Courts

27. All departures from the bases of the Judicial Statute of November 20, 1864, which separated judicial from administrative power (irremovability of judges, independence of courts, and equality of all citizens before the court) as well as the introduction of subsequent novelties are to be abolished . . . Courts with class representatives are abolished. Matters of *volost* justice are subject to the competence of an elected justice of the peace. The *volost* court and the institution of *zemskii nachalniks* [land administrators] are abolished. The demand for property qualifications to perform the functions of a Justice of the Peace as well as that of a sworn deputy is abolished. The principle of the unity of appelate court is reestablished. Advocacy is organized on the foundation of true self-administration.

28. In addition to this, the aim of penal policy should consist of: (a) unconditional abolishment forever of the death penalty; (b) introduction of conditional conviction; (c) establishment of protection during preliminary investigation; and (d) introduction into court proceedings of controvertible rule.

29. The immediate task centers in the full examination of the criminal code, the annulment of decrees which are contrary to the foundations of political freedom, and the reworking of the project of the civil code.

V. Financial and Economic Policy

30. There should be reexamination of government expenditure in order to eliminate unproductive expenses, and to bring about an appreciable increase of state resources for the real needs of the people.

31. The redemption payments should be repealed.

32. There should be replacement of indirect by direct taxes, general lowering of indirect taxes, and gradual repeal of indirect taxes on items of general consumption.

33. There should be a reform of direct taxes on the basis of progressive income, a reform of property taxation, and a progressive tax on inheritance.

34. In conformity with the condition of individual industries, there should be a lowering of custom duties in order to cut down the cost of products of general consumption and to improve the technical level of industry and agriculture.

35. Saving banks should be used for the development of small loans.

VI. Agrarian Legislation

36. There should be an increase of arable land for that part of the population which works the land with its own labor, namely landless and petty peasants—as well as other peasants—by state, princely, cabinet, monastery, and private estates at the state's expense, with private owners being compensated at a fair (not market) price for their land.

37. Expropriated land should be transfered to a state and land reserve. Rules by which the land from this reserve should be given to a needy population (ownership, or personal or communal use, and so forth) should be determined in accordance with peculiarities of land ownership and land usage in different parts of Russia.

38. There should be broad organization of government aid to migration, resettlement, and arrangement of the economic life of peasants. There should be reorganization of the Boundary Office, termination of surveying, and introduction of other measures for bringing prosperity to the rural population and improving the rural economy.

39. Legislation dealing with the lease relationship should be promulgated in order to protect the right of tenants and the right to re-lease . . .

40. The existing rules on hiring of agricultural workers should be repealed and labor legislation should be extended to agricultural workers. . . .

VII. Labor Legislation

41. There should be freedom of labor unions and assemblies.

42. The right to strike should be granted. Punishment for violations of law which occur during or as a result of strikes should be determined in general terms and under no circumstances should be extreme.

43. Labor legislation and independent inspection of labor should be extended to all forms of hired labor; there should be participation of workers'

elected representatives in inspections aimed at safeguarding the interests of workers.

44. Legislation should introduce the eight-hour working day. Where possible, this norm should be immediately realized everywhere, and systematically introduced in other industries. Night work and overtime work should be prohibited except where technically and socially indispensible.

45. Protection of female and child labor and the establishment of special measures to protect male labor should be developed in dangerous enterprises.

46. Arbitration offices, consisting of an equal number of representatives of labor and capital to regulate all kinds of hiring which are not regulated by labor legislation, and solving of disputes which may arise between workers and employers, should be established.

47. Obligatory state medical care (for a definite period), accident and work-connected illness compensations, which are to be contributed to by the employers, should be established.

48. State old age security and disability allowances for all individuals who make a living by their own work should be introduced.

49. Criminal responsibility for violation of laws dealing with the protection of labor should be established.

VIII. Problems of Education

Public education should be founded on freedom, democracy, and decentralization in order to realize the following goals:

50. The elimination of all restrictions on school admissions based on sex, origin, or religion.

51. Freedom of private and public initiative to found and organize all sorts of educational institutions, including education outside the school; freedom of instruction.

52. Better liaison should be organized between various school classes in order to make easier a transfer from one school to another.

53. There should be full autonomy and freedom of instruction in universities and other institutions of higher learning. Their numbers should increase. The fee for attending lectures should be lowered. Institutions of higher learning should organize education to meet the needs of broad layers of society. Students should have freedom to organize themselves.

54. The number of institutions of secondary learning should increase in accordance with public needs; the fee for these should be reduced. Local public institutions should have the right to participate in the formulation of the education curriculum.

55. A universal, free, and obligatory system of education should be intro-

duced in elementary schools. Local self-government should extend material aid to those who need it.

56. Local self-government should organize institutions for the education of the adult population—elementary schools for the adult, as well as public libraries and public universities.

57. Professional education should be developed.

Program of the Union of the Russian People, 1905

Russian People!

The great manifesto of October 30 granted us civil freedom on the basis of inviolability of person, freedom of expression, conscience, meetings and unions. In spite of this Tsarist grace, under the cover of promised freedom, many of us in fact have joined the darkest slavery of a mysterious, unknown, coarse, and all-destructive force which arbitrarily determines our fate without any legal authority, issues its own "manifestos" and openly advocates a whole series of impractical demands, such as complete destruction of the Russian army and its replacement by militia subordinate to city administration, organization of a social democratic republic, and so forth. The enemies of the Tsar and of the country, by means of deception, threats, and violence, cause strikes in factories and mills, stop trains, disrupt trade, inflict tremendous loss to the entire state, and deprive hundreds of thousands of poor people of work in order to force them into violence through hunger. Our children are deprived of the possibility of education, the sick are dying, not being able to obtain medicine. . . . The trouble has not stopped in spite of the fact that we have received freedom, the same "freedom" which everyone has demanded so ardently. God only knows how far this anarchy will lead. One thing, however, is certain: we are proceeding directly to the downfall and destruction of the Russian state. This is why we call upon all those honest Russian people, irrespective of their profession or status, who are loyal to the Tsar, the country, and traditional Russian principles, to unite in order to conduct an active struggle by every legal means against arbitrariness, violence, and other repulsive manifestations of the recently granted freedom.

The ultimate aim which this Union of the Russian People must seek is the introduction of a firm, durable, legal order, on the basis of the following foundations:

1. Unity and indivisibility of the Russian Empire and stability of the basic foundations of Russian statehood, because only firm Tsarist authority, based on a direct union between the Tsar and the people, or their elected representatives, can provide unconditional guarantees for a durable legal order in such a multi-national state as Russia.

2. Establishment of a State Duma with the right to report directly to the Sovereign, the right to address an inquiry to the ministers, the right to control the activity of the ministers, and the right to petition the Emperor that the former be dismissed and tried in the courts.

3. Coordination of the activity of ministers and establishment of their firm, actual responsibility, similar to the responsibility of all other officials, for every irregularity connected with their service and for damages suffered by private individuals, including bringing them to the attention of the Procurator.

4. Allowing the election of Jews to the State Duma, not more than three persons, elected by the entire Jewish population of the Russian Empire to present in the Duma the special needs of the Jewish population. Such limitation is necessary because of the disruptive, anti-state activity of the united Jewish masses, their unceasing hatred of everything Russian, and the unscrupulousness which they so openly demonstrated during the recent revolutionary movement.

5. The realization of freedom and inviolability granted by the Manifesto of October 30; that is, protection of individuals from the arbitrariness and violence of officials, of private individuals as well as of all sorts of societies, unions, and committees, both open and secret.

6. Establishment of a firm criminal responsibility of the press to protect the basic foundation of the state system, based on special legislation similar to that which exists in the countries of Western Europe.

7. Firm, severe, and actual protection of property rights of private individuals, of societies, and of the state.

The basis of our Union is brotherly love towards neighbors, and we therefore do not allow any of the arbitrariness, force, falsehoods, rumors, distortions, secret or similar means of struggle used by our enemies, by the Tsar's enemies, or by enemies of the country.

The Statute of the Union of the Russian People

I. *The Aim of the Union*

1. The Union of the Russian People sets as its undeviating goal a durable unity of the Russian people of all classes and professions to work for the general good of our fatherland—a Russia united and indivisible.

II. *Program*

2. The well being of the country should consist of a firm preservation of Russian autocracy, orthodoxy, and nationality, and of the establishment of a State Duma, order, and legality.

3. Russian autocracy was created by national wisdom, sanctified by the Church, and justified by history. Our autocracy consists of unity between the Tsar and the people.

Note: Convinced that national well being consists of the unity between the Russian Tsar and the people, the Union acknowledges that the present ministerial bureaucratic system, which separates the pure soul of the Russian Tsar from the people, and which has appropriated a number of rights that truly belongs to the Russian autocratic power, has brought our country to grave troubles and should therefore be changed fundamentally. At the same time the Union firmly believes that a change of the existing order should be accomplished not through the introduction of certain restrictive institutions such as constitutional or constituent assemblies, but rather through convocation of a State Duma as an institution which would represent a direct tie between the autocratic will of the Tsar and the right of the people.

4. The Russian people are Orthodox people and therefore the Orthodox faith remains steadfastly the official religion of the Russian Empire. All subjects of the Empire, however, have the freedom of religious worship.

5. The Russian nation, as the gatherer of Russian lands and the creator of the great might of the state, enjoys a preferential position in national life and in national administration.

Note: All institutions of the Russian state should be united and should constantly strive to maintain the greatness of Russia and the preferential rights of the Russian nation that legally belong to them, so that the numerous minorities that inhabit our country would consider it their privilege to be a part of the Russian Empire and would not consider themselves oppressed.

Note: The Russian language is and should be the official language of the Russian Empire for all of its people.

6. The State Duma, the bulwark of autocracy, should not demand any limitations on the supreme authority of the Tsar. It should only inform him of the real needs of the people and of the state and help the Lawgiver to realize the necessary reforms.

7. The immediate activity of authorities should be directed toward the introduction of a firm order and legality guaranteeing freedom of speech, press, assembly, and unions, and the inviolability of the individual. There should be established a rule that would determine the limits of these freedoms in order to prevent the violation of the established system, the endangering of the rights of other individuals, and thus to protect freedom itself.

III. *The Activity of the Union*

8. The Union sets as its continuous aim active participation in elections, from among its midst, of members to the State Duma to realize the aims to which the Union subscribes.

Note: Problems which the Union believes should be dealt with as soon as possible by the State Duma have been listed in Appendix 1 of the present statute.

9. The Union intends to assume the responsibility of providing people with sound education, of developing among the people consciousness in the spirit of autocracy, and of spreading among them Christian foundations, thereby strengthening their patriotism and feelings of debt to the nation, society, and family.

Note: The proposed educational activity of the Union will be accomplished through the opening of a greater number of schools, through the preparation of readings, meetings, talks, distribution of appropriate books and pamphlets, and through the publication of newspapers and journals. The foundation of educational activity of Union schools are included in Appendix 2 of the present charter.

10. Within the limits of its possibilities, the Union intends to build churches and to open hospitals, shelters, industries, and similar useful buildings, and to aid in the founding of mutual banks and other industrial-protective unions.

11. The Union considers as its immutable obligation the extension, within its capabilities, of brotherly help to all of its members; that is, material and moral support.

12. The Union has the right to enter into relations with governmental and public institutions on matters that relate to the aims of the Union.

13. The Union has the right to appropriate in its own name, using legal means, immovable property and operate these as legally its own.

IV. *The Organization of the Union*

14. Members of the Union can be only native Russians of both sexes, of all classes and professions, who are dedicated to the aims of the Union, who show an indication that they are firmly acquainted with the aims of the Union and who, when they join the Union, will promise not to enter into any association with a secret organization or an organization that pursues aims that are contrary to those of the Union.

15. All other persons can be accepted as members of the Union only by the decision of the General Meeting of the members of the Union.

Note: Jews cannot become members of the Union.

16. Members of the Union pay membership dues of fifty *kopecks* annually, and any payment above the indicated sum is considered a gift; the name of a person making such a gift will be listed on a special list to be published twice a year indicating the amount given.

Note: Persons who cannot afford membership dues are freed from the payment.

17. Members of the Union who distinguish themselves by their useful work, either for the well-being of the nation or in executing the goals of the Union, as well as those who contribute appreciable gifts, will receive the title

of Distinguished Members of the Union to be designated by the General Meeting of the members of the Union.

18. The Union is governed by a Council consisting of twelve members of the Union elected by a general meeting which also elects three candidate members of the Council. Candidates in turn replace absent members of the Council. Members of the Council elect from their members a Chairman of the Council of the Union and two Associate Chairmen. The Chairman is obligated to execute the decision of the Council and of the General Meeting.

19. The first membership of the Council of the Union is to be elected by the founding members from among their midst for a period of three years. Subsequently, at the expiration of three years, three members of the Council will be replaced annually by new members of the Council elected by the General Meeting. Retired members of the Council may be reelected at the next General Meeting.

20. The Council of the Union is responsible for the organization of provincial branches of the Union in *gubernias, oblasts,* cities, settlements, villages, and hamlets. Members of the Council of the Union may delegate this activity to individual members of the Union.

Note: Members of the Union pledge not to assume any organizational activity without the decision of the Council of the Union, and have no right to act without such a decision in behalf of the Union.

21. Members of the Council elect from their midst a Secretary of the Council.

22. All matters in the Council of the Union are decided by a simple majority of votes. The Chairman of the Council, in case of a tie vote, casts the deciding vote.

23. Members of the Council elect from their membership a clerk of the Council of the Union, and a Treasurer of the Union.

24. The Council of the Union has its own press, and the Chairman of the Council of the Union is responsible for it.

25. Upon joining the Union every member receives the insignia of the Union, which is uniform throughout the Russian Empire.

26. Members of the Union form a General Meeting which can be called by the Council twice a year or more if necessary. The General Meeting can also be called on demand of the members themselves if the number of those desiring a General Meeting is more than fifty members.

27. The Union may enter into relations with other Unions or societies if the latters' aims do not contradict the aims and activities of the Union of the Russian People.

V. *Resources of the Union*

28. Resources of the Union Consist of membership dues and other offerings.

29. Monetary funds of the Union, upon the decision of the Council, are deposited in either government or private banks.

30. Monetary funds of the Union are safe deposited to draw interest, but they can be converted into securities, guaranteed by the government, if the Council deems it more useful.

31. Monetary funds of the Union are disposed of by the decision of the Council; their withdrawal from the bank must be done only by a check bearing three signatures, including that of the Chairman or his assistant.

32. The decisions of the Council of the Union are considered binding if the meeting of the Council is attended by not fewer than seven members.

VI. *The Accountability of the Union*

33. The Council will present before every General Meeting an account of its revenues and expenditures, the finances of the Union, and will account for the activity of the Union and of individual members.

34. The General Meeting has the right to audit finances of the Union. To do so it selects an Auditing Commission consisting of three members of the Union for every individual audit.

Appendix 1 (to Article 8 of the Statute) Of the problems that the State Duma should first consider, the Union lists among others: the peasant problem; the improvement of living conditions of all the toiling classes, irrespective of their profession; the responsibility of all officials for illegal acts in the performance of their duties.

1. The Union believes that one of the most important national problems is to resolve whether the village commune among the peasants should be retained or abolished. The Union, believing that the peasants themselves, without any outside compulsion, express themselves on this issue, publicly states that it will not assume any initiative in resolving this problem; until the peasants themselves resolve this problem, the Union considers its obligation to be to provide the peasants a peaceful atmosphere for an absolutely free solution of the communal organization without any outside interference, whether by institutions or individuals.

While limiting its support to advocating free expression by the peasants on the commune problem until its solution by the peasants themselves, the Union, to improve peasant conditions, considers that its immediate task is to advocate that poor peasants be given more land, or that such peasants be either resettled or permitted to transfer their land to other peasants by a freely reached bargain.

The Union also takes note of the extreme unproductivity of Russian agriculture and suggests that a broad program of education be instituted to acquaint the Russian agricultural population with a more rational form of farming and to provide them with every needed assistance for a more rational increase of the productivity of land.

2. The Union considers that its special obligation is to do everything possible to improve the condition of all the toiling classes regardless of their occupation; toward the workers the Union considers that its particular obligation is to declare that their difficult situation in many enterprises demands that relations between the workers and employers be regulated without delay by means of legislation, taking into account the location and the nature of the enterprise.

3. The Union believes that the existing system of accountability for responsible officials is one of the causes of the current difficult situation in Russia. Presently, all those who have suffered from abuses and illegal acts by responsible officials have no recourse against them in the courts to seek legal compensations for their losses from the guilty ones, and can only complain to administrators who, by virtue of the powers vested in them by the law, take note only of those cases which have endangered the interests of the Treasury. The impunity of present officials has given rise to an infinite abuse which can easily be stopped by repealing the appropriate articles of the law and by allowing every individual who has suffered the right to turn freely and directly to the Procurator's Office and/or to the Court with his complaint against illegal acts of officials, and to demand compensation for the losses suffered as a result of official negligence. To prevent abuses of this system the law should severely punish those who accuse unjustly or report falsely.

Appendix 2 (to Article 9 of the Statute) The elementary school does not at all correspond either to the spirit or the needs of the Russian people.

The Union sets as one of its main objectives the education of peasant, city, and working population on firm foundations and the development in them of political consciousness and principles of Christianity. Village schools should equip the peasant for the necessities of rural life, agriculture, crafts, and domestic industry.

60

Witte's Account of His Premiership and His Views of the Jewish Problem

Sergei Iu. Witte (1849–1915), who was of Dutch ancestry, emerged as one of Russia's great statesmen. During his career he held numerous government posts, including those of Minister of Finance (1892–1903) and Russia's first constitutional Prime Minister (1905–06). As Minister of Finance, Witte successfully promoted Russia's industrial development through protective tariffs, government purchase orders, foreign investments, increased taxes, stable currency, and peaceful foreign policy. As Prime Minister he was instrumental in convincing Nicholas II to project Russia along a path of constitutional reforms that promised her subjects political freedoms and a representative form of government.

While many of Witte's policies were intended to benefit Russia in the long run, the immediate effect was infringement on influential conservative and extreme-radical interests. Russian conservatives intrigued against him because they felt Witte was moving the country towards liberalism. Russian radicals despised him because, by promoting stability and progress, he was undermining their *cause celebre.*

It also should be noted that Witte was Russia's first major political figure who understood the complexity of the country's ethnic problem and the first to advocate tolerance toward its religious and national minorities.

Witte's Account of His Premiership

Shortly after my arrival from my peace mission in the United States, I had a heart-to-heart talk with Count Dimitry Solski, President of the Imperial Council, about Russian home affairs. "Count," he repeated, "you alone can save the situation." When I declared that it was my intention to keep aloof by all means, and to go abroad for a few months' rest, he burst into tears and reproached me for my egoism and lack of patriotism. "Go abroad!" he exclaimed. "In the meantime we shall all perish here!"

Reprinted with permission of Avrahm Yarmolinsky from *The Memoirs of Count Witte.* Translated from the original Russian manuscript and edited by Abraham Yarmolinsky. (Garden City, N.Y.: Doubleday, Page & Company, 1921), pp. 285–298, 307–309.

Unwilling to shirk the duty I owed to my Monarch and country, I did not go abroad. Although I had no illusions about the difficulty and thanklessness of the task, I assumed the burden of power and bore it for six months. My appointment as President took place immediately upon the publication of the historical manifesto of October 17th, which granted the Russian people civic liberties and a parliamentary regime.

In October 1905, the Government had neither troops nor funds with which to fight the revolution. I soon perceived that only two things could save the dynasty and enable Russia to weather the revolutionary storm, namely, a large foreign loan and the return of the army from Transbaikalia and Manchuria to the European part of the country. These two measures, coupled with a determination on the part of the Government to carry out in good faith the promises of the constitutional manifesto, I was certain, would pacify the country.

At the time when I assumed the task of ruling the country, the bulk of the army, about a million men, was in far Manchuria. Those units which remained in Russia were largely depleted, both in their personnel and military equipment. As a matter of fact, the whole vast body of the Russian army was in a state of complete physical and moral prostration. Owing its existence, as it did, to universal military conscription, the army could not help being affected by the spirit of general discontent which prevailed in the country. Indeed, the most extreme subversive ideas found a fertile soil among the military, who felt more keenly than the civilian population the pain and disgrace of the disastrous war into which the country had been dragged by its irresponsible rulers. It should be noted that actual cases of mutinies in the army were rather infrequent, this being perhaps due to the energy Grand Duke Nikolai Nikolaievich displayed in dealing with the outbreaks.

Several days before my appointment I conferred with the Minister of War and General Trepov, then commander of the St. Petersburg garrison, for the purpose of ascertaining to what extent we could depend on the troops in case it should be decided to crush the revolution by armed force. The impression I gained from that conference was that the army was unreliable for two reasons, namely, because of its numerical weakness and its dangerous state of mind. This circumstance perhaps accounts for His Majesty's decision in preferring the road of reforms to the unstinted application of sheer force. I cannot explain His Majesty's choice otherwise, for like all weak people, he believes most in physical force.

After the ratification of the Portsmouth treaty, in accordance with the letter of the law, it was necessary to discharge the reservists who had been called to the colours for the duration of the war. Since these solidiers were the most troublesome element of the army and had infected with revolutionary ideas both the Transbaikalian troops and the units stationed in European Russia, I had them demobilized immediately. As a result, the army at my disposal diminished in numbers, but it was purged of the troublesome element, which was at any moment liable to break out in uncontrollable mutinies. Thus, European Russia was practically denuded of troops. A sufficient number of them was available only in the St. Petersburg, Warsaw, and Caucasian military districts, but as the situation in those regions was threatening the commanders there were extremely reluctant to part with their units for the benefit of other regions. Central Russia was almost completely deprived of troops. The disorganization was so great that the military authorities themselves did not know how many men were available and where they were stationed. Most of the units in the rear were far below their normal strength, but the military authorities were in many cases ignorant of the extent to which the units had been depleted. At the request of the local administration, a battalion would be dispatched, after long delay, to quell a peasant riot. We would next hear that, instead of a battalion no more than, say, a dozen men had arrived. We would then turn to the army authorities and learn that most of the personnel of the battalion in question was at the front. Such cases, I remember, were by no means exceptional. This chaotic condition, I later found out, was the result of General Kuropatkin's activity as Minister of War.

As we had at our disposal neither troops nor rural police, it was impossible to combat the agrarian disorders with any degree of efficiency. In the course of my premiership I succeeded in increasing and improving the police force, both municipal and rural. But at the height of the disturbances in some places there was no police at all, and even in Moscow the force was poorly armed. The policemen often reported for duty with empty revolver cases for all arms.

Since the local administration was in many places demoralized, I conceived the plan of sending His Majesty's Adjutant Generals to those districts where the situation was most alarming. Thus, Adjutant General Sakharov was sent to the government of Saratov, Adjutant General Strukov to the governments of Tambov and Voronezh, and Adjutant General Dubasov to the governments of Chemigov and Kursk. General Dubasov acted very energetically, but in such a way as not to arouse anyone's animosity. He was profoundly impressed by the extent and importance of the agrarian disturbances. He urged me, I recall, without waiting for the opening of the Duma to enact a law whereby the land forcefully seized by the peasants would be made their legitimate property. This, he argued, would pacify the peasants. As for the landowners, he said, it would be best for them, too, for otherwise the peasants would seize all the private estates and leave nothing to their owners.

The peasant riots were caused by Russian conditions and also, to a certain extent, by the propaganda of the socialists.

In shaping the course of the revolution an exceedingly important role was played by the whole gamut of socialistic doctrines, from Tolstoy's Christian communism to "anarchistic socialism," which served as a disguise for plain robbery—all these teachings having in common a denial of property rights as defined in Roman law. During the last fifty years the ideas of socialism have advanced with vigorous strides throughout the whole of Europe. They found a fertile soil in Russia, owing to the constant violation of every right, especially of property rights, on the part of the authorities, and also because of the lack of culture among the population. The revolutionists promised the factories to the workmen and the land of *pomieshchiki* (landowners) to the peasants, declaring that these commodities belong to the people by right, and had been unjustly taken away from them. The workers naturally responded with strikes, while the peasants began to practise what, in imitation of an orator of the French Revolution, Deputy Herzenstein in the First Duma called "the illumination" of the landowners' estates; that is, they began to burn and loot the property of the landed gentry.

The Manchurian armies were naturally anxious to get home. Owing to the railroad strikes in European Russia and in Siberia, the Far East was oftentimes cut off from the rest of Russia for weeks together. As a result the most fantastic rumours spread among the troops like wildfire. Making his way home through Siberia, after the conclusion of the Portsmouth treaty, Prince Vasilchikov did not know, until he reached Cheliabinsk, whether the Emperor was still in Russia, for he had heard rumours to the effect that the Imperial family had escaped abroad and that my colleagues and myself had been strung up on lamp posts on the Champ de Mars in St. Petersburg. This story I have from His Majesty himself.

I am under the impression that toward the end of 1905 the army at the front was thoroughly demoralized and revolutionary. If this was not a matter of common knowledge, it is because it was the policy of the military authorities to hide the plagues which were corroding the very heart of the army.

The first revolutionary wave, originating in the West, moved eastward and infected the Transbaikalian army. A movement in the opposite direction began toward the end of 1905, some of the discharged soldiers from the front bringing the revolutionary germ into the interior of the country. Alarming news of the state of mind of the Manchurian army had reached St. Petersburg in previous months. Under the influence of this news, the Minister of Agriculture, Schwanebach, laid before the Committee of Ministers a plan for allotting the crown lands in Siberia to the soldiers in active service who would consent to settle there. After a short discussion of this singular scheme, the committee declined to consider it further, and the whole matter came to nothing.

The strike on the Great Siberian Railroad, coupled with the eagerness of the troops to return home, completely disorganized the Eastern Chinese Railway, which circumstance added to the dissatisfaction of the army. The railroad strikes were responsible for the delay in assembling recruits and in transporting the Manchurian armies home. At one time the Siberian railroads were in the hands of self-constituted bands and organizations which refused to obey the governmental authorities. The revolutionists perceived that no sooner did the troops reach their homes than they lost all their revolutionary ardor and turned into a bulwark of law and order. For that reason they made every effort to keep up the railroad strikes in Siberia.

Traffic on the Siberian and Eastern Chinese Railways oftentimes ceased completely, and the troops indulged in rioting as they made their way westward. Then the strike of the telegraph operators came to increase the confusion. Day after day passed and the armies were still far away from Central Russia, their absence complicating both the internal and international position of the country. I repeatedly pointed out the seriousness of the situation to Grand Duke Nikolai Nikolaievich, to the Minister of War, and to the Chief of the General Staff, General Palitzyn. They replied quite correctly that the matter was within the province of General Linevich, Commander-in-Chief of the armies in active service. The only official communication I received from the Commander-in-chief throughout the six months of my premiership was a dispatch informing me that fourteen (I remember that number very distinctly) anarchist-revolutionists had arrived at the front to stir up trouble in the army. I showed this telegram to His Majesty and he returned it to me with the following words written on the margin: "I hope they will be hanged."

At this juncture, I hit upon the idea of dispatching two military trains, one from Kharbin westward, the other from European Russia eastward, under the command of two firm and resolute generals, instructed to open up normal traffic on the Siberian roads and remove the causes which hindered the regular functioning of the roads. His Majesty was pleased by this idea and adopted my plan. General Meller-Zakomelski was placed at the head of the expedition which had Moscow as its starting-point, while the train dispatched from Kharbin was put under the command of General Rennenkampf. The two generals were ordered to reopen normal traffic and restore order along the Siberian railways *at any price.* They acquitted themselves of their task with eminent success, and the two trains effected a junction near Chita. Naturally enough, this extraordinary measure could not be carried into effect without severe repressions. On reaching Chita, which was entirely in the hands of revolutionists, General Rennenkampf proceeded to execute a number of people. While he was restoring order at Chita, my wife once came to me in alarm and showed me a telegram sent to her from Brussels, in the name of the Russian revolutionary group of that city. It read as follows: "If your husband does not immediately cancel Rennenkampf's death sentences, he and the following men (names follow) will be executed; your daughter and grandson will be killed on the same day." As a matter of fact, my daughter lived in Brussels with her husband, K. V. Naryshkin, who served at our Embassy, and they had a one-year-old boy for whom both my wife and myself had an affection almost morbid in its intensity. Of course, I paid no heed to this threat, which, by the way, the revolutionists failed to carry out. This incident illustrates the perfection to which the revolutionists carried their system of underground communication, and also the difficult position in which we were in those days.

Simultaneously, Commander-in-Chief Linevich was dismissed and General Grodekov appointed in his stead, at my recommendation. He succeeded in restoring order in the army and transporting the Manchurian armies into the interior of the county. At my suggestion, the location of the troops was altered, with a view to the most effective suppression of local insurrections and riots. My principle was to oppose force to force and to take the most drastic measures against an open uprising, but at the same time I was against the practice of mass executions months and years after order had been restored.

My next great task was to secure a foreign loan. As early as 1904, the need for a foreign loan became apparent. At that time our financial system was already giving way under the pressure of the war expenditures. In concluding our second commercial treaty with Germany in 1904, I succeeded in securing Germany's permission to float our loan in that country. The next year I made an effort to prepare the ground for the loan in France and in the United States, where I went on the Portsmouth peace mission. My intention was to conclude the loan before the opening of the Imperial Duma. As I felt sure that the first Duma would be unbalanced and to a certain extent revengeful, I was afraid that its interference might thwart the loan negotiations and render the bankers less tractable. As a result, the Government, without funds, would lose the freedom of action which is so essential during a period of upheaval.

I had a keen personal interest in the loan. It must be borne in mind that I was responsible for the adoption by Russia (in 1896) of the gold standard of currency, and it was doubly painful for me to see this standard seriously threatened by the financial crisis brought about by the war, on the one hand, and by the nearsighted policy of the Minister of Finances, on the other. He waited for the end of the war to conclude a large loan, but he failed to foresee the outbreak of the revolution, with its disastrous effect on our credit.

France was willing to open its money market to us, but as a preliminary condition the French Government demanded the conclusion of peace with Japan. When the Portsmouth treaty was concluded, new obstacles presented themselves, notably the Franco-German conflict over Morocco, and the Paris Government made the conclusion of the loan contingent upon the peaceable settlement of that conflict. Elsewhere, in my remarks on the Kaiser, I tell the story of how I succeeded in having the clash arbitrated by an international conference at Algeciras. The conference lasted till the end of March 1906, and until its termination the conclusion of the loan was out of the question.

The loan was to be an international one, but in view of its large amount the French group of bankers was to play the leading part. In 1905, I opened preliminary negotiations with Neutzlin, the head of the Banque de Paris et des Pays Bas. After the death of Germain, of the Crédit Lyonnais, the Banque de Paris et des Pays Bas became the chief banking institution in the so-called Christian group of bankers' syndicates. The other group of banks, known as the Jewish group, was headed by the Rothschild firm. Old Baron Alphonse Rothschild, with whom I had been on very friendly terms, was already dead, and Lord Rothschild of London was now the head of the family. Consequently, I instructed Rafalovich, our financial agent in Paris, to go to London and find out what was the attitude of the Rothschilds toward our loan. Rafalovich's reply was to the effect that out of respect for Count Witte as a statesman they would willingly render full assistance to the loan, but that they would not be in a position to do so until the Russian Government had enacted legal measures tending to improve the conditions of the Jews in Russia. As I deemed it beneath our dignity to connect the solution of our Jewish question with the loan, I decided to give up my intention of securing the participation of the Rothschilds.

The Constitutional Democrats ("Cadets") were fully aware of the stabilizing effect the loan would have upon the Government. Consequently, they sought to defeat my efforts to conclude the loan before the opening of the Duma. Their representatives, chiefly Prince Dolgoruki and Maklakov, acted in Paris, trying to persuade the French Government that it was illegal for the Imperial Government to conclude the loan without the sanction of the Duma. It is not without shame, I am sure, that these public leaders, who were very decent men for all that, recall this activity of theirs, which could hardly be termed patriotic. Their only excuse lies in the fact that in those days the greater part of thinking Russia was in a state of intoxication. People were actually drunk with the old wine of freedom, which had been brewing for many generations.

As for our press, it did nothing to inspire the foreign investor with confidence. For instance, nearly all the papers printed the appeal of the revolutionists to the population enjoining it to withdraw their deposits from the banks and local treasuries, so as to force the Government to cease the exchange of credit bills and reduce the Treasury to a state of insolvency. On the other hand, the foreign press displayed a great deal of hostility toward us. . . .

Already in November 1905, our money circulation was in a very critical state and I found it necessary to keep the financial committee informed about the situation. With my approval, the committee appointed two of its members, V. N. Kokovtzev and Schwanebach, Minister of Agriculture, together with the Minister of Finances, I. P. Shipov, to watch the transactions of the Imperial Bank, but, of course, they were unable to suggest anything to improve matters. As the situation was rapidly growing worse and as some of the members of the financial committee thought it was possible to conclude a foreign loan immediately, I proposed to Kokovtzev that he go abroad with full powers to contract a loan. I knew very well that before the settlement of the Morocco conflict, this was out of the question, but I did not judge it possible to take the financial committee into my confidence with regard to the political aspect of the situation.

Kokovtzev went to Paris late in December 1905, and was told, of course, by Rouvier that we could not conclude the loan before the peaceable termination of the Morocco affair. He also had an interview with President Loubet. Kokovtzev succeeded in getting an advance of 100 million *rubles* on account of the future loan. This sum was but a drop in the bucket, for the short-term bonds issued by Kokovtzev in Berlin were soon to fall due. Accordingly, I asked Kokovtzev to stop in Berlin on his way back and try to obtain an extension of time for these bonds. This extension he secured, for the reason that the German Government was still undecided as to what course I would follow in matters pertaining to Russia's external policy. For, though I was instrumental in annulling the monstrous Björke agreement, I nevertheless made it clear that I was in favour of a coalition between Russia, Germany, and France, which would dominate the whole of Europe, if not the world, If this plan, which was my chief political idea, was not realized, it was because of insufficient political farsightedness on our part and also on the part of Emperor William of Germany. . . .

In January 1906, I decided to push further the negotiations for the loan, which I had initiated in Paris on my way back from the United States. As I could not go abroad and as there was no one who could be entrusted with the task of conducting the negotiations, I asked Neutzlin to come to Russia. It was a matter of extreme importance that his visit should be a secret to the public, for otherwise it would have had an undesirable effect upon the course of the Algeciras Conference and upon the Russian Stock Exchange. I may mention in passing that since I had left the post of Minister of Finances in 1903, the Russian securities had fallen twenty percent. Accordingly, Neutzlin came to Russia incognito and put up at the palace of Grand Duke Vladimir Alexandrovich, at Tsarskoye Selo. He arrived on February 2nd, and his visit lasted five days. In the course of that period I had several conferences with

Neutzlin, and in the presence of the Minister of Finance, Shipov, we agreed upon the terms of the loan. At first, Neutzlin insisted that the loan should not be realized before the opening of the Duma, but I succeeded in convincing him of the undesirability of such an arrangement, and it was then agreed that the loan should be effected immediately upon the termination of the Algeciras Conference. It was also agreed that the amount of the loan should be made as large as possible, so as to enable us to get along for a considerable period of time without new loans and also in order to cancel the temporary loans contracted by Kokovtzev in France and in Germany. I insisted on 2,750,000,000 *francs*—as the nominal amount of the loan. Anticipating upon the course of events, I may say that, owing to the treachery of Germany and of the American syndicate of bankers headed by Morgan, we had to reduce the amount to 2,250,000,000 *francs*—843,750,000 *rubles.* Neutzlin insisted on six and a quarter percent, but I could not agree to that rate of interest, and it was fixed at six percent, the loan certificates becoming convertible after ten years. The syndicate which was to handle the loan was to be made up, we agreed, of French, Dutch, English, German, American, and Russian banking firms. Austrian banks were also permitted to partiipate in the loan. The sums realized were to be left in the hands of the syndicate at one-and-a-quarter percent and then transferred to the Russian Government in definite instalments in the course of one year. Not less than half of the amount of the loan the syndicate was to take upon itself. We also agreed upon the secondary details. Neutzlin returned home, conferred with the other members of the syndicate, and they all indorsed the main terms of the agreement which was formulated at Tsarskoye Selo. I continued to advise him all the while, and until the very conclusion of the loan he turned to me personally for instructions. . . .

The loan was indeed an achievement of the highest importance. It was the largest foreign loan in the history of the modern nations. After the Franco-Prussian War, Thiers succeeded in securing a somewhat greater loan, but it was largely an internal loan, while this one was almost exclusively subscribed abroad. By means of it Russia maintained intact its gold standard of currency, which I introduced in 1896. This, in its turn, served to sustain all the basic principles of our financial system, which were mostly inaugurated by myself, and which Kokovtzev preserved with laudable firmness. It was these principles that enabled Russia to recover after that ill-starred war and the subsequent senseless turmoil, known as the Russian revolution. This loan enabled the Imperial Government to weather all the vicissitudes of the period extending from 1906 to 1910 by providing it with funds, which together with the troops recalled from Transbaikalia restored consistency and assurance to the acts of the Government.

In view of all this, what was the Emperor's attitude toward the loan? His Majesty fully appreciated how important it was to conclude the loan and what a disaster failure to secure it would mean. In all financial matters throughout the time when I held the office of Minister of Finances he had full confidence in me and did not in the least thwart my activity. In this case, too, as on previous occasions, he granted me full liberty of action, as far as this financial operation depended upon political action. He stood there like a spectator, as it were, watching a great politico-financial game of chess, but a spectator fully cognizant of the momentous importance of the game's outcome for Russia and deeply engrossed in its course.

In the months of February and March, I had already begun to lose patience with the reactionary attacks directed against the reform of October 17th. In certain circles people began to brand me as a traitor. At the same time, Durnovo, the Temporary Governors-General and others carried out many measures without my knowledge, although the responsibility for those measures fell upon me as the head of the Government. As a result I began to intimate that I had no objection to surrendering my post to a man enjoying more confidence. The invariable reply was to the effect that this was impossible before the conclusion of the loan. The Emperor was fully aware of the fact that I alone could negotiate it: first, because of my prestige in financial circles abroad; second, because of my vast experience in financial affairs. The following is from a letter written to me by His Majesty in his own hand and dated April 15th:

> The successful conclusion of the loan forms the best page in the history of your ministerial activity. It is for the Government a great moral triumph and a pledge of Russia's undisturbed and peaceful development in the future.

Witte's Views of the Jewish Problem

Stolypin's treatment of the thorny Jewish question is a striking illustration of his unprincipled policies and reckless methods. His views of this problem were almost diametrically opposed to mine. It has always been my conviction that the policy of restrictions cannot bring any results, for the reason that, in the long run, this policy cannot be followed out. The history of the Jewish people in western countries bears out this assertion with sufficient clearness. It is possible to assume various attitudes towards Jews. One may hate them, or be indifferent to them. That is a matter of personal feeling. But our

Source: *The Memoirs of Count Witte.* Translated from the Original Russian Manuscript and edited by Abraham Yarmolinsky (Garden City: Doubleday, Page & Co., 1921), pp. 375–385.

emotional attitude cannot alter the natural course of events, in virtue of which the Jews, since they are human beings after all, acquire the full measure of civic rights. I believe, however, that the abolition of Jewish disabilities must be gradual and as slow as possible.

This view was held by both Nicholas I and Alexander II. Emperor Alexander III somewhat deviated from this tendency and entered upon the road of anti-Jewish restrictions. But like everything done by Alexander III, his anti-Jewish policy was firm but moderate and judicious.

Emperor Alexander III asked me on one occasion: "Is it true that you are in sympathy with the Jews?" "The only way I can answer this question," I replied to the Emperor, "is by asking Your Majesty whether you think it possible to drown all the Russian Jews in the Black Sea. To do so would, of course, be a radical solution of the problem. But if your Majesty will recognize the right of the Jews to live, then conditions must be created which will enable them to carry on a human existence. In that case, gradual abolition of the disabilities is the only adequate solution of the Jewish problem."

His Majesty said nothing, but he never showed that he disapproved of my attitude toward the Russian Jews. It has remained substantially the same throughout my career. As Minister of Finance, I vigorously opposed all measures intended to restrict the rights of the Jews, but it was not in my power to repeal the existing laws against the Jews. Many of these laws were unjust, and, upon the whole these laws did much harm to Russia and Russians. In dealing with the Jewish legislation, I did not consider primarily the advantages to be derived from a certain measure by the Jewish race. What was foremost in my mind was the effect of this or that measure upon Russia as a whole.

All the more important legal provisions relating to the Jews, which have become effective in the course of the last decade, were enacted as temporary measures. The decrees usually opened with the Pharisaic formula: "Pending the revision of the laws relating to the Jews, we order, and so forth," the intimation being that such a revision would be favourable to the Jewish population. The truth of the matter is that the authors of the anti-Jewish laws did not have the courage to offer a radical and statesmanlike solution of the problem. As it was known that the Imperial Council was likely to oppose these restrictive measures, or, at least, tell the Ministers a few unpleasant truths, the anti-Jewish regulations were enacted either by the Committee of Ministers, by special commissions, or else by Imperial decrees.

Among the most implacable enemies of the Russian Jews was Grand Duke Sergey Alexandrovich, the man who, by his ultra-reactionary and near-sighted policy, drove Moscow into the arms of the revolutionists. The measures which the Grand Duke adopted against the Jews of Moscow the Committee of

Ministers refused to sanction, so that they had to be passed either by special commissions or directly by Imperial decrees.

It will take decades or, more probably, centuries to do away altogether with the Jewish question. The racial peculiarities of the Jews will disappear only gradually and slowly. Had the Government followed Alexander II's policy toward the Jews, they would not have become one of the evil factors of our accursed revolution. The Jewish question would have lost its peculiar acuteness and would have assumed the form in which it exists at present in all those countries where Jews live in considerable numbers.

The whole mass of the legislation regarding the Jews consists of legal provisions of an extremely vague character. This circumstance led to a number of arbitrary and conflicting interpretations, which became a source of all manner of graft. No element of the population is so thoroughly mulcted by the Administration as the Jews are. In some regions the graft has assumed the form of a veritable tax upon the Jews. Under these conditions, the whole burden of the anti-Jewish policy falls upon the poorer class of the Jews, for the more opulent a Jew is, the easier it is for him to smooth his way by means of graft and the less he feels the pressure of the restrictive measures. Not only do the wealthy Jews not feel the oppression of their legal disabilities, but they are, to a certain extent, in a domineering position, inasmuch as they exert influence upon the high local officials.

In the early 1880s the Senate combatted this state of affairs, seeking to eliminate all arbitrary interpretations of the laws and all illegal restrictions upon the Jewish population. The result was that some of the senators were denounced by the Minister of the Interior for interfering with the Administration. They were subjected to abuse and some of the more refractory were even removed and replaced by more obedient members. Consequently, the Senate, too, began to interpret the laws relating to the Jews in a manner distinctly anti-Jewish.

All this naturally rendered the Jewish masses revolutionary, especially the younger element, the process being furthered by the Russian schools. From the pusillanimous people that the Jews were some thirty years ago there sprang men and women who threw bombs, committed political murders and sacrificed their lives for the revolution. Of course, all the Jews have not become revolutionists, but it is certain that no nationality in Russia has yielded such a large percentage of extreme radicals as the Jewish. Nearly the entire Jewish intellectual class, including graduates of the institutions of higher learning, joined the "Party of the People's Freedom" (the Constitutional Democrats), which promised them equal rights. This political party owes much of its influence to the Jews, who lent it both intellectual and financial support.

I repeatedly warned the Jewish leaders, both in Russia and abroad, that they had entered upon a hazardous road and were likely to add to the acuteness of the Jewish problem in Russia. I told them that they must show an example of loyalty to the existing regime, and to seek to better their condition by appealing to the Tsar's Government. I advised them, instead of dreaming of revolutionary freedom, to adopt the motto: "The only thing we beg is not to be discriminated against." But I pleaded in vain. Blinded by revolutionary ardour and deluded by the Cadet leaders, they disregarded my well-intentioned counsel.

Indeed, how could they heed the voice of prudence and loyalty to the Tsar at the moment when, as they thought, they stood on the threshold of the triumph of the revolution, which meant also the triumph of the principle of equal rights for the Jews!

The outcome was a strong reaction. Many people who formerly either sympathized with the Jews or were indifferent to them, turned pronounced Jew-haters. Russian Jews never had as many enemies as they have now, nor was the outlook for the Jews ever more sombre than it is at the present. Such a state of affairs is highly unfavorable to the pacification of the country. It is my profound conviction that as long as the Jewish problem is handled in an unstatesmanlike, vindictive, and non-humanitarian fashion, Russia will remain in a state of unrest and upheaval. On the other hand, I fear that the immediate granting of full rights to the Jews may lead to new disturbances and complications, thus defeating its purpose. I repeat, problems involving the historical prejudices of the masses which are based on race peculiarities, can be solved only by degrees and slowly. In these matters one should avoid disturbing the equilibrium, even though it should be a temporary and artificial equilibrium. A body politic is a living organism, and one must be exceedingly cautious in operating upon it.

The anti-Jewish legislation of 1882 is identified with the name of Count N. P. Ignatyev. He did much harm to the country by pursuing a ruthless anti-Jewish policy. Such an ultra-conservative but intelligent statesman as was Count Tolstoy, Minister of the Interior under Alexander III, would not have committed this mistake. He did not succeed in undoing Ignatyev's work, but he refrained from following in his footsteps. After Tolstoy's death, I. K. Durnovo resumed Ignatyev's policy, although he was on the best of terms with some of the Jewish millionaires. A man of very limited intelligence, he was prompted to take this course of action by his desire to please the Court *camarilla*, where the spirit of Jew-baiting was at that time predominant. But it is Plehve who was the leading spirit of the anti-Jewish policy and the author of all the anti-Jewish laws and administrative measures both under Ignatyev and Durnovo. Personally he had nothing against the Jews. This I know from my numerous talks with him on the subject of the Jewish question. He possessed enough intelligence to understand that he was following an essentially wrong policy. But it pleased Grand Duke Sergey Alexandrovich and apparently His Majesty. Consequently, Plehve exerted himself to the utmost.

The "pogroms," that peculiar feature of the Jewish question in Russia, raged with particular violence under Ignatyev. Count Tolstoy at once put an end to them. Under Plehve the tide of pogroms again rose high. Especially brutal and revolting was the anti-Jewish outbreak at Kishinev. I would not venture to say that Plehve personally and directly organized these pogroms, but he did not oppose these, in his opinion, counter-revolutionary outbreaks. When the Kishinev pogroms roused the public opinion of the whole civilized world, Plehve entered into negotiations with the Jewish leaders in Paris and also with the Russian rabbis. What he told them amounted to the following: "Make your people stop their revolutionary activity, and I will stop the pogroms and abolish the Jewish disabilities." "The situation is beyond our control," was the reply. "The young element, crazed by hunger, is out of hand. But should a policy of relieving the oppression of the Jews be inaugurated, we believe that the unrest among the people will subside." Plehve appears to have heeded these words and assumed a more liberal attitude about the Jews, but he was soon assassinated.

I should like to say a word about the status of the Jews during my administration. It must be admitted that the Jews played a prominent part in leading the forces of unrest and in fanning the flame of discontent. Of course, this circumstance may be accounted for and, to a considerable extent, justified by the intolerable legal status of the Jews and the pogroms which the Government not only tolerated, but even organized itself. However that may be, the outstanding part of the Jews in the revolution is an indisputable fact.

Immediately after my appointment, a Jewish deputation headed by Baron Ginzburg, a very respectable and wealthy man, called upon me. I received them. I remember, besides Ginzburg, the deputation included: Vinaver, a lawyer, later a prominent delegate of the First Imperial Duma from the city of St. Petersburg, Sliozberg and Kulisher, also legal lights, and Varshawski, son of the celebrated railroad builder. They came to plead the cause of full rights for their people, and they begged me to lay the matter before the Emperor. I stated frankly my views on the subject, emphasizing the point that the removal of the legal disabilities must proceed by degrees, for otherwise in some rural localities genuine, not artificial, pogroms might break out. In order that I might be able to raise the question of granting substantial rights to the Jews, I told them, and that I might advance the principle of equalizing the Jews with the rest of the population, before the law, it was necessary for the Jews to change their mode of behaviour. They must publicly declare, I said, to the Monarch—and substantiate their declaration by actual deeds—that they beg of His Majesty nothing else than to be treated on an equal footing with his other subjects. "Of late years," I told the delegation, "the Jews have come to the fore as leaders of various political parties and advocates of the most extreme political ideas. Now, it is not your business to teach us. Leave that to Russians by birth and civil status, and mind your own affairs. I assure you that your present conduct is fraught with harmful consequences both to you and your children."

Baron Ginzburg declared that he completely shared my opinion. Sliozberg and Kulisher also agreed with me. The rest of the deputation, however, were not impressed by my arguments. Vinaver, for instance, declared that the moment had now come when the Russian people were going to obtain political freedom and full rights for all the citizens irrespective of race or faith, and that it was the duty of the Jews to offer every possible support to those Russians who were fighting for the political emancipation of the country. Thus the conference came to nothing.

When, in the summer of 1907, I came to Frankfort-on-the-Main, the local Jewish leaders met me in the house of a wealthy citizen by the name of Askenazi, whom I had known for a long time. The chief representatives of the German Jewry, including the celebrated Dr. Nathan of Berlin, were present there. I reiterated to them substantially what I told the Jewish delegation in St. Petersburg. In this case Dr. Nathan played Vinaver's part. From Frankfort I went to Paris, where I had a conference with a number of prominent French Jews. I repeated to them the views which I had previously offered to their Russian and German co-religionists. The French Jews assured me that they agreed with me but that they were helpless to influence the Russian Jewry. At present, I think the Jews see clearly who was right, I or their tactless, to speak mildly, counsellors.

When Stolypin assumed power, narrow nationalism was predominant in the Court circles. Accordingly, he decided that it would be advantageous for him to adopt a policy of persecuting all the Russian subjects of non-Russian stock, that is, one-third of the entire population of the Empire (about 60,000,000). New anti-Jewish restrictions followed. On September 16, 1908, His Majesty confirmed a bill drafted by the Council of Ministers "about the percentage of persons of Jewish faith admitted to educational institutions." This measure, being of a legislative character, should have passed through the Duma and the Imperial Council, but all that time Stolypin treated the Duma not as a legislative body but as a bureaucratic office subordinate to the Minister of the Interior. This act was the first shot in Stolypin's war against the Jews.

It is noteworthy that during my premiership the question of the percentage of Jewish students was raised by the Minister of Education, Count Tolstoy, but his purpose was to remove the measures which restricted the educational opportunities of the Jews. Count Tolstoy laid before the Council of Ministers a bill for the abolition of these restrictions. He argued from the premise, which to my mind is perfectly correct, that the most natural solution of the Jewish question is the assimilation of the race through Russian education. After a lengthy discussion, the Council of Ministers decided in favour of the bill. But the Emperor refused to sanction it and returned it to the Council with a resolution that he would issue instructions on the subject at a later period. This case aptly illustrates the difference between the Jewish policy of my Cabinet and that of Stolypin's. It is true that at the beginning of his administration Stolypin was inclined to abolish some of the existing Jewish disabilities. He drafted a memorandum on the subject and submitted it to His Majesty, but the Emperor again postponed the matter. In 1907 the Council of Ministers, under Stolypin's presidency, took up the question of Jewish disabilities and adopted a resolution that it was necessary to enter upon the road of gradual abolition of the existing restrictions. The minutes of this session His Majesty refused to sign.

A year later Stolypin reversed his policy and gradually there arose in Russia an intense movement against the Jews, which is both un-Christian and politically indefensible. At present Jew-baiting is at its worst, and I believe that the baiters themselves hardly know whither they are headed and what they intend to achieve by this ruthless persecution. One may not sympathize with the Jews, one may consider them an accursed nation. Nevertheless, they are human beings and Russian subjects, and there is no other method of treating them than that which is adopted in all the civilized countries, that is, the method of gradually making them full-fledged members of the communities where they reside.

In November, 1907, St. Petersburg was visited by Taft, then Secretary of War and now President of the United States. I remember having heard Roosevelt speak of him in friendly and commending terms. In fact, it was Roosevelt who has made him President in the hope that he would be faithful to him, but, as it oftern happens, the two men are now in opposite political camps, and right now the question is debated as to who of the two is to be elected President, should the Republican party gain the upper hand. On my part, I can say that, no doubt, Roosevelt is a much abler man than Taft. It is known that during the Spanish-American War Colonel Roosevelt commanded a military detachment in Porto Rico, although neither Roosevelt nor Taft are military men. It is said that during his stay in the capital Taft had an audience with the Emperor, in the course of which he took up the question of the right of American citizens of Jewish faith to enter Russia.

As early as April 1905, Minister of the Interior Bulygin recommended that together with the introduction of new passport regulations all the restrictions upon the right of foreign Jews to enter the Empire should be removed. He pointed out that these restrictions served no purpose and merely complicated international relations. With the creation of the Duma, many of the legislative projects filling the dossiers of the Imperial Council were returned to the respective Ministers that they might be laid before the Duma. Such was also the fate of Bulygin's recommendation; it was returned to the Ministry of the Interior, and there it was permanently buried.

I have told elsewhere how President Roosevelt handed me a letter to His Majesty, asking him to remove the restrictions upon the right of American Jews to enter Russia. Five years passed, and the President's letter remained unanswered. I do not know whether any further negotiations took place, but the practice objectionable to the United States continued. As a result several months ago the American Government lost its patience and denounced its old commerical treaty with Russia. Our jingoists are naturally thundering against America. There is no doubt, however, that we ourselves have driven the United States Government to this step.

61

The Russo-English Treaty on Persia, Afghanistan, and Tibet, August 31, 1907

The Japanese defeat of Russia in the war of 1904–1905 produced several far-reaching repercussions. On the domestic front the defeat strengthened the popular contempt for the government, increased the violence, and forced the Tsar to make a number of important concessions, such as calling of the Duma into existence, approving a new constitution, and agrarian and school reforms. In the realm of foreign policy the repercussions were equally great. The defeat revealed not only Russia's weakness but that of the Franco-Russian Alliance as well. Since this revelation increased the stature of the German-led Triple Alliance, immediately

From the *American Journal of International Law, Supplement.* (1907), vol. I, pp. 400–405.

after hostilities ceased there occurred a major big power realignment aimed at restoring the "balance of power." In July 1907, Russia and Japan signed the first of a series of secret agreements aimed at the division of China; and in August of the same year Russia and England reached an understanding over areas that had been a major cause of their antagonism throughout most of the nineteenth century; namely, Persia, Afghanistan, and Tibet.

Arrangement Concerning Persia

The Governments of Great Britain and Russia having mutually engaged to respect the integrity and independence of Persia, and sincerely desiring the preservation of order throughout that country and its peaceful development, as well as the permanent establishment of equal advantages for the trade and industry of all other nations;

Considering that each of them has, for geographical and economic reasons, a special interest in the maintenance of peace and order in certain provinces of Persia adjoining, or in the neighbourhood of, the Russian frontier on the one hand, and the frontiers of Afghanistan and Baluchistan on the other hand; and being desirous of avoiding all cause of conflict between their respective interests in the above-mentioned Provinces of Persia;

Have agreed on the following terms:

Article 1

Great Britain engages not to seek for herself, and not to support in favor of British subjects, or in favor of the subjects of third Powers, any Concessions of a political or commercial nature—such as Concessions for railways, banks, telegraphs, roads, transport, insurance, and so forth—beyond a line starting from Kasr-i-Shirin, passing through Isfahan, Yezd, Kakhk, and ending at a point on the Persian frontier at the intersection of the Russian and Afghan frontiers, and not to oppose, directly or indirectly, demands for similar Concessions in this region which are supported by the Russian Government. It is understood that the above-mentioned places are included in the region in which Great Britain engages not to seek the Concessions referred to.

Article 2

Russia, on her part, engages not to seek for herself and not to support, in favour of Russian subjects, or in favour of the subjects of third Powers, any Concessions of a political or commercial nature—such as Concessions for railways, banks, telegraphs, roads, transport, insurance and so forth—beyond a line going from the Afghan frontier by way of Gazik, Birjand, Kerman, and ending at Bunder Abbas, and not to oppose, directly or indirectly, demands for similar Concessions in this region which are supported by the British Government. It is understood that the above-mentioned places are included in the region in which Russia engages not to seek the Concessions referred to.

Article 3

Russia, on her part, engages not to oppose, without previous arrangement with Great Britain, the grant of any Concessions whatever to British subjects in the regions of Persia situated between the lines mentioned in Articles 1 and 2.

Great Britain undertakes a similar engagement as regards the grant of Concessions to Russian subjects in the same regions of Persia.

All Concessions existing at present in the regions indicated in Articles 1 and 2 are maintained.

Article 4

It is understood that the revenues of all the Persian customs, with the exception of those of Farsistan and of the Persian Gulf, revenues guaranteeing the amortization and the interest of the loans concluded by the Government of the Shah with the "Banque d'Escompte et des Prets de Perse" up to the date of the signature of the present Arrangement, shall be devoted to the same purpose as in the past.

It is equally understood that the revenues of the Persian customs of Farsistan and of the Persian Gulf, as well as those of the fisheries on the Persian shore of the Caspian Sea and those of the Posts and Telegraphs, shall be devoted, as in the past, to the services of the loans concluded by the Government of the Shah with the Imperial Bank of Persia up to the date of the signature of the present Arrangement.

Article 5

In the event of irregularities occurring in the amortization or the payment of the interest of the Persian loans concluded with the "Banque d'Escompte et des Prets de Perse" and with the Imperial Bank of Persia up to the date of the signature of the present Arrangement, and in the event of the necessity arising for Russia to establish control over the sources of revenue guaranteeing the regular service of the loans concluded with the first-named bank, and situated in the region mentioned in Article 2 of the present Arrangement, or for Great Britain to establish control over the sources of revenue guaranteeing the regular service of the loans concluded with the second-named bank, and situated in the region mentioned in Article 1 of the present Arrangement, the British and Russian Governments undertake to enter beforehand into a friendly exchange of ideas with a view to determine, in agreement with each other, the measures of control in question and to avoid all interference which would not be in conformity with the principles governing the present Arrangement.

Convention Concerning Afghanistan

The High Contracting Parties, in order to ensure perfect security on their respective frontiers in Central Asia and to maintain in these regions a solid and lasting peace, have concluded the following Convention:

Article 1

His Britannic Majesty's Government declare that they have no intention of changing the political status of Afghanistan.

His Britannic Majesty's Government further engage to exercise their influence in Afghanistan only in a pacific sense, and they will not themselves take, nor encourage Afghanistan to take, any measures threatening Russia.

The Russian Government, on their part, declare that they recognize Afghanistan as outside the sphere of Russian influence, and they engage that all their political relations with Afghanistan shall be conducted through the intermediary of His Britannic Majesty's Government; they further engage not to send any Agents into Afghanistan.

Article 2

The Government of His Britannic Majesty having declared in the Treaty signed at Kabul on the 21st March, 1905, that they recognize the Agreement and the engagements concluded with the late Ameer Abdur Rahman, and that they have no intention of interfering in the internal government of Afghan territory, Great Britain engages neither to annex nor to occupy in contravention of that Treaty any portion of Afghanistan or to interfere in the internal administration of the country, provided that the Ameer fulfils the engagements already contracted by him towards His Britannic Majesty's Government under the above-mentioned Treaty.

Article 3

The Russian and Afghan authorities, specially designated for the purpose on the frontier or in the frontier provinces, may establish direct relations with each other for the settlement of local questions of a non-political character.

Article 4

His Britannic Majesty's Government and the Russian Government affirm their adherence to the principle of equality of commercial opportunity in Afghanistan, and they agree that any facilities which may have been, or shall be hereafter obtained for British and British-Indian trade and traders, shall be equally enjoyed by Russian trade and traders. Should the progress of trade establish the necessity for Commercial Agents, the two Governments will agree as to what measures shall be taken, due regard, of course, being had to the Ameer's sovereign rights.

Article 5

The present Arrangements will only come into force when His Britannic Majesty's government shall have notified to the Russian Government the consent of the Ameer to the terms stipulated above.

Arrangement Concerning Tibet

The Governments of Great Britain and Russia recognizing the suzerain rights of China in Tibet, and considering the fact that Great Britain, by reason of her geographical position, has a special interest in the maintenance of the *status quo* in the external relations of Tibet, have made the following Arrangement:—

Article 1

The two High Contracting Parties engage to respect the territorial integrity of Tibet and to abstain from all interference in its internal administration

Article 2

In conformity with the admitted principle of the suzerainty of China over Tibet, Great Britain and Russia engage not to enter into negotiations with Tibet except through the intermediary of the Chinese Government. This engagement does not exclude the direct relations between British Commercial Agents and the Tibetan authorities provided for in Article 5 of the Convention between Great Britain and Tibet of the 7th September, 1904, and confirmed by the Convention between Great Britain and China of the 27th April, 1906; nor does it modify the engagements entered into by Great Britain and China in Article 1 of the said Convention of 1906.

It is clearly understood that Buddhists, subjects of Great Britain or of Russia, may enter into direct relations on strictly religious matters with the Dalai Lama and the other representatives of Buddhism in Tibet; the Governments of Great Britain and Russia engage, as far as they are concerned, not to allow those relations to infringe the stipulations of the present Arrangement.

Article 3

The British and Russian Governments respectively engage not to send Representatives to Lhassa.

Article 4

The two High Contracting Parties engage neither to seek nor to obtain, whether for themselves of their subjects, any Concessions for railways, roads, telegraphs, and mines, or other rights in Tibet.

Article 5

The two Governments agree that no part of the revenues of Tibet, whether in kind or in cash, shall be pledged or assigned to Great Britain or Russia or to any of their subjects.

Annex to the Arrangement between Great Britain and Russia Concerning Tibet

Great Britain reaffirms the Declaration, signed by his Excellency the Viceroy and Governor-General of India and appended to the ratification of the Convention of the 7th September, 1904, to the effect that the occupation of the Chumbi Valley by British forces shall cease after the payment of three annual instalments of the indemnity of 25,000,000 *rupees,* provided that the trade marts mentioned in Article 2 of that Convention have been effectively opened for three years, and that in the meantime the Tibetan authorities have faithfully complied in all respects with the terms of the said Convention of 1904. It is clearly understood that if the occupation of the Chumbia Valley by the British forces has, for any reason, not been terminated at the time anticipated in the above Declaration, the British and Russian Governments will enter upon a friendly exchange of views on this subject.

The present Convention shall be ratified, and the ratifications exchanged at St. Petersburgh as soon as possible.

In witness whereof the respective Plenipotentiaries have signed the present Convention and affixed thereto their seals.

Done in duplicate at St. Petersburgh, the 18th (31st) August, 1907.

Nicolson
Iswolsky

62

Russia and Japan on the Division of China, 1907–1916

Between the Treaty of Nerchinsk in 1689 and about 1850, imperial Russia's policy in the Far East had been generally peaceful. After 1850, however, she assumed an aggressive attitude. Two basic facts seem to have contributed to this change. The first was the defeat, humiliation, and partial territorial dismemberment of China by West European powers in a series of wars beginning with the Opium War (1839–1842) and ending with the Boxer Rebellion in 1900. The second was the sudden rise of Japanese power and ambitions in the Far East. To remove Russia's opposition to the Japanese advance into Korea and Manchuria, Japanese forces attacked Russia early in 1904 and in a series of spectacular moves inflicted a humiliating defeat.

The war was formally ended by the Treaty of Portsmouth on September 5, 1905, but the terms of the treaty were unpopular with both sides. Between 1907 and 1916, however, the two former adversaries, through a series of secret agreements, divided Manchuria and northern China between themselves and pledged to cooperate fully to prevent any third power from seeking a "sphere of influence" at China's expense. The overthrow of the tsarist government in the March 1917 Revolution prevented realization of these ambitious schemes.

Secret Convention of July 30, 1907

The Government of His Majesty the Emperor of All the Russias and the Government of His Majesty the Emperor of Japan, desiring to obviate for the future all causes of friction or misunderstanding with respect to certain questions relating to Manchuria, Korea and Mongolia, have agreed upon the following provisions:

Article 1

Having in view the natural gravitation of interests and of political and economic activity in Manchuria, and desiring to avoid all complications which might arise from competition, Japan undertakes not to seek to obtain on its own account, or for the benefit of Japanese or other subjects, any concession in the way of railways or telegraphs in Manchuria to the north of a line defined in the Additional Article of the present Convention, and not to obstruct, either directly or indirectly, any intiatives supported by the Russian Government with a view to concessions of that sort in those regions; and Russia, on its part, inspired by the same pacific motive, undertakes not to seek to obtain on its own account, or for the benefit of Russian or other subjects, any concession in the way of railways or telegraphs in Manchuria to the south of the above-mentioned line, and not to obstruct, either directly or indirectly, any initiatives supported by the Japanese Government with a view to concessions of that sort in those regions.

It is fully understood that all the rights and privileges belonging to the Chinese Eastern Railway Company by virtue of the contracts for the construction of this railway, dated August 28, 1896 and June 25, 1898, will remain in force on the section of the railway lying to the south of the line of demarcation defined in the Additional Article.

Article 2

Russia, recognizing the relations of political solidarity between Japan and Korea resulting from the conventions and arrangements at present in force between them, copies of which have been communicated to the Russian Government by the Japanese Government, undertakes not to interfere with nor to place any obstacle in the way of the further development of those relations; and Japan, on its part, undertakes to extend in all respects most-favored-nation treatment to the Russian Government, consular officers, subjects, commerce, industry and navigation in Korea, pending the conclusion of a definitive treaty.

Article 3

The Imperial Government of Japan, recognizing the special interest of Russia in Outer Mongolia, undertakes to refrain from any interference which might prejudice those interests.

Article 4

The present Convention shall be strictly confidential between the two High Contracting Parties.

Additional Article

The line of demarcation between North Manchuria and South Manchuria mentioned in Article 1 of the present convention is established as follows:

Starting from the northwestern point of the Russo-Korean frontier, and forming a succession of straight lines, the line runs, by way of Hunchun and the northern extremity of Lake Pirteng, to Hsiushuichan; thence it follows the Sungari to the mouth of the Nunkiang, thereupon ascending the course of that river to the confluence of the Tola River. From that point, the line follows the course of that river to its intersection with Meridian 122° East of Greenwich.

Secret Convention of July 4, 1910

The Imperial Government of Russia and the Imperial Government of Japan, desiring to consolidate and develop the provisions of the secret Convention signed at St. Petersburg July 30, 1907, have agreed upon the following:

Article 1

Russia and Japan recognize the line of demarcation fixed by the Additional Article of the secret Convention of 1907 as delimiting the respective spheres of their special interests in Manchuria.

Article 2

The two High Contracting Parties undertake to respect reciprocally their special interests in the spheres above indicated. They consequently recognize the right of each, within its own sphere, freely to take all measures necessary for the safeguarding and the defense of those interests.

Article 3

Each of the two High Contracting Parties undertakes not to hinder in any way the consolidation and further development of the special interests of the other Party within the limits of the above—mentioned spheres.

Article 4

Each of the two High Contracting Parties undertakes to refrain from all political activity within the sphere of special interests of the other in Manchuria. It is furthermore understood that Russia will not seek in the Japanese sphere—and Japan will not seek in the Russian sphere—any privilege or any concession of a nature to prejudice their reciprocal special interests, and that both the Russian and Japanese Governments will respect all the rights acquired by

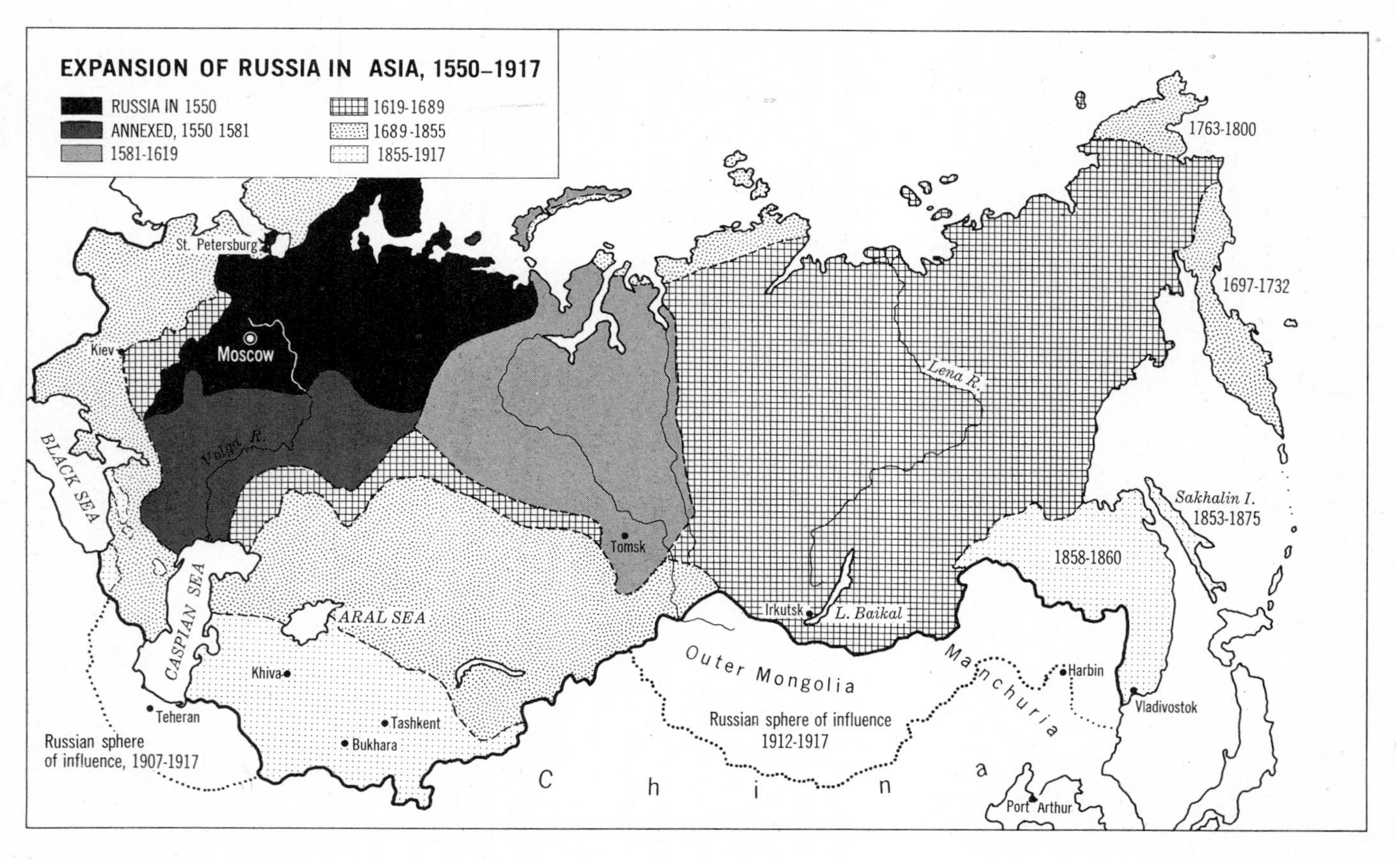
EXPANSION OF RUSSIA IN ASIA, 1550–1917
RUSSIA IN 1550
ANNEXED, 1550 1581
1581-1619
1619-1689
1689-1855
1855-1917
St. Petersburg
Moscow
Kiev
Volga R.
BLACK SEA
CASPIAN SEA
ARAL SEA
Khiva
Bukhara
Tashkent
Teheran
Russian sphere
of influence, 1907-1917
Tomsk
Irkutsk
L. Baikal
Lena R.
Outer Mongolia
Russian sphere of influence
1912-1917
China
Manchuria
Harbin
Port Arthur
Vladivostok
1858-1860
Sakhalin I.
1853-1875
1763-1800
1697-1732

each of them within its sphere by virtue of the treaties, conventions or other arrangements mentioned in Article 2 of the public Convention of today's date.

Article 5

In order to insure the good working of their reciprocal engagements, the two High Contracting Parties will at all times frankly and loyally enter into communication with regard to anything that concerns matters affecting in common their special interests in Manchuria.

In the event that these special interests should come to be threatened, the two High Contracting Parties will agree upon the measures to be taken with a view to common action or to the support to be accorded for the safeguarding and the defense of those interests.

Article 6

The present Convention shall be strictly confidential between the two High Contracting Parties.

Secret Convention of July 8, 1912

The Imperial Government of Russia and the Imperial Government of Japan, desirous of making precise and completing the provisions of the secret Conventions concluded between them July 30, 1907 and July 4, 1910, in order to avoid all cause of misunderstanding concerning their special interests in Manchuria and in Mongolia, have decided to prolong the line of demarcation fixed by the additional article to the above—cited Convention of July 30, 1907, and to define their spheres of special interests in Inner Mongolia, and have agreed upon the following:

Article 1

Starting from the point of intersection of the Tola River and Meridian 122° East of Greenwich, the above—mentioned line of demarcation follows the course of the Oulountchourh River and the Moushisha River up to the line of the watershed between the Moushisha River and the Haldaitai River; thence it follows the frontier line between the Province of Heilungkiang and Inner Mongolia until reaching the extreme point of the frontier between Inner Mongolia and Outer Mongolia.

Article 2

Inner Mongolia is divided into two parts: one to the West, and the other to the East, of the meridian of Peking (116° 27′ East of Greenwich).

The Imperial Government of Russia undertakes to recognize and to respect the Japanese special interests in the part of Inner Mongolia to the East of the meridian above indicated, and the Imperial Government of Japan undertakes to recognize and to respect the Russian special interests in the part of Inner Mongolia to the West of the said meridian.

Article 3

The present Convention shall be strictly confidential between the two High Contracting Parties. . . .

Tibet Convention of July 3, 1916

The Imperial Government of Russia and the Imperial Government of Japan, desiring to consolidate the sincerely friendly relations established by their secret Conventions of July 30, 1907, July 4, 1910, and July 8, 1912, have agreed on the following clauses designed to complete the above—mentioned agreements:

Article 1

The two High Contracting Parties, recognizing that their vital interests demand that China should not fall under the political domination of any third Power hostile to Russia or Japan, will frankly and loyally enter into communication whenever circumstances may demand, and will agree upon the measures to be taken to prevent such a situation being brought about.

Article 2

In the event that, in consequence of the measures taken by mutual agreement as provided in the preceding article, war should be declared between one of the Contracting Parties and one of the third Powers contemplated by the preceding article, the other Contracting Party will, upon the demand of its ally, come to its aid, and in that case each of the High Contracting Parties undertakes not to make peace without a previous agreement with the other Contracting Party.

Article 3

The conditions in which each of the High Contracting Parties will lend its armed cooperation to the other Contracting Party, as stipulated in the preceding article, and the means by which this cooperation will be effected, will be established by the competent authorities of the two High Contracting Parties.

Article 4

It is fully understood, however, that neither of the High Contracting Parties will be bound to lend its ally the armed assistance contemplated by Article

2 of the present Convention unless it has assured itself of cooperation, on the part of its allies, corresponding to the gravity of the impending conflict.

Article 5

The present Convention will come into force immediately after the date of signature, and will continue in effect until July 14, 1921.

In case neither of the High Contracting Parties should have given notice, twelve months prior to the expiration of that period, of its intention to bring the effectiveness of the Convention to an end, it will continue in force until the expiration of one year from the date on which one or the other of the High Contracting Parties shall have denounced it.

Article 6

The present Convention shall remain strictly confidential between the two High Contracting Parties. . . .

63

Rasputin: The Holy Devil

The last years of imperial Russian history are closely linked with the name of Gregory Efimovich Rasputin (1872–1916). To his admirers Rasputin was a "holy man" whose mission was to save the Romanov dynasty. To his opponents he was a pernicious pervert whose activity accelerated the downfall of imperial Russia. A Siberian peasant by birth, Rasputin was a half-literate, unordained religious teacher who wandered through rural Russia and lived on donations from simple-minded believers. The essence of his preaching seems to have been a belief that "sexual indulgence is the true path to humility and, through humility, to eternal salvation." In 1905, through the efforts of a group of ladies of St. Petersburg society, he was introduced to the imperial family. His apparent hypnotic and clairvoyant powers and his seeming ability to control the bleeding of the hemophilic heir to the Russian throne immediately captured the imagination of Empress Alexandra, who felt him

---

Reprinted with permission of the publisher from M. V. Rodzianko, *The Reign of Rasputin: An Empire's Collapse.* Translated by Catherine Zvegintzoff. Introduction by Sir Bernard Pares (London: Philpot, 1927), pp. 41–47, 49–59, 61–62.

to be an instrument of Providence sent to save Russia and the Romanov dynasty. She sought his advice on all matters, family as well as state, and denounced criticism of his loose morals and crude manners as slanderous. Because he wielded such powerful influence, Rasputin attracted as followers all kinds of adventurers and their activities soon became a national scandal. In 1911 and 1912 he was severely criticized by the leaders of the Duma and bitterly indicted by M. V. Rodzianko (1859–1924), the President of the Duma, whose charges against Rasputin are presented below.

"Your Majesty, my report today [February 26, 1912, O. S.][1] extends to matters far beyond its usual scope. Granted the gracious permission of your Majesty, I intend to lay before you the detailed and documentary evidence concerning a process of destruction which has begun, pregnant with the most disastrous consequences to all concerned. . . ."

The Tsar glanced at me in some astonishment.

I continued:

"I refer to the *starets* Rasputin and to the inadmissible fact of his presence at your Majesty's Court. I beseech you, Sire, as your Majesty's most loyal subject—will it be your pleasure to hear me to the end? If not, say but one word, and I will remain silent."

With bowed head and averted gaze the Tsar murmured in a low voice:

"Speak."

"Your Majesty, the presence of this man of more than tarnished reputation in the most intimate Court circles is an event unparalleled in the history of the Russian Monarchy. The entire nation, all circles of the community, view with profound apprehension the influence this man exercises on the affairs of Church and State. The whole machinery of government, from Ministers to the inferior ranks of the secret police, is mobilized for the purpose of shielding this adventurer. Rasputin is a tool in the hands of Russia's enemies; he is their instrument for undermining the Church and the Monarchy itself. No revolutionary propaganda could achieve as much as Rasputin's mere presence at Court. Everyone fears his intimacy with the Imperial Family. Public feeling is running very high."

"But why such attacks on Rasputin?" interrupted the Tsar; "why is he considered so harmful?"

"Your Majesty, the fact that Rasputin has created a split in the Synod has become common knowledge, both by hearsay and through the Press. Everyone knows that bishops are being transferred from their posts owing to his intrigues."

"Which bishops?" asked the Tsar.

"The case of Mgr. Hermogen aroused universal indignation, as being an undeserved insult to a prelate. Mgr. Hermogen has many supporters. I have received a petition signed by ten thousand people, begging me to intercede on his behalf before your Majesty."

"I think Mgr. Hermogen is a good man," said the Tsar; "he will soon be permitted to return. Still, I could not allow him to remain unpunished for his flagrant disobedience to my Imperial order."

"Your Majesty, according to the canons of the Church, an episcopal court can alone sit in judgment on a bishop. Mgr. Hermogen was sentenced to banishment on the sole charge of the High Procurator and on the strength of his personal report. It was an infringement of the canons of the Church."

The Tsar listened in silence.

"The case of Iliodor, too, has made a most painful impression on the people. After the inquiry held by order of your Majesty, his trial was cancelled a year ago. Now, without trial, he is confined in the Floristchevo hermitage—and this was done after he had dared to speak openly against Rasputin. These two were not the only ones to suffer. Bishop Feofan was deprived of his office of the Empress's confessor and removed to Simferopol. Bishop Anthony of Tobolsk, who was the first to inform the Synod of Rasputin's adherence to the *khlysty* sect and to demand his trial, was transferred to Tver. Anyone who dares utter a word against Rasputin is persecuted by the Synod. Such a state of affairs cannot be tolerated, your Majesty. How can Orthodox Christians stand by in silence, when Orthodoxy is being defiled and destroyed by the pernicious activities of this rogue? One may well understand the general outburst of indignation which followed the disclosure that Rasputin was a *khlyst*."

"What proofs have you?"

"The police discovered that he went to the baths with women. That is one of the peculiarities of their religious practices."

"What of that? It is merely a custom among common people."

"No, your Majesty, there is no such custom. Perhaps husbands and wives go together, but what we have here is sheer debauchery. Permit me, in the first place, to read you letters from those of his victims, who fell into the trap and repented afterwards. Here is a letter from a priest in Siberia, addressed to several members of the Duma [I did not like to mention Gutchkoff by name], and imploring them to inform the authorities of Rasputin's exploits, his immoral conduct and the rumours he circulated concerning his position and influence at the Imperial Court." (This letter I read out from end to end.)

"Here is another letter written by a lady confessing having been seduced and morally corrupted by Rasputin. She afterwards recoiled from him and repented of her fall . . . and met him one evening coming out of the baths in the company of her two daughters. . . . The wife of an engineer, Mme. L., also fell a victim to Rasputin's teachings. She became insane and is now in a lunatic asylum. Will your Majesty order this evidence to be verified?"

"I believe you," said the Tsar.

I read him other letters and extracts from Novoseloff's pamphlet; I laid stress on the painful impression which the prohibition of any publication in the Press concerning Rasputin had made on the public mind. He did not belong to the category of persons of whom it was forbidden to write. He occupied no exalted position, neither was he a member of the Imperial Family. Ministers of the Crown, the presidents of the Imperial Duma or of the Council of the Empire were freely criticized in the Press. Why, then, this enforced silence concerning Rasputin? Such a policy naturally led the public to suppose him to be intimately connected with the Imperial Family.

"But why do you assume him to be a *khlyst?*"

"Your Majesty should read Novoseloff's pamphlet. He made a special investigation of the case. He states that Rasputin was prosecuted on the charge of belonging to that sect, but that for some reason or other the prosecution was stopped. Moreover, as has been ascertained, meetings of Rasputin's followers were held at Sazonoff's flat, where Rasputin himself was staying at the time. Permit me to show you a foreign newspaper cutting, in which it is said that at the Masonic Congress in Brussels Rasputin was mentioned as being a useful instrument for carrying out the freemason's policy in Russia. The whole intrigue, with all its subsequent developments, is as clear as daylight. It is not the fate of the dynasty and the prestige of the Imperial Family alone which are involved."

"How?" inquired the Tsar, greatly agitated.

"Your Majesty, there is no serious or responsible person in charge of the Tsarevitch; he is entrusted to the care of a country yokel, Derevenko, who may be a very good man, but is a simple peasant. Ignorant folk are naturally inclined towards mysticism. What if anything were to happen to the Heir Apparent? This is a subject of profound anxiety to all. . . . Such a charming child, so universally beloved."

The Tsar was evidently struggling to overcome his emotion. He nervously lit one cigarette after another, then threw them down again.

I here decided to approach the subject from another side and to persuade the Emperor that Rasputin was a sycophant. I produced a photograph of the *starets* wearing a pectoral cross.

"Your Majesty knows Rasputin is not in holy orders; yet there he is depicted as a priest."

The Tsar replied:

"Yes, this is really going too far. He has no right to wear a pectoral cross."

"It is blasphemy, your Majesty. He is an illiterate peasant and not entitled to wear a cowl, which appertains to the priesthood. Here is another photograph. It is a '*khlysty* ship.' This was reproduced in the *Ogonek*[2] and circulated throughout the country. Here is Rasputin surrounded by young girls; there are also boys with him in their midst. Here he is with two young men. They are carrying a placard inscribed with *khlysty* texts, and he is holding a *khlysty* ikon of Our Lady in his hands. It is a 'ship' bearing its inmates towards fornication."

"What is that?" asked the Tsar.

"Read Novoseloff's pamphlet, which I will submit to you. Here is another photograph of Rasputin with two women, and inscribed: 'The Way to Salvation ' . . . "

"The suppression of any mention of Rasputin in the Press encourages the idea that the *khlysty* enjoy the patronage of the Tsar. What if a war broke out? Where is the prestige of the Tsar's name and authority? A number of persons closely connected with the Court are openly designated as Rasputin's followers. Rumours are current that the highest society is contaminated with his sectarian teachings. Thus a slur is cast on society and on the Court. In defiance of the censorship, all the rumours and stories about Rasputin are being feverishly seized upon and reproduced by the provincial Press."

"Have you read Stolypin's report?" asked the Emperor.

"No, I have heard it spoken of, but never read it."

"I rejected it," said the Tsar.

"It is a pity," I replied, "for all this would not have happened. Your Majesty, you witness my profound emotion. It pains me exceedingly to be obliged to speak the cruel truth. But I dared not keep silent, I had no right to conceal from my Sovereign the menacing state of affairs with their possible terrible consequences. I believe that God has placed me as a mediator between the Tsar and the representatives of the people summoned together by his august command. It is my duty, Sire, as a Russian and as your Majesty's loyal subject to warn you that our enemies are striving to undermine the Throne and the Church and to cast a shadow on the beloved name of the Tsar. I always bear in mind the text of the oath of allegiance. In the name of all you hold sacred, in the name of Russia, and for the sake of the welfare and happiness of your successors—I implore you to banish this villainous rogue, and so dispel the fears which assail those who are loyal to the Throne."

"He is not here now," replied the Tsar in a low voice.

"Will you authorize me to tell everyone that he will not return?"

The Tsar remained silent for a while, then said:

"No, I cannot promise you that. Nevertheless, I fully believe all you have told me."

"Do you believe, Sire, in the absolute loyalty and trustworthiness of all those who raised the question in the Duma? Will you believe that they were inspired by the same motives which prompted my coming to lay the whole case before you?"

"I feel the sincerity of your report, and I trust the Duma because I trust you."

I was anxious to learn whether the Emperor was pleased with my report. I continued:

"Your Majesty, I came here fully prepared to pay the penalty if I had the misfortune to incur your Majesty's displeasure. If I have overstepped my rights, you have but to say a word, and I will resign my office of President of the Imperial Duma. I sought but to do my duty in laying the whole matter before you. In view of the excitement raised by this affair in the Duma, I did not think it right to conceal it from my Sovereign."

"I thank you. You acted as an honourable man and a loyal subject." . . .

That same evening I drove to the Duma, where I was immediately surrounded by groups of deputies. I gave them a brief account of the interview and of the gracious reception accorded me by the Emperor. My narrative produced a most excellent impression on all. I gave a *verbatim* account of the whole interview to my most intimate associates.

On the morning of February 28, General V. N. Dediulin, Commandant of the Imperial Palace and A.D.C. to the Emperor, telephoned to me from Tsarskoe Selo, asking me to call on him at his flat in town. General Dediulin was an old schoolfellow of mine and a personal friend; hence the conversation which ensued was of an intimate nature. Dediulin imparted to me the following news.

"After your visit to Tsarskoe Selo," he said to me, "it became known that the Tsar has scarcely touched his dinner and remained all the time extremely taciturn and thoughtful. When I reported to him next morning I took the liberty of saying to him: 'Your Majesty, you have received Rodzianko. It appears he has fatigued you very much.' "

The Tsar replied: "No, I am not in the least tired. I see that Rodzianko is a loyal subject who is not afraid of speaking the truth. He told me much that I knew nothing about. You are an old schoolfellow of his. Tell him, from me, to investigate Rasputin's case. Let him take from the Synod all the secret documents concerning Rasputin, thoroughly examine them and report the results to me. But tell him to keep the whole affair secret for the time being."

I was astounded by the news. That same evening I invited V. I. Karpoff, a member of the Council of the Empire, and the members of the Duma Kamensky, Shubinsky, and Gutchkoff, to come to see me. We discussed far into the night the best means for proceeding with the mission entrusted to me by the Tsar. Next day I asked M. Damansky, Assistant High Procurator of the Synod, to come to the Duma and bring me the secret *dossier* on Rasputin's case. Damansky arrived. In order the better to draw him out, I decided to feign complete ignorance. This manoeuvre met with complete success. My informant divulged all I wished to know. In his endeavours to persuade me of Gregory's holiness and purity, he declared that the *starets* was honoured and respected by many highly placed persons, who enjoyed and found edification in his conversations. Damansky revealed many names and confirmed much evidence already familiar to me through other channels. He said that Rasputin lodged with the Sazonoffs, a very respectable family with whom he, Damansky, was on intimate terms; that the house was visited by M. Taneieff, Gentleman Usher to the Emperor, by the wife of General Orloff, Countess Witte,[3] "such a universally respected man" as Bishop Barnabas, and many others. I expressed my astonishment at all this, and nodded in assent.

All this time Damansky kept a firm hold on the file of documents in his hands, and kept repeatedly assuring me that the case was in itself too trivial to be worth looking into. While dwelling on the virtues of the *starets,* Damansky professed profound indignation at the gossip and calumny of which he was the subject. "He is accused of being a *khlyst* and a libertine. Some people go so far as to allege an intimacy between him and the Empress Alexandra Feodorovna . . . "

Here I dropped the mask, struck the table with my fist, drew myself up to my full height,[4] and looking as ferocious as I could, shouted at the top of my voice so as to be heard in the adjoining room:

"Are you mad, sir? How dare you utter such abominations in my presence? You forget of whom and to whom you are speaking! I refuse to listen to you any further."

My outburst was so unexpected that he turned pale, cowered, and hastened to excuse himself. The object of his mean behaviour was obvious. He imagined me to be his dupe, and hoped to lead me on to talk scandal with the intention of reporting it in certain quarters afterwards. He expected to convince me by his explanations, and prevent my claiming the documents. He was, therefore, completely taken aback when I wrenched the file from his grasp, locked it up in my desk and, placing the key in my pocket, declared: "By order of his Majesty the Emperor, I shall examine these documents, and inform you later of the results."

Having obtained possession of these important documents, I at once ordered the clerical staff of the Duma and the sworn-in lady typists to make complete copies of them. With the aid of J. V. Glinka, the head of the Duma clerks' office, I myself proceeded to draft a plan of procedure for the task in hand—

a task demanding great circumspection in view of the extremely delicate nature of the case.

The very next day Damansky telephoned asking for a private interview at my flat. Suspecting a trap, I replied that I did not give private interviews on matters of State; I therefore requested his presence in my room at the Duma at three o'clock that afternoon, and to avoid any further explanations I immediately hung up the receiver.

On my arrival at the Duma I found Damansky waiting for me. To my astonishment he was accompanied by the Archpriest Alexander Vasilieff, the religious teacher of the Imperial children. The reverend father's presence at the Duma was rather surprising. I at once realized that some plan for putting pressure on me was afoot, and decided to separate them. They were, therefore, shown into different rooms.

First I tackled Damansky. He explained that he was entrusted with a mission to reclaim from me the file containing the documents on Rasputin. I expressed surprise at this request, and replied that the documents had been placed in my keeping by the Emperor's orders, and that their surrender could only be claimed by a similar act, that is, by an Imperial order transmitted either verbally through an adjutant-general or a Secretary of State, or by written decree. At this juncture, looking somewhat perturbed and agitated, and lowering his voice, Damansky explained that though he did not bear an order from the Emperor, the demand came from a very exalted person.

"Who was it?" I asked. "Sabler?"

Damansky made a deprecating gesture.

"No, someone much more highly placed," he replied.

"Who was it, then?" I repeated, putting on an expression of astonishment.

"The Empress Alexandra Feodorovna."

"If that is the case, will you kindly inform her Majesty that she is as much a subject of her August Consort as myself, and that it is the duty of us both to obey his commands. I am, therefore, not in a position to comply with her wishes."

"What!" exclaimed Damansky, "must I really tell her that? But it is her desire."

"I am very sorry," I replied, "but nevertheless I am unable to accede to it." And to prevent further insistence on Damansky's part, I ended the interview.

I then passed on to Father Vasilieff. He was instructed by the Empress Alexandra Feodorovna, he said, to communicate to me his opinion on the *starets*.

"He really is a God-fearing and pious man, absolutely harmless and even rather useful to the Imperial Family," said Father Vasilieff.

"What part does he play in the intimate life of the Imperial Family, particularly in relation to the children?"

"He has talks with them about God and about religion . . . "

At these words I flew into a passion.

"You dare tell me that! You, an orthodox priest and the religious teacher of the Tsar's children! You tolerate that a stupid, ignorant *mouzhik* should speak to them on matters of faith; you tolerate his pernicious hypnotic influence on their pure childish souls? You are a witness to the part played by this sectarian *khlyst* in the family life of the Tsar, and yet you keep silent. By countenancing this man's criminal activities you betray your holy office and your oath of allegiance. You know everything that is going on, and yet out of cowardice and servility you prefer to hold your tongue when, as a servant of the Church of God, your duty bids you to raise your voice in defence of our faith. By your criminal connivance you, too, become a sectarian and a participator in the devilish conspiracy engineered by the enemies of Russia and of the Tsar, who aim at defiling the Throne and the Orthodox Church."

The unfortunate priest, completely taken aback by my vehemence, grew pale and murmured tremulously:

"No one has ever spoken to me like this before. You have opened my eyes. Tell me what I am to do."

"Go and tell the Empress from me, that if she does not want to see the ruin of her husband and son and the collapse of the Throne, she must dismiss this obscene *khlyst* from her presence for ever. The position is serious. No revolutionary propaganda could inflict greater injury on the Monarchy nor degrade the prestige of the Imperial House as does Rasputin's presence at the Palace. If you continue to be silent and fail to disclose the truth—then the cross you wear upon your breast will brand your very heart and soul."

He told Prince Volkonsky afterwards: "When I left the President I was trembling all over, and fully realized the force and truth of his arguments."

Father Vasilieff, however, as I was subsequently informed, gave a completely distorted account of our interview to the Empress, thereby merely strengthening the disfavour in which she already held me. He continued to encourage her infatuation for Rasputin, and persevered in his ambiguous behaviour.

From Gutchkoff I learnt that my prolonged interview with the Tsar had seriously agitated all Rasputin's followers, and that they had decided to recall him to St. Petersburg.

Princess Z. N. Yusupoff informed us by telephone that the Empress was so distressed by Rasputin's dismissal that she took to her bed. It is interesting to recall that after the questions on Rasputin in the Duma, the Empress wrote a despairing letter of eight pages to Princess Yusupoff complaining of the unjust attacks and calumnies of which they were the object. "No one loves us," wrote the Empress; "everyone is trying to do us harm. This interpellation was a revolutionary act."

The Empress's complaints of their tragic position were so bitter that Princess Yusupoff felt sorry for her and sent a telephone message that she would come to see her next day. Owing, however, in all probability to some intrigue on the part of Mme. Vyrubova, Princess Yusupoff was informed that the Empress was indisposed and unable to receive her.

It was not till March 9, 1912, that Princess Yusupoff was admitted to see the Empress. Her visit took place after Gutchkoff's speech in the Duma on the Synod estimates, in which he made a further allusion to Rasputin. Princess Yusupoff spoke very gravely on the subject and tried to impress the Empress with the same arguments I had submitted to the Tsar, but in vain. The Empress remained obdurate, working herself into a state of great indignation and excitement. She expressed her displeasure at the tenor of my report to the Tsar, and was particularly angry at my refusal to return the Rasputin documents.

"What right had he to keep them and refuse their surrender?" the Empress repeated.

Princess Yusupoff tried to persuade her to believe the word of the President of the Duma.

"He is an honest and truthful man," she said.

"No, no! You don't know what he told Father Vasilieff! Hanging is too good for men like Rodzianko and Gutchkoff!"

"How can you say such things?" the Princess exclaimed indignantly. "You ought to thank God for sending you honest men who speak the truth to the Tsar. Rasputin must be turned out. He is a *khlyst* who abuses your confidence."

"No, no, that is a calumny. He is a holy man."

A thorough examination of the documents produced by Damansky revealed the history of Rasputin in all its sordid reality.

The first time that Rasputin was arraigned as a *khlyst* was as far back as 1902, when, on the strength of an official intimation from the parish priest of Pokrovskoe, the head of the district police denounced him to the Governor of Tobolsk. The Governor handed over the case to the local bishop, Mgr. Anthony, who ordered one of the diocesan missionaries to carry out a detailed investigation. The latter, being an energetic man, made a domiciliary search in Rasputin's house, carried off various material proofs, and brought to light numerous obscure facts, all tending to prove irrefutably Rasputin's adherence to the *khlysty* sect. A detailed report on the case, supported by important circumstantial evidence, was presented to the bishop. Some of the details mentioned in the report were of so obscene and revolting a nature, that it was impossible to read them without a feeling of repulsion.

On receiving the report, Mgr. Anthony handed it over for study to an expert on sectarianism, a M. Berezkin, inspector of the Theological Seminary at Tobolsk. The affair dragged on indefinitely. Rasputin, meanwhile, had made his way to St. Petersburg, where, as I have previously described, he gradually wormed himself into the confidence of highly placed persons and was introduced at the Palace.

A survey of the very thorough and conscientious investigation carried out by Berezkin, confirmed, moreover, by the evidence of numerous witnesses, letters and references to the teachings of the *khlysty,* revealed beyond the shadow of a doubt Rasputin's adherence to that disgusting sect. He was, moreover, a *khlyst* of a superior order, a clever propagandist, and a pernicious corrupter of souls of simpleminded Orthodox folk. The evidence in hand established beyond doubt his connection with many of the *khlysty "prophets,"* among whom he occupied a more or less important position.

In his report to the Bishop of Tobolsk, M. Berezkin declared that he had no doubt whatever that Rasputin belonged to the *khlysty,* and recommended that the whole case should be referred to the civil authorities in order that Rasputin might be prosecuted. Before doing so, however, M. Berezkin advised the Bishop to collect certain additional evidence on the case. Acting on the strength of this report, Bishop Anthony ordered the consistory of Tobolsk to carry out M. Berezkin's injunctions and hand over the case of Gregory Efimoff Rasputin to the judicial authorities.

While this inter-departmental procedure was going on, Rasputin returned from St. Petersburg to his native village. He brought with him considerable sums of money and proceeded to build himself a large, well-furnished house. He openly boasted of favors received from members of the Imperial Family, and exhibited to everyone the presents they had given him—for instance, a richly ornamented gold cross on a golden chain, a medallion containing a portrait of the Empress Alexandra Feodorovna, and photographs of exalted personages with appropriate inscriptions. He flaunted about in expensive sable-lined coats. In a word, the prosecuted sectarian was transformed into an influential personage, whose patronage was already beginning to be sought by many.

After Bishop Anthony's resolution recommending Rasputin's prosecution, the affair was brought to an end by an *ukase* of the Holy Synod appointing, by Imperial warrant, Bishop Anthony of Tobolsk to the archbishopric of Tver and Kashin, that is, the removal of Mgr. Anthony from his former diocese. As I learnt afterwards from competent sources, to avoid a public scandal over the Rasputin case, Bishop Anthony was given the choice of two alternatives: either to withdraw his charge against Rasputin and receive promotion to the see of Tver, or to retire to a monastery. He chose the former, and Rasputin's prosecution was suppressed.

Having completed a thorough and all-round examination of the documents submitted to my investigation, I drew up a comprehensive and concise summary of the case, and on March 8, 1912, presented a request for an audience with the Emperor for the purpose of reporting on the result of the mission entrusted by me by his Majesty.

For a long time my petition remained unanswered. The Empress Alexandra Feodorovna, I learned, was absolutely opposed to my having a second interview with the Emperor, particularly as I should confront him with official and incriminating evidence against Rasputin. . . .

In the meantime Rasputin again made his appearance at St. Petersburg and, according to the papers, received a great welcome from his admirers assembled at the flat of Mme. Golovina. This time he was closely tracked both by the police and by pressmen. Rasputin was brought by his friends to Tsarskoe Selo, but their attempts to gain him admittance to the Empress suffered a defeat.

In the sixth week of Lent the Imperial Family left for the Crimea. Mme. Vyrubova succeeded in smuggling Rasputin on the suite's train, where he was concealed in Prince Tumanoff's compartment. Someone informed the Emperor, who was exceedingly angry at such flagrant disobedience to his command and ordered the train to be stopped at Tosno. Rasputin was removed from the train and, under surveillance of a secret service official, conveyed to the province of Tobolsk.

My words had struck home. After that Rasputin ceased for some time to appear at Court. Now and again he returned to St. Petersburg, never daring to remain for more than two or three days. The chief of the police department used to complain to me: "I am utterly sick of him. He has to be watched. Directly he arrives, off he goes, straight from the station to the baths, with two ladies."

The Empress, I feel sure, never forgave me for my interference. No news reached me concerning the fate of my report; I received neither reply nor reproof. Had the Tsar read it? I did not know. A rumour was current that he read it in the Crimea with his brother-in-law, the Duke of Hesse.

Notes

1. All dates given here are according to the Julian Calendar.
2. An illustrated weekly.
3. Wife of the ex-Prime Minister.
4. M. Rodzianko was an exceptionally tall and powerful man.

64

Durnovo's Memorandum, February 1914

In historical literature Peter N. Durnovo (1844–1915) is cursorily dismissed as either "an experienced policeman" or "a vicious reactionary." Durnovo acquired his reputation through his unswerving insistence on maintaining the *status quo,* first as an official of the Ministry of Justice (1872–1883), then as head of the Police Department of the Ministry of Interior (1884–1893), later as Deputy Minister of Interior (1900–1905), subsequently as Minister of Interior (1905–1907), and finally as a prominent member of the State Council, Russia's upper legislative chamber.

But while he was a reactionary—a fact that made him unpopular with liberals as well as revolutionaries—Durnovo was at the same time one of the most astute observers of Russia's domestic ills and her international position on the eve of World War I. This is clearly evident from the February 1914 memorandum he submitted to Nicholas II. In it, he pleaded for a thorough reappraisal of the goals of Russia's foreign policy, for abandonment of her association with France and England (which he called "an artificial combination") and, above all, that she stay out of any European war, not only because she was inadequately prepared but primarily because she would have to carry the main burden of fighting. Russia's probable defeat, Durnovo argued, would result in "hopeless anarchy, the issue of which cannot be foreseen." Because his analysis turned out to be remarkably correct, it is reproduced here in its entirety.

A Future Anglo-German War Will Become an Armed Conflict between Two Groups of Powers

The central factor of the period of world history through which we are now passing is the rivalry between England and Germany. This rivalry must inevitably lead to an armed struggle between them, the issue of which will, in all probability, prove fatal to the vanquished side. The interests of these two powers are far too incompatible, and their simultaneous existence as world powers will sooner or later prove impossible. On the one hand, there is an

---

From Frank Alfred Golder, ed. *Documents of Russian History, 1914–1917.* Translated by Emanuel Aronsberg (New York: The Century Co., 1927), pp. 3–23.

insular State, whose world importance rests upon its domination of the sea, its world trade, and its innumerable colonies. On the other, there is a powerful continental empire, whose limited territory is insufficient for an increased population. It has therefore openly and candidly declared that its future is on the seas. It has, with fabulous speed, developed an enormous world commerce, built for its protection a formidable navy, and, with its famous trademark, "Made in Germany," created a mortal danger to the industrial and economic prosperity of its rival. Naturally, England cannot yield without a fight, and between her and Germany a struggle for life or death is inevitable.

The armed conflict impending as a result of this rivalry cannot be confined to a duel between England and Germany alone. Their resources are far too unequal, and, at the same time, they are not sufficiently vulnerable to each other. Germany could provoke rebellion in India, in South Africa, and, especially, a dangerous rebellion in Ireland, and paralyze English sea trade by means of privateering and, perhaps, submarine warfare, thereby creating for Great Britain difficulties in her food supply; but, in spite of all the daring of the German military leaders, they would scarcely risk landing in England, unless a fortunate accident helped them to destroy or appreciably to weaken the English navy. As for England, she will find Germany absolutely invulnerable. All that she may achieve is to seize the German colonies, stop German sea trade, and, in the most favorable event, annihilate the German navy, but nothing more. This, however, would not force the enemy to sue for peace. There is no doubt, therefore, that England will attempt the means she has more than once used with success, and will risk armed action only after securing participation in the war, on her own side, of powers stronger in a strategical sense. But since Germany, for her own part, will not be found isolated, the future Anglo-German war will undoubtedly be transformed into an armed conflict between two groups of powers, one with a German, the other with an English orientation.

It Is Hard to Discover Any Real Advantages to Russia in Rapprochement with England

Until the Russo-Japanese War, Russian policy has neither orientation. From the time of the reign of Emperor Alexander III, Russia had a defensive alliance with France, so firm as to assure common action by both powers in the event of attack upon either, but, at the same time, not so close as to obligate either to support unfailingly, with armed force, all political actions and claims of the ally. At the same time, the Russian Court maintained the traditional friendly relations, based upon ties of blood, with the Court of Berlin. Owing precisely to this conjuncture, peace among the great powers was not disturbed in the course of a great many years, in spite of the presence of abundant combustible material in Europe. France, by her alliance with Russia, was guaranteed against attack by Germany; the latter was safe, thanks to the tried pacifism and friendship of Russia, from *revanche* ambitions on the part of France; and Russia was secured, thanks to Germany's need of maintaining amicable relations with her, against excessive intrigues by Austria-Hungary in the Balkan peninsula. Lastly, England, isolated and held in check by her rivalry with Russia in Persia, by her diplomats' traditional fear of our advance on India, and by strained relations with France, especially notable at the time of the well-known Fashoda incident, viewed with alarm the increase of Germany's naval power, without, however, risking an active step.

The Russo-Japanese War radically changed the relations among the great powers and brought England out of her isolation. As we know, all through the Russo-Japanese War, England and America observed benevolent neutrality toward Japan, while we enjoyed a similar benevolent neutrality from France and Germany. Here, it would seem, should have been the inception of the most natural political combination for us. But after the war, our diplomacy faced abruptly about and definitely entered upon the road toward rapprochement with England. France was drawn into the orbit of British policy; there was formed a group of powers of the Triple Entente, with England playing the dominant part; and a clash, sooner or later, with the powers grouping themselves around Germany became inevitable.

Now, what advantages did the renunciation of our traditional policy of distrust of England and the rupture of neighborly, if not friendly, relations with Germany promise us then and at present?

Considering with any degree of care the events which have taken place since the Treaty of Portsmouth, we find it difficult to perceive any practical advantages gained by us in rapproachement with England. The only benefit—improved relations with Japan—is scarcely a result of the Russo-English rapproachement. There is no reason why Russia and Japan should not live in peace; there seems to be nothing over which they need quarrel. All Russia's objectives in the Far East, if correctly understood, are entirely compatible with Japan's interests. These objectives, in their essentials, are very modest. The too broad sweep of the imagination of overzealous executive officials, without basis in genuine national interests, on the one hand, and the excessive nervousness and impressionability of Japan, on the other, which erroneously regarded these dreams as a consistently executed policy—these were the things that provoked a clash which a more capable diplomacy would have managed to avoid.

Russia needs neither Korea nor even Port Arthur. An outlet to the open sea is undoubtedly useful, but the sea in itself is, after all, not a market, but merely a road to a more advantageous delivery of goods at the consuming markets. As a matter of fact, we do not possess, and shall not for a long time possess any goods in the Far East that promise any considerable profits in exportation abroad. Nor are there any markets for the export of our products. We cannot expect a great supply of our export commodities to go to industrially and agriculturally developed America, to poor, but likewise industrial, Japan, or even to the maritime sections of China and remoter markets, where our exports would inevitably meet the competition of goods from the industrially stronger rival powers. There remains the interior of China, with which our trade is carried on, chiefly overland. Consequently, an open port would aid the import of foreign merchandise more than the export of our own products.

Japan, on her part, no matter what is said, has no desire for our Far Eastern possessions. The Japanese are by nature a southern people, and the harsh environment of our Far Eastern borderland cannot attract them. We know that even within Japan itself, northern Yezo is sparsely populated, while apparently Japanese colonization is making little headway even in the southern part of Sakhalin Island, ceded to Japan under the Treaty of Portsmouth. After taking possession of Korea and Formosa, Japan will hardly go farther north, and her ambitions, it may be assumed, will turn rather in the direction of the Philippine Islands, Indo-China, Java, Sumatra, and Borneo. The most she might desire would be the acquisition, for purely commercial reasons, of a few more sections of the Manchurian railway.

In a word, peaceable coexistence, nay, more, a close rapprochement, between Russia and Japan in the Far East is perfectly natural, regardless of any mediation by England. The grounds for agreement are self-evident. Japan is not a rich country, and the simultaneous upkeep of a strong army and a powerful navy is hard for her. Her insular situation drives her to strengthen her naval power, and alliance with Russia would allow her to devote all her attention to her navy, especially vital in view of her imminent rivalry with America, leaving the protection of her interests on the continent to Russia. On our part, we, having the Japanese navy to protect our Pacific coast, could give up once for all the dream, impossible to us, of creating a navy in the Far East.

Thus, so far as our relations with Japan are concerned, the rapprochement with England has yielded us no real advantage. And it has gained us nothing in the sense of strengthening our position in Manchuria, Mongolia, or even the Ulianghai territory, where the uncertainty of our position bears witness that the agreement with England has certainly not freed the hands of our diplomats. On the contrary, our attempt to establish relations with Tibet met with sharp opposition from England.

In Persia, also, our position has been no better since the conclusion of this agreement. Every one recalls our predominant influence in that country under the Shah Nasr-Eddin, that is, exactly at a time when our relations with England were most strained. From the moment of our accord with the latter, we have found ourselves drawn into a number of strange attempts to impose upon the Persian people an entirely needless constitution, with the result that we ourselves contributed to the overthrow, for the benefit of our inveterate enemies, of a monarch who was devoted to Russia. That is, not only have we gained nothing, but we have suffered a loss all along the line, ruining our prestige and wasting many millions of *rubles*, even the precious blood of Russian soldiers, who were treacherously slain and, to please England, not even avenged.

The worst results, however, of the accord with England—and of the consequent discord with Germany—have been felt in the Near East. As we know, it was Bismarck who coined that winged phrase about the Balkan problem not being worth to Germany the bones of a single Pomeranian grenadier. Later the Balkan complications began to attract much more attention from German diplomacy, which had taken the "Sick Man" under its protection, but even then Germany, for a long time, failed to show any inclination to endanger relations with Russia in the interests of Balkan affairs. The proofs are patent. During the period of the Russo-Japanese War and the ensuing turmoil in our country, it would have been very easy for Austria to realize her cherished ambitions in the Balkan peninsula. But at that time Russia had not yet linked her destinies with England, and Austria-Hungary was forced to lose an opportunity most auspicious for her purposes.

No sooner had we taken the road to closer accord with England, however, than there immediately followed the annexation of Bosnia and Herzegovina, a step which might have been taken so easily and painlessly in 1905 or 1906. Next came the Albanian question and the combination with the Prince of Wied. Russian diplomacy attempted to answer Austrian intrigue by forming a Balkan league, but this combination, as might have been expected, proved to be quite unworkable. Intended to be directed against Austria, it immediately turned on Turkey and fell apart in the process of dividing the spoils taken from the latter. The final result was merely the definite attachment of Turkey to Germany, in whom, not without good reason, she sees her sole protector. In short, the Russo-British rapproachement evidently seems to Turkey as tantamount to England's renouncing her traditional policy of closing the Dardanelles to us, while the creation of the Balkan league, under the auspices of Russia, appeared as a direct threat to the continued existence of Turkey as a European power.

To sum up, the Anglo-Russian accord has brought us nothing of practical value up to this time, while for the future, it threatens us with an inevitable armed clash with Germany.

Fundamental Alignments in the Coming War

Under what conditions will this clash occur and what will be its probable consequences? The fundamental groupings in a future war are self-evident: Russia, France, and England, on the one side, with Germany, Austria, and Turkey, on the other. It is more than likely that other powers, too, will participate in that war, depending upon circumstances as they may exist at the war's outbreak. But, whether the immediate cause for the war is furnished by another clash of conflicting interests in the Balkans, or by a colonial incident, such as that of Algeciras, the fundamental alignment will remain unchanged.

Italy, if she has any conception of her real interests, will not join the German side. For political as well as economic reasons, she undoubtedly hopes to expand her present territory. Such an expansion may be achieved only at the expense of Austria, on one hand, and Turkey, on the other. It is, therefore, natural for Italy not to join that party which would safeguard the territorial integrity of the countries at whose expense she hopes to realize her aspirations. Furthermore, it is not out of the question that Italy would join the anti-German coalition, if the scales of war should incline in its favor, in order to secure for herself the most favorable conditions in sharing the subsequent division of spoils.

In this respect, the position of Italy is similar to the probable position of Rumania, which, it may be assumed, will remain neutral until the scales of fortune favor one or another side. Then, animated by normal political self-interest, she will attach herself to the victors, to be rewarded at the expense of either Russia or Austria. Of the other Balkan States, Serbia, and Montenegro will unquestionably join the side opposing Austria, while Bulgaria and Albania (if by that time they have not yet formed at least the embryo of a State) will take their stand against the Serbian side. Greece will in all probability remain neutral or make common cause with the side opposing Turkey, but that only after the issue has been more or less determined. The participation of other powers will be incidental, and Sweden ought to be feared, of course, in the ranks of our foes.

Under such circumstances, a struggle with Germany presents to us enormous difficulties, and will require countless sacrifices. War will not find the enemy unprepared, and the degree of his preparedness will probably exceed our most exaggerated calculations. It should not be thought that this readiness is due to Germany's own desire for war. She needs no war, so long as she can attain her object—the end of exclusive domination of the seas. But, once this vital object is opposed by the coalition, Germany will not shrink from war, and, of course, will even try to provoke it, choosing the most auspicious moment.

The Main Burden of the War Will Fall on Russia

The main burden of the war will undoubtedly fall on us, since England is hardly capable of taking a considerable part in a continental war, while France, poor in man power, will probably adhere to strictly defensive tactics, in view of the enormous losses by which war will be attended under present conditions of military technique. The part of a battering-ram, making a breach in the very thick of the German defense, will be ours, with many factors against us to which we shall have to devote great effort and attention.

From the sum of these unfavorable factors we should deduct the Far East. Both America and Japan—the former fundamentally, and the latter by virtue of her present political orientation—are hostile to Germany, and there is no reason to expect them to act on the German side. Furthermore, the war, regardless of its issue, will weaken Russia and divert her attention to the West, a fact which, of course, serves both Japanese and American interests. Thus, our rear will be sufficiently secure in the Far East, and the most that can happen there will be the extortion from us of some concessions of an economic nature in return for benevolent neutrality. Indeed, it is possible that America or Japan may join the anti-German side, but, of course, merely as usurpers of one or the other of the unprotected German colonies.

There can be no doubt, however, as to an outburst of hatred for us in Persia, and a probable unrest among the Moslems of the Caucasus and Turkestan; it is possible that Afghanistan, as a result of that unrest, may act against us; and, finally, we must foresee very unpleasant complications in Poland and Finland. In the latter, a rebellion will undoubtedly break out if Sweden is found in the ranks of our enemies. As for Poland, it is not to be expected that we can hold her against our enemy during the war. And after she is in his power, he will undoubtedly endeavor to provoke an insurrection which, while not in reality very dangerous, must be considered, nevertheless, as one of the factors unfavorable to us, especially since the influence of our allies may induce us to take such measures in our relations with Poland as will prove more dangerous to us than any open revolt.

Are we prepared for so stubborn a war as the future war of the European nations will undoubtedly become? This question we must answer, without evasion, in the negative. That much has been done for our defense since the Japanese war, I am the last person to deny, but even so, it is quite inadequate considering the unprecedented scale on which a future war will inevitably be fought. The fault lies, in a considerable measure, in our young legislative institutions, which have taken a dilettante interest in our defenses, but are far from grasping the seriousness of the political situation arising from the new orientation which, with the sympathy of the public, has been followed in recent years by our Ministry of Foreign Affairs.

The enormous number of still unconsidered legislative bills of the war and navy departments may serve as proof of this: for example, the plan of the organization of our national defense proposed to the Duma as early as the days of Secretary of State Stolypin. It cannot be denied that, in the matter of military instruction, according to the reports of specialists, we have achieved substantial improvements, as compared with the time before the Japanese War. According to the same specialists, our field artillery leaves nothing to be desired; the gun is entirely satisfactory, and the equipment convenient and practical. Yet, it must be admitted that there are substantial shortcomings in the organization of our defenses.

In this regard we must note, first of all, the insufficiency of our war supplies, which, certainly, cannot be blamed upon the war department, since the supply schedules are still far from being executed, owing to the low productivity of our factories. This insufficiency of munitions is the more significant since, in the embryonic condition of our industries, we shall, during the war, have no opportunity to make up the revealed shortage by our own efforts, and the closing of the Baltic as well as the Black Sea will prevent the importation from abroad of the defense materials which we lack.

Another circumstance unfavorable to our defense is its far too great dependence, generally speaking, upon foreign industry, a fact which, in connection with the above noted interruption of more or less convenient communications with abroad, will create a series of obstacles difficult to overcome. The quantity of our heavy artillery, the importance of which was demonstrated in the Japanese War, is far too inadequate, and there are few machine guns. The organization of our fortress defenses has scarcely been started, and even the fortress of Reval, which is to defend the road to the capital, is not yet finished.

The network of strategic railways is inadequate. The railways possess a rolling stock sufficient, perhaps, for normal traffic, but not commensurate with the collossal demands which will be made upon them in the event of a European war. Lastly, it should not be forgotten that the impending war will be fought among the most civilized and technically most advanced nations. Every previous war has invariably been followed by something new in the realm of military technique, but the technical backwardness of our industries does not create favorable conditions for our adoption of the new inventions.

The Vital Interests of Germany and Russia Do Not Conflict

All these factors are hardly given proper thought by our diplomats, whose behavior toward Germany is, in some respects, even aggressive, and may unduly hasten the moment of armed conflict, a moment which, of course, is really inevitable in view of our British orientation.

The question is whether this orientation is correct, and whether even a favorable issue of the war promises us such advantages as would compensate us for all the hardships and sacrifices which must attend a war unparalleled in its probable strain.

The vital interests of Russia and Germany do not conflict. There are fundamental grounds for a peaceable existence of these two States. Germany's future lies on the sea; that is, in a realm where Russia, essentially the most continental of the great powers, has no interests whatever. We have no overseas colonies, and shall probably never have them, and communication between the various parts of our empire is easier overland than by water. No surplus population demanding territorial expansion is visible, but, even from the viewpoint of new conquests, what can we gain from a victory over Germany? Posen, or East Prussia? But why do we need these regions, densely populated as they are by Poles, when we find it difficult enough to manage our own Russian Poles? Why encourage centripetal tendencies, that have not ceased even to this day in the Vistula territory, by incorporating in the Russian State the restless Posnanian and East Prussian Poles, whose national demands even the German Government, which is more firm than the Russian, cannot stifle?

Exactly the same thing applies to Galicia. It is obviously disadvantageous to us to annex, in the interests of national sentimentalism, a territory that has lost every vital connection with our fatherland. For, together with a negligible handful of Galicians, Russian in spirit, how many Poles, Jews, and Ukrainian Uniates we would receive! The so-called Ukrainian, or Mazeppist, movement is not a menace to us at present, but we should not enable it to expand by increasing the number of turbulent Ukrainian elements, for in this movement there undoubtedly lies the seed of an extremely dangerous Little Russian separatism which, under favorable conditions, may assume quite unexpected proportions.

The obvious aim of our diplomacy in the rapprochement with England has been to open the Straits. But a war with Germany seems hardly necessary for the attainment of this object, for it was England, and not Germany at all, that closed our outlet from the Black Sea. Was it not because we made sure of the cooperation of the latter power, that we freed ourselves in 1871 from the humiliating restrictions imposed upon us by England under the Treaty of Paris?

Also, there is reason to believe that the Germans would agree sooner than the English to let us have the Straits, in which they have only a slight interest, and at the price of which they would gladly purchase our alliance.

Moreover, we should not cherish any exaggerated hopes from our occupation of the Straits. Their acquisition would be advantageous to us only as they served to close the Black Sea to others, making it an inland sea for us, safe from enemy attack.

The Straits would not give us an outlet to the open sea, however, since on the other side of them there lies a sea consisting almost wholly of territorial waters, a sea dotted with numerous islands where the British navy, for instance, would have no trouble whatever in closing to us every inlet and outlet, irrespective of the Straits. Therefore, Russia might safely welcome an arrangment which, while not turning the Straits over to our direct control, would safeguard us against a penetration of the Black Sea by an enemy fleet. Such an arrangement, attainable under favorable circumstances without any war, has the additional advantage that it would not violate the interests of the Balkan States, which would not regard our seizure of the Straits without alarm and quite natural jealousy.

In Trans-Caucasia we could, as a result of war, expand territorially only at the expense of regions inhabited by Armenians, a move which is hardly desirable in view of the revolutionary character of present Armenian sentiment, and of its dream of a greater Armenia; and in this region, Germany, were we allied to her, would certainly place even fewer obstacles in our way than England. Those territorial and economic acquisitions which might really prove useful to us are available only in places where our ambitions may meet opposition from England, but by no means from Germany. Persia, the Pamir, Kuldja, Kashgar, Dzungaria, Mongolia, the Ulianghai territory—all these are regions where the interests of Russia and Germany do not conflict, whereas the interests of Russia and England have clashed there repeatedly.

And Germany is in exactly the same situation with respect to Russia. She could seize from us, in case of a successful war, only such territories as would be of slight value to her, and because of their population, would prove of little use for colonization; the Vistula territory, with a Polish-Lithuanian population, and the Baltic provinces, with a Lettish-Estonian population, are all equally turbulent and anti-German.

Russia's Economic Advantages and Needs Do Not Conflict with Germany's

It may be argued, however, that, under modern conditions in the various nations, territorial acquisitions are of secondary importance, while economic interests take first rank. But in this field, again, Russia's advantages and needs do not conflict with Germany's as much as is believed. It is, of course, undeniable that the existing Russo-German trade agreements are disadvantageous to our agriculture and advantageous to Germany's, but it would be hardly fair to ascribe this circumstance to the treachery and unfriendliness of Germany.

It should not be forgotten that these agreements are in many of their sections advantageous to us. The Russian delegates who concluded these agreements were confirmed protagonists of a development of Russian industry at any cost, and they undoubtedly made a deliberate sacrifice, at least to some extent, of the interests of Russian agriculture to the interests of Russian industry. Furthermore, we ought not to forget that Germany is far from being the direct consumer of the greater share of our agricultural exports abroad. For the greater share of our agricultural produce, Germany acts merely as middleman, and so it is for us and the consuming markets to establish direct relations and thus avoid the expensive German mediation. Lastly, we should keep in mind that the commercial relations of States depend on their political understandings, for no country finds advantage in the economic weakening of an ally but, conversely, profits by the ruin of a political foe. In short, even though it be obvious that the existing Russo-German commercial treaties are not to our advantage, and that Germany in concluding them, availed herself of a situation that happened to be in her favor—in other words, forced us to the wall—this action should have been expected from Germany and thought of. It should not, however, be looked upon as a mark of hostility toward us, but rather as an expression of healthy national self-interest, worthy of our emulation. Aside from that, we observe, in the case of Austria-Hungary, an agricultural country that is in a far greater economic dependence upon Germany than ours, but nevertheless, is not prevented from attaining an agricultural development such as we may only dream of.

In view of what has been said, it would seem that the conclusion of a commercial treaty with Germany, entirely acceptable to Russia, by no means requires that Germany first be crushed. It will be quite sufficient to maintain neighborly relations with her, to make a careful estimate of our real interests in the various branches of national economy, and to engage in long, insistent bargaining with German delegates, who may be expected to protect the interests of their own fatherland and not ours.

But I would go still further and say that the ruin of Germany, from the viewpoint of our trade with her, would be disadvantageous to us. Her defeat would unquestionably end in a peace dictated from the viewpoint of England's economic interests. The latter will exploit to the farthest limit any success that falls to her lot, and we will only lose, in a ruined Germany without sea routes, a market which, after all, is valuable to us for our otherwise unmarketable products.

In respect to Germany's economic future, the interests of Russia and England are diametrically opposed. For England, it is profitable to kill Germany's maritime trade and industry, turning her into a poor and, if possible, agricultural country. For us, it is of advantage for Germany to develop her seagoing commerce and the industry which serves it, so as to supply the remotest world markets, and at the same time open her domestic market to our agricultural products, to supply her large working population.

But, aside from the commercial treaties, it has been customary to point out the oppressive character of German domination in Russian economic life, and the systematic penetration of German colonization into our country, as representing a manifest peril to the Russian State. We believe, however, that fears on these grounds are considerably exaggerated. The famous "Drang nach Osten" was in its own time natural and understandable, since Germany's land could not accommodate her increased population, and the surplus was driven in the direction of the least resistance; that is, into a less densely populated neighboring country. The German Government was compelled to recognize the inevitability of this movement, but could hardly look upon it as to its own interests. For, after all, it was Germans who were being lost to the influence of the German State, thus reducing the man power of their own country. Indeed, the German Government made such strenuous efforts to preserve the connection between its emigrants and their old fatherland that it adopted even the unusual method of tolerating dual citizenship. It is certain, however, that a considerable proportion of German emigrants definitely and irrevocably settled in their new homes, and slowly broke their ties with the old country. This fact, obviously incompatible with Germany's State interests, seems to have been one of the incentives which started her upon a colonial policy and maritime commerce, previously so alien to her. And at present, as the German colonies increase and there is an attendant growth of German industry and naval commerce, the German colonization movement decreases, in a measure, and the day is not remote when the "Drang nach Osten" will become nothing more than a subject for history.

In any case, the German colonization, which undoubtedly conflicts with our State interests, must be stopped, and here, again, friendly relations with Germany cannot harm us. To express a preference for a German orientation does not imply the advocacy of Russian vassalage to Germany, and, while maintaining friendly and neighborly intercourse with her, we must not sacrifice our State interests to this object. But Germany herself will not object to measures against the continued flow of German colonists into Russia. To her, it is of greater benefit to turn the wave of emigration toward her own colonies.

Moreover, even before Germany had colonies, when her industry was not yet sufficiently developed to employ the entire population, the German Government did not feel justified in protesting against the restrictive measures that were adopted against foreign colonization during the reign of Alexander III.

As regards the German domination in the field of our economic life, this phenomenon hardly justifies the complaints usually voiced against it. Russia is far too poor, both in capital and in industrial enterprise, to get along without a large import of foreign capital. A certain amount of dependence upon some kind of foreign capital is, therefore, unavoidable, until such time as the industrial enterprise and material resources of our population develop to a point where we may entirely forego the services of foreign investors and their money. But as long as we do require them, German capital is more advantageous to us than any other.

First and foremost, this capital is cheaper than any other, being satisfied with the lowest margin of profit. This, to a large extent, explains the relative cheapness of German products, and their gradual displacement of British products in the markets of the world. The lower demands of German capital, as regards returns, have for their consequence Germany's readiness to invest in enterprises which, because of their relatively small returns, are shunned by other foreign investors. Also, as a result of that relative cheapness of German capital, its influx into Russia is attended by a smaller outflow of investors' profits from Russia, as compared with French and English investments, and so a larger amount of rubles remain in Russia. Moreover, a considerable proportion of the profits made on German investments in Russian industry do not leave our country at all, but are spent in Russia.

Unlike the English or French, the German capitalists, in most cases, come to stay in Russia, themselves, with their money. It is this very German characteristic which explains in a considerable degree the amazing number of German industrialists, manufacturers, and mill owners in our midst, as compared with the British and French.

The latter live in their own countries, removing from Russia the profits produced by their enterprises, down to the last *kopek*. The German investors, on the contrary, live in Russia for long periods, and not infrequently settle down permanently. Whatever may be said to the contrary, the fact is that the Germans, unlike other foreigners, soon feel at home in Russia and rapidly become Russianized. Who has not seen Frenchmen and Englishmen, for example, who have spent almost their whole lives in Russia and yet do not speak a word of Russian? On the other hand, are there many Germans here who cannot make themselves understood in Russian, even though it be with a strong accent and in broken speech? Nay, more—who has not seen genuine Russians, orthodox, loyal with all their hearts dedicated to the principles of the Russian State, and yet only one or two generations removed from their German emigrant ancestry? Lastly, we must not forget that Germany herself is, to a certain extent, interested in our economic well-being. In this regard, Germany differs, to our advantage, from other countries, which are interested exclusively in obtaining the largest possible returns from capital invested in Russia, even at the cost of the economic ruin of this country. Germany however, in her capacity of permanent—although, of course, not unselfish—middleman for our foreign trade, has an interest in preserving the productive resources of our country, as a source of profitable intermediary operations for her.

Even a Victory over Germany Promises Russia an Exceedingly Unfavorable Prospect

In any case, even if we were to admit the necessity for eradicating German domination in the field of our economic life, even at the price of a total banishment of German capital from Russian industry, appropriate measures could be taken, it would seem, without war against Germany. Such a war will demand such enormous expenditures that they will many times exceed the more than doubtful advantages to us in the abolition of the German [economic] domination. More than that, the result of such a war will be an economic situation compared with which the yoke of German capital will seem easy.

For there can be no doubt that the war will necessitate expenditures which are beyond Russia's limited financial means. We shall have to obtain credit from allied and neutral countries, but this will not be granted gratuitously. As to what will happen if the war should end disastrously for us, I do not wish to discuss now. The financial and economic consequences of defeat can be neither calculated nor foreseen, and will undoubtedly spell the total ruin of our entire national economy.

But even victory promises us extremely unfavorable financial prospects; a totally ruined Germany will not be in a position to compensate us for the cost involved. Dictated in the interest of England, the peace treaty will not afford Germany opportunity for sufficient economic recuperation to cover our war expenditures, even at a distant time. The little which we may perhaps succeed in extorting from her will have to be shared with our allies, and to our share ther will fall but negligible crumbs, compared with the war cost. Meantime, we shall have to pay our war loans, not without pressure by the allies. For, after the destruction of German power, we shall no longer be necessary to them. Nay, more, our political might, enhanced by our victory, will induce them to weaken us, at least economically. And so it is inevitable that, even after a victorious conclusion of the war, we shall fall into the same sort of financial and economic dependence upon our creditors, compared with which our present dependence upon German capital will seem ideal.

However, no matter how sad may be the economic prospects which face us as a result of union with England, and, by that token, of war with Germany, they are still of secondary importance when we think of the political consequences of this fundamentally unnatural alliance.

A Struggle Between Russia and Germany Is Profoundly Undesirable to Both Sides, as It Amounts to a Weakening of the Monarchist Principle

It should not be forgotten that Russia and Germany are the representatives of the conservative principle in the civilized world, as opposed to the democratic principle, incarnated in England and, to an infinitely lesser degree, in France. Strange as it may seem, England, monarchistic and conservative to the marrow at home, has in her foreign relations always acted as the protector of the most demagogical tendencies, invariably encouraging all popular movements aiming at the weakening of the monarchical principle.

From this point of view, a struggle between Germany and Russia, regardless of its issue, is profoundly undesirable to both sides, as undoubtedly involving the weakening of the conservative principle in the world of which the abovenamed two great powers are the only reliable bulwarks. More than that, one must realize that under the exceptional conditions which exist, a general European war is mortally dangerous both for Russia and Germany, no matter who wins. It is our firm conviction, based upon a long and careful study of all contemporary subversive tendencies, that there must inevitably break out in the defeated country a social revolution which, by the very nature of things, will spread to the country of the victor.

During the many years of peaceable neighborly existence, the two countries have become united by many ties, and a social upheaval in one is bound to affect the other. That these troubles will be of a social, and not a political, nature cannot be doubted, and this will hold true, not only as regards Russia, but for Germany as well. An especially favorable soil for social upheavals is found in Russia, where the masses undoubtedly profess, unconsciously, the principles of Socialism. In spite of the spirit of antagonism to the Government in Russian society, as unconscious as the Socialism of the broad masses of the people, a political revolution is not possible in Russia, and any revolutionary movement inevitably must degenerate into a Socialist movement. The opponents of the government have no popular support. The people see no difference between a government offical and an intellectual. The Russian masses, whether workmen or peasants, are not looking for political rights, which they neither want nor comprehend.

The peasant dreams of obtaining a gratuitous share of somebody else's land; the workman, of getting hold of the entire capital and profits of the manufacturer. Beyond this, they have no aspirations. If these slogans are scattered far and wide among the populace, and the Government permits agitation along these lines, Russia will be flung into anarchy, such as she suffered in the ever-memorable period of troubles in 1905–1906. War with Germany would create exceptionally favorable conditions for such agitation. As already stated, this war is pregnant with enormous difficulties for us, and cannot turn out to be a mere triumphal march to Berlin. Both military disasters—partial ones, let us hope—and all kinds of shortcomings in our supply are inevitable. In the excessive nervousness and spirit of opposition of our society, these events will be given an exaggerated importance, and all the blame will be laid on the Government.

It will be well if the Government does not yield, but declares directly that in time of war no criticism of the governmental authority is to be tolerated, and resolutely suppresses all opposition. In the absence of any really strong hold on the people by the opposition, this would settle the affair. The people did not heed the writers of the Wiborg Manifesto, in its time, and they will not follow them now.

But a worse thing may happen: the government authority may make concessions, may try to come to an agreement with the opposition, and thereby weaken itself just when the Socialist elements are ready for action. Even though it may sound like a paradox, the fact is that agreement with the opposition in Russia positively weakens the Government. The trouble is that our opposition refuses to reckon with the fact that it represents no real force. The Russian opposition is intellectual throughout, and this is its weakness, because between the intelligentsia and the people there is a profound gulf of mutual misunderstanding and distrust. We need an artificial election law, indeed, we require the direct influence of the governmental authority, to assure the election to the State Duma of even the most zealous champions of popular rights. Let the Government refuse to support the elections, leaving them to their natural course, and the legislative institutions would not see within their walls a single intellectual, outside of a few demagogic agitators. However insistent the members of our legislative institutions may be that the people confide in them, the peasant would rather believe the landless government official than the Octobrist landlord in the Duma, while the workingman treats the wage-earning factory inspector with more confidence than the legislating manufacturer, even though the latter professes every principle of the Cadet party.

It is more than strange, under these circumstances, that the governmental authority should be asked to reckon seriously with the opposition, that it should for this purpose renounce the role of impartial regulator of social relationships, and come out before the broad masses of the people as the obedient organ of the class aspirations of the intellectual and propertied minority of the population. The opposition demands that the Government should be responsible to it, representative of a class, and should obey the parliament which it artificially created. (Let us recall that famous expression of V. Nabokov: "Let the executive power submit to the legislative power!") In other words, the opposition demands that the Government should adopt the psychology of a savage, and worship the idol which he himself made.

Russia Will be Flung into Hopeless Anarchy, the Issue of Which Will be Hard to Foresee

If the war ends in victory, the putting down of the Socialist movement will not offer any insurmountable obstacles. There will be agrarian troubles, as a result of agitation for compensating the soldiers with additional land allotments; there will be labor troubles during the transition from the probably increased wages of war time to normal schedules; and this, it is to be hoped, will be all, so long as the wave of the German social revolution has not reached us. But in the event of defeat, the possibility of which in a struggle with a foe like Germany cannot be overlooked, social revolution in its most extreme form is inevitable.

As has already been said, the trouble will start with the blaming of the Government for all disasters. In the legislative institutions a bitter campaign against the Government will begin, followed by revolutionary agitations throughout the country, with Socialist slogans, capable of arousing and rallying the masses, beginning with the division of the land and succeeded by a division of all valuables and property. The defeated army, having lost its most dependable men, and carried away by the tide of primitive peasant desire for land, will find itself too demoralized to serve as a bulwark of law and order. The legislative institutions and the intellectual opposition parties, lacking real authority in the eyes of the people, will be powerless to stem the popular tide, aroused by themselves, and Russia will be flung into hopeless anarchy, the issue of which cannot be foreseen.

Germany, in Case of Defeat, is Destined to Suffer Social Upheavals No Less than those of Russia

No matter how strange it may appear at first sight, considering the extraordinary poise of the German character, Germany, likewise, is destined to suffer, in case of defeat, no lesser social upheavals. The effect of a disastrous war upon the population will be too severe not to bring to the surface destructive tendencies, now deeply hidden. The peculiar social order of modern Germany rests upon the actually predominant influence of the agrarians, Prussian Junkerdom, and propertied peasants.

These elements are the bulwark of the profoundly conservative German regime, headed by Prussia. The vital interests of these classes demand a protective economic policy towards agriculture, import duties on grain, and consequently, high prices for all farm products. But Germany, with her limited territory and increasing population, has long ago turned from an agricultural into an industrial State, so that protection of agriculture is, in effect, a matter of taxing the larger part of the population for the benefit of the smaller. To this majority, there is a compensation in the extensive development of the export of German industrial products to the most distant markets, so that the advantages derived thereby enable the industrialists and working people to pay the higher prices for the farm products consumed at home.

Defeated, Germany will lose her world markets and maritime commerce, for the aim of the war—on the part of its real instigator, England—will be the destruction of German competition. After this has been achieved, the laboring masses, deprived not only of higher but of any and all wages, having suffered greatly during the war, and being, naturally, embittered, will offer fertile soil for anti-agrarian and later anti-social propaganda by the Socialist parties.

These parties, in turn, making use of the outraged patriotic sentiment among the people, owing to the loss of the war, their exasperation at the militarists and the feudal burgher regime that betrayed them, will abandon the road of peaceable evolution which they have thus far been following so steadily, and take a purely revolutionary path. Some part will also be played, especially in the event of agrarian troubles in neighboring Russia, by the class of landless farmhands, which is quite numerous in Germany. Apart from this, there will be a revival of the hitherto concealed separatist tendencies in southern Germany, and the hidden antagonism of Bavaria to domination by Prussia will emerge in all its intensity. In short, a situation will be created which (in gravity) will be little better than that in Russia.

Peace Among the Civilized Nations is Imperiled Chiefly by the Desire of England to Retain Her Vanishing Domination of the Seas

A summary of all that has been stated above must lead to the conclusion that a rapprochement with England does not promise us any benefits, and that the English orientation of our diplomacy is essentially wrong. We do not travel the same road as England; she should be left to go her own way, and we must not quarrel on her account with Germany.

The Triple Entente is an artificial combination, without a basis of real interest. It has nothing to look forward to. The future belongs to a close and incomparably more vital rapprochement of Russia, Germany, France (reconciled with Germany), and Japan (allied to Russia by a strictly defensive union). A political combination like this, lacking all aggressiveness toward other States, would safeguard for many years the peace of the civilized nations, threatened, not by the militant intentions of Germany, as English diplomacy is trying to show, but solely by the perfectly natural striving of England to retain at all costs her vanishing domination of the seas. In this direction, and not in the fruitless search of a basis for an accord with England, which is in its very nature contrary to our national plans and aims, should all the efforts of our diplomacy be concentrated.

It goes without saying that Germany, on her part, must meet our desire to restore our well-tested relations and friendly alliance with her, and to elaborate, in closest agreement with us, such terms of our neighborly existence as to afford no basis for anti-German agitation on the part of our constitutional-liberal parties, which, by their very nature, are forced to adhere, not to a Conservative German, but to a liberal English orientation.

February, 1914 P. N. Durnovo

65

Imperial Russia in World War I, 1914–1917

Imperial Russia entered World War I unprepared—militarily, economically, and psychologically. This soon became apparent at all levels of activity, as a few simple facts can illustrate. On the eve of the war, for example, Russia's regular armed forces numbered 1,423,000 men. By December 1914, mobilization had increased that figure to 6,553,00. At

---

Source: *Riech*, No. 193, August 4, 1914, as reproduced in Frank Alfred Golder, *Documents of Russian History, 1914–1917* (New York: The Century Company, 1927), pp. 29–30.

that time the country had only 4,652,000 available rifles. These shortages reflected themselves in the great reverses on the battlefield as well as in the development of chaos on the home front. The scope of that chaos is best illustrated by the fact that between July 1914 and March 1917, Russia had four prime ministers; four ministers of war; three ministers of foreign affairs; four ministers of justice; four ministers of agriculture; and six ministers of internal affairs!

These constant changes produced instability, frustration, alienation, and loss of confidence in the government and in the throne itself. The authorities deepened the crisis by intensifying the presecution of their critics for alleged unpatriotism and treason and by encouraging mass outbursts of "antiforeign" hysteria. They also turned down all constructive suggestions aimed at solving complex and pressing problems. By their obstructionism they pushed Imperial Russia to the brink of revolution.

Nicholas II's Manifesto on the Declaration of War, August 2, 1914

By the Grace of God, We, Nicholas II, Emperor and Autocrat of all Russia, Tsar of Poland, Grand Duke of Finland, and so forth, and so forth, and so forth, proclaim to all Our loyal subjects:

Following her historical traditions, Russia, united in faith and blood with the Slav nations, has never regarded their fate with indifference. The unanimous fraternal sentiments of the Russian people for the Slavs have been aroused to special intensity in the past few days, when Austria-Hungary presented to Serbia demands which she foresaw would be unacceptable to a Sovereign State.

Having disregarded the conciliatory and peaceable reply of the Serbian Government, and having declined Russia's well-intentioned mediation, Austria hastened to launch an armed attack in a bombardment of unprotected Belgrad.

Compelled, by the force of circumstances thus created, to adopt the necessary measures of precaution, We commanded that the army and the navy be put on a war footing, but, at the same time, holding the blood and the treasure of Our subjects dear, We made every effort to obtain a peaceable issue of the negotiations that had been started.

In the midst of friendly communications, Austria's ally, Germany, contrary to our trust in century-old relations of neighborliness, and paying no heed to Our assurances that the measures We had adopted implied no hostile aims whatever, insisted upon their immediate abandonment, and, meeting with a rejection of this demand, suddenly declared war on Russia.

We have now to intercede not only for a related country, unjustly attacked, but also to safeguard the honor, dignity, and integrity of Russia, and her position among the Great Powers. We firmly believe that all Our loyal subjects will rally self-sacrificingly and with one accord to the defense of the Russian soil.

At this hour of threatening danger, let domestic strife be forgotten. Let the union between the Tsar and His people be stronger than ever, and let Russia, rising like one man, repel the insolent assault of the enemy.

With a profound faith in the justice of Our cause, and trusting humbly in Almighty Providence, We invoke prayerfully the Divine blessing for Holy Russia and our valiant troops.

Given at St. Petersburg, on the second day of August, in the year of Our Lord one thousand nine hundred and fourteen, and the twentieth year of Our reign.

NICHOLAS.

M. V. Rodzianko's Statement at Nicholas II's Reception of Duma Deputies, August 7, 1914

YOUR IMPERIAL MAJESTY!

All Russia has heard with great pride and deep enthusiasm the words of the Russian Tsar, summoning his people to join him in a perfect union at this difficult hour of sore trials which has come upon our country.

Sire! Russia knows that your thoughts and desires have always been to bring about conditions which would make it possible for the nation to live and work in peace, and that your loving heart strove for a stable peace in order to protect the lives of your subjects that are dear to you.

But the terrible hour has struck. All of us, young and old, have seized the significance and profundity of the historical events which have unfolded themselves. A threat has been made against the prosperity and integrity of the State; national honor has been offended; and national honor is dearer to us than life. It is time to show the world how terrible the Russian people, who surrounds their crowned leader with a firm faith in Divine Providence, like an impenetrable wall, can be to the enemy.

Sire! The time has come for a stubborn fight to protect our national dignity, a fight for the integrity and inviolability of the Russian land. There is neither doubt nor hesitation among us. Summoned to participate in the life of the State, at Your Majesty's will, the people's representatives now stand before

Source: *Reich,* August 8, 1914, as repruduced in Frank Alfred Golder, *Documents of Russian History, 1914–1917* (New York: The Century Company, 1927), pp. 31–32.

you. The State Duma, reflecting the unanimous impulse of every section of Russia, and joined together in the single thought which unifies us all, has charged me to say to you, Sire, that your people are ready to fight for the honor and glory of the fatherland.

Without differences of opinions, views, or convictions, the State Duma, speaking in the name of the Russian country, is calmly and firmly saying to its Tsar: "Dare, Sire! The Russian people are with you and, trusting firmly in Divine mercy, will stop at no sacrifice until the enemy is crushed, and the dignity of our native land secured."

An Appeal to Poles by Grand Duke Nikolai Mikhailovich, Russia's Supreme Commander-in-Chief, August 14, 1914

POLES!

The hour has struck for the cherished dreams of your fathers and forefathers to be realized.

A century-and-a-half ago the living body of Poland was torn into parts, but her soul did not die. She lived in the hope that the hour of the resurrection of the Polish nation, of its fraternal reconciliation with Great Russia, would arrive.

The Russian armies are bringing you the glad message of this reconciliation.

Let the boundary lines which have cut the Polish nation asunder be obliterated. Let the Poles be reunited under the scepter of the Russian Tsar.

Under that scepter Poland will be reborn, free in her faith, language, and self-government.

There is only one thing that Russia expects of you—an equal regard for the rights of those nationalities with which history has linked you.

With an open heart, with an extended, brotherly hand, Great Russia greets you. She trusts that the sword that beat the foe at Grunewald has not rusted.

From the shores of the Pacific to the seas of the North, the Russian hosts are on the march.

The dawn of a new life is breaking for you.

Let there shine forth in this dawn the sign of the Cross, the symbol of the Passion and resurrection of nations.

The Supreme Commander-in-Chief,
General-Adjutant NICHOLAS

Source: *Riech,* August 15, 1914, as reproduced in Frank Alfred Golder, *Documents of Russian History, 1914–1917* (New York: The Century Company, 1927), pp. 37–38.

A Decree Authorizing the Russification Policy for Finland, November 1914

His Imperial Majesty has sanctioned a program of measures of law concerning Finland which was elaborated by a commission specially named by His Imperial Majesty. The commission wishes to point out that the present program has in view two principal groups of measures:

(1) Appropriate measures for reinforcing the authority of the Imperial Government in Finland, to assure the proper execution of the laws and the maintenance of order in Finland;

(2) Measures tending to establish a stricter policy and economic union between Finland and the rest of the Empire.

In the first group the following measures are enumerated:

1. The revision of the laws concerning the disciplinary responsibility of the authorities in Finland;

2. The transfer to the tribunals of the Empire of all cases relative to offenses committed by civil functionaries in their service;

3. The revision of the law at present in force in Finland, relative to civil officials and, particularly, the restriction of the irremovability of Finnish civil servants and the modification of the formula of the oath taken by them, as well as the restriction of their right to belong to political parties;

4. The preparation of a personnel with a view to filling vacant posts in the Finnish administration, and, above all, the creation of chairs of Finnish law in the establishments of higher education of the Empire; the introduction of the Finnish and Swedish languages in the schools of the Empire and the addition of the Russian language as an indispensable subject for students' entrance examinations at the University of the Emperor Alexander (at Helsingfors);

5. The revision of the laws in force for the Governor-General in Finland and, at the same time, the creation of an Imperial Finnish Senate;

6. The reorganization of the principal Government services, now administered by colleagues collectively, and their transformation into institutions directed by the authority of a single person;

7. The reorganization of the *bureau* of the Public Ministry in Finland;

8. The promulgation of a law with a view to applying to Finland the system of exceptional law;

9. The revision of the regulations concerning the police and *gendarmerie* in Finland;

Source: *Riech,* November 18, 1914, as reproduced in Malbone W. Graham, Jr. *New Government of Eastern Europe* (New York: Henry Holt and Company, 1927), pp. 621–623.

10. The promulgation of laws to be put in force conjointly in the Empire and in Finland in regard to the press, asembly, association and public meetings;

11. The extension of the control of the Ministry of Public Instruction to Finnish educational establishments and to the University of the Emperor Alexander at Helsingfors;

12. The participation of the Finnish treasury in the expenses occasioned by the defense of the Empire;

13. The unification of the Finnish posts and telegraphs in a single district organized on the general basis of the same service in the Empire;

14. The adoption of measures against the introduction of arms and munitions into Finland;

15. The coordination of the technical conditions of the Finnish railroads with those existing in the Empire, the establishment of direct communications between the Imperial and Finnish railroads, and the subjection of these to the regulations of the laws governing the Russian railways.

In the second group the following measures are enumerated:

1. The regulation of questions concerning the Orthodox religion and Church in Finland, the submission of the schools of the Orthodox Church in Finland to the authority of the Department of the Russian Orthodox Church;

2. The introduction into Finland of customs duties uniform with those of the rest of the Empire, and, in particular, the regulation of the question of assuring to certain Russian products such as sugar, meat, and so forth, a privileged position on the Finnish market;

3. The opening of savings banks in Finland; the right of private banks and other like credit establishments situated in the Empire to open branches and conduct their business in Finland;

4. The guarantee to commercial, industrial, transport, and other companies and societies already established in other parts of the Empire to carry on their business in Finland;

5. The reform of the law on railway rates in Finland;

6. The regulation of the monetary system in Finland, with a view to making it uniform with that of the Empire;

7. The distribution of land under privileged conditions to those who are deprived of it, and the extension to Finland of the Peasants' Land Bank;

8. The participation of the Finnish treasury in the expenses of the Empire in addition to the expenditures occasioned by the military defenses and, particularly, its sharing of the expenses of the Ministry of Foreign Affairs;

9. The promulgation of a law common to the Empire and to Finland in relation to the acquisition or loss of Russian citizenship;

10. The regulation of the question relative to Russians becoming Finnish subjects;

11. The revision of the maritime laws of Finland, as well as other ordinances relating to navigation;

12. Finally, the extension to Finland of the law in force in the Empire regarding copyright.

Program of the Progressive Bloc, September 1915

The undersigned representatives of factions and groups of the State Council and of the State Duma, convinced that only a strong, firm, and active authority can lead the fatherland to victory, and that such an authority can be only that which rests upon popular confidence and is capable of organizing the active cooperation of all citizens, have arrived at the unanimous conclusion that the most important and essential task, that of creating such an authority, cannot be realized without the fulfillment of the following conditions:

1. The formation of a united government, composed of individuals who enjoy the confidence of the country and who have agreed with the legislative institutions upon the fulfillment, at the earliest possible time, of a definite program.

2. Decisive change in the methods of administration employed thus far, which have been based upon a distrust of public initiative. In particular:

(a) Strict observance of the principles of legality in administration.
(b) Abolition of the dual authority of civil and military power in problems which have no direct relation to the conduct of war.
(c) Reestablishment of local administrations.
(d) A sensible and consistent policy aimed at the maintenance of internal peace and the removal of differences between nationalities and classes.

For the realization of such a policy the following measures must be adopted, by means of administration as well as legislation:

1. By means of Imperial clemency, a termination of cases initiated on charges of purely political and religious transgressions not aggravated by transgressions of a generally felonious nature; the release from punishment and the restoration of rights, including the right of participation in elections to the State Duma, *zemstvo*, city institutions, and so forth, of persons convicted of such crimes; and the amelioration of the condition of others sentenced for political and religious crimes, with the exception of spies and traitors.

From *Riech* [Talk], No. 234 (3257) September 8, 1915, p.6. Translation mine. Words in brackets are mine.

2. The return of those who were exiled by administrative decree for matters of a political and religious nature.

3. Complete and decisive cessation of persecution on religious grounds, under any pretext whatsoever, and repeal of circulars aimed at limitation and perversion of the *ukaz* of April 30, 1905.

4. Solution of the Russo-Polish problem; namely, removal of limitations of the rights of Poles throughout Russia; the immediate drafting and presentation to the legislative institutions of a bill for autonomy of the Kingdom of Poland, and a simultaneous review of the laws concerning Polish land ownership.

5. Inauguration of a program aimed at abolition of restrictions upon the rights of Jews; in particular, further steps towards the abolition of the Pale of Settlement, facilitation of admission to educational institutions, removal of obstacles to choosing professions, and restoration of the Jewish press.

6. A policy of conciliation regarding the Finnish question; in particular, changes in the composition of the administration and Senate, and cessation of persecution of officials.

7. Restoration of the Little Russian [Ukrainian] press; immediate disposition of cases of confined or exiled inhabitants of Galicia, and the release of those wrongfully subjected to persecution.

8. Restoration of activity of trade unions and termination of persecution of hospital workers' representatives on suspicion of membership in an illegal party. Restoration of the labor press.

9. Agreement between the government and the legislative institutions regarding early introduction of:

(a) All bills related to national defense, the supply of the army, welfare of the wounded, care of refugees, and other problems directly related to the war.

(b) The following legislative program aimed at the organization of the country to realize victory and maintain internal peace:

Equalization of peasants' rights with those of other classes.

Establishment of *volost zemstvo.*

Repeal of the land statute of 1890.

Repeal of the municipal statute of 1892.

Establishment of *zemstvo* institutions in the border regions, such as Siberia, Archangel *Gubernia,* Don *Oblast,* the Caucasus, etc.

Legislation concerning the cooperative societies.

Legislation concerning rest for business employees.

Improvement of the material condition of the post and telegraph employees.

Confirmation of temperance for all time.
[Legislation] concerning land and city congresses and unions.
Statutes concerning census.
Introduction of Justices of the Peace in those *gubernias* where their establishment was prevented by financial considerations.
Inauguration of legislative measures that may be indispensable to the administrative execution of the above outlined program of action.

For the progressive group of Nationalists, Count V. Bobrinskii.
For the faction of the Center, V. Lvov.
For the faction of Zemstvo-Octobrists, I. Dmitriukov.
For the group of the Union of October 17th, S. Shidlovskii.
For the faction of Progressivists, I. Efremov.
For the faction of Popular Freedom, P. Miliukov.

A Resolution of the Congress of Representatives of the Provincial Zemstvos, *September 1915*

At this dreadful hour of national trial, we, the Representatives of the Provincial *Zemstvos*, united in the All-Russian Union of *Zemstvos* and assembled at Moscow, reaffirm our unshaken faith in the strength and courage of our army, and our firm trust in ultimate victory, before which there should and could not be any thought of peace.

In the consciousness of the great responsibility to our fatherland which ought to unite all of its sons, we shall continue and expand with unflagging energy our work for the benefit of the army. But, although convinced of the possibility of utterly defeating the enemy, we see with alarm the approaching danger of a fatal disruption of that internal unity which, at the very beginning of the war, was proclaimed from the heights of the Throne as the true pledge of victory.

This peril can be averted only by a reformation of the Government, which will be powerful only if it has the confidence of the nation and is in unity with its lawful representatives.

The indispensable work of the State Duma in strengthening our defenses inspired courage and confidence not only among the popular masses, but in the army itself.

Source: *Izvestiia Glavnogo Komiteta po Snabzheniiu Armii,* Nos. 2–3, October 14, 1915, pp. 16–17, as reproduced in Frank Alfred Golder, *Documents of Russian History, 1914–1917* (New York: The Century Company, 1927), pp. 150–152.

In accord with the wishes of the nation, the State Duma indicated the road that would lead Russia out of the trials which have been visited upon her. In this unprecedented unanimity of purpose in the Duma, the Government failed to join. It rejected the indicated program, and suspended the activities of the Duma. Cooperation of the representative and governmental forces has not been realized, although ardently desired by the whole country and indispensable to victory. We know how profoundly the public mind has been disturbed as a result of this.

It compels us once more to point out the need of the speediest resumption of the work of the State Duma, which alone can afford a reliable basis for a strong government. Then, and then only, will the powers of the Russian people be manifested in all their fullness, and Russia's capacity to bear the most difficult trials.

In the consciousness of our great responsibility and duty to our native country, let each one of us redouble his efforts to attain our common object, victory; and may concerted and zealous work preserve the order and tranquillity that are needed for the salvation of Russia.

The following resolution was also unanimously passed:

To instruct a deputation of three persons, specially selected by this Convention, to report to His Imperial Majesty the views which appeared at the Convention of Representatives in connection with current events, and were expressed in the above resolution.

Considering the fact that the Congress of Representatives of Cities has also resolved to appoint a special deputation to report to His Imperial Majesty the resolution passed by that Congress, it is desirable that the deputations be presented to the Emperor together.

A Resolution of the Congress of Representatives of Russian Cities, September 1915

The Congress of Representatives of the Cities of Russia considers it a sacred duty at this moment of sore trial to salute warmly our steadfast, valiant army. May it rest assured that all the thoughts and sentiments of Russia's citizens are united in the effort to win a victory in the fervent desire to assist our heroes with all our means in the trying struggle that has fallen to their lot. As heretofore, the Russian people are determined to prosecute the war to final victory, in perfect accord with our faithful Allies.

Source: *Izvestiia Glavnogo Komiteta po Snabzheniiu Armii,* Nos. 2–3, October 14, 1915, pp. 38–39, as reproduced in Frank Alfred Golder, *Documents of Russian History, 1914–1917* (New York: The Century Company, 1927), pp. 149–150.

But fatal obstacles in the path of final victory, the old faults of our State organization are still here: the irresponsibility of the Government, and its lack of real contact with the people. A determined and real turning toward a new path is indispensable. It is demanded by patriotic duty.

In the place of the present Government, there should be summoned persons possessing the confidence of the nation; the construction work of the popular representatives should be resumed without delay; and internal peace and solidarity of spirit—those important conditions of victory—should be assured in our country by reconciliation, the forgetting of the political strife of the past, and the equality of all citizens before the law.

The Representatives of the Cities of Russia, inspired by a firm belief in the future of our country, in perfect self-control and the calm assurance or the righteousness of their cause and power, will continue, in common with the whole nation, their tireless and concerted activity in aid of the army, mindful of the fact that every hour of interruption in this work would defer the achievement of victory. . . .

The Congress of Representatives of the Cities of Russia has appointed a special deputation of three persons, together with representatives of the All-Russian Union of *Zemstvos*, to bring to the notice of the Emperor the alarms and hopes which are agitating the nation, and to express the view of this Congress on the necessity of carrying the war to a victorious conclusion, the immediate resumption of work in the legislative institutions, and the summoning to the Government of such persons as enjoy the confidence of the nation. [The Emperor refused to receive the special deputation].

A Letter to Nicholas II from Grand Duke Nikolai Mikhailovich Concerning Rural Conditions, December 1916

In accordance with my promise, I am writing about my impressions here. My estate represents an immense area of 75,000 *desiatins*. It is situated in three *uiezds* of three *guberniias*: Kherson and Ekaterinoslav, *uiezds* of the same names, and Taurida *guberniia*, *uiezd* of Melitopol. There are sixteen villages on the estate, and seven German colonies, one of which moved away last year on its own initiative. The remaining colonies are waiting for the decision of the Government; most of them are Mennonites, who are inclined to stay, and one, of Wurtembergers, intends to move. Thus far there have been no misunderstandings with them.

Source: *Nikolai II i Velikie Kniazia,* pp. 75–79, as reproduced in Frank Alfred Golder, *Documents of Russian History, 1914–1917* (New York: The Century Compaany, 1927), pp. 179–181.

The Mennonites emphasize the fact that they left Germany two-hundred years ago, spent a long time in Poland, migrated to us under Emperor Alexander II, and have been dwelling here over fifty years. Although they do not believe in war, they furnished soldiers who serve as hospital orderlies. In conversation, they stress their anti-German attitude, even though everywhere in their homes there are protraits of the Kaiser, and also old Vasili Fedorovich, [Kaiser Wilhelm I], as well as of Bismarck and Moltke. Personally, I hope that they will clear out, bag and baggage, after the war.

Complete statistics of losses in men in our Russian villages could not be obtained. For the present, I have data only for one village, that of Grushevka. The figures are: 115 (10 killed, 34 wounded, 71 missing or in captivity) out of 829 souls mobilized. Consequently, for the village of Grushevka the losses amount to thirteen per cent of the total population of 3,307 souls, of whom 829 souls were in the army. In the village of Grushevka alone, more than five-hundred petitions have been presented by widows, wives, and mothers of soldiers in active duty. They are getting allowances regularly, but the widows of the killed soldiers decorated with the order of St. George have thus far received nothing. I have collected all the information and turned it over to the proper authorities. We have also a goodly number of refugees: the largest percentage comes from Kholm *guberniia,* but there are also refugees from Grodno and Minsk *guberniias*. They all receive allowances regularly.

The grain harvest is good—in some places all that can be desired. Harvesting and threshing are going on everywhere, and there is hope that the work will be finished on time in the fall. In addition to women, children, and the aged, I have working for me thirty-six people from the Kherson jail, and 947 Austrian war prisoners. There are no Germans. The Austrians are made up of Czechs, Ruthenians, Slovaks, Croatians, Poles, and Transylvania Rumanians. The latter are lazy and grumbling; the others work well and without driving. . . .

I shall probably remain at Grushevka until the 20th of August, that is, three whole weeks. The air here is incomparable. Space galore. Cannot see the horizon. Fields, fields . . . without end. At dawn I hunt anything that comes along. So far, with the aid of six urchins who beat the bushes, I have bagged six foxes, fourteen quail, and eight partridges.

I ask Alix and you to accept my best wishes for the birthday of Alexei. May the Lord God protect you all.

Sincerely yours,
Nikolai M[ikhailovich]

A Resolution of the Congress of the Nobility, December 1916

The Twelfth Congress of the united associations of nobles, always devoted to their sovereigns, notes with deep sorrow that in the terrible historical moment through which Russia is passing, when the monarchist principle is especially vital to the solidity and unity of the State, this ancient basis of the State is being shaken to its foundations.

In the administration of the State, irresponsible, dark powers, alien to the legitimate authority, are gaining influence. These powers are subjecting the heights of the Government to their influence and are even encroaching upon the administration of the Church.

The worthiest pastors of the Church are troubled by the shameful deeds that are taking place in the view of all. The Church, guardian of the truth of Christ, does not hear the free word of its bishops and knows that they are oppressed.

It is necessary to assure to the Church its internal administration as established by the canons.

The civil administration of the country is not less shaken. Moreover, subjected to the same fatal influences, it lacks the necessary solidity, singleness of thought and purpose, and does not enjoy the confidence of the people.

Such a situation, ruinous at any time, is especially fatal at this time of world war; and it has caused chaos in every branch of the national life.

It is necessary to eliminate, once for all, the influence of the dark powers in the affairs of State.

It is necessary to form a strong Government, Russian in thought and feeling, enjoying popular confidence, and capable of working in common with the legislative institutions, but responsible to the Monarch alone. It should be armed with the fullness of authority, in the person of the President of the Council of Ministers, and firmly united in a common program.

Only such a Government can assure the prosecution of the war to final victory, without which the popular conscience does not admit any conclusive peace.

Source: *Riech,* December 15, 1916, as reproduced in Frank Afred Golder, *Documents of Russian History, 1914–1917* (New York: The Century Company, 1927), pp. 177–178.

Nicholas II's Special Order of the Day, January 7, 1917

More than two years ago, in time of profound peace, Germany, who had long been secretly preparing to subjugate all the peoples of Europe, attacked Russia and her faithful ally, France, which obliged England to join us and take part in the struggle. The complete contempt for all bases of law, which manifested itself by Germany's infringement of the neutrality of Belgium, and the merciless cruelty of the Germans in regard to the peaceful populations of the provinces occupied by their troops, gradually united all the Great Powers of Europe against Germany, and her ally, Austria-Hungary.

Under the pressure of the German armies, inordinately strong owing to the superiority of their technical means, Russia, as well as France, were obliged, in the first year of the war, to cede a part of their territory to the foe. This temporary reverse, however, did not crush the spirit of our brave allies, or yours, my gallant troops. Meanwhile, by the united efforts of all the forces of the Empire, the difference in our technical means and those of the Germans was gradually disappearing. But, long before this, even since the autumn of the past year of 1915, our enemy was unable to occupy another foot of Russian territory, and in the spring and summer of this current year, the German troops experienced a series of severe defeats, and passed from aggression to a state of defense on the whole of our front. Their forces are obviously wearing themselves out, while the might and power of Russia and her valorous allies surely and steadily grow. Germany feels that she will be completely routed, that the hour of retaliation for all her cruelties and violations of the law is near. And so—similarly to her sudden declaration of war at a time when she felt her military superiority over her neighbors, Germany, feeling her weakness, suddenly comes forward with an offer to peace to the allies, strongly united against her in an indissoluble bond. She, very naturally, wishes to begin peace negotiations before the measure of her weakness becomes evident to all, before she definitely loses her fighting capacity. At the same time, [taking] advantage of her temporary victory over Rumania—due to the latter's want of military experience—she endeavors to give her enemies a false idea of the strength of her armies. But, if Germany could declare war and attack Russia and her ally, France, at the most unfavorable moment for them—at the present moment these two countries, supported by noble Italy and powerful England, and fortified by the struggle, are able, in their turn, to enter into peace negotiations with Germany when they consider the time favorable for it, this time has

Source: A. Loukomsky, *Memoirs of the Russian Revolution,* pp. 47–48, as reproduced in Frank Alfred Golder, *Documents of Russian History, 1914–1917* (New York: The Century Company, 1927), pp. 51–53.

not yet come. The enemy has not yet been expelled from the provinces which have been seized by him; Russia has not yet attained the aim created by this war—the possession of Tsargrad [Constantinople] and the Straits; the formation of a whole and independent Poland out of its three existing, but as yet separate parts, is still not assured. To conclude a peace with Germany at present would mean not to profit fully by the heroic efforts of the Russian Army and Fleet. These efforts, and the sacred memory of those gallant sons of Russia who have perished on the field of battle, forbid us even to think of making peace before achieving a final and complete victory over the foe; who dares to think that, if he could begin the war, he can end it whenever he likes.

I do not doubt for a moment that every loyal son of Russia, whether forming part of my glorious Army, or working for the might of that Army in the interior of the country, or pursuing his own peaceful labor, is imbued with this sentiment, and thinks alike on the subject. Peace can only be granted to the enemy when he is definitely broken and defeated, and gives us and the allies solid proofs of the impossibility for him to renew his treacherous attack . . . when we may rest assured that he will be obliged, by the very force of circumstances, to keep his engagements, and fulfil the obligations laid upon him by the Treaty of Peace.

Let us then remain firm and immovable in our assurance of victory, and the Almighty will bless our banners; He will cover them once more with undying glory, and will grant us a peace worthy of your heroic deeds, my glorious troops—a peace for which the coming generations will bless you, and which will render your memory forever sacred to them.

NICHOLAS.

66

Abdication of the Romanovs, March 1917

Imperial Russia came to an abrupt end on March 12, 1917, when the old government, overrun by a revolutionary civilian mob and defiant soldiers, ceased to function. The remarkable ease with which the monarchy

---

From *London Times,* March 19, 1917, p. 10, col. 4.

collapsed, first in the capital and then throughout the country, stunned everyone. Immediately, two revolutionary institutions emerged to deal with the resulting confusion: the *soviets* or self-appointed committees representing the victorious revolutionary mob; and the *Provisional Government,* whose self-appointed members represented a solid cross section of the educated public.

Technically, between March 12 and 16, Russia still had a tsar. Nicholas II stayed at the General Headquarters at Mogilev until March 13, when he left for Petrograd. His train never reached its destination, for it was rerouted to Pskov, the Headquarters of the Northern Front. All military leaders the tsar consulted, including his uncle the Grand Duke Nicholas, urged him to abdicate in favor of his son Alexei with the tsar's brother Grand Duke Michael, acting as regent. In the afternoon of March 15, Nicholas II signed documents to this effect. In the evening, pleading inability to part with his "beloved son," he changed his mind and abdicated in favor of his brother. Michael was willing to accept "only if and when our great people, having elected by universal suffrage a Constituent Assembly to determine the form of government and lay down the fundamental law of the new Russian State, invest me with such a power." The Russian people had no desire to make such an offer. The three-hundred-year-old Romanov dynasty, which had been founded by a Michael, technically expired with another Michael.

Abdication of Nicholas II, March 15, 1917

By the Grace of God, We, Nicholas II, Emperor of All the Russias, Tsar of Poland, Grand Duke of Finland, and so forth, to all our faithful subjects be it known:

In the days of a great struggle against a foreign enemy who has been endeavoring for three years to enslave our country, it pleased God to send Russia a further painful trial.

Internal troubles threatened to have a fatal effect on the further progress of this obstinate war. The destinies of Russia, the honor of her heroic Army, the happiness of the people, and the whole future of our beloved country demand that the war should be conducted at all costs to a victorious end.

The cruel enemy is making his last efforts and the moment is near when our valiant Army, in concert with our glorious Allies, will finally overthrow the enemy.

In these decisive days in the life of Russia we have thought that we owed to our people the close union and organization of all its forces for the realization of a rapid victory; for which reason, in agreement with the Imperial Duma, we have recognized that it is for the good of the country that we should abdicate the Crown of the Russian State and lay down the Supreme Power.

Not wishing to separate ourself from our beloved son, we bequeath our heritage to our brother, the Grand Duke Michael Alexandrovitch, with our blessing for the future of the Throne of the Russian State.

We bequeath it our brother to govern in full union with the national representatives sitting in the Legislative Institutions, and to take his inviolable oath to them in the name of our well-beloved country.

We call upon all faithful sons of our native land to fulfill their sacred and patriocic duty of obeying the Tsar at the painful moment of national trials and to aid them, together with the representatives of the nation, to conduct the Russian State in the way of prosperity and glory.

May God help Russia.

Declaration from the Throne by Grand Duke Michael, March 16, 1917

A heavy task has been intrusted to me by the will of my brother, who has given me the Imperial Throne at a time of unprecedented war and domestic strife.

Animated by the same feelings as the entire nation—namely, that the welfare of the country overshadows all other interests—I am firmly resolved to accept the Supreme Power only if this should be the desire of our great people, who must, by means of a plebiscite, through their representatives in the Constituent Assembly, establish the form of government and the new fundamental laws of the Russian State.

Invoking God's blessing, I therefore request all citizens of Russia to obey the Provisional Government, set up on the initiative of the Duma and invested with plenary powers, until, within as short a time as possible, the Constituent Assembly, elected on a basis of universal, equal, and secret suffrage, shall express the will of the nation regarding the form of government to be adopted.

PETER I

CATHERINE I

PETER II

Anna

ELIZABETH

PETER III

CATHERINE II

PAUL I

ALEXANDER I

Nicholas I

ALEXANDER II

ALEXANDER III

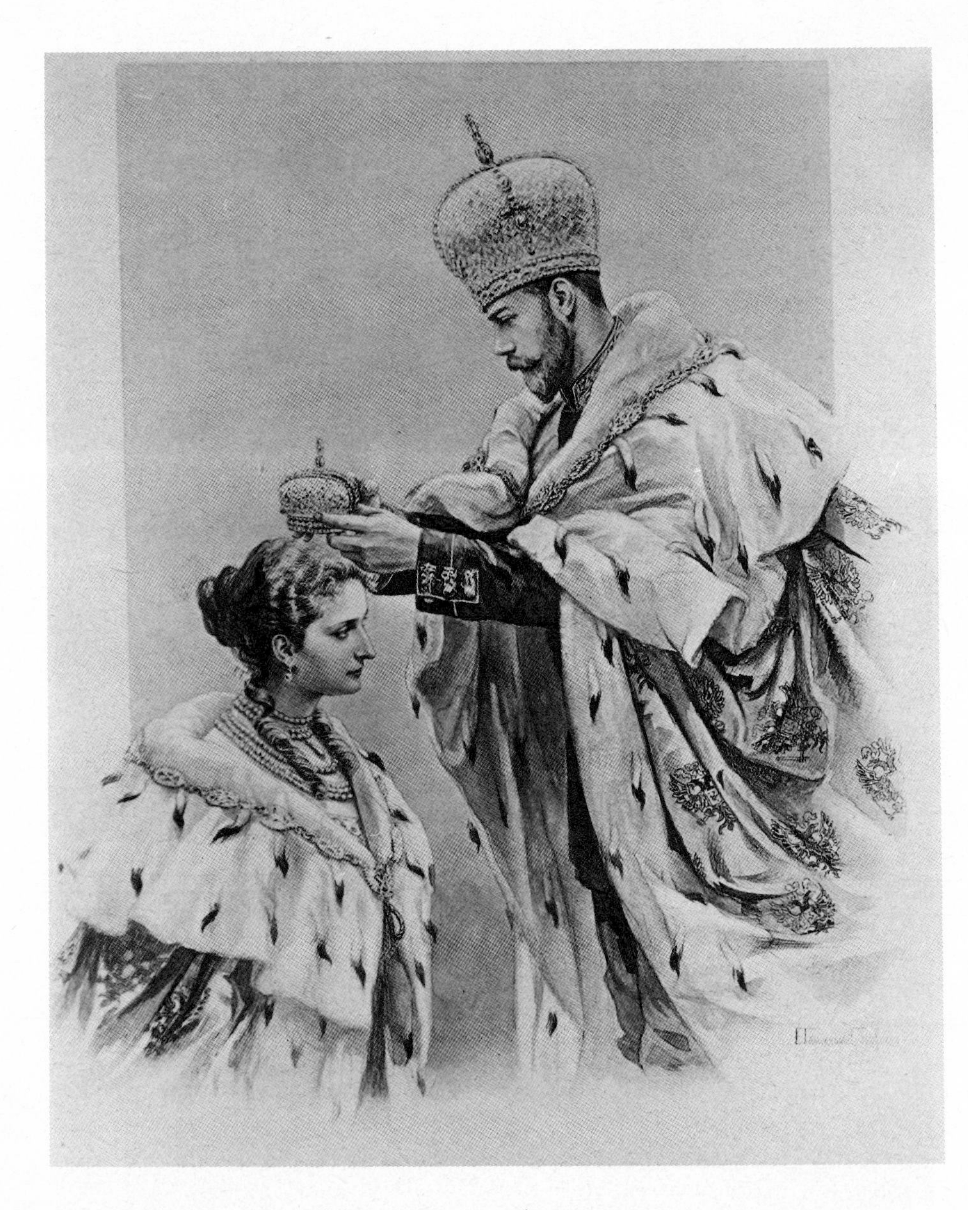

NICHOLAS AND ALEXANDRA

Chronological Table

1689–1725	Reign of Peter I, the Great (sole ruler after the death of Ivan V in 1696).
1695–1696	Azov campaigns of Peter the Great and the seizure of the town of Azov.
1695–1697	Russian conquest of Kamchatka.
1697–1698	Peter the Great's first journey abroad (Prussia, Holland, England, Holy Roman Empire, and Poland).
1698	Revolt of the *streltsy* crushed; Peter the Great begins modernization of Russia by ordering the shaving of beards and wearing of Western clothes.
1700	Peter the Great adopts the Julian Calendar for Russia and suspends the patriarchate.
1700–1721	Northern War between Russia and Sweden over control of the Baltic ends in Treaty of Nystadt, giving Russia a "Window to the West," the Baltic region.
1703	Founding of St. Petersburg; the first Russian newspaper, *Vedomosti* (News) appears in Moscow.
1704	Reform of the alphabet.
1705	Beard tax introduced.
1705–1708	Revolts against Peter the Great's policies in Astrakhan, Bashkiria, and the Don region.
1708	Local government reforms; eight *gubernias* organized.
1709	Russian victory over Charles XII and *Hetman* Mazepa at Poltava; Ukraine loses its autonomy.
1710	Population census.
1711	Pruth campaign against the Turks; Russia loses Azov; monetary reform; establishment of the Senate to supervise administration.
1713	Capital of Russia transferred from Moscow to St. Petersburg.

1714	Decrees on primogeniture and education of nobles.
1715	Naval Academy founded in St. Petersburg.
1715–1717	Russian expedition to Central Asia.
1716–1717	Peter the Great's second visit to Western Europe (Holland and France).
1718	Trial and death of Tsarevich Alexei; establishment of the collegium system of central administration.
1719	Construction of the Ladoga Canal begun (completed in 1731).
1721	Peter the Great assumes the title of Emperor; Holy Synod established.
1721–1723	Russo-Persian War.
1722	Table of Ranks introduced; law on imperial succession.
1724	Russian Academy of Sciences chartered; Pososhkov completes *A Book on Poverty and Wealth.*
1725	Death of Peter the Great.
1725–1727	Reign of Catherine I.
1725–1729	First expedition of Captain Bering to find the limits of America (second expedition from 1732–1741).
1727–1730	Reign of Peter II (grandson of Peter the Great).
1730–1740	Reign of Anna (daughter of Ivan V) and her favorite, Biron (Bühren).
1733–1743	Kamchatka scientific expedition headed by G. F. Müller, J. G. Gmelin, S. P. Krasheninnikov, and others.
1736–1739	War with Turkey ending in Treaty of Belgrade; Russia regains Azov.
1736	Term of military service for nobles reduced to twenty-five years.
1740–1741	Reign of the infant emperor, Ivan VI.
1741–1761	Reign of Elizabeth, youngest daughter of Peter the Great.
1741–1743	War with Sweden; Treaty of Abö gives Russia a portion of Finland.
1744	Death penalty abolished in Russia.
1747–1762	Architect Rastrelli beautifies St. Petersburg with such structures as Winter Palace, Smolny Convent, and Peterhof Palace.
1753	Abolition of internal customs.
1755	University of Moscow chartered.
1756–1762	Russia's participation in the Seven Years' War.
1760	Nobles granted the right to exile their serfs to Siberia; Russian forces invade Berlin.
1761–1762	Reign of Peter III.
1762	Nobles freed from obligatory state service.
1762–1796	Reign of Catherine II, the Great.

1764	Final secularization of church lands; church lands placed under management of the Economic College; Russo-Prussian alliance and secret convention concerning Poland; abolition of the office of *hetman* in the Ukraine.
1765	The Free Economic Society founded in St. Petersburg; nobles granted the right to exile their serfs to hard labor.
1766	Annexation of the Aleutian Islands.
1767–1768	Legislative Commission works unsuccessfully to prepare a new code of laws.
1768–1774	War with Turkey ends in Treaty of Kutchuk-Kainardzhi ceding Black Sea steppes to Russia.
1772	First partition of Poland by Russia, Prussia, and Austria; uprising of the Iaik or Ural cossacks.
1773–1775	Peasant revolt led by Pugachev engulfs the Volga region and the Don basin.
1775	*Gubernia* reforms; breakup of the Zaporozhian or Ukrainian cossacks.
1781–1786	Absorption of the Ukraine and the Crimea into the Russian Empire.
1782–1785	Architect Quarenghi builds the Hermitage.
1783–1784	Architect Starov builds the Taurida Palace.
1785	Charter to the Nobility and Charter to the Towns issued.
1787–1792	War with Turkey; Treaty of Jassy.
1790–1792	Radishchev sentenced to death for writing *A Journey from St. Petersburg to Moscow,* then exiled to Siberia instead.
1793	Second partition of Poland by Russia and Prussia.
1795	Third partition of Poland by Russia, Prussia, and Austria.
1796–1801	Reign of Paul.
1797	Law issued on succession to the throne according to genealogical seniority.
1798	Russia joins the Second Coalition against France.
1799	Russian forces under Suvorov campaign in North Italy and Switzerland; Russian-American Company chartered (liquidated in 1868).
1800	Paul allies with Napoleon against England; import of foreign books into Russia prohibited.
1801	Paul assassinated; Georgia annexed by Russia.
1801–1825	Reign of Alexander I.
1801–1804	Internal reforms.
1802	Reorganization of Senate; establishment of Ministries and Committee of Ministers.

1804	University Code granted; Universities of Kazan and Kharkov chartered.
1805	Russia joins the Third Coalition against France; defeat at Austerlitz.
1806–1812	War with Turkey ends in Treaty of Bucharest and annexation of Bessarabia.
1807	Treaty of Tilsit with Napoleon; Russia joins the Continental System.
1807–1811	Reforms of Speranskii.
1809	Russian conquest of Finland.
1812	Napoleon's invasion of and retreat from Russia.
1814	Alexander I enters Paris in triumph.
1814–1815	Congress of Vienna.
1815	Holy Alliance and Quadruple Alliance conceived; Russia acquires the Duchy of Warsaw.
1816–1819	Serfdom abolished in Baltic provinces (landless emancipation).
1816	Union of Salvation, the first Decembrist Society, organized.
1817	Union of Welfare, the second Decembrist Society, organized.
1819	University of St. Petersburg chartered.
1821	Division of Decembrist Societies into Northern and Southern Branches.
1822	Reforms of Speranskii in Siberia.
1825	Death of Alexander I; Decembrist Revolt.
1825–1855	Reign of Nicholas I.
1826	Trial and punishment of the Decembrist leaders.
1826–1828	War with Persia ends in Treaty of Turkmanchai and annexation of Armenia.
1828–1829	War with Turkey ends in Treaty of Adrianople and Greek independence.
1830–1831	Polish uprising against Russian rule.
1832	Uvarov enunciates the three principles of autocracy, Orthodoxy, and nationality; duchy of Warsaw incorporated into Russia.
1833	Publication of the *Polnoe Sobranie Zakonov* (Complete Collection of the Laws).
1834	Kiev University founded.
1835–1844	216 peasant uprisings recorded.
1836	Gogol's *Inspector General* and Chadaev's *Philosophical Letters* appear.
1837	Pushkin fatally wounded in duel; first railway opened in Russia, linking St. Petersburg and Tsarskoe Selo.
1837–1841	Kiselev introduces reforms affecting state peasants.

1842	Gogol's *Dead Souls* appears.
1845	Russian Geographic Society founded.
1847	Herzen exiles himself permanently from Russia; arrest and trial of members of the Society of Saints Cyril and Methodious; Belinskii writes *Letter to Gogol.*
1849	Dostoevskii sentenced to forced labor in Siberia; Russian forces intervene in Hungary.
1853–1856	Crimean War ends in Treaty of Paris and diplomatic humiliation of Russia.
1855–1881	Reign of Alexander II.
1857	Alexander appoints Secret Committee to plan steps toward abolishment of serfdom.
1858	Russia annexes the Amur Basin and Maritime Provinces by terms of the Treaty of Aigun.
1860	Treaty of Peking confirms Russia's gains; city of Vladivostok founded; State Bank chartered.
1861	Manifesto on emancipation of serfs published; reestablishment of local government in Polish provinces.
1861–1862	Peasant unrest and student revolutionary agitation.
1861–1863	Activity of the secret revolutionary organization *Zemlia i Volia* (Land and Freedom).
1861–1876	Activity of Bakunin in Western Europe.
1862	Turgeniev's *Fathers and Sons* published; Rumiantsev Public Library (now Lenin State Public Library) opened in Moscow; arrest of Chernyshevskii and Pisarev; closing of Sunday Schools.
1863	Uprising in Poland, Lithunia, and Belorussia against Russian rule; new University Statute promulgated.
1864	Judicial reform; *Zemstvo* Statute; Dostoevskii's *Memoirs from Underground.*
1865–1885	Russian conquest of Central Asia.
1865	Censorship relaxed; University of Odessa chartered.
1866	Attempt on Alexander II's life by Karakozov.
1867	Alaska and the Aleutian Islands sold to the United States; meeting of a Panslav Congress in Moscow; Katkov turns to Russification.
1869	Tolstoy's *War and Peace*; University of Warsaw chartered; Bakunin and Nechaev write *Catechism of the Revolutionary.*
1870	Municipal reforms; repudiation of Black Sea clauses of the Treaty of Paris of 1856; Lenin (Ulianov) born in Simbirsk.
1871	Danilevskii's *Russia and Europe* published; London Convention on the Straits.

1872	Translation of Marx's *Das Kapital* published in Russia.
1873	Three Emperor's League formed.
1874	Military reform; compulsory military service introduced; Mussorgskii's *Boris Godunov* produced.
1876	"Land and Freedom," populist secret society organized.
1877–1878	Russo-Turkish War.
1878	Treaty of San Stefano; Congress of Berlin; Tolstoy's *Anna Karenina.*
1879	"Land and Freedom" split into "People's Will" and "Black Partition"; Stalin (Dzhugashvili) born.
1880	Dostoevskii's *Brothers Karamozov*; Plekhanov, father of Russian Marxism, flees to Western Europe.
1881	Alexander II assassinated; Three Emperors" League revived (renewed in 1884 for three years).
1881–1894	Reign of Alexander III.
1882	Foundation of the Peasant Bank; reduction of peasant redemption payments; establishment of factory inspection.
1883	Plekhanov organizes first Russian Marxist group, "The Emancipation of Labor," in Geneva.
1884	Reactionary regulations for universities.
1885	Land Bank for the Nobility founded.
1886	Abolition of soul tax throughout the Empire (except Siberia).
1887	Reinsurance Treaty between Russia and Germany signed; attempted assassination of Alexander III by Lenin's brother.
1888	University of Tomsk chartered.
1891–1905	Construction of Trans-Siberian Railway.
1891–1892	The great famine in Russian agricultural regions.
1891	Secret Franco-Russian military convention against the Triple Alliance concluded.
1892–1903	Witte serves as Minister of Communication, Finance, and Commerce.
1894–1917	Reign of Nicholas II.
1896	Russo-Chinese alliance against Japan signed.
1897	First general population census in Russia; working day limited to eleven and one-half hours; Russia adopts gold standard; Lenin exiled to Siberia.
1898	First conference of the Russian Social Democratic party in Minsk; Nicholas II launches a drive for world peace and disarmament; Russians lease Port Arthur from the Chinese.
1900	Boxer Rebellion in China against foreign influence; Russian forces occupy Manchuria.

1902	Socialist Revoluntionary party is formed to protect peasant interests; wave of peasant unrest; Lenin's *What Is to Be Done?* and Gorky's *Lower Depths* appear.
1903	Wave of industrial strikes hits Russia; Russian Social Democratic party splits into *Bolshevik* and *Menshevik* factions.
1904	Japan attacks Russian forces at Port Arthur without declaration of war; Plehve assassinated; Baltic fleet sails for Far East and meets disaster at Tsushima Strait.
1905	Surrender of Port Arthur; outbreak of general strike in St. Petersburg; "Bloody Sunday"; formation of first Soviet of Workers: mutiny on battleship *Potemkin*; Treaty of Portsmouth signed; October Manifesto promises a Duma for Russia and extends suffrage rights, freedom of speech, press, and assembly; Moscow uprising; cancellation of peasant redemption payments.
1905–1906	Witte's Prime Ministership.
1906	France grants Russia a loan of two and one-half billion *francs*; First Duma opened and dissolved; Witte dismissed; Stolypin forms Cabinet; Vyborg Manifesto; beginning of the Stolypin agrarian reforms.
1907	Meeting and dissolution of Second Duma; new electoral law published; Anglo-Russian Entente divides spheres of influence in Persia, Afghanistan and Tibet; meeting of the Third Duma.
1908	Bosnian Crisis.
1910	Death of Tolstoy.
1911	Stolypin assassinated in Kiev.
1912	Bolshevik newspaper *Pravda* makes first appearance; election of Fourth Duma.
1912–1913	Balkan Wars.
1914	Outbreak of World War I; military disaster at the Mazurian Lakes; victory in Galicia; arrest of Bolshevik deputies of the Duma.
1915	Retreat of Russian forces from Galicia; formation of the "Progressive bloc" in the Duma.
1916	Rasputin murdered.
1917	General strike and uprising in Petrograd; Romanov dynasty toppled; Nicholas II abdicates; imperial period of Russian history ends; Soviet period begins.

Selected Bibliography

There is an impressive amount of literature in English on the history of Imperial Russia. Some of this material (and in many ways the best of it) has been written by American, Canadian, and English scholars. Some (by German, French, Soviet, and other scholars) has been made available to readers of English through translations.

The items listed below are representative of the fine works (most recently published and older classics) that deal with the complexities of Imperial Russian history. They have been selected not because I necessarily agree with their views but because they might provide the reader with valuable insights for a fair and accurate understanding of problems that have either been touched on in this collection or treated in various basic texts.

The selected bibliography is divided into two parts: 1) Monographic Literature, and 2) Periodical Literature. Persons interested in pursuing specific topics that have been dealt with in this volume should consult library card catalogues, references cited within each work listed in this bibliography, or other available sources.

Monographic Literature

Alexander, John T. *Bubonic Plague in Early Modern Russia: Public Health and Urban Disaster.* Baltimore: The Johns Hopkins University Press, 1980.

———. *Catherine the Great. Life and Legend.* New York: Oxford University Press, 1989.

Alston, Patrick L. *Education and State in Tsarist Russia.* Stanford: Stanford University Press, 1969.

Andrew, Joe. *Russian Writers and Society in the Second Half of the Nineteenth Century.* London: Macmillan, 1982.

Ascher, Abraham. *The Revolution of 1905.* Stanford: Stanford University Press, 1988.

Balmuth, Daniel. *Censorship in Russia, 1865–1905.* Washington: University Press of America, 1979.

Barratt, Glynn. *Russia in Pacific Waters, 1715–1825.* Vancouver: University of British Columbia Press, 1980.

Bartlett, Roger P. *Human Capital: The Settlement of Foreigners in Russia, 1762–1804.* Cambridge: Cambridge University Press, 1980.

Berlin, Isaiah. *Russian Thinkers.* New York: Viking, 1978.

Billington, James H. *The Icon and the Axe.* New York: Vintage Books, 1970.

Black, Joseph L. *Nicholas Karamzin and Russian Society in the Nineteenth Century.* Toronto: University of Toronto Press, 1975.

Blackwell, William L. *The Beginnings of Russian Industrialization, 1800–1860.* Princeton: Princeton University Press, 1968.

Blum, Jerome. *Lord and Peasant in Russia from the 9th to the 19th Century.* Princeton: Princeton University Press, 1961.

Bolkhovitinov, Nikolai N. *The Beginnings of Russian-American Relations, 1775–1815.* Transl. by Elena Levin. Cambridge: Harvard University Press, 1975.

Bowman, H. E. *Vissarion Belinski: A Study in the Origin of Social Criticism in Russia.* Cambridge: Harvard University Press, 1954.

Brennan, James F. *Enlightened Despotism in Russia: The Reign of Elizabeth, 1741–1762.* New York: American University Studies, 1987.

Brooks, Jeffrey. *When Russians Learned to Read: Literacy and Popular Literature, 1861–1917.* Princeton: Princeton University Press, 1986.

Brown, William E. *A History of Eighteenth-Century Russian Literature.* Ann Arbor: Ardis, 1980.

———. *A History of Russian Literature of the Romantic Period.* Ann Arbor: Ardis, 1986.

Brower, Daniel R. *Training of Nihilists: Education and Radicalism in Tsarist Russia.* Ithaca: Cornell University Press, 1975.

Christoff, Peter K. *K. S. Aksakov: A Study in Ideas.* Princeton: Princeton University Press, 1982.

Chyzhevskyi, Dmytro. *History of Nineteenth-Century Russian Literature.* 2 vols. Nashville: Vanderbilt University Press, 1974.

Cracroft, James. *The Church Reform of Peter the Great.* Stanford: Stanford University Press, 1971.

———. *The Petrine Revolution in Russian Architecture.* Chicago: University of Chicago Press, 1988.

Crankshaw, Edward. *The Shadow of the Winter Palace: Russia's Drift to Revolution, 1825–1917.* New York: Viking, 1976.

Cross, A. G. *"By the Banks of the Thames": The Russians in 18th Century Britain.* Newtonville: Oriental Research Partners, 1980.
Curtiss, John S. *Church and State in Russia . . . 1900–1917.* New York: Columbia University Press, 1940.
———. *Russia's Crimean War.* Durham: Duke University Press, 1979.
———. *The Russian Army Under Nicholas I (1825–1855).* Durham: Duke University Press, 1965.
Curtiss, Minna. *A Forgotten Empress: Anna Ivanovna and Her Era, 1730–1740.* New York: Ungar, 1974.
de Custine, Marquis. *The Empire of the Tsars: A Journey Through Eternal Russia.* New York: Doubleday, 1989.
de Madariaga, Isabel. *Russia in the Age of Catherine the Great.* New Haven: Yale University Press, 1980.
Dmytryshyn, Basil, ed. *Modernization of Russia Under Peter I and Catherine II.* New York: Wiley, 1974.
———, E. A. P. Crownhart-Vaughan and Thomas Vaughan, eds. *Russian Penetration of the North Pacific Ocean, 1700–1797: A Documentary Record.* Portland: Oregon Historical Society Press, 1988.
———. *The Russian-American Colonies, 1798–1867: A Documentary Record.* Portland: Oregon Historical Society Press, 1989.
Dukes, Paul. *Catherine the Great and the Russian Nobility.* Cambridge: Cambridge University Press, 1967.
Edelman, Robert. *Gentry Politics on the Eve of the Russian Revolution: The Nationalist Party, 1907–1917.* New Brunswick: Rutgers University Press, 1980.
Emmons, Terence. *The Formation of Political Parties and the First National Elections in Russia.* Cambridge: Harvard University Press, 1983.
———. *Russian Landed Gentry and the Peasant Emancipation of 1861.* Cambridge: Cambridge University Press, 1968.
———, and Wayne S. Vucinich, eds. *The Zemstvo in Russia: An Experiment in Local Self-Government.* Cambridge: Cambridge University Press, 1982.
Field, Daniel. *Rebels in the Name of the Tsar.* Boston: Houghton Mifflin, 1976.
Fisher, Raymond H. *Bering's Voyages: Whither and Why?* Seattle: University of Washington Press, 1977.
Florinsky, *Michael T. Russia: A History and an Interpretation.* vol. 2. New York: Macmillan, 1954.
Foust, Clifford M. *Muscovite and Mandarin.* Chapel Hill: University of North Carolina Press, 1969.
Geyer, Dietrich. *Russian Imperialism: The Interaction of Domestic and Foreign Policy, 1860–1914.* New Haven: Yale University Press, 1987.

Gibson, James R. *Imperial Russia in Frontier America . . . 1784–1867.* New York: Oxford University Press, 1976.

Gleason, Abbott. *Young Russia: The Genesis of Russian Radicalism in the 1860s.* New York: Viking, 1980.

Gleason, Walter J. *Moral Idealists, Bureaucracy and Catherine the Great.* New Brunswick: Rutgers University Press, 1981.

Grey, Ian. *Catherine the Great.* Philadelphia: Lippincott, 1962.

———. *Peter the Great.* Philadelphia: Lippincott, 1960.

Grimstead, Patricia K. *The Foreign Ministers of Alexander I, 1801–1825.* Berkeley: University of California Press, 1969.

Hamburg, G. M. *Politics of the Russian Nobility, 1881–1905.* New Brunswick: Rutgers University Press, 1984.

Hamm, Michael F. ed. *The City in Late Imperial Russia.* Bloomington: Indiana University Press, 1986.

Harcave, Sidney. *Years of the Golden Cockerel: The Last Romanov Tsars, 1814–1917.* New York: Macmillan, 1968.

Herlihy, Patricia. *Odessa: A History, 1794–1914.* Cambridge: Harvard University Press, 1987.

Hingley, Ronald. *Russian Writers and Society in the 19th Century.* 2nd ed. London: Weidenfeld & Nicholson, 1977.

Jelavich, Barbara. *A Century of Russian Foreign Policy, 1814–1914.* Philadelphia: Lippincott, 1964.

Jensen, Ronald. *The Alaska Purchase and Russian-American Relations.* Seattle: University of Washington Press, 1976.

Johanson, Christine. *Women's Struggle for Higher Education in Russia, 1855–1900.* Montreal: McGill University Press, 1987.

Jones, Robert E. *The Emancipation of the Russian Nobility, 1762–1785.* Princeton: Princeton University Press, 1974.

Katz, Martin. *Mikhail N. Katkov, 1818–1887: A Political Biography.* The Hague: Mouton, 1966.

Keep, John L. H. *The Rise of Social Democracy in Russia.* Oxford: Oxford University Press, 1963.

Klier, John D. *Russia Gathers Her Jews . . . 1772–1825.* DeKalb: Northern Illinois University Press, 1986.

Kliuchevsky, Vasili. *Peter the Great.* New York: Vintage Books, 1958.

Lang, David M. *The First Russian Radical: Alexander Radishchev, 1749–1802.* London: G. Allen, 1959.

Lensen, George A. *The Russian Push Toward Japan . . . 1697–1875.* Princeton: Princeton University Press, 1959.

Lincoln, W. Bruce. *In the Vanguard of Reform: Russia's Enlightened Bureaucrats, 1825–1861.* DeKalb: Northern Illinois University Press, 1982.

———. *In War's Dark Shadow: The Russians Before the Great War.* New York: Dial, 1983.
———. *Nicholas I. Emperor and Autocrat of All the Russias.* Bloomington: Indiana University Press, 1978.
Longworth, Philip. *The Art of Victory: The Life and Achievements of Field Marshal Suvorov, 1729–1800.* New York: Holt, Rinehart and Winston, 1965.
———. *The Three Empresses: Catherine I, Anna and Elizabeth.* New York: Holt, Rinehart and Winston, 1972.
Macey, David A. J. *Government and Peasants in Russia, 1861–1906.* DeKalb: Northern Illinois University Press, 1987.
Malia, Martin E. *Alexander Herzen and the Birth of Russian Socialism.* Cambridge: Harvard University Press, 1961.
Manning, Roberta Th. *The Crisis of the Old Order in Russia: Gentry and Government.* Princeton: Princeton University Press, 1982.
McConnell, Allen. *Tsar Alexander I.* New York: Crowell, 1970.
Marker, Gary. *Publishing, Printing and the Origins of Intellectual Life in Russia, 1700–1800.* Princeton: Princeton University Press, 1985.
Masaryk, Thomas G. *The Spirit of Russia.* New edition. 2 vols. London: Macmillan, 1955.
Massie, Robert K. *Nicholas and Alexandra.* New York: Dell, 1967.
———. *Peter the Great. His Life and World.* New York: Knopf, 1980.
Mathewson, R. W. *The Positive Hero in Russian Literature.* New York: Columbia University Press, 1958.
Mazour, Anatole G. *The First Russian Revolution, 1825.* Berkeley: University of California Press, 1937.
McConnell, A. *A Russian "Philosophe": Alexander Radishchev.* The Hague: Mouton, 1964.
Menshutkin, B. N. *Russia's Lomonosov: Chemist, Courtier, Physicist, Poet.* Princeton: Princeton University Press, 1952.
Miller, Martin A. *The Russian Revolutionary Emigres, 1825–1870.* Baltimore: The Johns Hopkins University Press, 1986.
Monas, Sidney. *The Third Section: Police and Society in Russia Under Nicholas I.* Cambridge: Harvard University Press, 1961.
Mosse, W. E. *Alexander II and the Modernization of Russia.* New York: Macmillan, 1958.
Muller, Alexander V. ed. *The Spiritual Regulations of Peter the Great.* Seattle: University of Washington Press, 1972.
Offord, Derek. *Portraits of Early Russian Liberals.* Cambridge: Cambridge University Press, 1985.

Okun, Semeon B. *The Russian-American Company*. Trans. by Carl Ginsburg. Cambridge: Harvard University Press, 1951.

Palmer, Alan. *Alexander I. Tsar of War and Peace*. London: Weidenfeld & Nicholson, 1974.

Pearson, Thomas S. *Russian Officialdom in Crisis: Autocracy and Local Self-Government, 1861–1900*. New York: Cambridge University Press, 1988.

Petrovich, Michael B. *The Emergence of Russian Panslavism, 1856–1870*. New York: Columbia University Press, 1956.

Pierce, Richard A. *Russian Central Asia, 1867–1917*. Berkeley: University of California Press, 1960.

———, ed. *Russia's Hawaiian Adventure, 1815–1817*. Berkeley: University of California Press, 1965.

Pipes, Richard. *Russia Under the Old Regime*. New York: Scribners, 1975.

———, ed. *The Russian Intelligentsia*. New York: Columbia University Press, 1961.

Pomper, Philip. *The Russian Revolutionary Intelligentsia*. New York: Crowell, 1970.

Pushkarev, Sergei. *The Emergence of Modern Russia, 1801–1917*. New York: Holt, Rinehart & Winston, 1963.

Questead, R. K. I. *The Expansion of Russia in East Asia, 1857–1860*. Singapore: University of Malaya Press, 1968.

Raeff, Marc. *Michael Speransky: Statesman of Imperial Russia*. The Hague: Nijhoff, 1957.

———. *Origins of Russian Intelligentsia*. New York: Harcourt, 1966.

Ragsdale, Hugh. *Tsar Paul and the Question of Madness*. New York: Greenwood Press, 1988.

Riasanovsky, Nicholas V. *A Parting of Ways: Government and the Educated Public in Russia, 1801–1855*. Oxford: Clarendon Press, 1976.

———. *The Images of Peter the Great in Russian History and Thought*. New York: Oxford University Press, 1985.

———. *Nicholas I and Official Nationality in Russia, 1825–1855*. Berkeley: University of California Press, 1959.

Rice, Tamara T. *Elizabeth: Empress of Russia*. London: Weidenfeld & Nicholson, 1970.

Rieber, Alfred J. *Merchants and Entrepreneurs in Imperial Russia*. Chapel Hill: University of North Carolina Press, 1982.

Robinson, Geroid T. *Rural Russia Under the Old Regime*. New York: Longmans, 1949.

Rogger, Hans. *National Consciousness in Eighteenth-Century Russia*. Cambridge: Harvard University Press, 1960.

Ruud, Charles A. *Fighting Words: Imperial Censorship and the Russian Press, 1804–1906.* Toronto: University of Toronto Press, 1982.

Rywkin, Michael, ed. *Russian Colonial Expansion to 1917.* London: Mansell, 1988.

Sablinsky, Walter. *The Road to Bloody Sunday.* Princeton: Princeton University Press, 1976.

Saunders, David. *The Ukranian Impact on Russian Culture, 1750–1850.* Edmonton: University of Alberta Press, 1985.

Seaton, Albert. *The Crimean War: A Russian Chronicle.* London: Batsford, 1977.

Seaton-Watson, Hugh. *The Russian Empire, 1801–1917.* Oxford: Oxford University Press, 1967.

Staar, S. Frederick, ed. *Russia's American Colony.* Durham: Duke University Press, 1987.

Stavrou, Theophanis G. *Russian Interests in Palestine, 1882–1914.* Thessaloniki: Institute for Balkan Studies, 1963.

———. ed. *Russia Under the Last Tsars.* Minneapolis: University of Minnesota Press, 1969.

Thaden, Edward C. *Russia Since 1801.* New York: Wiley, 1971.

———. *Russia's Western Borderlands, 1710–1870.* Princeton: Princeton University Press, 1984.

Tikhmenev, Peter A. *A History of the Russian-American Company.* Trans. and edited by Richard A. Pierce and Alton S. Donnelly. Seattle: University of Washington Press, 1978.

Todd, William Mills, ed. *Literature and Society in Imperial Russia, 1800–1914.* Stanford: Stanford University Press, 1978.

Venturi, Franco. *Roots of Revolution.* New York: Knopf, 1960.

von Haxthausen, Baron. *The Russian Empire. Its People, Institutions and Resources.* 2 vols. London: F. Cass & Co., 1962.

von Laue, Theodore. *Sergei Witte and the Industrialization of Russia.* New York: Columbia University Press, 1963.

Vucinich, Alexander. *Science in Russian Culture: A History to 1860.* Stanford: Stanford University Press, 1963.

———. *Science in Russian Culture, 1867–1917.* Stanford: Stanford University Press, 1970.

Vucinich, Wayne, ed. *The Peasant in Nineteenth-Century Russia.* Stanford: Stanford University Press, 1970.

Ulam, Adam B. *In the Name of the People.* New York: Viking, 1977.

Walicki, Andrzej. *A History of Russian Thought from the Enlightenment to Marxism.* Stanford: Stanford University Press, 1979.

———. *The Legal Philosophies of Russian Liberalism.* New York: Oxford University Press, 1987.

Wheeler, Mary E. *The Origins and Formation of the Russian-American Company.* Chapel Hill: University of North Carolina Press, 1966.

Wolfe, Bertram. *Three Who Made a Revolution: Lenin, Trotsky, Stalin.* New York: Dial, 1948.

Yaney, George L. *The Systematization of Russian Government.* Urbana: University of Illinois Press, 1973.

Yarmolinsky, Avraham. *Road to Revolution: A Century of Russian Radicalism.* London: Cassell, 1957.

Zipperstein, Steven J. *The Jews of Odessa: A Cultural History, 1794–1881.* Stanford: Stanford University Press, 1986.

Periodical Literature

Adams, Arthur E., "The Character of Pestel's Thought," *The American Slavic and East European Review,* vol. 12, no. 2 (April 1953), 153–161.

———, "Pobedonostsev and the Rule of Firmness," *Slavonic Review,* vol. 32, no. 78 (December 1953), 132–139.

Aldanov, Mark, "P. N.Durnovo: Prophet of War and Revolution," *Russian Review,* vol. 2, no. 1 (Autumn 1942), 31–45.

Anderson, M. S., "English Views of Russia in the Age of Peter the Great," *The American Slavic and East European Review,* vol. 13, no. 2 (April, 1954), 200–214.

———, "The Great Powers and the Russian Annexation of the Crimea, 1783–84," *Slavonic Review,* vol. 38, no. 2 (April 1958), 17–41.

Aronson, I. Michael, "The Attitude of Russian Officials in the 1880s Toward Jewish Assimilation and Emigration," *Slavic Review,* vol. 34, no. 1 (March 1975), 1–18.

Baron, Samuel H., "Plekhanov and the Origins of Russian Marxism," *Russian Review,* vol. 13, no. 1 (January 1954), 38–51.

Berlin, Isaiah, "Russia and 1848," *Slavonic Review,* vol. 26, no. 67 (April 1948), 341–360.

Billington, James H., "The Intelligentsia and the Religion of Humanity," *The American Historical Review,* vol. 65, no. 4 (July 1960), 807–821.

Black, Cyril E., "The Nature of Imperial Russian Society," *Slavic Review,* vol. 20, no. 4 (December 1961), 565–582.

Black, J. L., "G. F. Muller and the Russian Academy of Sciences Contingent in the Second Kamchatka Expedition, 1733–43," *Canadian Slavonic Papers,,* vol. 25, no. 2 (June 1983), 235–252.

Blumberg, Arnold, "Russian Policy and the Franco-Austrian War of 1859," *Journal of Modern History,* vol. 26, no. 2 (June 1954), 137–153.

Bolkhovitinov, Nikolai N., "The Adventures of Dr. Schaffer in Hawaii, 1815–1819," *The Hawaiian Journal of History,* 7 (1973), 55–78.

———, "Russia and the Declaration of the Non-Colonization Principle: New Archival Evidence,: *Oregon Historical Quarterly,* vol. 72 (1971), 101–127.

Bolsover, G. H., "Nicholas I and the Partition of Turkey," *Slavonic Review,* vol. 27, no. 68 (December 1948), 115–145.

Bowman, Herbert E., "Revolutionary Elitism in Cernysevskij," *The American Slavic and East European Review,* vol. 13, no. 2 (April 1954), 185–199.

Brown, Edward J., "The Circle of Stankevich," *The American Slavic and East European Review,* vol. 16, no. 3 (October 1957), 349–368.

Burgess, M., "Fairs and Entertainers in 18th Century Russia," *Slavonic Review,* vol. 38, no. 90 (December 1959), 95–113.

Brooks, E. Willis, "Reform in the Russian Army, 1856–1861," *Slavic Review,* vol. 43, no. 1 (Spring 1984), 63–82.

Brower, Daniel R., "Labor Violence in Russia in the Late 19th Century," *Slavic Review,* vol. 41, no. 3 (Fall 1982), 417–431.

———, "Urbanization and Autocracy: Russian Urban Development in the First Half of the 19th Century," *Russian Review,* vol. 42, no. 4 (October 1983), 377–402.

Crisp, Olga, "State Peasants Under Nicholas I," *Slavonic Review,* vol. 37, no. 89 (June 1959), 387–412.

de Madariaga, Isabel, "Catherine II and the Serfs: A Reconsideration of Some Problems," *Slavonic and East European Review,* vol. 52, no. 126 (January 1974), 34–62.

———, "The Foundation of the Russian Educational System by Catherine II," *Slavonic and East European Review,* vol. 57, no. 3 (July 1979), 369–395.

Dmytryshyn, Basil, "The Economic Content of the 1767 *Nakaz* of Catherine II," *The American Slavic and East European Review,* vol. 14, no. 1 (February 1960), 1–9.

———, "Nikolai S. Mordvinov: Russia's Forgotten Liberal," *Russian Review,* vol. 30, no. 1 (January 1971), 54–63.

Dziewanowski, M. K., "Herzen, Bakunin and the Polish Insurrection of 1863," *Journal of Central European Affairs,* vol. 8, no. 1 (April 1948), 58–78.

Edwards, David W., "Count Joseph Marie de Maistre and Russian Educational Policy, 1803–1828," *Slavic Review,* vol. 36, no. 1 (March 1977), 54–75.

Emmons, Terence, "The Russian Landed Gentry," *Russian Review,* vol. 33, no. 3 (July 1974), 269–283.

Flynn, James T., "Tuition and Social Class in the Russian Universities: S.S. Uvarov and 'Reaction" in the Russia of Nicholas I," *Slavic Review,* vol. 35, no. 2 (June 1976), 232–248.

Freeze, Gregory L., "Social Mobility and the Russian Parish Clergy in the 18th Century," *Slavic Review,* vol. 33, no. 4 (December 1974), 641–662.

———, "The Orthodox Church and Serfdom in Prereform Russia," *Slavic Review,* vol. 48, no. 3, (Fall, 1989), pp. 361–387.

Gibson, James R., "Russia in California, 1833: Report of Governor Wrangel," *Pacific Northwest Quarterly,* (January, 1972), 1–13.

———, "The Sale of Russian America to the United States," *Acta Slavica Iaponica,* vol. 1 (1983), 15–37.

Godwin, Robert, "Russia and the Portsmouth Peace Conference," *The American Slavic and East European Review,* vol. 9, no. 4 (December 1950), 279–291.

Hammer, Oscar J., "Free Europe Versus Russia, 1830–1854," *The American Slavic and East European Review,* vol. 11, no. 1 (February 1952), 27–41.

Hardy, Deborah, "The Lonely Emigre: Peter Tkachev and the Russian Colony in Switzerland," *Russian Review,* vol. 35, no. 4 (October 1976), 400–416.

Harjan, George, "Dobroliubov's 'What is Oblomovism?' " *Canadian Slavonic Papers,* vol. 18, no. 3 (September 1976), 284–292.

Heilbronner, Hans, "The Russian Plague of 1878-79," *Slavic Review,* vol. 21, no. 1 (March 1962), 89–112.

Hodgson, John H., "Finland's Position in the Russian Empire, 1905–1910," *Journal of Central European Affairs,* vol. 20, no. 2 (July 1960), 158–173.

Kahan, Arcadius, "The Cost of 'Westernization" in Russia: The Gentry and the Economy in the 18th Century," *Slavic Review,* vol. 25, no. 1 (March 1966), 40–66.

Keep, J. L. H., "Russian Social Democracy and the First State Duma," *Slavonic Review,* vol. 34, no 82 (December 1955), 180–199.

Kenez, Peter, "A Profile of the Prerevolutionary Officer Corps," *California Slavic Studies,* vol. 7 (1973), 121–158.

Kimball, Stanley B., "The Prague 'Slav Congress' of 1848," *Journal of Central European Affairs,* vol. 22, no. 2 (July 1962), 174–199.

Kirchner, Walther, "Emigration to Russia," *The American Historical Review,* vol. 55, no. 3 (April 1950), 552–561.

Klier, John D., "The Jewish Question in the Reform Era Russian Press, 1855–1865," *Russian Review,* vol. 39, no. 3 (July 1980), 301–319.

Knight, Amy, "Female Terrorists in the Russian Socialist Revolutionary Party," *Russian Review,* vol. 38, no. 2 (April 1979), 139–159.

Kucherov, Samuel, "Administration of Justice Under Nicholas I of Russia,"

The American Slavic and East European Review, vol. 7, no. 2 (April 1948), 125–138.

Lavrin, Janko, "Chaadayev and the West," *Russian Review,* vol. 22, no. 3 (July 1963), 274–288.

Leighton, Laureen G., "Freemasonry in Russia: The Grand Lodge of Astraea (1815–1822)," *Slavonic and East European Review,* vol. 60, no. 2 (April 1982), 244–261.

Letiche, John M. and Basil Dmytryshyn, "The Adam Smith Russian Angle: Student Years of Ivan A. Tretiakov and Simeon E. Desnitskii," *International Review of Economics and Business,* (Milan), vol. 33, no. 1 (January 1986), 7–22.

Lewin, Moshe, "Customary Law and Russian Rural Society in the Post-Reform Era," *Russian Review,* vol. 44, no. 1 (January 1985), 1–20.

MacKenzie, David, "Pan-Slavism in Practice: Cherniaev in Serbia (1876), *Journal of Modern History,* vol. 36, no. 3 (September 1964), 279–297.

McKinsey, Pamela S., "From City Workers to Peasantry: The Beginnings of Russian Movement 'To the People'," *Slavic Review,* vol. 38, no. 4 (December 1979), 629–649.

McNally, Raymond T., "Chaadaev's Evaluation of Peter the Great," *Slavic Review,* vol. 23, no. 1 (March 1964), 31–44.

Mosse, Werner E., "Russian Bureaucracy at the End of the *Ancient Regime:* The Imperial Council, 1897–1915," *Slavic Review,* vol. 39, no. 4 (December 1980), 616–632.

O'Brien, C. Bickford, "Ivan Pososhkov: Russian Critic of Mercantilist Principles," *The American Slavic and East European Review,* vol. 14, no. 4 (December 1955), 503–511.

Pereira, N. G. O., "N. G. Chernyshevsky as Architect of the Politics of Anti-Liberalism in Russia," *Russian Review,* vol. 32, no. 3 (July 1973), 264–277.

Pinter, Walter M., "The Burden of Defense in Imperial Russia, 1725–1914," *Russian Review,* vol. 43, no. 3 (July 1984), 231–259.

Pipes, Richard, "The Russian Military Colonies, 1810–1831," *Journal of Modern History,* vol. 22, no. 3 (September 1950), 205–219.

Pomper, Philip, "Nechaev and Tsaricide: The Conspiracy with Conspiracy," *Russian Review,* vol. 33, no. 2 (April 1974), 123–138.

Raeff, Marc, "The Political Philosophy of Speranskij," *The American Slavic and East European Review,* vol. 12, no. 1 (February 1953), 1–21.

Ragsdale, Hugh, "Evaluating the Traditions of Russian Aggression: Catherine II and the Greek Preject," *Slavonic and East European Review,* vol. 66, no. 1 (January 1985), 97–117.

Raun, Toivo U., "The Latvian and Estonian National Movements, 1860–

1914," *Slavonic and East European Review,* vol. 64, no. 1 (January 1986), 66–80.

Rogger, Hans, "Russian Ministers and the Jewish Question, 1881–1917," *California Slavic Studies,* vol. 8 (1975), 15–76.

Ruud, Charles A., "Censorship and the Peasant Question: The Contingencies of Reform Under Alexander II (1855–59)," *California Slavic Studies,* vol. 5 (1970), 137–168.

Saunders, David B., "Historians and Concept of Nationality in Early 19th Century Russia," *Slavonic and East European Review,* vol. 60, no. 1 (January 1982), 44–62.

Schmidt, Albert J., "The Restoration of Moscow After 1812," *Slavic Review,* vol. 40, no. 1 (Spring, 1981), 37–48.

Sokol, A. E., "Russian Expansion and Explorations in the Pacific," *The American Slavic and East European Review,* vol. 2 no. 2 (1952), 85–105.

Spring, D. W., "Russia and the Franco-Russian Alliance, 1905–1914: Dependence or Interdependence?" *Slavonic and East European Review,* vol. 66, no. 4 (October 1988), 564–592.

———, "The Trans-Persian Railway Project and Anglo-Russian Relations, 1909–1914," *Slavonic and East European Review,* vol. 54, no. 1 (January 1976), 60–82.

Stephan, John J., "The Crimean War in the Far East," *Modern Asian Studies,* vol. 3, no. 3 (1969), 257–277.

Strakhovsky, L. I., "Count N. P. Ignat'yev: Reformer of Russian Education," *Slavonic Review,* vol. 36, no. 86 (December 1957), 1–26.

———, "The Statesmanship of Peter Stolypin: A Reappraisal," *Slavonic Review,* vol. 37, no. 89 (June 1959), 348–70.

Taranovski, Theodore, "Alexander III and His Bureaucracy: The Limitations on Autocratic Power," *Canadian Slavonic Papers,* vol. 26, nos. 2–3 (June–September 1984), 207–219.

Taylor, G. P., "Spanish-Russian Rivalry in the Pacific, 1769–1820," *Americas,* vol. 25 (1958), 109–127.

Treadgold, Donald W., "Was Stolypin in Favor of the Kulaks?" *The American Slavic and East European Review,* vol. 14, no. 1 (February 1955), 1–14.

Violette, Aurele J., "The Grand Duke Constantine Nikolaevich and the Reform of Naval Administration, 1855–1870," *Slavonic and East European Review,* vol. 52, no. 129 (October 1974), 584–601.

———, "Judicial Reforms in the Russian Navy During the 'Era of Great Reforms': The Reform Act of 1867 and the Abolition of Corporal Punishment," *Slavonic and East European Review,* vol. 56, no. 4 (October 1978), 586–603.

von Herzen, Michael, "Catherine II—Editor of *Vsiakaia Vsiachina?* A Reappraisal," *Russian Review,* vol. 38, no. 3 (July 1979), 283–297.

von Laue, Theodore H., "Count Witte and the Russian Revolution of 1905," *The American Slavic and East European Review,* vol. 17, no. 1 (February 1958), 25–46.

Walicki, Andrzej, "Russian Social Thought: An Introduction to the Intellectual History of 19th Century Russia," *Russian Review,* vol. 36, no. 1 (January, 1977), 1–45.

Weissman, Neil, "Regular Police in Tsarist Russia, 1900–1914," *Russian Review,* vol. 44, no. 1 (January 1985), 45–68.

Yaney, George L., "The Concept of the Stolypin Land Reform," *Slavic Review,* vol. 23, no. 2 (June 1964), 275–293.

Zeldin, Mary Barbara, "Chaadayev as Russia's First Philosopher," *Slavic Review,* vol. 37, no. 3 (September, 1978), 473–480.